The Abridged Edersheim

The Life And Times of Jesus The Messiah
Books 4, 5 & Appendices

Alfred Edersheim

(1825-1889)

Edited and Abridged by

Michael Steele

To order additional copies of this book, contact:
Xlibris Corporation
1-888-795-4274
www.Xlibris.com
Orders@Xlibris.com
66085

The Abridged
Edersheim

Contents

BOOK 4—The Valley of Humiliation and Death

BOOK 5—The Cross and the Crown

Appendices

Chapter 1

The Transfiguration

(Matthew 15:1-8; Mark 9:2-8; Luke 9:28-36)

The great confession of Peter, as the representative Apostle, had laid the foundations of the Church as such. In contradistinction to the varying opinions of even those best disposed towards Christ, it openly declared that Jesus was the Very Christ of God, the fulfillment of all Old Testament prophecy, the heir of Old Testament promise, the realization of the Old Testament hope for Israel, and, in Israel, for all mankind. Without this confession, Christians might have been a Jewish sect, a religious party, or a school of thought, and Jesus a Teacher, Rabbi, Reformer, or Leader of men. But the confession which marked Jesus as the Christ, also constituted His followers, the Church. It separated them, as it separated Him, from all around; it gathered them into one, even Christ; and it marked out the foundation on which the building made without hands was to rise. Never was illustrative answer so exact as this: On this Rock, bold, outstanding, well defined, immovable, will I build My Church.

Without doubt this confession also marked the high point of the Apostle's faith. Never afterwards, until His Resurrection, did it reach so high. What followed seems rather a retrogression from it: beginning with their unwillingness to receive the announcement of His decease, and ending with their unreadiness to share His sufferings or to believe in His Resurrection. And if we realize the circumstances, we shall understand at least, their initial difficulties. Their highest faith had been followed by the most crushing disappointment; the confession that He was the Christ, by the announcement of His approaching Sufferings and death at Jerusalem. The proclamation that He was the Divine Messiah had not been met by promises of the near glory of the Messianic Kingdom, but by announcements of certain, public rejection and seeming terrible defeat. Such possibilities had never seriously entered into their thoughts of the Messiah; and the declaration of the very worst, and that in the near future, made at such a moment, must have been a staggering blow to all their hopes. It was as if they had reached the topmost height, only to be cast from there into the lowest depth.

On the other hand, it was necessary that at this stage in the History of the Christ, and immediately after His proclamation, the sufferings and the rejection of the Messiah should be prominently brought forward. It was needful for the Apostles, as the protest of Peter showed; and, with reverence be it added, it was needful for the Lord Himself, as even His words to Peter seem to imply: Get you behind Me; you are a stumbling block to me. For, as we have said, was not the protest of the disciple in measure a re-enactment of the great initial Temptation by Satan after the forty days fast in the wilderness? And, in view of all this, and of what immediately afterwards followed, we venture to say, it was fitting that an interval of six days should intervene, or, as Luke puts it, including the day of Peter's confession and the night of Christ's Transfiguration, about eight days. The Chronicle of these days is significantly left blank in the Gospels, but we cannot doubt, that it was filled up with thoughts and teaching concerning that death, leading up to the revelation on the Mount of Transfiguration.

There are other blanks in the narrative besides that just referred to. We shall try to fill them up, as best we can. Perhaps it was the Sabbath when Peter's great confession was made; and the six days of Matthew and Mark become the about eight days of Luke, when we figure from that Sabbath to the close of another, and suppose that at even Jesus ascended the Mount of Transfiguration with the three Apostles: Peter, James, and John. There can scarcely be a reasonable doubt that Christ and His disciples had not left the neighborhood of Caesarea, and therefore, that the mountain must have been one of the slopes of gigantic, snowy Hermon. In that quiet semi-Gentile retreat of Caesarea Philippi could He best teach them, and they best learn, without interruption or temptation from Pharisees and Scribes, that terrible mystery of His Suffering. And on that gigantic mountain barrier which divided Jewish and Gentile lands, and while surveying, as Moses of old, the land to be occupied in all its extent, amid the solemn solitude and majestic grandeur of Hermon, did it seem most fitting that, both by anticipatory fact and declamatory word, the Divine attestation should be given to the proclamation that He was the Messiah, and to this also, that, in a world that is in the power of sin and Satan, God's Elect must suffer, in order that, by ransoming, He may conquer it to God. But what a background, here, for the Transfiguration; what surroundings for the Vision, what echoes for the Voice from heaven!

It was evening, and, as we have suggested, the evening after the Sabbath, when the Master and those three of His disciples, who were most closely linked to Him in heart and thought, climbed the path that led up to one of the heights of Hermon. In all the most solemn transactions of earth's history, there has been this selection and separation of the few to witness God's great doings. Alone with his son, as the destined sacrifice, did Abraham climb Moriah; alone did Moses look at, amid the awful loneliness of the wilderness, the burning bush, and alone on Sinai's height did he commune with God; alone was Elijah at Horeb, and with no other companion to view it than Elisha did he ascend into heaven. But Jesus, the Savior of His people, could not be quite alone, save in those innermost transactions of His soul: in the great contest of His first Temptation, and in the solitary communing of His heart with God. These are mysteries which the outspread wings of Angels, as reverently they hide their faces, conceal from earth's, and even heaven's vision. But otherwise, in the most solemn turning points of this history, Jesus could not be alone, and yet was alone with those three chosen ones, most receptive of Him, and most representative of the Church. It was so in the house of Jairus, on the Mount of Transfiguration, and in the Garden of Gethsemane.

As Luke alone informs us, it was to pray that Jesus took them apart up into that mountain. To pray, no doubt in connection with those sayings; since their reception required quite as much the direct teaching of the Heavenly Father, as had the previous confession of Peter, of which it was, the complement, the other aspect, the twin height. And the Transfiguration, with its attendant glorified Ministry and Voice from heaven, was God's answer to that prayer.

What has already been stated, has convinced us that it could not have been to one of the highest peaks of Hermon, as most modern writers suppose, that Jesus led His companions. There are three such peaks: those north and south, of about equal height (9,400 feet above the sea, and nearly 11,000 above the Jordan valley), are only 500 paces distant from each other, while the third, to the west (about 100 feet lower), is separated from the others by a narrow valley. Now, to climb the top of Hermon is, even from the nearest point, an Alpine ascent, trying and fatiguing, which would occupy a whole day (six hours in the ascent and four in the descent), and require provisions of food and water; while, from the keenness of the air, it would be impossible to spend the night on the top. To all this there is no allusion in the text, nor slightest hint of either difficulties or preparations, such as otherwise would have been required. Indeed, a contrary impression is left on the mind.

Up into a high mountain apart, to pray. The Sabbath sun had set, and a delicious cool hung in the summer air, as Jesus and the three commenced their ascent. From all parts of the land, far as Jerusalem or Tyre, the one great object in view must always have been snow clad Hermon. And now it stood out before them, as, to the memory of the traveler in the West, Monte Rosa or Mont Blanc, in all the wondrous glory of a sunset: first rose colored, then deepening red, next the death-like pallor, and the darkness relieved by the snow, in quick succession. From high up there, as one describes it, a deep ruby flush came over all the scene, and warm purple shadows crept slowly on. The sea of Galilee was lit up with a delicate greenish yellow hue, between its dim walls of hill. The flush died out in a few minutes, and a pale, steel colored shade succeeded . . . . A long pyramidal shadow slid down to the eastern foot of Hermon, and crept across the great plain; Damascus was swallowed up by it; and finally the pointed end of the shadow stood out distinctly against the sky, a dusky cone of dull color against the flush of the afterglow. It was the shadow of the mountain itself, stretching away for seventy miles across the plain, the most marvelous shadow perhaps to be seen anywhere. The sun underwent strange changes of shape in the thick vapors, now almost square, now like a domed Temple, until at length it slid into the sea, and went out like a blue spark. And overhead shone out in the blue summer sky, one by one, the stars in Eastern brilliancy. We do not know the exact direction which the climbers took, nor how far their journey went. But there is only one road that leads from Caesarea Philippi to Hermon, and we cannot be mistaken in following it. First, among vine clad hills stocked with mulberry, apricot and fig trees; then, through grain fields where the pear tree supplants the fig; next, through oak grove, and up rocky ravines to where the soil is dotted with dwarf shrubs. And if we pursue the ascent, it still becomes steeper, until the first ridge of snow is crossed, after which turf banks, gravelly slopes, and broad snow patches alternate. The top of Hermon in summer, and it can only be ascended in summer or autumn, is free from snow, but broad patches run down the sides expanding as they descend. To the very summit it is well earthed; to 500 feet below it, studded with countless plants, higher up with dwarf clumps.

As they ascend in the cool of that Sabbath evening, the keen mountain air must have breathed strength into the climbers, and the scent of snow, for which the parched tongue would long in summer's heat, have refreshed them. We do not know what part may have been open to them of the glorious panorama from Hermon embracing as it does a great part of Syria from the sea to Damascus, from the Lebanon and the gorge of the Litany to the mountains of Moab; or down the Jordan valley to the Dead Sea; or over Galilee, Samaria, and on to Jerusalem and beyond it. But such darkness as that of a summers night would creep on. And now the moon shone out in dazzling splendor, cast long shadows over the mountain, and lit up the broad patches of snow, reflecting their brilliancy on the objects around.

On that mountain top He prayed. Although the text does not expressly state it, we can scarcely doubt, that He prayed with them, and still less, that He prayed for them, as did the Prophet for his servant, when the city was surrounded by Syrian horsemen: that his eyes might be opened to behold heavens host, the far more that are with us than they that are with them. And, with deep reverence be it said, for Himself also did Jesus pray. For, as the pale moonlight shone on the fields of snow in the deep passes of Hermon, so did the light of the coming night shine on the cold glitter of death in the near future. He needed prayer, that in it His Soul might lie calm and still, perfect, in the unruffled quiet of His Self surrender, the absolute rest of His Faith, and the victory of His Sacrificial Obedience. And He needed prayer also, as the introduction to, and preparation for, His Transfiguration. Truly, He stood on Hermon. It was the highest ascent, the widest prospect into the past, present, and future, in His Earthly Life. Yet was it but Hermon at night. And this is both the divine and human view of this prayer, and of its consequence.

As we understand it, the prayer with them had ceased, or it had merged into silent prayer of each, or Jesus now prayed alone and apart, when what gives this scene such a truly human and truthful aspect ensued. It was but natural for these men of simple habits, at night, and after the long ascent, and in the strong mountain air, to be heavy with sleep. And we also know it as a psychological fact, that, in quick reaction after the overpowering influence of the strongest emotions, drowsiness would creep over their limbs and senses. They were heavy, weighted, with sleep, as afterwards at Gethsemane their eyes were weighted. Yet they struggled with it, and it is quite consistent with experience, that they should continue in that state of semi-stupor, during what passed between Moses and Elijah and Christ, and also be fully awake, to see His Glory, and the two men who stood with Him. In any case this descriptive trait, so far from being (as negative critics would have it), a later embellishment, could only have formed part of a primitive account, since it is impossible to conceive any rational motive for its later addition.

What they saw was their Master, while praying, transformed. The form of God shone through the form of a servant; the appearance of His Face became other, it did shine as the sun. The whole Figure seemed bathed in light, the very garments whiter far than the snow on which the moon shone, so as no fuller on earth can white them, glittering, white as the light. And more than this they saw and heard. They saw with Him two men, whom, in their heightened sensitiveness to spiritual phenomena, they could have no difficulty in recognizing, by such of their conversation as they heard, as Moses and Elijah. The column was now complete: the base in the Law; the shaft in that Prophetism of which Elijah was the great Representative, in his first Mission, as fulfilling the primary object of the Prophets: to call Israel back to God; and, in his second Mission, this other aspect of the Prophets work, to prepare the way for the Kingdom of God; and the apex in Christ Himself, a unity completely fitting together in all its parts. And they heard also, that they spoke of His Exodus, outgoing, which He was about to fulfill at Jerusalem. Although the term Exodus, outgoing, occurs otherwise for death, we must bear in mind its meaning as contrasted with that in which the same Evangelic writer designates the Birth of Christ, as His incoming. In truth, it implies not only His death, but its manner, and even His Resurrection and Ascension. In that sense we can understand the better, as on the lips of Moses and Elijah, this about His fulfilling that Exodus: accomplishing it in all its fullness, and so completing Law and Prophecy, type and prediction.

And still that night of glory had not ended. A strange peculiarity has been noticed about Hermon in the extreme rapidity of the formation of cloud on the summit. In a few minutes a thick cap forms over the top of the mountain, and as quickly disperses and entirely disappears. It almost seems as if this, like the natural position of Hermon itself, was, if not to be connected with, yet, so to speak, to form the background to what was to be enacted. Suddenly a cloud passed over the clear brow of the mountain, not an ordinary, but a luminous cloud, a cloud lit up, filled with light. As it laid itself between Jesus and the two Old Testament Representatives, it parted, and now enwrapped them. Most significant is it, suggestive of the Presence of God, revealing, yet concealing, a cloud, yet luminous. And this cloud overshadowed the disciples: the shadow of its light fell upon them. A nameless terror seized them. Gladly would they have held what seemed forever to escape their grasp. Such vision had never before been granted to mortal man as had fallen on their sight; they had already heard Heaven's converse; they had tasted Angel's Food, the Bread of His Presence. Could the vision not be perpetuated, at least prolonged? In the confusion of their terror they did not know how otherwise to word it, than by an expression of ecstatic longing for the continuance of what they had, of their earnest readiness to do their little best, if they could but secure it, make booths for the heavenly Visitors, and themselves wait in humble service and reverent attention on what their dull heaviness had prevented their enjoying and profiting by, to the full. They knew and felt it: Lord, Rabbi, Master, it is good for us to be here, and they longed to have it; yet how to secure it, their terror could not suggest, save in the language of ignorance and semiconscious confusion. They did not understand what they said. In presence of the luminous cloud that enwrapped those glorified Saints, they spoke from out of that darkness which surrounded them about.

And now the light cloud was spreading; now its fringe fell upon them. Heaven's awe was upon them: for the touch of the heavenly strains, almost to breaking, the bond between body and soul. And a Voice came out of the cloud, saying, This is My Beloved Son: hear Him. It had needed only One other Testimony to seal it all; One other Voice, to give both meaning and music to what had been the subject of Moses' and Elijah's speaking. That Voice had now come, not in testimony to any fact, but to a Person, that of Jesus as His Beloved Son, and in gracious direction to them. They heard it, falling on their faces in awestruck worship.

How long the silence had lasted, and the last rays of the cloud had passed, we do not know. Now it was a gentle touch that roused them. It was the Hand of Jesus, as with words of comfort He reassured them: Arise, and do not be afraid. And as, startled, they looked round about them, they saw no man save Jesus only. The Heavenly Visitors had gone, the last glow of the light cloud had faded away, the echoes of Heaven's Voice had died out. It was night, and they were on the Mount with Jesus, and with Jesus only.

Is it truth or falsehood; was it reality or vision, or part of both, this Transfiguration scene on Hermon? One thing, at least, must be evident: if it was a true narrative, it cannot possibly describe a merely subjective vision without objective reality. But, in that case, it would not be only difficult, but impossible, to separate one part of the narrative, the appearance of

Moses and Elijah, from the other, the Transfiguration of the Lord, and to assign to the latter objective reality, while regarding the former as merely a vision. But is the account true? It certainly represents primitive tradition, since it is not only told by all the three Evangelists, but referred to in 2 Peter 1:16-18, and evidently implied in the words of John, both in his Gospel, and in the opening of his First Epistle. Few, if any would be so bold as to assert that the whole of this history had been invented by the three Apostles, who professed to have been its witnesses. Nor can any adequate motive be imagined for its invention. It could not have been intended to prepare the Jews for the Crucifixion of the Messiah, since it was to be kept a secret until after His Resurrection; and, after the event, it could not have been necessary for the assurance of those who believed in the Resurrection, while to others it would carry no weight. Again, the special traits of this history are inconsistent with the theory of its invention. In a legend, the witnesses of such an event would not have been represented as scarcely awake, and not knowing what they said. Manifestly, the object would have been to convey the opposite impression. Lastly, it cannot be too often repeated, that, in view of the many witness of the Evangelists, amply confirmed in all essentials by the Epistles, preached, lived, and blood sealed by the primitive Church, and handed down as primitive tradition, the most untenable theory seems that which imputes intentional fraud to their narratives, or, to put it otherwise, non-belief on the part of the narrators of what they related.

But can we suppose, if not fraud, yet mistake on the part of these witnesses, so that an event, otherwise naturally explainable, may, through their ignorance or imaginativeness, have assumed the proportions of this narrative? The investigation will be the more easy, that, as regards all the main features of the narrative, the three Evangelists are entirely agreed. Instead of examining in detail the various rationalistic attempts made to explain this history on natural grounds, it seems sufficient for refutation to ask the intelligent reader to attempt imagining any natural event, which by any possibility could have been mistaken for what the eyewitnesses related, and the Evangelists recorded.

There still remains the mythical theory of explanation, which, if it could be supported, would be the most attractive among those of a negative character. But we cannot imagine a legend without some historical motive or basis for its origination. The legend must be in character, that is, in agreement to the ideas and expectancies entertained. Such a history as that of the Transfiguration could not have been a pure invention; but if such or similar expectancies had existed about the Messiah, then such a legend might, without intentional fraud, have, by gradual enlargement, gathered around the Person of Him Who was regarded as the Christ. And this is the rationale of the so called mythical theory. But all such ideas vanish at the touch of history. There was absolutely no Jewish expectancy that could have bodied itself forth in a narrative like that of the Transfiguration. To begin with the accessories, the idea, that the coming of Moses was to be connected with that of the Messiah, rests not only on an exaggeration, but on a dubious and difficult passage in the Jerusalem Targum. It is quite true, that the face of Moses shone when he came down from the Mount; but, if this is to be regarded as the basis of the Transfiguration of Jesus, the presence of Elijah would not be in point. On the other hand, to pass over other inconsistencies, anything more un-Jewish could scarcely be imagined than a Messiah crucified, or that Moses and Elijah should appear to converse with Him on such a death! If it be suggested, that the purpose was to represent the Law and the Prophets as bearing testimony to the Dying of the Messiah, we fully admit it. Certainly, this is the New Testament and the true idea concerning the Christ; but equally certainly, it was not and is not, that of the Jews concerning the Messiah.

If it is impossible to regard this narrative as a fraud; hopeless, to attempt explaining it as a natural event; and utterly unaccountable, when viewed in connection with contemporary thought or expectancy, in short, if all negative theories fail, let us see whether, and how on the supposition of its reality, it will fit into the general narrative. To begin with: if our previous investigations have rightly led us up to this result, that Jesus was the Very Christ of God, then this event can scarcely be described as miraculous, at least in such a history. If we would not expect it, it is certainly that which might have been expected. For, first, it was (and at that particular period) a necessary stage in Jesus' History, viewed in the light in which the Gospels present Him. Secondly, it was needful for His own strengthening, even as the Ministry of the Angels after the Temptation. Thirdly, it was good for these three disciples to be there: not only for future witness, but for present help, and also with special reference to Peter's protest against Christ's death message. Lastly, the Voice from heaven, in hearing of His disciples, was of the deepest importance. Coming after the announcement of His death and Passion, it sealed that testimony, and, in view of it, proclaimed Him as the Prophet to Whom Moses had commanded Israel to listen, while it repeated the heavenly utterance concerning Him made at His Baptism.

But, for us all, the interest of this history lies not only in the past; it is in the present also, and in the future. To all ages it is like the vision of the bush burning, in which was the Presence of God. And it points us forward to that transformation, of which that of Christ was the pledge, when this corruptible shall put on incorruption. As in olden times the beacon fires, lighted from hill to hill, announced to them far away from Jerusalem the advent of solemn feast, so does the glory kindled on the Mount of Transfiguration shine through the darkness of the world, and tell of the Resurrection Day.

On Hermon the Lord and His disciples had reached the highest point in this history. From here on it is a descent into the Valley of Humiliation and death!

End Notes:

[1]   According to an old tradition, Christ had left Caesarea Philippi, and the scene of the Transfiguration was Mount Tabor. But (1) there is no notice of His departure, such as in generally made by Mark; (2) on the contrary, it is mentioned by Mark as after the Transfiguration (9:30); (3) Mount Tabor was at that time crowned by a fortified city, which would render it unsuitable for the scene of the Transfiguration.

[2]   Meyer's arguments for regarding the appearance of Moses and Elijah as merely a vision, because the former at least had no resurrection body, are very weak. Are we sure, that disembodied spirits have no kind of corporeity, or that they cannot assume a visible appearance?

Chapter 2

The Day After the Transfiguration

(Matthew 15:9-21; Mark 9:9-29; Luke 9:37-43)

It was the early dawn on another summer's day when the Master and His disciples turned their steps once more towards the plain. They had seen His Glory; they had had the most solemn witness which, as Jews, they could have; and they had gained a new knowledge of the Old Testament. It all bore reference to the Christ, and it spoke of His death. Perhaps on that morning better than in the previous night they realized the vision, and feel its calm happiness. It was to their souls like the morning air which they breathed on that mountain.

It would be only natural, that their thoughts should also wander to the companions and fellow disciples whom, on the previous evening, they had left in the valley beneath. How much they had to tell them, and how glad they would be of the news they would hear! That one night had forever answered so many questions about that most hard of all His sayings: concerning His Rejection and violent death at Jerusalem; it had shed heavenly light into that terrible gloom! They, at least these three, had formerly simply submitted to the saying of Christ because it was His, without understanding it; but now they had learned to see it in quite another light. How they must have longed to tell it to those whose difficulties were at least as great, perhaps greater, who perhaps had not yet recovered from the rude shock which their Messianic thoughts and hopes had so lately received. We think here especially of those, whom, so far as individuality of thinking is concerned, we may designate as the representative three, and the counterpart of the three chosen Apostles: Philip, who ever sought firm

23

standing ground for faith; Thomas, who wanted evidence for believing; and Judas, whose burning Jewish zeal for a Jewish Messiah had already begun to consume his own soul, as the wind had driven back upon himself the flame that had been kindled. Every question of a Philip, every doubt of a Thomas, every despairing wild outburst of a Judas, would be met by what they had now to tell.

But it was not to be so. Evidently, it was not an event to be made generally known, either to the people or even to the great body of the disciples. They could not have understood its real meaning; they would have misunderstood, and in their ignorance misapplied to carnal Jewish purposes, its heavenly lessons. But even the rest of the Apostles must not know of it: that they were not qualified to witness it, proved that they were not prepared to hear of it. We cannot for a moment imagine, that there was favoritism in the selection of certain Apostles to share in what the others might not witness. It was not because these were better loved, but because they were better prepared—more fully receptive, more readily accepting, more entirely self surrendering. Too often we commit in our estimate the error of thinking of them exclusively as Apostles, not as disciples; as our teachers, not as His learners, with all the failings of men, the prejudices of Jews, and the unbelief natural to us all, but assuming in each individual special forms, and appearing as characteristic weaknesses.

And so it was that, when the silence of that morning descent was broken, the Master laid on them the command to tell no man of this vision, until after the Son of Man was risen from the dead. This mysterious injunction of silence affords another presumptive evidence against the invention, or the rationalistic explanations, or the mythical origin of this narrative. It also teaches two further lessons. The silence thus enjoined was the first step into the Valley of Humiliation. It was also a test, whether they had understood the spiritual teaching of the vision. And their strict obedience, not questioning even the grounds of the injunction, proved that they had learned it. So entire, was their submission, that they dared not even ask the Master about a new and seemingly greater mystery than they had yet heard: the meaning of the Son of Man rising from the Dead. Did it refer to the general Resurrection; was the Messiah to be the first to rise from the dead, and to awaken the other sleepers—or was it only a figurative expression for His triumph and vindication? Evidently, they knew as yet nothing of Christ's Personal Resurrection as separate from that of others, and on the third day after His death. And yet it was so near! So ignorant were they, and so unprepared! And they dared not ask Jesus of it.

This much they had already learned: not to question the mysteries of the future, but simply to receive them. But in their inmost hearts they kept that saying, as the Virgin Mother had kept many a like saying, carrying it about with them as a precious living germ that would now spring up and bear fruit, or as that which would kindle into light and chase all darkness. But among themselves, then and many times afterwards, in secret conversation, they questioned what the rising again from the dead should mean.

There was another question, and it they might ask of Jesus, since it concerned not the mysteries of the future, but the lessons of the past. Thinking of that vision, of the appearance of Elijah and of his speaking of the death of the Messiah, why did the Scribes say that Elijah should first come, and, as was the universal teaching, for the purpose of restoring all things? If, as they had seen, Elijah had come, but only for a brief season, not to abide, along with Moses, as they had fondly wished when they proposed to rear them booths; if he had come not to the people but to Christ, in view of only the three—and they were not even to tell of it; and, if it had been, not to prepare for a spiritual restoration, but to speak of what implied the opposite: the Rejection and violent death of the Messiah, then, were the Scribes right in their teaching, and what was its real meaning? The question afforded the opportunity of presenting to the disciples not only a solution to their difficulties, but another insight into the necessity of His Rejection and death. They had failed to distinguish between the coming of Elijah and its alternative sequence. Truly Elijah comes first, and Elijah had come already in the person of John the Baptist. The Divinely intended object of Elijah's coming was to restore all things. This implied a moral element in the submission of the people to God, and their willingness to receive his message. Otherwise there was this Divine alternative in the prophecy of Malachi: For fear that I come to strike the land with the ban (Cherem). Elijah had come; if the people had received his message, there would have been the promised restoration of all things. As the Lord had said on a previous occasion: If you are willing to receive him, this is Elijah, which is to come. Similarly, if Israel had received the Christ, He would have gathered them as a hen her chicks for protection; He would not only have been, but have visibly appeared as, their King. But Israel did not know their Elijah, and did to him what ever they desired; and so, in logical sequence, would the Son of Man also suffer from them. And thus has the other part of Malachi's prophecy been fulfilled: and the land of Israel been struck with the ban.

Amid such conversation the descent from the mountain was accomplished. Now they found themselves in view of a scene, which only too clearly showed that unfitness of the disciples for the heavenly vision of the preceding night, to which reference has been made. For, amid the divergence of details between the narratives of Matthew and Mark, and, so far as it goes, that of Luke, the one point in which they almost literally and emphatically agree is, when the Lord speaks of them, in language of bitter disappointment and sorrow, as a generation with whose lack of faith, in spite of all that they had seen and learned, He had still to bear, expressly attributing their failure in restoring the demoniac, to their unbelief.

It was, a terrible contrast between the scene below and that vision of Moses and Elijah, when they had spoken of the Exodus of the Christ, and the Divine Voice had attested the Christ from out the radiant cloud. A concourse of excited people, among them once more Scribes, who had tracked the Lord and come upon His weakest disciples in the hour of their greatest weakness, is gathered about a man who had in vain brought his demonized son for healing. He is eagerly questioned by the multitude, and moodily answers; or, as it might almost seem from Matthew, he is leaving the crowd and those from whom he had vainly sought help. This was the hour of triumph for these Scribes. The Master had refused the challenge in Dalmanutha, and the disciples, accepting it, had signally failed. There they were, questioning with them noisily, discussing this and all similar phenomena, but chiefly the power, authority, and reality of Jesus. It reminds us of Israel's temptation in the wilderness, and we should scarcely wonder, if they had even questioned the return of Jesus, as those in olden days did that of Moses.

At that very moment, Jesus appeared with the three. We cannot wonder that, when they saw Him, they were greatly amazed, and running to Him greeted Him. He came, as always, and to us also, unexpectedly, most opportunely, and for the real decision of the question at hand. There was immediate calm, preceding victory. Before Jesus' inquiry about the cause of this violent discussion could be answered, the man who had been its occasion came forward. With lowliest gesture (kneeling to Him) he addressed Jesus. At last he had found Him, Whom he had come to seek; and, if possibility of help there were, oh! let it be granted. Describing the symptoms of his son's condition, which were those of epilepsy and mania, although both the father and Jesus rightly attributed the disease to demoniac influence, he told, how he had come in search of the Master, but only found the nine disciples, and how they had presumptuously attempted, and signally failed in the attempted cure.

Why had they failed? For the same reason, that they had not been taken into the Mount of Transfiguration, because they were faithless, because of their unbelief. They had that outward faith of the probatum est (it is proved); they believed because, and what, they had seen; and they were drawn closer to Christ, at least almost all of them, though in varying measure, as to Him Who, and Who alone, spoke the words of eternal life, which, with wondrous power, had swayed their souls, or laid them to heaven's rest. But that deeper, truer faith, which consisted in the spiritual view of that which was the unseen in Christ, and that higher power, which flows from such apprehension, they had not. In such faith as they had, they spoke, repeated forms of exorcism, tried to imitate their Master. But they signally failed, as did those seven Jewish Priest sons at Ephesus. And it was intended that they should fail, that so to them and to us the higher meaning of faith as contrasted with power, the inward as contrasted with the merely outward qualification, might appear. In that hour of crisis, in the presence of questioning Scribes and a wondering populace, and in the absence of the Christ, only one power could prevail, that of spiritual faith; and that kind could not come out but by prayer.

It is this lesson, viewed also in organic connection with all that had happened since the great temptation at Dalmanutha, which furnishes the explanation of the whole history. For one moment we have a glimpse into Jesus' soul: the poignant sorrow of His disappointment at the unbelief of the faithless and perverse generation, with which He had so long borne; the infinite patience and condescension, the Divine need be of His having thus to bear even with His own, together with the deep humiliation and keen pang which it involved; and the almost home longing, as one has called it, of His soul. These are mysteries to adore. The next moment Jesus turns to the father. At His command the demonized is brought to Him. In the Presence of Jesus, and in view of the coming contest between Light and Darkness, one of those convulsions of demoniac operation ensues, such as we have witnessed on all similar occasions. This was allowed to pass in view of all. But both this, and the question as to the length of time the demonized had been afflicted, together with the answer, and the description of the dangers involved, which it elicited, were evidently intended to point the lesson of the need of a higher faith. To the father, however, who did not know the mode of treatment by the Heavenly Physician, they seemed like the questions of an earthly healer who must consider the symptoms before he could attempt to cure. If You can do anything, have compassion on us, and help us.

It was but natural, and yet it was the turning point in this whole history, as regarded the healing of the demonized, the better leading of his father, the teaching of the disciples, and that of the multitude and the Scribes. There is all the calm majesty of Divine self consciousness, yet without trace of self assertion, when Jesus, utterly ignoring the if You can, turns to the man and tells him that, while with the Divine Helper there is the possibility of all help, it is conditioned by a possibility in ourselves, by man's receptiveness, by his faith. Not, if the Christ can do anything or even everything, but, If you can believe, all things are possible to him that believes. The question is not, it can never be, as the man had put it; it must not even be answered, but ignored. It must ever be, not what He can, but what we can. When the infinite fullness is poured forth, as it ever is in Christ, it is not the oil that is weak, but the vessels which fail. He gives richly, inexhaustibly, but not mechanically; there is only one condition, the moral one of the presence of absolute faith, our receptiveness. And so these words have for all time remained the teaching to every individual striver in the battle of the higher life, and to the Church as a whole, the victory that overcomes the world, even our faith.

It was a lesson, of which the reality was attested by the hold which it took on the man's whole nature. While by one great outgoing of his soul he leaped over all, to lay hold on the one fact set before him, he felt all the more the dark chasm of unbelief behind him, but he also clung to that Christ, Whose teaching of faith had shown him, together with the possibility, the source of faith. Thus through the felt unbelief of faith he attained true faith by laying hold on the Divine Savior, when he cried out and said: Lord, I believe; help my unbelief. These words have remained historic, marking all true faith, which, even as faith, is conscious of, implies, unbelief, but brings it to Christ for help. The most bold leap of faith and the timid resting at His Feet, the first beginning and the last ending of faith, have this as their watchword.

Such cry could not be, and never is, unheard. It was real demoniac influence which, continuing with this man from childhood onwards, had well near crushed all moral individuality in him. In his many coherent intervals these many years, since he had grown from a child into a youth, he had never sought to shake off the yoke and regain his moral individuality, nor would he even now have come, if his father had not brought him. If any, this narrative shows the view which the Gospels and Jesus took of what are described as the demonized. It was a reality, and not accommodation to Jewish views, when, as He saw the multitude running together, He rebuked the unclean spirit, saying to him: Dumb and deaf spirit, I command you, come out of him, and no more come into him. Another and a more violent convulsion, so that the bystanders almost thought him dead. But the unclean spirit had come out of him. And with strong gentle Hand Jesus lifted him, and with loving gesture delivered him to his father.

All things had been possible to faith; not to that external belief of the disciples, which failed to reach that kind, and ever fails to reach such kind, but to true spiritual faith in Him. And so it is to each of us individually, and to the Church, for all time. That kind, whether it is of sin, of lust, of the world, or of science falsely so called, of temptation, or of materialism, does not come out by any of our ready made formulas or dead dogmas. Not so are the flesh and the Devil vanquished; not so is the world overcome. It comes out by nothing but by prayer: Lord, I believe; help my unbelief. Then, although our faith was only what in popular language was described as the smallest, like a grain of mustard seed, and the result to be achieved the greatest, most difficult, seemingly transcending human ability to compass it, what in popular language was designated as removing mountains, nothing shall be impossible to us. And these eighteen centuries of suffering in Christ, and deliverance through Christ, and work for Christ, have proved it. For all things are ours, if Christ is ours.

End Notes:

[3]   The question, whether there is to be a literal reappearance of Elijah before the Second Advent of Christ does not seem to be answered in the present passage. Perhaps it is purposely left unanswered.

[4]   The Rabbinic use of the expression, grain of mustard seed, has already been noted. The expression tearing up or removing mountains was also proverbial among the Rabbis. Thus, a great Rabbi might be designated as one who uprooted mountains (Ber., last page, line 5 from top; and Horay, 14 a), or as one who pulverized them (Sanh. 24 a). The expression is also used to indicate apparently impossible things, such as those which a pagan government may order a man to do (Baba B. 3 b).

Chapter 3

The Consequent Teaching of Christ

(Matthew 15:22, 16:22; Mark 9:30-50; Luke 9:43-50)

Now that Jesus' retreat in the utmost borders of the land, at Caesarea Philippi, was known to the Scribes, and that He was again surrounded and followed by the multitude, there could be no further object in His retirement. The time was coming that He should meet that for which He had been, and was still, preparing the minds of His disciples, His death at Jerusalem. Accordingly, we find Him once more with His disciples in Galilee, not to live there, nor to travel over it as formerly for Missionary purposes, but preparatory to His journey to the Feast of Tabernacles. The few events of this brief stay, and the teaching connected with it, may be summed up as follows.

1. Prominently, perhaps, as the summary of all, we have now the clear and emphatic repetition of the prediction of His death and Resurrection. While He would keep His present stay in Galilee as private as possible, He would gladly so emphasize this teaching to His disciples, that it should sink down into their ears and memories. For it was, the most needful for them in view of the immediate future. Yet the announcement only filled their loving hearts with great sorrow; they did not comprehend it; they were, perhaps not unnaturally, afraid to ask Him about it. We remember, that even the three who had been with Jesus on the Mount, did not understand what the rising from the dead should mean, and that, by direction of the Master, they kept the whole Vision from their fellow disciples; and, thinking of it all, we scarcely wonder that, from

their standpoint, it was hid from them, so that they might not perceive it.

2. It is to the depression caused by His insistence on this terrible future, to the constant apprehension of near danger, and the consequent desire not to offend, and so provoke those at whose hands, Christ had told them, He was to suffer, that we trace the incident about the tribute money. We can hardly believe, that Peter would have answered as he did, without previous permission of his Master, had it not been for such thoughts and fears. It was another mode of saying, That be far from You, or, rather, trying to keep it as far as he could from Christ. Indeed, we can hardly repress the feeling, that there was a certain amount of secretiveness on the part of Peter, as if he had understood that Jesus would not have wished him to act as he did, and would gladly have kept the whole transaction from the knowledge of his Master.

It is well known that, on the ground of the injunction in Exodus 30:13 etc., every male in Israel, from twenty years upwards, was expected annually to contribute to the Temple Treasury the sum of one half shekel of the Sanctuary, that is, one common shekel, or two Attic drachms, equivalent to about 1s. 2d. or 1s. 3d. of our money. Whether or not the original Biblical ordinance had been intended to institute a regular annual contribution, the Jews of the Dispersion would probably regard it in the light of a patriotic as well as religious act.

To the particulars previously given on this subject a few others may be added. The family of the Chief of the Sanhedrin (Gamaliel) seems to have enjoyed the curious distinction of bringing their contributions to the Temple Treasury, not like others, but to have thrown them down before him who opened the Temple Chest, when they were immediately placed in the box from which, without delay, sacrifices were provided. Again, the commentators explain a certain passage in the Mishnah and the Talmud as implying that, although the Jews in Palestine had to pay the tribute money before the Passover, those from neighboring lands might bring it before the Feast of Weeks, and those from such remote countries as Babylonia and Media as late as the Feast of Tabernacles. Lastly, although the Mishnah lays it down, that the goods of those might be seized, who had not paid the Temple tribute by the 25th Adar, it is hardly credible that this obtained at the time of Christ, at any rate in Galilee. This seems implied in the statement of the Mishnah and the Talmud, that one of the thirteen trumpets in the Temple, into which contributions were cast, was destined for the shekels of the current, and another for those of the preceding, year. Finally, these Temple contributions were in the first place devoted to the purchase of all public sacrifices, that is, those which were offered in the name of the whole congregation of Israel, such as the morning and evening sacrifices. It will be remembered, that this was one of the points in fierce dispute between the Pharisees and Sadducees, and that the former perpetuated their triumph by marking its anniversary as a festive day in their calendar. It seems a terrible irony of judgment when Vespasian ordered, after the destruction of the Temple, that this tribute should from then on be paid for the rebuilding of the Temple of Jupiter Capitolinus.

It will be remembered that, shortly before the previous Passover, Jesus with His disciples had left Capernaum, that they returned to the latter city only for the Sabbath, and that, as we have suggested, they passed the first Paschal days on the borders of Tyre. We have, no means of knowing where Jesus had waited during the ten days between the 15th and the 25th Adar, supposing the Mishnic arrangements to have been in force in Capernaum. He was certainly not at Capernaum, and it must also have been known, that He had not gone up to Jerusalem for the Passover. Accordingly, when it was told in Capernaum, that the Rabbi of Nazareth had once more come to what seems to have been His Galilean home, it was only natural, that they who collected the Temple tribute should have applied for its payment. It is quite possible, that their application may have been, if not prompted, yet quickened, by the wish to involve Him in a breach of so well known an obligation, or else by a hostile curiosity. Would He, Who took so strangely different views of Jewish observances, and Who made such extraordinary claims, own the duty of paying the Temple tribute? Had it been owing to His absence, or from principle, that He had not paid it last Passover season? The question which they put to Peter implies, at least, their doubt.

We have already seen what motives prompted the hasty reply of Peter. He might, also otherwise, in his rashness, have given an affirmative answer to the inquiry, without first consulting the Master. For there seems little doubt, that Jesus had on former occasions complied with the Jewish custom. But matters were now wholly changed. Since the first Passover, which had marked His first public appearance in the Temple at Jerusalem, He had stated, and quite lately in most explicit terms, that He was the Christ, the Son of God. To have now paid the Temple tribute, without explanation, might have involved a very serious misapprehension. In view of all this, the history before us seems simple and natural. There is no pretext for the artificial construction put upon it by commentators, any more than for the suggestion, that such was the poverty of the Master and His disciples, that the small sum required for the Temple tribute had to be miraculously supplied.

We picture it to ourselves this way. Those who received the Tribute money had come to Peter, and perhaps met him in the court or corridor, and asked him: Your Teacher (Rabbi), does He not pay the didrachma? While Peter hastily responded in the affirmative, and then entered into the house to procure the coin, or else to report what had passed, Jesus, Who had been in another part of the house, but was aware of all, anticipated him. Addressing him in kindly language as Simon, He pointed out the real state of matters by an illustration which must not be too literally pressed, and of which the meaning was: Whom does a King intend to tax for the maintenance of his palace and officers? Surely not his own family, but others. The inference from this, as regarded the Temple tribute, was obvious. As in all similar Jewish parabolic teaching, it was only indicated in general principle: Then the children are free. But even so, was it as Peter had wished, although not from the same motive. Let no needless offence be given; for, assuredly, they would not have understood the principle on which Christ would have refused the Tribute money, and all misunderstanding on the part of Peter was now impossible. Yet Christ would still further vindicate His royal title. He will pay for Peter also, and pay, as heaven's King, with a Stater, or four drachm piece, miraculously provided.

Thus viewed, there is, we submit, a moral purpose and spiritual instruction in the provision of the Stater out of the fish's mouth. The rationalistic explanation of it need not be seriously considered; for any mythical interpretation there is not the shadow of support in Biblical precedent or Jewish expectancy. But the narrative in its literality has a true and high meaning. And if we wished to mark the difference between its sober simplicity and the extravagances of legend, we would remind ourselves, not only of the well known story of the Ring of Polycrates, but of two somewhat kindred Jewish Haggadahs. They are both intended to glorify the Jewish mode of Sabbath observance. One of them bears that one Joseph, known as the honored of the Sabbath, had a wealthy pagan neighbor, to whom the Chaldeans had prophesied that all his riches would come to Joseph. To render this impossible, the wealthy man converted all his property into one magnificent gem, which he carefully concealed within his head gear. Then he took a ship, so as forever to avoid the dangerous vicinity of the Jew. But the wind blew his head gear into the sea, and the gem was swallowed by a fish. And lo! it was the holy season, and they brought to the market a splendid fish. Who would purchase it but Joseph, for none as he would prepare to honor the day by the best which he could provide. But when they opened the fish, the gem was found in it, the moral being: He that borrows for the Sabbath, the Sabbath will repay him.

The other legend is similar. It was in Rome (in the Christian world) that a poor tailor went to market to buy a fish for a festive meal. Only one was on sale, and for it there was intense competition between the servant of a Prince and the Jew, the latter at last buying it for not less than twelve dinars. At the banquet, the Prince inquired of his servants why no fish had been provided. When he ascertained the cause, he sent for the Jew with the threatening inquiry, how a poor tailor could afford to pay twelve dinars for a fish? My Lord, replied the Jew, there is a day on which all our sins are remitted us, and should we not honor it? The answer satisfied the Prince. But God rewarded the Jew, for, when the fish was opened, a precious gem was found in it, which he sold, and forever afterwards lived of the proceeds. The reader can hardly fail to mark the absolute difference between even the most beautiful Jewish legends and any trait in the Evangelic history.

3. The event next recorded in the Gospels took place partly on the way from the Mount of Transfiguration to Capernaum, and partly in Capernaum itself, immediately after the scene connected with the Tribute money. It is recorded by the three Evangelists, and it led to explanations and admonitions, which are told by Mark and Luke, but chiefly by Matthew. This circumstance seems to indicate, that the latter was the chief actor in that which occasioned this special teaching and warning of Christ, and that it must have sunk very deeply into his heart.

As we look at it, in the light of the then mental and spiritual state of the Apostles, not in that in which, perhaps naturally, we regard them, what happened seems not difficult to understand. As Mark puts it, by the way they had disputed among themselves which of them would be the greatest, as Matthew explains, in the Messianic Kingdom of Heaven. They might now the more confidently expect its near Advent from the mysterious announcement of the Resurrection on the third day, which they would probably connect with the beginning of the last Judgment, following upon the violent death of the Messiah. Of a dispute, serious and even violent, among the disciples, we have evidence in the exhortation of

Jesus, as reported by Mark, in the direction of the Lord how to deal with an offending brother, and in the answering inquiry of Peter. Nor can we be at a loss to understand its occasion. The distinction just bestowed on the three, in being taken up the Mount, may have roused feelings of jealousy in the others perhaps of self exaltation in the three. The spirit which John displayed in his harsh prohibition of the man that did not follow with the disciples, and the self righteous bargaining of Peter about forgiving the supposed or real offences of a brother, give evidence of anything but the frame of mind which we would have expected after the Vision on the Mount.

In truth, most incongruous as it may appear to us, looking back on it in the light of the Resurrection, day almost incredible, evidently, the Apostles were still greatly under the influence of the old spirit. It was the common Jewish view, that there would be distinctions of rank in the Kingdom of Heaven. It can hardly be necessary to prove this by Rabbinic quotations, since the whole system of Rabbinism and Pharisaism, with its separation from the common and ignorant, rests upon it. But even within the charmed circle of Rabbinism, there would be distinctions, due to learning, merit, and even to favoritism. In this world there were His special favorites, who could command anything at His hand, to use the Rabbinic illustration, like a spoiled child from its father. And in the Messianic age God would assign booths to each according to his rank. On the other hand, many passages could be quoted bearing on the duty of humility and self abasement. But the stress laid on the merit attaching to this shows too clearly, that it was the pride that copies humility. One instance, previously referred to, will suffice by way of illustration. When the child of the great Rabbi Jochanan ben Zakkai was dangerously ill, he was restored through the prayer of one Chanina ben Dosa. On this the father of the child remarked to his wife: If the son of Zakkai had all day long put his head between his knees, no attention would have been given to him. How is that? asked his wife; is Chanina greater than you? No, was the reply, he is like a servant before the King, while I am like a prince before the King (he is always there, and has thus opportunities which I, as a lord, do not enjoy).

How deep rooted were such thoughts and feelings, appears not only from the dispute of the disciples by the way, but from the request offered by the mother of Zebedee's children and her sons at a later period, in terrible contrast to the near Passion of Jesus. It does, indeed come upon us as a most painful surprise, and as sadly incongruous, this constant self promoting, self assertion, and low, carnal self seeking; this Judaistic trifling in face of the utter self negation and self sacrifice of the Son of Man. Surely, the contrast between Christ and His disciples seems at times almost as great as between Him and the other Jews. If we would measure His Stature, or comprehend the infinite distance between His aims and teaching and those of His contemporaries, let it be by comparison with even the best of His disciples. It must have been part of His humiliation and self examination to bear with them. And is it not, in a sense, still so as regards us all?

We have already seen, that there was quite sufficient occasion and material for such a dispute on the way from the Mount of Transfiguration to Capernaum. We suppose Peter to have been only at the first with the others. To judge by the later question, how often he was to forgive the brother who had sinned against him, he may have been so deeply hurt, that he left the other disciples, and hurried on with the Master, Who would, at any rate, stay in his house. For, neither he nor Christ seem to have been present when John and the others had forbid the man, who would not follow with them, to cast out demons in Christ's name. Again, the other disciples only came into Capernaum, and entered the house, just as Peter had gone for the Stater, with which to pay the Temple tribute for the Master and himself. And, if speculation be permissible, we would suggest that the brother, whose offences Peter found it so difficult to forgive, may have been none other than Judas. In such a dispute by the way, he, with his Judaistic views, would be especially interested; perhaps he may have been its chief instigator; certainly, he, whose natural character, amid its sharp contrasts to that of Peter, presented so many points of resemblance to it, would, on many grounds, be especially jealous of, and antagonistic to him.

Quite natural in view of this dispute by the way is another incident of the journey, which is afterwards related. As we judge, John seems to have been the principal actor in it; perhaps, in the absence of Peter, he claimed the leadership. They had met one who was casting out demons in the Name of Christ, whether successfully or not, we need scarcely inquire. So widely had faith in the power of Jesus extended; so real was the belief in the subjection of the demons to Him; so reverent was the acknowledgment of Him. A man, who, thus forsaking the methods of Jewish exorcists, owned Jesus in the face of the Jewish world, could not be far from the Kingdom of Heaven; at any rate, he could not quickly speak evil of Him. John had, in name of the disciples, forbidden him, because he had not cast in his lot wholly with them. It was quite in the spirit of their ideas about the Messianic Kingdom, and of their dispute, which of His close followers would be greatest there. And yet, they might deceive themselves as to the motives of their conduct. If it were not almost impertinence to use such terms, we would have said that there was infinite wisdom and kindness in the answer which Jesus gave, when referred to on the subject. To forbid a man, in such circumstances, would be either prompted by the spirit of the dispute by the way, or else must be grounded on evidence that the motive was, or the effect would ultimately be (as in the case of the sons of Sceva) to lead men to speak evil of Christ, or to hinder the work of His disciples. Assuredly, such could not have been the case with a man, who invoked His Name, and perhaps experienced its efficacy. More than this, and here is an eternal principle: He that is not against us is for us; he that does not oppose the disciples, really is for them, a saying still more clear, when we adopt the better reading in Luke, He that is not against you is for you.

There was admonition in this, as well as instruction, deeply consistent with that other, though seemingly different, saying: He that is not with Me is against Me. The distinction between them is twofold. In the one case it is not against, in the other it is not with; but chiefly it lies in this: in the one case it is not against the disciples in their work, while in the other it is, not with Christ. A man who did what he could with such knowledge of Christ as he possessed, even although he did not absolutely follow with them, was not against them. Such a one should be regarded as thus far with them; at least be let alone, left to Him Who knew all things. Such a man would not lightly speak evil of Christ, and that was all the disciples should care for, unless, they sought their own. Quite other was it as regarded the relation of a person to the Christ Himself. There neutrality was impossible, and that which was not with Christ, by this very fact was against Him. The lesson is of the most deep reaching character, and the distinction, unfortunately still overlooked, perhaps, because ours is too often the spirit of those who journeyed to Capernaum. Not, that it is unimportant to follow with the disciples, but that it is not ours to forbid any work done, however imperfectly, in His Name, and that only one question is really vital, whether or not a man is decidedly with Christ.

Such were the incidents along the way. And now, while withholding from Christ their dispute, and, anything that might seem personal in the question, the disciples, on entering the house where He was in Capernaum, addressed to Him this question (which should be inserted from the opening words of Matthew's narrative): Who, then, is greatest in the Kingdom of Heaven? It was a general question, but Jesus perceived the thought of their hearts; He knew about what they had argued along the way, and now asked them concerning it. The account of Mark is most graphic. We almost see the scene. Conscience stricken they held their peace. As we read the further words: And He sat down, it seems as if Jesus had at first gone to welcome the disciples on their arrival, and they, full of their dispute, had, without delay, addressed their question to him in the court or antechamber, where they met Him, when, reading their thoughts, He had first put the searching counter question, what had been the subject of their dispute. Then, leading the way into the house, He sat down, not only to answer their inquiry, which was not a real inquiry, but to teach them what so much they needed to learn. He called a little child, perhaps Peter's little son, and put him in the midst of them. Not to struggle as to who was to be greatest, but to be utterly without self consciousness, like a child, thus, to become turned and entirely changed in mind: converted, was the condition for entering into the Kingdom of Heaven. Then, as to the question of greatness there, it was really one of greatness of service, and that was greatest service which implied most self denial. Suiting the action to the teaching, the Blessed Savior took the happy child in His arms. Not, to teach, to preach, to work miracles, nor to do great things, but to do the humblest service for Christ's sake, lovingly, earnestly, wholly, self forgetfully, simply for Christ, was to receive Christ to receive the Father. And the smallest service, as it might seem, even the giving a cup of cold water in such spirit, would not lose its reward. Blessed teaching this to the disciples and to us; blessed lesson, which, these many centuries of scorching heat, has been of unspeakable refreshing, to the giver and the receiver of the cup of water in the Name of Christ, in the love of Christ, and for the sake of Christ.

These words about receiving Christ, and receiving in the Name of Christ, had stirred the memory and conscience of John, and made him half wonder, half fear, whether what they had done by the way, in forbidding the man to do what he could in the name of Christ, had been right. And so he told it, and received the further and higher teaching on the subject. And, more than this, Mark and, more fully, Matthew, record some further instruction in connection with it, to which Luke refers, in a slightly different form, at a somewhat later period. But it seems so in agreement to the present occasion, that we conclude it was then spoken, although, like other sayings, it may have been afterwards repeated under similar circumstances. Certainly, no more effective continuation, and application to Jewish minds, of the teaching of Jesus could be conceived than that which follows. For, the love of Christ goes deeper than the condescension of receiving a child, utterly un-Pharisaic and un-Rabbinic as this is. To have regard to the weaknesses of such a child, to its mental and moral ignorance and folly, to adapt ourselves to it, to restrain our fuller knowledge and forego our felt liberty, so as not to offend, not to give occasion for stumbling to one of these little ones, that so through our knowledge the weak brother for whom Christ died should not perish: this is a lesson which reaches even deeper than the question, what is the condition of entrance into the Kingdom, or what service constitutes real greatness in it. A man may enter into the Kingdom and do service, yet, if in so doing he disregard the law of love to the little ones, far better his work should be abruptly cut short; better, one of those large millstones, turned by a donkey, were hung about his neck and he cast into the sea! We pause to note, once more, the Judaic, and, therefore, evidential, setting of the Evangelic narrative. The Talmud also speaks of two kinds of millstones, the one turned by hand, referred to in Luke 15:35; the other turned by a donkey (mlos nils), just as the Talmud also speaks of the donkey of the millstone. Similarly, the figure about a millstone hung round the neck occurs also in the Talmud, although there as figurative of almost impossible difficulties. Again, the expression, it was better for him, is a well known Rabbinic expression (Mutabh hayah lo). Lastly, according to Jerome, the punishment which seems alluded to in the words of Christ, and which we know to have been inflicted by Augustus, was actually practiced by the Romans in Galilee on some of the leaders of the insurrection under Judas of Galilee.

And yet greater guilt would only too surely be incurred! Judgment to the world! Occasions of stumbling and offence will surely come, but judgment to the man through whom such havoc was performed. What then is the alternative? If it be a question as between offence and some part of ourselves, a limb or member, however useful, the hand, the foot, the eye, then let it rather be severed from the body, however painful, or however seemingly great the loss. It cannot be so great as that of the whole being in the eternal fire of Gehenna, where their worm does not die, and the fire is not quenched. Hand, foot, or eye, practice, pursuit, or research, which consciously leads us to occasions of stumbling, must be resolutely put aside in view of the incomparably greater loss of eternal remorse and anguish.

Here Mark abruptly breaks off with a saying in which Jesus makes general application, although the narrative is further continued by Matthew. The words reported by Mark are so remarkable, so brief, we had almost said abbreviated, as to require special consideration. It seems to us that, turning from this thought that even members which are intended for useful service may, in certain circumstances, have to be cut off to avoid the greatest loss, Jesus gave to His disciples this as the final summary and explanation of all: For everyone shall be salted with the fire, or, as a very early gloss, which has strangely crept into the text, paraphrased and explained it, Every sacrifice shall be salted with salt. No one is fit for the sacrificial fire, no one can himself be, nor offer anything as a sacrifice, unless it have been first, according to the Levitical Law, covered with salt, symbolic of the incorruptible. Salt is good; but if the salt, with which the spiritual sacrifice is to be salted for the fire, have lost its savor, with what will you season it? Therefore, have salt in yourselves, but do not let that salt be corrupted by making it an occasion of offence to others, or among yourselves, as in the dispute by the way, or in the disposition of mind that led to it, or in forbidding others to work who do not follow with you, but be at peace among yourselves.

To this explanation of the words of Christ it may, perhaps, be added that, from their form, they must have conveyed a special meaning to the disciples. It is a well known law, that every sacrifice burned on the Altar must be salted with salt. According to the Talmud, not only every such offering, but even the wood with which the sacrificial fire was kindled, was sprinkled with salt. Salt symbolized to the Jews of that time the incorruptible and the higher. Thus, the soul was compared to the salt, and it was said concerning the dead: Shake off the salt, and throw the flesh to the dogs. The Bible was compared to salt; so was acuteness of intellect.

Lastly, the question: If the salt has lost its savor, with what will you season it? seems to have been proverbial, and occurs in exactly the same words in the Talmud, apparently to denote a thing that is impossible.

Most thoroughly anti-Pharisaic and anti-Rabbinic as all this was, what Matthew further reports leads still farther in the same direction. We seem to see Jesus still holding this child, and, with evident reference to the Jewish contempt for that which is small, point to him and apply, in quite another manner than they had ever heard, the Rabbinic teaching about the Angels. In the Jewish view, only the chief of the Angels were before the Face of God within the curtained Veil, or Pargod, while the others, ranged in different classes, stood outside and awaited his command. The distinction which the former enjoyed was always to see His Face, and to hear and know directly the Divine counsels and commands. This distinction was, therefore, one of knowledge; Christ taught that it was one of love. Not the more exalted in knowledge, and merit, or worth, but the simpler, the more unconscious of self, the more receptive and clinging, the nearer to God. Look up from earth to heaven; those representative, it may be, guardian, Angels nearest to God, are not those of deepest knowledge of God's counsel and commands, but those of simple, humble grace and faith, and so learn, not only not to despise one of these little ones, but who is truly greatest in the Kingdom of Heaven!

Viewed in this light, there is nothing incongruous in the transition: For the Son of Man has come to save that which was lost. This, His greatest condescension when He became the Babe of Bethlehem, is also His greatest exaltation. He Who is nearest the Father, and, in the most special and unique sense, always sees His Face, is He that became a Child, and, as the Son of Man, stoops lowest, to save that which was lost. The words are, regarded as spurious by most critics, because certain leading manuscripts omit them, and they are supposed to have been imported from Luke 19:10. But such a transference from a context wholly unconnected with this section seems unaccountable, while, on the other hand, the verse in question forms, not only an apt, but almost necessary, transition to the Parable of the Lost Sheep. It seems, therefore, difficult to eliminate it without also striking out that Parable; and yet it fits most beautifully into the whole context. Suffice it for the present to note this. The Parable itself is more fully repeated in another connection, in which it will be more convenient to consider it.

Yet a further depth of Christian love remained to be shown, which, all self forgetful, sought not its own, but the things of others. This also bore on the circumstances of the time, and the dispute between the disciples, but went far beyond it, and set forth eternal principles. To this point it had been a question of not seeking self, nor minding great things, but Christ-like and God-like, to condescend to the little ones. What if actual wrong had been done, and just offence given by a brother? In such case, also, the principle of the Kingdom, which, negatively, is that of self forgetfulness, positively, that of service of love, would first seek the good of the offending brother. We mark, here, the contrast to Rabbinism, which directs that the first overtures must be made by the offender, not the offended; and even prescribes this to be done in the presence of numerous witnesses, and, if needful, repeated three times. As regards the duty of showing to a brother his fault, and the delicate tenderness of doing this in private, so as not to put him to shame, Rabbinism speaks the same as the Master of Nazareth. In fact, according to Jewish criminal law, punishment could not be inflicted unless the offender (even the woman suspected of adultery) had previously been warned before witnesses. Yet, in practice, matters were very different: and neither could those be found who would take admonition, nor yet such as were worthy to administer it.

Quite other was it in the Kingdom of Christ, where the theory was left undefined, but the practice clearly marked. Here, by loving dealing, to convince of his wrong, him who had done it, was not humiliation nor loss of dignity or of right, but real gain: the gain of our brother to us, and eventually to Christ Himself. But even if this should fail, the offended must not discontinue his service of love, but adjoin in it others with himself so as to give weight and authority to his complaints, as not being the outcome of personal feeling or prejudice, perhaps, also, to be witnesses before the Divine tribunal. If this failed, a final appeal should be made on the part of the Church as a whole, which could only be done through her representatives and rulers, to whom Divine authority had been committed. And if that were rejected, the offer of love would, as always in the Gospel, pass into danger of judgment. Not, that such was to be executed by man, but that such an offender, after the first and second admonition, was to be rejected. He was to be treated as was the custom in regard to a pagan or a publican, not persecuted, despised, or avoided, but not received in Church fellowship (a pagan), nor admitted to close familiar association (a publican). And this, as we understand it, marks out the mode of what is called Church discipline in general, and specifically as regards wrongs done to a brother. Discipline so exercised (which may God restore to us) has the highest Divine sanction, and the most earnest reality attaches to it. For, in virtue of the authority which Christ has committed to the Church in the persons of her rulers and representatives, what they bound or loosed, declared obligatory or non-obligatory, was ratified in heaven. Nor was this to be wondered at. The incarnation of Christ was the link which bound earth to heaven: through it whatever was agreed upon in the fellowship of Christ, as that which was to be asked, would be done for them of his Father Which was in heaven. Thus, the power of the Church reached up to heaven through the power of prayer in His Name Who made God our Father. And so, beyond the exercise of discipline and authority, there was the omnipotence of prayer—if two of you shall agree . . . as touching anything . . . it shall be done for them, and, with it, also the infinite possibility of a higher service of love. For, in the smallest gathering in the Name of Christ, His Presence would be, and with it the certainty of nearness to, and acceptance with, God.

It is bitterly disappointing that, after such teaching, even a Peter could, either immediately afterwards, or perhaps after he had had time to think it over, and apply it, come to the Master with the question, how often he was to forgive an offending brother, imagining that he had more than satisfied the new requirements, if he extended it to seven times. Such traits show better than elaborate discussions the need of the mission and the renewing of the Holy Spirit. And yet there is something touching in the simplicity and honesty with which Peter goes to the Master with such a misapprehension of His teaching, as if he had fully entered into its spirit. Surely, the new wine was bursting the old bottles. It was a principle of Rabbinism that, even if the wrongdoer had made full restoration, he would not obtain forgiveness until he had asked it of him whom he had wronged, but that it was cruelty in such circumstances to refuse pardon. The Jerusalem Talmud adds the beautiful remark: Let this be a token in your hand, each time that you show mercy, God will show mercy on you; and if you do not show mercy, neither will God show mercy on you. And yet it was a settled rule, that forgiveness should not be extended more than three times. Even so, the practice was terribly different. The Talmud relates, without blame, the conduct of a Rabbi, who would not forgive a very small slight of his dignity, though asked by the offender for thirteen successive years, and that on the Day of Atonement, the reason being, that the offended Rabbi had learned by a dream that his offending brother would attain the highest dignity, whereupon he pretended himself irreconcilable, to force the other to migrate from Palestine to Babylon, where, unenvied by him, he might occupy the chief place!

And so it must have seemed to Peter, in his ignorance, quite a stretch of charity to extend forgiveness to seven, instead of three offences. It did not occur to him, that the very act of numbering offences marked an externalism which had never entered into, nor comprehended the spirit of Christ. Until seven times? No, until seventy times seven! The evident purpose of these words was to destroy all such landmarks. Peter had yet to learn, what we, unfortunately too often forget: that as Christ's forgiveness, so too that of the Christian, must not be computed by numbers. It is qualitative, not quantitative: Christ forgives sin, not sins, and he who has experienced it, follows in His footsteps.

End Notes:

[5]   The expression in Matthew abode, but a temporary stay—a going to (15:22) does not imply permanent abode, but a temporary stay, a going to and fro.

[6]   According to Nehemiah 10:32, immediately after the return from Babylon the contribution was a third of a shekel, probably on account of the poverty of the people.

[7]   In Succ. 30 a, we read a parable of a king who paid toll, and being asked the reason, replied that travelers were to learn by his example not to seek to withdraw themselves from paying all dues.

[8]   It is both curious and interesting to find that the question, whether the Priests exercised their functions as the sent of God or the sent of the congregation, that is, held their commission directly from God, or only as being the representatives of the people, is discussed already in the Talmud (Yoma 18 b & c.; Nedar. 35 b). The Talmud replies that, as it is impossible to delegate what one does not possess, and since the laity might neither offer sacrifices nor do any like service, the Priests could not possibly have been the delegates of the Church, but must be those of God. (See the essay by Delitzsch in the Zeitschr. fur Luther. Theol. for 1854, pp. 446-449.)

[9]   The Mishnah (Ab. 3:2), and the Talmud (Ber. 6 a), infer from Malachi 3:16, that, when two are together and occupy themselves with the Law, the Shechinah is between them. Similarly, it is argued from Lamentations 3:28, and Exodus 20:21, that if even one alone is engaged in such pursuits, God is with him and will bless him.

Chapter 4

The Journey to Jerusalem

(John 5:1-16; Luke 9:1-56; 57-62; Matthew 8:19-22)

The part in the Evangelic History which we have now reached has this peculiarity and difficulty, that the events are now recorded by only one of the Evangelists. The section in Luke from 9:51 to 16:14 stands absolutely alone. From the circumstance that Luke omits throughout his narrative all notation of time or place, the difficulty of arranging here the chronological succession of events is so great, that we can only suggest what seems most probable, without feeling certain of the details. Happily, the period embraced is a short one, while at the same time the narrative of Luke remarkably fits into that of John. John mentions three appearances of Christ in Jerusalem at that period: at the Feast of Tabernacles, at that of the Dedication, and His final entry, which is referred to by all the other Evangelists. But, while the narrative of John confines itself exclusively to what happened in Jerusalem or its immediate neighborhood, it also either mentions or gives sufficient indication that on two out of these three occasions Jesus left Jerusalem for the country east of the Jordan (John 10:19-21; John 10:39-43, where the words in ver. 39, they sought again to take Him, point to a previous similar attempt and flight). Besides these, John also records a journey to Bethany, though not to Jerusalem, for the raising of Lazarus, and after that a council against Christ in Jerusalem, in consequence of which He withdrew out of Judean territory into a district near the wilderness, as we infer, that in the north, where John had been baptizing and Christ been tempted, and where He had afterwards withdrawn. We regard this wilderness as on the western bank of the Jordan, and extending northward towards the eastern shore of the Lake of Galilee.

If John relates three appearances of Jesus at this time in Jerusalem, Luke records three journeys to Jerusalem, the last of which agrees, in regard to its starting point, with the notices of the other Evangelists, always supposing that we have correctly indicated the locality of the wilderness where, according to John 10:54, Christ retired previous to His last journey to Jerusalem. In this respect, although it is impossible with our present information to localize the City of Ephraim, the statement that it was near the wilderness, affords us sufficient general notice of its situation. For, the New Testament speaks of only two wilderness, that of Judea in the far South, and that in the far North of Perea, or perhaps in the Decapolis, to which Luke refers as the scene of the Baptist's labors, where Jesus was tempted, and where He afterwards withdrew. We can, therefore, have little doubt that John refers to this district. And this entirely accords with the notices by the other Evangelists of Christ's last journey to Jerusalem, as through the borders of Galilee and Samaria, and then across the Jordan, and by Bethany to Jerusalem.

It follows (as previously stated) that Luke's account of the three journeys to Jerusalem fits into the narrative of Christ's three appearances in Jerusalem as described by John. And the unique section in Luke supplies the record of what took place before, during, and after those journeys, of which the upshot is told by John. This much seems certain; the exact chronological succession must be, in part, matter of suggestion. But we have now some insight into the plan of Luke's Gospel, as compared with that of the others. We see that Luke forms a kind of transition, is a sort of connecting link between the other two Synoptists and John. This is admitted even by negative critics. The Gospel by Matthew has for its main object the discourses or teaching of the Lord, around which the History groups itself. It is intended as a demonstration, primarily addressed to the Jews, and in a form peculiarly suited to them, that Jesus was the Messiah, the Son of the Living God. The Gospel by Mark is a rapid survey of the History of the Christ as such. It deals mainly with the Galilean Ministry. The Gospel by John, which gives the highest, the reflective, view of the Eternal Son as the Word, deals almost exclusively with the Jerusalem Ministry. And the Gospel by Luke complements the narratives in the other two Gospels (Matthew and Mark), and it supplements them by tracing, what is not done otherwise: the Ministry in Perea. Thus, it also forms a transition to the Fourth Gospel of the Judean Ministry. If we may venture a step further:

The Gospel by Mark gives the general view of the Christ; that by Matthew the Jewish, that by Luke the Gentile, and that by John the Church's view. Imagination might, go still further, and see the impress of the number five, that of the Pentateuch and the Book of Psalms—in the First Gospel; the numeral four (that of the world) in the Second Gospel (4x4=16 chapters); that of three in the Third (8x3=24 chapters); and that of seven, the sacred Church number, in the Fourth Gospel (7x3=21 chapters). And perhaps we might even succeed in arranging the Gospels into corresponding sections. But this would lead, not only beyond our present task, but from solid history and exegesis into the regions of speculation.

The subject, then, primarily before us, is the journeying of Jesus to Jerusalem. In that wider view which Luke takes of this whole history, he presents what really were three separate journeys as one, that towards the great end. In its conscious aim and object, all—from the moment of His finally leaving Galilee to His final Entry into Jerusalem, formed, in the highest sense, only one journey And this Luke designates in a peculiar manner. Just as he had spoken, not of Christ's death but of His Exodus, or outgoing, which included His Resurrection and Ascension, so he now tells us that, when the days of His up taking, including and pointing to His Ascension, were being fulfilled, He also firmly set His Face to go to Jerusalem.

John, goes farther back, and speaks of the circumstances which preceded His journey to Jerusalem. There is an interval, or, as we might term it, a blank, of more than half a year between the last narrative in the Fourth Gospel and this. For, the events chronicled in the sixth chapter of John's Gospel took place immediately before the Passover, which was on the fifteenth day of the first ecclesiastical month (Nisan), while the Feast of Tabernacle began on the same day of the seventh ecclesiastical month (Tishri). But, except in regard to the beginning of Christ's Ministry, that sixth chapter is the only one in the Gospel of John which refers to the Galilean Ministry of Christ. We would suggest, that what it records is partly intended to exhibit, by the side of Christ's fully developed teaching, the fully developed hostility of the Jerusalem Scribes, which led even to the defection of many former disciples. Thus, chapter 6: would be a connecting link (both as regards the teaching of Christ and the opposition to Him) between chapter 5, which tells of His visit at the Unknown Feast, and chapter 7, which records that at the Feast of Tabernacles. The six or seven months between the Feast of Passover and that of Tabernacles, and all that passed within them, are covered by this brief remark: After these things

Jesus traveled in Galilee: for He would not travel in Judea, because the Jews [the leaders of the people] sought to kill Him.

But now the Feast of Tabernacles was at hand. The pilgrims would probably arrive in Jerusalem before the opening day of the Festival. For, besides the needful preparations, which would require time, especially on this Feast, when booths had to be constructed in which to live during the festive week, it was (as we remember) the common practice to offer such sacrifices as might have previously become due at any of the great Feasts to which the people might go up. Remembering that five months had elapsed since the last great Feast (that of Weeks), many such sacrifices must have been due. Accordingly, the ordinary festive companies of pilgrims, which would travel slowly, must have started from Galilee some time before the beginning of the Feast. These circumstances fully explain the details of the narrative. They also afford another most painful illustration of the loneliness of Christ in His Work. His disciples had failed to understand, they misapprehended His teaching. In the near prospect of His death they either displayed gross ignorance, or else disputed about their future rank. And His own brothers did not believe in Him. The whole course of late events, especially the unmet challenge of the Scribes for a sign from heaven, had deeply shaken them. What was the purpose of works, if done in the privacy of the circle of Christ's Apostles, in a house, a remote district, or even before an ignorant multitude? If, claiming to be the Messiah, He wished to be openly known as such, He must use other means. If He really did these things, let Him show Himself before the world, in Jerusalem, the capital of their world, and before those who could test the reality of His Works. Let Him come forward, at one of Israel's great Feasts, in the Temple, and especially at this Feast which pointed to the Messianic ingathering of all nations. Let Him now go up with them in the festive company into Judea, that so His disciples, not the Galileans only, but all, might have the opportunity of gazing on His Works.

As the challenge was not new, so, from the worldly point of view, it can hardly be called unreasonable. It is, in fact, the same in principle as that to which the world would now submit the claims of Christianity to men's acceptance. It has only this one fault, that it ignores the world's hostility to the Christ. Discipleship is not the result of any outward manifestation by evidences or demonstration. It requires the conversion of a child-like spirit. To manifest Himself! This truly would He do, though not in their way. For this the season had not yet come, though it would soon arrive. Their season, that for such Messianic manifestations as they contemplated—was always ready. And this naturally, for the world could not hate them; they and their demonstrations were quite in accordance with the world and its views. But towards Him the world cherished personal hatred, because of their contrariety of principle, because Christ was manifested, not to restore an earthly kingdom to Israel, but to bring the Heavenly Kingdom upon earth, to destroy the works of the Devil. Therefore, He must provoke the hostility of that world which lay in the Wicked One. Another manifestation than that which they sought would He make, when His season was fulfilled; soon, beginning at this very Feast, continued at the next, and completed at the last Passover; such manifestation of Himself as the Christ, as could alone be made in view of the essential hostility of the world.

And so He let them go up in the festive company, while Himself waited. When the noise and publicity (which He wished to avoid) were no longer in mind, He also went up, but privately, not publicly, as they had suggested. Here Luke's account begins. It almost reads like a commentary on what Jesus had just said to His brethren, about the hostility of the world, and His mode of manifestation, who would not, and who would receive Him, and why. He came to His own, and His own did not receive Him. But as many as received Him, to them gave He power to become children of God . . . which were born . . . of God.

The first purpose of Christ seems to have been to take the more direct road to Jerusalem, through Samaria, and not to follow that of the festive pilgrim bands, which traveled to Jerusalem through Perea, in order to avoid the band of their hated rivals. But His intention was soon frustrated. In the very first Samaritan village to which the Christ had sent beforehand to prepare for Himself and His company, His messengers were told that the Rabbi could not be received; that neither hospitality nor friendly treatment could be extended to One Who was going up to the Feast at Jerusalem. The messengers who brought back this strangely un-Oriental answer met the Master and His followers on the road. It was not only an outrage on common manners, but an act of open hostility to Israel, as well as to Christ, and the Son's of Thunder, whose feelings for their Master were, perhaps, the more deeply stirred as opposition to Him grew more fierce, proposed to vindicate the cause, of Israel and its Messiah King, by the open and Divine judgment of fire called down from heaven to destroy that village. Did they in this connection think of the vision of Elijah, ministering to Christ on the Mount of Transfiguration, and was this their application of it? Truly, they did not know of what Spirit they were to be the children and messengers. He Who had come, not to destroy, but to save, turned

and rebuked them, and passed from Samaritan into Jewish territory to
pursue His journey. Perhaps, He had only passed into Samaria to teach His
disciples this needful lesson. The view of this event just presented seems
confirmed by the circumstance, that Matthew lays the scene immediately
following on the other side, that is, in the Decapolis.

It was a journey of deepest interest and importance. For, it was decisive
not only as regarded the Master, but those who followed Him. From here
on it must not be, as in former times, but wholly and exclusively, as into
suffering and death. It is thus that we view the next three incidents of the
way. Two of them find, also, a place in the Gospel by Matthew, although in
a different connection, in accordance with the plan of that Gospel, which
groups together the Teaching of Christ, with but secondary attention to
chronological succession.

It seems that, as, after the rebuff of these Samaritans, they were going
towards another, and a Jewish village, one of the company, and, as we
learn from Matthew, a Scribe, in the generous enthusiasm of the moment,
perhaps, stimulated by the wrong of the Samaritans, perhaps, touched by
the love which would rebuke the zeal of the disciples, but had no word of
blame for the unkindness of others, broke into a spontaneous declaration of
readiness to follow Him absolutely and everywhere. Like the benediction of
the woman who heard Him, it was one of these outbursts of an enthusiasm
which His Presence awakened in every susceptible heart. But there was one
eventuality which that Scribe, and all of like enthusiasm, did not reckoned
with, the utter homelessness of the Christ in this world, and this, not from
accidental circumstances, but because He was the Son of Man. And there
is here also material for still deeper thought in the fact that this man was a
Scribe, and yet had not gone up to the Feast, but waited near Christ, was
one of those that followed Him now, and was capable of such feelings!
How many whom we regard as Scribes, may be in analogous relation to
the Christ, and yet how much of fair promise has failed to ripen into reality
in view of the homelessness of Christ and Christianity in this world, the
stranger ship of suffering which it involves to those who would follow, not
somewhere, but absolutely, and everywhere?

The intenseness of the self denial involved in following Christ, and its
opposition to all that was commonly received among men, was, purposely,
immediately further brought out. This Scribe had offered to follow Jesus.
Another of his disciples He asked to follow Him, and that in peculiar
circumstances and difficulty. The expression to follow a Teacher would, in
those days be universally understood as implying discipleship. Again, no

other duty would be regarded as more sacred than that they, on whom the obligation naturally entrusted, should bury the dead. To this everything must give way, even prayer, and the study of the Law. Lastly, we feel morally certain, that, when Christ called this disciple to follow Him, He was fully aware that at that very moment his father lay dead. Thus, He called him not only to homelessness, for this he might have been prepared, but to set aside what natural feeling and the Jewish Law seemed to impose on him as the most sacred duty. In the seemingly strange reply, which Christ made to the request to be allowed first to bury his father, we pass over the consideration that, according to Jewish law, the burial and mourning for a dead father, and the subsequent purifications, would have occupied many days, so that it might have been difficult, perhaps impossible, to overtake Christ. We would rather stand by the simple words of Christ. They teach us this very solemn and searching lesson, that there are higher duties than either those of the Jewish Law, or even of natural reverence, and a higher call than that of man. No doubt Christ had here in view the near call to the Seventy, of whom this disciple was to be one, to go and preach the Kingdom of God. When the direct call of Christ to any work comes, that is, if we are sure of it from His own words, and not (as, unfortunately too often we do) only infer it by our own reasoning on His words, then every other call must give way. For, duties can never be in conflict, and this duty about the living and life must take precedence of that about death and the dead. Nor must we hesitate, because we do not know in what form this work for Christ may come. There are critical moments in our inner history, when to postpone the immediate call, is really to reject it; when to go and bury the dead, even though it was a dead father, were to die ourselves!

Yet another hindrance to following Christ was to be faced. Another in the company that followed Christ would go with Him, but he asked permission first to go and bid farewell to those whom he had left in his home. It almost seems as if this request had been one of those tempting questions, addressed to Christ. But, even if otherwise, the farewell proposed was not like that of Elisha, nor like the supper of Levi Matthew. It was rather like the year which Jephtha's daughter would have with her companions, before fulfilling the vow. It shows, that to follow Christ was regarded as a duty, and to leave those in the earthly home as a trial; and it betokens, not merely a divided heart, but one not fit for the Kingdom of God. For, how can he draw a straight furrow in which to cast the seed, who, as he puts his hand to the plough, looks around or behind him?

Thus, these are the three vital conditions of following Christ: absolute self denial and homelessness in the world; immediate and entire self surrender to Christ and His Work, and a heart and affections simple, undivided, and set on Christ and His Work, to which there is no other trial of parting like that which would involve parting from Him, no other or higher joy than that of following Him. In such spirit let them now go after Christ in His last journey, and to such work as He will appoint them!

End Notes:

[10]   According to Babha K. 113 a, regular festive lectures commenced in the Academies thirty days before each of the great Feasts. Those who attended them were called Beney Rigla, in distinction to the Beney Khallah, who attended the regular Sabbath lectures.

[11]   Godet infers from the word secretly, that the journey of Luke 9:51 could not have been that referred to by John. But the qualified expression, as it were in secret, conveys to my mind only a contrast to the public pilgrim bands, in which it was the custom to travel to the Feasts, a publicity, which His brethren especially desired at this time. Besides, the in secret of John might refer not so much to the journey as to the appearance of Christ at the Feast: comp. John 5:11, 14.

[12]   It does not necessarily follow, that the company at starting was a large one. But they would have no host nor quarters ready to receive them in Samaria. Therefore the dispatch of messengers.

[13]   We mark, that the designation Son of Man is here for the first time applied to Christ by Matthew. May this history have been inserted in the First Gospel in that particular connection for the purpose of pointing out this contrast in the treatment of the Son of Man by the sons of men, as if to say: Learn the meaning of the representative title: Son of Man, in a world of men who would not receive Him? It is the more marked, that it immediately precedes the first application on the part of men of the title Son of God to Christ in this Gospel (Matthew 5:29).

Chapter 5

The Mission of the Seventy and at Bethany

(Luke 10:1-16; Matthew 9:36-38; 10:20-24; Luke 10:17-24; Matthew 10:25-30; 13:16; Luke 10:25; 38-42.)

Although, for the reasons explained in the previous chapter, the exact succession of events cannot be absolutely determined, it seems most likely, that it was on His progress southwards at this time that Jesus designated those seventy others, who were to announce His arrival in every town and village. Even the circumstance, that the instructions to them are so similar to, and yet distinct from, those formerly given to the Twelve, seems to point to them as those from whom the Seventy are to be distinguished as other. We judge, that they were sent forth at this time, first, from the Gospel of Luke, where this whole section appears as a distinct and separate record, presumably, chronologically arranged; secondly, from the fitness of such a mission at that particular period, when Jesus made His last Missionary progress towards Jerusalem; and, thirdly, from the unlikelihood, if not impossibility, of taking such a public step after the persecution which broke out after His appearance at Jerusalem on the Feast of Tabernacles. At any rate, it could not have taken place later than in the period between the Feast of Tabernacles and that of the Dedication of the Temple, since, after that, Jesus no longer walked openly among the Jews.

With all their similarity, there are notable differences between the Mission of the Twelve and this of the other Seventy. The former is recorded by the three Evangelists, so that there could have been no confusion on the part of Luke. But the mission of the Twelve was at the time of their appointment to the Apostolate; it was evangelistic and missionary; and it was in confirmation and manifestation of the power and authority given to them. We regard it, therefore, as symbolical of the Apostolate just instituted, with its work and authority. On the other hand, no power or authority was formally conferred on the Seventy, their mission being only temporary, and, for one definite purpose; its primary object was to prepare for the coming of the Master in the places to which they were sent; and their selection was from the wider circle of disciples, the number being now Seventy instead of Twelve. Even these two numbers, as well as the difference in the functions of the two classes of messengers, seem to indicate that the Twelve symbolized the princes of the tribes of Israel, while the Seventy were the symbolical representatives of these tribes, like the seventy elders appointed to assist Moses. This symbolical meaning of the number Seventy continued among the Jews. We can trace it in the LXX (supposed) translators of the Bible into Greek, and in the seventy members of the Sanhedrin, or supreme court.

There was something very significant in this appearance of Christ's messengers, by two and two, in every place He was about to visit. As John the Baptist had, at the first, heralded the Coming of Christ, so now two heralds appeared to solemnly announce His Advent at the close of His Ministry; as John had sought, as the representative of the Old Testament Church, to prepare His Way, so they, as the representatives of the New Testament Church. In both cases the preparation sought was a moral one. It was the national summons to open the gates to the rightful King, and accept His rule. Only, the need was now the greater for the failure of John's mission, through the misunderstanding and disbelief of the nation. This conjunction with John the Baptist and the failure of his mission, as regarded national results, accounts for the insertion in Matthew's Gospel of part of the address delivered on the Mission of the Seventy, immediately after the record of Christ's rebuke of the national rejection of the Baptist. For Matthew, who (as well as Mark) does not record the Mission of the Seventy, simply because (as before explained) the whole section, of which it forms part, is peculiar to Luke's Gospel, reports the discourses connected with it in other, and to them appropriate, connections.

We mark, that, what may be termed the Preface to the Mission of the Seventy, is given by Matthew (in a somewhat fuller form) as that to the appointment and mission of the Twelve Apostles; and it may have been, that similar words had preceded both. Partially, the expressions reported in Luke 10:2 had been employed long before. Those multitudes throughout Israel those also which are not of that flock, appeared to His view like sheep without a true shepherd's care, distressed and prostrate, and their mute misery and only partly conscious longing appealed, and not in vain, to His Divine compassion. This constituted the ultimate ground of the Mission of the Apostles, and now of the Seventy, into a harvest that was truly great. Compared with the extent of the field, and the urgency of the work, how few were the laborers! Yet, as the field was God's, so also could He alone thrust forth laborers willing and able to do His work, while it must be ours to pray that He would be pleased to do so.

On these introductory words, which ever since have formed the inviting prayer of the Church in her work for Christ, followed the commission and special directions to the thirty five pairs of disciples who went on this task force. In almost every particular they are the same as those formerly given to the Twelve. We mark, however, that both the introductory and the concluding words addressed to the Apostles are lacking in what was said to the Seventy. It was not necessary to warn them against going to the Samaritans, since the direction of the Seventy was to those cities of Perea and Judea, on the road to Jerusalem, through which Christ was about to pass. Nor were they armed with precisely the same supernatural powers as the Twelve. Naturally, the personal directions as to their conduct were in both cases substantially the same. We mark only three peculiarities in those addressed to the Seventy. The direction to salute no man by the way was suitable to a temporary and rapid mission, which might have been sadly interrupted by making or renewing acquaintances. Both the Mishnah and the Talmud lay it down, that prayer was not to be interrupted to salute even a king to uncoil a serpent that had wound round the foot. On the other hand, the Rabbis discussed the question, whether the reading of the Shema and of the portion of the Psalms called the Hallel might be interrupted at the close of a paragraph, from respect for a person, or interrupted in the middle, from motives of fear. All agreed, that immediately before prayer no one should be saluted, to prevent distraction, and it was advised rather to summarize or to cut short than to break into prayer, though the latter might be admissible in case of absolute necessity. None of these provisions, however, seems to have been in the mind of Christ. If any parallel is to be sought, it would be found in the similar direction of Elisha to Gehazi, when sent to lay the prophets staff on the dead child of the Shunammite.

The other two peculiarities in the address to the Seventy seem verbal rather than real. The expression, if the Son of Peace is there, is a Hebraism, equivalent to if the house is worthy, and refers to the character of the head of the house and the tone of the household. Lastly, the direction to eat and drink such things as were set before them is only a further explanation of the command to stay in the house which had received them, without seeking for better entertainment. On the other hand, the whole most important close of the address to the Twelve, which, forms by far the largest part of it, is lacking in the commission to the Seventy, thus clearly marking its merely temporary character.

In Luke's Gospel, the address to the Seventy is followed by a denunciation of Chorazin and Bethsaida. This is evidently in its right place there, after the Ministry of Christ in Galilee had been completed and finally rejected. In Matthew's Gospel, it stands (for a reason already indicated) immediately after Jesus' rebuke of the popular rejection of the Baptist's message. The judgment pronounced on those cities, in which most of His mighty works were done, is in proportion to the greatness of their privileges. The denunciation of Chorazin and Bethsaida is the more remarkable, that Chorazin is not otherwise mentioned in the Gospels, nor yet any miracles recorded as having taken place in (the western) Bethsaida. From this two inferences seem inevitable. First, this history must be real. If the whole were legendary, Jesus would not be represented as selecting the names of places, which the writer had not connected with the legend. Again, apparently no record has been preserved in the Gospels of most of Christ's miracles, only those being narrated which were necessary in order to present Jesus as the Christ, in accordance with the respective plans on which each of the Gospels was constructed.

As already stated, the denunciations were in proportion to the privileges, and therefore to the guilt, of the unbelieving cities. Chorazin and Bethsaida are compared with Tyre and Sidon, which under similar admonitions would have repented, while Capernaum, which, as for so long the home of Jesus, had truly been exalted to heaven, is compared with Sodom. And such guilt involved greater punishment. The very site of Bethsaida and Chorazin cannot be fixed with certainty. The former probably represents the Fisherton of Capernaum, the latter seems to have almost disappeared from the shore of the Lake. Jerome places it two miles from Capernaum. If so, it may be represented by the modern Kerazeh, somewhat to the northwest of Capernaum. The site would correspond with the name. For Kerazeh is at present a spring with an insignificant ruin above it, and the name Chorazin may well be derived from Keroz a water jar, Cherozin, or Chorazin, the water jars. If so, we can readily understand that the Fisherton on the south side of Capernaum, and the well known springs, Chorazin, on the other side of it, may have been the frequent scene of Christ's miracles. This explains also, in part, why the miracles there performed had not been told as well as those done in Capernaum itself. In the Talmud a Chorazin, or rather Chorzim, is mentioned as celebrated for its wheat. But as for Capernaum itself, standing on that vast field of ruins and upturned stones which marks the site of the modern Tell Hum, we feel that no description of it could be more pictorially true than that in which Christ prophetically likened the city in its downfall to the desolateness of death and Hades.

Whether or not the Seventy actually returned to Jesus before the Feast of Tabernacles, it is convenient to consider in this connection the result of their Mission. It had filled them with the joy of assurance; the result had exceeded their expectations, just as their faith had gone beyond the mere letter to the spirit of His Words. As they reported it to Him, even the demons had been subject to them through His Name. In this they had exceeded the letter of Christ's commission; but as they made experiment of it, their faith had grown, and they had applied His command to heal the sick to the worst of all sufferers, those grievously vexed by demons. And, as always, their faith was not disappointed. Nor could it be otherwise. The great contest had been long decided; it only remained for the faith of the Church to gather the fruits of that victory. The Prince of Light and Life had vanquished the Prince of Darkness and death. The Prince of this world must be thrown out. In spirit, Christ gazed on Satan fallen as lightning from heaven. As one has aptly paraphrased it: While you throw out his subjects, I saw the prince himself fall. It has been asked, whether the words of Christ referred to any particular event, such as His Victory in the Temptation. But any such limitation would imply grievous misunderstanding of the whole. So to speak, the fall of Satan is to the bottomless pit; ever going on to the final triumph of Christ. As the Lord sees him, he is fallen from heaven, from the seat of power and of worship; for, his mastery is broken by One Stronger than he. And he is fallen like lightning, in its rapidity, dazzling splendor, and destructiveness. Yet as we perceive it, it is only demons thrown out in His Name. For still is this fight and sight continued, and to all ages of the present dispensation. Each time the faith of the Church throws out demons, whether as formerly, or as they now vex men, whether in the lighter combat about possession of the body, or in the greater fight about possession of the soul, as Christ sees it, it is ever Satan fallen. For, he sees of the travail of His soul, and is satisfied. And so also is there joy in heaven over every sinner that repents.

The authority and power over the demons, attained by faith, was not to pass away with the occasion that had called it forth. There were Seventy representatives of the Church in her work of preparing for the Advent of Christ. As already indicated, the sight of Satan fallen from heaven is the continuous history of the Church. What the faith of the Seventy had attained was now to be made permanent to the Church, whose representatives they were. For, the words in which Christ now gave authority and power to tread on serpents and scorpions, and over all the power of the Enemy, and the promise that nothing should hurt them, could not have been addressed to the Seventy for a Mission which had now come to an end, except in so far as they represented the Church Universal. It is almost needless to add, that those serpents and scorpions are not to be literally but symbolically understood. Yet it is not this power or authority which is to be the main joy either of the Church or the individual, but the fact that our names are written in heaven. And so Christ brings us back to His great teaching about the need of becoming children, and wherein lies the secret of true greatness in the Kingdom.

It is beautifully in the spirit of all this, when we read that the joy of the disciples was met by that of the Master, and that His teaching now merged into a prayer of thanksgiving. Throughout the occurrences since the Transfiguration, we have noticed an increasing antithesis to the teaching of the Rabbis. But it almost reached its climax in the thanksgiving, that the Father in heaven had hid these things from the wise and the understanding, and revealed them to babes. As we view it in the light of those times, we know that the wise and understanding, the Rabbi and the Scribe, could not, from their standpoint, have perceived them; that it is matter of never ending thanks that, not what they, but what the babes, understood, was, as alone it could be, the subject of the Heavenly Father's revelation. We even tremble to think how it would have fared with the babes, if the wise and understanding had had part with them in the knowledge revealed. And so it must ever be, not only the Law of the kingdom and the fundamental principle of Divine Revelation, but matter for thanksgiving, that, not as wise and understanding, but only as babes, as converted, like children, we can share in that knowledge which makes wise to salvation. And this truly is the Gospel, and the Father's good pleasure.

The words, with which Christ turned from this address to the Seventy and thanksgiving to God, seem almost like the Father's answer to the prayer of the Son. They refer to, and explain, the authority which Jesus had bestowed on His Church: All things were delivered to Me of My Father;

and they afford the highest rationale for the fact, that these things had been hid from the wise and revealed to babes. For, as no man, only the Father, could have full knowledge of the Son, and, conversely, no man, only the Son, had true knowledge of the Father, it followed, that this knowledge came to us, not of Wisdom or learning, but only through the Revelation of Christ: No one knows Who the Son is, except the Father; and Who the Father is, except the Son, and he to whom ever the Son wills to reveal Him.

Matthew, who also records this, although in a different connection, immediately after the denunciation of the unbelief of Chorazin, Bethsaida, and Capernaum, concludes this section by words which have ever since been the grand text of those who following in the wake of the Seventy, have been ambassadors for Christ. On the other hand, Luke concludes this part of his narrative by adducing words equally agreeable to the occasion, which, are not new in the mouth of Jesus. From their suitableness to what had preceded, we can have little doubt that both that which Matthew, and that which Luke, report was spoken on this occasion. Because knowledge of the Father came only through the Son, and because these things were hidden from the wise and revealed to babes, did the gracious Lord open His Arms so wide, and called all that labored and were heavy laden come to Him. These were the sheep, distressed and prostrate, whom to gather, that He might give them rest, He had sent forth the Seventy on a work, for which He had prayed the Father to thrust forth laborers, and which He has since entrusted to the faith and service of love of the Church. And the true wisdom, which qualified for the Kingdom, was to take up His yoke, which would be found easy, and a lightsome burden, not like that unbearable yoke of Rabbinic conditions; and the true understanding to be sought, was by learning of Him. In that wisdom of entering the Kingdom by taking up its yoke, and in that knowledge which came by learning of Him, Christ was Himself the true lesson and the best Teacher for those babes. For He is meek and lowly in heart. He had done what He taught, and He taught what He had done; and so, by coming to Him, would true rest be found for the soul.

These words, as recorded by Matthew, the Evangelist of the Jews, must have sunk the deeper into the hearts of Christ's Jewish hearers, that they came in their own old familiar form of speech, yet with such contrast of spirit. One of the most common figurative expressions of the time was that of the yoke, to indicate submission to an occupation or obligation. Thus, we read not only of the yoke of the Law, but of that to earthly governments, and ordinary civil obligations. Very instructive for the understanding of the figure is this paraphrase of Song of Solomon 1:10: How beautiful is their neck for bearing the yoke of Your statues; and it shall be upon them like the yoke on the neck of the ox that ploughs in the field, and provides food for himself and his master. This yoke might be thrown off, as the ten tribes had thrown off that of God, and thus brought on themselves their exile. On the other hand, to take upon oneself the yoke meant to submit to it of free choice and deliberate resolution. Thus, in the allegorism of the Midrash, in the inscription, Proverbs 30:1, concerning Agur, the son of Jakeh—which is viewed as a symbolical designation of Solomon, the word Massa, rendered in the KJV prophecy, is thus explained in reference to Solomon: Massa, because he lifted on himself (Nasa) the yoke of the Holy One, blessed is He. And of Isaiah it was said, that he had been privileged to prophesy of so many blessings, because he had taken upon himself the yoke of the Kingdom of Heaven with joy. And, as previously stated, it was set forth that in the Shema, or Creed, which was repeated every day, the words, Deuteronomy 6:4-9, were recited before those in 10:13-21, so as first generally to take upon ourselves the yoke of the Kingdom of Heaven, and only afterwards that of the commandments. And this yoke all Israel had taken upon itself, thereby gaining the merit ever afterwards attributed to them.

Yet, practically, the yoke of the Kingdom was none other than that of the Law and of the commandments; one of laborious performances and of impossible self righteousness. It was unbearable, not the easy and light yoke of Christ, in which the Kingdom of God was of faith, not of works. And, as if themselves to bear witness to this, we have this saying of theirs, terribly significant in this connection: Not like those formerly (the first), who made for themselves the yoke of the Law easy and light; but like those after them (those afterwards), who made the yoke of the Law upon them heavy! And, this voluntary making of the yoke as heavy as possible, the taking on themselves as many obligations as possible, was the ideal of Rabbinic piety. There was, therefore, peculiar teaching and comfort in the words of Christ; and well might He add, as Luke reports, that blessed were they who saw and heard these things. For, that Messianic Kingdom, which had been the object of enthralled vision and earnest longing to prophets and kings of old had now become reality.

As plentiful as this history is in contrasts, it seems not unlikely, that the scene next recorded by Luke stands in its right place. Such an inquiry on the part of a certain lawyer, as to what he should do to inherit eternal life, together with Christ's parabolic teaching about the Good Samaritan, is evidently in agreement to the previous teaching of Christ about entering into the Kingdom of Heaven. Possibly, this Scribe may have understood the words of Jesus about these things being hid from the wise, and the need of taking up the yoke of the Kingdom, as enforcing the views of those Rabbinic teachers, who laid more stress upon good works than upon study. Perhaps himself belonged to that minority, although his question was intended to tempt, to try whether Jesus would stand the Rabbinic test, morally and dialectically. And, without at present entering on the Parable which gives Christ's final answer (and which will best be considered together with the others belonging to that period), it will be seen how peculiarly suited it was to the state of mind just supposed.

From this interruption, which, but for the teaching of Christ connected with it, would have formed a terrible dispute in the heavenly harmony of this journey, we turn to another scene. It follows in the course of Luke's narrative, and we have no reason to consider it out of its proper place. If so, it must mark the close of Christ's journey to the Feast of Tabernacles, since the home of Martha and Mary, to which it introduces us, was in Bethany, close to Jerusalem, almost one of its suburbs. Other indications, confirmatory of this note of time, are not lacking. Thus, the history which follows that of the home of Bethany, when one of His disciples asks Him to teach them to pray, as the Baptist had similarly taught his followers, seems to indicate, that they were then on the scene of John's former labors, northeast of Bethany; and, therefore, that it occurred on Christ's return from Jerusalem. Again, from the narrative of Christ's reception in the house of Martha, we gather that Jesus had arrived in Bethany with His disciples, but that He alone was the guest of the two sisters. We infer that Christ had dismissed His disciples to go into the neighboring City for the Feast, while Himself waited in Bethany. Lastly, with all this agrees the notice in John 5:14, that it was not at the beginning, but about the midst of the feast, that Jesus went up into the Temple. Although traveling on the two first festive days was not actually unlawful, yet we can hardly conceive that Jesus would have done so, especially on the Feast of Tabernacles; and the inference is obvious, that Jesus had waited in the immediate neighborhood, as we know He did at Bethany in the house of Martha and Mary.

Other things, also, do so explain themselves, notably, the absence of the brother of Martha and Mary, who probably spent the festive days in the City itself. It was the beginning of the Feast of Tabernacles, and the scene recorded by Luke would take place in the open leafy booth which served as the sitting apartment during the festive week. For, according to law, it was duty during the festive week to eat, sleep, pray, study, in short, to live, in these booths, which were to be constructed of the boughs of living trees. And, although this was not absolutely obligatory on women, yet, the rule which called all make the booth the principal, and the house only the secondary dwelling, would induce them to make this leafy tent at least the sitting apartment for men and women. And, those autumn days were just the season when it would be joy to sit in these delightful cool retreats, the memorials of Israel's pilgrim days! They were high enough, and yet not too high; chiefly open in front; close enough to be shady, and yet not so close as to exclude sunlight and air. Such would be the apartment in which what is recorded passed; and, if we add that this booth stood probably in the court, we can picture to ourselves Martha moving forwards and backwards on her busy errands, and seeing, as she passed again and again, Mary still sitting a absorbed listener, not pay attention to what passed around; and, lastly, how the elder sister could, as the language of verse 40 implies, enter so suddenly Jesus' Presence, bringing her complaint.

To understand this history, we must dismiss from our minds preconceived, though, perhaps, attractive thoughts. There is no evidence that the household of Bethany had previously belonged to the circle of Christ's professed disciples. It was, as the whole history shows, a wealthy home. It consisted of two sisters, the elder, Martha (a not uncommon Jewish name, being the feminine of Mar, and equivalent to our word mistress); the younger, Mary; and their brother Lazarus, or, Laazar. Although we do not know how it came, yet, evidently, the house was Martha's, and into it she received Jesus on His arrival in Bethany. It would have been no uncommon occurrence in Israel for a pious, wealthy lady to receive a great Rabbi into her house. But the present was not an ordinary case. Martha must have heard of Him, even if she had not seen Him. But, the whole narrative implies, that Jesus had come to Bethany with the view of accepting the hospitality of Martha, which probably had been offered when some of those Seventy, sojourning in the worthiest house at Bethany, had announced the near arrival of Jesus. Still, her bearing affords only indication of being drawn towards Christ—at most, of a sincere desire to learn the good news, not of actual discipleship.

And so Jesus came, and, with Him and in Him, heaven's own Light and Peace. He was to lodge in one of the booths, the sisters in the house, and the great booth in the middle of the courtyard would be the common living apartment of all. It could not have been long after His arrival, it must have been almost immediately, that the sisters felt they had received more than an Angel unawares. How best to do Him honor, was equally the thought of both. To Martha it seemed, as if she could not do enough in showing Him all hospitality. And, this festive season was a busy time for the mistress of a wealthy household, especially in the near neighborhood of Jerusalem, from which her brother might, after the first two festive days, bring with him, any time that week, honored guests from the City. To these cares was now added that of doing sufficient honor to such a Guest, for she, also, deeply felt His greatness. And so she hurried to and fro through the courtyard, literally, distracted about much serving.

Her younger sister, also, would do Him all highest honor; but, not as Martha. Her homage consisted in forgetting all else but Him, Who spoke as none had ever done. As truest courtesy or affection consists, nor in its demonstrations, but in being so absorbed in the object of it as to forget its demonstration, so with Mary in the Presence of Christ. And then a new Light, another Day had risen upon her; a fresh life had sprung up within her soul: She sat at Jesus' Feet, and heard his Word. We dare not inquire, and yet we well know, of what it would be. And so, time after time, perhaps, hour after hour, as Martha passed on her busy way, she still sat listening and living. At last, the sister who, in her impatience, could not think that a woman could, in such manner, fulfill her duty, or show forth her religious profiting, broke in with what sounds like a irritable complaint: Lord, do You not care that my sister left me to serve alone? Mary had served with her, but she had now left her to do the work alone. Would Jesus direct her to resume her neglected work? But, with tone of gentle reproof and admonition, the affectionateness of which appeared even in the repetition of her name, Martha, Martha, as, similarly, on a later occasion, Simon, Simon, did He teach her in words which, however simple in their primary meaning, are so full, that they have ever since borne the most many sided application: You are careful and anxious about many things; but one thing is needful; and Mary has chosen that good part, which shall not be taken away from her.

It was, as we imagine, perhaps the first day of, or else the preparation for, the Feast. More than that one day did Jesus wait in the home of Bethany. Whether Lazarus came then to see Him, and, still more, what both Martha and Mary learned, either then, or afterwards, we reverently refrain to search into. Suffice it, that though the natural disposition of the sisters remained what it had been, yet from then on, Jesus loved Martha and her sister.

End Notes:

[14]   In Bemidb. R. 15, ed. Warsh. p. 64 b, the mode of electing these Seventy is thus described. Moses chose six from every tribe, and then put into an urn seventy two lots, of which seventy had the word Zaqen (Elder) inscribed on them, while two were blanks. The latter are supposed to have been drawn by Eldad and Medad.

[15]   Martha occurs, however, also as a male name (in the Aramaic).

[16]   The name Laazar, or Lazar, occurs frequently in Talmudic writings as an abbreviated form of Elazar or Eleazar.

Chapter 6

At The Feast of Tabernacles

(John 5:11-36)

It was Chol ha Moed, as the non-sacred part of the festive week, the half holy days were called. Jerusalem, the City of Solemnities, the City of Palaces, the City of beauty and glory, wore quite another than its usual aspect; other, even, than when its streets were thronged by festive pilgrims during the Passover week, or at Pentecost. For this was pre-eminently the Feast for foreign pilgrims, coming from the farthest distance, whose Temple contributions were then received and counted. Despite the strange costumes of Media, Arabia, Persia, or India, and even further; or the Western speech and bearing of the pilgrims from Italy, Spain, the modern Crimea, and the banks of the Danube, if not from yet more strange and barbarous lands, it would not be difficult to recognize the characteristics of the Jew, nor to perceive that to change one's climate was not to change one's mind. As the Jerusalemite would look with proud self consciousness, not unmingled with kindly patronage, on the common strangers, yet fellow countrymen, or the eager eyed Galilean curiously stare after them, the pilgrims would, in turn, gaze with mingled awe and wonderment on the novel scene. Here was the realization of their fondest dreams ever since childhood, the home and spring of their holiest thoughts and best hopes, that which gave inward victory to the vanquished, and converted persecution into anticipated triumph.

They could come at this season of the year, not during the winter for the Passover, nor yet quite so readily in summer's heat for Pentecost. But now, in the delicious cool of early autumn, when all harvest operations, the gathering in of luscious fruit and the vintage were past, and the first streaks of gold were tinting the foliage, strangers from far off, and countrymen from Judea, Perea, and Galilee, would mingle in the streets of Jerusalem, under the ever present shadow of that glorious Sanctuary of marble, cedar wood, and gold, up there on high Moriah, symbol of the infinitely more glorious overshadowing Presence of Him, Who was the Holy One in the midst of Israel. How all day long, even until the stars lit up the deep blue canopy over head, the smoke of the burning, smoldering sacrifices rose in slowly widening column, and hung between the Mount of Olives and Zion; how the chant of Levites, and the solemn responses of the Hallel were borne on the breeze, or the clear blast of the Priest's silver trumpets seemed to awaken the echoes far away! And then, at night, how all these vast Temple buildings stood out, illuminated by the great Candelabras that burned in the Court of the Women, and by the glare of torches, when strange sound of mystic hymns and dances came floating over the intervening darkness! Truly, well might Israel designate the Feast of Tabernacles as the Feast (ha Chag), and the Jewish historian describe it as the holiest and greatest.

Early on the 14th Tishri (corresponding to our September or early October), all the festive pilgrims had arrived. Then it was, a scene of bustle and activity. Hospitality had to be sought and found; guests to be welcomed and entertained; all things required for the feast to be got ready. Above all, booths must be erected everywhere, in court and on housetop, in street and square, for the lodgment and entertainment of that vast multitude; leafy dwellings everywhere, to remind of the wilderness journey, and now of the goodly land. Only that fierce castle, Antonia, which frowned above the Temple, was undecked by the festive spring into which the land had burst. To the Jew it must have been a hateful sight, that castle, which guarded and dominated his own City and Temple, hateful sight and sounds, that Roman garrison, with its foreign, pagan, vulgar speech and manners. Yet, for all this, Israel could not read on the lowering sky the signs of the times, nor yet knew the day of their merciful visitation. And this, although of all festivals, that of Tabernacles should have most clearly pointed them to the future.

The whole symbolism of the Feast, beginning with the completed harvest, for which it was a thanksgiving, pointed to the future. The Rabbis themselves admitted this. The strange number of sacrificial bullocks, seventy in all, they regarded as referring to the seventy nations of pagandom. The ceremony of the outpouring of water, which was considered of such vital importance as to give to the whole festival the name of House of Outpouring, was symbolical of the outpouring of the Holy Spirit. As the brief night of the great Temple illumination closed, there was solemn testimony made before Jehovah against paganism. It must have been a stirring scene, when from out of the mass of Levites, with their musical instruments, who crowded the fifteen steps that led from the Court of Israel to that of the Women, stepped two priests with their silver trumpets. As the first rooster crowing announced the dawn of morning, they blew a threefold blast; another on the tenth step, and yet another threefold blast as they entered the Court of the Women. And still sounding their trumpets, they marched through the Court of the Women to the Beautiful Gate. Here, turning round and facing westwards to the Holy Place, they repeated: Our fathers, who were in this place, they turned their backs on the Sanctuary of Jehovah, and their faces eastward, for they worshipped eastward, the sun; but we, our eyes are towards Jehovah. We are Jehovah's, our eyes are towards Jehovah. The whole of this night and morning scene was symbolical: the Temple illumination, of the light which was to shine from out the Temple into the dark night of pagandom; then, at the first dawn of morn the blast of the priests silver trumpets, of the army of God, as it advanced, with festive trumpet sound and call, to awaken the sleepers, marching on to quite the farthest limits of the Sanctuary, to the Beautiful Gate, which opened upon the Court of the Gentiles, and, then again, facing round to utter solemn protest against paganism, and make solemn confession of Jehovah!

But Jesus did not appear in the Temple during the first two festive days. The pilgrims from all parts of the country, perhaps, they from abroad also, had expected Him there, foreveryone would now speak of Him, not openly, in Jerusalem, for they were afraid of their rulers. It was hardly safe to speak of Him without reserve. But they sought Him, and inquired after Him, and they did speak of Him, though there was only a murmuring, a low, confused discussion of the pros and cons, in this great controversy among the multitudes, or festive bands from various parts. Some said: He is a good man, while others declared that He only led astray the common, ignorant populace. And now, all at once, in Chol ha Moed, Jesus Himself appeared in the Temple, and taught. We know that, on a later occasion, He walked and taught in Solomon's Porch, and, from the circumstance that the early disciples made this their common meeting place, we may draw the inference that it was here the people now found Him. Although neither Josephus nor the Mishnah mention this Porch by name, we have every reason for believing that it was the eastern colonnade, which abutted against the Mount of Olives and faced the Beautiful Gate, that formed the principal entrance into the Court of the Women, and so into the Sanctuary. For, all along the inside of the great wall which formed the Temple enclosure ran a double colonnade, each column a monolith of white marble, 25 cubits high, covered with cedar beams. That on the south side (leading from the western entrance to Solomon's Porch), known as the Royal Porch, was a threefold colonnade, consisting of four rows of columns, each 27 cubits high, and surmounted by Corinthian capitals. We infer that the eastern was Solomon's Porch, from the circumstance that it was the only relic left of Solomon's Temple. These colonnades, which, from their ample space, formed places for a quiet walk and for larger gatherings, had benches in them, and, from the liberty of speaking and teaching in Israel, Jesus might here address the people in the very face of His enemies.

We do not know what the subject was of Christ's teaching on this occasion. But the effect on the people was one of general astonishment. They knew what common unlettered Galilean tradesmen were, but this, from where did it come? How does this one know literature (letters, learning), never having learned? To the Jews there was only one kind of learning, that of Theology; and only one road to it, the Schools of the Rabbis. Their major was true, but their minor false, and Jesus hurried to correct it. He had, learned, but in a School quite other than those which alone they recognized. Yet, on their own showing, it claimed the most absolute submission. Among the Jews a Rabbis teaching derived authority from the fact of its accordance with tradition, that it accurately represented what had been received from a previous great teacher, and so on upwards to Moses, and to God Himself. On this ground Christ claimed the highest authority. His doctrine was not His own invention, it was the teaching of Him that sent Him. The doctrine was God received, and Christ was sent direct from God to bring it. He was God's messenger of it to them. Of this twofold claim there was also twofold evidence. Did He assert that what He taught was God received? Let trial be made of it. Everyone who in his soul felt drawn towards God; each one who really wills to do His Will, would know concerning this teaching, whether it is of God, or whether it was of man. It was this felt, though unrealized influence which had drawn all men after Him, so that they hung on His lips. It was this which, in the hour of greatest temptation and mental difficulty, had led Peter, in name of the others, to end the great inner contest by laying hold on this fact: To whom shall we go? You have the words of eternal life, and we have believed and know, that You are the Holy One of God. Marking, as we pass, that this inward connection between that teaching and learning and the present occasion, may be the deeper reason why, in the Gospel by John, the one narrative is immediately followed by the other, we pause to say, how real it has proved in all ages and to all stages of Christian learning, that the heart makes the truly God taught (pectus facit Theologum), and that inward, true aspiration after the Divine prepares the eye to behold the Divine Reality in the Christ. But, if it be so is there not evidence here, that He is the God sent, that He is a real, true Ambassador of God? If Jesus' teaching meets and satisfies our moral nature, if it leads up to God, is He not the Christ?

And this brings us to the second claim which Christ made, that of being sent by God. There is yet another logical link in His reasoning. He had said: He shall know of the teaching, whether it is of God, or whether I speak from Myself. From Myself? Why, there is this other test of it: Who speaks from himself, seeks his own glory, there can be no doubt or question of this, but do I seek My own glory?, But He Who seeks the glory of Him Who sent Him, He is true (a faithful messenger), and unrighteousness is not in Him. Thus did Christ appeal and prove it: My doctrine is of God, and I am sent of God!

Sent of God, no unrighteousness in Him! And yet at that very moment there hung over Him the charge of defiance of the Law of Moses of that of God, in an open breach of the Sabbath commandment, there, in that very City, the last time He had been in Jerusalem; for which, as well as for His Divine claims, the Jews were even then seeking to kill Him. And this forms the transition to what may be called the second part of Christ's address. If, in the first part, the Jewish form of rationalization was already apparent, it seems almost impossible for anyone acquainted with those forms to understand how it can be overlooked in what follows. It is exactly the mode in which a Jew would argue with Jews, only the substance of the reasoning is to all times and people. Christ is defending Himself against a charge which naturally came up, when He claimed that His Teaching was of God and Himself God's real and faithful Messenger. In His reply the two threads of the former argument are taken up. Doing is the condition of knowledge, and a messenger had been sent from God! Admittedly, Moses was such, and yet everyone of them was breaking the Law which he had given them; for, were they not seeking to kill Him without right or justice? This, put in the form of a double question, represents a peculiarly Jewish mode of argumentation, behind which lay the terrible truth, that those, whose hearts were so little longing to do the Will of God, not only must remain ignorant of His Teaching as that of God, but had also rejected that of Moses.

A general disclaimer, a cry You have a demon (are possessed), who seeks to kill You? here broke in upon the Speaker. But He would not be interrupted, and continued: One work I did, and all you wonder on account of it, referring to His healing on the Sabbath, and their utter inability to understand His conduct. Well, then, Moses was a messenger of God, and I am sent of God. Moses gave the law of circumcision, not, that it was of his authority, but had long before been God given, and, to observe this law, no one hesitated to break the Sabbath, since, according to Rabbinic principle, a positive ordinance superseded a negative. And yet, when Christ, as sent from God, made a man every bit whole on the Sabbath (made a whole man sound) they were angry with Him! Every argument which might have been urged in favor of the postponement of Christ's healing to a week day, would equally apply to that of circumcision; while every reason that could be urged in favor of Sabbath circumcision, would tell a hundredfold in favor of the act of Christ. Oh, then, let them not judge after the mere outward appearance, but judge the right judgment. And, had it not been to convince them of the externalism of their views, that Jesus had on that Sabbath opened the great controversy between the letter that kills and the spirit that makes alive, when He directed the impotent man to carry home the bed on which he had reclined?

If any doubt could obtain, how truly Jesus had gauged the existing state of things, when He contrasted heart willingness to do the Will of God, as the necessary preparation for the reception of His God sent Teaching, with their murderous designs, springing from blind literalism and ignorance of the spirit of their Law, the reported remarks of some Jerusalemites in the crowd would suffice to convince us. The fact that He, Whom they sought to kill, was suffered to speak openly, seemed to them incomprehensible. Could it be that the authorities were shaken in their former idea about Him, and now regarded Him as the Messiah? But it could not be. It was a settled popular belief, and, in a sense, not quite unfounded, that the appearance of the Messiah would be sudden and unexpected. He might be there, and not be known; or He might come, and be again hidden for a time. As they put it, when Messiah came, no one would know from where He was; but they all knew from where this One was. And with this rough and ready argument of a coarse realism, they, like so many among us, settled off hand and once for all the great question. But Jesus could not, even for the sake of His poor weak disciples, let it rest there. Therefore He lifted up His voice, so that it reached the dispersing, receding multitude. Yes, they thought they knew both Him and from which He came. It would have been so had He come from Himself. But He had been sent, and He that sent Him was real; it was a real Mission, and Him, who had thus sent the Christ, they did not know. And so, with a reaffirmation of His twofold claim, His discourse closed. But they had understood His allusions, and in their anger would gladly have laid hands on Him, but His hour had not come. Yet others were deeply stirred to faith. As they parted they spoke of it among themselves, and the sum of it all was: The Christ, when He comes, will He do more miracles (signs) than this One did?

So ended the first teaching of that day in the Temple. And as the people dispersed, the leaders of the Pharisees, who, no doubt aware of the presence of Christ in the Temple, yet unwilling to be in the number of His hearers, had watched the effect of His Teaching, overheard the low, cautious, half outspoken remarks (the murmuring) of the people about Him. Now they conferred with the heads of the priesthood and the chief Temple officials. Although there was neither meeting, nor decree of the Sanhedrin about it, nor, could be, orders were given to the Temple guard on the first possible occasion to seize Him. Jesus was aware of it, and as, either on this or another day, He was moving in the Temple, watched by the spies of the rulers and followed by a mingled crowd of disciples and enemies, deep sadness in view of the end filled His heart. Jesus therefore said, no doubt to His disciples, though in the hearing of all, yet a little while am I with you, then I go away to Him that sent Me. You shall seek Me, and not find Me; and where I am, there you cannot come. Mournful words, these, which were only too soon to become true. But those who heard them naturally failed to comprehend their meaning. Was He about to leave Palestine, and go to the Diaspora of the Greeks, among the dispersed who lived in pagan lands, to teach the Greeks? Or what could be His meaning? But we, who hear it across these centuries, feel as if their question, like the suggestion of the High Priest at a later period, like so many suggestions of men, had been, all unconsciously, prophetic of the future.

End Notes:

[17] This was a well recognized Rabbinic principle. Comp. for example Shabb. 132 a, where the argument runs that, if circumcision, which applies to one of the 248 members, of which, according to the Rabbis, the human body consists, superseded the Sabbath, how much more the preservation of the whole body.

[18]   The word lethins has not an exact English equivalent, scarcely a Germa
       one (wahrhaftig ?). It is a favorite word of John's, who uses it eight times
       in his Gospel, or, if the Revised reading 8:16 be adopted, nine times (1:9;
       4:23, 37; 6:32; 5:28; 8:16 ?; 15:1; 15:3; 19:35); and four times in his
       First Epistle (2:8, and three times in ch. 5:20). Its Johannine meaning is
       perhaps best seen when in combination with leths (for example, 1 John
       2:8). But in the Book of Revelation, where it occurs ten times (3:7, 14;
       6:10; 15:3; 15:7; 19:2, 9, 11; 20:5; 22:6), it has another meaning, and
       can scarcely be distinguished from our English true. It is used, in the same
       sense as in John's Gospel and Epistle, in Luke 15:11, in 1 Thessalonians
       1:9; and three times in the Epistle to the Hebrews (8:2; 9:24; 10:22).
       We may, therefore, regard it as a word to which a Grecian, not a Judean
       meaning attaches. In our view it refers to the true as the real, and the real
       as that which has become outwardly true. I do not quite understand, and,
       so far as I understand it, I do not agree with, the view of Cremer (Bibl.
       Theol. L Exodus, Engl. ed. p. 85), that lethins is related to leths as form
       to contents or substance. The distinction between the Judean and the
       Grecian meaning is not only borne out by the Book of Revelation (which
       uses it in the Judean sense), but by Ecclus. 42:2, 11. In the LXX it stands
       for not fewer than twelve Hebrew words.

[19]   Only those unacquainted with the judicial procedure of the Sanhedrin
       could imagine that there had been a regular meeting and decree of that
       tribunal. That would have required a formal accusation, witnesses,
       examination, etc.

Chapter 7

The Great Day of the Feast

(John 5:37, 8:11)

It was the last, the great day of the Feast, and Jesus was once more in the Temple. We can scarcely doubt that it was the concluding day of the Feast, and not, as most modern writers suppose, its Octave (eighth), which, in Rabbinic language, was regarded as a festival by itself. But such solemn interest attaches to the Feast, and this occurrence on its last day, that we must try to realize the scene. We have here the only Old Testament type yet unfulfilled; the only Jewish festival which has no counterpart in the cycle of the Christian year, just because it points forward to that great, yet unfulfilled hope of the Church: the ingathering of Earth's nations to the Christ.

The celebration of the Feast corresponded to its great meaning. Not only did all the priestly families minister during that week, but it has been calculated that not fewer than 446 Priests, with a corresponding number of Levites, were required for its sacrificial worship. In general, the services were the same every day, except that the number of bullocks offered decreased daily from thirteen on the first, to seven on the seventh day. Only during the first two, and on the last festive day (as also on the Octave of the Feast), was strict Sabbatic rest required. On the intervening half holidays (Chol ha Moed), although no new labor was to be undertaken, unless in the public service, the ordinary and necessary labors of the home and of life were carried on, and especially all done that was required for the festive season. But the last, the Great Day of the Feast, was marked by special observances.

Let us suppose ourselves in the number of worshippers, who on the last, the Great Day of the Feast, are leaving their booths at daybreak to take part in the service. The pilgrims are all in festive array. In his right hand each carries what is called the Lulabh, which, although properly meaning a branch, or palm branch, consisted of a myrtle and willow branch tied together with a palm branch between them. This was supposed to be in fulfillment of the command, Leviticus 23:40. The fruit (KJV boughs) of the goodly trees, mentioned in the same verse of Scripture, was supposed to be the Ethrog, the so called Paradise apple (according to Ber. R. 15, the fruit of the forbidden tree), a species of citron. This Ethrog each worshipper carries in his left hand. It is scarcely necessary to add, that this interpretation of Leviticus 23:40 was given by the Rabbis; perhaps more interesting to know, that this was one of the points in controversy between the Pharisees and Sadducees.

Thus armed with Lulabh in their right, and Ethrog in their left hands, the festive multitude would divide into three bands. Some would remain in the Temple to attend the preparation of the Morning Sacrifice. Another band would go in procession below Jerusalem to a place called Moza, the Kolonia of the Jerusalem Talmud, which some have sought to identify with the Emmaus of the Resurrection Evening. At Moza they cut down willow branches, with which, amid the blasts of the Priests trumpets, they adorned the altar, forming a leafy canopy about it. Yet a third company were taking part in a still more interesting service. To the sound of music a procession started from the Temple. It followed a Priest who carried a golden pitcher, capable of holding three log. Onwards it passed, probably, through Ophel, which recent investigations have shown to have been covered with buildings to the very verge of Siloam, down the edge of the Tyropeon Valley, where it merges into that of the Kedron. To this day terraces mark where the gardens, watered by the living spring, extended from the Kings Gardens by the spring Rogel down to the entrance into the Tyropeon. Here was the so called Fountain Gate, and still within the City wall the Pool of Siloam, the overflow of which fed a lower pool. As already stated it was at the merging of the Tyropeon into the Kedron Valley, in the southeastern angle of Jerusalem. The Pool of Siloam was fed by the living spring farther up in the narrowest part of the Kedron Valley, which now bears the name of the Virgins Fountain, but represents the ancient En Rogel and Gihon. The very canal which led from the one to the other, with the inscription of the workmen upon it, has lately been excavated. Though chiefly of historical interest, a sentence may be added. The Pool of Siloam is the same as the

Kings Pool of Nehemiah 2:14. It was made by King Hezekiah, in order both to divert from a sieging army the spring of Gihon, which could not be brought within the City wall, and yet to bring its waters within the City. This explains the origin of the name Siloam, sent, a conduit, or Siloah, as Josephus calls it. Lastly, we remember that it was down in the valley at Gihon (or En Rogel), that Solomon was proclaimed, while the opposite faction held revel, and would have made Adonijah king, on the cliff Zoheleth (the modern Zahweileh) right over against it, not a hundred yards distant, where they must have distinctly heard the sound of the trumpets and the shouts of the people as Solomon was proclaimed king.

But to return. When the Temple procession had reached the Pool of Siloam, the Priest filled his golden pitcher from its waters. Then they went back to the Temple, so timing it, that they should arrive just as they were laying the pieces of the sacrifice on the great Altar of Burnt offering, towards the close of the ordinary Morning Sacrifice service. A threefold blast of the Priests trumpets welcomed the arrival of the Priest, as he entered through the Water gate, which obtained its name from this ceremony, and passed straight into the Court of the Priests. Here he was joined by another Priest, who carried the wine for the drink offering. The two Priests ascended the rise of the altar, and turned to the left. There were two silver funnels here, with narrow openings, leading down to the base of the altar. Into that at the east, which was somewhat wider, the wine was poured, and, at the same time, the water into the western and narrower opening, the people shouting to the Priest to raise his hand, so as to make sure that he poured the water into the funnel. For, although it was held, that the water pouring was an ordinance instituted by Moses, a Halakhah of Moses from Sinai, this was another of the points disputed by the Sadducees. And, to give practical effect to their views, the High Priest Alexander Jannaeus had on one occasion poured the water on the ground, when he was nearly murdered, and in the riot, that ensued, six thousand persons were killed in the Temple.

Immediately after the pouring of water, the great Hallel, consisting of Psalms 113 to 116 (inclusive), was chanted antiphonally, or rather, with responses, to the accompaniment of the flute. As the Levites intoned the first line of each Psalm, the people repeated it; while to each of the other lines they responded by Hallelu Yah (Praise you the Lord). But in Psalm 116 the people not only repeated the first line, O give thanks to the Lord, but also these, O then, work now salvation, Jehovah, O Lord, send now prosperity; and again, at the close of the Psalm, O give thanks to the Lord.

As they repeated these lines, they shook towards the altar the Lulabh which they held in their hands, as if with this token of the past to express the reality and cause of their praise, and to remind God of His promises. It is this moment which should be chiefly kept in view.

The festive morning service was followed by the offering of the special sacrifices for the day, with their drink offerings, and by the Psalm for the day, which, on the last, the Great Day of the Feast, was Psalm 82 from verse 5. The Psalm was chanted, as always, to instrumental accompaniment, and at the end of each of its three sections the Priests blew a threefold blast, while the people bowed down in worship. In further symbolism of this Feast, as pointing to the ingathering of the pagan nations, the public services closed with a procession around the Altar by the Priests, who chanted O then, work now salvation, Jehovah! O Jehovah, send now prosperity. But on the last, the Great Day of the Feast, this procession of Priests made the circuit of the altar, not only once, but seven times, as if they were again compassing, but now with prayer, the Gentile

Jericho which barred their possession of the promised land. Therefore the seventh or last day of the Feast was also called that of the Great Hosannah. As the people left the Temple, they saluted the altar with words of thanks, and on the last day of the Feast they shook off the leaves on the willow branches round the altar, and beat their palm branches to pieces. On the same afternoon the booths were dismantled, and the Feast ended.

We can have little difficulty in determining at what part of the services of the last, the Great Day of the Feast, Jesus stood and cried, If anyone thirst, let Him come to Me and drink! It must have been with special reference to the ceremony of the outpouring of the water, which, as we have seen, was considered the central part of the service. Moreover, all would understand that His words must refer to the Holy Spirit, since the rite was universally regarded as symbolical of His outpouring. The pouring forth of the water was immediately followed by the chanting of the Hallel. But after that there must have been a short pause to prepare for the festive sacrifices (the Musaph). It was then, immediately after the symbolic rite of water pouring, immediately after the people had responded by repeating those lines from Psalm 116: given thanks, and prayed that Jehovah would send salvation and prosperity, and had shaken their Lulabh towards the altar, thus praising with heart, and mouth, and hands, and then silence had fallen upon them, that there rose, so loud as to be heard throughout the Temple, the Voice of Jesus. He did not interupt the services, for they had for the moment ceased: He interpreted, and He fulfilled them.

Whether we realize it in connection with the deeply stirring rites just concluded, and the song of praise that had scarcely died out of the air; or think of it as a vast step in advance in the history of Christ's Manifestation, the scene is equally wondrous. But yesterday they had been divided about Him, and the authorities had given directions to take Him; today He is not only in the Temple, but, at the close of the most solemn rites of the Feast, asserting, within the hearing of all, His claim to be regarded as the fulfillment of all, and the true Messiah! And yet there is neither harshness of command nor violence of threat in His proclamation. It is the King, meek, gentle, and loving; the Messiah, Who will not break the bruised reed, Who will not lift up His Voice in tone of anger, but speak in accents of loving, condescending compassion, Who now invites, who ever is thirsty, come to Him and drink. And so the words have for all time remained the call of Christ to all that are thirsty, from what ever their need and longing of soul may be. But, as we listen to these words as originally spoken, we feel how they mark that Christ's hour was indeed coming: the preparation past; the manifestation in the present, unmistakable, urgent, and loving; and the final conflict at hand.

Of those who had heard Him, none but must have understood that, if the invitation were indeed real, and Christ the fulfillment of all, then the promise also had its deepest meaning, that he who believed on Him would not only receive the promised fullness of the Spirit, but give it to the fertilizing of the barren waste around. It was, truly, the fulfillment of the Scripture promise, not of one but of all: that in Messianic times the Nabhi, prophet, literally the weller forth, namely, of the Divine, should not be one or another select individual, but that He would pour out on all His handmaidens and servants of His Holy Spirit, and thus the moral wilderness of this world is changed into a fruitful garden. This is expressly stated in the Targum which thus paraphrases Isaiah 44:3: Look, as the waters are poured on arid ground and spread over the dry soil, so will I give the Spirit of My Holiness on your sons, and My blessing on your children's children. What was new to them was, that all this was treasured up in the Christ, that out of His fullness men might receive, and grace for grace. And yet even this was not quite new. For, was it not the fulfillment of that old prophetic cry: The Spirit of the Lord Jehovah is upon Me: therefore has He Messiahed (anointed) Me to preach good news to the poor? So then, it was nothing new, only the happy fulfillment of the old, when He thus spoke of the Holy Spirit, which they who believed on Him should receive, not then, but upon His Messianic exaltation.

And so we scarcely wonder that many, on hearing Him, said, though not with that heart conviction which would have led to self surrender, that He was the Prophet promised of old, even the Christ, while others, by their side, regarding Him as a Galilean, the Son of Joseph, raised the ignorant objection that He could not be the Messiah, since the latter must be of the seed of David and come from Bethlehem. Such was the anger of some against what they regarded a dangerous seducer of the poor people, that they would gladly have laid violent hands on Him. But amid all this, the strongest testimony to His Person and Mission remains to be told. It came, as so often, from a quarter from which it could least have been expected. Those Temple officers, whom the authorities had commissioned to watch for an opportunity for seizing Jesus, came back without having done their job, and that, when, manifestly, the scene in the Temple might have offered the desired ground for His imprisonment. To the question of the Pharisees, they could only give this reply, which has ever since remained unquestionable fact of history, admitted by friend and foe: Never has man spoken as this man. For, as all spiritual longing and all upward tending, not only of men but even of systems, consciously or unconsciously tends towards Christ, so can we measure and judge all systems by this, which no sober student of history will argue with, that no man or system ever so spoke.

It was not this which the Pharisees now argued with, but rather the obvious, and, we may add, logical, inference from it. The scene which followed is so thoroughly Jewish, that it alone would suffice to prove the Jewish, and therefore Johannine, authorship of the Fourth Gospel. The harsh sneer: Are you also led astray? is succeeded by pointing to the authority of the learned and great, who with one accord were rejecting Jesus. But this people, the country people (Am ha arez), the ignorant, unlettered rabble, are cursed. Sufficient has been shown in previous parts of this book to explain the Pharisaic claim of authority and their almost unutterable contempt of the unlettered. So far did the latter go, that it would refuse, not only all family connection and friendly interaction, but even the bread of charity, to the unlettered; that, in theory at least, it would have regarded their murder as no sin, and even cut them off from the hope of the Resurrection. But is it not true, that, even in our days, this double sneer, rather than argument, of the Pharisees is the main reason of the disbelief of so many: Which of the learned believe on Him? but the ignorant multitude are led by superstition to ruin.

There was one standing among the Temple authorities, whom an uneasy conscience would not allow to remain quite silent. It was the Sanhedrist

Nicodemus, still a night disciple, even in brightest noon light. He could not hold his peace, and yet he dared not speak for Christ. So he made compromise of both by taking the part of, and speaking as, a righteous, rigid Sanhedrist. Does our Law judge (pronounce sentence upon) a man, except it first hear from himself and know what he does? From the Rabbinic point of view, no sounder judicial saying could have been uttered. Yet such common places impose not on anyone, nor even serve any good purpose. It did not help the cause of Jesus, and it did not disguise the advocacy of Nicodemus. We know what was thought of Galilee in the Rabbinic world. Are you also of Galilee? Search and see, for out of Galilee arises no prophet.

And so ended this incident, which, to all concerned, might have been so fruitful of good. Once more Nicodemus was left alone, as everyone who had dared and yet not dared for Christ is after all such bootless compromises; alone, with great heart, stricken conscience, and a great longing.

End Notes:

[20]   The benediction said at the beginning of every Feast is not only said on the first of that of Tabernacles, but also on the octave of it (Sukk. 48 a). The sacrifices for that occasion were quite different from those for Tabernacles; the booths were removed; and the peculiar rites of the Feast of Tabernacles no longer observed. This is distinctly stated in Sukk. 4:1, and the diverging opinion of R. Jehudah on this and another point is formally rejected in Tos. Sukk. 3:16. For the six points of difference between the Feast of Tabernacles and its Octave, see end note of ch. 8.

[21]   The reader will observe, that the narrative of the woman taken in adultery, as also the previous verse (John 5:53-8:11) have been left out in this History, although with great reluctance. By this it is not intended to characterize that section as Apocryphal, nor indeed to pronounce any opinion as to the reality of some such occurrence. For, it contains much which we instinctively feel to be like the Master, both in what Christ is represented as saying and as doing. All that we reluctantly feel bound to maintain is, that the narrative in its present form did not exist in the Gospel of John, and, could not have existed. For a summary of the external evidence against the Johannine authorship of the passage, I would refer to Canon Westcotts Note, ad loc., in the Speakers Commentary. But there is also internal evidence, and, to my mind at least, most rational, against its authenticity, at any rate, in its present form. From first to last it is

utterly un-Jewish. Accordingly, unbiased critics who are conversant either with Jewish legal procedure, or with the habits and views of the people at the time, would feel obliged to reject it, even if the external evidence had been as strong in its favor as it is for its rejection. Archdeacon Farrar has, devoted to the illustration of this narrative some of his most pictorial pages. But, with all his ability and eloquence, his references to Jewish law and observances are not such as to satisfy the requirements of criticism. To this general objection to their correctness I must add a protest against the views which he presents of the moral state of Jewish society at the time. On the other hand, from whatever point we view this narrative, the accusers, the witnesses, the public examination, the bringing of the woman to Jesus, or the punishment claimed—it presents insuperable difficulties. That a woman taken in the act of adultery should have been brought before Jesus (and apparently without the witnesses to her crime); that such an utterly un-Jewish, as well as illegal, procedure should have been that of the Scribes and Pharisees; that such a breach of law, and of what Judaism would regard as decency, should have been perpetrated to tempt Him; or that the Scribes should have been so ignorant as to substitute stoning for strangulation, as the punishment of adultery; lastly, that this scene should have been enacted in the Temple, presents a veritable climax of impossibilities. I can only express surprise that Archdeacon Farrar should have suggested that the Feast of Tabernacles had grown into a kind of vintage festival, which would often degenerate into acts of license and immorality, or that the lives of the religious leaders of Israel were often stained with such sins. The first statement is quite ungrounded; and as for the second, I do not recall a single instance in which a charge of adultery is brought against a Rabbi of that period. The quotations in Sepps Leben Jesu (vol. v. p. 183), which Archdeacon Farrar adduces, are not to cases in point, however much, from the Christian point of view, we may reprobate the conduct of the Rabbis there mentioned.

Chapter 8

Teaching in the Temple

(John 8:12-59)

The startling teaching on the last, the Great Day of the Feast was not the only one delivered at that season. The impression left on the mind is, that after silencing, as they thought, Nicodemus, the leaders of the Pharisees had dispersed. The addresses of Jesus which followed must, therefore, have been delivered, either later on that day, or, what on every account seems more likely, chiefly, or all, on the next day, which was the Octave of the Feast, when the Temple would be once more crowded by worshippers.

On this occasion we find Christ, first in the Treasury, and then in some unnamed part of the sacred building, in all probabilities one of the Porches. Greater freedom could be here enjoyed, since these Porches, which enclosed the Court of the Gentiles, did not form part of the Sanctuary in the stricter sense. Discussions might take place, in which not, as in the Treasury, only the Pharisees, but the people generally, might offer questions, answer, or assent. Again, as regards the requirements of the present narrative, since the Porches opened upon the Court, the Jews might there pick up stones to throw at Him (which would have been impossible in any part of the Sanctuary itself), while lastly, Jesus might easily pass out of the Temple in the crowd that moved through the Porches to the outer gates.

But the narrative first transports us into the Treasury, where the Pharisees, or leaders, would alone venture to speak. It ought to be especially marked, that if they laid not hands on Jesus when He dared to teach in this sacred locality, and that such unwelcome doctrine, His immunity must be ascribed to the higher appointment of God: because His hour had not yet come. An archaeological question may here be raised as to the exact localization of the Treasury, whether it was the colonnade around the Court of the Women, in which the receptacles for charitable contributions, the so called Shopharoth, or trumpets, were placed, or one of the two chambers in which, respectively, secret gifts and votive offerings were deposited. The former seems the most likely. In any case, it would be within the Court of the Women, the common meeting place of the worshippers, and, as we may say, the most generally attended part of the Sanctuary. Here, in the hearing of the leaders of the people, took place the first dialogue between Christ and the Pharisees.

It opened with what probably was an allusion to one of the great ceremonies of the Feast of Tabernacles, to its symbolic meaning, and to an express Messianic expectation of the Rabbis. As the Mishnah states: On the first, or, as the Talmud would have it, on every night of the festive week, the Court of the Women was brilliantly illuminated, and the night spent in the demonstrations already described. This was called the joy of the feast. This festive joy, of which the origin is obscure, was no doubt connected with the hope of earth's great harvest joy in the conversion of the pagan world, and so pointed to the days of the Messiah. In connection with this we mark, that the term light was especially applied to the Messiah. In a very interesting passage of the Midrash we are told, that, while commonly windows were made wide within and narrow without, it was the opposite in the Temple of Solomon, because the light issuing from the Sanctuary was to illumine that which was without. This reminds us of the language of devout old Simeon in regard to the Messiah, as a light to illumine the Gentiles, and the glory of His people Israel. The Midrash further explains, that, if the light in the Sanctuary was to be always burning before Jehovah, the reason was, not that He needed such light, but that He honored Israel with this as a symbolic command. In Messianic times God would, in fulfillment of the prophetic meaning of this rite, kindle for them the Great Light, and the nations of the world would point to them, who had lit the light for Him Who illumined the whole world. But even this is not all. The Rabbis speak of the original light in which God had wrapped Himself as in a garment, and which could not shine by day, because it would have dimmed the light of the sun. From this light that of the sun, moon, and stars had been kindled. It was now reserved under the throne of God for the Messiah, in Whose days it would shine forth once more. Lastly, we ought to refer to a passage in another Midrash, where, after a remarkable discussion on such names of the Messiah as the Lord our Righteousness, the Branch, the Comforter, Shiloh, Compassion, His Birth is connected with the destruction, and His return with the restoration of the Temple. But in that very passage the Messiah is also especially designated as the Enlightener, the words: the light dwells with Him, being applied to Him.

What has just been stated shows, that the Messianic hope of the aged Simeon most truly expressed the Messianic thoughts of the time. It also proves, that the Pharisees could not have mistaken the Messianic meaning in the words of Jesus, in their reference to the past festivity: I am the Light of the world. This circumstance is itself evidential as regards this discourse of Christ, the truth of this narrative, and even the Jewish authorship of the Fourth Gospel. But, the whole address, the argumentation with the Pharisees which follows, as well as the subsequent discourse to, and argumentation with, the Jews, are peculiarly Jewish in their form of reasoning. Substantially, these discourses are a continuation of those previously delivered at this Feast. But they carry the argument one important step both backwards and forwards. The situation had now become quite clear, and neither party cared to conceal it. What Jesus had gradually communicated to the disciples, who were so unwilling to receive it, had now become an acknowledged fact. It was no longer a secret that the leaders of Israel and Jerusalem were compassing the death of Jesus. This underlies all His Words. And He sought to turn them from their purpose, not by appealing to their pity nor to any lower motive, but by claiming as His right that, for which they would condemn Him. He was the Sent of God, the Messiah; although, to know Him and His Mission, it needed moral kinship with Him that had sent Him. But this led to the very root of the matter. It needed moral kinship with God: did Israel, as such, possess it? They did not; no man possessed it, until given him of God. This was not exactly new in these discourses of Christ, but it was now far more clearly stated and developed, and in that sense new.

We also are too apt to overlook this teaching of Christ, perhaps have overlooked it. It is concerning the corruption of our whole nature by sin, and therefore the need of God teaching, if we are to receive the Christ, or understand His doctrine. That which is born of the flesh is flesh; that which is born of the Spirit is Spirit; wherefore, do not marvel that I said, You must be born again. That had been Christ's initial teaching to Nicodemus, and it became, with growing emphasis, His final teaching to the teachers of Israel. It is not Paul who first sets forth the doctrine of our entire moral ruin: he had learned it from the Christ. It forms the very basis of Christianity; it is the ultimate reason of the need of a Redeemer, and the rationale of the work which Christ came to do. The Priesthood and the Sacrificial Work of Christ, as well as the higher aspect of His Prophetic Office, and the true meaning of His Kingship, as not of this world, are based upon it. Very markedly, it constitutes the starting point in the fundamental divergence between the leaders of the Synagogue and Christ, we might say, for all time between Christians and non-Christians. The teachers of Israel did not know, nor believed in the total corruption of man, Jew as well as Gentile, and, therefore, felt not the need of a Savior. They could not understand it, how Except a man, at least a Jew, were born again, and, from above, he could not enter, nor even see, the Kingdom of God. They did not understand their own Bible: the story of the Fall, not Moses and the Prophets; and how could they understand Christ? They did not believe them, and how could they believe Him? And yet, from this point of view, but only from this, does all seem clear: the Incarnation, the history of the Temptation and Victory in the Wilderness, and even the Cross. Only he who has, in some measure, himself felt the agony of the first garden, can understand that of the second garden. Had they understood, by that personal experience which we must all have of it, the Proto-Evangel of the great contest, and of the great conquest by suffering, they would have followed its lines to their final goal in the Christ as the fulfillment of all. And so, here also, were the words of Christ true, that it needed heavenly teaching, and kinship to the Divine, to understand His doctrine.

This underlies, and is the main object of these discourses of Christ. As a corollary He would teach, that Satan was not a merely malicious, impish being, working outward destruction, but that there was a moral power of evil which held us all, not the Gentile world only, but even the most favored, learned, and exalted among the Jews. Of this power Satan was the concentration and impersonation; the prince of the power of darkness. This opens up the reasoning of Christ, as expressed and implied. He presented Himself to them as the Messiah, and therefore as the Light of the World. It resulted, that only in following Him would a man not walk in the darkness, but have the light, and that, be it marked, not the light of knowledge, but of life. On the other hand, it also followed, that all, who were not within this light, were in darkness and in death.

It was an appeal to the moral in His hearers. The Pharisees sought to turn it aside by an appeal to the external and visible. They asked for some witness, or palpable evidence, of what they called His testimony about Himself, well knowing that such could only be through some external, visible, miraculous manifestation, just as they had formerly asked for a sign from heaven. The Bible, and especially the Evangelic history, is full of what men ordinarily, and often thoughtlessly, call the miraculous. But, in this case, the miraculous would have become the magical, which it never is. If Christ had yielded to their appeal, and transferred the question from the moral to the coarsely external sphere, He would have ceased to be the Messiah of the Incarnation, Temptation, and Cross, the Messiah Savior. It would have been to un-Messiah the Messiah of the Gospel, for it was only, in another form, a repetition of the Temptation. A miracle or sign would at that moment have been a moral relic, as much as any miracle would be in our days, when the Christ makes His appeal to the moral, and is met by a demand for the external and material evidence of His Witness.

The interruption of the Pharisees was thoroughly Jewish, and so was their objection. It had to be met, and that in the Jewish form in which it had been raised, while the Christ must at the same time continue His former teaching to them concerning God and their own distance from Him. Their objection had proceeded on this fundamental judicial principle, A person is not accredited by himself. Harsh and unjust as this principle sometimes was, it evidently applied only in judicial cases, and therefore implied that these Pharisees sat in judgment on Him as one suspected, and charged with guilt. The reply of Jesus was plain. Even if His testimony about Himself were unsupported, it would still be true, and He was competent to bear it, for He knew, as a matter of fact, from where He came and where He went, His own part in this Mission, and its goal, as well as God's, whereas they did not know either. But, more than this: their demand for a witness had proceeded on the assumption of their being the judges, and He the panel, a relation which only arose from their judging after the flesh. Spiritual judgment upon that which was within belonged only to Him, that searches all secrets. Christ, while on earth, judged no man; and, even if He did so, it must be remembered that He did it not alone, but with, and as the Representative of, the Father. Therefore, such judgment would be true. But, as for their main charge, was it either true, or good in law? In accordance with the Law of God, there were two witnesses to the fact of His Mission: His own, and the frequently shown attestation of His Father. And, if it were objected that a man could not bear witness in his own cause, the same Rabbinic canon laid it down, that this only applied if his testimony stood alone. But if it were corroborated (even in a matter of greatest delicacy), although by only one male or female slave, who ordinarily were unfit for testimony, it would be credited.

The reasoning of Christ, without for a moment quitting the higher ground of His teaching, was quite unanswerable from the Jewish standpoint. The Pharisees felt it, and, though well knowing to Whom He referred, tried to evade it by the sneer, where (not Who) His Father was? This gave occasion for Christ to return to the main subject of His address, that the reason of their ignorance of Him was, that they did not know the Father, and, in turn, that only acknowledgment of Him would bring true knowledge of the Father.

Such words would only ripen in the hearts of such men the murderous resolve against Jesus. Yet, not until His, not their, hour had come! Now we find Him again, now in one of the Porches, probably that of Solomon, teaching, this time, the Jews. We imagine they were chiefly, if not all, Judeans, perhaps Jerusalemites, aware of the murderous intent of their leaders, not His own Galileans, whom He addressed. It was in continuation of what had gone before, of what He had said to them and of what they felt towards Him. The words are intensely sad, Christ's farewell to His rebellious people, His tear words over lost Israel; abrupt also, as if they were torn sentences, or, else, headings for special discourses: I go My way, You shall seek Me, and in your sin shall you die, Where I go, you cannot come! And is it not all most true? These many centuries has Israel sought its Christ, and perished in its great sin of rejecting Him; and where Christ and His kingdom tended, the Synagogue and Judaism never came. They thought that He spoke of His dying, and not, as He did, of that which came after it. But, how could His dying establish such separation between them? This was the next question which rose in their minds. Would there be anything so peculiar about His dying, or, did His expression about going indicate a purpose of taking away His Own life?

It was this misunderstanding which Jesus briefly but emphatically corrected by telling them, that the ground of their separation was the difference of their nature: they were from beneath, He from above; they of this world, He not of this world. Therefore they could not come where He would be, since they must die in their sin, as He had told them, if you do not believe that I am.

The words were intentionally mysteriously spoken, as to a Jewish audience. Do not believe that You are! But Who are You? Whether or not the words were spoken in scorn, their question condemned themselves. In His broken sentence, Jesus had tried them, to see how they would complete it. Then it was so! All this time they had not yet learned Who He was; had not even a conviction on that point, either for or against Him, but were ready to be swayed by their leaders! Who I am?, am I not telling you it even from the beginning; has My testimony by word or deed ever swerved on this point? I am what all along, from the beginning, I tell you. Then, putting aside this interruption, He resumed His argument. Many other things had He to say and to judge concerning them, besides the bitter truth of their perishing if they did not believe that it was He, but He that had sent Him was true, and He must ever speak into the world the message which He had received. When Christ referred to it as that which He heard from Him, He evidently wished thereby to emphasize the fact of His Mission from God, as constituting His claim on their obedience of faith. But it was this very point which, even at that moment, they were not understanding. And they would only learn it, not by His Words, but by the event, when they had lifted Him up, as they thought, to the Cross, but really on the way to His Glory. They would then perceive the meaning of the designation He had given of Himself, and the claim founded on it: Then shall you perceive that I am. Meantime: And of Myself I do nothing, but as the Father taught Me, these things I speak. And He that sent Me is with Me. He has not left Me alone, because what pleases Him I do always.

If the Jews failed to understand the expression lifting up, which might mean His Exaltation, though it did mean, in the first place, His Cross, there was that in His Appeal to His Words and Deeds as bearing witness to His Mission and to the Divine Help and Presence in it, which by its sincerity, earnestness, and reality, found its way to the hearts of many. Instinctively they felt and believed that His Mission must be Divine. Whether or not this found clear expression, Jesus now addressed Himself to those who thus far, at least for the moment, believed on Him. They were at the crisis of their spiritual history, and He must press home on them what He had sought to teach at the first. By nature far from Him, they were bondsmen. Only if they lived in His Word would they know the truth, and the truth would make them free. The result of this knowledge would be moral, and therefore that knowledge consisted not in merely believing on Him, but in making His Word and teaching their dwelling, living in it. But it was this very moral application which they resisted. In this also Jesus had used their own forms of thinking and teaching, only in a much higher sense. For their own tradition had it, that he only was free who labored in the study of the Law. Yet the liberty of which He spoke came not through study of the Law, but from living in the Word of Jesus. But it was this very thing which they resisted. And so they ignored the spiritual, and fell back upon the national, application of the words of Christ. As this is once more evidential of the Jewish authorship of this Gospel, so also the characteristically Jewish boast, that as the children of Abraham they had never been, and never could be, in real servitude. It would take too long to enumerate all the benefits supposed to be derived from descent from Abraham. Suffice here the almost fundamental principle: All Israel are the children of Kings, and its application even to common life, that as the children of Abraham, Isaac, and Jacob, not even Solomon's feast could be too good for them.

However, would the Lord would not allow them to pass it by. He pointed them to another servitude which they did not know, that of sin, and, entering at the same time also on their own ideas, He told them that continuance in this servitude would also lead to national bondage and rejection: For the servant does not live in the house forever. On the other hand, the Son lives there forever; whom He made free by adoption into His family, they would be free in reality and essentially. Then for their very dullness, He would turn to their favorite conceit of being Abraham's seed. There was, an obvious sense in which, by their natural descent, they were such. But there was a moral descent, and that alone was of real value. Another, and to them wholly new, and heavenly teaching this, which Jesus now applied in a manner they could neither misunderstand nor argue with, while He at the same time connected it with the general drift of His teaching. Abraham's seed? But they entertained purposes of murder, and that, because the Word of Christ did not have free course, made no way in them. His Word was what He had seen with (before) the Father, not heard, for His presence was there Eternal. Their deeds were what they had heard from their father, the word seen in our common text depending on a wrong reading. And thus He showed them, in answer to their interpretation, that their father could not have been Abraham, so far as spiritual descent was concerned. They had now a glimpse of His meaning, but only to misapply it, according to their Jewish prejudice. Their spiritual descent, they urged, must be of God, since their descent from Abraham was legitimate. But Jesus dispelled even this conceit by showing, that if theirs were spiritual descent from God, then they would not reject His Message, nor seek to kill Him, but recognize and love Him.

But from where this misunderstanding of His speech? Because they are morally incapable of hearing it, and this because of the sinfulness of their nature: an element which Judaism had never taken into account. And so, with infinite Wisdom, Christ once more brought back His discourse to what He would teach them concerning man's need, whether he be Jew or Gentile, of a Savior and of renewing by the Holy Spirit. If the Jews were morally unable to hear His Word and cherished murderous designs, it was because, morally speaking, their descent was of the Devil. Very differently from Jewish ideas He spoke concerning the moral evil of Satan, as both a murderer and a liar—a murderer from the beginning of the history of our race, and one who did not stand in the truth, because truth is not in him. Therefore whenever he speaks a lie, whether to our first parents, or now concerning the Christ, he speaks from out his own (things), for he (Satan) is a liar, and the father of such a one (who tells or believes lies). Which of them could convict Him of sin? If therefore He spoke truth, and they did not believe Him, it was because they were not of God, but, as He had shown them, of their father, the Devil.

The argument was unanswerable, and there seemed only one way to turn it aside, a Jewish Tu quoque, an adaptation of the Physician, heal yourself: Do we not rightly say, that You are a Samaritan, and have a demon? It is strange that the first clause of this reproach should have been so misunderstood and yet its direct explanation lies on the surface. We have only to translate it into the language which the Jews had used. By no strain of ingenuity is it possible to account for the designation Samaritan, as given by the Jews to Jesus, if it is regarded as referring to nationality. Even at the very Feast they had made it an objection to His Messianic claims, that He was (as they supposed) a Galilean. Nor had He come to Jerusalem from Samaria; nor could He be so called (as Commentators suggest) because He was a foe to Israel, or a breaker of the Law, or unfit to bear witness, for neither of these circumstances would have led the Jews to designate Him by the term Samaritan. But, in the language which they spoke, what is rendered into Greek by Samaritan, would have been either Kuthi, which, while literally meaning a Samaritan, is almost as often used in the sense of heretic, or else Shomroni. The latter word deserves special attention. Literally, it also means, Samaritan; but, the name Shomron (perhaps from its connection with Samaria), is also sometimes used as the equivalent of Ashmedai, the Prince of the demons.

According to the Kabbalists, Shomron was the father of Ashmedai, and therefore the same as Sammael, or Satan. That this was a wide spread Jewish belief, appears from the circumstance that in the Koran (which, in such matters, would reproduce popular Jewish tradition), Israel is said to have been seduced into idolatry by Shomron, while, in Jewish tradition, this is attributed to Sammael. If, therefore, the term applied by the Jews to Jesus was Shomroni, and not Kuthi, heretic, it would literally mean, Child of the Devil.

This would also explain why Christ only replied to the charge of having a demon, since the two charges meant substantially the same: You are a child of the devil and have a demon. In wondrous patience and mercy He almost passed it by, dwelling rather, for their teaching, on the fact that, while they dishonored Him, He honored His Father. He did not listen to their charges. His concern was the glory of His Father; the vindication of His own honor would be brought about by the Father, though, unfortunately in judgment on those who were putting such dishonor on the Sent of God. Then, as if lingering in deep compassion on the terrible issue, He once more pressed home the great subject of His discourse, that only if a man keeps, both have regard to, and observes, His Word, he shall not gaze at death [intently behold it] to eternity, forever shall he not come within close and terrible gaze of what is really death, of what became such to Adam in the hour of his Fall.

It was, as repeatedly observed, this death as the consequence of the Fall, of which the Jews did not know a thing. And so they once more misunderstood it as of physical death, and, since Abraham and the prophets had died, regarded Christ as setting up a claim higher than theirs. The discourse had contained all that He had wished to bring before them, and their objections were degenerating into squabbling. It was time to break it off by a general application. The question, He added, was not of what He said, but of what God said of Him, that God, Whom they claimed as theirs, and yet did not know, but Whom He knew, and Whose Word He kept. But, as for Abraham, he had exulted in the thought of the coming day of the Christ, and, seeing its glory, he was glad. Even Jewish tradition could scarcely argue with this, since there were two parties in the Synagogue, of which one believed that, when that horror of great darkness fell on him, Abraham had, in vision, been shown not only this, but the coming world, and not only all events in the present age, but also those in Messianic times. And now, theirs was not misunderstanding, but willful misinterpretation. He had spoken of Abraham seeing His day; they took it of His seeing Abraham's day, and challenged its possibility. Whether or not they intended thus to elicit an declaration of His claim to eternal duration, and therefore to Divinity, it was not time any longer to withhold the full statement, and, with Divine emphasis, He spoke the words which could not be mistaken: Truly, truly, I say to you, before Abraham was, I Am.

It was as if they had only waited for this. Furiously they rushed from the Porch into the Court of the Gentiles, with symbolic significance, even in this, to pick up stones, and to throw them at Him. But, once more, His hour had not yet come, and their fury proved powerless. Hiding Himself for the moment, as might so easily be done, in one of the many chambers, passages, or gateways of the Temple, He now exited.

It had been the first plain disclosure and declaration of His Divinity, and it was in the midst of His enemies, and when most contempt was thrown upon Him. Now would that declaration be renewed both in Word and by Deed; for the end of mercy and judgment had not yet come, but was drawing terribly near.

End Notes:

[22]   It is not unlikely that the first address (vv. 12-19) may have been delivered on the afternoon of the Last Day of the Feast, when the cessation of preparations for the Temple illumination may have given the outward occasion for the words: I am the light of the world. The sense of vv. 12 and 21 seems in each case to indicate a fresh period of time. Besides, we can scarcely suppose that all from 5:37 to 8:59 had taken place the same day. For this and other arguments on the point, see Luecke, vol. 2: pp. 279-281.

[23]   The so called chamber of the silent (Chashaim), Sheqal. v. 6.

[24]   The chamber of the vessels (Kelim). It was probably over, or in this chamber that Agrippi hung up the golden memorial chain of his captivity (Jos. Antiq. 19:6. 1).

[25]   The Court of the Women (gunaikons), Jos. Jew. War 5:5. 3; comp. also 5:5. 2), so called, because women could not penetrate further. It was the real Court of the Sanctuary. Here Jeremiah also taught (19:14; 25:2). But it is not correct to state (Westcott), that the Council Chamber of the Sanhedrin (Gazith) was between the Court of the Women and the inner court. It was in the southeastern angle of the Court of the Priests, and therefore at a considerable distance from the Court of the Women. But, not to speak of the circumstance that the Sanhedrin no longer met in that Chamber, even if it had been nearer, Christ's teaching in the Treasury could not (at any period) have been within earshot of the Sanhedrin, since it would not sit on that day.

[26]   Although Rabbi Joshua tells (in the Talmud) that during all the nights of the festive week they did not taste sleep, this seems scarcely credible, and the statement of the Mishnah is the more rational. Maimonides, however, adopts the view of the Talmud (Hilch. Lul. v3:12).

[27]   I imagine a more thorough misunderstanding of the character and teaching
        of Christianity than, for example, the proposal to test the efficacy of prayer,
        by asking for the recovery of those in a hospital ward! This would represent
        paganism, not Christianity.

[28]   Generally this is understood as referring to the supposed Jewish belief,
        that suicides occupied the lowest place in Gehenna. But a glance at the
        context must convince that the Jews could not have understood Christ as
        meaning, that He would be separated from them by being sent to the lowest
        Gehenna. Besides, this supposed punishment of suicides is only derived
        from a rhetorical passage in Josephus (Jew. War 3:8. 5), but unsupported by
        any Rabbinic statements. The Rabbinic definition, or rather limitation, of
        what constitutes suicide is remarkable. Thus, neither Saul, nor Ahithophel,
        nor Zimri, are regarded as suicides, because they did it to avoid falling into
        the hands of their enemies. For premeditated, real suicide the punishment
        is left with God. Some difference is to be made in the burial of such, yet
        not such as to put the survivors to shame.

[29]   As Canon Westcott rightly points out (John 12:32), the term lifting up
        includes both the death and the glory. The verb Nasa naturally occurs
        (comp. Gen 40:19 with ver. 13). For we suppose, that the word used by
        Christ at this early part of His Ministry could not have necessarily involved
        a prediction of His Crucifixion, and that they who heard it rather imagined
        it to refer to His Exaltation. There is a curiously illustrative passage here (in
        Pesiqta R. 10), when a king, having given orders that the head of his son
        should be lifted up, that it should be hanged up, is exhorted by the tutor to
        spare what was his moneginos (only begotten). On the kings replying that
        he was bound by the orders he had given, the tutor answers by pointing
        out that the verb Nasa means lifting up in the sense of exalting, as well as
        of executing. But, besides the verb Nasa, there is also the verb Zeqaph,
        which in the Aramaic and in the Syriac is used both for lifting up and
        for hanging—specifically for crucifying; and, lastly, the verb Tela, which
        means in the first place to lift up, and secondarily to hang or crucify (see
        Levy, Targum, Woerterb. 2: p. 539 a and b). It this latter verb was used,
        then the Jewish expression Taluy, which is still given to Jesus, would after
        all represent the original designation by which He described His own death
        as the lifted up One.

[30]   He spoke of seeing, they of tasting death (vv. 51, 52). The word taste, is used
        in precisely the same manner by the Rabbis. Thus, in the Jeremiah Targum
        on Deuteronomy 32:1. In Ber. R. 9, we are told, that it was originally
        destined that the first man should not taste death. Again, Elijah did not

taste the taste of death (Ber. R. 21). And, tropically, in such a passage as this: If anyone would taste a taste (here: have a foretaste) of death, let him keep his shoes on while he goes to sleep (Yom. 78 l). It is also used of sleep, as: All the days of the joy of the house of drawing [Feast of Tabernacles] we did not taste the taste of sleep (Succ. 53 a). It is needless to add other quotations.

[31]   In the Targum Jerusalem on Genesis 15 also it seems implied that Abraham saw in vision all that would happen to his children in the future, and also Gehenna and its torments. So far as I can gather, only the latter, not the former, seems implied in the Targ. Pseudo-Jonathan. Note on the differences between the Feast of Tabernacles and that of its Octave (see p. 156, note 1). The six points of difference which mark the Octave as a separate feast are indicated by the memorial words and letters, and are as follows: (1) During the seven days of Tabernacles the Priests of all the courses officiated, while on the Octave the sacrificial services were appointed, as usually, by lot. (2) The benediction at the beginning of a feast was spoken again at the Octave. (3) The Octave was designated in prayer, and by special ordinances, as a separate feast. (4) Difference in the sacrifices. (5) Difference in the Psalms, on the Octave (Soph. 19:2) probably Psalm 12. (6) According to 1 Kings 8:66, difference as to the blessing.

Chapter 9

Healing the Man Born Blind

(John 9)

After the scene in the Temple described in the last chapter, and Christ's consequent withdrawal from His enemies, we can hardly suppose any other great event to have taken place on that day within or near the precincts of the Sanctuary. And yet, from the close connection of the narratives, we are led to infer that no long interval of time can have elapsed before the healing of the man born blind. Probably it happened the day after the events just recorded. We know that it was a Sabbath, and this fresh mark of time, as well as the multiplicity of things done, and the whole style of the narrative, confirm our belief that it was not on the evening of the day when He had spoken to them first in the Treasury, and then in the Porch.

On two other points there is strong presumption, though we cannot offer actual proof. Remembering, that the entrance to the Temple or its Courts was then, as that of churches is on the Continent, the chosen spot for those who, as objects of pity, solicited charity; remembering, also, how rapidly the healing of the blind man became known, and how soon both his parents and the healed man himself appeared before the Pharisees, presumably, in the Temple; lastly, how readily Jesus knew where again to find him, we can scarcely doubt that the miracle took place at the entering to the Temple, or on the Temple Mount. Secondly, both the Work, and especially the Words of Christ, seem in such close connection with what had preceded, that we can scarcely be mistaken in regarding them as intended to form a continuation of it.

It is not difficult to realize the scene, nor to understand the remarks of all who had part in it. It was the Sabbath, the day after the Octave of the Feast, and Christ with His disciples was passing, presumably when going into the Temple, where this blind beggar was accustomed to sit, probably soliciting alms, perhaps in some such terms as these, which were common at the time: Gain merit by me; or, O tenderhearted, by me gain merit, to your sown benefit. But on the Sabbath he would, neither ask nor receive alms, though his presence in the conspicuous place would secure wider notice and perhaps lead to many private gifts. The blind were regarded as especially entitled to charity; and the Jerusalem Talmud relates some touching instances of the delicacy displayed towards them. As Jesus and His disciples passed the blind beggar, Jesus saw him, with that look which they who followed Him knew to be full of meaning. Yet, so thoroughly Judaized were they by their late contact with the Pharisees, that no thought of possible mercy came to them, only a truly and characteristically Jewish question, addressed to Him expressly, and as Rabbi: through whose guilt has this blindness come upon him, through his own, or that of his parents.

For, thoroughly Jewish the question was. Many instances could be cited, in which one or another sin is said to have been punished by some immediate stroke, disease, or even by death; and we constantly find Rabbis, when meeting such unfortunate persons, asking them, how or by what sin this had come to them. But, as this man was blind from his birth, the possibility of some actual sin before birth would suggest itself, at least as a speculative question, since the evil impulse (Yetser ha Ra), might even then be called into activity. At the same time, both the Talmud and the later charge of the Pharisees, In sins were you born altogether, imply that in such cases the alternative explanation would be considered, that the blindness might be caused by the sin of his parents. It was a common Jewish view, that the merits or demerits of the parents would appear in the children. In fact, up to thirteen years of age a child was considered, as it were, part of his father, and as suffering for his guilt. More than that, the thoughts of a mother might affect the moral state of her unborn offspring, and the terrible apostasy of one of the greatest Rabbis had, in popular belief, been caused by the sinful delight his mother had taken when passing through an idol grove. Lastly, certain special sins in the parents would result in specific diseases in their offspring, and one is mentioned as causing blindness in the children. But the impression left on our minds is, that the disciples felt unsure as to either of these solutions of the difficulty. It seemed a mystery, inexplicable on the supposition of God's infinite goodness, and to which they sought to apply the common Jewish solution. Many similar mysteries meet us in the administration of God's Providence, questions, which seem unanswerable, but to which we try to give answers, perhaps, not much wiser than the explanations suggested by disciples.

But why seek to answer them at all, since we possess not all, perhaps very few of, the data requisite for it? There is one aspect, however, of adversity, and of a strange dispensation of evil, on which the light of Christ's Words here shines with the brightness of a new morning. There is a physical, natural reason for them. God has not especially sent them, in the sense of His interference or primary causation, although He has sent them in the sense of His knowledge, will, and reign. They have come in the ordinary course of things, and are traceable to causes which, if we only knew them, would appear to us the sequence of the laws which God has imposed on His creation, and which are necessary for its orderly continuance. And, further, all such evil consequences, from the operation of God's laws, are in the last instance to be traced back to the curse which sin has brought upon man and on earth. With these His Laws, and with their evil sequences to us through the curse of sin, God does not interfere in the ordinary course of His Providence; although he would be daring, who would negate the possibility of what may seem, though it is not, interference, since the natural causes which lead to these evil consequences may so easily, naturally, and rationally be affected. But there is another and a higher aspect of it, since Christ has come, and is really the Healer of all disease and evil by being the remover of its ultimate moral cause. This is indicated in His words, when, putting aside the clumsy alternative suggested by the disciples, He told them that it was so in order that the works of God might be made manifest in him. They wanted to know the why, He told them the in order to, of the man's calamity; they wished to understand its reason as regarded its origin, He told them its reasonableness in regard to the purpose which it, and all similar suffering, should serve, since Christ has come, the Healer of evil, because the Savior from sin. Thus He transferred the question from intellectual ground to that of the moral purpose which suffering might serve. And this not in itself, nor by any destiny or appointment, but because the Coming and Work of the Christ has made it possible to us all. Sin and its sequences are still the same, for the world is established so that it cannot move. But over it all has risen the Sun of Righteousness with healing in His wings; and, if we but open ourselves to His influence, these evils may serve this purpose, and so have this for their reason, not as, regards their genesis, but their continuance, that the works of God may be made manifest.

To make this the reality to us, was the work of Him Who sent, and for which He sent, the Christ. And rapidly now must He work it, for perpetual example, during the few hours still left of His brief working day. This figure was not unfamiliar to the Jews, though it may well be that, by thus emphasizing the briefness of the time, He may also have anticipated any objection to His healing on the Sabbath. But it is of even more importance to notice, how the two leading thoughts of the previous days discourse were now again taken up and set forth in the miracle that followed. These were, that He did the Work which God had sent Him to do, and that He was the Light of the world. As its Light He could not but shine so long as He was in it. And this He now symbolized (and is not every miracle a symbol?) in the healing of the blind.

Once more we notice, how in His Deeds, as in His Words, the Lord adopted the forms known and used by His contemporaries, while He filled them with quite other substance. It has already been stated, that saliva was commonly regarded as a remedy for diseases of the eye, although not for the removal of blindness. With this He made clay, which He now used, adding to it the direction to go and wash in the Pool of Siloam, a term which literally meant sent. A symbolism, this, of Him Who was the Sent of the Father. For, all is here symbolical: the cure and its means. If we ask ourselves why means were used in this instance, we can only suggest, that it was partly for the sake of him who was to be healed, partly for theirs who afterwards heard of it. For, the blind man seems to have been ignorant of the character of his Healer, and it needed the use of some means to make him, so to speak, receptive. On the other hand, not only the use of means, but their inadequacy to the object, must have impressed all.

Symbolical, also, were these means. Sight was restored by clay, made out of the ground with the spittle of Him, Whose breath had at the first breathed life into clay; and this was then washed away in the Pool of Siloam, from whose waters had been drawn on the Feast of Tabernacles that which symbolized the pouring forth of the new life by the Spirit. Lastly, if it is asked why such miracle should have been performed on one who did not have previous faith, who did not even seem to have known about the Christ, we can only repeat, that the man himself was intended to be a symbol, that the works of God should be made manifest in him.

And so, what the Pharisees had sought in vain, was freely granted when there was need for it. With unmatched simplicity, itself evidence that no legend is told, the man's obedience and healing are recorded. We judge, that his first impulse when healed must have been to seek for Jesus, naturally, where he had first met Him. On his way, probably past his own house to tell his parents, and again on the spot where he had so long sat begging, all who had known him must have noticed the great change that had passed over him. So marvelous, did it appear, that, while part of the crowd that gathered would acknowledge his identity, others would say: No, but he is like him; in their suspiciousness looking for some masquerade. For there can be little doubt, that on his way he must have learned more about Jesus than merely His Name, and in turn have communicated to his informants the story of his healing. Similarly, the formal question now put to him by the Jews was as much, if not more, a preparatory inquisition than the outcome of a wish to learn the circumstances of his healing. And so we notice in his answer the cautious desire not to say anything that could incriminate his Benefactor. He tells the facts truthfully, plainly; he accentuates by what means he had recovered, not received, sight; but otherwise gives no clue by which either to discover or to incriminate Jesus.

Now they bring him to the Pharisees, not to take notice of his healing, but to found on it a charge against Christ. Such must have been their motive, since it was universally known that the leaders of the people had, of course informally, agreed to take the strictest measures, not only against the Christ, but against anyone who professed to be His disciple. The ground on which the present charge against Jesus would rest was plain: the healing involved a manifold breach of the Sabbath Law. The first of these was that He had made clay. Next, it would be a question whether any remedy might be applied on the holy day. Such could only be done in diseases of the internal organs (from the throat downwards), except when danger to life or the loss of an organ was involved. It was, declared lawful to apply, for example, wine to the outside of the eyelid, on the ground that this might be treated as washing; but it was sinful to apply it to the inside of the eye. And as regards saliva, its application to the eye is expressly forbidden, on the ground that it was evidently intended as a remedy.

There was, therefore, abundant legal ground for a criminal charge. And, although on the Sabbath the Sanhedrin would not hold any formal meeting, and, even had there been such, the testimony of one man would not have sufficed, yet the Pharisees set the inquiry regularly on foot. First, as if not satisfied with the report of those who had brought the man, they made him repeat it. The simplicity of the man's language left no room for evasion or subterfuge. Rabbinism was on its great trial. The wondrous fact could neither be denied nor explained, and the only ground for resisting the legitimate inference as to the character of Him Who had done it, was its inconsistence with their traditional law. The alternative was: whether their traditional law of Sabbath observance, or else He Who had done such miracles, was Divine? Was Christ not of God, because He did not keep the Sabbath in their way? But, then; could an open transgressor of God's Law do such miracles? In this dilemma they turned to the simple man before them. Seeing that He opened his eyes, what did he say of Him? what was the impression left on his mind, who had the best opportunity for judging?

There is something very peculiar, and, in one sense, most instructive, as to the general opinion entertained even by the best disposed, who had not yet been taught the higher truth, in his reply, so simple and solemn, so comprehensive in its sequences, and yet so utterly inadequate by itself: He is a Prophet. One possibility still remained. After all, the man might not have been really blind; and they might, by cross examining the parents, elicit that about his original condition which would explain the pretended cure. But on this most important point, the parents, with all their fear of the anger of the Pharisees, remained unshaken. He had been born blind; but as to the manner of his cure, they declined to offer any opinion. Thus, as so often, the plots of the enemies of Christ led to results the opposite of those wished for. For, the evidential value of their testimony of their sons blindness was manifestly proportional to their fear of committing themselves to any testimony for Christ, well knowing what it would entail.

For to persons so wretchedly poor as to allow their son to live by begging, the consequence of being un-Synagogued, or put outside the congregation, which was to be the punishment of any who confessed Jesus as the Messiah, would have been dreadful. Talmudic writings speak of two, or rather, we should say, of three, kinds of excommunication, of which the two first were chiefly disciplinary, while the third was the real casting out, un-Synagoguing, cutting off from the congregation. The general designation for excommunication was Shammatta, although, according to its literal meaning, the term would only apply to the severest form of it. The first and lightest degree was the so called Neziphah or Neziphutha; properly, a rebuke, a verbal attack. Ordinarily, its duration extended over seven days; but, if pronounced by the Nasi, or Head of the Sanhedrin, it lasted for thirty days. In later times, however, it only rested for one day on the guilty person. Perhaps Paul referred to this rebuke in the expression which he used about an offending Elder. He certainly adopted the practice in Palestine, when he would not have an Elder rebuked although he went far beyond it when he would have such an earnest appeal. In Palestine it was ordered, that an offending Rabbi should be scourged instead of being excommunicated. Yet another direction of Paul's is evidently derived from these arrangements of the Synagogue, although applied in a far different spirit. When the Apostle wrote: A heretic after the first and second admonition reject; there must have been in his mind the second degree of Jewish excommunication, the so called Niddui (from the verb to thrust, thrust out, cast out). This lasted for thirty days at the least, although among the Babylonians only for seven days. At the end of that term there was a second admonition, which lasted other thirty days. If still unrepentant, the third, or real excommunication, was pronounced, which was called the Cherem, or ban, and of which the duration was indefinite. Any three persons, or even one duly KJV, could pronounce the lowest sentence. The greater excommunication (Niddui), which, happily, could only be pronounced in a assembly of ten, must have been terrible, being accompanied by curses, and, at a later period, sometimes proclaimed with the blast of the horn. If the person so visited occupied an honorable position, it was the custom to intimate his sentence in a euphemistic manner, such as: It seems to me that your companions are separating themselves from you. He who was so, or similarly addressed, would only too well understand its meaning. From here on he would sit on the ground, and bear himself like one in deep mourning. He would allow his beard and hair to grow wild and shaggy; he would not bathe, nor anoint himself; he would not be admitted into a assembly of ten men, neither to public prayer, nor to the Academy; though he might either teach, or be taught by, single individuals. As if he were a leper, people would keep at a distance of four cubits from him. If he died, stones were tossed on his coffin, nor was he allowed the honor of the ordinary funeral, nor were they to mourn for him. Still more terrible was the final excommunication, or Cherem, when a ban of indefinite duration was laid on a man. From here on he was like one dead. He was not allowed to study with others, no association was to be held with him, he was not even to be shown the road. He might buy the necessaries of life but it was forbidden to eat or drink with such a one.

We can understand, how everyone would dread such an anathema. But when we remember, what it would involve to persons in the rank of life, and so miserably poor as the parents of that blind man, we no longer wonder at their evasion of the question put by the Sanhedrin. And if we ask ourselves, on what ground so terrible a punishment could be inflicted to all time and in every place, for the ban once pronounced applied everywhere, simply for the confession of Jesus as the Christ, the answer is not difficult.

The Rabbinics enumerate twenty four grounds for excommunication, of which more than one might serve the purpose of the Pharisees. But in general, to resist the authority of the Scribes, or any of their decrees, or to lead others either away from the commandments, or to what was regarded as profaning of the Divine Name, was sufficient to incur the ban, while it must be borne in mind that excommunication by the President of the Sanhedrin extended to all places and persons.

As nothing could be elicited from his parents, the man who had been blind was once more summoned before the Pharisees. It was no longer to inquire into the reality of his alleged blindness, nor to ask about the cure, but simply to demand of him recantation, though this was put in the most baseless manner. You have been healed: own that it was only by God's Hand miraculously stretched forth, and that this man had nothing to do with it, save that the coincidence may have been allowed to try the faith of Israel. It could not have been Jesus Who had done it, for they knew Him to be a sinner. Of the two alternatives they had chosen that of the absolute rightness of their own Sabbath traditions as against the evidence of His Miracles. Virtually, then, this was the condemnation of Christ and the glorification of traditionalism. And yet, false as their conclusion was, there was this truth in their premises, that they judged of miracles by the moral evidence in regard to Him, Who was represented as working them.

But he who had been healed of his blindness was not to be so betrayed into a denunciation of his great Physician. The simplicity and earnestness of his convictions enabled him to gain even a logical victory. It was his turn now to bring back the question to the issue which they had originally raised; and we admire it all the more, as we remember the consequences to this poor man of thus daring the Pharisees. As against their opinion about Jesus, as to the correctness of which neither he nor others could have direct knowledge, there was the unquestionable fact of his healing of which he had personal knowledge. The renewed inquiry now by the Pharisees, as to the manner in which Jesus had healed him, might have had for its object to betray the man into a positive confession, or to elicit something demoniacal in the mode of the cure. The blind man had now fully the advantage. He had already told them; why the renewed inquiry? As he put it half ironically: Was it because they felt the wrongness of their own position, and that they should become His disciples? It stung them to the quick; they lost all self possession, and with this their moral defeat became complete. You are the disciple of that man, but we (according to the favorite phrase) are the disciples of Moses. Of the Divine Mission of Moses they knew, but of the Mission of Jesus they did not knowing. The unlettered man had now the full advantage in the controversy. In this, there was the marvelous, that the leaders of Israel should confess themselves ignorant of the authority of One, Who had power to open the eyes of the blind, a marvel which had never before been witnessed. If He had that power, from where had He obtained it, and why? It could only have been from God. They said, He was a sinner, and yet there was no principle more frequently repeated by the Rabbis, than that answers to prayer depended on a man being devout and doing the Will of God. There could therefore by only one inference: If Jesus had not Divine Authority, He could not have had Divine Power.

The argument was unanswerable, and in its unanswerableness shows us, not indeed the purpose, but the evidential force of Christ's Miracles. In one sense they had no purpose, or rather were purpose to themselves, being the bursting forth of His Power and the manifestation of His Being and Mission, of which latter, as applied to things physical, they were part. But the truthful reasoning of that untutored man, which confounded the acuteness of the sages, shows the effect of these manifestations on all whose hearts were open to the truth. The Pharisees had nothing to answer, and, as not infrequently in similar cases, could only, in their fury, throw him out with bitter reproaches. Would he teach them, he, whose very disease showed him to have been a child conceived and born in sin, and who, ever since his birth, had been among ignorant, Law neglecting sinners?

But there was Another, Who watched and knew him: He Whom, so far as he knew, he had dared to confess, and for Whom he was content to suffer. Let him now have the reward of his faith, even its completion; and so shall it become manifest to all time, how, as we follow and cherish the better light, it rises upon us in all its brightness, and that faithfulness in little brings the greater stewardship. Tenderly did Jesus seek him out, wherever it may have been: and, as He found him, this one question did He ask, whether the conviction of his experience was not growing into the higher faith of the yet unseen: Do you believe on the Son of God? He had had personal experience of Him, was not that such as to lead up to the higher faith? And is it not always so, that the higher faith is based on the conviction of personal experience, that we believe on Him as the Son of God, because we have experience of Him as the God sent, Who has Divine Power, and has opened the eyes of the blind born, and Who has done to us what had never been done by any other in the world? Thus is faith always the child of experience, and yet its father also; faith not without experience, and yet beyond experience; faith not superseded by experience, but made reasonable by it.

To such a soul it needed only the directing Word of Christ. And Who is He, Lord, that I may believe on Him? It seems as if the question of Jesus had kindled in him the conviction of what was the right answer. We almost see how, like a well of living water, the words sprang joyfully from his inmost heart, and how he looked up expectantly on Jesus. To such readiness of faith there could be only one answer. In language more plain than He had ever before used, Jesus answered, and with immediate confession of implicit faith the man lowly worshipped. And so it was, that the first time he saw his Deliverer, it was to worship Him. It was the highest stage yet attained. What contrast this faith and worship of the poor unlettered man, once blind, now in every sense seeing, to the blindness of judgment which had fallen on those who were the leaders of Israel! The cause of the one and the other was the Person of the Christ. For our relationship to Him determines sight or blindness, as we either receive the evidence of what He is from what He unquestionably does, or reject it, because we hold by our own false conceptions of God, and of what His Will to us is. And so is Christ also for judgment.

There were those who still followed Him, not convinced by, nor as yet decided against Him, Pharisees, who well understood the application of His Words. Formally, it had been a contest between traditionalism and the Work of Christ. They also were traditionalists, were they also blind? But they had misunderstood Him by leaving out the moral element, thus showing themselves blind indeed. It was not the calamity of blindness; but it was a blindness in which they were guilty, and for which they were responsible, which indeed was the result of their deliberate choice: therefore their sin, not their blindness only, remained!

End Notes:

[32] It would lead too far to set these forth in detail. But the shrinking from receiving alms was in proportion to the duty of giving them. Only extreme necessity would warrant begging, and to solicit charity needlessly, or to simulate any disease for the purpose, would, deservedly, bring the reality in punishment on the guilty.

[33] The common view (Meyer, Watkins, Westcott) is, that the expression, Give glory to God was merely a formula of solemn adjuration, like Joshua

5:19. But even so, as Canon Westcott remarks, it implies that the cure was due directly to God.

[34]   proseknesen. The word is never used by John of mere respect for man, but always implies Divine worship. In the Gospel it occurs ch. 4:20-24; 9:38; 12:20; and twenty three times in the Book of Revelation, but always in the sense of worship.

Chapter 10

The Good Shepherd

(John 10:1-21)

The closing words which Jesus had spoken to those Pharisees who followed Him breath the sadness of expected near judgment, rather than the hopefulness of challenge. And the discourse which followed, before He once more left Jerusalem, is of the same character. It seems, as if Jesus could not part from the City in holy anger, but ever, and only, with tears. All the topics of the former discourses are now resumed and applied. They are not in any way softened or modified, but uttered in accents of loving sadness rather than of reproving warning. This connection with the past proves, that the discourse was spoken immediately after, and in connection with, the events recorded in the previous chapters. At the same time, the tone adopted by Christ prepares us for His Perean Ministry, which may be described as that of the last and fullest outgoing of His most intense pity. This, in contrast to what was exhibited by the rulers of Israel, and which would so soon bring terrible judgment on them. For, if such things were done in the green tree of Israel's Messiah King, what would the end be in the dry wood of Israel's commonwealth and institutions?

It was in accordance with the character of the discourse now under consideration, that Jesus spoke it, not, in Parables in the strict sense (for none such are recorded in the Fourth Gospel), but in an allegory in the Parabolic form, hiding the higher truths from those who, having eyes, had not seen, but revealing them to such whose eyes had been opened. If the scenes of the last few days had made anything plain, it was the utter unfitness of the teachers of Israel for their professed work of feeding the flock of God.

The Rabbinics also called their spiritual leaders feeders, Parnasin, a term by which the Targum renders some of the references to the Shepherds in Ezekiel 34:and Zechariah 10: The term comprised the two ideas of leading and feeding, which are separately insisted on in Jesus' allegory. As we think of it, no better illustration, nor more apt, could be found for those to whom the flock of God was entrusted. It needed not therefore that a sheepfold should have been in view, to explain the form of Christ's address. It only required to recall the Old Testament language about the shepherding of God, and that of evil shepherds, to make the application to what had so lately happened. They were, surely, not shepherds, who had thrown out the healed blind man, or who so judged of the Christ, and would throw out all His disciples. They had entered into God's Sheepfold, but not by the door by which the owner, God, had brought His flock into the fold. To it the entrance had been His free love, His gracious provision, His thoughts of pardoning, His purpose of saving mercy. That was God's Old Testament door into His Sheepfold. Not by that door, as had so lately fully appeared, had Israel's rulers come in. They had climbed up to their place in the fold some other way, with the same right, or by the same wrong, as a thief or a robber. They had wrongfully taken what did not belong to them, cunningly and undetected, like a thief; they had allotted it to themselves, and usurped it by violence, like a robber. What more accurate description could be given of the means by which the Pharisees and Sadducees had attained the rule over God's flock, and claimed it for themselves? And what was true of them holds equally so of all, who, like them, enter by some other way.

How different He, Who comes in and leads us through God's door of covenant mercy and Gospel promise, the door by which God had brought, and ever brings, His flock into His fold! This was the true Shepherd. The allegory must not be too closely pressed; but, as we remember how in the East the flocks are at night driven into a large fold, and charge of them is given to an under shepherd, we can understand how, when the shepherd comes in the morning, the doorkeeper or guardian opens to him. In interpreting the allegory, stress must be laid not so much on any single phrase, be it the porter, the door, or the opening, as on their combination. If the shepherd comes to the door, the porter hurries to open it to him from within, that he may obtain access to the flock; and when a true spiritual Shepherd comes to the true spiritual door, it is opened to him by the guardian from within, that is, he finds ready and immediate access. Equally pictorial is the progress of the allegory. Having thus gained access to His flock, it has not been to steal or rob, but the Shepherd knows and calls them, each by his name, and leads them out. We mark that in the expression: when He has put forth all His own, the word is a strong one. For they have to go each singly, and perhaps they are not willing to go out each by himself, or even to leave that fold, and so he puts or thrusts them forth, and He does so to all His own. Then the Eastern shepherd places himself at the head of his flock, and goes before them, guiding them, making sure of their following simply by his voice, which they know. So would His flock follow Christ, for they know His Voice, and in vain would strangers seek to lead them away, as the Pharisees had tried. It was not the known Voice of their own Shepherd, and they would only flee from it.

We can scarcely wonder, that they who heard it did not understand the allegory, for they were not of His flock and did not know His Voice. But His own knew it then, and would know it forever. Therefore, both for the sake of the one and the other, He continued, now dividing for greater clearness the two leading ideas of His allegory, and applying each separately for better comfort. These two ideas were: entrance by the door, and the characteristics of the good Shepherd, thus affording a twofold test by which to recognize the true, and distinguish it from the false.

I. The door, Christ was the Door. The entrance into God's fold and to God's flock was only through that, of which Christ was the reality. And it had ever been so. All the Old Testament institutions, prophecies, and promises, so far as they referred to access into God's fold, meant Christ. And all those who went before Him, pretending to be the door, whether Pharisees, Sadducees, or Nationalists, were only thieves and robbers: that was not the door into the Kingdom of God. And the sheep, God's flock, did not hear them; for, although they might pretend to lead the flock, the voice was that of strangers. The transition now to another application of the allegorical idea of the door was natural and almost necessary, though it appears somewhat abrupt. Even in this it is peculiarly Jewish. We must understand this transition as follows: I am the Door; those who professed otherwise to gain access to the fold have climbed in some other way. But if I am the only, I am also truly the Door. And, dropping the figure, if any man enters by Me, he shall be saved, securely go out and in (where the language is not to be closely pressed), in the sense of having liberty and finding pasture.

II. This forms also the transition to the second leading idea of the allegory: the True and Good Shepherd. Here we mark a fourfold progression of thought, which reminds us of the poetry of the Book of Psalms. There the thought expressed in one line or one couplet is carried forward and developed in the next, forming what are called the Psalms of Ascent (of Degrees). And in the discourse of Christ also the final thought of each couplet of verses is carried forward, or rather leads upward in the next. Thus we have here a Psalm of Degrees concerning the Good Shepherd and His Flock, and, at the same time, a New Testament version of Psalm 23: Accordingly its analysis might be formulated as follows:

1. Christ, the Good Shepherd, in contrast to others who falsely claimed to be the shepherds. Their object had been self, and they had pursued it even at the cost of the sheep, of their life and safety. He came for them, to give, not to take, that they may have life and have abundance. Life that they may have it, I lay down Mine: so does it appear that I am the Good Shepherd.

2. The Good Shepherd Who lays down His life for His Sheep! What a contrast to a mere hireling, whose are not the sheep, and who flees at sight of the wolf (danger), and the wolf seizes them, and scatters (namely, the flock): (he flees) because he is a hireling, and does not care for the sheep. The simile of the wolf must not be too closely pressed, but taken in a general sense, to point the contrast to Him Who lays down His Life for His sheep. Truly He is, is seen to be, the fair Shepherder, Whose are the sheep, and as such, I know Mine, and Mine know Me, even as the Father knows Me, and I know the Father. And I lay down My Life for the sheep.

3. For the sheep that are Mine, whom I know, and for whom I lay down My Life! But those sheep, they are not only of this fold, not all of the Jewish fold, but also scattered sheep of the Gentiles. They have all the characteristics of the flock: they are His; and they hear His Voice; but as yet they are outside the fold. Them also the Good Shepherd must lead, and, in evidence that they are His, as He calls them and goes before them, they shall hear His Voice, and so, O most glorious consummation, they shall become one flock and one Shepherd.

And thus is the great goal of the Old Testament reached, and the good news of great joy which issue from Israel are to all people. The Kingdom of David, which is the Kingdom of God, is set up upon earth, and opened to all believers. We cannot help noticing, though it almost seems to detract from it, how different from the Jewish ideas of it is this Kingdom with its

Shepherd King, Who knows and Who lays down His Life for the sheep, and Who leads the Gentiles not to subjection nor to inferiority, but to equality of faith and privileges, taking the Jews out of their special fold and leading up the Gentiles, and so making of both one flock. From where did Jesus of Nazareth obtain these thoughts and views, towering so far aloft of all around?

But, on the other hand, they are utterly un-Gentile also, if by the term Gentile we mean the Gentile Churches, in antagonism to the Jewish Christians, as a certain school of critics would represent them, which traces the origin of this Gospel to this separation. A Gospel written in that spirit would never have spoken on this wise of the mutual relation of Jews and Gentiles towards Christ and in the Church. The magnificent words of Jesus are only compatible with one supposition: that He was indeed the Christ of God. Although men have studied or quibbled at these words for eighteen and a half centuries, they have not yet reached to this: They shall become one flock, one Shepherd.

4. In the final Step of Ascent the leading thoughts of the whole discourse are taken up and carried to the last and highest thought. The Good Shepherd that brings together the One Flock! Yes—by laying down His Life, but also by taking it up again. Both are necessary for the work of the Good Shepherd the life is laid down in the surrender of sacrifice, in order that it may be taken up again, and much more fully, in the Resurrection Power. And, therefore, His Father loves Him as the Messiah Shepherd, Who so fully does the work committed to Him, and so entirely surrenders Himself to it. His death, His Resurrection, let no one imagine that it comes from without! It is His own act. He has power in regard to both, and both are His own, voluntary, Sovereign, and Divine acts. And this, all this, in order to be the Shepherd Savior, to die, and rise for His Sheep, and thus to gather them all, Jews and Gentiles, into one flock, and to be their Shepherd. This, neither more nor less, was the Mission which God had given Him; this, the commandment which He had received of His Father, that which God had given Him to do.

It was a noble close of the series of those discourses in the Temple, which had it for their object to show, that He was truly sent of God. And, in a measure, they attained that object. To some, it all seemed unintelligible, incoherent, madness; and they fell back on the favorite explanation of all this strange drama, He has a demon! But others there were, let us hope, many, not yet His disciples, to whose hearts these words went straight. And how could they resist the impression? These utterances are not of a demonized, and, then, it came back to them: Can a demon open the eyes of the blind? And so, once again, the Light of His Words and His Person fell upon His Works, and, as ever, revealed their character, and made them clear.

Note. It seems right here, in a kind of Postscript Note, to call attention to what could not have been inserted in the text without breaking up its unity, and yet seems too important to be relegated to an ordinary foot note. In Yoma 66 b, lines 18 to 24 from top, we have a series of questions addressed to Rabbi Eliezer ben Hyrcanos, designed, as it seems to me, to test his views about Jesus and his relation to the new doctrine. Rabbi Eliezer, one of the greatest Rabbis, was the brother-in-law of Gamaliel II, the son of that Gamaliel at whose feet Paul sat. He may, therefore, have been acquainted with the Apostle. And we have unquestionable evidence that he had communication with Jewish Christians, and took pleasure in their teaching; and, further, that he was accused of favoring Christianity. Under these circumstances, the series of covered, enigmatic questions, reported as addressed to him, gains a new interest. I can only repeat, that I regard them as referring to the Person and the Words of Christ. One of these questions is to this effect: Is it [right, proper, duty] for the Shepherd to save a lamb from the lion? To this the Rabbi gives (as always in this series of questions) an evasive answer, as follows: You have only asked me about the lamb. On this the following question is next put, I presume by way of forcing an express reply: Is it [right, proper, duty] to save the Shepherd from the lion? and to this the Rabbi once more evasively replies: You have only asked me about the Shepherd. Thus, as the words of Christ to which covert reference is made have only meaning when the two ideas of the Sheep and the Shepherd are combined, the Rabbi, by dividing them, cleverly evaded giving an answer to his questioners. But these inferences come to us, all of deepest importance: 1. I regard the questions above quoted as containing a distinct reference to the words of Christ in John 10:11. The whole string of questions, of which the above form part, refers to Christ and His Words. 2. It casts a peculiar light, not only upon the personal history of this great Rabbi, the brother-in-law of the

Patriarch Gamaliel II, but a side light also, on the history of Nicodemus. Of course, such evasive answers are utterly unworthy of a disciple of Christ, and quite incompatible with the boldness of confession which must characterize them. But the question arises—now often seriously discussed by Jewish writers: how far many Rabbis and laymen may have gone in their belief of Christ, and yet, at least in too many instances, fallen short of discipleship; and, lastly, as to the relation between the early Church and the Jews, on which not a few things of deep interest have to be said, though it may not be on the present occasion. 3. Critically also, the quotation is of the deepest importance. For, does it not furnish a reference, and that on the lips of Jews, to the Fourth Gospel, and that from the close of the first century? There is here something which the opponents of its genuineness and authenticity will have to meet and answer.

Another series of similar allegorical questions in connection with R. Joshua b.Chananyah is recorded in Bekhor. 8 a and b, but answered by the Rabbi in an anti-Christian sense. See Mandelstamm, Talmud. Stud. i. But Mandelstamm goes too far in his view of the purely allegorical meaning, especially of the introductory part.

End Notes:

[35] This would be all the more striking that, according to Rabbinic law, a shepherd was not called upon to expose his own life for the safety of his flock, nor responsible in such a case. The opposite view depends on a misunderstanding of a sentence quoted from Bab. Mez. 93 b. As the context there shows, if a shepherd leaves his flock, and in his absence the wolf comes, the shepherd is responsible, but only because he ought not to have left the flock, and his presence might have prevented the accident. In case of attack by force superior he is not responsible for his flock.

Chapter 11

The First Perean Discourses

(Matthew 12:22-45; Luke 10:14-36)

It was well that Jesus should, for the present, have parted from Jerusalem with words like these. They would cling about His hearers like the odor of incense that had ascended. Even the schism that had come among them concerning His Person made it possible not only to continue His Teaching, but to return to the City once more before His final entrance. For, His Perean Ministry, which extended from after the Feast of Tabernacles to the week preceding the last Passover, was, so to speak, cut in half by the brief visit of Jesus to Jerusalem at the Feast of the Dedication. Thus, each part of the Perean Ministry would last about three months; the first, from about the end of September to the month of December; the second, from that period to the beginning of April. Of these six months we have (with the solitary exception of Matthew 12:22-45), no other account than that furnished by Luke, although, as usually, the Jerusalem and Judean incidents of it are described by John. After that we have the account of His journey to the last Passover, recorded, with more or less detail, in the three Synoptic Gospels.

This section is peculiarly lacking in incident. It consists almost exclusively of discourses and Parables, with but few narrative portions interspersed. And this, not only because the season of the year must have made itinerancy difficult, and thus have hindered the introduction to new scenes and of new persons, but chiefly from the character of His Ministry in Perea. We remember that, similarly, the beginning of Christ's Galilean Ministry had been chiefly marked by discourses and Parables. Besides, after what had passed, and must now have been so well known, illustrative Deeds could scarcely have been so essential in Perea. In fact, His Perean was, substantially, a resumption of His early Galilean Ministry, only modified and influenced by the much fuller knowledge of the people concerning Christ, and the greatly developed hostility of their leaders. This accounts for the recurrence, although in fuller, or else in modified, form, of many things recorded in the earlier part of this History. Thus, to begin with, we can understand how He would, at this initial stage of His Perean, as in that of His Galilean Ministry, repeat, when asked for instruction concerning prayer, those sacred words ever since known as the Lord's Prayer. The variations are so slight as to be easily accounted for by the individuality of the reporter. They afford, however, the occasion for remarking on the two principal differences. In Luke the prayer is for the forgiveness of sins, while Matthew uses the Hebraic term debts, which has passed even into the Jewish Liturgy, denoting our guilt as indebtedness. Again, the day by day of Luke, which further explains the petition for daily bread, common both to Matthew and Luke, may be illustrated by the beautiful Rabbinic teaching, that the Manna fell only for each day, in order that thought of their daily dependence might call forth constant faith in our Father Who is in heaven. Another Rabbinic saying places our nourishment on the same level with our redemption, as regards the thanks due to God and the fact that both are day by day. Yet a third Rabbinic saying notes the peculiar manner in which both nourishment and redemption are always mentioned in Scripture (by repeated expressions), and how, while redemption took place by an Angel, nourishment is attributed directly to God.

But to return. From the introductory expression: When (or whenever) you pray, say, we venture to infer, that this prayer was intended, not only as the model, but as furnishing the words for the future use of the Church. Yet another suggestion may be made. The request, Lord, teach us to pray, as John also taught his disciples, seems to indicate what was the certain place, which, now consecrated by Jesus' prayer, became the school for ours. It seems at least likely, that the allusion of the disciples to the Baptist may have been prompted by the circumstance, that the locality was that which had been the scene of John's labors, of course, in Perea. Such a note of place is the more interesting, that Luke so rarely indicates localities. In fact, he leaves us in ignorance of what was the central place in Christ's Perean Ministry, although there must have been such. In the main, the events are, most likely narrated in their chronological order. But, as discourses, Parables, and incidents are so closely mixed up, it will be better, in a work like the present, for clearness and briefness sake, to separate and group them, so far as possible. Accordingly, this chapter will be devoted to the briefest summary of Jesus' discourses in Perea, previous to His return to Jerusalem for the Feast of the Dedication of the Temple.

The first of these was on the occasion of His casting out a demon, and restoring speech to the demonized; or if, as seems likely, the cure is the same as that recorded in Matthew 12:22, both sight and speech, which had probably been paralyzed. This is one of the cases in which it is difficult to determine whether narratives in different Gospels, with slightly varying details, represent different events or only differing modes of narration. It needs no argument to prove, that substantially the same event, such as the healing of a blind or dumb demonized person, may, and probably would, have taken place on more than one occasion, and that, when it occurred, it would elicit substantially the same remarks by the people, and the same charge against Christ of superior demoniac agency which the Pharisees had now distinctly formulated. Again, when recording similar events, the Evangelists would naturally come to tell them in much the same manner. Therefore, it does not follow that two similar narratives in different Gospels always represent the same event. But in this instance, it seems likely. The earlier place which it occupies in the Gospel by Matthew may be explained by its position in a group denunciating the Pharisees; and the notice there of their blasphemous charge of His being the instrument of Satan probably indicates the outcome of their council, how they might destroy Him.

It is this charge of the Pharisees which forms the main subject of Christ's address, His language being now much more explicit than formerly, even as the opposition of the Pharisees had more fully ripened. In regard to the slight difference in the narratives of Matthew and Luke, we mark that, as always, the Words of the Lord are more fully reported by the former, while the latter supplies some vivid pictorial touches. The following are the leading features of Christ's reply to the Pharisaic charge: First, It was utterly unreasonable, and inconsistent with their own premises, showing that their attribution of Satanic agency to what Christ did was only prompted by hostility to His Person. This mode of turning the argument against the arguer was peculiarly Hebraic, and it does not imply any assertion on the part of Christ, as to whether or not the disciples of the Pharisees really cast out demons. Mentally, we must supply, according to your own professions, your disciples cast out demons. If so, by whom are they doing it?

But, secondly, beneath this logical argumentation lies deep and spiritual instruction, closely connected with the late teaching during the festive days in Jerusalem. It is directed against the flimsy, superstitious, and unspiritual views entertained by Israel, of the Kingdom of evil and of that of God. For, if we ignore the moral aspect of Satan and his kingdom, all degenerates into the absurdities and superstitions of the Jewish view concerning demons and Satan, which are fully described in another place. On the other hand, introduce the ideas of moral evil, of the concentration of its power in a kingdom of which Satan is the representative and ruler, and of our own inherent sinfulness, which makes us his subjects, and all becomes clear. Then, truly, can Satan not cast out Satan, or else how could his kingdom stand; then, also, is the casting out of Satan only by God's Spirit, or Finger, and this is the Kingdom of God. By their own admission, the casting out of Satan was part of the work of Messiah. Then had the Kingdom of God, come to them, for in this was the Kingdom of God; and He was the God sent Messiah, come not for the glory of Israel, nor for anything outward or intellectual, but to engage in mortal conflict with moral evil, and with Satan as its representative. In that contest Christ, as the Stronger, binds the strong one, spoils his house (divides his spoil), and takes from him the armor in which his strength lay (he trusted) by taking away the power of sin. This is the work of the Messiah, and, therefore also, no one can be indifferent towards Him, because all, being by nature in a certain relation towards Satan, must, since the Messiah had commenced His Work, occupy a definite relationship towards the Christ Who combats Satan.

It follows, that the work of the Christ is a moral contest waged through the Spirit of God, in which, from their position, all must take a part. But it is conceivable that a man may not only try to be passively, but even be actively on the enemy's side, and this not by merely speaking against the Christ, which might be the outcome of ignorance or unbelief, but by representing that as Satanic which was the object of His Coming. Such perversion of all that is highest and holiest, such opposition to, and denunciation of, the Holy Spirit as if He were the manifestation of Satan, represents sin in its absolute completeness, and for which there can be no pardon, since the state of mind of which it is the outcome admits not the possibility of repentance, because its essence lies in this, to call that Satanic which is the very object of repentance. It were unduly to press the Words of Christ, to draw from them such inferences as, whether sins unforgiven in this world might or might not be forgiven in the next, since, manifestly, it was not the intention of Christ to teach on this subject. On the other hand, His Words seem to imply that, at least as regards this sin, there is no room for forgiveness in the other world. For, the expression is not the age to come, but, the world to come which, as we know, does not strictly refer to Messianic times, but to the future and eternal, as distinguished both from this world, and from the days of the Messiah.

3. But this recognition of the spiritual, which was the opposite of the sin against the Holy Spirit, was, as Christ had so lately explained in Jerusalem, only to be attained by spiritual kinship with it. The tree must be made good, if the fruit were to be good; tree and fruit would correspond to each other. How, then, could these Pharisees speak good things, since the state of the heart determined speech and action? Therefore, a man would have to give an account even of every idle word, since, however trifling it might appear to others or to oneself, it was really the outcome of the heart, and showed the inner state. And thus, in reality, would a man's future in judgment be determined by his words; a conclusion the more solemn, when we remember its bearing on what His disciples on the one side, and the Pharisees on the other, said concerning Christ and the Spirit of God.

4. Both logically and morally the Words of Christ were unanswerable; and the Pharisees fell back on the old device of challenging proof of His Divine Mission by some visible sign. But this was to avoid the appeal to the moral element which the Lord had made; it was an attempt to shift the argument from the moral to the physical. It was the moral that was at fault, or rather, lacking in them; and no amount of physical evidence or demonstration could have supplied that. All the signs from heaven would not have supplied the deep sense of sin and of the need for a mighty spiritual deliverance, which alone would lead to the reception of the Savior Christ. Therefore, as under previous similar circumstances, He would offer them only one sign, that of Jonah the prophet. But whereas on the former occasion Christ chiefly referred to Jonah preaching (of repentance), on this He rather pointed to the allegorical history of Jonah as the Divine attestation of his Mission. As he appeared in Nineveh, he was himself a sign to the Ninevites; the fact that he had been three days and nights in the whale's belly, and that from there he had, so to speak, been sent forth alive to preach in Nineveh, was evidence to them that he had been sent of God. And so would it be again. After three days and three nights in the heart of the earth, which is a Hebraism for in the earth, would His Resurrection Divinely attest to this generation His Mission. The Ninevites did not

question, but received this testimony of Jonah; an authentic report of the wisdom of Solomon had been sufficient to bring the Queen of Sheba from so far; in the one case it was, because they felt their sin; in the other, because she felt need and longing for better wisdom than she possessed. But these were the very elements lacking in the men of this generation; and so both Nineveh and the Queen of Sheba would stand up, not only as mute witnesses against, but to condemn, them. For, the great Reality of which the preaching of Jonah had been only the type, and for which the wisdom of Solomon had been only the preparation, had been presented to them in Christ.

5. And so, having put aside this complaint, Jesus returned to His former teaching concerning the Kingdom of Satan and the power of evil; only now with application, not, as before, to the individual, but, as prompted by a view of the unbelieving resistance of Israel, to the Jewish commonwealth as a whole. Here, also, it must be remembered, that, as the words used by Jesus were allegorical and illustrative, they must not be too closely pressed. As compared with the other nations of the world, Israel was like a house from which the demon of idolatry had gone out with all his attendants, really the Beel Zibbul whom they dreaded. And then the house had been swept of all the foulness and uncleanness of idolatry, and garnished with all manner of Pharisaic adornments. Yet all this while the house was left really empty; God was not there; the Stronger One, Who alone could have resisted the Strong One, did not hold rule in it. And so the demon returned to it again, to find the house from which he had come out, swept and garnished indeed, but also empty and defenseless. The folly of Israel lay in this, that they thought of only one demon, him of idolatry, Beel Zibbul, with all his foulness. That was all very repulsive, and they had carefully removed it. But they knew that demons were only manifestations of demoniac power, and that there was a Kingdom of evil. So this house, swept of the foulness of paganism and adorned with all the self righteousness of Pharisaism, but empty of God, would only become a more suitable and more secure habitation of Satan; because, from its cleanness and beauty, his presence and rule there as an evil spirit would not be suspected. So, to continue the illustrative language of Christ, he came back with seven other spirits more wicked than himself, pride, self righteousness, unbelief, and the like, the number seven being general, and thus the last state, Israel without the foulness of gross idolatry and garnished with all the adornments of Pharisaic devotion to the study and practice

of the Law, was really worse than had been the first with all its open repulsiveness.

6. Once more was the discourse interrupted, this time by a truly Jewish incident. A woman in the crowd burst into exclamations about the blessedness of the Mother who had borne and nurtured such a Son. The phraseology seems to have been not uncommon, since it is equally applied by the Rabbis to Moses, and even to a great Rabbi. More striking, perhaps, is another Rabbinic passage (previously quoted), in which Israel is described as breaking forth into these words on beholding the Messiah: Blessed the hour in which Messiah was created; blessed the womb from which He issued; blessed the generation that sees Him; blessed the eye that is worthy to behold Him.

And yet such praise must have been peculiarly unwelcome to Christ, as being the exaltation of only His Human Personal excellence, intellectual or moral. It quite looked away from that which He would present: His Work and Mission as the Savior. Therefore it was, although from the opposite direction, as great a misunderstanding as the Personal depreciation of the Pharisees. Or, to use another illustration, this praise of the Christ through His Virgin Mother was as unacceptable and unsuitable as the depreciation of the Christ, which really, though unconsciously, underlay the loving care of the Virgin Mother when she would have arrested Him in His Work, and which (perhaps for this very reason) Matthew relates in the same connection. Accordingly, the answer in both cases is substantially the same: to point away from His merely Human Personality to His Work and Mission, in the one case: Who ever shall do the Will of My Father Which is in heaven, the same is My brother, and sister, and mother; in the other: Yes rather, blessed are they that hear the Word of God and keep it.

7. And now the discourse draws to a close by a fresh application of what, in some other form or connection, Christ had taught at the outset of His public Ministry in the Sermon on the Mount. Rightly to understand its present connection, we must pass over the various interruptions of Christ's discourse, and join this as the conclusion to the previous part, which contained the main subject. This was, that spiritual knowledge presupposed spiritual kinship. Here, as becomes the close of a discourse, the same truth is practically applied in a more popular and plain, one might almost say realistic, manner. As here put, it is, that spiritual receptiveness is ever the condition of spiritual

reception. What was the object of lighting a lamp? Surely, that it may give light. But if so, no one would put it into a vault, nor under the bushel, but on the stand. Should we then expect that God would light the spiritual lamp, if it is put in a dark vault? Or, to take an illustration for it from the eye, which, as regards the body, serves the same purpose as the lamp in a house. Does it not depend on the state of the eye whether or not we have the sensation, enjoyment, and benefit of the light? Let us, therefore, take care, for fear that, by placing, as it were, the lamp in a vault, the light in us is really only darkness. On the other hand, if by means of a good eye the light is transmitted through the whole system, if it is not turned into darkness, like a lamp that is put into a vault or under a bushel, instead of being set up to spread light through the house, then shall we be wholly full of light. And this, finally, explains the reception or rejection of Christ: how, in the words of an Apostle, the same Gospel would be both a savor of life to life, and of death to death.

It was a blessed lesson with which to close His discourse, and one full of light, if only they had not put it into the vault of their darkened hearts. Yet now would it shine forth again, and give light to those whose eyes were opened to receive it; for, according to the Divine rule and spiritual order, to him that has shall be given, and from him that has not shall be taken away even that he has.

End Notes:

[36] It marks the chronological place of this miracle that it seems suitably to follow the popular charge against Jesus, as expressed in John 8:48 and 10:20.

[37] This is simply a Hebraism of which, as similar instances, may be quoted, Exodus 15:8 (the heart of the sea); Deuteronomy 4:11 (the heart of heaven); 2 Samuel 16:14 (the heart of the terebinth). Therefore, I cannot agree with Dean Plumptre, that the expression heart of the earth bears any reference to Hades.

[38] In view of such teaching, it is indeed difficult to understand the cultus of the Virgin, and even much of that tribute to the exclusively human in Christ which is so characteristic of Romanism.

Chapter 12

Meals and Feasts Among the Jews

(Luke 10:37-54)

Bitter as was the hostility of the Pharisaic party against Jesus, it had not yet so far spread, nor become so avowed, as in every place to supersede the ordinary rules of courtesy. It is thus that we explain that invitation of a Pharisee to the morning meal, which furnished the occasion for the second recorded Perean discourse of Christ. Alike in substance and tone, it is a continuation of His former address to the Pharisees. And it is probably here inserted in order to mark the further development of Christ's anti-Pharisaic teaching. It is the last address to the Pharisees, recorded in the Gospel of Luke. A similar last appeal is recorded in a much later portion of Matthew's Gospel, only that Luke reports that spoken in Perea, Matthew that made in Jerusalem. This may also partly account for the similarity of language in the two discourses. Not only were the circumstances parallel, but the language held at the end may naturally have recurred to the writer, when reporting the last controversial discourse in Perea. Thus it may well have been, that Christ said substantially the same things on both occasions, and yet that, in the report of them, some of the later modes of expression may have been transferred to the earlier occasion. And because the later both represents and presents the fullest anti-Pharisaic discourse of Jesus, it will be better to postpone our analysis until we reach that period of His Life.

Some distinctive points, however, must here be made. The remarks already made will explain, how some time may have elapsed between this and the former discourse, and that the expression And as He spoke must not be pressed as a mark of time (referring to the immediately preceding discourse), but rather be regarded as indicating the circumstances under which a Pharisee had invited Him to the meal. Indeed, we can scarcely imagine that, immediately after such a charge by the Pharisees as that Jesus acted as the representative of Beelzebul, and such a reply on the part of Jesus, a Pharisee would have invited Him to a friendly meal, or that Lawyers, or, to use a modern term, Canonists, would have been present at it. How different their feelings were after they had heard His denunciations, appears from the bitterness with which they afterwards sought to provoke Him into saying what might serve as ground for a criminal charge. And there is absolutely no evidence that, as commentators suggest, the invitation of the Pharisee had been hypocritically given, for the purpose of getting up an accusation against Christ. More than this, it seems entirely inconsistent with the unexpressed astonishment of the Pharisee, when he saw Jesus sitting down to food without having first washed hands. Up to that moment, then, it would seem that he had only regarded Him as a celebrated Rabbi, though perhaps one who taught strange things.

But what makes it almost certain, that some time must have elapsed between this and the previous discourse (or rather that, as we believe, the two events happened in different places), is, that the invitation of the Pharisee was to the morning meal. We know that this took place early immediately after the return from morning prayers in the Synagogue. It is, therefore, scarcely conceivable, that all that is recorded in connection with the first discourse should have occurred before this first meal. On the other hand, it may well have been, that what passed at the Pharisees table may have some connection with something that had occurred just before in the Synagogue, for we conjecture that it was the Sabbath day. We infer this from the circumstance that the invitation was not to the principal meal, which on a Sabbath the Lawyers (and, all householders) would, at least ordinarily, have in their own homes. We can picture to ourselves the scene. The week day family meal was simple enough, whether breakfast or dinner, the latter towards evening, although sometimes also in the middle of the day, but always before actual darkness, in order, as it was expressed, that the sight of the dishes by daylight might excite the appetite. The Babylonian Jews were content to make a meal without meat; not so the Palestinians. With the latter the favorite food was young meat: goats, lambs, calves. Beef was not so often used, and still more rarely fowls. Bread was regarded as the mainstay of life, without which no entertainment was considered as a meal. Indeed, in a sense it constituted the meal. For the blessing was spoken over the bread, and this was supposed to cover all the rest of the food that followed, such as the meat, fish or vegetables, in short, all that made up the dinner, but not the dessert. Similarly, the blessing spoken over the wine included all other kinds of drink. Otherwise it would have been necessary to pronounce a separate benediction over each different article eaten or drunk. He who neglected the prescribed benedictions was regarded as if he had eaten of things dedicated to God, since it was written: The earth is the Lord's, and the fullness thereof. Beautiful as this principle is, it degenerated into tedious questions of dishonest deception. Thus, if one kind of food was eaten as an addition to another, it was settled that the blessing should be spoken only over the principal kind. Again, there are elaborate disagreements as to what should be regarded as fruit, and have the corresponding blessing, and how, for example, one blessing should be spoken over the leaves and blossom, and another over the berries of the caper. That bush gave rise to a serious controversy between the Schools of Hillel and Shammai: Another series of elaborate discussions arose, as to what blessing should be used when a dish consisted of various ingredients, some the product of the earth, others, like honey, derived from the animal world. Such and similar questions, giving rise to endless argument and controversy, busied the minds of the Pharisees and Scribes.

Let us suppose the guests assembled. To such a morning meal they would not be summoned by slaves, nor be received in such solemn state as at feasts. First, each would observe, as a religious rite, the washing of hands. Next, the head of the house would cut a piece from the whole loaf, on the Sabbath there were two loaves, and speak the blessing. But this, only if the company reclined at table, as at dinner. If they sat, as probably always at the early meal, each would speak the benediction for himself. The same rule applied in regard to the wine. Jewish scheme had it, that one blessing sufficed for the wine intended as part of the meal. If other wine were brought in during the meal, then each one would have to say the blessing anew over it; if after the meal (as was done on Sabbaths and feast days, to prolong the feast by drinking), one of the company spoke the benediction for all.

At the entertainment of this Pharisee, as indeed generally, Jesus omitted the prescribed washing of hands before the meal. But as this rite was in itself indifferent, He must have had some definite object, which will be explained in the sequel. The externalism of all these practices will best appear from the following account which the Talmud gives of a feast. As the guests enter, they sit down on chairs, and water is brought to them, with which they wash one hand. After this the cup is taken, when each speaks the blessing over the wine partaken of before dinner. Now they all lie down at table. Water is again brought them, with which they now wash both hands, preparatory to the meal, when the blessing is spoken over the bread, and then over the cup, by the chief person at the feast, or else by one selected by way of distinction. The company responded by Amen, always supposing the benediction to have been spoken by an Israelite, not a pagan, slave, nor law breaker. Nor was it lawful to say it with an unlettered man, although it might be said with a Cuthean (heretic, or else Samaritan), who was learned. After dinner the crumbs, if any, are carefully gathered, hands are again washed, and he who first had done so leads in the prayer of thanksgiving. The formula in which he is to call on the rest to join him, by repeating the prayers after him, is prescribed, and differs according to the number of those present. The blessing and the thanksgiving are allowed to be said not only in Hebrew, but in any other language.

In regard to the position of the guests, we know that the uppermost seats were occupied by the Rabbis. The Talmud formulates it in this manner: That the worthiest lies down first, on his left side, with his feet stretching back. If there are two cushions (divans), the next worthiest reclines above him, at his left hand; if there are three cushions, the third worthiest lies below him who had lain down first (at his right), so that the chief person is in the middle (between the worthiest guest at his left and the less worthy one at his right hand). The water before eating is first handed to the worthiest, and so in regard to the washing after meat. But if a very large number are present, you begin after dinner with the least worthy, until you come to the last five, when the worthiest in the company washes his hands, and the other four after him. The guests being thus arranged, the head of the house, or the chief person at table, speaks the blessing, and then cuts the bread. By some it was not deemed etiquette to begin eating until after he who had said the prayer had done so, but this does not seem to have been the rule among the Palestinian Jews. Then, generally, the bread was dipped into salt, or something salted, etiquette demanding that where there were two they should wait one for the other, but not where there were three or more.

This is not the place to furnish what may be termed a list of menus at Jewish tables. In earlier, times the meal was, no doubt, very simple. It became otherwise when association with Rome, Greece, and the East made the people familiar with foreign luxury, while commerce supplied its requirements. Indeed, it would scarcely be possible to enumerate the various articles which seem to have been imported from different, and even distant, countries.

To begin with: the wine was mixed with water, and, some thought that the benediction should not be pronounced until the water had been added to the wine. According to one statement, two parts, according to another, three parts, of water were to be added to the wine. Various vintages are mentioned: among them a red wine of Saron, and a black wine. Spiced wine was made with honey and pepper. Another mixture, chiefly used for invalids, consisted of old wine, water, and balsam; yet another was wine of myrrh; we also read of a wine in which capers had been soaked. To these we should add wine spiced, either with pepper, or with absinthe; and what is described as vinegar, a cooling drink made either of grapes that had not ripened, or of the remains. Besides these, palm wine was also in use. Of foreign drinks, we read of wine from Ammon, and from the province Asia, the latter a kind of must be boiled down. Wine in ice came from the Lebanon; a certain kind of vinegar from Idumea; beer from Media and Babylon; a barley wine (zythos) from Egypt. Finally, we ought to mention Palestinian apple cider, and the juice of other fruits. If we adopt the rendering of some, even liquors were known and used.

Long as this catalogue is, that of the various articles of food, whether native or imported, would occupy a much larger space. Suffice it that, as regarded the various kinds of grain, meat, fish, and fruits. either in their natural state or preserved, it embraced almost everything known to the ancient world. At feasts there was an introductory course, consisting of appetizing salted meat, or of some light dish. This was followed by the dinner itself, which finished with dessert (Aphiqomon or terugima) consisting of pickled olives, radishes and lettuce, and fruits, among which even preserved ginger from India is mentioned. The most diverse and even strange statements are made as to the healthiness, or the reverse, of certain articles of diet, especially vegetables. Fish was a favorite dish, and never lacking at a Sabbath meal. It was a saying, that both salt and water should be used at every meal, if health was to be preserved. Condiments, such as mustard or pepper, were to be sparingly used. Very different were the meals of the poor. Locusts, fried in flour or honey, or preserved, required, according to the Talmud, no blessing, since the animal was really among the curses of the land. Eggs were a common article of food, and sold in the shops. Then there was a milk dish into which people dipped their bread. Others, who were better off, had a soup made of vegetables, especially onions, and meat, while the very poor would satisfy the cravings of hunger with bread and cheese, or bread and fruit, or some vegetables, such as cucumbers, lentils, beans, peas, or onions.

At meals the rules of etiquette were strictly observed, especially as regarded the sages. Two tractates are added to the Talmud, of which the one describes the general etiquette, the other that of sages, and the title of which may be translated by The Way of the World (Derekh Erets), being a sort of code of good manners. According to some, it was not good breeding to speak while eating. The learned and most honored occupied not only the chief places, but were sometimes distinguished by a double portion. According to Jewish etiquette, a guest should conform in everything to his host, even though it were unpleasant. Although hospitality was the greatest and most prized social virtue, which, to use a Rabbinic expression, might make every home a sanctuary and every table an altar, an uninvited guest, or a guest who brought another guest, was proverbially an unwelcome spirit. Sometimes, by way of self righteousness, the poor were brought in, and the best part of the meal ostentatiously given to them. At ordinary entertainments, people were to help themselves. It was not considered good manners to drink as soon as you were asked, but you ought to hold the cup for a little in your hand. But it would be the height of rudeness, either to wipe the plates, to scrape together the bread, as though you had not had enough to eat, or to drop it, to the inconvenience of your neighbor. If a piece were taken out of a dish, it must of course not be put back; still less must you offer from your cup or plate to your neighbor. From the almost religious value attaching to bread, we scarcely wonder that these rules were laid down: not to steady a cup or plate upon bread, nor to throw away bread, and that after dinner the bread was to be carefully swept together. Otherwise, it was thought, demons would sit upon it. The Way of the World for Sages, lays down these as the marks of a Rabbi: that he does not eat standing; that he does not lick his fingers; that he sits down only beside his equals, in fact, many regarded it as wrong to eat with the unlearned; that he begins cutting the bread where it is best baked, nor ever breaks off a bit with his hand; and that, when drinking, he turns away his face from the company. Another saying was that the sage was known by four things: at his cups, in money matters, when angry, and in his jokes. After dinner, the formalities concerning hand washing and prayer, already described, were gone through, and then frequently aromatic spices burnt, over which a special benediction was pronounced. We have only to add, that on Sabbaths it was deemed a religious duty to have three meals, and to procure the best that money could obtain, even though one were to save and fast for it all the week. Lastly, it was regarded as a special obligation and honor to entertain sages.

We have no difficulty now in understanding what passed at the table of the Pharisee. When the water for purification was presented to Him, Jesus would either refuse it; or if, as seems more likely at a morning meal, each guest repaired by himself for the prescribed purification, He would omit to do so, and sit down to meat without this formality. No one, who knows the stress which Pharisaism laid on this rite would argue that Jesus might have conformed to the practice. The controversy was long and bitter between the Schools of Shammai and Hillel, on such a point as whether the hands were to be washed before the cup was filled with wine, or after that, and where the towel was to be deposited. With such things the most serious ritual inferences were connected on both sides. A religion which spent its energy on such trivialities must have lowered the moral tone. All the more that Jesus insisted so earnestly, as the substance of His Teaching, on that corruption of our nature which Judaism ignored, and on that spiritual purification which was needful for the reception of His doctrine, would He publicly and openly set aside ordinances of man which diverted thoughts of purity into questions of the most childish character. On the other hand, we can also understand what bitter thoughts must have filled the mind of the Pharisee, whose guest Jesus was, when he observed His neglect of the cherished rite. It was an insult to himself, a defiance of Jewish Law, a revolt against the most cherished traditions of the Synagogue. Remembering that a Pharisee ought not to sit down to a meal with such, he might feel that he should not have asked Jesus to his table. All this, as well as the terrible contrast between the thoroughness of Pharisaism in outward purifications, and the inward defilement which it never sought to remove, must have been open before Him Who read the inmost secrets of the heart, and kindled His holy wrath. Probably taking occasion (as previously suggested) from something that had passed before, He spoke with the point and emphasis which a last appeal to Pharisaism demanded.

What Jesus said on this occasion will be considered in detail in another place. Suffice it hear to mark, that He first exposed the mere externalism of the Pharisaic law of purification, to the utter ignoring of the higher need of inward purity, which lay at the foundation of all. If the primary origin of the ordinance was to prevent the eating of sacred offerings in defilement, were these outward offerings not a symbol of the inward sacrifice, and was there not an inward defilement as well as the outward? To consecrate what we had to God in His poor, instead of selfishly enjoying it, would not, be a purification of them (for such was not needed), but it would, in the truest sense, be to eat God's offerings in cleanness. We mark here a progress and a development, as compared with the former occasion when Jesus had publicly spoken on the same subject. Formerly, He had treated the ordinance of the Elders as a matter not binding; now, He showed how this externalism militated against thoughts of the internal and spiritual. Formerly, He had shown how traditionalism came into conflict with the written Law of God: now, how it superseded the first principles which underlay that Law. Formerly, He had laid down the principle that defilement came not from without inwards, but from within outwards; now, He unfolded this highest principle that higher consecration imparted purity.

The same principle, would apply to other things, such as to the Rabbinic law of tithing. At the same time it may have been, as already suggested, that something which had previously taken place, or was the subject of conversation at table, had given occasion for the further remarks of Christ. Thus, the Pharisee may have wished to convey his rebuke of Christ by referring to the subject of tithing. And such covert mode of rebuking was very common among the Jews. It was regarded as utterly defiling to eat of that which had not been tithed. The three distinctions of a Pharisee were: not to make use nor to partake of anything that had not been tithed; to observe the laws of purification; and, as a consequence of these two, to abstain from familiar interaction with all non-Pharisees. This separation formed the ground of their claim to distinction. Observe that it is exactly to these three things Jesus adverts: so that these sayings of His are not, as might seem, unconnected, but in the strictest internal relationship. Our Lord shows how Pharisaism, as regarded the outer, was connected with the opposite tendency as regarded the inner man: outward purification with ignorance of the need of that inward purity, which consisted in God consecration, and with the neglect of it; strictness of outward tithing with ignorance and neglect of the principle which underlay it, namely, the acknowledgment of God's right over mind and heart (judgment and the love of God); while, lastly, the Pharisaic pretence of separation, and consequent claim to distinction, issued only in pride and self assertion. Thus, tried by its own tests, Pharisaism terribly failed. It was hypocrisy, although that word was not mentioned until afterwards; and that both negatively and positively: the concealment of what it was, and the pretension to what it was not. And the Pharisaism which pretended to the highest purity, was, really, the greatest impurity, the defilement of graves, only covered up, not to be seen of men!

It was at this point that one of the Scribes at table broke in. Remembering in what contempt some of the learned held the ignorant bigotry of the

Pharisees, we can understand that he might have listened with secret enjoyment to denunciations of their folly. As the common saying had it, the silly pietist, a woman Pharisee, and the (self inflicted) blows of Pharisaism, were among the plagues of life. And we cannot help feeling, that there is sometimes a touch of quiet humor in the accounts which the Rabbis give of the encounters between the Pharisees and their opponents. But, as the Scribe rightly remarked, by attacking, not merely their practice, but their principles, the whole system of traditionalism, which they represented, was condemned. And so the Lord assuredly meant it. The Scribes were the exponents of the traditional law; those who bound and loosed in Israel. They bound on heavy burdens, but they never loosed one; all those grievous burdens of traditionalism they laid on the poor people, but not the slightest effort did they make to remove any of them. Tradition, yes! the very profession of it bore witness against them. Tradition, the ordinances that had come down, they would not reform nor put aside anything, but claim and proclaim all that had come down from the fathers as a sacred inheritance to which they clung. So be it! let them be judged by their own words. The fathers had murdered the prophets, and they built their tombs; that, also, was a tradition, that of guilt which would be avenged. Tradition, learning, exclusiveness, unfortunately it was only taking away from the poor the key of knowledge; and while they themselves did not enter by the door into the Kingdom, they hindered those who would have gone in. And truly so did they prove that theirs was the inheritance, the tradition, of guilt in hindering and banishing the Divine teaching of old, and murdering its Divine messengers.

There was a terrible truth and solemnity in what Jesus spoke, and in the Judgment which He denounced on them. The history of the next few months would bear witness how truly they had taken upon them this tradition of guilt; and all the after history of Israel shows how fully this Judgment has come upon them. But, after such denunciations, the entertainment in the Pharisees house must have been broken up. The Christ was too terribly in earnest, too mournfully so over those whom they hindered from entering the Kingdom, to bear with the awful guilt of their trivialities. With what feelings they parted from Him, appears from the sequel.

And when He was come out from there, the Scribes and the Pharisees began to press upon Him vehemently, and to provoke Him to speak of many things; laying wait for Him, to catch something out of His Mouth.

End Notes:

[39]   The expression one of the Lawyers (ver. 45) seems to imply that there were several at table.

[40]   To take the first meal later in the day was deemed very unwholesome: like throwing a stone into a skin.

[41]   As always in the East, there were many kinds of baked food, from the coarse barley bread or rice cake to the finest pastry. We read even of a kind of biscuit, imported from India (the Teritha, Ber. 37 b).

[42]   So rigid was this, that it was deemed duty to speak a blessing over a drink of water, if one was thirsty, Ber. v1:8.

[43]   The arrangement indicated in the text is of importance as regards the places taken at the Last Supper, when there was a dispute among the disciples about the order in which they were to sit (comp. pp. 493-495).

Chapter 13

Teaching the Disciples

(Luke 12:1, 13:17)

The record of Christ's last warning to the Pharisees, and of the feelings of murderous hate which it called forth, is followed by a summary of Christ's teaching to His disciples. The tone is still that of warning, but entirely different from that to the Pharisees. It is a warning of sin that threatened, not of judgment that awaited; it was for prevention, not in denunciation. That such warnings were most seasonable, requires scarcely proof. They were prompted by circumstances around. The same teaching, because prompted by the same causes, had been mostly delivered, also, on other occasions. Yet there are notable, though seemingly slight, divergences, accounted for by the difference of the writers or of the circumstances, and which mark the independence of the narratives.

1. The first of these discourses naturally connects itself with what had passed at the Pharisees table, an account of which must soon have spread. Although Jesus is reported as having addressed the same language chiefly to the Twelve when sending them on their first Mission, we shall now mark several characteristic variations. The address, or so much of it as is reported, probably only its summary, is introduced by the following notice of the circumstances: In the mean time, when the many thousands of the people were gathered together, so that they stepped on each other, He began to say to His disciples: "First [above all], beware of the leaven of the Pharisees, which is hypocrisy." There is no need to point out the connection between

this warning and the denunciation of Pharisaism and traditionalism at the Pharisee's table. Although the word hypocrisy had not been spoken there, it was the sum and substance of His contention, that Pharisaism, while pretending to what it was not, concealed what it was. And it was this which, like leaven, pervaded the whole system of Pharisaism. Not that as individuals they were all hypocrites, but that the system was hypocrisy. And here it is characteristic of Pharisaism, that Rabbinic Hebrew has not even a word equivalent to the term hypocrisy. The only expression used refers either to flattery of, or pretence before men, not to that unconscious hypocrisy towards God which Jesus so truly describes as the leaven that pervaded all the Pharisees said and did. It is against this that He warned His disciples, and in this, rather than conscious deception, pretence, or flattery, lies the danger of the Church. Our common term, unreality, but partially describes it. Its full meaning can only be gathered from Christ's teaching. But what precise term He may have used, it is impossible to suggest.

After all, hypocrisy was only self deception. But, there is nothing covered that shall not be revealed. Therefore, what they had said in the darkness would be revealed, and what they had spoken about in the store rooms would be proclaimed on the housetops. Nor should fear influence them. Fear of whom? Man could only kill the body, but God held body and soul. And, as fear was foolish, so was it needless in view of that wondrous Providence which watched over even the most common of God's creatures. Rather let them, in the impending struggle with the powers of this world, rise to consciousness of its full importance, how earth's voices would find their echo in heaven. And then this contest, what was it! Not only opposition to Christ, but, in it inmost essence, blasphemy against the Holy Spirit. Therefore, to succumb in that contest, implied the deepest spiritual danger. But let them not be apprehensive; their acknowledgment would not be only in the future; even now, in the hour of their danger, would the Holy Spirit help them, and give them an answer before their accusers and judges, whoever they might be—Jews or Gentiles. Thus, if they fell victims, it would be with the knowledge, not by neglect, of their Father; here, there, everywhere, in their own hearts, before the Angels, before men, would He give testimony for those who were His witnesses.

Before proceeding, we briefly mark the differences between this and the previous kindred address of Christ, when sending the Apostles on their Mission. There (after certain personal directions), the discourse began with what it here closes. There it was in the form of warning prediction, here in that of comforting reassurance; there it was near the beginning, here near the close, of His Ministry. Again, as addressed to the Twelve on their Mission, it was followed by personal directions and consolations, and then, transition was made to the admonition to dismiss fear, and to speak out publicly what had been told them privately. On the other hand, when addressing His Perean disciples, while the same admonition is given, and partly on the same grounds, yet, as spoken to disciples rather than to preachers, the reference to the similarity of their fate with that of Christ is omitted, while, to show the real character of the struggle, an admonition is added, which in His Galilean Ministry was given in another connection. Lastly, whereas the Twelve were admonished not to fear, and, therefore, to speak openly what they had learned privately, the Perean disciples are forewarned that, although what they had spoken together in secret would be dragged into the light of greatest publicity, yet they were not to be afraid of the possible consequences to themselves.

2. The second discourse recorded in this connection was occasioned by a request for judicial intervention on the part of Christ. This He answered by a Parable, which will be explained in conjunction with the other Parables of that period. The outcome of this Parable, as to the utter uncertainty of this life, and the consequent folly of being so careful for this world while neglectful of God, led Him to make warning application to His Perean disciples. Only here the negative injunction that preceded the Parable, beware of covetousness, is, when addressed to the disciples, carried back to its positive underlying principle: to dismiss all anxiety, even for the necessaries of life, learning from the birds and the flowers to have absolute faith and trust in God, and to labor for only one thing, the Kingdom of God. But, even in this, they were not to be careful, but to have absolute faith and trust in their Father, Who was well pleased to give them the Kingdom.

With but slight variations the Lord had used the same language, even as the same admonition had been needed, at the beginning of His Galilean Ministry, in the Sermon on the Mount. Perhaps we may here, also, regard the allusion to the springing flowers as a mark of time. Only, whereas in Galilee this would mark the beginning of spring, it would, in the more favored climate of certain parts of Perea, indicate the beginning of December, about the time of the Feast of the Dedication of the Temple.

More important, perhaps, is it to note, that the expression rendered in the KJV and Revised Versions, neither be you of doubtful mind, really means, neither be you uplifted, in the sense of not aiming, or seeking after great things. This rendering the Greek word (meteorzein) is in accordance with its uniform use in the LXX, and in the Apocrypha; while, on the other hand, it occurs in Josephus and Philo, in the sense of being of a doubtful mind. But the context here shows, that the term must refer to the disciples coveting great things, since only to this the remark could apply, that the Gentile world sought such things, but that our Father knew what was really needful for us.

Of deepest importance is the final consolation, to dismiss all care and anxiety, since the Father was pleased to give to this little flock the Kingdom. The expression flood carries us back to the language which Jesus had held before parting from Jerusalem. From here on this designation would mark His people. Even its occurrence fixes this discourse as not a repetition of that which Matthew had formerly reported, but as spoken after the Jerusalem visit. It designates Christ's people in distinction to their ecclesiastical (or outward) organization in a fold, and marks their individuality and their conjunction, their need and dependence, and their relation to Him as the Good Shepherd. Small and despised though it is in the eyes of men, the little flock is unspeakably noble, and rich in the gift of the Father.

These admonitions, as against covetousness, and as to absolute trust and a self surrender to God, which would count all loss for the Kingdom, are finally set forth, in their present application and their ultimate and permanent principle, in what we regard as the concluding part of this discourse. Its first sentence: Sell what you have, and give alms, which is only recorded by Luke, indicates not a general principle, but its application to that particular period, when the faithful disciple required to follow the Lord, unencumbered by worldly cares or possessions. The general principle underlying it is that expressed by Paul, and finally resolves itself into this: that the Christian should not have as holding, and not use what he has for self nor sin, but for necessity. This conclusion of Christ's discourse, also, confirms the inference that it was delivered near the terrible time of the end. Most seasonable would be here the repetition, though in slightly different language, of an admonition, given in the beginning of Christ's Galilean Ministry, to provide treasure in heaven, which could neither fail nor be taken away, for, assuredly, where the treasure was, there also would the heart be.

3.   Closely connected with, and yet quite distinct from, the previous discourse is that about the waiting attitude of the disciples in regard to their Master. Wholly detached from the things of the world, their hearts set on the Kingdom, only one thing should seem worthy of their whole attention, and engage all their thoughts and energies: their Master! He was away at some joyous feast, and the uncertainty of the hour of His return must not lead the servants to indulge in surplusing, nor to lie down in idleness, but to be faithful to their trust, and eagerly expectant of their Master. The discourse itself consists of three parts and a practical application, itself consists of three parts and a practical application.

1.   The Disciples as Servants in the absence of their Master: their duty and their reward. This part, containing what would be so needful to these Perean disciples, is peculiar to Luke. The Master is supposed to be absent, at a wedding, a figure which must not be closely pressed, not being one of the essentials in the Parable. At most, it points to a joyous occasion, and its mention may chiefly indicate that such a feast might be protracted, so that the exact time of Jesus' return could not be known to the servants who waited at home. In these circumstances, they should hold themselves in readiness, that, whatever hour it might be, they should be able to open the door at the first knocking. Such eagerness and devotion of service would naturally meet its reward, and Jesus would, in turn, consult the comfort of those who had not allowed themselves their evening meal, nor lain down, but watched for His return. Hungry and weary as they were from their zeal for Him, He would now, in turn, minister to their personal comfort. And this applied to servants who so watched—it did not mattered how long, whether into the second or the third of the watches into which the night was divided.

The Parable now passes into another aspect of the case, which is again referred to in the last discourses of Christ. Conversely, suppose the other case, of people sleeping: the house might be broken into. Of course, if one had known the hour when the thief would come, sleep would not have been indulged in; but it is just this uncertainty and suddenness, and the Coming of the Christ into His Kingdom would be equally sudden, which should keep the people in the house ever on their watch until Christ came.

It was at this particular point that a question of Peter interrupted the discourse of Christ. To whom did this Parable apply about the good man and the servants who were to watch: to the Apostles, or also to all? From the implied, for it is not stated, answer of the Lord, we infer, that Peter expected some difference between the Apostles and the rest of the disciples, whether as regarded the attitude of the servants that waited, or the reward. From the words of Christ the former seems the more likely. We can understand how Peter might entertain the Jewish notion, that the Apostles would come with Jesus from the marriage supper, rather than wait for His return, and work while waiting. It is to this that the reply of Christ refers. If the Apostles or others are rulers, it is as stewards, and their reward of faithful and wise stewardship will be advance to higher administration. But as stewards they are servants, servants of Christ, and ministering servants in regard to the other and general servants. What becomes them in this twofold capacity is faithfulness to the absent, yet ever near, Lord, and to their work, avoiding, on the one hand, the masterfulness of pride and of harshness, and, on the other, the self degradation of conformity to evil manners, either of which would entail sudden and deserved punishment in the sudden and righteous reckoning at His appearing. The Parable, therefore, as to the waiting and the reckoning, applied to work for Christ, as well as to personal relationship towards Him.

Thus far this solemn warning would naturally be afterwards repeated in Christ's last discourses in Judea, as equally needful, in view of His near departure. But in this Perean discourse, as reported by Luke, there now follows what must be regarded, not, as a further answer to Peter's inquiry, but as specifically referring to the general question of the relation between special work and general discipleship which had been raised. For, in one sense, all disciples are servants, not only to wait, but to work. As regarded those who, like the professed stewards or laborers, knew their work, but neither made ready, nor did according to His Will, their punishment and loss (where the illustrative figure of many and few stripes must not be too closely pressed) would naturally be greater than that of them who did not know, though this also involves guilt, that their Lord had any will towards them, that is, any work for them. This, according to a well understood principle, universally, almost instinctively, acted upon among men.

2. In the absence of their master! A period this of work, as well as of waiting; a period of trial also. Here, also, the two opening verses, in their evident connection with the subject matter under the first

head of this discourse, but especially with the closing sentences about work for Jesus, are peculiar to Luke's narrative, and fit only into it. The Church had a work to do in His absence, the work for which He had come. He came to cast fire on earth, that fire which was kindled when the Risen Savior sent the Holy Spirit, and of which the tongues of fire were the symbol. Oh, how He longed, that it were already kindled! But between Him and it lay the cold flood of His Passion, the terrible Passion in which He was to be baptized. Oh, how He felt the burden of that coming agony! That fire must they spread: this was the work in which, as disciples, each one must take part. Again, in that Baptismal Agony of His they also must be prepared to share. It was fire: burning up, as well as purifying and giving light. And here it was in place to repeat to His Perean disciples the prediction already addressed to the Twelve when going on their Mission, as to the certain and necessary trials connected with carrying the fire which Christ had cast on earth, even to the burning up of the closest bonds of association and kinship.

3. Thus far to the disciples. And now for its application to the multitudes, although here also He could only repeat what on a former occasion He had said to the Pharisees. Let them not think that all this only concerned the disciples. No; it was a question between Israel and their Messiah, and the struggle would involve the widest consequences, to the people and the Sanctuary. Were they so blinded as not to know how to interpret the time? Could they not read its signs, they who had no difficulty in interpreting it when a cloud rose from the sea, or the sirocco blew from the south? Why then, and here Luke is again alone in his report—did they not, in the circumstances, of themselves judge what was right and fitting and necessary, in view of the gathering tempest?

What was it? Even that he had told them before in Galilee, for the circumstances were the same. What common sense and common prudence would dictate to everyone whom his accuser or creditor hauled before the magistrate: to come to an agreement with him before it was too late, before sentence had been pronounced and executed. Although the illustration must not be pressed as to details, its general meaning would be the more readily understood that there was a similar Rabbinic proverb, although with very different practical application.

4. Besides these discourses, two events are recorded before Christ's departure to the Feast of the Dedication. Each of these led to a brief discourse, ending in a Parable.

The first records two circumstances not mentioned by the Jewish historian Josephus, nor in any other historical notice of the time, either by Rabbinic or other writers. This shows, on the one hand, how terribly common such events must have been, when they could be so generally omitted from the long catalogue of Pilate's misdeeds towards the Jews. On the other hand it also evidences that the narrative of Luke was derived from independent, authentic sources, in other words, the historical character of his narrative, when he could refer as well known to facts, which are not mentioned in any other record of the times; and, lastly, that we are not warranted in rejecting a notice, simply because we find no other mention of it than on the pages of the Third Gospel.

It appears that, just then, or quite soon afterwards, some persons told Christ about a number of His own Galileans, whom Pilate had ordered to be cut down, as we infer, in the Temple, while engaged in offering their sacrifices, so that, in the pictorial language of the East, their blood had mingled with that of their sacrifices. Clearly, their narration of this event must be connected with the preceding discourse of Jesus. He had asked them, whether they could not discern the signs of the terrible national storm that was nearing. And it was in reference to this, as we judge, that they repeated this story. To understand their object, we must attend to the answer of Christ. It is intended to refute the idea, that these Galileans had in this been visited by a special punishment of some special sin against God. Two questions here arise. Since between Christ's visit to Jerusalem at the Feast of Tabernacles and that at the Dedication of the Temple no Festival took place, it is most probable that this event had happened before Christ's visit to Jerusalem. But in that case it seems most likely, almost certain, that Christ had heard of it before. If so, or, at any rate, if it was not quite a recent event, why did these men tell Him of it then and there? Again, it seems strange that, although the Jews connected special sins with special punishments, they should have regarded it as the Divine punishment of a special sin to have been martyred by a Pilate in the Temple, while engaged in offering sacrifices.

All this becomes quite plain, if we regard these men as trying to turn the edge of Jesus' warning by a kind of Tu quoque argument. Very probably these Galileans were thus ruthlessly murdered, because of their real or suspected connection with the Nationalist movement, of which Galilee was the focus. It is as if these Jews had said to Jesus: Yes, signs of the times and of the coming storm! These Galileans of yours, your own countrymen, involved in a kind of Pseudo-Messianic movement, a kind of signs of the times rising, something like that towards which you want us to look, was not their death a deserved punishment? This latter inference they did not express in words, but implied in their narration of the fact. But Jesus read their thoughts and refuted their reasoning. For this purpose He cited another instance, when a tower at the Siloam Pool had fallen on eighteen persons and killed them, perhaps in connection with that construction of an aqueduct into Jerusalem by Pilate, which called forth, on the part of the Jews, the violent opposition, which the Roman so terribly avenged. As good Jews, they would probably think that the fall of the tower, which had buried in its ruins these eighteen persons, who were perhaps engaged in the building of that cursed structure, was a just judgment of God! For Pilate had used for it the sacred money which had been devoted to Temple purposes (the Qorban), and many there were who perished in the tumult caused by the Jewish resistance to this act of profaning. But Christ argued, that it was as wrong to infer that Divine judgment had overtaken His Galilean countrymen, as it would be to judge that the Tower of Siloam had fallen to punish these Jerusalemites. Not one party only, nor another; not the supposed Messianic tendency (in the shape of a national rising), nor, on the other hand, the opposite direction of absolute submission to Roman domination, was in fault. The whole nation was guilty; and the coming storm, to the signs of which He had pointed, would destroy all unless there were spiritual repentance on the part of the nation. And yet wider than this, and applying to all time, is the underlying principle, that, when a calamity befalls a district or an aggregation of individuals, we ought not to take to ourselves judgment as to its special causation, but to think spiritually of its general application, not so much seek to trace what is the character of its connection with a district or individuals, as to learn its lessons and to regard them as a call addressed to all. And conversely, also, this holds true in regard to deliverances.

Having thus answered the implied objection, Jesus next showed, in the Parable of the Fig tree, the need and urgency of national repentance.

The second event recorded by Luke in this connection recalls the incidents of the early Judean and of the Galilean Ministry. We observe the same narrow views and externalism as before in regard to the Sabbath on the part of the Jewish authorities, and, on the part of Christ, the same wide principles and spiritual application. If we were in search of evidence of the Divine Mission of Jesus, we would find it in this contrariety on so fundamental a point, since no teacher in Israel nor Reformer of that time, not the most advanced Sadducee, would have defended, far less originated, the views as to the Sabbath which Christ now propounded. Again, if we were in quest of evidence of the historical truthfulness of the Gospel narratives, we would find it in a comparison of the narratives of the three Sabbath controversies: in Jerusalem, in Galilee, and in Perea. In all the spirit was the same. And, although the differences between them may seem slight, they are characteristic, and mark, as if they pointed to it with the finger, the locality and circumstances in which each took place. In Jerusalem there is neither reasoning nor rebuke on the part of the Jews, but absolute persecution. There also Jesus enters on the higher exposition of His action, motives, and Mission. In Galilee there is questioning, and cunning intrigue against Him on the part of the Judeans who dogged His steps. But while no violence can be attempted against Him, the people do not venture openly to take His part. But in Perea we are confronted by the clumsy zeal of a country Archisynagogos (Chief Ruler of a Synagogue), who is very angry, but not very wise; who admits Christ's healing power, and does not dare to attack Him directly, but, instead, rebukes, not Christ, not even the woman who had been healed, but the people who witnessed it, at the same time telling them to come for healing on other days, not perceiving, in his narrow minded bigotry, what this admission implied. This rustic Ruler did not have the cunning, nor even the courage, of the Judean Pharisees in Galilee, whom Jesus had formerly convicted and silenced. Enough, to show this obscure Perean partisan of Pharisaism and the like of him their utter folly, and that by their own admissions. And now, not only were His adversaries ashamed, while in Galilee they went out and held a council against Him, but the people were not afraid, as the Galileans had been in presence of their rulers, and openly rejoiced in the glorious working of the Christ.

Little more requires to be added about this incident in one of the Synagogues of Perea. Let us only briefly recall the scene. Among those present in this Synagogue had been a poor woman, who for eighteen years had been a sufferer, as we learn, through demoniac agency. It is quite true that most, if not all, such diseases were connected with moral distemper, since demoniac possession was not permanent, and resistance might have been made in the lucid intervals, if there had been moral soundness. But it is ungrounded to distinguish between the spirit of infirmity as the moral and psychical, and her being bent, as indicating the physical disease, or even to describe the latter as a permanent curvature of the spine. The Greek word here rendered infirmity has passed into Rabbinic language (Isteniseyah,), and there means, not any particular disease, but sickliness, sometimes weakliness. In fact, she was, both physically and morally, not sick, but sickly, and most truly was hers a spirit of infirmity, so that she was bowed together, and could in no wise lift herself up. For, we mark that hers was not demoniac possession at all, and yet, though she had not yielded, she had not effectually resisted, and so she was bound by a spirit of infirmity, both in body and soul.

We recognize the same spirit of infirmity in the circumstances of her healing. When Christ, seeing her, probably a fit symbol of the Pereans in that Synagogue, called her, she came; when He said to her, Woman, you have been loosed from your sickliness, she was unbound, and yet in her weakliness she did not answer, nor straightened herself, until Jesus laid His Hands on her, and so strengthened her in body and soul, and then she was immediately made straight, and glorified God.

As for the Archisynagogos, we have, as already hinted, such characteristic portrail of him that we can almost see him: confused, irresolute, perplexed, and very angry, bustling forward and scolding the people who had done nothing, yet not venturing to silence the woman, now no longer infirm, far less, to reprove the great Rabbi, Who had just done such a glorious thing, but speaking at Him through those who had been the astounded eye witnesses. He was easily and effectually silenced, and all who sympathized with him put to shame. Hypocrites! spoke Jesus, on your own admissions your practice and your Law condemn your speech. Every one on the Sabbath looses his ox or donkey, and leads him to the watering. The Rabbinic law expressly allowed this, and even to draw the water, provided the vessel were not carried to the animal. If, as you admit, I have the power of loosing from the bonds of Satan, and she has been so bound these eighteen years, should she, a daughter of Abraham, not have that done for her which you do for your beasts of burden?

The retort was unanswerable and irresistible; it did what was intended: it covered the adversaries with shame. And the Pereans in that Synagogue felt also, at least for the time, the blessed freedom which had come to that woman. They took up the echoes of her hymn of praise, and rejoiced for all the glorious things that were done by Him. And He answered their joy by rightly directing it, by setting before them the Kingdom, which He had come both to preach and to bring, in all its freeness, reality, power, and all pervading energy, as exhibited in the two Parables of the Mustard seed and the Leaven, spoken before in Galilee. These were now repeated, as especially suited to the circumstances: first, to the Miracle they had witnessed; then, to the contention that had passed; and, lastly, to their own state of feeling. And the practical application of these Parables must have been obvious to all.

End Notes:

[44] Luke seems to use tameon in that sense (here and in ver. 24), Matthew in the sense of inner chamber (Matthew 6:6; 24:26). In the LXX it is used chiefly in the latter sense; in the Apocr. once in the sense of inner chamber (Tob. 5:16), and once in that of storeroom (Ecclus. 29:12).

[45] The observant reader will notice how characteristic the small differences are. Thus, the sirocco would not be expected in Galilee, but in Perea, and in the latter also the first flowers would appear much earlier.

Chapter 14

The Feast of Dedication

(Luke 13:22; John 10:22-42)

About two months had passed since Jesus had left Jerusalem after the Feast of Tabernacles. Although we must not commit ourselves to such calculations, we may here mention the computation which identifies the first day of the Feast of Tabernacles of that year with Thursday the 23rd September; the last, the Great Day of the Feast, with Wednesday the 29th; the Octave of the Feast with the 30th September; and the Sabbath when the man born blind was healed with the 2nd of October. In that case, the Feast of the Dedication of the Temple, which commenced on the 25th day of Chislev, and lasted eight days, would have begun on Wednesday the 1st, and closed on Wednesday the 8th December. But, possibly, it may have been a week or two later. At that Feast, or about two months after He had left the City, we find Christ once more in Jerusalem and in the Temple. His journey there seems indicated in the Third Gospel (Luke 13:22), and is at least implied in the opening words with which John prefaces his narrative of what happened on that occasion.

As we think of it, there seems special fitness, now to be pointed out, in Christ's spending what we regard as the last anniversary season of His Birth in the Temple at that Feast. It was not of Biblical origin, but had been instituted by Judas Maccabaeus in 164 BC, when the Temple, which had been desecrated by Antiochus Epiphanes, was once more purified, and re-dedicated to the Service of Jehovah. Accordingly, it was designated as the Dedication of the Altar. Josephus calls it The Lights, from one of the principal observances at the Feast, though he speaks in hesitating language of the origin of the festival as connected with this observance, probably because, while he knew, he was ashamed to declare, and yet afraid to deny his belief in the Jewish legend connected with it. The Jews called it Chanukkah, dedication or consecration, and, in much the same sense, Enkainia in the Greek of the LXX, and in the New Testament. During the eight days of the Feast the series of Psalms known as at the Hallel was chanted in the Temple, the people responding as at the Feast of Tabernacles. Other rites resembled those of the latter Feast. Thus, originally, the people appeared with palm branches. This, however, does not seem to have been after wards observed, while another rite, not mentioned in the Book of Maccabees, that of illuminating the Temple and private houses, became characteristic of the Feast. Thus, the two festivals, which indeed are put in union in 2 Maccabees 10:6, seem to have been both externally and internally connected. The Feast of the Dedication, or of Lights, derived from that of Tabernacles its duration of eight days, the chanting of the Hallel, and the practice of carrying palm branches. On the other hand, the rite of the Temple illumination may have passed from the Feast of the Dedication into the observances of that of Tabernacles. Tradition had it, that, when the Temple Services were restored by Judas Maccabeus, the oil found to have been desecrated. Only one flagon was discovered of that which was pure, sealed with the very signet of the High Priest. The supply proved just sufficient to feed for one day the Sacred Candlestick, but by a miracle the flagon was continually replenished during eight days, until a fresh supply could be brought from Thekoah. In memory of this, it was ordered the following year, that the Temple be illuminated for eight days on the anniversary of its Dedication. The Schools of Hillel and Shammai differed in regard to this, as on most other observances. The former would have begun the first night with the smallest number of lights, and increased it every night until on the eighth it was eight times as large as on the first. The School of Shammai, on the other hand, would have begun with the largest number, and diminished, until on the last night it amounted to an eighth of the first. Each party had its own, not very satisfactory—reasons for its distinctive practice, and its own adherents. But the Lights in honor of the Feast were lit not only in the Temple, but in every home. One would have sufficed for the whole household on the first evening, but pious householders lit a light for every person in the home, so that, if ten burned on the first, there would be eighty on the last night of the Festival. According to the Talmud, the light might be placed at the entrance to the house or room, or, according to circumstances, in the window, or even on the table. According to modern practice the light is placed at the left on entering a room (the Mezuzah is on the right). Certain benedictions are spoken on lighting these lights, all work is discontinued, and the festive time spent in merriment. The first night is especially kept in memory of Judith, who is supposed then to have slain Holofernes, and cheese is freely partaken of as the food of which, according to legend, she gave him so largely, to incite him to thirst and drunkenness. Lastly, during this Festival, all fasting and public mourning were prohibited, though some minor acts of private mourning were allowed.

More interesting, perhaps, than this description of the outward observances is the meaning of this Festival and its connection with the Feast of Tabernacles, to both of which reference has already been made. Like the Feast of Tabernacles, it commemorated a Divine Victory, which again gave to Israel their good land, after they had once more undergone sorrows like those of the wilderness; it was another harvest feast, and pointed forward to yet another ingathering. As the once extinguished light was relit in the Temple, and, according to Scriptural imagery, might that not mean the Light of Israel, the Lamp of David?, it grew day by day in brightness, until it shone quite out into the pagan darkness, that once had threatened to quench it. That He Who purified the Temple, was its True Light, and brought the Great Deliverance, should (as hinted) have spent the last anniversary season of His Birth at that Feast in the Sanctuary, shining into their darkness, seems most fitting, especially as we remember the Jewish legend, according to which the making of the Tabernacle had been completed on the 25th Chislev, although it was not set up until the 1st of Nisan (the Paschal month).

Thoughts of the meaning of this Feast, and of what was associated with it, will be helpful as we listen to the words which Jesus spoke to the people in Solomon's Porch. There is a pictorialness in the description of the circumstances, which marks the eyewitness. It is winter, and Christ is walking in the covered Porch, in front of the Beautiful Gate, which formed the principal entrance into the Court of the Women. As he walks up and down, the people are literally barring His Way, came round about Him. From the whole circumstances we cannot doubt, that the question which they put: How long will You hold us in suspense? had not in it an element of truthfulness or genuine inquiry. Their desire, that He should tell them plainly if He were the Christ, had no other motive than that of grounding on it an accusation. The more clearly we see this, the more wonderful appears the restraint of Christ and the wisdom of His answer. Briefly he puts aside their hypocrisy. What need is there of fresh speech? He told them before, and they did not believe. From words He appeals to the mute but indisputable witness of deeds: the works which He performed in His Father's Name. Their non-belief in presence of these facts was due to their not being of His Sheep. As he had said to them before, it was characteristic of His Sheep (as generally of every flock in regard to its own shepherd) to hear, recognize, listen to, His Voice and follow Him. We mark in the words of Christ, a triplet of double parallelisms concerning the Sheep and the Shepherd, in ascending climax, as follows:

Richer or more comforting assurance than that recorded above could not have been given. But something special has here to be marked. The two first parallelisms always link the promise of Christ to the attitude of the sheep; not, perhaps, conditionally, for the relation is such as not to admit conditionalness, either in the form of because, therefore, or even of if, then, but as a matter of sequence and of fact. But in the third parallelism there is no reference to anything on the part of the sheep; it is all promise, and the second clause only explains and intensifies what is expressed in the first. If it indicates attack of the fiercest kind and by the strongest and most cunning of enemies, be they men or devils, it also marks the watchfulness and absolute superiority of Him Who has them, as it were, in His Hand, perhaps a Hebraism for power, and therefore their absolute safety. And, as if to carry twofold assurance of it, He reminds His hearers that His Work being the Father's Commandment, it is really the Father's Work, given to Christ to do, and no one could snatch them out of the Father's Hand. It is a poor hair splitting, to try to limit these assurances by seeking to grasp and to comprehend them in the hollow of our human logic. Do they convey what is commonly called the doctrine of perseverance? No! But they teach us, not about our faith but about His faithfulness, and convey to us assurance concerning Him rather than ourselves; and this is the only aspect in which the doctrine of perseverance is either safe, true, or Scriptural.

But one logical sequence is unavoidable. Rightly understood, it is not only the last and highest announcement, but it contains and implies everything else. If the Work of Christ is really that of the Father, and His Working also that of the Father, then it follows that He and the Father are One (one is in the neuter). This identity of work (and purpose) implies the identity of Nature (Essence); that of working, the identity of power. And so, evidently, the Jews understood it, when they again took up stones with the intention of stoning Him, no doubt, because He expressed, in yet more plain terms, what they regarded as His blasphemy.

Once more Jesus appealed from His Words, which were doubted, to His Works, which were unquestionable. And so He does to all time. His Divine Mission is evidence of His Divinity. And if His Divine Mission be doubted, He appeals to the many excellent works (kal rga) which He has showed from the Father, anyone of which might, and, in the case of not a few, had, served as evidence of His Mission. And when the Jews ignored, as so many in our days, this line of evidence, and insisted that He had been guilty of blasphemy, since, being a man, He had made Himself God, Jesus replied in a manner that calls for our special attention. From the peculiarly

Hebraic mode of designating a quotation from the Psalms as written in the Law, we gather that we have here a literal transcript of the very words of Jesus. But what we especially wish, is, emphatically, to disclaim any interpretation of them, which would seem to imply that Christ had wished to evade their inference: that He claimed to be One with the Father, and to convey to them, that nothing more had been meant than what might lawfully be applied to an ordinary man. Such certainly is not the case. He had claimed to be One with the Father in work and working: from which the necessary inference was, that He was also One with Him in Nature and Power. Let us see whether the claim was strange. In Psalm 82:6 the titles God (Elohim) and Son's of the Highest (Beney Elyon) had been given to Judges as the Representatives and Deputies of God, wielding His delegated authority, since to them had come His Word of authorization. But here was authority not transmitted by the word, but personal and direct consecration, and personal and direct Mission on the part of God. The comparison made was not with prophets, because they only told the word and message from God, but with Judges, who, as such, did the very act of God. If those who, in so acting, had received an indirect commission, were gods, the very representatives of God, could it be blasphemy when He claimed to be the Son of God, Who had received, not authority through a word transmitted through long centuries, but direct personal command to do the Father's Work; had been directly and personally consecrated to it by the Father, and directly and personally sent by Him, not to say, but to do, the work of the Father? Was it not rather the true and necessary inference from these premises?

All would depend on this, whether Christ really did the works of the Father. That was the test; and, as we instinctively perceive, both rationally and truly. But if He did the works of His Father, then let them believe, if not the words yet the works, and thus would they arrive at the knowledge, and understand, distinguishing here the act from the state, that in Me is the Father, and I in the Father. In other words, recognizing the Work as that of the Father, they would come to understand that the father worked in Him, and that the root of His Work was in the Father.

The stones, that had been taken up, were not thrown, for the words of Christ rendered impossible the charge of explicit blasphemy which alone would, according to Rabbinic law, have warranted such summary vengeance. But they sought again to seize Him, so as to drag Him before their tribunal. His time, however, had not yet come, and He went forth out of their hand, how, we do not know.

Once more the Jordan rolled between Him and His bitter persecutors. Far north, over against Galilee, in the place of John's early labors, probably close to where Jesus Himself had been baptized, was the scene of His last labors. And those, who so well remembered both the Baptist and the testimony which he had there borne to the Christ, recalled it all as they listened to His Words and saw His Works. As they crowded around Him, both the difference and the unity between John and Jesus carried conviction to their minds. The Baptist had done no sign, such as those which Jesus performed: but all things which John had spoken of Him, they felt it, were true. And, undisturbed by the hair splitting of Pharisees and Scribes, many of these simple minded, true hearted men, far away from Jerusalem, believed on Him. To adapt a saying of Bengel: they were the posthumous children of the Baptist. Thus did he, being dead, yet speak. And so will all that is sown for Christ, though it lie buried and forgotten of men, spring up and ripen, as in one day, to the deep, grateful, and external joy of them who had labored in faith and gone to rest in hope.

End Notes:

[46]   In Rabbinic writings the word for Law (Torah, or Oreya, or Oreyan) is very frequently used to denote not only the Law, but the whole Bible. Let one example suffice: Blessed be the Merciful Who has given the threefold Law (Pentateuch, Prophets, and Hagiographa) to a threefold people (priests, Levites, laity) by the hands of a third (Moses, being the third born of his parents) on the third day (after the preparation) in the third month (Sivan), Shabb. 88 a.

[47]   We would call attention to the words The Scripture cannot be broken (ver. 35) as evidential of the views which Jesus took of the authority of the Old Testament, as well as of its inspiration.

[48]   The circumstance, that, according to the Gospels, no miracle was performed by John, is not only evidential of the trustworthiness of their report of Jesus' miracles, but otherwise also deeply significant. It shows that there is no craving for the miraculous, as in the Apocryphal and legendary narratives, and it proves that the Gospel narratives were not cast in the mold of Jewish contemporary expectation, which would certainly have assigned another role to Elijah as the Forerunner of the Messiah than, first, that of solitary testimony, then of forsakenness, and, lastly, of cruel and unavenged murder at the hands of a Herodian. Truly, the history of Jesus is not that of the Messiah of Judaic conception!

Chapter 15

The Second Series of Parables

(Luke 10:25-37; 10:5-13)

The period between Christ's return from the Feast of the Dedication and His last entry into Jerusalem, may be arranged into two parts, divided by the brief visit to Bethany for the purpose of raising Lazarus from the dead. Even if it were possible, with any certainty, chronologically to arrange the events of each of these periods, the variety and briefness of what is recorded would prevent our closely following them in this narrative. Accordingly, we prefer grouping them together as the Parables of that period, its discourses, and its Events. And the record of the raising of Lazarus may serve as a landmark between our Summary of the Parables and that of the discourses and Events which preceded Jesus' final appearance in Jerusalem.

These last words help us to understand the necessary difference between the Parables of this and of the preceding and the following periods. The Parables of this period look back upon the past, and forward into the future. Those spoken by the Lake of Galilee were purely symbolical. They presented unseen heavenly realities under emblems which required to be translated into earthly language. It was quite easy to do so, if you possessed the key to the heavenly mysteries; otherwise, they were dark and mysterious. So to speak, they were easily read from above downwards. Viewed from below upwards, only most dim and strangely intertwining outlines could be perceived. It is quite otherwise with the second series of Parables. They could, as they were intended, be understood by all. They required no translation. They were not symbolical but typical, using the word type, not in the sense of involving a predictive element, but as indicating an example, or, perhaps, more correctly, an exemplification. Accordingly, the Parables of this series are also intensely practical. Lastly, their prevailing character is not descriptive, but exhortation; and they bring the Gospel, in the sense of glad news to the lost, most closely and touchingly to the hearts of all who hear them. They are signs in words, as the miracles are signs in works, of what Christ has come to do and to teach. Most of them bear this character openly; and even those which do not, but seem more like warning, have still an undertone of love, as if Divine compassion lingered in tender pity over that which threatened, but might yet be averted.

Of the Parables of the third series it will for the present suffice to say, that they are neither symbolical nor typical, but their prevailing characteristic is prophetic. As befits their historical place in the teaching of Christ, they point to the near future. They are the fast falling, lengthening shadows cast by the events which are near at hand,

The Parables of the second (or Perean) series, which are typical and exhortation, and Evangelical in character, are thirteen in number, and, with the exception of the last, are either peculiar to, or else most fully recorded in, the Gospel by Luke.

1. The Parable of the Good Samaritan., This Parable is connected with a question, addressed to Jesus by a lawyer, not one of the Jerusalem Scribes or Teachers, but probably an expert in Jewish Canon Law, who possibly made it more or less a profession in that district, though perhaps not for gain. Accordingly, there is a marked absence of that animosity and hatred which characterized his colleagues of Judea. In a previous chapter it has been shown, that this narrative probably stands in its proper place in the Gospel of Luke. We have also suggested, that the words of this lawyer referred, or else that himself belonged, to that small party among the Rabbinics who, at least in theory, attached greater value to good works than to study. At any rate, there is no occasion to impute directly evil motives to him. Knowing the habits of his class, we do not wonder that he put his question to tempt, test, try, the great Rabbi of Nazareth. There are many similar instances in Rabbinic writings of meetings between great Teachers, when each tried to involve the other in dialectic difficulties and subtle disputations. This was part of Rabbinism, and led to that painful and fatal trifling with truth, when everything became matter of argumentive subtlety, and nothing was really sacred. What we require to keep in view is, that to this lawyer the question which he propounded was only one of

theoretic, not of practical interest, nor matter of deep personal concern, as it was to the rich young ruler, who, not long afterwards, addressed a similar inquiry to Jesus.

We seem to witness the opening of a regular Rabbinic contest, as we listen to this speculative problem: Teacher, what having done shall I inherit eternal life? At the foundation lay the notion, that eternal life was the reward of merit, of works: the only question was, what these works were to be. The idea of guilt had not entered his mind; he had no conception of sin within. It was the old Judaism of self righteousness speaking without disguise: that which was the ultimate ground of the rejecting and crucifying of the Christ. There certainly was a way in which a man might inherit eternal life, not indeed as having absolute claim to it, but (as the Schoolmen might have said: de congruo) in consequence of God's Covenant on Sanai: And so Jesus, using the common Rabbinic expression what read you?, pointed him to the Scriptures of the Old Testament.

The reply of the lawyer is remarkable, not only on its own account, but as substantially, and even literally, that given on two other occasions by Jesus Himself. The question therefore naturally arises, from which did this lawyer, who certainly had not spiritual insight, derive his reply? As regarded the duty of absolute love to God, indicated by the quotation of Deuteronomy 6:5, there could be no hesitation in the mind of a Jew. The primary obligation of this is frequently referred to, and, taken for granted, in Rabbinic teaching. The repetition of this command, which in the Talmud receives the most elaborate and strange interpretation, formed part of the daily prayers. When Jesus referred the lawyer to the Scriptures, he could scarcely fail to quote this first paramount obligation. Similarly, he spoke as a Rabbinic lawyer, when he referred in the next place to love to our neighbor, as enjoined in Leviticus 19:18. Rabbinism is never weary of quoting as one of the characteristic sayings of its greatest teacher, Hillel (who lived before this time), that he had summed up the Law, in briefest compass, in these words: What is hateful to you, that do not to another. This is the whole Law; the rest is only its explanation. Similarly, Rabbi Akiba taught, that Leviticus 19:18 was the principal rule, we might almost say, the chief summary of the Law. Still, the two principles just mentioned are not enunciated in conjunction by Rabbinism, nor seriously propounded as either containing the whole Law or as securing heaven. They are also, as we shall now see, subjected to grave modifications. One of these, as regards the negative form in which Hillel put it, while Christ put it positively, has been previously noticed. The existence of such Rabbinic modifications, and the circumstance, already mentioned, that on two other occasions the answer of Christ Himself to a similar inquiry was precisely that of this lawyer, suggests the inference, that this question may have been occasioned by some teaching of Christ, to which they had just listened, and that the reply of the lawyer may have been prompted by what Jesus had preached concerning the Law.

If it be asked, why Christ seemed to give His assent to the lawyers answer, as if it really pointed to the right solution of the great question, we reply: No other answer could have been given him. On the ground of works, if that had been tenable, this was the way to heaven. To understand any other answer, would have required a sense of sin; and this could not be imparted by reasoning: it must be experienced. It is the preaching of the Law which awakens in the mind a sense of sin. Besides, if not morally, yet mentally, the difficulty of this way would soon suggest itself to a Jew. Such, at least, is one aspect of the counter question with which the lawyer now sought to retort on Jesus.

Whatever complexity of motives there may have been, for we do not know of the circumstances, and there may have been that in the conduct or heart of the lawyer which was especially touched by what had just passed, there can be no doubt as to the main object of his question: But who is my neighbor? He wished to justify himself, in the sense of vindicating his original question, and showing that it was not quite so easily settled as the answer of Jesus seemed to imply. And here it was that Christ could in a Parable show how far orthodox Judaism was from even a true understanding, much more from such perfect observance of this Law as would gain heaven. Thus might He bring even this man to feel his shortcomings and sins, and awaken in him a sense of his great need. This would be the negative aspect of this Parable; the positive is to all time and to all men.

That question: Who is my neighbor? has ever been at the same time the outcome of Judaism (as distinguished from the religion of the Old Testament), and also its curse. On this point it is duty to speak plainly, even in face of the wicked persecutions to which the Jews have been exposed on account of it. Whatever modern Judaism may say to the contrary, there is a foundation of truth in the ancient pagan charge against the Jews of odium generis humani (hatred of mankind). God had separated Israel to Himself by purification and renovation, and this is the original meaning of the word holy and sanctify in the Hebrew. They separated themselves in self righteousness and pride, and that is the original meaning of the word

Pharisee and Pharisaism. In so saying no blame is cast on individuals; it is the system which is at fault. This question: Who is my neighbor? frequently engages Rabbinism. The answer to it is only too clear. If a hypercriticism were to interpret away the passage which directs that idolaters are not to be delivered when in imminent danger, while heretics and apostates are even to be led into it, the painful discussion on the meaning of Exodus 23:5 would place it beyond question. The sum of it is, that, except to avert hostility, a burden is only to be unloaded, if the beast that lies under it belongs to an Israelite, not if it belong to a Gentile; and so the expression, the donkey of him that hates you, must be understood of a Jewish, and not of a Gentile enemy.

It is needless to follow the subject further. But more complete rebuke of Judaistic narrowness, as well as more full, generous, and spiritual world teaching than that of Christ's Parable could not be imagined. The scenery and coloring are purely local. And here we should remember, that, while admitting the lawfulness of the widest application of details for homiletical purposes, we must take care not to press them in a strictly exegetical interpretation.

Someone coming from the Holy City, the Metropolis of Judaism, is pursuing the solitary desert road, those twenty one miles to Jericho, a district notoriously insecure, when he fell among robbers, who, having both stripped and inflicted on him strokes, went away leaving him just as he was, half dead. This is the first scene. The second opens with an expression which, theologically, as well as exegetically, is of the greatest interest. The word rendered by chance (sunkura) occurs only in this place, for Scripture commonly views matters in relation to agents rather than to results. As already noted, the real meaning of the word is concurrence, much like the corresponding Hebrew term. And better definition could not be given, not, of Providence, which is a pagan abstraction for which the Bible has no equivalent, but for the concrete reality of God's providing. He provides through a concurrence of circumstances, all in themselves natural and in the succession of ordinary causation (and this distinguishes it from the miracle), but the concurring of which is directed and overruled by Him. And this helps us to put aside those coarse tests of the reality of prayer and of the direct rule of God, which men sometimes propose. Such stately ships ride not in such shallow waters.

It was by such a concurrence, that, first a priest, then a Levite came down that road, when each, successively, when he saw him, passed by over against (him). It was the principle of questioning, Who is my neighbor?

which led both priest and Levite to such heartless conduct. Who knew what this wounded man was, and how he came to lie there: and were they called upon, in ignorance of this, to take all the trouble, perhaps incur the risk of life, which care of him would involve? Thus Judaism (in the persons of its chief representatives) had, by its exclusive attention to the letter, come to destroy the spirit of the Law. Happily, there came yet another that way, not only a stranger, but one despised, a semi-pagan Samaritan. He did not ask who the man was, but what was his need. Whatever the wounded Jew might have felt towards him, the Samaritan proved a true neighbor. He came towards him, and seeing him, he was moved with compassion. His resolution was soon taken. He first bound up his wounds, and then, taking from his traveling provision wine and oil, made of them, what was regarded as the common dressing for wounds. Next, having set (lifted) him on his own beast, he walked by his side, and brought him to one of those houses of rest and entertainment, whose designation (pandocheon) has passed into Rabbinic language. These khans, or inns, by the side of unfrequented roads, afforded free lodgment to the traveler. But generally they also offered entertainment, in which case the host, commonly a non-Israelite, charged for the food supplied to man or beast, or for the care taken. In the present instance the Samaritan seems himself to have tended the wounded man all that evening. But even thus his care did not end. The next morning, before continuing his journey, he gave to the host two dinars, about one shilling and three pence of our money, the amount of a laborers wages for two days, as it were, two days wages for his care of him, with this provision, that if any further expense were incurred, either because the wounded man was not sufficiently recovered to travel, or else because something more had been supplied to him, the Good Samaritan would pay it when he next came that way.

So far the Parable: its lesson the lawyer is made himself to pronounce. Which of these three seems to you to have become neighbor of him that fell among the robbers? Though unwilling to take the hated name of Samaritan on his lips, especially as the meaning of the Parable and its anti-Rabbinic bearing were so evident, the lawyer was obliged to reply, He that showed mercy on him, when Jesus finally answered, Go, and do you likewise.

Some further lessons may be drawn. The Parable implies not a mere enlargement of the Jewish ideas, but a complete change of them. It is truly a Gospel Parable, for the whole old relationship of mere duty is changed into one of love. Thus, matters are placed on an entirely different basis from that of Judaism. The question now is not Who is my neighbor? but Whose neighbor am I? The Gospel answers the question of duty by pointing us to love. Would you know who is your neighbor? Become a neighbor to all by the utmost service you can do them in their need. And so the Gospel would not only abolish man's hostility, but bridge over man's separation. Thus is the Parable truly Christian, and, more than this, points up to Him Who, in our great need, became Neighbor to us, even at the cost of all He had. And from Him, as well as by His Word, are we to learn our lesson of love.

2. The Parable which follows in Luke's narrative seems closely connected with that just commented upon. It is also a story of a good neighbor who gives in our need, but presents another aspect of the truth to which the Parable of the Good Samaritan had pointed. Love bends to our need: this is the objective manifestation of the Gospel. Need looks up to love, and by its cry elicits the benefit which it seeks. And this is the subjective experience of the Gospel. The one underlies the story of the first Parable, the other that of the second.

Some such internal connection between the two Parables seems, indicated even by the loose manner in which this second Parable is strung to the request of some disciples to be taught what to pray. Like the Parable of the Good Samaritan, it is typical, and its application would be the more felt, that it not only points to an exemplification, but appeals to every man's consciousness of what himself would do in certain given circumstances. The latter are as follows. A man has a friend who, long after nightfall, unexpectedly comes to him from a journey. He has nothing in the house, yet he must provide for his need, for hospitality demands it. Accordingly, though it is so late, he goes to his friend and neighbor to ask him for three loaves, stating the case. On the other hand, the friend so asked refuses, since, at that late hour, he has retired to bed with his children, and to grant his request would imply not only inconvenience to himself, but the disturbing of the whole household. The main circumstances therefore are: Sudden, unthought of sense of imperative need, obliging to make what seems an unseasonable and unreasonable request, which, on the face of it, offers difficulties and has no claim upon compliance. It is, therefore, not ordinary but, so to speak, extraordinary prayer, which is here alluded to.

To return to the Parable: the question (abruptly broken off from the beginning of the Parable in ver. 5), is what each of us would do in the circumstances just detailed. The answer is implied in what follows. It points

to continued insistence, which would at last obtain what it needs. I tell
you, even if he will not give him, rising up, because he is his friend, yet at
least on account of his insistence, he will rise up and give him as many as he
needs. This literal rendering will, it is hoped, remove some of the seeming
difficulties of the Parable. It is a gross misunderstanding to describe it as
presenting a mechanical view of prayer: as if it implied, either that God
was unwilling to answer; or else, that prayer, otherwise unheard, would be
answered merely for its insistence. It must be remembered, that he who is
within is a friend, and that, under circumstances, he would at once have
complied with the request. But, in this case, there were special difficulties,
which are represented as very great; it is midnight; he has retired to bed,
and with his children; the door is locked. And the lesson is, that where, for
some reasons, there are, or seem, special difficulties to an answer to our
prayers (it is very late, the door is no longer open, the children have already
been gathered in), the insistence arising from the sense of our absolute
need, and the knowledge that He is our Friend, and that He has bread, will
ultimately prevail. The difficulty is not as to the giving, but as the giving
then, rising up, and this is overcome by perseverance, so that (to return to
the Parable), if he will not rise up because he is his friend, yet at least he
will rise because of his insistence, and not only give him three loaves, but,
in general, as many as he needs.

So important is the teaching of this Parable, that Christ makes detailed
application of it. In the circumstances described a man would persevere
with his friend, and in the end succeed. And, similarly, the Lord invites us
to ask, and that earnestly and believingly; seek, and that energetically and
instantly; knock, and that intently and loudly. Ask, He is a Friend, and we
shall receive; seek, it is there, and we shall find; knock, our need is absolute,
and it shall be opened to us. But the emphasis of the Parable and its lesson
are in the word everyone. Not only this or that, but everyone, shall so
experience it. The word points to the special difficulties that may be in
the way of answer to prayer, the difficulties of the rising up, which have
been previously indicated in the Parable. These are met by perseverance
which indicates the reality of our need (ask), the reality of our belief that
the supply is there (seek), and the intensity and energy of our spiritual
longing (knock). Such insistence applies to everyone, whoever he be,
and whatever the circumstances which would seem to render his prayer
especially difficult to answer. Though he feel that he has not and needs, he
asks; though he have lost, time, opportunities, mercies, he seeks; though
the door seem shut, he knocks. Thus the Lord is helper to everyone; but, as

for us, let us learn the lesson from what we ourselves would do in analogous circumstances.

More than this, God will not deceive by the appearance of what is not reality. He will even give the greatest gift. The Parabolic relation is now not that of friends, but of father and son. If the son asks for bread, will the father give what seems such, but is only a stone? If he asks for a fish, will he give him what looks like such, but is a serpent? If he seeks an egg, will he hand to him what breeds a scorpion? The need, the hunger, of the child will not, in answer to its prayer, receive at the Father's Hands, that which seems, but gives not the reality of satisfaction, rather is poison. Let us draw the inference. Such is our conduct, how much more shall our heavenly Father give His Holy Spirit to them that ask Him. That gift will not disappoint by the appearance of what is not reality; it will not deceive either by the promise of what it does not give, or by giving what would prove fatal. As we follow Christ's teaching, we ask for the Holy Spirit; and the Holy Spirit, in leading us to Him, leads us into all truth, to all life, and to what satisfies all need.

End Notes:

[49] A distinction between different classes of Scribes, of whom some gave themselves to the study of the Law, while others included with it that of the Prophets, such as Dean Plumptre suggests (on Matthew 22:35), did not exist.

[50] Thus: "With all your heart", with both your impulses, that to good and that to evil; "with all your soul", even if it takes away your soul; "with all your might", "with all your money." Another interpretation: "With all your might", in regard to every measure with which He measures to you are you bound to praise Him (there is here a play on the words which cannot be rendered), Ber. 54 a, about the middle.

Chapter 16

The Three Parables of Warning

(Luke 12:13-21; 13:6-9; 14:16-24)

The three Parables, which successively follow in Luke's Gospel, may generally be designated as those of warning. This holds especially true of the last two of them, which refer to the civil and the ecclesiastical polity of Israel. Each of the three Parables is set in a historical frame, having been spoken under circumstances which gave occasion for such illustration.

1. The Parable of the foolish rich man. It appears, that someone among them that listened to Jesus conceived the idea, that the authority of the Great Rabbi of Nazareth might be used for his own selfish purposes. This was all he had profited, that it seemed to open possibilities of gain, stirred thoughts of covetousness. But other inferences also come to us. Evidently, Christ must have attracted and deeply moved multitudes, or His interjection would not have been sought; and, equally evidently, what He preached had made upon this man the impression, that he might possibly enlist Him as his champion. The presumptive evidence which it affords as regards the effect and the subject matter of Christ's preaching is exceedingly interesting. On the other hand, Christ had not only no legal authority for interfering, but the Jewish law of inheritance was so clearly defined, and, we may add, so just, that if this person had any just or good cause, there could have been no need for appealing to Jesus. Therefore it must have been covetousness, in the strictest sense, which prompted it, perhaps, a wish to have, besides his own share as a younger brother, half of that additional portion which, by law, came to

the eldest son of the family. Such an attempt for covetous purposes to make use of the pure unselfish preaching of love, and to derive profit from His spiritual influence, accounts for the severity with which Christ rejected the demand, although, as we judge, He would, under any circumstances, have refused to interfere in purely civil disputes, with which the established tribunals were sufficient to deal.

All this accounts for the immediate reference of Jesus to covetousness, the folly of which He showed by this almost self evident principle, too often forgotten, that not in the super abounding to anyone [not in that wherein he has more than enough] consists his life, from the things which he possesses. In other words, that part of the things which a man possesses by which his life is sustained, consists not in what is superabundant; his life is sustained by that which he needs and uses; the rest, the superabundance, forms no part of his life, and may, perhaps, never be of use to him. Why, then, be covetous, or long for more than we need? And this folly also involves danger. For, the love of these things will engross mind and heart, and care about them will drive out higher thoughts and aims. The moral as regarded the Kingdom of God, and the warning not to lose it for thought of what perishes with the using, are obvious.

The Parable itself bears on all these points. It consists of two parts, of which the first shows the folly, the second the sin and danger, of that care for what is beyond our present need, which is the characteristic of covetousness. The rich man is surveying his land, which is bearing plentifully, evidently beyond its former yield, since the old provision for storing the grain appears no longer sufficient. It seems implied, or, we may at least conjecture, that this was not only due to the labor and care of the master, but that he had devoted to it his whole thought and energy. More than this, it seems as if, in the calculations which he now made, he looked into the future, and saw there progressive increase and riches. As yet, the harvest was not reaped; but he was already considering what to do, reckoning upon the riches that would come to him. And so he resolved to pull down the old, and build larger barns, where he would store his future possessions. From one aspect there would have been nothing wrong in an act of almost necessary foresight, only great folly in thinking, and speaking, and making plans, as if that were already absolutely his which might never come to him at all, which, was still unreaped, and might be garnered long after he was dead. His life was not sustained by that part of his possessions which were the super abounding. But to this folly was also added sin. For,

God was not in all his thoughts. In all his plans for the future, and it was his folly to make such absolutely, he thought not of God. His whole heart was set on the acquisition of earthly riches, not on the service of God. He did not remember his responsibility; all that he had, was for himself, and absolutely his own to profit upon; Soul, you have much goods laid up for many years; take your ease, eat, drink, be merry. He did not even remember, that there was a God Who might cut short his years.

So had he spoken in his heart, proud, selfish, self indulgent, God forgetting, as he looked forth upon what was not yet, even in an inferior sense, his own, but which he already treated as such, and that in the most absolute sense. And now comes the quick, sharp, contrast, which is purposely introduced quite abruptly. But God said to Him, not by revelation nor through inward presentiment, but, with awful suddenness, in those unspoken words of fact which cannot be contradicted or answered: You fool! this very night, which follows on your plans and purposings, your soul is required of you. But, the things which you have prepared, whose shall they be? Here, with the obvious evidence of the folly of such state of mind, the Parable breaks off. Its sinfulness and beyond this negative aspect of it, the wisdom of righteousness in laying up the good treasure which cannot be taken from us, appears in this concluding remark of Christ, So is he who lays up treasure (treasures) for himself, and is not rich towards God.

It was a barbed arrow, we might say, out of the Jewish quiver, but directed by the Hand of the Lord. For, we read in the Talmud that a Rabbi told his disciples, Repent the day before your death; and when his disciples asked him: Does a man know the day of his death? He replied, that on that very ground he should repent today, for fear that he should die tomorrow. And so would all his days be days of repentance. Again, the son of Sirach wrote: There is that waxes rich by his wariness and pinching, and this is the portion of his reward; whereas he says, I have found rest, and now will eat continually of my goods; and yet he does not know what time shall come upon him, and that he must leave those things to others, and die. But we sadly miss in all this the spiritual application which Christ made. Similarly, the Talmud, by a play on the last word, in the first verse of Psalm 49, compares man to the weasel, which laboriously gathers and deposits, not knowing for whom, while the Midrash tells a story, how, when a Rabbi returned from a feast where the Host had made plans of storing his wine for a future occasion, the Angel of death appeared to him, grieved for man, since you say, thus and thus shall we do in the future, while no one knows how soon he shall be called to die, as would be the case with the host of that evening, who would die after the lapse of thirty days. But once more we ask, where is the spiritual application, such as was made by Christ? So far from it, the Midrash adds, that when the Rabbi challenged the Angel to show him the time of his own death, he received this reply, that he had no dominion over the like of him, since God took pleasure in their good works, and added to their days!

2. The special warning intended to be conveyed by the Parable of the Barren Fig tree sufficiently appears from the context. As explained in a previous chapter, Jesus had not only corrected the erroneous interpretation which the Jews were giving to certain recent national occurrences, but pointed them to this higher moral of all such events, that, unless speedy national repentance followed, the whole people would perish. This Parable offers not merely an exemplification of this general prediction of Christ, but sets before us what underlies it: Israel in its relation to God; the need of repentance; Israel's danger; the nature of repentance, and its urgency; the relation of Christ to Israel; the Gospel; and the final judgment on impenitence.

As regards the details of this Parable, we mark that the fig tree had been especially planted by the owner in his vineyard, which was the choicest situation. This, we know, was not unusual. Fig trees, as well as palm and olive trees, were regarded as so valuable, that to cut them down if they yielded even a small measure of fruit, was popularly deemed to deserve death at the Hand of God. Ancient Jewish writings supply interesting particulars of this tree and its culture. According to Josephus, in favored localities the ripe fruit hung on the tree for ten months of the year, the two barren months being probably April and May, before the first of the three crops which it bore had ripened. The first figs ripened towards the end of June, sometimes earlier. The second, which are those now dried and exported, ripened in August; the third, which were small and of comparatively little value, in September, and often hung all winter on the trees. A species (the Benoth Shuach) is mentioned, of which the fruit required three years for ripening. The fig tree was regarded as the most fruitful of all trees. On account of its repeated crops, it was declared not subject to the ordinance which enjoined that fruit should be left in the corners for the poor. Its artificial injection was known. The practice mentioned in the Parable, of digging about the tree, and dunging it, is frequently mentioned in Rabbinic writings, and by the same designations. Curiously, Maimonides mentions three years as the utmost limit within which a tree should bear fruit in the land of Israel. Lastly, as trees were regarded as by their roots undermining and deteriorating the land, a barren tree would be of threefold disadvantage: it would yield no fruit; it would fill valuable space, which a fruit bearer might occupy; and it would needlessly deteriorate the land. Accordingly, while it was forbidden to destroy fruit bearing trees, it would, on the grounds above stated, be duty to cut down a barren or empty tree (Ilan seraq).

These particulars will enable us more fully to understand the details of the Parable. Allegorically, the fig tree served in the Old Testament as emblem of the Jewish nation, in the Talmud, rather as that of Israel's lore, and therefore of the leaders and the pious of the people. The vineyard is in the New Testament the symbol of the Kingdom of God, as distinct from the nation of Israel. Thus far, then, the Parable may be thus translated: God called Israel as a nation, and planted it in the most favored spot: as a fig tree in the vineyard of His own Kingdom. And He came seeking, as He had every right to do, fruit thereon, and found none. It was the third year that He had vainly looked for fruit, when He turned to His Vinedresser, the Messiah, to Whom the vineyard is committed as its King, with this direction: Cut it down, why does it also deteriorate the soil? It is barren, though in the best position; as a fig tree it ought to bear figs, and here the best; it fills the place which a good tree might occupy; and besides, it deteriorates the soil (literally). And its three years barrenness has established (as before explained) its utterly hopeless character. Then it is that the Divine Vinedresser, in His infinite compassion, pleads, and with far deeper reality than either Abraham or Moses could have entreated, for the fig tree which Himself had planted and tended, that it should be spared this year also, until then that I shall dig about it, and dung it, until He labor otherwise than before, even by His Own Presence and Words by laying to its roots His most precious Blood. And if then it bear fruit, here the text abruptly breaks off, as implying that in such case it would be allowed to remain; but if not, then against the future (coming) year shall you cut it down. The Parable needs no further comment. In the words of a recent writer: Between the tree and the axe nothing intervenes but the intercession of the Gardener, Who would make a last effort, and even His petition applies only to a short and definite period, and, in case it pass without result, this petition itself merges in the proposal, "But if not, then cut it down." How speedily and terribly the warning came true, not only students of history, but all men and in all ages have been made to know.

Of the lawfulness of a further application of this Parable to all kindred circumstances of nation, community, family even of individuals, it is not necessary to speak.

3. The third Parable of warning, that of the Great Supper, refers not to the political state of Israel, but to their ecclesiastical status, and their continuance as the possessors and representatives of the Kingdom of God. It was spoken after the return of Jesus from the Feast of the Dedication, and therefore carries us beyond the point in this history which we have reached. Accordingly, the attendant circumstances will be explained in the sequel. In regard to these we only note, how appropriately such a warning of Israel's spiritual danger, in consequence of their hardness of heart, misrepresentation, and perversion of God's truth, would come at a Sabbath meal of the Pharisees, when they lay in wait against Him, and He first challenged their externalizing of God's Day and Law to the subversion of its real meaning, and then rebuked the self assertion, pride, and utter lack of all real love on the part of these leaders of Israel.

What led up to the Parable of the Great Supper happened after these things: after His healing of the man with the dropsy in sight of them all on the Sabbath, after His twofold rebuke of their perversion of the Sabbath Law, and of those marked characteristics of Pharisaism, which showed how far they were from bringing forth fruit worthy of the Kingdom, and how, instead of representing, they represented the Kingdom, and were utterly unfit ever to do otherwise. The Lord had spoken of making a feast, not for ones kindred, nor for the rich, whether such outwardly, or mentally and spiritually from the standpoint of the Pharisees, but for the poor and afflicted. This would imply true spirituality, because that fellowship of giving, which descends to others in order to raise them as brethren, not condescends, in order to be raised by them as their Master and Superior. And He had concluded with these words: And you shall be blessed, because they have not to render back again to you, for it shall be rendered back to you again in the Resurrection of the Just.

It was this last clause, but separated, in true Pharisaic spirit, from that which had preceded, and indicated the motive, on which one of those present now commented, probably with a covert, perhaps a provocative, reference to what formed the subject of Christ's constant teaching: Blessed is he who shall eat bread in the Kingdom of Heaven. An expression this, which to the Pharisee meant the common Jewish expectancy of a great feast at the beginning of the Messianic Kingdom. So far he had rightly understood, and yet he had entirely misunderstood, the words of Christ. Jesus had, referred to the future retribution of (not, for) deeds of love, among which He had named as an instance, suggested by the circumstances, a feast for, or rather brotherly love and fellowship towards, the poor and suffering. But although the Pharisee referred to the Messianic Day, his words show that he did not own Jesus as the Messiah. Whether or not it was the object of his exclamation, as sometimes religious commonplaces or platitudes are in our days, to interrupt the course of Christ's rebukes, or, as before hinted, to provoke Him to unguarded speech, must be left undetermined. What is chiefly apparent is, that this Pharisee separated what Christ said about the blessings of the first Resurrection from that with which He had connected them, we do not say as their condition, but as logically their moral predecessor: namely, love, in opposition to self assertion and self seeking. The Pharisees words imply that, like his class, he, at any rate, fully expected to share in these blessings, as a matter of course, and because he was a Pharisee. Thus to leave out Christ's preceding words was not only to set them aside, but to pervert His saying, and to place the blessedness of the future on the very opposite basis from that on which Christ had rested it. Accordingly, it was to this man personally that the Parable was addressed.

There can be no difficulty in understanding the main ideas underlying the Parable. The man who made the Great Supper was He Who had, in the Old Testament, prepared a feast of fat things. The inviting many preceded the actual announcement of the day and hour of the feast. We understand by it a preliminary intimation of the feast then preparing, and a general invitation of the guests, who were the chief people in the city; for, as we shall now see, the scene is set in a city. This general announcement was made in the Old Testament institutions and prophecies, and the guests invited were those in the city, the chief men, not the ignorant and those out of the way, but the men who knew, and read, and expounded these prophecies. At last the preparations were ended, and Jesus sent out His Servant, not necessarily to be understood of anyone individual in particular, such as John the Baptist, but referring to whomever He would employ in His Service for that purpose. It was to intimate to the person's formerly invited, that everything was now ready. Then it was that, however differing in their special grounds for it, or expressing it with more or less courtesy, they were all at one in declining to come. The feast, to which they had been invited some time before, and to which they had apparently agreed to come (at least, this was implied), was, when actually announced as ready, not what they had expected, at any rate not what they regarded as more desirable than what they had, and must give up in order to come to it. For, and this seems one of the principal points in the Parable, to come to that feast, to enter into the Kingdom, implies the giving up of something that seems if not necessary yet most desirable, and the enjoyment of which appears only reasonable. Be it possession, business, and pleasure (Stier), or the priesthood, the magistracy, and the people generally (Augustine), or the priesthood, the Pharisees, and the Scribes, or the Pharisees, the Scribes, and the self righteously virtuous, with reference to whom we are especially to think of the threefold excuse, the main point lies in this, that, when the time came, they all refused to enter in, each having some valid and reasonable excuse. But the ultimate ground of their refusal was, that they felt no real desire, and saw nothing attractive in such a feast; had no real reverence for the host; in short, that to them it was not a feast at all, but something much less to be desired than what they had, and would have been obliged to give up, if they had complied with the invitation.

Then let the feast, for it was prepared by the goodness and liberality of the Host, be for those who were in need of it, and to whom it would be a feast: the poor and those afflicted, the maimed, and blind, and lame, on whom those great citizens who had been first invited would look down. This, with reference to, and in higher spiritual explanation of, what Christ had previously said about inviting such to our feast of fellowship and love. Accordingly, the Servant is now directed to go out quickly into the (larger) streets and the (narrow) lanes of the City, a trait which shows that the scene is laid in the City, the professed habitation of God. The importance of this circumstance is evident. It not only explains who the first invited chief citizens were, but also that these poor were the despised ignorant, and the maimed, lame, and blind, such as the publicans and sinners. These are they in the streets and lanes; and the Servant is directed, not only to invite, but to bring them in, as otherwise they might naturally shrink from coming to such a feast. But even so, there is yet room; for the great Lord of the house has, in His great liberality, prepared a very great feast for very many. And so the Servant is once more sent, so that the Lord's house may be filled. But now he is invited to go out, outside the City, outside the Theocracy, into the highways and hedges, to those who travel along the world's great highway, or who have fallen down weary, and rest by its hedges; into the busy, or else weary, pagan world. This reference to the pagan world is the more apparent that, according to the Talmud, there were commonly no hedges around the fields of the Jews. And this time the direction to the Servant is not, as in regard to those naturally bashful outcasts of the City, who would scarcely venture to the great house, to bring them in, but constrain [without a pronoun] to come in, Not certainly as indicating their resistance and implying force, but as the moral constraint of earnest, pressing invitation, coupled with assurance both of the reality of the feast and of their welcome to it. For, these wanderers on the world's highway had, before the Servant came to them, not known anything of the Master of the house, and all was quite new and unexpected. Their being invited by a Lord Whom they had not known, perhaps never heard of before, to a City in which they were strangers, and to a feast for which, as wayfarers, or as resting by the hedges, or else as working within their enclosure, they were wholly unprepared, required special urgency, a constraining, to make them either believe in it, or come to it from where the messengers found them, and that without preparing for it by dress or otherwise. And so the house would be filled!

Here the Parable abruptly breaks off. What follows are the words of Jesus in explanation and application of it to the company then present: For I say to you, that none of those men which were invited shall taste of My supper. And this was the final answer to this Pharisee and to those with him at that table, and to all such perversion of Christ's Words and misapplication of God's Promises as he and they were guilty of.

End Notes:

[51]   Cases might, however, arise when the claim was doubtful, and then the inheritance would be divided (Baba B. 9:2). The double part of an eldest son was computed in the following manner. If five sons were left, the property was divided into six parts, and the eldest son had two parts, or one third of the property. If nine sons were left, the property was divided into ten parts, and the eldest son had two parts, or a fifth of the property. But there were important limitations to this. Thus, the law did not apply to a posthumous son, nor yet in regard to the mother's property, nor to any increase or gain that might have accrued since the father's death. For a brief summary, see Saalschuetz, Mos

[52]   Not after three years, but evidently in the third year, when the third years crop should have appeared.

[53]   Dean Plumptre regards the fig tree as the symbol of a soul making fruitless profession; the vineyard as that of Israel. For homiletical purposes, or for

practical application, this is perfectly fair; but not in strict exegesis. To waive other and obvious objections, it was to introduce modern, Christian ideas, which would have been wholly unintelligible to Christ's hearers.

[54] The expression eating bread is a well known Hebraism, used both in the Old Testament and in Rabbinic writings for taking part in a meal.

[55] The principal meal, which was towards evening.

[56] It is most sad, and seems almost incredible, that this constrain to come in has from early times been quoted in justification of religious persecution.

Chapter 17

The Three Parables of the Gospel

(Luke 15)

A simple examination of the three Parables, grouped together in the fifteenth chapter of Luke's Gospel, will convince us of their connection. Although they address repentance, we can scarcely call them The Parables of Repentance; for, except in the last of them, the aspect of repentance is subordinate to that of restoration, which is the moral effect of repentance. They are rather peculiarly Gospel Parables of the recovery of the lost: in the first instance, through the unwearied labor; in the second, through the anxious care, of the owner; and in the third Parable, through the never ceasing love of the Father.

Properly to understand these Parables, the circumstance which elicited them must be kept in view. As Jesus preached the Gospel of God's call, not to those who had, as they imagined, prepared themselves for the Kingdom by study and good works, but as that to a door open, and a welcome free to all, all the publicans and sinners were [constantly] drawing near to Him. It has formerly been shown, that the Jewish teaching concerning repentance was quite other than contrary to, that of Christ. Theirs was not a Gospel to the lost: they had nothing to say to sinners. They called upon them to do penitence, and then Divine Mercy, or rather Justice, would have its reward for the penitent. Christ's Gospel was to the lost as such. It told them of forgiveness, of what Jesus was doing, and the Father purposed and felt for them; and that, not in the future and as reward of their penitence, but now in the immediate present. From what we know of the Pharisees, we can scarcely wonder that they were murmuring at Him, saying, This man receives "sinners," and eat with them. Whether or not Christ had on this, as on other occasions, joined at a meal with such persons, which in the eyes of the Pharisees would have been a great aggravation to His offence, their charge was so far true, that this One, in contrariety to the principles and practice of Rabbinism, received sinners as such, and consorted with them. There was even more than they charged Him with: He not only received them when they sought Him, but He sought them, so as to bring them to Him; not, that they might remain sinners, but that, by seeking and finding them, they might be restored to the Kingdom, and there might be joy in heaven over them. And so these are truly Gospel Parables, although presenting only some aspects of it.

Besides their subject matter, these three Parables have some other points in common. Two things are here of chief interest. They all proceed on the view that the work of the Father and of Christ, as regards the Kingdom, is the same; that Christ was doing the work of the Father, and that they who know Christ know the Father also. That work was the restoration of the lost; Christ had come to do it, and it was the longing of the Father to welcome the lost home again. Further, and this is only second in importance, the lost was still God's property; and he who had wandered farthest was a child of the Father, and considered as such. And, although this may, in a wider sense, imply the general propriety of Christ in all men, and the universal Fatherhood of God, yet, remembering that this Parable was spoken to Jews, we, to whom these Parables now come, can scarcely be wrong in thinking, as we read them, with special thankfulness of our Christian privileges, as by Baptism numbered among the sheep of His Flock, the treasure of His Possession, and the children of His Home.

In other particulars there are, however, differences, all the more marked that they are so finely shaded. These concern the lost, their restoration, and its results.

1. The Parable of the Lost Sheep. At the outset we remark that this Parable and the next, that of the Lost Drachm, are intended as an answer to the Pharisees. Therefore they are addressed to them: What man of you? or what woman? just as His late rebuke to them on the subject of their Sabbath hair splitting had been couched: Which of you shall have a son or an ox fallen into a well? Not so the last Parable, of the Lost Son, in which He passed from defense, or rather explanation, of His conduct, to its higher reason, showing that He was doing the work of the Father. Therefore, while the element of comparison (with that which had

not been lost) appears in most detailed form in the first Parable, it is generalized in the second, and wholly omitted in the third.

Other differences have to be marked in the Parables themselves. In the first Parable (that of the Lost Sheep) the main interest centers in the lost; in the second (that of the Lost Drachm), in the search; in the third, in the restoration. And although in the third Parable the Pharisees are not addressed, there is the highest personal application to them in the words which the Father speaks to the elder son—an application, not so much of warning, as of loving correction and entreaty, and which seems to imply, what otherwise these Parables convey, that at least these Pharisees had murmured, not so much from bitter hostility to Christ, as from spiritual ignorance and misunderstanding.

Again, these Parables, and especially that of the Lost Sheep, are evidently connected with the preceding series, that of warnings. The last of these showed how the poor, the blind, lame, and maimed even the wanderers on the world's highway, were to be the guests at the heavenly Feast. And this, not only in the future, and after long and laborious preparation, but now, through the agency of Jesus. As previously stated, Rabbinism placed acceptance at the end of repentance, and made it its wages. And this, because it did not know, nor felt the power of sin, nor yet the free grace of God. The Gospel places acceptance at the beginning of repentance, and as the free gift of God's love. And this, because it not only knows the power of sin, but points to a Savior, provided of God.

The Lost Sheep is only one among a hundred: not a very great loss. Yet which among us would not, even from the common motives of ownership, leave the ninety and nine, and go after it, all the more that it has strayed into the wilderness? And, to take these Pharisees on their own ground, should not the Christ have done likewise to the straying and almost lost sheep of His own flock? Quite generally and to all time, is this not the very work of the Good Shepherd, and may we not, each of us, thus draw from it precious comfort? As we think of it, we remember that it is natural for the foolish sheep so to wander and stray. And we think not only of those sheep which Jewish pride and arrogance had left to go astray, but of our own natural tendency to wander. And we recall the saying of Peter, which, no doubt, looked back upon this Parable: You were as sheep going astray; but are now returned to the Shepherd and Bishop of your souls. It is not difficult in imagination to follow the Parabolic picture: how in its folly and ignorance the sheep strayed further and further, and at last was lost in solitude and among stony places; how the shepherd followed and found it, weary and footsore; and then with tender care lifted it on his shoulder, and carried it home, joyfully that he had found the lost. And not only this, but when, after long absence, he returned home with his found sheep, that now nestled close to its Savior, he called together his friends, and called them rejoice with him over the once lost and now found treasure.

It needs not, and would only diminish the pathos of this exquisite Parable, were we to attempt interpreting its details. They apply wherever and to whatever they can be applied. Of these three things we think: of the lost sheep; of the Good Shepherd, seeking, finding, bearing, rejoicing; and of the sympathy of all who are truly friends, like minded with Him. These, then, are the emblems of heavenly things. In heaven, oh, how different the feeling from that of Pharisaism! View the flock as do the Pharisees, and divide them into those who need and who do not need repentance, the sinners and the righteous, as regards man's application of the Law, does not this Parable teach us that in heaven there shall be joy over the sinner that repents more than over the ninety and nine righteous, which have no need of repentance? And to mark the terrible contrast between the teaching of Christ and that of the Pharisees; to mark also, how directly from heaven must have been the message of Jesus, and how poor sinners must have felt it such, we put down in all its nakedness the message which Pharisaism brought to the lost. Christ said to them: There is joy in heaven over one sinner that repents. Pharisaism said, and we quote here literally, There is joy before God when those who provoke Him perish from the world.

2. In proceeding to the second Parable, that of the Lost Drachm, we must keep in mind that in the first the danger of being lost arose from the natural tendency of the sheep to wander. In the second Parable it is no longer our natural tendency to which our loss is attributable. The drachm (about 7 1/2d. of our money) has been lost, as the woman, its owner, was using or counting her money. The loss is the more sensible, as it is one out of only ten, which constitute the owner's property. But it is still in the house, not like the sheep that had gone astray, only covered by the dust that is continually accumulating from the work and accidents around. And so it is more and more likely to be buried under it, or swept into chinks and corners, and less and less likely to be found as time passes. But the woman lights a lamp, sweeps the house, and seeks diligently, until she has found it. And then she calls together those around, and invites them to rejoice with her over the finding of

the lost part of her possessions. And so there is joy in the presence of the Angels over one sinner that repents. The comparison with others that need not such is now dropped, because, whereas formerly the sheep had strayed, though from the stubbornness of its nature, here the money had simply been lost, fallen among the dust that accumulates, practically, was no longer money, or of use; became covered, hidden, and was in danger of being forever out of sight, not serviceable, as it was intended to be and might have been.

We repeat, the interest of this Parable centers in the search, and the loss is caused, not by natural tendency, but by surrounding circumstances, which cover up the bright silver, hide it, and render it useless as regards its purpose, and lost to its owner.

3. If it has already appeared that the two first Parables are not merely a repetition, in different form, of the same thought, but represent two different aspects and causes of the being lost—the essential difference between them appears even more clearly in the third Parable, that of the Lost Son. Before indicating it in detail, we may mark the similarity in form, and the contrast in spirit, of analogous Rabbinic Parables. The thoughtful reader will have noted this even in the Jewish parallel to the first Parable, where the reason of the man following the straying animal is Pharisaic fear and distrust, for fear that the Jewish wine which it carried should become mingled with that of the Gentiles. Perhaps, however, this is a more apt parallel, when the Midrash relates how, when Moses fed the sheep of Jethro in the wilderness, and a kid had gone astray, he went after it, and found it drinking at a spring. As he thought it might be weary, he laid it on his shoulder and brought it back, when God said that, because he had shown pity on the sheep of a man, He would give him His own sheep, Israel, to feed. As a parallel to the second Parable, this may be quoted as similar in form, though very different in spirit, when a Rabbi notes, that, if a man had lost a Sela (drachm) or anything else of value in his house, he would light ever so many lights until he had found what provides for only one hour in this world. How much more, then, should he search, as for hidden treasures, for the words of the Law, on which depends the life of this and of the world to come! And in regard to the high place which Christ assigned to the repenting sinner, we may note that, according to the leading Rabbis, the penitents would stand nearer to God than

the perfectly righteous, since, in Isaiah 55:19, peace was first invited to those who had been far off, and then only to those near. This opinion was, however, not shared by all, and one Rabbi maintained, that, while all the prophets had only prophesied with reference to penitents (this had been the sole object of their mission), yet, as regarded the perfectly righteous, eye has not seen O God, beside You, what He has prepared for them. Lastly, the expression there is joy before Him is not uncommon in Jewish writings with reference to events which take place on earth.

To complete these notes, it may be added that, besides illustrations, to which reference will be made in the sequel, Rabbinic tradition supplies a parallel to at least part of the third Parable, that of the Lost Son. It tells us that, while prayer may sometimes find the gate of access closed, it is never shut against repentance, and it introduces a Parable in which a king sends a tutor after his son, who, in his wickedness, had left the palace, with this message: Return, my son! To which the latter replied: With what face can I return? I am ashamed! On which the father sends this message: My son, is there a son who is ashamed to return to his father, and shall you not return to your father? You shall return. So, continues the Midrash, had God sent Jeremiah after Israel in the hour of their sin with the call to return, and the comforting reminder that it was to their Father.

In the Parable of the Lost Son, the main interest centers in his restoration. It is not now to the innate tendency of his nature, nor yet to the work and dust in the house that the loss is attributable, but to the personal, free choice of the individual. He does not stray; he does not fall aside, he willfully departs, and under aggravated circumstances. It is the younger of two sons of a father, who is equally loving to both, and kind even to his hired servants, whose home, moreover, is one not only of sufficiency, but of superabundance and wealth. The demand which he makes for the portion of property falling to him is founded on the Jewish Law of Inheritance. Presumably, the father had only these two sons. The eldest would receive two portions, the younger the third of all movable property. The father could not have disinherited the younger son, although, if there had been several younger sons, he might have divided the property falling to them as he wished, provided he expressed only his disposition, and did not add that such or such of the children were to have a less share or none at all. On the other hand, a man might, during his lifetime, dispose of all his property by gift, as he chose, to the disadvantage, or even the total loss, of the first born, or of any other children; he might give all to strangers. In such cases, as, in regard to all such dispositions, greater latitude was allowed if the donor was regarded as dangerously ill, than if he was in good health. In the latter case a legal formality of actual seizure required to be gone through. With reference to the two eventualities just mentioned, that of diminishing or taking away the portion of younger children, and the right of gift, the Talmud speaks of Testaments, which bear the name Diyatiqi, as in the New Testament. These dispositions might be made either in writing or orally. But if the share of younger children was to be diminished or taken away, the disposition must be made by a person presumably near death (Shekhibh mera). But no one in good health (Bari) could diminish (except by gift) the legal portion of a younger son.

It thus appears that the younger son was, by law, fully entitled to his share of the possessions, although he had no right to claim it during the lifetime of his father. That he did so, might have been due to the feeling that, after all, he must make his own way in the world; to dislike of the order and discipline of his home; to estrangement from his elder brother; or, most likely, to a desire for liberty and enjoyment, with the latent belief that he would succeed well enough if left to himself. At any rate, his conduct, whatever his motives, was most heartless as regarded his father, and sinful as before God. Such a disposition could not prosper. The father had yielded to his demand, and, to be as free as possible from control and restraint, the younger son had gone into a far country. There the natural sequences soon appeared, and his property was wasted in riotous living. Regarding the demand for his inheritance as only a secondary trait in the Parable, designed, on the one hand, more forcibly to bring out the guilt of the son, and, on the other, the goodness, and afterwards the forgiveness, of the Father, we can scarcely doubt that by the younger son we are to understand those publicans and sinners against whose reception by, and fellowship with, Christ the Pharisees had murmured.

The next scene in the history is misunderstood when the objection is raised, that the young man's misery is there represented as the result of Providential circumstances rather than of his own misdoing. To begin with, he would not have been driven to such straits in the famine, if he had not wasted his substance with riotous living. Again, the main object is to show, that absolute liberty and indulgence of sinful desires and passions ended in anything but happiness. The Providence of God had an important part in this. Far more frequently are folly and sin punished in the ordinary course of Providence than by special judgments. Indeed, it is contrary to the teaching of Christ, and it would lead to an unmoral view of life, to regard such direct interjections as necessary, or to substitute them for the ordinary government of God. Similarly, for our awakening also we are frequently indebted to what is called the Providence, but what is really the manifold working together of the grace, of God. And so we find special meaning in the occurrence of this famine. That, in his lack, he stayed close (kollthe) to one of the citizens of that country, seems to indicate that the man had been unwilling to engage the dissipated young stranger, and only yielded to his desperate insistence. This also explains how he employed him in the lowest menial service, that of feeding swine. To a Jew, there was more than degradation in this, since the keeping of swine (although perhaps the ownership rather than the feeding) was prohibited to Israelites under a curse. And even in this demeaning service he was so evil entreated, that for very hunger he would gladly have filled his belly with the carob pods that the pigs ate. But here the same harshness, which had sent him to such employment, met him on the part of all the people of that country: and no man gave to him, even sufficient of such food. What perhaps gives additional meaning to this description is the Jewish saying: When Israel is reduced to the carob tree, they become repentant.

It was this pressure of extreme lack which first showed to the younger son the contrast between the country and the circumstances to which his sin had brought him, and the plentiful provision of the home he had left, and the kindness which provided bread enough and to spare for even the hired servants. There was only a step between what he said, having come into himself, and his resolve to return, though its felt difficulty seems implied in the expression: I will arise. Nor would he go back with the hope of being reinstated in his position as son, seeing he had already received, and wasted in sin, his portion of the inheritance. All he sought was to be made as one of the hired servants. And, from true feeling, and to show that this was all his pretence, he would preface his request by the confession, that he had sinned against heaven, a frequent Hebraism for against God, and in the sight of his father, and therefore could no longer lay claim to the name of son. The provision of the son he had, as stated, already spent, the name he no longer deserved. This favor only would he seek, to be as a hired servant in his fathers house, instead of in that terrible, strange land of famine and harshness.

But the result was far other than he could have expected. When we read that, while he was yet far off, his father saw him, we must evidently understand it in the sense, that his father had been always on the lookout for him, an impression which is strengthened by the later command to the servants to bring the calf, the fatted one, as if it had been especially fattened against his return. As he now saw him, he was moved with compassion, and he ran, and he fell on his neck, and covered him with kisses. Such a reception rendered the purposed request, to be made as one of the hired servants, impossible, and its spurious insertion in the text of some important manuscripts affords sad evidence of the lack of spiritual tact and insight of early copyists. The father's love had anticipated his confession, and rendered its self spoken sentence of condemnation impossible. Perfect love casts out fear, and the hard thoughts concerning himself and his deserts on the part of the returning sinner were banished by the love of the father. And so he only made confession of his sin and wrong, not now as preface to the request to be taken in as a servant, but as the outgoing of a humbled, grateful, truly penitent heart. Him whom lack had humbled, thought had brought to himself, and mingled need and hope led a suppliant servant, the love of a father, which anticipated his confession, and did not even speak the words of pardon, conquered, and so morally fathered him a second time as his son. Here it deserves special notice, as marking the absolute contrast between the teaching of Christ and Rabbinism, that we have in one of the oldest Rabbinic works a Parable exactly the reverse of this, when the son of a friend is redeemed from bondage, not as a son, but to be a slave, that so obedience might be demanded of him. The inference drawn is, that the obedience of the redeemed is not that of filial love of pardoned, but the enforcement of the claim of a master. How otherwise in the Parable and teaching of Christ!

But even so the story of love has not come to an end. They have reached the house. And now the father would not only restore the son, but convey to him the evidence of it, and he would do so before, and by the servants. The three tokens of wealth and position are to be furnished him. Quickly the servants are to bring forth the stola, the upper garment of the higher classes, and that the first, the best, and this instead of the tattered, coarse garment of the foreign swineherd. Similarly, the finger ring for his hand, and the sandals for his unshod feet, would indicate the son of the house. And to mark this still further, the servants were not only to bring these articles, but themselves to put them on the son, so as thereby to own his mastership. And yet further, the calf, the fatted one for this very occasion, was to be killed, and there was to be a joyous feast, for this his son was dead, and is come to life again; was lost, and is found.

Thus far for the reception of publicans and sinners, and all in every time whom it may concern. Now for the other aspect of the history. While this was going on, so continues the Parable, the elder brother was still in the field. On his return home, he inquired of a servant the reason of the festivities which he heard within the house. Informed that his younger brother had come, and the calf long prepared against a feast had been killed, because his father had recovered him safe and sound, he was angry, would not go in, and even refused the request to that effect of the father, who had come out for the purpose. The harsh words of reproach with which he set forth his own apparent wrongs could have only one meaning: his father had never rewarded him for his services. On the other hand, as soon as this his son, whom he will not even call his brother, had come back, notwithstanding all his disservice, he had made a feast of joy!

But in this very thing lay the error of the elder son, and, to apply it, the fatal mistake of Pharisaism. The elder son regarded all as of merit and reward, as work and return. But it is not so. We mark, first, that the same tenderness which had welcomed the returning son, now met the elder brother. He spoke to the angry man, not in the language of merited reproof, but addressed him lovingly as son, and reasoned with him. And then, when he had shown him his wrong, he would gladly recall him to better feeling by telling him of the other as his brother. But the main point is this. There can be here no question of desert. So long as the son is in His Father's house He gives in His great goodness to His child all that is the Father's. But this poor lost one, still a son and a brother, he has not got any reward, only been taken back again by a Father's love, when he had come back to Him in the deep misery of his felt need. This son, or rather, as the other should view him, this brother, had been dead, and was come to life again; lost, and was found. And over this it was appropriate to make merry and be glad, not to murmur. Such murmuring came from thoughts of work and pay, wrong in themselves, and foreign to the proper idea of Father and son; such joy, from a Father's heart. The elder brother's were the thoughts of a servant: of service and return; the younger brother's was the welcome of a son in the mercy and everlasting love of a Father. And this to us, and to all time!

End Notes:

[57]   There is to some extent a Rabbinic parallel Parable (Ber. R. 86, ed. Warsh. p. 154 b, about the middle), where one who is driving twelve animals laden with wine, leaves the eleven and follows the twelfth into the shop of a Gentile, for fear that the wine which it bears might be mixed there.

[58]   But in regard to such disinheriting of children, even if they were bad, it
       was said, that the Spirit of Wisdom did not rest on them who made such
       disposition (Baba B. v3:5).

[59]   The fruit of the carob tree is regarded in Jewish and pagan literature as the
       poorest, and, only fit for animals. See Wetstein ad loc. According to Jewish
       ideas, it took seventy years before the carob tree bore fruit (Bekhor. 8 a).
       It is at least doubtful whether the tree is mentioned in the Old Testament
       (the of 2 Samuel 5:23, 24). In the Mishnah it is frequently referred to
       (Peah 1:5; Shabb. 24:2; Baba B. 2:7). Its fruit seems to have been the food
       of ascetics, such as Chanina b. Dosa, etc. (Ber. 17 b), and Simeon b. Jochai
       (Shabb. 33 b), even as it had been that of John the Baptist. Its leaves seem
       on occasions to have been used as writing material (Tos. Gitt. 2).

[60]   It may be worth mentioning a somewhat similar parable in Bemidb. R. 15
       (ed. Warsh. p. 62 b, near beginning). Reference is made to the fact, that,
       according to Numbers 7, all the twelve tribes brought gifts, except Levi:
       Upon that follows in Numbers 8: the consecration of the Levites to the
       service of the Lord. The Midrash likens it to a feast which a king had made
       for all the people, but to which he does not invite his special friend. And
       while the latter seems to fear that this exclusion may imply disfavor, the
       king has a special feast for his friend only, and shows him that while the
       common meal was for all, the special feast is for those he especially loves.

Chapter 18

Kingdom Parables

(Luke 16)

Although widely differing in their object and teaching, the last group of Parables spoken during this part of Christ's Ministry are, at least outwardly, connected by a leading thought. The word by which we would string them together is Righteousness. There are three Parables of the Unrighteous: the Unrighteous Steward, the Unrighteous Owner, and the Unrighteous Dispenser, or Judge. And these are followed by two other Parables of the Self righteous: Self righteousness in its Ignorance, and its dangers as regards oneself; and Self righteousness in its Harshness, and its dangers as regards others. But when this outward connection has been marked, we have gone the utmost length. Much more close is the internal connection between some of them.

We note it, first and chiefly, between the two first Parables. Recorded in the same chapter, and in the same connection, they were addressed to the same audience. True, the Parable of the Unjust Steward was primarily spoken to His disciples, that of the Rich Man and Lazarus to the Pharisees. But then the audience of Christ at that time consisted of disciples and Pharisees. And these two classes in the audience stood in peculiar relation to each other, which is exactly met in these two Parables, so that the one may be said to have sprung out of the other. For, the disciples, to whom the first Parable was addressed, were not primarily the Apostles, but those publicans and sinners whom Jesus had received, to the great displeasure of the Pharisees. Them He would teach concerning the material wealth of unrighteousness. And, when the Pharisees sneered at this teaching, He would turn it against them, and show that, beneath the self justification, which made them forget that now the Kingdom of God was opened to all, and imagine that they were the sole vindicators of a Law which in their everyday practice they notoriously broke, there lay as deep sin and as great alienation from God as that of the sinners whom they despised. Theirs might not be the material wealth of, yet it might be that for unrighteousness; and, while they sneered at the idea of such men making of their material wealth friends that would receive them into everlasting tabernacles, themselves would experience that in the end a terrible readjustment before God would follow on their neglect of using for God, and their employment only for self of such material wealth as was theirs, coupled as it was with harsh and proud neglect of what they regarded as wretched, great covered Lazarus, who lay forsaken and starving at their very doors.

It will have been observed, that we lay once more special stress on the historical connection and the primary meaning of the Parables. We would read them in the light of the circumstances in which they were spoken, as addressed to a certain class of hearers, and as referring to what had just passed. The historical application once ascertained, the general lessons may afterwards be applied to the widest range. This historical view will help us to understand the introduction, connection, and meaning, of the two Parables which have been described as the most difficult: those of the Unjust Steward, and of the Rich Man and Lazarus.

At the outset we must recall, that they were addressed to two different classes in the same audience. In both the subject is Unrighteousness. In the first, which is addressed to the recently converted publicans and sinners, it is the Unrighteous Steward, making unrighteous use of what had been committed to his administration by his Master; in the second Parable, which is addressed to the self justifying, sneering Pharisees, it is the Unrighteous Possessor, who uses only for himself and for time what he has, while he leaves Lazarus, who, in his view, is wretched and great covered, to starve or perish, ignored, at his very door. In agreement with its object, and as suited to the part of the audience addressed, the first Parable points a lesson, while the second furnishes a warning. In the first Parable we are told, what the sinner when converted should learn from his previous life of sin; in the second, what the self deceiving, proud Pharisee should learn as regarded the life which to him seemed so fair, but was in reality so empty of God and of love. It follows, and this is of greatest importance, especially in the interpretation of the first Parable, that we must not expect to find spiritual equivalents for each of the persons or incidents introduced. In each case, the Parable itself forms only an illustration of the lessons, spoken or implied, which Christ would convey to the one and the other class in His audience.

I. The Parable of the Unjust Steward., In accordance with the canon of interpretation just laid down, we distinguish, 1. The illustrative Parable. 2. Its moral. 3. Its application in the combination of the moral with some of the features of the Parable.

1. The illustrative Parable. This may be said to converge to the point brought out in the concluding verse: the prudence which characterizes the dealings of the children of this world in regard to their own generation, or, to translate the Jewish forms of expression into our own phraseology, the wisdom with which those who care not for the world to come choose the means most effectual for attaining their worldly objects. It is this prudence by which their aims are so effectually secured, and it alone, which is set before the children of light, as that by which to learn. And the lesson is the more practical, that those primarily addressed had up to this point been among these men of the world. Let them learn from the serpent its wisdom, and from the dove its harmlessness; from the children of this world, their prudence as regarded their generation, while, as children of the new light, they must remember the higher aim for which that prudence was to be employed. Thus would that material wealth which is of unrighteousness, and which certainly fails, become to us treasure in the world to come, welcome us there, and, so far from failing, prove permanent—welcome us in everlasting tabernacles. Thus, also, shall we have made friends of the material wealth of unrighteousness, and that, which from its nature must fail, become eternal gain, or, to translate it into Talmudic phraseology, it will be of the things of which a man enjoys the interest in this world, while the capital remains for the world to come.

It cannot now be difficult to understand the Parable. Its object is simply to show, in the most striking manner, the prudence of a worldly man, who is unrestrained by any other consideration than that of attaining his end. At the same time, with singular wisdom, the illustration is so chosen as that its matter (materia), the material wealth of unrighteousness, may serve to point a life lesson to those newly converted publicans and sinners, who had formerly sacrificed all for the sake, or in the enjoyment of, that material wealth. All else, such as the question, who is the master and who the steward, and such like, we dismiss, since the Parable is only intended as an illustration of the lesson to be afterwards taught.

The connection between this Parable and what Jesus had previously said concerning returning sinners, to which our remarks have already pointed, is further evidenced by the use of the term wasting (diaskorpzon), in the charge against the steward, just as the prodigal son had wasted (dieskrpise) his substance. Only, in the present instance, the property had been entrusted to his administration. As regards the owner, his designation as rich seems intended to mark how large was the property committed to the steward. The steward was not, as in Luke 12:42-46, a slave, but one employed for the administration of the rich man's affairs, subject to notice of dismissal. He was accused, the term implying wickedness, but not necessarily a false charge, not of fraud, but of wasting, probably by riotous living and carelessness, his masters goods. And his master seems to have convinced himself that the charge was true, since he at once gives him notice of dismissal. The latter is absolute, and not made dependent on the account of his stewardship, which is only asked as necessary, when he gives up his office. Nor does the steward either deny the charge or plead any extenuation. His great concern rather is, during the time still left of his stewardship, before he gives up his accounts, to provide for his future support. The only alternative before him in the future is that of manual labor or begging. But for the former he has not strength; from the latter he is restrained by shame.

Then it is that his prudence suggests a device by which, after his dismissal, he may, without begging, be received into the houses of those whom he has made friends. It must be borne in mind, that he is still steward, and, as such, has full power of disposing of his master's affairs. When, therefore, he sends for one after another of his master's debtors, and tells each to alter the sum in the bond, he does not suggest to them forgery or fraud, but, in remitting part of the debt, whether it had been incurred as rent in kind, or as the price of produce purchased, he acts, although unrighteously, yet strictly within his rights. Thus, neither the steward nor the debtors could be charged with criminality, and the master must have been struck with the cleverness of a man who had thus secured a future provision by making friends, so long as he had the means of so doing (before his material wealth of unrighteousness failed).

A few archaeological notices may help the interpretation of details. From the context it seems more likely, that the bonds, or rather writings, of these debtors were written acknowledgements of debt, than, as some have supposed that they were, leases of farms. The debts over which the steward variously disposed, according as he wished to gain more or less favor, were considerable. In the first case they are stated at a hundred Bath of oil, in the second as a hundred Cor of wheat. In regard to these quantities we have the preliminary difficulty, that three kinds of measurement were in use in Palestine, that of the Wilderness, or, the original Mosaic; that of Jerusalem, which was more than a fifth larger; and that of Sepphoris, probably the common Galilean measurement, which, in turn, was more than a fifth larger than the Jerusalem measure. To be more precise, one Galilean was equal to 3/2 Wilderness measures. Assuming the measurement to have been the Galilean, one Bath would have been equal to an Attic Metretes, or about 39 liters. On the other hand, the so called Wilderness measurement would correspond with the Roman measures, and, in that case, the Bath would be the same as the Amphora, or amount to a little less than 26 liters. The latter is the measurement adopted by Josephus. In the Parable, the first debtor was owing 100 of these Bath, or, according to the Galilean measurement, about 3,900 liters of oil. As regards the value of a Bath of oil, little information can be derived from the statements of Josephus, since he only mentions prices under exceptional circumstances, either in particularly plentiful years, or else at a time of war and siege. In the former, an Amphora, or 26 liters, of oil seems to have fetched about 9d.; but it must be added, that, even in such a year, this represents a rare stroke of business, since the oil was immediately afterwards re-sold for eight times the amount, and this, 3s. for half an Amphora of about 13 liters—would probably represent an exceptionally high war price. The fair price for it would probably have been 9d. For the Mishnah informs us, that the ordinary earthenware casks (the Gerabh) held each 2 Seah, or 48 Log, or about 26 liters. Again, according to a notice in the Talmud, 100 such casks, or, 200 Seah, were sold for 10 (presumably gold) dinars, or 250 silver dinars, equal to about 7l. 10s. of our money. And as the Bath (= 3 Seah) held a third more than one of those casks, or Gerabhin, the value of the 100 Bath of oil would probably amount to about 10l. of our money, and the remission of the steward, to 5l.

The second debtor owed a hundred Cor of wheat, that is, in dry measure, ten times the amount of the oil of the first debtor, since the Cor was ten Ephah or Bath, the Ephah three Seah, the Seah six Qabh, and the Qabh four Log. This must be borne in mind, since the dry and the fluid measures were precisely the same; and here, also, their threefold computation (the Wilderness, the Jerusalem, and the Galilean) obtained. As regards the value of wheat, we learn that, on an average, four Seah of seed were expected to produce one Cor, that is, seven and a half times their amount; and that a field 1,500 cubits long and 50 wide was expected to grow a Corinthians The average price of a Cor of wheat, bought uncut, amounted to about 25 dinars, or 15s. Striking an average between the lowest prices mentioned and the highest, we infer that the price of 3 Seah or an Ephah would be from two shillings to half a crown, and accordingly of a Cor (or 10 Ephah) from 20 to 25 shillings (probably this is rather more than it would cost). On this computation the hundred Cor would represent a debt of from 100l. to 125l., and the remission of the steward (of 20 Cor), a sum of from 20l. to 25l. Comparatively small as these sums may seem, they are in reality large, remembering the value of money in Palestine, which, on a low computation, would be five times as great as in our own country. These two debtors are only mentioned as instances, and so the unjust steward would easily secure for himself friends by the material wealth of unrighteousness, the term material wealth, we may note, being derived from the Syriac and Rabbinic word of the same kind (from = to apportion).

Another point on which acquaintance with the history and habits of those times throws light is, how the debtors could so easily alter the sum mentioned in their respective bonds. For, the text implies that this, and not the writing of a new bond, is intended; since in that case the old one would have been destroyed, and not given back for alteration. It would be impossible, within the present limits, to enter fully on the interesting subject of writing, writing materials, and written documents among the ancient Jews. Suffice it to give here the briefest notices.

The materials on which the Jews wrote were of the most divers kind: leaves, as of olives, palms, the carob, etc.; the rind of the pomegranate, the shell of walnuts, etc.; the prepared skins of animals (leather and parchment); and the product of the papyrus, used long before the time of Alexander the Great for the manufacture of paper, and known in Talmudic writings by the same name, as Papir or Apipeir, but more frequently by that of Nayyar, probably from the stripes (Nirin) of the plant of which it was made. But what interests us more, as we remember the tablet (pinakdion) on which Zacharias wrote the name of the future Baptist, is the circumstance that it bears not only the same name, Pinaqes or Pinqesa, but that it seems to have been of such common use in Palestine. It consisted of thin pieces of wood (the Luach) fastened or strung together. The Mishnah enumerates three kinds of them: those where the wood was covered with papyrus, those where it was covered with wax, and those where the wood was left plain to be written on with ink. The latter was of different kinds. Black ink was prepared of soot (the Deyo), or of vegetable or mineral substances. Gum Arabic and Egyptian (Qumos and Quma) and vitriol (Qanqanthos) seem also to have been used in writing. It is curious to read of writing in colors and with red ink or Siqra, and even of a kind of sympathetic ink, made from the bark of the ash, and brought out by a mixture of vitriol and gum. We also read of a gold ink, as that in which the copy of the Law was written which, according to the legend, the High Priest had sent to Ptolemy Philadelphus for the purpose of being translated into Greek by the LXX. But the Talmud prohibits copies of the Law in gold letters, or more probably such in which the Divine Name was written in gold letters. In writing, a pen, Qolemos, made of reed (Qaneh) was used, and the reference in an Apostolic Epistle to writing with ink and pen (di mlanos ka kalmou) finds even its verbal counterpart in the Midrash, which speaks of Milanin and Qolemin (ink and pens). The public writer, a trade very common in the East, went about with a Qolemos, or reed pen, behind his ear, as a badge of his employment. With the reed pen we ought to mention its necessary accompaniments: the penknife, the inkstand (which, when double, for black and red ink, was sometimes made of earthenware, Qalamarim), and the ruler, it being regarded by the stricter set as unlawful to write any words of Holy Writ on any unlined material, no doubt to ensure correct writing and reading.

In all this we have not referred to the practice of writing on leather especially prepared with salt and flour, nor to the Qelaph, or parchment in the stricter sense. For we are here chiefly interested in the common mode of writing, that on the Pinaqes, or tablet, and especially on that covered with wax. Indeed, a little vessel holding wax was generally attached to it (Pinaqes sheyesh bo beth Qibbul shaavah). On such a tablet they wrote not with a reed pen, but with a stylus, generally of iron. This instrument consisted of two parts, which might be detached from each other: the hard pointed writer (Kothebh), and the blotter (Mocheq) which was flat and thick for smoothing out letters and words which had been written or rather engraved in the wax. There can be no question that acknowledgments of debt, and other transactions, were ordinarily written down on such wax covered tablets; for not only is direct reference made to it, but there are special provisions in regard to documents where there are such erasures, or rather effacements: such as, that they require not to be in the document, under what conditions and how the witnesses are in such cases to affix their signatures, just as there are particular injunctions how witnesses who could not write are to affix their mark.

But although we have thus ascertained that the bonds in the Parable must have been written on wax, or else, possibly, on parchment—where the Mocheq, or blotter, could easily efface the numbers, we have also evidence that they were not, as so often, written on tablets (the Pinaques). For, the Greek term, by which these bonds or writings are designated in the Parable (grmmata), is the same as is sometimes used in Rabbinic writings (Gerammation) for an acknowledgment of debt; the Hebraized Greek word corresponding to the more commonly used (Syriac) term Shitre (Shetar), which also primarily denotes writings, and is used specifically for such acknowledgments. Of these there were two kinds. The most formal Shetar was not signed by the debtor at all, but only by the witnesses, who were to write their names (or marks) immediately (not more than two lines) below the text of the document, to prevent fraud. Otherwise, the document would not possess legal validity. Generally, it was further attested by the Sanhedrin of three, who signed in such manner as not to leave even one line vacant. Such a document contained the names of creditor and debtor, the amount owing, and the date, together with a clause attaching the property of the debtor. In fact, it was a kind of mortgage; all sale of property being, as with us, subject to such a mortgage, which bore the name Acharayuth (probably, guarantee) When the debt was paid, the legal obligation was simply returned to the debtor; if paid in part, either a new bond was written, or a receipt given, which was called Shobher or Tebhara, because it broke the debt.

But in many respects different were those bonds which were acknowledgements of debt for purchases made, such as we suppose those to have been which are mentioned in the Parable. In such cases it was not uncommon to dispense altogether with witnesses, and the document was signed by the debtor himself. In bonds of this kind, the creditor had not the benefit of a mortgage in case of sale. We have expressed our belief that the Parable refers to such documents, and we are confirmed in this by the circumstance that they not only bear a different name from the more formal bonds (the Shitre), but one which is perhaps the most exact rendering of the Greek term (a writing of hand, note of hand). For completeness sake we add, in regard to the farming of land, that two kinds of leases were in use. Under the first, called Shetar Arisuth, the lessee (Aris = oros) received a certain portion of the produce. He might be a lessee for life, for a specified number of years, or even a hereditary tiller of the ground; or he might sub-let it to another person. Under the second kind of lease, the farmer, or Meqabbel, entered into a contract for payment either in kind, when he undertook to pay a stipulated and unvarying amount of produce, in which case he was called a Chokher (Chakhur or Chakhira), or else a certain annual rental in money, when he was called a Sokher.

2. From this somewhat lengthened digression, we return to notice the moral of the Parable. It is put in these words: Make to yourselves friends out of [by means of] the material wealth of unrighteousness, that, when it shall fail, they may receive you into everlasting tabernacles. From what has been previously stated, the meaning of these words offers little serious difficulty. We must again recall the circumstances, that they were primarily addressed to converted publicans and sinners, to whom the expression material wealth of unrighteousness, of which there are close analogies, and even an exact transcript in the Targum, would have an obvious meaning. Among us, also, there are not a few who may feel its aptness as they look back on the past, while to all it carries a much needed warning. Again, the addition of the definite article leaves no doubt, that the everlasting tabernacles mean the well known heavenly home; in which sense the term tabernacle is, already used in the Old Testament. But as a whole we regard it (as previously hinted) as an adaptation to the Parable of the well known Rabbinic saying, that there were certain graces of which a man enjoyed the benefit here, while the capital, so to speak, remained for the next world. And if a more literal interpretation were demanded, we cannot but feel the duty incumbent on those converted publicans in a sense, on us all, to seek to make for ourselves of the material wealth, be it of money, of knowledge, of strength, or opportunities, which to many has, and to all may so easily, become that of unrighteousness, such lasting and spiritual application: gain such friends by means of it, that, when it fails, as fail it must when we die, all may not be lost, but rather meet us in heaven. Thus would each deed done for God with this material wealth become a friend to greet us as we enter the eternal world.

3. The suitableness both of the Parable and of its application to the audience of Christ appears from its similarity to what occurs

in Jewish writings. Thus, the reasoning that the Law could not have been given to the nations of the world, since they have not observed the seven Noachic commandments (which Rabbinism supposes to have been given to the Gentiles), is illustrated by a Parable in which a king is represented as having employed two administrators (Apiterophin); one over the gold and silver, and the other over the straw. The latter rendered himself suspected, and, continues the Parable, when he complained that he had not been set over the gold and silver, they said to him: You fool, if you had rendered yourself suspected in regard to the straw, shall they commit to you the treasure of gold and silver? And we almost seem to hear the very words of Christ: He that is faithful in that which is least, is faithful also in much, in this of the Midrash: The Holy One, blessed be His Name, does not give great things to a man until he has been tried in a small matter; which is illustrated by the history of Moses and of David, who were both called to rule from the faithful guiding of sheep.

Considering that the Jewish mind would be familiar with such modes of illustration, there could have been no misunderstanding of the words of Christ. These converted publicans might think, and so may some of us, that theirs was a very narrow sphere of service, one of little importance; or else, like the Pharisees, and like so many others among us, that faithful administration of the things of this world (the material wealth of unrighteousness) had no bearing on the possession of the true riches in the next world. In answer to the first difficulty, Christ points out that the principle of service is the same, whether applied to much or to little; that the one was, proper preparation for, and, in truth, the test of the other. He that is faithful, or, to paraphrase the word (pists), he that has proved himself, is accredited (answering to), in the least, is also faithful [accredited] in much; and who in the least is unjust is also in much unjust. Therefore, if a man failed in faithful service of God in his worldly matters, in the language of the Parable, if he were not faithful in the material wealth of unrighteousness, could he look for the true material wealth, or riches of the world to come? Would not his unfaithfulness in the lower stewardship imply unfitness for the higher? And, still in the language of the Parable, if they had not proved faithful in mere stewardship, in that which was another's, could it be expected that they would be exalted from stewardship to proprietorship? And the ultimate application of all was this, that dividedness was impossible in the service of God. It is impossible for the disciple to make separation between spiritual matters and worldly, and to attempt serving God in the one and material wealth in the other. There is absolutely no such distinction to the disciple, and our common usage of the words secular and spiritual is derived from a terrible misunderstanding and mistake. To the secular, nothing is spiritual; and to the spiritual, nothing is secular: No servant can serve two Masters; you cannot serve God and material wealth.

II. The Parable of The Rich Man and Lazarus. Although primarily spoken to the Pharisees, and not to the disciples, yet, as will now appear, it was spoken for the disciples. The words of Christ had touched more than one great spot in the hearts of the Pharisees. This consecration of all to God as the necessary condition of high spiritual service, and then of higher spiritual standing, as it were ownership, such as they claimed, was a very hard saying. It touched their covetousness. They would have been quite ready to hear they believed that the true treasure had been committed to their trust. But that its condition was, that they should prove themselves God devoted in the unrighteous material wealth, faithful in the employment of it in that for which it was entrusted to their stewardship, this was not to be borne. Nor yet, that such prospects should be held out to publicans and sinners, while they were withheld from those who were the custodians of the Law and of the Prophets. But were they faithful to the Law? And as to their claim of being the owners, the Parable of the Rich Owner and of his bearing would exhibit how unfaithful they were in much as well as in little, in what they claimed as owners as well as in their stewardship, and this, on their own showing of their relations to publicans and sinners: the Lazarus who lay at their doors.

Thus viewed, the verses which introduce the second Parable (that of the Rich Man and Lazarus) will appear, not detached sayings, as some commentators would have us believe, but most closely connected with the Parable to which they form the Preface. Only, here especially, must we remember, that we have only Notes of Christ's discourse, made years before by one who had heard it, and containing the barest outline, as it were, the stepping stones, of the argument as it proceeded. Let us try to follow it. As the Pharisees heard what Christ said, their covetousness was touched. It is said, moreover, that they derided Him, literally, turned up their noses at Him. The mocking gestures, with which they pointed to His publican disciples, would be accompanied by mocking words in which they would extol and favorably compare their own claims and standing with that of those new disciples of Christ. Not only to refute but to confute, to convict, and, if possible, to convince them, was the object of Christ's discourse and Parable. One by one their pleas were taken up and shown to be utterly untenable. They were persons who by outward righteousness and pretences sought to appear just before men, but God knew their hearts; and that which was exalted among men, their Pharisaic standing and standing aloof, was abomination before Him. These two points form the main subject of the Parable. Its first object was to show the great difference between the before men and the before God; between the Rich Man as he appears to men in this world, and as he is before God and will be in the next world. Again, the second main object of the Parable was to illustrate that their Pharisaic standing and standing aloof, the bearing of the Rich Man in reference to a Lazarus, which was the glory of Pharisaism before men, was an abomination before God. Yet a third object of the Parable was in reference to their covetousness, the selfish use which they made of their possessions, their material wealth. But a selfish was an unrighteous use; and, as such, would meet with greater retribution than in the case of an unfaithful steward.

But we leave for the present the comparative analysis of the Parable to return to the introductory words of Christ. Having shown that the claims of the Pharisees and their standing aloof from poor sinners were an abomination before God, Christ combats these grounds of their bearing, that they were the custodians and observers of the Law and of the Prophets, while those poor sinners had no claims upon the Kingdom of God. Yes, but the Law and the Prophets had their terminus ad quem in John the Baptist, who brought the good news of the Kingdom of God. Since then everyone had to enter it by personal resolution and force. Yes, it was true that the Law could not fail in one tittle of it. But, notoriously and in everyday life, the Pharisees, who thus spoke of the Law and appealed to it, were the constant and open breakers of it. Witness here their teaching and practice concerning divorce, which really involved a breach of the seventh commandment.

Thus, when bearing in mind that, as previously stated, we have here only the heads, or rather the stepping stones, of Christ's argument, from notes by a hearer at the time, which were afterwards given to Luke, we clearly perceive, how closely connected are the seemingly disjointed sentences which preface the Parable, and how aptly they introduce it. The Parable itself is strictly of the Pharisees and their relation to the publicans and sinners whom they despised, and to whose stewardship they opposed thoughts of their own proprietorship. With infinite wisdom and depth the Parable tells in two directions: in regard to their selfish use of the literal riches, their covetousness, and in regard to their selfish use of the figurative riches: their Pharisaic righteousness, which left poor Lazarus at their door to the dogs and to famine, not bestowing on him anything whatever from their supposed rich festive banquets.

On the other hand, it will be necessary in the interpretation of this Parable to keep in mind, that its Parabolic details must not be exploited, nor doctrines of any kind derived from them, either as to the character of the other world, the question of the duration of future punishments, or the possible moral improvement of those in Gehinnom. All such things are foreign to the Parable, which is only intended as a type, or exemplification and illustration, of what is intended to be taught. And, if proof were required, it would surely be enough to remind ourselves, that this Parable is addressed to the Pharisees, to whom Christ would scarcely have communicated details about the other world, on which He was so silent in His teaching to the disciples. The Parable naturally falls into three parts.

1. The Rich Man and Lazarus before and after death, or the contrast between before men and before God; the unrighteous use of riches, literal and figurative; and the relations of the Pharisaic the Rich Man to the publican Lazarus, as before men and as before God: the exalted among men an abomination before God. And the application of the Parable is here the more telling, that alms were so highly esteemed among the Pharisees, and that the typical Pharisee is thus set before them as, on their own showing, the typical sinner.

The Parable opens by presenting to us a rich man clothed in purple and byssus, joyously faring every day in splendor. All here is in character. His dress is described as the finest and most costly, for byssus and purple were the most expensive materials, only inferior to silk, which, if genuine and unmixed, for at least three kinds of silk are mentioned in ancient Jewish writings, was worth its weight in gold. Both byssus, of which it is not yet quite certain, whether it was of hemp or cotton, and purple were indeed manufactured in Palestine, but the best byssus (at least at that time) came from Egypt and India. The white garments of the High Priest on the Day of Atonement were made of it. To pass over exaggerated accounts of its costliness, the High Priests dress of Pelusian linen for the morning service of the Day of Atonement was said to have cost about 36l.; that of Indian linen for the evening of the same day about 24l. Of course, this stuff would, if of home manufacture, whether made in Galilee or in Judea, be much cheaper. As regarded purple, which was obtained from the coasts of Tyre, wool of violet purple was sold about that period by weight at the rate of about 3l. the Roman pound, though it would considerably vary in price.

Quite in accordance with this luxuriousness, unfortunately not uncommon among the very high placed Jews, since the Talmud (though, no doubt, exaggeratedly) speaks of the dress of a corrupt High Priest as having cost upwards of 300l., was the feasting every day, the description of which conveys the impression of company, merriment, and splendor. All this is intended to set forth the selfish use which this man made of his wealth, and to point the contrast of his bearing towards Lazarus. Here also every detail is meant to mark the pitiableness of the case, as it stood out before the Rich Man. The very name, not often mentioned in any other real, and never in any other Parabolic story, tells it: Lazarus, Laazar, a common abbreviation of Elazar, as it were, God help him! Then we read that he was cast (bbleto) at his gateway, as if to mark that the bearers were glad to throw down their unwelcome burden. Laid there, he was in full view of the Pharisee as he went out or came in, or sat in his courtyard. And as he looked at him, he was covered with a loathsome disease; as he heard him, he uttered a piteous request to be filled with what fell from the rich man's table. Yet nothing was done to help his bodily misery, and, as the word desiring (pithumn) implies, his longing for the crumbs remained unsatisfied. So selfish in the use of his wealth was the Rich Man, so wretched Lazarus in his view; so self satisfied and unpitying was the Pharisee, so miserable in his sight and so needy the publican and sinner. Yes, even the dogs came and licked his sores, for it is not to be understood as an alleviation, but as an aggravation of his ills, that he was left to the dogs, which in Scripture are always represented as unclean animals.

So it was before men. But how was it before God? There the relation was reversed. The beggar died, no more of him here. But the Angels carried him away into Abraham's bosom. Leaving aside for the present the Jewish teaching concerning the after death, we are struck with the magnificent simplicity of the figurative language used by Christ, as compared with the wild and sensuous fancies of later Rabbinic teaching on the subject. It is, true, that we must not look in this Parabolic language for Christ's teaching about the after death. On the other hand, while He would say nothing that was essentially divergent from, at least, the purest views entertained on the subject at that time, since otherwise the object of the Parabolic illustration would have been lost, yet, whatever He did say must, when stripped of its Parabolic details, be consistent with fact. Thus, the carrying up of the soul of the righteous by Angels is certainly in accordance with Jewish teaching, though stripped of all legendary details, such as about the number and the greetings of the Angels. But it is also fully in accordance with Christian thought of the ministry of Angels. Again, as regards the expression Abraham's bosom, it occurs, although not frequently, in Jewish writings. On the other hand, the appeal to Abraham as our father is so frequent, his presence and merits are so constantly invoked; notably, he is so expressly designated as he who receives the penitent into Paradise, that we can see how in agreement especially to the higher Jewish teaching, which did not deal in coarsely sensuous descriptions of Gan Eden, or Paradise, the phrase Abraham's bosom must have been. Nor surely can it be necessary to vindicate the accord with Christian thinking of a figurative expression, that likens us to children lying lovingly in the bosom of Abraham as our spiritual father.

2. The Rich Man and Lazarus after death: The great contrast fully realized, and how to enter into the Kingdom. Here also the main interest centers in the Rich Man. He also has died and been buried. Thus ends all his exaltedness before men. The next scene is in Hades or Sheol, the place of the disembodied spirits before the final Judgment. It consists of two divisions: the one of consolation, with all the faithful gathered to Abraham as their father; the other of fiery torment. Thus far in accordance with the general teaching of the New Testament. As regards the details, they evidently represent the views current at the time among the Jews. According to them, the Garden of Eden and the Tree of Life were the abode of the blessed. In common belief, the words of Genesis 2:10: a river went out of Eden to water the garden, indicated that this Eden was distinct from, and superior to, the garden in which Adam had been originally placed. With reference to it, we read that the righteous in Gan Eden see the wicked in Gehinnom, and rejoice; and, similarly, that the wicked in Gehinnom see the righteous sitting beautified

in Gan Eden, and their souls are troubled. Still more marked is the parallelism in a legend told about two wicked companions, of whom one had died impenitent, while the other on seeing it had repented. After death, the impenitent in Gehinnom saw the happiness of his former companion, and murmured. When told that the difference of their fate was due to the others penitence, he wished to have space assigned for it, but was informed that this life (the eve of the Sabbath) was the time for making provision for the next (the Sabbath). Again, it is consistent with what were the views of the Jews, that conversations could be held between dead persons, of which several legendary instances are given in the Talmud. The torment, especially of thirst, of the wicked, is repeatedly mentioned in Jewish writings. Thus, in one place, the fable of Tantalus is apparently repeated. The righteous is seen beside delicious springs, and the wicked with his tongue parched at the brink of a river, the waves of which are constantly receding from him. But there is this very marked and characteristic contrast, that in the Jewish legend the beatified is a Pharisee, while the sinner tormented with thirst is a Publican! Above all, and as marking the vast difference between Jewish ideas and Christ's teaching, we notice that there is no analogy in Rabbinic writings to the statement in the Parable, that there is a wide and impassable gulf between Paradise and Gehenna.

To return to the Parable. When we read that the Rich Man in torments lifted up his eyes, it was, no doubt, for help, or, at least, alleviation. Then he first perceived and recognized the reversed relationship. The text emphatically repeats here: And he, literally, this one (ka atos), as if now, for the first time, he realized, but only to misunderstand and misapply it, how easily superabundance might minister relief to extreme need, calling (namely, upon = invoking) said: "Father Abraham, have mercy upon me, and send Lazarus." The invocation of Abraham, as having the power, and of Abraham as Father, was natural on the part of a Jew. And Jesus does not here express what really was, but only introduces Jews as speaking in accordance with the popular notions. Accordingly, it does not necessarily imply on the part of the Rich Man either glorification of carnal descent (gloriatio carnis, as Bengel has it), nor a latent idea that he might still dispose of Lazarus. A Jew would have appealed to Father Abraham under such or like circumstances, and many analogous statements might be quoted in proof. But all the more telling is it, that the rich Pharisee should behold in the bosom of Abraham, whose child he especially claimed to be, what, in his sight, had been poor Lazarus, covered with moral sores, and, religiously speaking, thrown down outside his gate, not only not admitted to the fellowship of his religious banquet, but not even to be fed by the crumbs that fell from his table, and to be left to the dogs. And it was the climax of the contrast that he should now have to invoke, and that in vain, his ministry, seeking it at the hands of Abraham. And here we also recall the previous Parable about making, before it fail, friends by means of the material wealth of unrighteousness, that they may welcome us in the everlasting tabernacles.

It should be remembered that the Rich Man now limits his request to the humblest dimensions, asking only that Lazarus might be sent to dip the tip of his finger in the cooling liquid, and thus give him even the smallest relief. To this Abraham replies, though in a tone of pity: Child, yet decidedly, showing him, first, the rightness of the present position of things; and, secondly, the impossibility of any alteration, such as he had asked. The Rich Man had, in his lifetime, received his good things; that had been his things, he had chosen them as his part, and used them for self, without communicating of them. And Lazarus had received evil things. Now Lazarus was comforted, and the Rich Man in torment. It was the right order, not that Lazarus was comforted because in this world he had suffered, nor yet that the Rich Man was in torment because in this world he had had riches. But Lazarus received there the comfort which had been refused to him on earth, and the man who had made this world his good, and obtained there his portion, of which he had refused even the crumbs to the most needy, now received the appropriate reward of his unpitying, unloving, selfish life. But, besides all this, which in itself was right and proper, the Rich Man had asked what was impossible: no intercourse could be held between Paradise and Gehenna, and on this account a great and impassable chasm existed between the two, so that, even if they would, they could not, pass from heaven to hell, nor yet from hell to those in bliss. And, although doctrinal statements should not be drawn from Parabolic illustrations, we would suggest that, at least so far as this Parable goes, it seems to preclude the hope of a gradual change or transition after a life lost in the service of sin and self.

3. Application of the Parable, showing how the Law and the Prophets cannot fail, and how we must now press into the Kingdom. It seems a strange misconception on the part of some commentators, that

the next request of the Rich Man indicates a commencing change of mind on his part. To begin with, this part of the Parable is only intended to illustrate the need, and the sole means of conversion to God—the appeal to the Law and the Prophets being the more apt that the Pharisees made their boast of them, and the refusal of any special miraculous interjection the more emphatic, that the Pharisees had been asking for a sign from heaven. Besides, it would require more than ordinary charity to discover a moral change in the desire that his brothers might, not be converted, but not come to that place of torment!

Dismissing, therefore, this idea, we now find the Rich Man pleading that Lazarus might be sent to his five brothers, who, as we infer, were of the same disposition and life as himself had been, to testify to them, the word implying more than ordinary, even earnest, testimony. Presumably, what he so earnestly asked to be attested was, that he, the Rich Man, was in torment; and the expected effect, not of the testimony but of the mission of Lazarus, whom they are supposed to have known, was, that these, his brothers, might not come to the same place. At the same time, the request seems to imply an attempt at self justification, as if, during his life, he had not had sufficient warning. Accordingly, the reply of Abraham is no longer couched in a tone of pity, but implies stern rebuke of the Rich Man. They need no witness bearer: they have Moses and the Prophets, let them hear them. If testimony be needed, their has been given, and it is sufficient, a reply this, which would especially appeal to the Pharisees. And when the Rich Man, now, perhaps, as much bent on self justification as on the message to his brothers, objects that, although they had not received such testimony, yet if one come to them from the dead, they would repent, the final, and, as, unfortunately history has shown since the Resurrection of Christ, the true answer is, that if they hear not [give not hearing to] Moses and the Prophets, neither will they be influenced [moved: their intellects to believe, their wills to repent], if one rose from the dead.

And here the Parable, and the warning to the Pharisees, abruptly break off. When next we hear Jesus' voice, it is in loving application to the disciples of some of the lessons which were implied in what He had spoken to the Pharisees.

End Notes:

[61]   A somewhat similar parable occurs in Vayyik. R. 5 (towards the close) about a prudent farmer. When matters go badly with his farm, he dresses himself in his best, puts on a cheerful expression, and so appears before his landlord. By well turned, flattering replies to the inquiries about the cattle and the crops, he so appeases favor, that when the landlord finally inquires what he wished, and he requests a loan, he receives double the sum he had asked.

[62]   This difference between the Wilderness, or Mosaic, and the Galilean measure removes the difficulty (raised by Thenius) about the capacity of the brazen sea in Solomon's Temple (1 Kings 5:23, 26). The Bath should be calculated, not according to the Galilean (Metretes = about thirty nine liters), but according to the Wilderness measure (amphora = about twenty six liters).

[63]   Loew, u. s. vol. 1: pp.97, 98. It is curious to learn that in those days also waste paper went to the grocer. (Baba M. 56 b.)

[64]   From earlier times comes to us notice of the Gillayon (Isaiah 8:1), a smooth tablet of wood, metal, or stone, and of the Cheret, or stylus (Isaiah 8:1), and the Et, which means probably not only a stylus but also a calamus (Psalm 45:2; Jeremiah 8:8.)

[65]   The Deyo seems to have been a dry substance which was made into black ink. Ink from gall nuts appears to be of later invention.

[66]   But the learned Relandus asserts that there were in his country such texts written in gold letters, and that therefore the Talmudic prohibition could have only applied to the copies used in the Synagogues (Havercamps ed. of Josephus, vol. 1: p. 593, Note e.)

[67]   The codices of R. Meir seem to have embodied some variations of the common text. Thus, in the Psalms he wrote Halleluyah in one word, as it had been an interjection, and not in the orthodox way, as two words: Hallelu Yah (Jeremiah Meg. 72 a).

[68]   Similarly, the carpenter carried a small wooden rule behind his ear.

[69]   Letters, other documents, or bales of merchandise, were sealed with a kind of red clay.

[70]   In later times Palestinian byssus seems to have been in great repute. See Herzfeld, Handelsgesch. p. 107.

[71]   I cannot agree with Dean Plumptre that the name Lazarus had been chosen with special reference, and as a warning, to the brother of Martha and Mary. If Lazarus of Bethany was thus to be warned in regard to the proper

use of his riches, his name would have been given to the Rich Man, and not to the beggar. But besides, can we for one moment believe that Christ would in such manner have introduced the name of Lazarus of Bethany into such a Parable, he being alive at the time? Nothing, surely, could be further from His general mode of teaching than the introduction of such personalities.

Chapter 19

The Three Parables on the Religious Rulers

If we were to seek confirmation of the suggestion, that these last and the two preceding Parables are grouped together under a common viewpoint, such as that of Righteousness, the character and position of the Parables now to be examined would supply it. For, while the Parable of the Unjust Judge evidently bears close affinity to those that had preceded, especially to that of him who persisted in his request for bread, it evidently refers not, as the other, to man's present need, but to the Second Coming of Christ. The prayer, the perseverance, the delay, and the ultimate answer of which it speaks, are all connected with it. Indeed, it follows on what had passed on this subject immediately before, first, between the Pharisees and Christ, and then between Christ and the disciples.

Again, we must bear in mind that between the Parable of The Rich Man and Lazarus and that of the Unjust Judge, not indeed, a great interval of time, but most momentous events, had intervened. These were: the visit of Jesus to Bethany, the raising of Lazarus, the Jerusalem council against Christ, the flight to Ephraim, a brief stay and preaching there, and the beginning of His last journey to Jerusalem. During this last slow journey from the borders of Galilee to Jerusalem, we suppose the discourses and the Parable about the Coming of the Son of Man to have been spoken. And although such utterances will be best considered in connection with Christ's later and full discourses about The Last Things, we readily perceive, even at this stage, how, when He set His Face towards Jerusalem, there to be offered up, thoughts and words concerning the End may have entered

into all His teaching, and so have given occasion for the questions of the
Pharisees and disciples, and for the answers of Christ, by discourse and in
Parable.

The most common and specious, but also the most serious mistake in
reference to the Parable of the Unjust Judge, is to regard it as implying that,
just as the poor widow insisted in her petition and was righted because of
her insistence, so the disciples should persist in prayer and would be heard
because of their insistence. But this is an entirely false interpretation. When
treating of the Parable of the Unrighteous Steward, we disclaimed all merely
mechanical ideas of prayer, as if God heard us for our many repetitions.
This error must here also be carefully avoided. The inference from the
Parable is not, that the Church will be ultimately vindicated because she
perseveres in prayer, but that she so perseveres, because God will surely
right her cause: it is not, that insistence in prayer is the cause of its answer,
but that the certainty of that which is asked for should lead to continuance
in prayer, even when all around seems to forbid the hope of answer. This
is the lesson to be learned from a comparison of the Unjust Judge with the
Just and Holy God in His dealings with His own. If the widow persevered,
knowing that, although no other consideration, human or Divine, would
influence the Unjust Judge, yet her insistence would secure its object, how
much more should we not faint, but continue in prayer, who are appealing
to God, Who has His people and His cause at heart, even though He delay,
remembering also that even this is for their sakes who pray. And this is fully
expressed in the introductory words. He spoke also a Parable to them with
reference to the need be of their always praying and not fainting.

The remarks just made will remove what otherwise might seem another
serious difficulty. If it be asked, how the conduct of the Unjust Judge could
serve as illustration of what might be expected from God, we answer, that
the lesson in the Parable is not from the similarity but from the contrast
between the Unrighteous human and the Righteous Divine Judge. Hear
what the Unrighteous Judge says. But God [mark the emphatic position
of the word], shall He not indeed vindicate [the injuries of, do judgment
for] His elect . . . ? In truth, this mode of argument is perhaps the most
common in Jewish Parables, and occurs on almost every page of ancient
Rabbinic commentaries. It is called the Qal vaChomer, light and heavy,
and answers to our reasoning a fortiori or de minore ad majus (from the
less to the greater). According to the Rabbis, ten instances of such reasoning
occur in the Old Testament itself. Generally, such reasoning is introduced
by the words Qal vaChomer; often it is prefaced by, Al achath Kammah

veKammah, against one how much and how much, that is, how much more. Thus, it is argued that, if a King of flesh and blood did so and so, shall not the King of Kings, etc.; or, if the sinner received such and such, shall not the righteous, etc.? In the present Parable the reasoning would be: If the Judge of Unrighteousness said that he would vindicate, shall not the Judge of all Righteousness do judgment on behalf of His Elect? In fact, we have an exact Rabbinic parallel to the thought underlying, and the lesson derived from, this Parable. When describing, how at the preaching of Jonah Nineveh repented and cried to God, His answer to the loud persistent cry of the people is thus explained: The bold (he who is unabashed) conquers even a wicked person [to grant him his request], how much more the All Good of the world!

The Parable opens by laying down as a general principle the necessity and duty of the Disciples always to pray, the precise meaning being defined by the opposite, or limited clause: not to faint, that is, not to become weary. The word always must not be understood in respect of time, as if it meant continuously, but at all times, in the sense of under all circumstances, however apparently adverse, when it might seem as if an answer could not come, and we would therefore be in danger of fainting or becoming weary. This rule applies here primarily to that weariness which might lead to the cessation of prayer for the Coming of the Lord, or of expectancy of it, during the long period when it seems as if He delayed His return as if increasingly there were no likelihood of it. But it may also be applied to all similar circumstances, when prayer seems so long unanswered that weariness in praying threatens to overtake us. Thus, it is argued, even in Jewish writings, that a man should never be deterred from, nor cease praying, the illustration by Qal vaChomer being from the case of Moses, who knew that it was decreed he should not enter the land, and yet continued praying about it.

The Parable introduces to us a Judge in a city, and a widow. Except where a case was voluntarily submitted for arbitration rather than judgment, or judicial advice was sought of a sage, one man could not have formed a Jewish tribunal. Besides, his mode of speaking and acting is inconsistent with such an hypothesis. He must therefore have been one of the Judges, or municipal authorities, appointed by Herod or the Romans, perhaps a Jew, but not a Jewish Judge. Possibly, he may have been a police magistrate, or one who had some function of that kind delegated to him. We know that, at least in Jerusalem, there were two paid magistrates (Dayyaney Gezeroth whose duty it was to see to the observance of all police regulations and the prevention of crime. Unlike the regular Judges, who attended only on certain days and hours, and were unpaid, these magistrates were, so to speak, always on duty, and therefore unable to engage in any other occupation. It was probably for this reason that they were paid out of the Temple Treasury, and received so large a salary as 225l., or, if needful, even more. On account of this, perhaps also for their unjust exactions, Jewish wit designated them, by a play on the words, as Dayyaney Gezeloth, Robber Judges, instead of their real title of Dayyaney Gezeroth (Judges of Prohibitions, or else of Punishments). It may have been that there were such Jewish magistrates in other places also. Josephus speaks of local magistracies. At any rate there were in every locality police officials, who watched over order and law. The Talmud speaks in very depreciatory terms of these village Judges (Dayyaney deMegista), in opposition to the town tribunals (Bey Davar), and accuses them of ignorance, arbitrariness, and covetousness, so that for a dish of meat they would pervert justice. Frequent instances are also mentioned of gross injustice and bribery in regard to the non-Jewish Judges in Palestine.

It is to such a Judge that the Parable refers, one who was consciously, openly, and avowedly inaccessible to the highest motive, the fear of God, and not even restrained by the lower consideration of regard for public opinion. It is an extreme case, intended to illustrate the exceeding unlikelihood of justice being done. For the same purpose, the party seeking justice at his hands is described as a poor, unprotected widow. But we must also bear in mind, in the interpretation of this Parable, that the Church, whom she represents, is also widowed in the absence of her Lord. To return, this widow came to the Unjust Judge (the imperfect tense in the original indicating repeated, even continuous coming), with the urgent demand to be vindicated of her adversary, that is, that the Judge should make legal inquiry, and by a decision set her right as against him at whose hands she was suffering wrong. For reasons of his own he would not; and this continued for a while. At last, not from any higher principle, nor even from regard for public opinion, both of which, as he avowed to himself, had no weight with him, he complied with her request, as the text (literally translated) has it: Yet at any rate because this widow troubles me, I will do justice for her, for fear that, in the end, coming she bruise me, do personal violence to me, attack me bodily. Then follows the grand inference from it: If the Judge of Unrighteousness speak thus, shall not the Judge of all Righteousness, God, do judgment, vindicate [by His Coming to judgment and so setting right the wrong done to His Church] His Elect, which cry to Him day and night, although He suffer long on account of them, delay

His final interjection of judgment and mercy, and that, not as the Unjust Judge, but for their own sakes, in order that the number of the Elect may all be gathered in, and they fully prepared?

Difficult as the rendering of this last clause admittedly is, our interpretation of it seems confirmed by the final application of this Parable. Taking the previous verse along with it, we would have this double Parallelism: But God, shall He not vindicate [do judgment on behalf of] His Elect? I tell you, that He will do judgment on behalf of them shortly, this word being chosen rather than speedily (as in the KJV and R.V.), because the latter might convey the idea of a sudden interjection, such as is not implied in the expression. This would be the first Parallelism; the second this: Although He suffer long [delay His final interjection] on account of them (verse 7), to which the second clause of verse 8 would correspond, as offering the explanation and vindication: But the Son of Man, when He have come, shall He find the faith upon the earth? It is a terribly sad question, as put by Him Who is the Christ: After all this long suffering delay, shall He find the faith upon the earth, intellectual belief on the part of one class, and on the part of the Church the faith of the heart which trusts in, longs, and prays, because it expects and looks for His Coming, all undisturbed by the prevailing unbelief around, only quickened by it to more intensity of prayer! Shall He find it? Let the history of the Church each man's heart, make answer!

2. The Parable of the Pharisee and the Publican, which follows, is only internally connected with that of the Unjust Judge. It is not unrighteousness, but of self righteousness, and this, both in its positive and negative aspects: as trust in ones own state, and as contempt of others. Again, it has also this connection with the previous Parable, that, whereas that of the Unrighteous Judge pointed to continuance, this to humility in prayer.

The introductory clause shows that it has no connection in point of time with what had preceded, although the interval between the two may, have been very short. Probably, something had taken place, which is not recorded, to occasion this Parable, which, if not directly addressed to the Pharisees, is to such as are of Pharisaic spirit. It brings before us two men going up to the Temple, whether at the hour of prayer, or otherwise, is not stated. Remembering that, with the exception of the Psalms for the day and the interval for a certain prescribed prayer, the service in the Temple was entirely sacrificial, we are thankful for such glimpses, which show that, both in the time of public service, and still more at other times, the Temple was made the place of private prayer. On the present occasion the two men, who went together to the entrance of the Temple, represented the two religious extremes in Jewish society. To the entrance of the Temple, but no farther, did the Pharisee and the Publican go together. Within the sacred enclosure, before God, where man should least have made it, began their separation. The Pharisee put himself by himself, and prayed thus: O God, I thank You that I am not as the rest of men, extortioners, unjust, adulterers, nor also as this Publican [there]. Never, perhaps, were words of thanksgiving spoken in less thankfulness than these. For, thankfulness implies the acknowledgement of a gift; therefore, a sense of not having had ourselves what we have received; in other words, then, a sense of our personal need, or humility. But the very first act of this Pharisee had been to separate himself from all the other worshippers, and notably from the Publican, whom, as his words show, he had noticed, and looked down upon. His thanksgiving referred not to what he had received, but to the sins of others by which they were separated from him, and to his own meritorious deeds by which he was separated from them. Thus, his words expressed what his attitude indicated; and both were the expression, not of thankfulness, but of boastfulness. It was the same as their bearing at the feast and in public places; the same as their contempt and condemnation of the rest of men, and especially the publicans; the same that even their designation, Pharisees, Separated ones, implied. The rest of men might be either the Gentiles, or, more probably, the common unlearned people, the Am haArets, whom they accused or suspected of every possible sin, according to their fundamental principle: The unlearned cannot be pious. And, in their sense of that term, they were right, and in this lies the condemnation of their righteousness. And, most painful though it be, remembering the downright earnestness and zeal of these men, it must be added that, as we read the Liturgy of the Synagogue, we come ever and again upon such and similar thanksgiving, that they are not as the rest of men.

But this was not all. From looking down upon others the Pharisee proceeded to look up to himself. Here Talmudic writings offer painful parallelisms. They are full of references to the merits of the just, to the merits and righteousness of the fathers, or else of Israel in taking upon itself the Law. And for the sake of these merits and of that righteousness, Israel, as a nation, expects general acceptance, pardon, and temporal benefits, for, all spiritual benefits Israel as a nation, and the pious in Israel individually, possess already, nor do they need to get them from heaven, since they can and do work them out for themselves. And here the Pharisee in the Parable significantly dropped even the form of thanksgiving. The religious performances which he enumerated are those which mark the Pharisee among the Pharisees: I fast twice a week, and I give tithes of all that I acquire. The first of these was in pursuance of the custom of some more righteous than the rest, who, as previously explained, fasted on the second and fifth days of the week (Mondays and Thursdays). But, perhaps, we should not forget that these were also the regular market days, when the country people came to the towns, and there were special Services in the Synagogues, and the local Sanhedrin met, so that these saints in Israel would, at the same time, attract and receive special notice for their fasts. As for the boast about giving tithes of all that he acquired, and not merely of his land, fruits, etc., it has already been explained, that this was one of the distinctive characteristics of the sect of the Pharisees. Their practice in this respect may be summed up in these words of the Mishnah: He tithes all that he eats, all that he sells, and all that he buys, and he is not a guest with an unlearned person [Am haArets, so as not possibly to partake of what may have been left untithed].

Although it may not be necessary, yet one or two quotations will help to show how truly this picture of the Pharisee was taken from life. Thus, the following prayer of a Rabbi is recorded: I thank You, O Lord my God, that You have put my part with those who sit in the Academy, and not with those who sit at the corners [money changers and traders]. For, I rise early and they rise early: I rise early to the words of the Law, and they to vain things. I labor and they labor: I labor and receive a reward, they labor and receive no reward. I run and they run: I run to the life of the world to come, and they to the pit of destruction. Even more closely parallel is this thanksgiving, which a Rabbi puts into the mouth of Israel: Lord of the world, judge me not as those who dwell in the big towns [such as Rome]: among whom there is robbery, and uncleanness, and vain and false swearing. Lastly, as regards the boastful spirit of Rabbinism, we recall such painful sayings as those of Rabbi Simeon ben Jochai, to which reference has already been made, notably this, that if there were only two righteous men in the world, he and his son were these; and if only one, it was he!

The second picture, or scene, in the Parable sets before us the reverse state of feeling from that of the Pharisee. Only, we must bear in mind, that, as the Pharisee is not blamed for his giving of thanks, nor yet for his good doing, real or imaginary, so the prayer of the Publican is not answered, because he was a sinner. In both cases what decides the rejection or acceptance of the prayer is, whether or not it was prayer. The Pharisee retains the righteousness which he had claimed for himself, whatever its value; and the Publican receives the righteousness which he asks: both have what they desire before God. If the Pharisee stood by himself, apart from others, so did the Publican: standing far off, namely from the Pharisee, quite far back, as became one who felt himself unworthy to mingle with God's people. In accordance with this: He would not so much as lift his eyes to heaven, as men generally do in prayer, but beat his breast, as the Jews still do in the most solemn part of their confession on the Day of Atonement, saying, God be merciful to me the sinner. The definite article is used to indicate that he felt, as if he alone were a sinner the sinner. Not only, as has been well remarked, does he not think of anyone else (de nemine alio homine cogitat), while the Pharisee had thought of everyone else; but, as he had taken a position not in front of, but behind, everyone else, so, in contrast to the Pharisee, who had regarded everyone but himself as a sinner, the Publican regarded everyone else as righteous compared with him the sinner. And, while the Pharisee felt no need, and uttered no petition, the Publican felt only need, and uttered only petition. The one appealed to himself for justice, the other appealed to God for mercy.

More complete contrast, therefore, could not be imagined. And once more, as between the Pharisee and the Publican, the seeming and the real, that before men and before God, there is sharp contrast, and the lesson which Christ had so often pointed is again set forth, not only in regard to the feelings which the Pharisees entertained, but also to the joyfully news of pardon to the lost: I say to you, This man went down to his house justified above the other [so according to the better reading, pa kenon]. In other words, the sentence of righteousness as from God with which the Publican went home was above, far better than, the sentence of righteousness as pronounced by himself, with which the Pharisee returned. This saying casts also light on such comparisons as between the righteous elder brother and the pardoned prodigal, or the ninety nine that need no repentance and the lost that was found, or, on such an utterance as this: Except your righteousness shall exceed the righteousness of the Scribes and Pharisees, you shall in no case enter into the Kingdom of Heaven. And so the Parable ends with the general principle, so often enunciated: For everyone that exalts himself shall be abased; and he that humbles himself shall be exalted. And with this general teaching of the Parable fully agrees the instruction of Christ to His disciples concerning the reception of little children, which immediately follows.

3. The Parable with which this series closes, that of the Unmerciful Servant, can be treated more briefly, since the circumstances leading up to it have already been explained in chapter 3 of this Book. We are now reaching the point where the solitary narrative of Luke again merges with those of the other Evangelists. That the Parable was spoken before Christ's final journey to Jerusalem, appears from Matthew's Gospel. On the other hand, as we compare what in the Gospel by Luke follows on the Parable of the Pharisee and Publican with the circumstances in which the Parable of the Unmerciful Servant is introduced, we cannot fail to perceive inward connection between the narratives of the two Evangelists, confirming the conclusion, arrived at on other grounds, that the Parable of the Unmerciful Servant belongs to the Perean series, and closes it.

Its connection with the Parable of the Pharisee and the Publican lies in this, that Pharisaic self righteousness and contempt of others may easily lead to unforgiveness and unmercifulness, which are utterly incompatible with a sense of our own need of Divine mercy and forgiveness. And so in the Gospel of Matthew this Parable follows on the exhibition of a self righteous, unmerciful spirit, which would instruct how often we should forgive, forgetful of our own need of absolute and unlimited pardon at the hands of God, a spirit, moreover, of harshness, that could look down upon Christ's little ones, in forgetfulness of our own need perhaps of cutting off even a right hand or foot to enter the Kingdom of Heaven.

In studying this Parable, we must once more remind ourselves of the general rule of the need of distinguishing between what is essential in a Parable, as directly bearing on its lessons, and what is merely introduced for the sake of the Parable itself, to give point to its main teaching. In the present instance, no sober interpreter would regard of the essence of the Parable the King's command to sell into slavery the first debtor, together with his wife and children. It is simply a historical trait, introducing what is analogous circumstances might happen in real life, in order to point the lesson, that a man's strict barrenness before God is utter hopeless, and eternal ruin and loss. Similarly, when the promise of the debtor is thus introduced: Have patience with me, and I will pay you all, it can only be to complete in a natural manner the first part of the Parabolic history and to prepare for the second, in which forbearance is asked by a fellow servant for the small debt which he owes. Lastly, in the same manner, the recall of the King's original forgiveness of the great debtor can only be intended to bring out the utter incompatibility of such harshness towards a brother on the part of one who has been consciously forgiven by God his great debt.

Thus keeping apart the essentials of the Parable from the accidents of its narration, we have three distinct scenes, or parts, in this story. In the first, our new feelings towards our brethren are traced to our new relation towards God, as the proper spring of all our thinking, speaking, and acting. Notably, as regards forgiveness, we are to remember the Kingdom of God: Therefore has the Kingdom of God become like, therefore: in order that thereby we may learn the duty of absolute, not limited, forgiveness, not that of seven, but of seventy times seven. And now this likeness of the Kingdom of Heaven is set forth in the Parable of a man, a King (as the Rabbis would have expressed it, a king of flesh and blood), who would make his reckoning (sunairein) with his servants, certainly not his bondservants, but probably the governors of his provinces, or those who had charge of the revenue and finances. But after he had begun to consider, not necessarily at the very beginning of it, one was brought to him, a debtor of ten thousand talents. Considering them only as Attic talents (1 talent = 60 minas = 6,000 dinars) this would amount to the enormous sum of about two and a quarter millions sterling. No wonder, that one who during his administration had been guilty of such dishonesty, or else culpable negligence, should, as the words brought to him imply, have been reluctant to face the king. The Parable further implies, that the debt was admitted; and therefore, in the course of ordinary judicial procedure, according to the Law of Moses, and the universal code of antiquity, that servant, with his family and all his property, was ordered to be sold, and the returns paid into the treasury.

Of course, it is not suggested that the payment thus made had met his debt. Even this would, if need were, confirm the view, previously expressed, that this trait belongs not to the essentials of the Parable, but to the details of the narrative. So does the promise, with which the now terrified servant, as he threw himself at the feet of the King, supported his plea for patience: I will pay you all. In truth, the narrative takes no notice of this, but, on the other hand, states: But, being moved with compassion, the lord of that servant released him [from the bondage decreed, and which had virtually begun with his sentence], and the debt he forgave him. A more accurate representation of our relation to God could not be made. We are the debtors of our heavenly King, Who has entrusted to us the administration of what is His, and which we have stolen or misused, incurring an unspeakable debt, which we can never discharge, and of which, in the course of justice, unending bondage, misery, and utter ruin would be the proper sequence. But, if in humble repentance we throw ourselves at His Feet, He is ready, in infinite compassion, not only to release us from deserved punishment, but, O blessed revelation of the Gospel!, to forgive us the debt.

It is this new relationship to God which must be the foundation and the rule for our new relationship towards our fellow servants. And this brings us to the second part, or scene in this Parable. Here the lately pardoned servant finds one of his fellow servants, who owes him the small sum of 100 dinars, about 4l. 10s. Mark now the sharp contrast, which is so drawn as to give point to the Parable. In the first case, it was the servant brought to account, and that before the King; here it is a servant finding and that his fellow servant; in the first case, he owed talents, in the second dinars (a six thousandth part of them); in the first, ten thousand talents; in the second, one hundred dinars. Again, in the first case payment is only demanded, while in the second the man takes his fellow servant by the throat, a not uncommon mode of harshness on the part of Roman creditors, and says: Pay what, or according to the better reading, if you owe anything. And, lastly, although the words of the second debtor are almost the same as those in which the first debtor urgently appealed to the King's patience, yet no mercy is shown, but he is thrown [with violence] into prison, until he had paid what was due.

It can scarcely be necessary to show the unreasonableness or the guilt of such conduct. But this is the object of the third part, or scene, in the Parable. Here, again for the sake of pictorialness, the other servants are introduced as exceedingly sorry, no doubt about the fate of their fellow servant, especially in the circumstances of the case. Then they come to their lord, and clearly set forth, or explain (diasaphen) what had happened, upon which the Unmerciful Servant is summoned, and addressed as wicked servant, not only because he had not followed the example of his lord, but because, after having received such immense favor as the entire remission of his debt on pleading to his master, to have refused to the pleading of his fellow servant even a brief delay in the payment of a small sum, argued lack of all mercy and positive wickedness. And the words are followed by the manifestations of righteous anger. As he has done, so is it done to him, and this is the final application of the Parable. He is delivered to the tormentors, not in the sense of being tormented by them, which would scarcely have been just, but in that of being handed over to such keepers of the prison, to whom criminals who were to be tortured were delivered, and who executed such punishment on them: in other words he is sent to the hardest and severest prison, there to remain until he should pay all that was due by him, that is, in the circumstances, forever. And here we may again remark, without drawing any dogmatic inferences from the language of the Parable, that it seems to proceed on these two assumptions: that suffering neither atones for guilt, nor in itself amends the guilty, and that as sin has incurred a debt that can never be discharged, so the banishment, or rather the loss and misery of it, will be endless.

We pause to notice, how near Rabbinism has come to this Parable, and yet how far it is from its magnificent teaching. At the outset we recall that unlimited forgiveness, or, for more than the farthest limit of three times, was not the doctrine of Rabbinism. It did, teach how freely God would forgive Israel, and it introduces a similar Parable of a debtor appealing to his creditor, and receiving the fullest and freest release of mercy, and it also draws from it the moral, that man should similarly show mercy: but it is not the mercy of forgiveness from the heart, but of forgiveness of money debts to the poor, or of various injuries, and the mercy of benevolence and beneficence to the wretched. But, however beautifully Rabbinism at times speaks on the subject, the Gospel conception of forgiveness, even as that of mercy, could only come by blessed experience of the infinitely higher forgiveness, and the incomparably greater mercy, which the pardoned sinner has received in Christ from our Father in Heaven.

But to us all there is the deepest seriousness in the warning against unmercifulness; and that, even though we remember that the case here referred to is only that of unwillingness to forgive from the heart an offending brother who actually asks for it. Yet, if not the sin, the temptation to it is very real to us all, perhaps rather unconsciously to ourselves than consciously. For, how often is our forgiveness in the heart, as well as from the heart, narrowed by limitations and burdened with conditions; and is it not of the very essence of sectarianism to condemn without mercy him who does not come up to our demands, and until he shall have come up to them to the uttermost farthing?

End Notes:

[72]   This, as the only possible rendering of the verb in this instance, is also vindicated by Meyer ad loc. The Judge seems afraid of bodily violence from the exasperated woman. For a significant pugilistic use of the verb, comp. 1 Corinthians 9:27.

[73]   For the philological vindication of this rendering, see Goebel, Parabeln
        (i.p. 327). The arguments in its favor are as follows: 1. It corresponds to the
        description of the position of the Publican, who also stood by himself far
        off. 2. Otherwise, the mention that the Pharisee stood would seem utterly
        idle. He could not have sat. 3. The rendering prayed with himself, is not
        correct. The words mean: to himself, and this would give no meaning.
        But even were we to render it with himself in the sense of silent prayer,
        the introduction of such a remark as that he prayed silently, would be
        both needless and aimless. But what decides us is the parallelism with the
        account of the posture of the Publican.

[74]   Of this spirit are even such Eulogies as these in the ordinary morning
        prayer: Blessed are You, Lord, our God, King of the world, that You have
        not made me a stranger (a Gentile) . . . a servant . . . a woman.

[75]   The merit of Zekhuth. On this subject we must refer, as far too large
        for quotation, to the detailed account in such works as Weber, System
        d. altsynag. Theol. pp. 280 etc. There is no limit to such extravagances.
        The world itself had been created on account of the merits of Israel, and
        is sustained by them, even as all nations only continue by reason of this
        (Shemoth R. 15, 28; Bemidb. R. 2). A most extraordinary account is
        given in Bemidb. R. 20 of the four merits for the sake of which Israel
        was delivered out of Egypt: they did not change their names; nor their
        language; nor reveal their secrets; nor were dissolute.

[76]   According to the better reading, the word all in ver. 29 should be left
        out, and the omission is significant. The servant who promised to pay all
        (ver. 26) promised more than he could possibly perform; while he who
        undertook what he might reasonably perform, did not say all.

[77]   The Rabbinic Law was much more merciful than this apparently harsh
        (Roman or Herodian) administration of it. It laid it down that, just as
        when a person had owed to the Sanctuary a certain sum or his property,
        his goods might be seized, but so much was to be deducted and left to the
        person, or given to him, as was needful for his sustenance, so was it to be
        between creditor and debtor. If a creditor seized the goods of his debtor,
        he was bound to leave to the latter, if he had been a rich man, a sofa [to
        recline at table] and a couch and pillow; if the debtor had been a poor man,
        a sofa and a couch with a reed mat [for coverlet] (Bab. Mets. 113 a and
        b). Certain tools had to be returned for his use, nor was either the Sheriff
        officer nor the creditor allowed to enter the house to make seizure. (As
        regards seizures for Vows, see Arach. 23 b, 24 a).

Chapter 20

Close of the Perean Ministry

From the Parables we now turn to such discourses of Jesus as belong to this period of His Ministry. Their consideration may be the more brief, that throughout we find points of correspondence with previous or later portions of His teaching.

Thus, the first of these discourses, of which we have an outline, recalls some passages in the Sermon on the Mount, as well as what Jesus had said on the occasion of healing the servant of the centurion. But, to take the first of these parallelisms, the differences are only the more marked for the similarity of form. These prove incontestably, not only the independence of the two Evangelists in their narratives, but, along with deeper underlying unity of thought in the teaching of Christ, its different application to different circumstances and persons. Let us mark this in the discourse as outlined by Luke, and so gain fresh evidential confirmation of the trustworthiness of the Evangelic records.

The words of Jesus, as recorded by Luke, are not spoken, as in The Sermon on the Mount, in connection with His teaching to His disciples, but are in reply to a question addressed to Him by someone, we can scarcely doubt, a representative of the Pharisees: Lord, are they few, the saved ones [that are being saved]? Viewed in connection with Christ's immediately preceding teaching about the Kingdom of God in its wide and deep spread, as the great Mustard Tree from the tiniest seed, and as the Leaven hidden, which pervaded three measures of meal, we can scarcely doubt that the word saved bore reference, not to the eternal state of the soul, but to admission to the benefits of the Kingdom of God, the Messianic Kingdom, with its privileges and its judgments, such as the Pharisees understood it.

The question, whether few were to be saved, could not have been put from the Pharisaic point of view, if understood of personal salvation; while, on the other hand, if taken as applying to part in the near expected Messianic Kingdom, it has its distinct parallel in the Rabbinic statement, that, as regarded the days of the Messiah (His Kingdom), it would be similar to what it had been at the entrance into the land of promise, when only two (Joshua and Caleb), out of all that generation, were allowed to have part in it. Again, it is only when understanding both the question of this Pharisee and the reply of Jesus as applying to the Kingdom of the Messiah, though each viewing the Kingdom from his own standpoint, that we can understand the answering words of Christ in their natural and obvious sense, without either straining or adding to them a dogmatic gloss, such as could not have occurred to His hearers at the time.

Thus viewed, we can mark the characteristic differences between this discourse and the parallels in the Sermon on the Mount, and understand their reason. As regarded entrance into the Messianic Kingdom, this Pharisee, and those whom he represented, are told, that this Kingdom was not theirs, as a matter of course, their question as to the rest of the world being only, whether few or many would share in it—but that all must struggle [agonize] to enter in through the narrow door. When we remember, that in the Sermon on the Mount the call was only to enter in, we feel that we have now reached a period, when the access to the narrow door was obstructed by the hostility of so many, and when it needed violence to break through, and take the Kingdom by force. This personal breaking through the opposing multitude, in order to enter in through the narrow door, was in opposition to the many, the Pharisees and Jews generally, who were seeking to enter in, in their own way, never doubting success, but who would discover their terrible mistake. Then, when once the Master of the house is risen up, to welcome His guests to the banquet, and has shut to the door, while they, standing without, vainly call upon Him to open it, and He replies: I know you not from where you are, would they begin to remind Him of those covenant privileges on which, as Israel after the flesh, they had relied (we have eaten and drunk in Your presence, and You have taught in our streets). To this He would reply by a repetition of His former words, now seen to imply a disavowal of all mere outward privileges, as constituting a claim to the Kingdom, grounding His disavowal and His refusal to open on their inward contrariety to the King and His Kingdom: Depart from Me, all you workers of iniquity. It was a banquet to the friends of the King: the inauguration of His Kingdom. When they found the door shut, they would, knock, in the confident expectation that their claims would at once be recognized, and they admitted. And when the Master of the house did not recognize them, as they had expected, and they reminded Him of their outward connection, He only repeated the same words as before, since it was not outward but inward relationship that qualified the guests, and theirs was not friendship, but antagonism to Him. Terrible would then be their sorrow and anguish, when they would see their own patriarchs (we have eaten and drunk in Your Presence) and their own prophets (You have taught in our streets) within, and yet themselves were excluded from what was peculiarly theirs, while from all parts of the pagan world the welcome guests would flock to the joyous feast. And here pre-eminently would the saying hold good, in opposition to Pharisaic claims and self righteousness: There are last which shall be first, and there are first which shall be last.

As a further characteristic difference from the parallel passage in the Sermon on the Mount, we note, that there the reference seems not to any special privileges in connection with the Messianic Kingdom, such as the Pharisees expected, but to admission into the Kingdom of Heaven generally. In regard to the latter also the highest outward claims would be found unavailing; but the expectation of admission was grounded rather on what was done, than on mere citizenship and its privileges. And here it deserves special notice, that in Luke's Gospel, where the claim is that of fellow citizenship (eaten and drunk in Your Presence, and You have taught in our streets), the reply is made, I know you not from where you are; while in the Sermon on the Mount, where the claim is of what they had done in His Name, they are told: I never knew you. In both cases the disavowal emphatically bears on the special plea which had been set up. With this, another slight difference may be connected, which is not brought out in the KJV or in the Revised Version. Both in the Sermon on the Mount and in Luke's Gospel, they who are invited depart are designated as workers of iniquity. But, whereas, in Matthew's Gospel the term (noma) really means lawlessness, the word used in that of Luke should be rendered unrighteousness (dika). Thus, the one class are excluded, despite the deeds which they plead, for their real contrariety to God's Law; the other, despite the plea of citizenship and privileges, for their unrighteousness. And here we may also note, as a last difference between the two Gospels, that in the prediction of the future bliss from which they were to be excluded, the Gospel of Luke, which had reported the plea that He had taught in their streets, adds, as it were in answer, to the names of the Patriarchs, mention of all the prophets.

2. The next discourse, noted by Luke, had been spoken in that very day, as the last. It was occasioned by a pretended warning of certain of the Pharisees to depart from Perea, which, with Galilee, was the territory of Herod Antipas, as else the Tetrarch would kill Him. We have previously shown reason for supposing secret intrigues between the Pharisaic party and Herod, and attributing the final imprisonment of the Baptist, at least in part, to their scheming. We also remember, how the conscience of the Tetrarch connected Christ with His murdered Forerunner, and that rightly, since, at least so far as the Pharisees performed on the fears of that intensely jealous and suspicious prince, the imprisonment of John was as much due to his announcement of the Messiah as to the hostility of Herodias. On these grounds we can easily understand that Herod should have wished to see Jesus, not merely to gratify curiosity, nor in obedience to superstitious impulses, but to convince himself, whether He was really what was said of Him, and also to get Him into his power. Probably, therefore, the danger of which these Pharisees spoke might have been real enough, and they might have special reasons for knowing of it. But their suggestion, that Jesus should depart, could only have proceeded from a ruse to get Him Out of Perea, where, evidently, His works of healing were largely attracting and influencing the people.

But if Jesus would not be deterred by the fears of His disciples from going into Judea, feeling that each one had his appointed working day, in the light of which he was safe, and during the brief duration of which he was bound to walk, far less would He recede before His enemies. Pointing to their secret intrigues, He called them, if they chose, go back to that fox, and give to his low cunning, and to all similar attempts to hinder or arrest His Ministry, what would be a decisive answer, since it unfolded what He clearly foresaw in the near future. Depart?, yes, depart you to tell that fox, I have still a brief and an appointed time to work, and then I am perfected, in the sense in which we all readily understand the expression, as applying to His Work and Mission. Depart! Yes, I must "depart," or go My brief appointed time: I know that at the goal of it is death, yet not at the hands of Herod, but in Jerusalem, the slaughter house of them that "teach in her streets."

And so, remembering that this message to Herod was spoken in the very day, perhaps the very hour that He had declared how falsely the workers of wickedness claimed admission on account of the teaching in their streets, and that they would be excluded from the fellowship, not only of the fathers, but of all the prophets whom they called their own, we see peculiar meaning in the reference to Jerusalem as the place where all the prophets perished. One, Who in no way indulged in illusions, but knew that He had an appointed time, during which He would work, and at the end of which He would perish, and where He would so perish, could not be deterred either by the intrigues of the Pharisees nor by the thought of what a Herod might attempt, not do, which latter was in far other hands. But the thought of Jerusalem—of what it was, what it might have been, and what would come to it—may well have forced from the lips of Him, Who wept over it, a cry of mingled anguish, love, and warning. It may, be, that these very words, which are reported by Matthew in another, and manifestly most suitable, connection, are here quoted by Luke, because they fully express the thought to which Christ here first gave distinct utterance. But some such words, we can scarcely doubt, He did speak even now, when pointing to His near death in Jerusalem.

3. The next in order of the discourses recorded by Luke is that which prefaced the Parable of the Great Supper, expounded in a previous chapter. The Rabbinic views on the Sabbath Law have been so fully explained, that a very brief comment will here suffice. It appears, that Jesus condescended to accept the invitation to a Sabbath meal in the house of one of the Rulers of the Pharisees, perhaps one of the Rulers of the Synagogue in which they had just worshipped, and where Christ may have taught. Without here discussing the motives for this invitation, its acceptance was certainly made use of to watch Him. And the man with the dropsy had, no doubt, been introduced for a treacherous purpose, although it is not necessary to suppose that he himself had been privy to it. On the other hand, it is characteristic of the gracious Lord, that, with full knowledge of their purpose, He sat down with such companions, and that He did His Work of power and love unrestrained by their evil thoughts. But, even so, He must turn their wickedness also to good account. Yet we mark, that He first dismissed the man healed of the dropsy before He reproved the Pharisees. It was better so, for the sake of the guests, and for the healed man himself, whose mind quite new and blessed Sabbath thoughts would fill, to which all controversy would be jarring.

And, after his departure, Jesus first spoke to them, as was His habit, concerning their misapplication of the Sabbath Law, to which, their own practice gave the lie. They deemed it unlawful to heal on the Sabbath day, though, when He read their thoughts and purposes as against Him, they would not answer His question on the point. And yet, if a son, or even an ox, of any of them, had fallen into a pit, they would have found some valid legal reason for pulling him out! Then, as to their Sabbath feast, and their invitation to Him, when thereby they wished to lure Him to evil, and, their much boasted hospitality: all was characteristic of these Pharisees, only external show, with utter absence of all real love; only self assumption, pride, and self righteousness, together with contempt of all who were regarded as religiously or intellectually beneath them, chiefly of the unlearned and sinners, those in the streets and lanes of their city, whom they considered as the poor, and the maimed, and the halt, and the blind. Even among themselves there was strife about the first places, such as, perhaps, Christ had on that occasion witnessed, amid mock professions of humility, when, perhaps, the master of the house had afterwards, in true Pharisaic fashion, proceeded to re-arrange the guests according to their supposed dignity. And even the Rabbis had given advice to the same effect as Christ's, and of this His words may have reminded them.

But further, addressing him who had so treacherously invited Him to this feast, Christ showed how the principle of Pharisaism consisted in self seeking, to the necessary exclusion of all true love. Referring, for the fuller explanation of His meaning, to a previous chapter, we content ourselves here with the remark, that this self seeking and self righteousness appeared even in what, perhaps, they most boasted of, their hospitality. For, if in an earlier Jewish record we read the beautiful words: Let your house be open towards the street, and let the poor be the sons of your house, we have, also, this later comment on them, that Job had thus had his house opened to the four quarters of the globe for the poor, and that, when his calamities came about him, he protested with God on the ground of his merits in this respect, to which answer was made, that he had in this matter come very far short of the merits of Abraham. So entirely self introspective and self seeking did Rabbinism become, and so contrary was its outcome to the spirit of Christ, the inmost meaning of Whose Work, as well as Words, was entire self forgetfulness and self surrender in love.

4.   In the fourth discourse recorded by Luke, we pass from the parenthetic account of that Sabbath meal in the house of the Ruler of the Pharisees, back to where the narrative of the Pharisees threat about Herod and the reply of Jesus had left us. And, if proof were required of the great

influence exercised by Jesus, and which, as we have suggested, led to the attempt of the Pharisees to induce Christ to leave Perea, it would be found in the opening notice, as well as in the discourse itself which He spoke. Christ departed, from that place, though not yet from Perea; but with Him went great multitudes. And, in view of their professed adhesion, it was needful, and now more emphatically than ever, to set before them all that discipleship really involved, of cost and of strength, the two latter points being illustrated by brief Parables (in the wider sense of that term). Substantially, it was only what Christ had told the Twelve, when He sent them on their first Mission. Only it was now cast in a far stronger mold, as befitted the altered circumstances, in the near prospect of Christ's condemnation, with all that this would involve to His followers.

At the outset we mark, that we are not here told what constituted the true disciple, but what would prevent a man from becoming such. Again, it was now no longer (as in the earlier address to the Twelve), that he who loved the nearest and dearest of earthly kin more than Christ—and therefore clung to such rather than to Him, was not worthy of Him; nor that he who did not take his cross and follow after Him was not worthy of the Christ. Since then the hostility had ripened, and discipleship become impossible without actual renunciation of the nearest relationship, and, more than that, of life itself. Of course, the term hate does not imply hatred of parents or relatives, or of life, in the ordinary sense. But it points to this, that, as outward separation, consequent upon men's antagonism to Christ, was before them in the near future, so, in the present, inward separation, a renunciation in mind and heart, preparatory to that outwardly, was absolutely necessary. And this immediate call was illustrated in twofold manner. A man who was about to begin building a tower, must count the cost of his undertaking. It was not enough that he was prepared to defray the expense of the foundations; he must look to the cost of the whole. So must they, in becoming disciples, look not on what was involved in the present following of Christ, but remember the cost of the final acknowledgement of Jesus. Again, if a king went to war, common prudence would lead him to consider whether his forces were equal to the great contest before him; or else it was far better to withdraw in time, even though it involved humiliation, from what, in view of his weakness, would end in miserable defeat. So, and much more, must the intending disciple make complete inward surrender of all, deliberately counting the cost, and, in view of the coming trial, ask himself whether he had, sufficient inward strength, the force of love to Christ, to conquer. And thus discipleship, then, and, in measure, to all time, involves the necessity of complete inward surrender of everything for the love of Christ, so that if, and when, the time of outward trial comes, we may be prepared to conquer in the fight. He fights well, who has first fought and conquered within.

Or else, and here Christ breaks once more into that pithy Jewish proverb, only, oh! how aptly, applying it to His disciples, Salt is good; salt, if it has lost its savor, with what shall it be salted? We have preferred quoting the proverb in its Jewish form, to show its popular origin. Salt in such condition was neither fit to improve the land, nor, on the other hand, to be mixed with the manure. The disciple who had lost his distinctiveness would neither benefit the land, nor was he even fit, as it were, for the dunghill, and could only be thrown out. And so, let him that has ears to hear, hear the warning!

5. We have still to consider the last discourses of Christ before the raising of Lazarus. As being addressed to the disciples, we have to connect them with the discourse just commented upon. In point of fact, part of these admonitions had already been spoken on a previous occasion, and that more fully, to the disciples in Galilee. Only we must again bear in mind the difference of circumstances. Here, they immediately precede the raising of Lazarus, and they form the close of Christ's public Ministry in Perea. Therefore they come to us as Christ's parting admonitions to His Perean followers.

Thus viewed, they are intended to impress on the new disciples these four things: to be careful to give no offence; to be careful to take no offence; to be simple and earnest in their faith, and absolutely to trust its all prevailing power; and yet, when they had made experience of it, not to be elated, but to remember their relation to their Master, that all was in His service, and that, after all, when everything had been done, they were but unprofitable servants. In other words, they urged upon the disciples holiness, love, faith, and service of self surrender and humility.

Most of these points have been already considered, when explaining the similar admonitions of Christ in Galilee. The four parts of this discourse are broken by the prayer of the Apostles, who had formerly expressed their difficulty in regard to these very requirements: Add to us faith. It was upon this that Jesus spoke to them, for their comfort, of the absolute power of even the smallest faith, and of the service and humility of faith. The latter was couched in a Parabolic form, well calculated to impress on them those feelings which would keep them lowly. They were but servants; and, even though they had done their work, the Master expected them to serve Him, before they sat down to their own meal and rested. Yet meal and rest there would be in the end. Only, let there not be self elation, nor weariness, nor impatience; but let the Master and His service be all in all. Surely, if ever there was emphatic protest against the fundamental idea of Pharisaism, as claiming merit and reward, it was in the closing admonition of Christ's public Ministry in Perea: When you shall have done all those things which are commanded you, say, We are unprofitable servants; we have done that which was our duty to do. And with these parting words did He most effectually and forever separate, in heart and spirit, the Church from the Synagogue.

End Notes:

[78]   Thus, Canon Cook makes this distinction: They who are said to seek, seek (i.e. desire and wish) and no more. They do not struggle for admission. But would anyone be refused who sought, in the sense of desiring, or wishing?

[79]   The word implies a real combat to get at the narrow door, not a large crowd . . . struggling for admission. The verb occurs besides in the following passages: John 16:36; 1 Corinthians 9:25; Colossians 1:29; 4:12; 1 Timothy 6:12; 2 Timothy 4:7.

[80]   The words today, and tomorrow, and the third day, must not be taken as a literal, but as a well known figurative expression. Thus we are told (Mechilta, Par. Bo, 18, towards end, ed. Weiss, p. 27 b), There is a "tomorrow" which is now [refers to the immediate present], and a "tomorrow" of a later time, indicating a fixed period connected with the present, The latter, for example, in the passage illustrated in the Rabbinic quotation just made: Exodus 13:14, It shall be when your son shall ask you [literally] tomorrow, in our KJV in time to come. So also Joshua 22:24. The third day in such connection would be.

Chapter 21

Raising Lazarus and Jewish Burial Rites

From listening to the teaching of Christ, we turn once more to follow His working. It will be remembered, that the visit to Bethany divides the period from the Feast of the Dedication to the last Paschal week into two parts. It also forms the prelude and preparation for the awful events of the End. For, it was on that occasion that the members of the Sanhedrin formally resolved on His death. It now only remained to settle and carry out the plans for giving effect to their purpose.

This is one aspect of it. There is yet another and more solemn one. The raising of Lazarus marks the highest point (not in the Manifestation, but) in the ministry of Jesus; it is the climax in a history where all is miraculous, the Person, the Life, the Words, the Work. As regards Himself, we have here the fullest evidence of His Divinity and Humanity; as regards those who witnessed it, the highest manifestation of faith and of unbelief. Here, on this height, the two ways finally meet and part. And from this high point, not only from the resolution of the Sanhedrists, but from the raising of Lazarus, we have our first clear outlook on the death and Resurrection of Christ, of which the raising of Lazarus was the typical prelude. From this height, also, have we an outlook upon the gathering of the Church at His empty Tomb, where the precious words spoken at the grave of Lazarus received their full meaning, until death shall be no more. But chiefly do we now think of it as the Miracle of Miracles in the history of the Christ. He had, before this raised the dead; but it had been in far off Galilee, and in circumstances essentially different. But now it would be one so well known as Lazarus, at the very gates of Jerusalem, in the sight of all men, and amid surroundings which admitted not of mistake or doubt. If this Miracle be true, we instinctively feel all is true; and Spinoza was right in saying, that if he could believe the raising of Lazarus, he would tear to shreds his system, and humbly accept the creed of Christians.

But is it true? We have reached a stage in this history when such a question, always most painful, might seem almost uncalled for. For, gradually and with increasing clearness, we have learned the trustworthiness of the Evangelic records; and, as we have followed Him, the conviction has deepened into joyous assurance, that He, Who spoke, lived, and performed as none other, is in very deed the Christ of God. And yet we ask ourselves here this question again, on account of its absolute and infinite importance; because this may be regarded as the highest and decisive moment in this History; because, in truth, it is to the historical faith of the Church what the great Confession of Peter was to that of the disciples. And, although such an inquiry may seem like the jarring of a discord in Heaven's own melody, we pursue it, feeling that, in so doing, we are not discussing what is doubtful, but rather setting forth the evidence of what is certain, for the confirmation of the faith of our hearts, and, as we humbly trust, for the establishment of the faith as it is in Jesus.

At the outset, we must here once more meet, however briefly, the preliminary difficulty in regard to Miracles, of which the raising of Lazarus is, we shall not say, the greatest, for comparison is not possible on such a point, but the most notable. Undoubtedly, a Miracle runs counter, not only to our experience, but to the facts on which our experience is grounded; and can only be accounted for by a direct Divine interjection, which also runs counter to our experience, although it cannot logically be said to run counter to the facts on which that experience is grounded. Beyond this it is impossible to go, since the argument on other grounds than of experience, be it phenomenal [observation and historical information] or real [knowledge of laws and principles], would necessitate knowledge of all the laws of Nature and of all the secrets of Heaven.

On the other hand (as indicated in a previous part), to argue this point only on the ground of experience (phenomenal or real), were not only reasoning `a priori, but in a vicious circle. It would really amount to this: A thing has not been, because it cannot be; and it cannot be, because, so far as I know, it is not and has not been. But, to deny on such `a priori prejudgment the possibility of Miracles, ultimately involves a denial of a Living, Reigning God. For, the existence of a God implies at least the possibility, in certain circumstances it may be the rational necessity, of Miracles. And the same grounds of experience, which tell against the occurrence of a Miracle, would equally apply against belief in a God. We have as little ground in experience (of a physical kind) for the one as for the other. This is not said to deter inquiry, but for the sake of our argument. For, we confidently assert and challenge experiment of it, that disbelief in a God, or Materialism, involves infinitely more difficulties, and that at every step and in regard to all things, than the faith of the Christian.

But we instinctively feel that such a Miracle as the raising of Lazarus calls for more than merely logical formulas. Heart and mind crave for higher than questions of what may be logically possible or impossible. We want, so to speak, living evidence, and we have it. We have it, first of all, in the Person of the Incarnate God, Who not only came to abolish death, but in Whose Presence the continuance of disease and death was impossible. And we have it also in the narrative of the event itself. It was, an absurd demand to prove a Miracle, since to do so was to show that it was not a Miracle. But we may be rationally asked these three things: first, to show, that no other explanation is rationally possible than that which proceeds on the ground of its being a Miracle; secondly, to show, that such a view of it is consistent with itself and with all the details of the narrative; and, thirdly, that it is harmonious with what precedes and what follows the narrative. The second and third of these arguments will be the outcome of our later study of the history of this event; the first, that no other explanation of the narrative is rationally possible, must now be briefly attempted.

We may here dismiss, as what would not be entertained by anyone familiar with historical inquiries, the idea that such a narrative could be an absolute invention, ungrounded on any fact. Again, we may put aside as repugnant to, at least English, common sense, the theory that the narrative is consistent with the idea that Lazarus was not really dead (so, the Rationalists). Nor would anyone, who had the faintest sympathy with the moral standpoint of the Gospels, entertain the view of M. Renan, that it was all a pious fraud concocted between all parties, and that, in order to convert Jerusalem by a signal miracle, Lazarus had himself dressed up as a dead body and laid in the family tomb. Scarcely more rational is M. Renan's latest suggestion, that it was all a misunderstanding: Martha and Mary having told Jesus the wish of friends, that He should do some notable miracle to convince the Jews, and suggesting that they would believe if one rose from the dead, when He had replied, that they would not believe even if Lazarus rose from his grave, and that tradition had transformed this conversation into an actual event! Nor, finally, would English common sense readily believe (with Baur), that the whole narrative was an ideal composition to illustrate what must be regarded as the metaphysical statement: I am the Resurrection and the Life. Among ourselves, at least, no serious refutation of these and similar views can be necessary.

Nor do the other theories advanced require lengthened discussion. The mythical explanation of Strauss is, that as the Old Testament had recorded instances of raising from the dead, so Christian tradition must necessarily ascribe the same to the Messiah. To this (without repeating the detailed refutation made by Renan and Baur), it is sufficient to reply: The previous history of Christ had already offered such instances, why needlessly multiply them? Besides, if it had been a legend, such full and minute details would not have been introduced, and while the human element would have been suppressed, the miraculous would have been far more accentuated. Only one other theory on the subject requires notice: that the writer of the Fourth Gospel, or rather early tradition, had transformed the Parable of The Rich Man and Lazarus into an actual event. In answer, it is sufficient to say: first, that (as previously shown) there is no connection between the Lazarus of the Parable and him of Bethany; secondly, that, if it had been a Parable transformed, the characters chosen would not have been real persons, and that they were such is evident from the mention of the family in different circumstances in the three Synoptic Gospels, of which the writer of the Fourth Gospel was fully aware. Lastly, as Godet remarks, whereas the Parable closes by declaring that the Jews would not believe even if one rose from the dead, the Narrative closes on this wise: Many therefore of the Jews, which came to Mary and saw that which He did, believed on Him.

In view of these proposed explanations, we appeal to the impartial reader, whether any of them rationally accounts for the origin and existence of this history in Apostolic tradition? On the other hand, everything is clear and consistent on the supposition of the historical truth of this narrative: the minuteness of details; the vividness and pictorialness of the narrative: the characteristic manner in which Thomas, Martha, and Mary speak and act, in accordance with what we read of them in the other Gospels or in other parts of this Gospel; the Human affection of the Christ; the magnificent simplicity and majesty of the manner of the Miracle; and the effects of it on friend and foe. There is, this one difficulty (not objection), that the event is not mentioned in the Synoptic Gospels. But we know too little of the plan on which the Gospels, viewed as Lives of Christ, were constructed, to allow us to draw any sufficient inference from the silence of the Synoptists, while we do know that the Judean and Jerusalem

Ministry of Christ, except so far as it was absolutely necessary to refer to
it, lay outside the plan of the Synoptic Gospels, and formed the special
subject of that by John. Lastly, we should remember, that in the then state
of thought the introduction of another narrative of raising from the dead
could not have seemed to them of such importance as it appears to us
in the present state of controversy, more especially, since it was soon to
be followed by another Resurrection, the importance and evidential value
of which far overshadowed such an event as the raising of Lazarus. Their
Galilean readers had the story of the raising of the window's son at Nain,
and of Jairus daughter at Capernaum; and the Roman world had not only
all this, but the preaching of the Resurrection, and of pardon and life in
the Name of the Risen One, together with visual demonstration of the
miraculous power of those who preached it. It remained for the beloved
disciple, who alone stood under the Cross, alone to stand on that height
from which he had first full and intense outlook upon His death, and the
Life which sprang from it, and flowed into all the world.

We may now, undisturbed by preliminary objections, surrender
ourselves to the magnificentness and seriousness of this narrative. Perhaps
the more briefly we comment on it the better.

It was while in Perea, that this message suddenly reached Jesus from the
well remembered home at Bethany, the village of Mary, who, although the
younger, is for obvious reasons first mentioned in this history, and her sister
Martha, concerning their (younger) brother Lazarus: Lord, consider he
whom You love is sick! They are apparently the very words which the sisters
called their messenger tell. We note as an important fact to be stored in our
memory, that the Lazarus, who had not even been mentioned in the only
account preserved to us of a previous visit of Christ to Bethany, is described
as he whom Christ loved. What a gap of untold events between the two
visits of Christ to Bethany, and what modesty should it teach us as regards
inferences from the circumstance that certain events are not recorded in
the Gospels! The messenger was apparently dismissed by Christ with this
reply: This sickness is not to death, but for the glory of God, in order that
the Son of God may be glorified thereby. We must here bear in mind, that
this answer was heard by such of the Apostles as were present at the time.
They would naturally infer from it that Lazarus would not die, and that his
restoration would glorify Christ, either as having foretold it, or prayed for
it, or effected it by His Will. Yet its true meaning, even, as we now see, its
literal interpretation, was, that its final upshot was not to be the death of
Lazarus, but that it was to be for the glory of God, in order that Christ as

the Son of God might be made manifest. And we learn, how much more full are the Words of Christ than they often appear to us; and how truly, and even literally, they may bear quite another meaning than appears to our honest misapprehension of them, a meaning which only the event, the future, will disclose.

And yet, probably at the very time when the messenger received his answer, and before he could have brought it to the sisters, Lazarus was already dead! Nor, and this should be especially marked, did this awaken doubt in the minds of the sisters. We seem to hear the very words which at the time they said to each other when each of them afterwards repeated it to Jesus: Lord, if You had been here, my brother would not have died. They probably thought the message had reached Him too late, that Lazarus would have lived if Christ had been appealed to in time, or had been able to come, at any rate, if He had been there. Even in their keenest anguish, there was no failure of trust, no doubt, no close weighing of words on their part, only the confidence of love. Yet all this while Christ knew that Lazarus had died, and still He continued two whole days where He was, finishing His work. And yet, and this is significantly noted before anything else, in regard to His delay and to His after conduct, He loved Martha, and her sister, and Lazarus. Had there been no after history, or had it not been known to us, or before it became known, it might have seemed otherwise, and in similar circumstances it often does seem otherwise to us. And again, what majestic calm, what Self restraint of Human affections and magnificent consciousness of Divine Power in this delay: it is once more Christ asleep, while the disciples are despairing, in the boat almost swamped in the storm! Christ is never in a hurry: least of all, on His errands of love. And He is never in a hurry, because He is always sure.

It was only after these two days that Christ broke silence as to His purposes and as to Lazarus. Though thoughts of him must have been present with the disciples, none dared ask anything whatever, although not from misgiving, nor yet from fear. This also of faith and of confidence. At last, when His work in that part had been completed, He spoke of leaving, but even so not of going to Bethany, but into Judea. For, in truth, His work in Bethany was not only geographically, but really, part of His work in Judea; and He told the disciples of His purpose, just because He knew their fears and would teach them, not only for this but for every future occasion, what principle applied to them. For when, in their care and affection, they reminded the Rabbi, and the expression here almost jars on us, that the Jews were even now seeking to stone Him, He replied by telling them, in figurative language, that we have each our working day from God, and that while it lasts no enemy can shorten it or break up or work. The day had twelve hours, and while these lasted no mishap would happen him that walked in the way [he does not stumble, because he sees the light of this world]. It was otherwise when the day was past and the night had come. When our God given day has set, and with it the light been withdrawn which up to this point prevented our stumbling, then, if a man went in his own way and at his own time, might such mishap happen to him, because, figuratively as to light in the night time, and really as to guidance and direction in the way, the light is not in him.

But this was only part of what Jesus said to His disciples in preparation for a journey that would issue in such tremendous consequences. He next spoke of Lazarus, their friend, as fallen asleep, in the frequent Jewish (as well as Christian) figurative sense of it, and of His going there to wake him out of sleep. The disciples would naturally connect this mention of His going to Lazarus with His proposed visit to Judea, and, in their eagerness to keep Him from the latter, interjected that there could be no need for going to Lazarus, since sleep was, according to Jewish notions, one of the six, or, according to others, five symptoms or crises in recovery from dangerous illness. And when Jesus then plainly stated it, Lazarus died, adding, what should have aroused their attention, that for their sakes He was glad He had not been in Bethany before the event, because now that would come which would work faith in them, and proposed to go to the dead Lazarus, even then, their whole attention was so absorbed by the certainty of danger to their loved Teacher, that Thomas had only one thought: since it was to be so, let them go and die with Jesus. So little had they understood the figurative language about the twelve hours on which God's sun shone to light us on our way; so much did they need the lesson of faith to be taught them in the raising of Lazarus!

We already know the quiet happy home of Bethany. When Jesus reached it, He found, probably from those who met Him on the way, that Lazarus had been already four days in the grave. According to custom, he would be buried the same day that he had died. Supposing his death to have taken place when the message for help was first delivered, while Jesus continued after that two whole days in the place where He was, this would leave about a day for His journey from Perea to Bethany. We do not, know the exact place of His stay; but it must have been some well known center of activity in Perea, since the sisters of Bethany had no difficulty in sending their messenger. At the same time we also infer that, at least at this period, some kind of communication must have existed between Christ and His more intimate disciples and friends, such as the family of Bethany, by which they were kept informed of the general plan of His Mission journeys, and of any central station of His temporary sojourn. If Christ at that time occupied such a central station, we can the more readily understand how some of His Galilean disciples may, for a brief space, have been absent at their Galilean homes when the news about Lazarus arrived. Their absence may explain the prominent position taken by Thomas; perhaps, also, in part, the omission of this narrative from the Synoptic Gospels. One other point may be of interest. Supposing the journey to Bethany to have occupied a day, we would suggest the following as the order of events. The messenger of the Sisters left Bethany on the Sunday (it could not have been on the Sabbath), and reached Jesus on the Monday. Christ continued in Perea other two days, until Wednesday, and arrived at Bethany on Thursday. On Friday the meeting of the Sanhedrists against Christ took place, while He rested in Bethany on the Friday, and on the Sabbath, and returned to Perea and Ephraim on the Sunday.

This may be a convenient place for adding to the account already given, in connection with the burying of the widows son at Nain, such further particulars of the Jewish observances and rites, as may illustrate the present history. Referring to the previous description, we resume, in imagination, our attendance at the point where Christ met the bier at Nain and again gave life to the dead. But we remember that, as we are now in Judea, the hired mourners, both mourning men (for there were such) and mourning women, would follow, and not, as in Galilee, precede, the body. From the narrative we infer that the burial of Lazarus did not take place in a common burying ground, which was never nearer a town than 50 cubits, dry and rocky places being chosen in preference. Here the graves must be at least a foot and a half apart. It was deemed a dishonor to the dead to stand on, or walk over, the turf of a grave. Roses and other flowers seem to have been planted on graves. But cemeteries, or common burying places, appear in earliest times to have been used only for the poor, or for strangers. In Jerusalem there were also two places where executed criminals were buried. All these, it is needless to say, were outside the City. But there is abundant evidence, that every place did not have its own burying ground; and that, not infrequently, provision had to be made for the transport of bodies. Indeed, a burying place is not mentioned among the ten requirements for every fully organized Jewish community. The names given, both to the graves and to the burying place itself, are of interest. As regards the former, we mention such as the house of silence; the house of stone; the hostelry, or, literally, place where you spend the night; the couch; the resting place; the valley of the multitude, or of the dead. The cemetery was called the house of graves; or the court of burying; and the house of eternity. By a euphemism, to die was designated as going to rest, been completed; being gathered to the world or to the home of light; being withdrawn, or hidden. Burial without coffin seems to have continued the practice for a considerable time, and rules are given how a pit, the size of the body, was to be dug, and surrounded by a wall of loose stones to prevent the falling in of earth. When afterwards earth burials had to be vindicated against the Parsee idea of cremation, Jewish scholars more fully discussed the question of burial, and described the committal of the body to the ground as a sort of penance. It was a curious later practice, that children who had died a few days after birth were circumcised on their graves. Children not a month old were buried without coffin or mourning, and, as some have thought, in a special place. In connection with a recent controversy it is interesting to learn that, for the sake of peace, just as the poor and sick of the Gentiles might be fed and nursed as well as those of the Jews, so their dead might be buried with those of the Jews, though not in their graves. On the other hand, a wicked person should not be buried close to a sage. Suicides were not accorded all the honors of those who had died a natural death, and the bodies of executed criminals were laid in a special place, from which the relatives might after a time remove their bones. The burial terminated by casting earth on the grave.

But, as already stated, Lazarus was, as became his station, not laid in a cemetery, but in his own private tomb in a cave, probably in a garden, the favorite place of interment. Though on terms of close friendship with Jesus, he was evidently not regarded as an apostate from the Synagogue. For, every indignity was shown at the burial of an apostate; people were even to array themselves in white festive garments to make demonstration of joy. Here, on the contrary, as we gather from the sequel, every mark of sympathy, respect, and sorrow had been shown by the people in the district and by friends in the neighboring Jerusalem. In such case it would be regarded as a privilege to obey the Rabbinic direction of accompanying the dead, so as to show honor to the departed and kindness to the survivors. As the sisters of Bethany were disciples, we may well believe that some of the more extravagant demonstrations of grief were, if not dispensed with, yet modified. We can scarcely believe, that the hired mourners would alternate between extravagant praises of the dead and calls upon the attendants to lament; or that, as was their habit, they would strike their breast, beat their hands, and dash about their feet, or break into wails and mournings songs, alone or in chorus. In all probability, however, the funeral oration would be delivered, as in the case of all distinguished persons—either in the house, or at one of the stations where the bearers changed, or at the burying place; perhaps, if they passed it, in the Synagogue. It has previously been noted, what extravagant value was, in later times, attached to these orations, as indicating both a man's life on earth and his place in heaven. The dead was supposed to be present, listening to the words of the speaker and watching the expression on the face of the hearers. It would serve no good purpose to reproduce fragments from these orations. Their character is sufficiently indicated by the above remarks.

When thinking of these tombs in gardens, we so naturally revert to that which for three days held the Lord of Life, that all details become deeply interesting. And it is, perhaps, better to give them here rather than afterwards to interrupt, by such inquiries, our solemn thoughts in presence of the Crucified Christ. Not only the rich, but even those moderately well to do, had tombs of their own, which probably were acquired and prepared long before they were needed, and treated and inherited as private and personal property. In such caves, or rock hewn tombs, the bodies were laid, having been anointed with many spices, with myrtle, aloes, and, at a later period, also with hyssop, rose oil, and rose water. The body was dressed and, at a later period, wrapped, if possible, in the worn cloths in which originally a Roll of the Law had been held. The tombs were either rock hewn or natural caves or else large walled vaults, with niches along the sides. Such a cave or vault of 4 cubits (6 feet) width, 6 cubits (9 feet) length, and 4 cubits (6 feet) height, contained niches for eight bodies, three on each of the longitudinal sides, and two at the end opposite the entrance. Each niche was 4 cubits (6 feet) long, and had a height of seven and a width of six handbreadths. As these burying niches were hollowed out in the walls they were called Kukhin. The larger caves or vaults were 6 cubits (9 feet) wide, and 8 cubits (12 feet) long, and held thirteen bodies, four along each side wall, three opposite to, and one on either side of the entrance. These figures apply only to what the Law required, when a vault had been contracted for. When a person constructed one for himself, the dimensions of the walls and the number of Kukhin might vary. At the entrance to the vault was a court 6 cubits (9 feet) square, to hold the bier and its bearers. Sometimes two caves opened on this court. But it is difficult to decide whether the second cave, spoken of, was intended as an crypt (ossarium). Certain it is, that after a

time the bones were collected and put into a box or coffin, having first
been anointed with wine and oil, and being held together by wrappings of
cloths. This circumstance explains the existence of the mortuary chests, or
osteophagi, so frequently found in the tombs of Palestine by late explorers,
who have been unable to explain their meaning. This unclearness is much
to be regretted, when we read, for example, of such a chest as found in a
cave near Bethany. One of the explorers has discovered on them fragments
of Hebrew inscriptions. Up to the present, only few Hebrew memorial
inscriptions have been discovered in Palestine. The most interesting are
those in or near Jerusalem, dating from the first century BC to the first AD.
There are, also, many inscriptions found on Jewish tombs out of Palestine
(in Rome, and other places), written in bad Greek or Latin, containing,
perhaps, a Hebrew word, and generally ending with shalom, peace, and
adorned with Jewish symbols, such as the Seven branched Candlestick, the
Ark, the festive emblems of the Feast of Tabernacles, and others. In general,
the advice not to read such inscriptions, as it would affect the sight, seems
to imply the common practice of having memorial inscriptions in Hebrew.
They appear to have been engraved either on the lid of the mortuary chest,
or on the Golel, or great stone rolled at the entrance to the vault, or to the
court leading into it, or else on the inside walls of yet another erection,
made over the vaults of the wealthy, and which was supposed to complete
the burying place, or Qebher.

These small buildings surmounting the graves may have served as
shelter to those who visited the tombs. They also served as monuments, of
which we read in the Bible, in the Apocrypha, and in Josephus. In Rabbinic
writings they are frequently mentioned, chiefly by the name Nephesh, soul,
person, transferred in the sense of monument, or, by the more Scriptural
name of bamah, or, by the Greco-Aramaic, or the Hebrew designation for a
building generally. But of gravestones with inscriptions we cannot find any
record in Talmudic works. At the same time, the place where there was a
vault or a grave was marked by a stone, which was kept whitened, to warn
the passer by against defilement.

We are now able fully to realize all the circumstances and surroundings
in the burial and raising of Lazarus. Jesus had come to Bethany. But in the
house of mourning they did not know. As Bethany was only about fifteen
furlongs, or about two miles, from Jerusalem, many from the City, who
were on terms of friendship with what was evidently a distinguished family,
had come in obedience to one of the most binding Rabbinic directions,
that of comforting the mourners. In the funeral procession the sexes had

been separated, and the practice probably prevailed even at that time for the women to return alone from the grave. This may explain why afterwards the women went and returned alone to the Tomb of Jesus. The mourning, which began before the burial, had been shared by the friends who sat silent on the ground, or were busy preparing the mourning meal. As the company left the dead, each had taken leave of the deceased with a Depart in peace! Then they had formed into lines, through which the mourners passed amid expressions of sympathy, repeated (at least seven times) as the procession halted on the return to the house of mourning. Then began the mourning in the house, which really lasted thirty days, of which the first three were those of greatest, the others, during the seven days, or the special week of sorrow, of less intense mourning. But on the Sabbath, as God's holy day, all mourning was intermitted, and so they rested on the Sabbath, according to the commandment.

In that household of disciples this mourning would not have assumed such violent forms, as when we read that the women were in the habit of tearing out their hair, or of a Rabbi who publicly scourged himself. But we know how the dead would be spoken of. In death the two world's were said to meet and kiss. And now they who had passed away beheld God. They were at rest. Such beautiful passages as Psalm 112:6, Proverbs 10:7, Isaiah 10:10, last clause, and Isaiah 55:2, were applied to them. The holy dead should be called living. In truth, they knew about us, and unseen still surrounded us. Nor should they ever be mentioned without adding a blessing on their memory.

In this spirit, we cannot doubt, the Jews were now comforting the sisters. They may have repeated words like those quoted as the conclusion of such a consolatory speech: May the Lord of consolations comfort you! Blessed is He Who comforts the mourners! But they could scarcely have imagined how literally a wish like this was about to be fulfilled. For, already, the message had reached Martha, who was probably in one of the outer apartments of the house: Jesus is coming! She hurried to meet Jesus. Not a word of complaint, not a murmur, nor doubt, escaped her lips, only what during those four bitter days these two sisters must have been so often saying to each other, when the luxury of solitude was allowed them, that if He had been there their brother would not have died. And even now, when it was all too late, when they had not received what they had asked of Him by their messenger, it must have been, because He had not asked it, though he had said that this sickness was not to death; or else because he had delayed to work it until He would come. And still she held fast by it, that even now God would give Him what ever He asked. Or, did they mean more: were they such words of unconscious prophecy, or sight and sound of heavenly things, as sometimes come to us in our passion of grief, or else winged thoughts of faith too soon beyond our vision? They could not have been the expression of any real hope of the miracle about to take place, or Martha would not have afterwards sought to stop Him, when He called them to roll away the stone. And yet is not even so, that, when that comes to us which our faith had once dared to suggest, if not to hope, we feel as if it were all too great and impossible, that a the physical world cannot separate us from it?

It was in very truth and literality that Jesus meant it, when He told Martha her brother would rise again, although she understood His Words of the Resurrection at the Last Day. In answer, Christ pointed out to her the connection between Himself and the Resurrection; and, what He spoke, that He did when He raised Lazarus from the dead. The Resurrection and the Life are not special gifts either to the Church or to humanity, but are connected with the Christ, the outcome of Himself. The Resurrection of the Just and the General Resurrection are the consequence of the relation in which the Church and humanity in general stand to the Christ. Without the Christ there would have been no Resurrection. Most literally He is the Resurrection and the Life, and this, the new teaching about the Resurrection, was the object and the meaning of the raising of Lazarus. And thus is this raising of Lazarus the outlook, also, upon His own Resurrection, Who is the first fruits from the dead.

And though the special, then present, application, or rather manifestation of it, would be in the raising of Lazarus, yet this teaching, that accompanied it, is to all believers: He that believes in Me, even if [though] he die, shall live; and who ever lives and believes in Me shall not die forever (to the eon)—where possibly we might, for comment, mentally insert the sign of a pause between the words die and forever, or to the eon. It is only when we think of the meaning of Christ's previous words, as implying that the Resurrection and the Life are the outcome of Himself, and come to us only through Him and in Him, that we can understand the answer of Martha to His question: Believe you this? Yes, Lord, I have believed that you are the Christ, the Son of God [with special reference to the original message of Christ], He that comes into the world [the Coming One into the world = the world's promised, expected, come Savior].

What else passed between them we can only gather from the context. It seems that Jesus called for Mary. This message Martha now hurried to deliver, although secretly. Mary was probably sitting in the chamber of mourning, with its upset chairs and couches, and other sad tokens of mourning, as was the custom; surrounded by many who had come to comfort them; herself, we can scarcely doubt, silent, her thoughts far away in that world to, and of which Jesus was to her the Way, the Truth, and the Life. As she heard of His coming and call, she rose quickly, and the Jews followed her, under the impression that she was again going to visit, and to weep at the tomb of her brother. For, it was the practice to visit the grave, especially during the first three days. When she came to Jesus, where He still stood, outside Bethany, she was forgetful of all around. It was, as if sight of Him melted what had frozen the tide of her feelings. She could only fall at His Feet, and repeat the poor words with which she and her sister had these four weary days tried to cover the nakedness of their sorrow: poor words of consolation, and poor words of faith, which she did not, like her sister, make still poorer of by adding the poverty of her hope to that of her faith, the poverty of the future to that of the past and present. To Martha that had been the maximum, to Mary it was the minimum of her faith; for the rest, it was far, far better to add nothing more, but simply to worship at His Feet.

It must have been a deeply touching scene: the outpouring of her sorrow, the absoluteness of her faith, the mute appeal of her tears. And the Jews who witnessed it were moved as she, and wept with her. What follows is difficult to understand; still more difficult to explain: not only from the choice of language, which is peculiarly difficult, but because its difficulty springs from the yet greater difficulty of expressing what it is intended to describe. The expression, groaned in spirit, cannot mean that Christ was moved with indignation in the spirit, since this could not have been the consequence of witnessing the tears of Mary and what, we feel sure, was the genuine emotion of the Jews. Of the various interpretations, that commends itself most to us, which would render the expression: He vehemently moved His Spirit and troubled Himself. One, whose insight into such questions is peculiarly deep, has reminded us that the miracles of Jesus were not performed by the simple word of power, but that in a mysterious way the element of sympathy entered into them. He took away the sufferings and diseases of men in some sense by taking them upon Himself. If, with this most just view of His Condescension to, and union with, humanity as its Healer, by taking upon Himself its diseases, we combine the statement formerly made about the Resurrection, as not a gift or windfall but the outcome of Himself, we may, in some way, not understand, but be able to gaze into, the unfathomed depth of the human fellow suffering which was both vicarious and redemptive, and which, before He became the Resurrection to Lazarus, shook His whole inner Being, when, in the words of John, He vehemently moved His Spirit and troubled Himself.

And now every trait is in accord. Where have you laid him? So truly human, as if He, Who was about to raise the dead, needed the information where he had been laid; so truly human, also, in the underlying tenderness of the personal address, and in the absorption of the whole divine-human energy on the mighty burden about to be lifted and lifted away. So, also, as they called Him come and see, were the tears that fell from Him (dkrusen), not like the violent lamentation (klausen) that burst from Him at sight and prophetic view of doomed Jerusalem. Yet we can scarcely think that the Jews rightly interpreted it, when they ascribed it only to His love for Lazarus. But surely there was not a touch either of ill will or of irony, only what we feel to be quite natural in the circumstances, when some of them asked it aloud: Could not this One, Who opened the eyes of the blind, have performed so that [in order] this one also should not die? Scarcely was it even unbelief. They had so lately witnessed in Jerusalem that Miracle, such as had not been heard since the world began; that it seemed difficult to understand how, seeing there was the will (in His affection for Lazarus), there was not the power, not to raise him from the dead, for that did not occur to them, but to prevent his dying. Was there, then, a barrier in death? And it was this, and not indignation, which once more caused that divine-human recurrence upon Himself, when again He vehemently moved His Spirit.

And now they were at the cave which was Lazarus' tomb. He told them to roll aside the great stone which covered its entrance. Amid the awful pause which preceded obedience, one voice only was raised. It was that of Martha. Jesus had not spoken of raising Lazarus. But what was about to be done? She could scarcely have thought that He merely wished to gaze once more upon the face of the dead. Something nameless had seized her. She dared not believe; she dared not disbelieve. Did she, perhaps, not dread a failure, but feel misgivings, when thinking of Christ as in presence of commencing corruption before these Jews, and yet, as we so often, still love Him even in unbelief? It was the common Jewish idea that corruption commenced on the fourth day, that the drop of gall, which had fallen from the sword of the Angel and caused death, was then working its effect, and that, as the face changed, the soul took its final leave from the resting place of the body. Only one sentence Jesus spoke of gentle reproof, of reminder of what He had said to her just before, and of the message He had sent when first He heard of Lazarus illness, but, oh so full of calm majesty and consciousness of Divine strength. And now the stone was rolled away. We all feel that the fitting thing here was prayer, yet not petition, but thanksgiving that the Father heard Him, not as regarded the raising of Lazarus, which was His Own Work, but in the ordering and arranging of all the circumstances, the petition and the thanksgiving having for their object them that stood by, for He knew that the Father always heard Him: that so they might believe, that the Father had sent Him. Sent of the Father, not come of Himself, not sent of Satan, and sent to do His Will!

And in doing this Will, He was the Resurrection and the Life. One loud command spoken into that silence; one loud call to that sleeper; one flash of God's Own Light into that darkness, and the wheels of life again moved at the outgoing of The Life. And, still bound hand and foot with grave clothes [bands, Takhrikhin], and his face with the napkin, Lazarus stood forth, shuddering and silent, in the cold light of earth's day. In that multitude, now more pale and shuddering than the man bound in the grave clothes, the Only One majestically calm was He, Who before had been so deeply moved and troubled Himself, as He now called them Loose him, and let him go.

We know no more. Holy Writ in this also proves its Divine authorship and the reality of what is here recorded. The momentarily lifted veil has again fallen over the darkness of the Most Holy Place, in which is only the Ark of His Presence and the cloudy incense of our worship. What happened afterwards, how they loosed him, what they said, what thanks, or praise, or worship, the sisters spoke, and what were Lazarus first words, we do not know. And better so. Did Lazarus remember anything whatever of the late past, or was not rather the rending of the grave a real rending from the past: the awakening so sudden, the transition so great, that nothing of the bright vision remained, but its impress, just as a marvelously beautiful Jewish legend has it, that before entering this world, the soul of a child has seen all of heaven and hell, of past, present, and future; but that, as the Angel strikes it on the mouth to awaken it into this world, all of the other has passed from the mind? Again we say: We do not know, and it is better so.

And here abruptly breaks off this narrative. Some of those who had seen it believed on Him; others hurried back to Jerusalem to tell it to the Pharisees. Then was hastily gathered a meeting of the Sanhedrists, not to judge Him, but to deliberate what was to be done. That He was really doing these miracles, there could be no question among them. Similarly, all but one or two had no doubt as to the source of these miracles. If real, they were of Satanic agency, and all the more tremendous they were, the more certainly so. But whether really of Satanic power, or merely a Satanic delusion, one thing, at least, was evident, that, if He were let alone, all men would believe on Him? And then, if He headed the Messianic movement of the Jews as a nation, the Jewish City and Temple, and Israel as a nation, would perish in the fight with Rome. But what was to be done? They had not the courage of, though the wish for, judicial murder, until he who was the High Priest, Caiaphas, reminded them of the well known Jewish adage, that it is better one man should die, than the community perish. Yet, even so, he who spoke was the High Priest; and for the last time, before in speaking the sentence he spoke it forever as against himself and the office he held, spoke through him God's Voice, not as regards the counsel of murder, but this, that His death should be for that nation as John adds, not only for Israel, but to gather into one fold all the now scattered children of God.

This was the last prophecy in Israel; with the sentence of death on Israel's true High Priest died prophecy in Israel, died Israel's High Priesthood. It had spoken sentence upon itself.

This was the first Friday of dark resolve. From here on it only needed to concert plans for carrying it out. Someone, perhaps Nicodemus, sent word of the secret meeting and resolution of the Sanhedrists. That Friday and the next Sabbath Jesus rested in Bethany, with the same majestic calm which He had shown at the grave of Lazarus. Then He withdrew, far away to the obscure bounds of Perea and Galilee, to a city of which the very location is now unknown. And there He continued with His disciples, withdrawn from the Jews, until He would make His final entrance into Jerusalem.

End Notes:

[81]   These were: a law court, provision for the poor, a synagogue, a public bath, a secessus, a doctor, a surgeon, a scribe, a butcher, and a schoolmaster.

[82]   On account of the poverty of some of the sages, it was declared that they needed not monuments; their deeds were their monuments (Jeremiah Shequal. 2:7, p. 47 a).

[83]   The city called Ephraim has not been localized. Most modern writers identify it with the Ephraim, or Ephron, of 2 Chronicles 13:19, in the neighborhood of Bethel, and near the wilderness of Bethaven. But the text seems to require a place in Perea and close to Galilee. Comp. p. 127.

Chapter 22

The Journey to Jerusalem

The brief time of rest and quiet conversation with His disciples in the retirement of Ephraim was past, and the Savior of men prepared for His last journey to Jerusalem. All the three Synoptic Gospels mark this, although with varying details. From the mention of Galilee by Matthew, and by Luke of Samaria and Galilee, or more correctly, between (along the frontiers of) Samaria and Galilee, we may conjecture that, on leaving Ephraim, Christ made a very brief detour along the northern frontier to some place at the southern border of Galilee, perhaps to meet at a certain point those who were to accompany him on his final journey to Jerusalem. This suggestion, for it is no more, is in itself not improbable, since some of Christ's immediate followers might naturally wish to pay a brief visit to their friends in Galilee before going up to Jerusalem. And it is further confirmed by the notice of Mark, that among those who had followed Christ there were many women which came up with Him to Jerusalem. For, we can scarcely suppose that these many women had gone with Him in the previous autumn from Galilee to the Feast of Tabernacles, nor that they were with Him at the Feast of the Dedication, or had during the winter followed Him through Perea, nor yet that they had been at Bethany. All these difficulties are averted if, as suggested, we suppose that Christ had passed from Ephraim along the border of Samaria to a place in Galilee, there to meet such of His disciples as would go up with Him to Jerusalem. The whole company would then form one of those festive bands which traveled to the Paschal Feast, nor would there be anything strange or unusual in the appearance of such a band, in this instance under the leadership of Jesus.

Another and deeply important notice, furnished by Matthew and Mark, is, that during this journey through Perea, great multitudes resorted to, and followed Him, and that He healed and taught them. This will account for the incidents and discourses on the way, and also how, from among many deeds, the Evangelists may have selected for record what to them seemed the most important or novel, or else best accorded with the plans of their respective narratives.

Thus, to begin with, Luke alone relates the very first incident by the way, and the first discourse. Nor is it difficult to understand the reason of this. To one who, like Matthew, had followed Christ in His Galilean Ministry, or, like Mark, had been the penman of Peter, there would not be anything so peculiar or novel in the healing of lepers as to introduce this on the overcrowded canvas of the last days. They had both already recorded what may be designated as a typical healing of lepers. But Luke had not recorded such healing before; and the restoration of ten at the same time would seem to the beloved physician matter, not only new in his narrative, but of the deepest importance. Besides, we have already seen, that the record of the whole of this East Jordan Ministry is peculiar to Luke; and we can scarcely doubt that it was the result of personal inquiries made by the Evangelist on the spot, in order to supplement what might have seemed to him a gap in the Gospels of Matthew and Mark. This would explain his fullness of detail as regards incidents, and, for example, the introduction of the history of Zaccheus, which to Mark, or rather to Peter, but especially to Matthew (himself once a publican), might appear so like that which they had so often witnessed and related, as scarcely to require special narration. On the same ground we account for the record by Luke of Christ's discourse predictive of the Advent of the Messianic Kingdom. This discourse is evidently in its place at the beginning of Christ's last journey to Jerusalem. But the other two Evangelists merge it in the account of the fuller teaching on the same subject during the last days of Christ's sojourn on earth.

It is a further confirmation of our suggestion as to the road taken by Jesus, that of the ten lepers whom, at the outset of His journey, He met when entering into a village, one was a Samaritan. It may have been that the district was infested with leprosy; or these lepers may, on news of Christ's approach, have hastily gathered there. It was, as fully explained in another place, in strict accordance with Jewish Law, that these lepers remained both outside the village and far from Him to Whom they now cried for mercy. And, without either touch or even command of healing, Christ called them go and show themselves as healed to the priests. For this it was, as will be remembered, not necessary to go to Jerusalem. Any priest might declare unclean or clean provided the applicants presented themselves singly, and not in company, for his inspection. And they went at Christ's inviting, even before they had actually experienced the healing! So great was their faith, and, may we not almost infer, the general belief throughout the district, in the power of the Master. And as they went, the new life coursed in their veins. Restored health began to be felt, just as it ever is, not before, nor yet after believing, but in the act of obedience of a faith that has not yet experienced the blessing.

But now the characteristic difference between these men appeared. Of the ten, equally recipients of the benefit, the nine Jews continued their way, presumably to the priests, while the one Samaritan in the number at once turned back, with a loud voice glorifying God. The whole event may not have occupied many minutes, and Jesus with his followers may still have stood on the same spot from which He called the ten lepers go show themselves to the priests. He may have followed them with his eyes, as, but a few steps on their road of faith, health overtook them, and the grateful Samaritan, with voice of loud thanksgiving, hurried back to his Healer. No longer now did he remain far off, but in humblest reverence fell on his face at the Feet of Him to Whom he gave thanks. This Samaritan had received more than new bodily life and health: he had found spiritual life and healing.

But why did the nine Jews not return? Assuredly, they must have had some faith when first seeking help from Christ, and still more when setting out for the priests before they had experienced the healing. But perhaps, regarding it from our own standpoint, we may overestimate the faith of these men. Bearing in mind the views of the Jews at the time, and what constant succession of miraculous cures, without a single failure, had been witnessed these years, it cannot seem strange that lepers should apply to Jesus. Not yet perhaps did it, in the circumstances, involve very much greater faith to go to the priests at His inviting, implying that they were or would be healed. But it was far different to turn back and to fall down at His feet in lowly worship and thanksgiving. That made a man a disciple.

Many questions here suggest themselves: Did these nine Jews separate from the one Samaritan when they felt healed, common misfortune having made them companions and brethren, while the bond was snapped so soon as they felt themselves free of their common sorrow? The History of the Church and of individual Christians furnishes, unfortunately not a few analogous instances. Or did these nine Jews, in their legalism and obedience to the letter, go on to the priests, forgetful that, in obeying the letter, they violated the spirit of Christ's command? Of this also there are, unfortunately only too many parallel cases which will occur to the mind. Or was it Jewish pride, which felt it had a right to the blessings, and attributed them, not to the mercy of Christ, but to God; or, rather, to their own relation as Israel to God? Or, what seems to us the most probable, was it simply Jewish ingratitude and neglect of the blessed opportunity now within their reach, a state of mind too characteristic of those who do not know the time of their visitation, and which led up to the neglect, rejection, and final loss of the Christ? Certain it is, that Jesus emphasized the terrible contrast in this between the children of the household and this stranger. And here another important lesson is implied in regard to the miraculous in the Gospels. The history shows how little spiritual value or efficacy they attach to miracles, and how essentially different in this respect their tendency is from all legendary stories. The lesson conveyed in this case is, that we may expect, and even experience, miracles, without any real faith in the Christ; with belief, in His Power, but without surrender to His Rule. According to the Gospels, a man might either seek benefit from Christ, or else receive Christ through such benefit. In the one case, the benefit sought was the object, in the other, the means; in the one, it was the goal, in the other, the road to it; in the one, it gave healing, in the other, brought salvation; in the one, it ultimately led away from, in the other, it led to Christ and to discipleship. And so Christ now spoke it to this Samaritan: Arise, go your way; your faith has made you whole. But for all time there are here to the Church lessons of most important distinction.

2. The discourse concerning the Coming of the Kingdom, which is reported by Luke immediately after the healing of the ten lepers, will be more conveniently considered in connection with the fuller statement of the same truths at the close of Jesus' Ministry. It was probably delivered a day or so after the healing of the lepers, and marks a farther stage in the Perean journey towards Jerusalem. For, here we meet once more the Pharisees as questioners. This circumstance, as will now appear, is of great importance, as carrying us back to the last mention of an interjection by the Pharisees.

3. This brings us to what we regard as, in point of time, the next discourse of Christ on this journey, recorded both by Matthew, and, in briefer form, by Mark. These Evangelist place it immediately after their notice

of the beginning of this journey. For reasons previously indicated, Luke inserts the healing of the lepers and the prophetic discourse, while the other two Evangelists omit them. On the other hand, Luke omits the discourse here reported by Matthew and Mark, because, as we can readily see, its subject matter would, from the standpoint of his Gospel, not appear of such supreme importance as to demand insertion in a narrative of selected events.

The subject matter of that discourse is, in answer to Pharisaic tempting, and exposition of Christ's teaching in regard to the Jewish law and practice of divorce. The introduction of this subject in the narratives of Matthew and Mark seems, to say the least, abrupt. But the difficulty is entirely removed, or, rather, changed into undesigned evidence, when we fit it into the general history. Christ had advanced farther on His journey, and now once more encountered the hostile Pharisees. It will be remembered that He had met them before in the same part of the country, and answered their taunts and objections, among other things, by charging them with breaking in spirit that Law of which they professed to be the exponents and representatives. And this He had proved by reference to their views and teaching on the subject of divorce. This seems to have irritated their minds. Probably they also imagined, it would be easy to show on this point a marked difference between the teaching of Jesus and that of Moses and the Rabbis, and to enlist popular feeling against Him. Accordingly, when these Pharisees again encountered Jesus, now on his journey to Judea, they resumed the subject precisely where it had been broken off when they had last met Him, only now with the object of tempting Him. Perhaps it may also have been in the hope that, by getting Christ to commit Himself against divorce in Perea—the territory of Herod, they might enlist against Him, as formerly against the Baptist, the merciless hatred of Herodias.

But their main object evidently was to involve Christ in controversy with some of the Rabbinic Schools. This appears from the form in which they put the question, whether it was lawful to put away a wife for every cause? Mark, who gives only a very condensed account, omits this clause; but in Jewish circles the whole controversy between different teachers turned upon this point. All held that divorce was lawful, the only question being as to its grounds. We will not here enter on the unsavory question of Divorce among the Jews, to which the Talmud devotes a special tractate. There can, however, be no question that the practice was discouraged by many of the better Rabbis, in word and by their example; nor yet, that the

Jewish Law took the most watchful care of the interests of the woman. In fact, if any doubt were raised as to the legal validity of the letter of divorce, the Law always pronounced against the divorce. At the same time, in popular practice, divorce must have been very frequent; while the principles underlying Jewish legislation on the subject are most objectionable. These were in turn due to a comparatively lower estimate of woman, and to an unspiritual view of the marriage relation. Christianity has first raised woman to her proper position, not by giving her a new one, but by restoring and fully developing that assigned to her in the Old Testament. Similarly, as regards marriage, the New Testament, which would have us to be, in one sense, eunuchs for the Kingdom of God, has also fully restored and finally developed what the Old Testament had already implied. And this is part of the lesson taught in this discourse, both to the Pharisees and to the disciples.

To begin with, divorce (in the legal sense) was regarded as a privilege accorded only to Israel, not to the Gentiles. On the question: what constituted lawful grounds of divorce, the Schools were divided. Taking their departure from the sole ground of divorce mentioned in Deuteronomy 24:1: a matter of shame [literally, nakedness], the School of Shammai applied the expression only to moral transgressions, and, exclusively to unchastity. It was declared that, if a woman were as mischievous as the wife of Ahab, or [according to tradition] as the wife of Korah, it was well that her husband should not divorce her, except it be on the ground of adultery. At the same time this must not be regarded as a fixed legal principle, but rather as an opinion and good counsel for conduct. The very passages, from which the above quotations are made, also afford only too painful evidence of the laxity of views and practices current. And the Jewish Law unquestionably allowed divorce on almost any grounds; the difference being, not as to what was lawful, but on what grounds a man should set the Law in motion, and make use of the absolute liberty which it accorded him. Therefore, it is a serious mistake on the part of Commentators to set the teaching of Christ on this subject by the side of that of Shammai.

But the School of Hillel proceeded on different principles. It took the words, matter of shame in the widest possible sense, and declared it sufficient ground for divorce if a woman had spoiled her husbands dinner. Rabbi Akiba thought, that the words, if she find no favor in his eyes, implied that it was sufficient if a man had found another woman more attractive than his wife. All agreed that moral blame made divorce a duty, and that in such cases a woman should not be taken back. According to the Mishnah, if they transgressed against the Law of Moses or of Israel. The former is explained as implying a breach of the laws of tithing, of setting apart the first of the dough, and of purification. The latter is explained as referring to such offences as that of going in public with uncovered head, of spinning in the public streets, or entering into talk with men, to which others add, that of brawling, or of disrespectfully speaking of her husbands parents in his presence. A troublesome, or quarrelsome wife might certainly be sent away; and ill repute, or childlessness (during ten years) were also regarded as valid grounds of divorce.

Incomparably as these principles differ from the teaching of Christ, it must again be repeated, that no real comparison is possible between Christ and even the strictest of the Rabbis, since none of them actually prohibited divorce, except in case of adultery, nor yet laid down those high eternal principles which Jesus enunciated. But we can understand how, from the Jewish point of view, tempting Him, they would put the question, whether it was lawful to divorce a wife for every cause. Avoiding their hair splitting, Jesus appealed straight to the highest authority, God's institution of marriage. He, Who at the beginning [from the first, originally,] had made them male and female, had in the marriage relation joined them together, to the breaking of every other, even the nearest, relationship, to be one flesh, that is, to a union which was unity. Such was the fact of God's ordering. It followed, that they were one, and what God had willed to be one, man might not put asunder. Then followed the natural Rabbinic objection, why, in such case, Moses had commanded a bill of divorcement. Our Lord replied by pointing out that Moses had not commanded divorce, only tolerated it on account of their hardness of heart, and in such case commanded to give a bill of divorce for the protection of the wife. And this argument would appeal the more forcibly to them, that the Rabbis themselves taught that a somewhat similar concession had been made by Moses in regard to female captives of war, as the Talmud has it, on account of the evil impulse. But such a separation, Jesus continued, had not been provided for in the original institution, which was a union to unity. Only one thing could put an end to that unity, its absolute breach. Therefore, to divorce ones wife (or husband) while this unity lasted, and to marry another, was adultery, because, as the divorce was null before God, the original marriage still subsisted, and, in that case, the Rabbinic Law would also have forbidden it. The next part of Jesus' inference, that whoever marries her which is put away commits adultery, is more difficult of interpretation. Generally, it is understood as implying that a woman divorced for adultery might not be married. But it has been argued, that, as the literal rendering is, whoever marries her when put away, it applies to the woman whose divorce had just before been prohibited, and not, as is sometimes thought, to a woman divorced [under any circumstances]. Be this as it may, the Jewish Law, which regarded marriage with a woman divorced under any circumstances as unadvisable, absolutely banned that of the adulterer with the adulteress.

Whatever, therefore, may be pleaded, on account of the hardness of heart in modern society, in favor of the lawfulness of relaxing Christ's law of divorce, which confines dissolution of marriage to the one ground (of adultery), because then the unity of God's making has been broken by sin, such a reversal was at least not in the mind of Christ, nor can it be considered lawful, either by the Church or for individual disciples. But, that the Pharisees had rightly judged, when tempting Him, what the popular feeling on the subject would be, appears even from what His disciples [not necessarily the Apostles] afterwards said to Him. They waited to express their dissent until they were alone with Him in the house, and then urged that, if it were as Christ had taught, it would be better not to marry at all. To which Jesus replied, that this saying of the disciples, it is not good to marry, could not be received by all men, but only by those to whom it was given. For, there were three cases in which abstinence from marriage might lawfully be contemplated. In two of these it was natural; and, where it was not so, a man might, for the Kingdom of Heaven's sake, that is, in the service of God and of Christ, have all his thoughts, feelings, and impulses so engaged that others were no longer existent. For, we must here beware of a twofold misunderstanding. It is not bare abstinence from marriage, together, perhaps, with what the German Reformers called immunda continentia (unchaste continency), which is here commended, but such inward preoccupation with the Kingdom of God as would remove all other thoughts and desires. It is this which requires to be given of God; and which he that is able to receive it, who has the moral capacity for it, is called upon to receive. Again, it must not be imagined that this involves any command of celibacy: it only speaks of such who in the active service of the Kingdom feel, that their every thought is so engrossed in the work, that wishes and impulses to marriage are no longer existent in them.

4.   The next incident is recorded by the three Evangelists. It probably occurred in the same house where the disciples had questioned Christ about His teaching on the Divinely sacred relationship of marriage. And

the account of His blessing of infants and little children most aptly follows on the former teaching. It is a scene of unspeakable sweetness and tenderness, where all is in character, unfortunately even the conduct of the disciples as we remember their late inability to sympathize with the teaching of Jesus. And it is all so utterly unlike what Jewish legend would have invented for its Messiah. We can understand how, when One Who so spoke and performed, rested in the house, Jewish mothers should have brought their little children, and some their infants, to Him, that He might touch, put His Hands on them, and pray. What power and holiness must these mothers have believed to be in His touch and prayer; what life to be in, and to come from Him; and what gentleness and tenderness must His have been, when they dared so to bring these little ones! For, how utterly contrary it was to all Jewish notions, and how incompatible with the supposed dignity of a Rabbi, appears from the rebuke of the disciples. It was an occasion and an act when, as the fuller and more pictorial account of Mark inform us, Jesus was much displeased, the only time this strong word is used of Jesus, and said to them: Allow the little children to come to Me, hinder them not, for of such is the Kingdom of God. Then He gently reminded His own disciples of their grave error, by repeating what they had apparently forgotten, that, in order to enter the Kingdom of God, it must be received as by a little child, that here there could be no question of intellectual qualification, nor of distinction due to a great Rabbi, but only of humility, receptiveness, meekness, and a simple application to, and trust in, the Christ. And so He folded these little ones in His Arms, put His Hands upon them, and blessed them, and thus forever consecrated that child life, which a parent's love and faith brought to Him; blessed it also by the laying on of His Hands, as it were, ordained it, as we fully believe to all time, strength because of His enemies.

End Notes:

[84] Any lengthened journeying, and for an indefinite purpose, would have been quite contrary to Jewish manners. Not so, the traveling in the festive band up to the Paschal Feast.

[85] Some have seen in the reference by Luke here, and in the Parable of the Good Samaritan, a peculiarly Pauline trait. But we remember John's reference to the Samaritans (4), and such sentiments in regard to the Gentiles as Matthew 8:11, 12.

[86]   The Talmudic tractate on Divorce, while insisting on its duty in case of sin, closes with the words: He who divorces his first wife, the very altar sheds tears over him (Gitt. 90 b, last lines; comp. Mal. 2:13-16.)

[87]   Two disgusting instances of Rabbis making proclamation of their wish to be married for a day (in a strange place, and then divorced), are mentioned in Yoma 18 b.

[88]   An extraordinary attempt has been made to explain the expression (burns his mess) as meaning brings dishonor upon him. But (1) in the two passages quoted as bearing out this meaning (Ber. 17 b, Sanh. 103 a, second line from bottom), the expression is not the precise equivalent for bringing dishonor, while in both cases the addition of the words in public marks its figurative use. The real meaning of the expression in the two passages referred to is: One who brings into disrepute (destroys) that which has been taught and learned. But (2) in Gitt. 9:10; 90 a; Bemidb. R. 9 there is no indication of any figurative use of the expression, and the commentators explain it, as burning the dish, either by fire or by salt; while (3), the expression is followed by an anti-climax giving permission of divorce if another woman more pleasing were found.

[89]   For, it is not merely to practice outward continence, but to become in mind and heart a eunuch.

Chapter 23

To Leave All For Christ

As we near the goal, the wondrous story seems to grow in tenderness and sorrow. It is as if all the loving condescension of the Master were to be crowded into these days; all the pressing need also, and the human weaknesses of His disciples. And with equal compassion He looks upon the difficulties of them who truly seek to come to Him, and on those which, springing from without, or even from self and sin, overwhelmed them who have already come. Let us try reverently to follow His steps, and learn of His words.

As He was going forth into the way, we owe this trait, as one and another in the same narrative, to Mark, probably in early morning, as He left the house where He had forever folded into His Arms and blessed the children brought to Him by believing parents, His progress was arrested. It was a young man, a ruler, probably of the local Synagogue, who came with all haste, running, and with lowliest gesture [kneeling], to ask what to him, to us all, is the most important question. Remembering that, while we owe to Mark the most graphic touches, Matthew most fully reports the words that had been spoken, we might feel inclined to adopt that reading of them in Matthew which is not only most strongly supported, but at first sight seems to remove some of the difficulties of exposition. This reading would omit in the address of the young ruler the word good before Master, what good thing shall I do that I may inherit eternal life? and would make Christ's reply read: Why do you ask Me concerning the good [that which is good]? There is One Who is good. This would meet not only the objection, that in no recorded instance was a Jewish Rabbi addressed as Good Master, but the obvious difficulties connected with the answer of Christ, according to the common reading: Why do you call Me good? none is good, save only One: God. But on the other side it must be urged, that the undoubted reading of the question and answer in Mark's and Luke's Gospels agrees with that of our KJV, and therefore that any difficulty of exposition would not be removed, only shifted, while the reply of Christ does far better with the words Good Master, the strangeness of such an address from Jewish lips giving only the more reason for taking it up in the reply: Why do you call Me good? none is good save only One: God. Lastly, the designation of God as the only One good agrees with one of the titles given Him in Jewish writings: The Good One of the world.

The actual question of the young Ruler is one which repeatedly occurs in Jewish writings, as put to a Rabbi by his disciples. Amid the different answers given, we scarcely wonder that they also pointed to observance of the Law. And the saying of Christ seems the more adapted to the young Ruler when we recall this sentence from the Talmud: There is nothing else that is good but the Law. But here again the similarity is only of form, not of substance. For, it will do not advantage, that, in the more full account by Matthew, Christ leads the young Ruler upwards through the table of the prohibitions of deeds to the first positive command of deed, and then, by a rapid transition, to the substitution for the tenth commandment in its negative form of this wider positive and all embracing command: You shall love your neighbor as yourself. Any Jewish Ruler, but especially one so earnest, would have at once answered a challenge on the first four commandments by Yes, and that not self righteously, but sincerely, though of course in ignorance of their real depth. And this was not the time for lengthened discussion and instruction; only for rapid awakening, to lead up, if possible, from earnestness and a heart drawing towards the master to real discipleship. Best here to start from what was admitted as binding, the ten commandments, and to lead from that in them which was least likely to be broken, step by step, upwards to that which was most likely to awaken consciousness of sin.

And the young Ruler did not, as that other Pharisee, reply by trying to raise a Rabbinic disputation over the Who is neighbor to me? but in the sincerity of an honest heart answered that he had kept, that is, so far as he knew them, all these things from his youth. On this Matthew puts into his mouth the question, What do I yet lack? Even if, like the other two Evangelists, he had not reported it, we would have supplied this from what follows. There is something intensely earnest, genuine, generous, even enthusiastic, in the higher cravings of the soul in youth, when that youth has not been poisoned by the breath of the world, or stricken with the rottenness of vice. The soul longs for the true, the higher, the better, and, even if strength fails of attainment, we still watch with keen sympathy the form of the climber upwards. Much more must all this have been the case with a Jewish youth, especially in those days; one, besides, like this young Ruler, in whose case affluence of circumstances not only allowed free play, but tended to draw out and to give full scope to the finer feelings, and where wealth was joined with religiousness and the service of a Synagogue. There was not in him that pride of riches, nor the self sufficiency which they so often engender; nor the pride of conscious moral purity and aim after righteousness before God and man; nor yet the pride of the Pharisee or of the Synagogue Ruler. What he had seen and heard of the Christ had quickened to greatest intensity all in him that longed after God and heaven, and had brought him in this supreme moral earnestness, lowly, reverently, to the Feet of Him in Whom, as he felt, all perfectness was, and from Whom all perfectness came. He had not been first drawn to Christ, and from there to the pure, as were the publicans and sinners; but, like so many, even as Peter, when in that hour of soul agony he said: To whom shall we go? You have the words of eternal life, he had been drawn to the pure and the higher, and therefore to Christ. To some the way to Christ is up the Mount of Transfiguration, among the shining Beings of another world; to some it is across dark Kedron, down the deep Garden of Gethsemane with its agonies. What does it matter, if it equally lead to Him, and equally bring the sense of need and experience of pardon to the seeker after the better, and the sense of need and experience of holiness to the seeker after pardon?

And Jesus saw it all: down, through that intense upward look; inwards, through that question, What do I yet lack? far deeper down than that young man had ever seen into his own heart, even into depths of weakness and need which he had never sounded, and which must be filled, if he would enter the Kingdom of Heaven. Jesus saw what he lacked; and what He saw, He showed him. For, looking at him in his sincerity and earnestness, He loved him, as He loves those that are His Own. One thing was needful for this young man: that he should not only become His disciple, but that, in so doing, he should come and follow Christ. We can all perceive how, for one like this young man, such absolute and entire coming and following Christ was needful. And again, to do this, it was in the then circumstances both of this young man and of Christ necessary, that he should go and part with all that he had. And what was an outward, was also, as we perceive it, an inward necessity; and so, as ever, Providence and Grace would work together. For, to many of us some outward step is often not merely the means of but absolutely needful for, spiritual decision. To some it is the first open profession of Christ; to others, the first act of self denial, or the first distinct No saying; to some, it may be, it is the first prayer, or else the first act of self consecration. Yet it seems, as if it needed not only the word of God but a stroke of some Moses rod to make the water gush forth from the rock. And thus would this young Ruler have been perfect; and what he had given to the poor had become, not through merit nor by way of reward, but really treasure in heaven.

What he lacked, was earth's poverty and heaven's riches; a heart fully set on following Christ: and this could only come to him through willing surrender of all. And so this was to him the means, the test, and the need. To him it was this; to us it may be something quite other. Yet each of us has a lack, something quite deep down in our hearts, which we may never yet have known, and which we must know and give up, if we would follow Christ. And without forsaking, there can be no following. This is the law of the Kingdom, and it is such, because we are sinners, because sin is not only the loss of the good, but the possession of something else in its place.

There is something deeply pathetic in the mode in which Mark describes it: he was sad, the word painting a dark gloom that overshadowed the face of the young man. Did he then not lack it, this one thing? We need scarcely here recall the almost extravagant language in which Rabbinism describes the miseries of poverty; we can understand his feelings without that. Such a possibility had never entered his mind: the thought of it was terribly startling. That he must come and follow Christ, then and there, and in order to do so, sell all that he had and give it away among the poor, and be poor himself, a beggar, that he might have treasure in heaven; and that this should come to him as the one thing needful from that Master in Whom he believed, from Whose lips he would learn the one thing needful, and who but a little before had been to him the All in All! It was a terrible surprise, a sentence of death to his life, and of life to his death. And that it should come from His lips, at Whose Feet he had run to kneel, and Who held for him the keys of eternal life! Rabbinism had never asked this; if it demanded almsgiving, it was in odious boastfulness; while it was declared even unlawful to give away all ones possessions, at most, only a fifth of them might be dedicated.

And so, with clouded face he gazed down into what he lacked, within; but also gazed up in Christ on what he needed. And, although we hear no more of him, who that day went back to his rich home very poor, because very sorrowful, we cannot but believe that he, whom Jesus loved, yet found in the poverty of earth the treasure of heaven.

Nor was this all. The deep pity of Christ for him, who had gone that day, speaks also in his warning to his disciples. But surely those are not only riches in the literal sense which make it so difficult for a man to enter into the Kingdom of Heaven—so difficult, as to amount almost to that impossibility which was expressed in the common Jewish proverb, that a man did not even in his dreams see an elephant pass through the eye of a needle. But when in their perplexity the disciples put to each other the saddened question: Who then can be saved? He pointed them onward, then upward, as well as inward, teaching them that, what was impossible of achievement by man in his own strength, God would work by His Almighty Grace.

It almost jars on our ears, and prepares us for still stranger and sadder to come, when Peter, perhaps as spokesman of the rest, seems to remind Jesus that they had forsaken all to follow Him. Matthew records also the special question which Simon added to it: What shall we have therefore? and therefore his Gospel alone makes mention of Jesus' reply, in so far as it applied only to the Apostles. For, that reply really bore on two points: on the reward which all who left everything to follow Christ would obtain; and on the special acknowledgment awaiting the Apostles of Christ. In regard to the former we mark, that it is twofold. They who had forsaken all for His sake and the Gospels, for the Kingdom of God's sake, and these three expressions explain and supplement each other—would receive in this time manifold more of new, and better, and closer relationships of a spiritual kind for those which they had surrendered, although, as Mark significantly adds, to prevent all possible mistakes, with persecutions. But by the side of this stands out unclouded and bright the promise for the world to come of everlasting life. As regarded the Apostles personally, some mystery lies on the special promise to them. We could quite understand, that the distinction of rule to be bestowed on them might have been worded in language taken from the expectations of the time, in order to make the promise intelligible to them. But, unfortunately, we have no explanatory information to offer. The Rabbis, speak of a renovation or regeneration of the world which was to take place after the 7,000 or else 5,000 years of the Messianic reign. Such a renewal of all things is not only foretold by the prophets, and dwelt upon in later Jewish writings, but frequently referred to in Rabbinic literature. But as regards the special rule or judgment of the Apostles, or ambassadors of the Messiah, we do not have, and cannot expect any parallel in Jewish writings. That the promise of such rule and judgment to the Apostles is not peculiar to what is called the Judaic Gospel of Matthew, appears from its renewal at a later period, as recorded by Luke. Lastly, that it is in accordance with Old Testament promise, will be seen by a reference to Daniel 5:9, 10, 14, 27; and there are few references in the New Testament to the blessed consummation of all things in which such renewal of the world, and even the rule and judgment of the representatives of the Church, are not referred to. However mysterious, therefore, in their details, these things seem clear, and may without undue curiosity or presumption be regarded as the teaching of Jesus: the renewal of earth; the share in His rule and judgment which He will in the future give to His saints; the special distinction which He will bestow on His Apostles, corresponding to the special gifts, privileges, and rule with which He had endowed them on earth, and to their nearness to, and their work and sacrifices for Him; and, lastly, we may add, the preservation of Israel as a distinct, probably tribal, nation. As for the rest, as so much else, it is behind the veil, and, even as we see it, better for the Church that the veil has not been further lifted.

The reference to the blessed future with its rewards was followed by a Parable, recorded, as, with one exception, all of that series, only by Matthew. It will best be considered in connection with the last series of Christ's Parables. But it was accompanied by what, in the circumstances, was also a most needful warning. Thoughts of the future Messianic reign, its glory, and their own part in it might have so engrossed the minds of the disciples as to make them forgetful of the terrible present, immediately before them. In such case they might not only have lapsed into that most fatal Jewish error of a Messiah King, Who was not Savior, the Crown without the Cross, but have even suffered shipwreck of their faith, when the storm broke on the Day of His Condemnation and Crucifixion. If ever, it was most needful in that hour of elation to remind and forewarn them of what was to be expected in the immediate future. How truly such preparation was required by the disciples, appears from the narrative itself.

There was something sadly mysterious in the words with which Christ had closed His Parable, that the last should be first and the first last, and it had carried dark misgivings to those who heard it. And now it seemed all so strange! Yet the disciples could not have indulged in illusions. His own sayings on at least two previous occasions, however ill or partially understood, must have led them to expect at any rate grievous opposition and tribulations in Jerusalem, and their endeavour to deter Christ from going to Bethany to raise Lazarus proves, that they were well aware of the danger which threatened Jesus in Judea. Yet not only was He now going up to Jerusalem, but there was that in His bearing which was quite unusual. As Mark writes, He was going before them, we infer, apart and alone, as One, busy with thoughts all engrossing, Who is setting Himself to do His great work, and goes to meet it. And going before them was Jesus; and they were amazed [utterly bewildered, namely the Apostles]; and those who were following, were afraid. It was then that Jesus took the Apostles apart, and in language more precise than ever before, told them how all things that were written by the prophets shall be accomplished on the Son of Man, not merely, that all that had been written concerning the Son of Man should be accomplished, but a far deeper truth, all comprehensive as regards the Old Testament: that all its true prophecy ran up into the sufferings of the Christ. As the three Evangelists report it, Jesus gave them full details of His Betrayal, Crucifixion, and Resurrection.

And yet we may, without irreverence, doubt whether on that occasion He had really entered into all those particulars. In such case it would seem difficult to explain how, as Luke reports, they understood none of these things, and the saying was hid from them, neither knew they the things which were spoken; and again, how afterwards the actual events and the Resurrection could have taken them so by surprise. Rather do we think, that the Evangelists report what Jesus had said in the light of after events. He did tell them of His Betrayal by the leaders of Israel, and that into the hands of the Gentiles; of His death and Resurrection on the third day, yet in language which they could, and actually did, misunderstand at the time, but which, when viewed in the light of what really happened, was perceived by them to have been actual prediction of those terrible days in Jerusalem and of the Resurrection morning. At the time they may have thought that it pointed only to His rejection by Jews and Gentiles, to Sufferings and death, and then to a Resurrection, either of His Mission or to such a reappearance of the Messiah, after His temporary disappearance, as Judaism expected.

But all this time, and with increasing fierceness, were terrible thoughts contending in the breast of Judas; and beneath the tramp of that fight was there only a thin covering of earth, to hide and keep from bursting forth the hellish fire of the master passion within.

One other incident, more strange and sad than any that had preceded, and the Perean stay is forever ended. It almost seems, as if the fierce blast of temptation, the very breath of the destroyer, was already sweeping over the little flock, as if the twilight of the night of betrayal and desertion were already falling around. And now it has fallen on the two chosen disciples, James and John, the sons of thunder, and one of them, the beloved disciple! Peter, the third in that band most closely bound to Christ, had already had his fierce temptation, and would have it more fiercely, to the uprooting of life, if the Great High Priest had not especially interceded for him. And, as regards these two sons of Zebedee and of Salome, we know what temptation had already come to them, how John had forbidden one to cast out devils, because he did not follow with them, and how both he and his brother, James, would have called down fire from heaven to consume the Samaritans who would not receive Christ. It was essentially the same spirit that now prompted the request which their mother Salome offered, not only with their full concurrence, but, as we are expressly told, with their active participation. There is the same faith in the Christ, the same allegiance to Him, but also the same unhallowed earnestness, the same misunderstanding, and, let us add, the same latent self exaltation, as in the two former instances, in the present request that, as the most honored of His guests, and also as the nearest to Him, they might have their places at His Right Hand and at His Left in His Kingdom. Terribly incongruous as is any appearance of self seeking at that moment and with that prospect before them, we cannot but feel that there is also an intenseness of faith and absoluteness of love almost magnificent, when the mother steps forth from among those who follow Christ to His Suffering and death, to offer such a request with her sons, and for them.

And so Jesus seems to have viewed it. With unspeakable patience and tenderness, He, Whose Soul is filled with the terrible contest before Him, bears with the weakness and selfishness which could cherish such thoughts and ambitions even at such a time. To correct them, He points to that near prospect, when the Highest is to be made low. You do not know what you ask! The King is to be King through suffering, are they aware of the road which leads to that goal? Those nearest to the King of sorrows must reach the place nearest to Him by the same road as He. Are they prepared for it; prepared to drink that cup of soul agony, which the Father will hand to Him, to submit to, to descend into that baptism of consecration, when the floods will sweep over Him? In their ignorance, and listening only to the promptings of their hearts, they imagine that they are. In some measure it would be so; yet, finally to correct their mistake: to sit at His Right and at His Left Hand, these were not marks of mere favor for Him to bestow, in His own words: it is not Mine to give except to them for whom it is prepared of My Father.

But as for the other ten, when they heard of it, it was only the pre-eminence which, in their view, James and John had sought, which stood out before them, to their envy, jealousy, and indignation. And so, in that tremendously solemn hour would the fierce fire of controversy have broken out among them, who should have been most closely united; would jealousy and ambition have filled those who should have been most humble, and fierce passions, born of self, the world and Satan, have distracted them, whom the thought of the great love and the great sacrifice should have filled. It was the rising of that storm on the sea, the noise and tossing of those angry billows, which He hushed into silence when He spoke to them of the grand contrast between the princes of the Gentiles as they lord it over them, or the great among them as they domineer over men, and their own aims, how, whoever would be great among them, must seek his greatness in service, not greatness through service, but the greatness of service; and, whosever would be chief or rather first among them, let it be in service. And had it not been thus, was it not, would it not be so in the Son of Man, and must it not therefore be so in them who would be nearest to Him, even His Apostles and disciples? The Son of Man, let them look back, let them look forward, He came not to be ministered to, but to minister. And then, breaking through the reserve that had held Him, and revealing to them the inmost thoughts which had occupied Him when He had been alone and apart, going before them on the way, He spoke for the first time fully what was the deepest meaning of His Life, Mission, and death: to give His Life a ransom for many, to pay with His Life Blood the price of their redemption, to lay down His Life for them: in their place and stead, and for their salvation.

These words must have sunk deep into the heart of one at least in that company. A few days later, and the beloved disciple tells us of this Ministry of His Love at the Last Supper, and ever afterwards, in his writings or in his life, does he seem to bear them about with him, and to re-echo them. Ever since also have they remained the foundation truth, on which the Church has been built: the subject of her preaching, and the object of her experience.

End Notes:

[90]   Of course, the expression twelve thrones (Matthew 19:28) must not be pressed to utmost literality, or it might be asked whether Paul or Matthias occupied the place of Judas. On the other hand, neither must it be frittered

away, as if the regeneration referred only to the Christian dispensation, and to spiritual relations under it.

[91]   It is very remarkable that, in Matthew 20:20, she bears the unusual title: the mother of Zebedee's children (comp. also for the mention of Zebedee, Mark x. 35). This, evidently, to emphasize that the distinction was not asked on the ground of earthly kinship, as through Salome, who was the aunt of Jesus.

[92]   I have chosen these two words because the verbs in the Greek (which are the same in the two Gospels) express not ordinary dominion and authority, but a forcible and tyrannical exercise of it. The first verb occurs again in Acts 19:16, and 1 Peter 5:3; the second only in this passage in the Gospels.

Chapter 24

In Jericho and Bethany

Once more, and now for the last time, were the fords of Jordan passed, and Christ was on the soil of Judea proper. Behind Him were Perea and Galilee; behind Him the Ministry of the Gospel by Word and Deed; before Him the final Act of His Life, towards which all had consciously tended. Rejected as the Messiah of His people, not only in His Person but as regarded the Kingdom of God, which, in fulfillment of prophecy and of the merciful Counsel of God, He had come to establish, He was of set purpose going up to Jerusalem, there to accomplish His death, to give His Life a Ransom for many. And He was coming, not, as at the Feast of Tabernacles, privately, but openly, at the head of His Apostles, and followed by many disciples, a festive band going up to the Paschal Feast, of which Himself was to be the Lamb of sacrifice.

The first station reached was Jericho, the City of Palms, a distance of only about six hours from Jerusalem. The ancient City occupied not the site of the present wretched hamlet, but lay about half an hour to the northwest of it, by the so called Elisha Spring. A second spring rose an hour further to the north northwest. The water of these springs, distributed by aqueducts, gave, under a tropical sky, unsurpassed fertility to the rich soil along the plain of Jericho, which is about twelve or fourteen miles wide. The Old Testament history of the City of Palms is sufficiently known. It was here also that King Zedekiah had, on his flight, been seized by the Chaldeans, and there a company of 345 men returned under Zerubbabel. In the war of liberation under the Maccabees the Syrians had attempted to fortify Jericho. These forts were afterwards destroyed by Pompey in his campaign. Herod the Great had first plundered, and then partially rebuilt, fortified, and adorned Jericho. It was here that he died. His son Archelaus also built there a palace. At the time of which we write, it was under Roman dominion. Long before, it had recovered its ancient fame for fertility and its prosperity. Josephus describes it as the richest part of the country, and calls it a little Paradise. Antony had bestowed the revenues of its balsam plantations as an Imperial gift upon Cleopatra, who in turn sold them to Herod. Here grew palm trees of various kinds, sycamores, the cypress flower, the myrobalsamum, which yielded precious oil, but especially the balsam plant. If to these advantages of climate, soil, and productions we add, that it was, so to speak, the key of Judea towards the east, that it lay on the caravan road from Damascus and Arabia, that it was a great commercial and military center, and lastly, its nearness to Jerusalem, to which it formed the last station on the road of the festive pilgrims from Galilee and Perea, it will not be difficult to understand either its importance or its prosperity.

We can picture to ourselves the scene, as Jesus on that afternoon in early spring beheld it. There it was, already summer, for, as Josephus tells us, even in winter the inhabitants could only bear the lightest clothing of linen. We are approaching it from the Jordan. It is protected by walls, flanked by four forts. These walls, the theater, and the amphitheater, have been built by Herod; the new palace and its splendid gardens are the work of Archelaus. All around wave groves of feathery palms, rising in stately beauty; stretch gardens of roses, and especially sweet scented balsam plantations, the largest behind the royal gardens, of which the perfume is carried by the wind almost out to sea, and which may have given to the city its name (Jericho, the perfumed). It is the Eden of Palestine, the very fairyland of the old world. And how strangely is this gem set! Deep down in that hollowed valley, through which tortuous Jordan winds, to lose his waters in the slimy mass of the Sea of Judgment. The river and the Dead Sea are nearly equidistant from the town, about six miles. Far across the river rise the mountains of Moab, on which lies the purple and violet coloring. Towards Jerusalem and northwards stretch those bare limestone hills, the hiding place of robbers along the desolate road towards the City. There, and in the neighboring wilderness of Judea, are also the lonely dwellings of anchorites, while over all this strangely varied scene has been flung the many colored mantle of a perpetual summer. And in the streets of Jericho a motley throng meets: pilgrims from Galilee and Perea, priests who have a station here, traders from all lands, who have come to purchase or to sell, or are on the great caravan road from Arabia and Damascus, robbers and anchorites, wild fanatics, soldiers, courtiers, and busy publicans, for Jericho was the central station for the collection of tax and custom, both on native produce and on that brought from across Jordan. And yet it was a place for dreaming also, under that glorious summer sky, in those scented groves, when these many figures from far off lands and that crowd of priests, numbering, according to tradition, half those in Jerusalem, seemed fleeting as in a vision, and (as Jewish legend had it) the sound of Temple music came from Moriah, borne in faint echoes on the breeze, like the distant sound of many waters.

It was through Jericho that Jesus, having entered, was passing. Tidings of the approach of the festive band, consisting of His disciples and Apostles, and headed by Jesus Himself, must have preceded Him, these six miles from the fords of Jordan. His Name, His Works, His Teaching, perhaps Himself, must have been known to the people of Jericho, just as they must have been aware of the feelings of the leaders of the people, perhaps of the approaching great contest between them and the Prophet of Nazareth. Was He a good man; had He performed those great miracles in the power of God or by Satanic influence, was He the Messiah or the Antichrist; would He bring salvation to the world, or entail ruin on His own nation? Conquer or be destroyed? Was it only one more in the long list of delusions and illusions, or was the long promised morning of heaven's own day at last to break? Close by was Bethany, from which news had come; most incredible yet unquestioned and unquestionable, of the raising of Lazarus, so well known to all in that neighborhood. And yet the Sanhedrin, it was well known, had resolved on His death! At any rate there was no concealment about Him; and here, in face of all, and accompanied by His followers, humble and unlettered, it must be admitted, but thoroughly convinced of His superhuman claims, and deeply attached, Jesus was going up to Jerusalem to meet His enemies!

It was the custom, when a festive band passed through a place, that the inhabitants gathered in the streets to bid their brethren welcome. And on that afternoon, surely, scarce anyone in Jericho but would go forth to see this pilgrim band. Men, curious, angry, half convinced; women, holding up their babes, it may be for a passing blessing, or pushing forward their children that in after years they might say they had seen the Prophet of Nazareth; traders, soldiers, a solid wall of onlookers before their gardens was this crowd along the road by which Jesus was to pass. Would He only pass through the place, or be the guest of some of the leading priests in Jericho; would He teach, or work any miracle, or silently go on His way to Bethany? Only one in all that crowd seemed unwelcome; alone, and out of place. It was the chief of the Publicans, the head of the tax and customs department. As his name shows, he was a Jew; but yet that very name Zaccheus, Zakkai, the just, or pure, sounded like mockery. We know in what repute Publicans were held, and what opportunities of wrong doing and oppression they possessed. And from his after confession it is only too evident, that Zaccheus had to the full used them for evil. And he had got that for which he had given up his nation and his soul: he was rich. If, as Christ had taught, it was harder for any rich man to enter the Kingdom of Heaven than for a camel to pass through the eye of a needle, what of him who had gotten his riches by such means?

And yet Zaccheus was in the crowd that had come to see Jesus. What had brought him? Certainly, not curiosity only. Was it the long working of conscience; or a dim, scarcely self avowed hope of something better; or had he heard Him before; or of Him, that He was so unlike those harsh leaders and teachers of Israel, who refused all hope on earth and in heaven to such as him, that Jesus received called to Him the publicans and sinners? Or was it only the nameless, deep, irresistible inward drawing of the Holy Spirit, which may perhaps have brought us, as it has brought many, we do not know why or how, to the place and hour of eternal decision for God, and of infinite grace to our souls? Certain it is, that, as so often in such circumstances, Zaccheus encountered only hindrances which seemed to render his purpose almost impossible. The narrative is singularly detailed and pictorial. Zaccheus, trying to push his way through the press, and repulsed; Zaccheus, little of stature, and unable to look over the shoulders of others: it reads almost like a symbolical story of one who is seeking to see Jesus, but cannot push his way because of the crowd, whether of the self righteous, or of his own conscious sins, that seem to stand between him and Jesus, and which will not make room for him, while he is unable to look over them because he is, so to speak, little of stature.

Needless questions have been asked as to the import of Zaccheus wish to see who Jesus was. It is just this vagueness of desire, which Zaccheus himself does not understand, which is characteristic. And, since he cannot otherwise succeed, he climbs up one of those wide spreading sycamores in a garden, perhaps close to his own house, along the only road by which Jesus can pass, to see Him. Now the band is approaching, through that double living wall: first, Jesus, viewing that crowd, with, ah! how different thoughts from theirs, surrounded by His Apostles, the face of each expressive of such feelings as were uppermost; conspicuous among them, he who carried the bag, with furtive, uncertain, wild glance here and there, as one who seeks to gather himself up to a terrible deed. Behind them are the disciples, men and women, who are going up with Him to the Feast. Of all persons in that crowd the least noted, the most hindered in coming, and yet the one most concerned, was the Chief Publican. It is always so, it is ever the order of the Gospel, that the last shall be first. Yet never more self unconscious was Zaccheus than at the moment when Jesus was entering that garden road, and passing under the overhanging branches of that sycamore, the crowd closing up behind, and following as He went along. Only one thought, without ulterior conscious object, temporal or spiritual, filled his whole being. The present absolutely held him, when those wondrous Eyes, out of which heaven itself seemed to look upon earth, were upturned, and that Face of infinite grace, never to be forgotten, beamed upon him the welcome of recognition, and He uttered the self spoken invitation in which the invited was the real Inviter, the guest the true Host. Did Jesus know Zaccheus before—or was it only all open to His Divine gaze as He looked up and saw him? This latter seems, indicated by the must of His abiding in the house of Zaccheus, as if His Father had so appointed it, and Jesus come for that very purpose. And herein, also, seems this story spiritually symbolical.

As invited by Christ, Zaccheus made haste and came down. Under the gracious influence of the Holy Spirit he received Him rejoicing. Nothing was as yet clear to him, and yet all was joyous within his soul. In that dim twilight of the new day, and at this new creation, the Angels sang and the Son's of God shouted together, and all was melody and harmony in his heart. But a few steps farther, and they were at the house of the Chief Publican. Strange hostelry this for the Lord; yet not stranger in that Life of absolute contrasts than that first hostelry, the same, even as regards its designation in the Gospel, as when the manager had been His cradle; not so strange, as at the Sabbath feast of the Pharisee Rulers of the Synagogue. But now the murmur of disappointment and anger ran through the accompanying crowd, which perhaps had not before heard what had passed between Jesus and the Publican, certainly, had not understood, or else not believed its import, because He was gone to be guest with a man who was a sinner. Oh, terribly fatal misunderstanding of all that was characteristic of the Mission of the Christ! Oh, terribly fatal blindness and jealousy! But it was this sudden shock of opposition which awoke Zaccheus to full consciousness. The hands so rudely and profanely thrust forward only served to rend the veil. It often needs some such sudden shock of opposition, some sudden sharp contest, to awaken the new convert to full consciousness, to bring before him, in clear outline, the past and the present. In that moment Zaccheus saw it all: what his past had been, what his present was, what his future must be. Standing forth, not so much before the crowd as before the Lord, and not ashamed scarcely conscious of the confession it implied, so much is the sorrow of the past in true repentance swallowed up by the joy of the present, Zaccheus vowed fourfold restoration, as by a thief, of what had become his through false accusation, as well as the half of all his goods to the poor. And so the whole current of his life had been turned, in those few moments, through his joyous reception of Christ, the Savior of sinners; and Zaccheus the public robber, the rich Chief of the Publicans, had become an almsgiver.

It was then, when it had been all done in silence, as mostly all God's great works, that Jesus spoke it to him, for his endless comfort, and in the hearing of all, for their and our teaching: This day became, arose, there salvation to this house, forasmuch as, truly and spiritually, this one also is a son of Abraham. And, as regards this man, and all men, so long as time endures: For the Son of Man came to seek and to save that which was lost.

The Evangelistic record passes with significant silence over that night in the house of Zaccheus. It forms not part of the public history of the Kingdom of God, but of that joy with which a stranger does not meddle. It was in the morning, when the journey in company with His disciples was resumed, that the next public incident occurred in the healing of the blind by the wayside. The small divergences in the narratives of the three Evangelists are well known. It may have been that, as Matthew relates, there were two blind men sitting by the wayside, and that Luke and Mark mention only one, the latter by name as Bar Timaeus, because he was the spokesman. But, in regard to the other divergence, trifling as it is, that Luke places the incident at the arrival, the other two Evangelists at the departure of Jesus from Jericho, it is better to admit our inability to reconcile these differing notes of time, than to make clumsy attempts at harmonizing them. We can readily believe that there may have been circumstances unknown to us, which might show these statements to not be really diverging. And, if it were otherwise, it would in no way affect the narrative itself. Historical information could only have been derived from local sources; and we have already seen reason to infer that Luke had gathered his from personal inquiry on the spot. And it may have been, either that the time was not noted, or wrongly noted, or that this miracle, as the only one in Jericho, may have been reported to him before mention was made of the reception by Christ of Zaccheus. In any case, it shows the independence of the account of Luke from that of the other two Evangelists.

Little need be said of the incident itself: it is so like the other Deeds of His Life. So to speak, it was left in Jericho as the practical commentary, and the seal on what Christ had said and done the previous evening in regard to Zaccheus. Once more the crowd was following Jesus, as in the morning He resumed the journey with His disciples. And, there by the wayside, begging, sat the blind men, there, where Jesus was passing. As they heard the tramp of many feet and the sound of many voices, they learned that Jesus of Nazareth was passing by. It is all deeply touching, and deeply symbolical. But what must their faith have been, when there, in Jericho, they not only owned Him as the true Messiah, but cried, in the deep significance of that special mode of address, as coming from Jewish lips: Jesus, You Son of David, have mercy on me! It was quite in accordance with what one might almost have expected, certainly with the temper of Jericho, as we learned it on the previous evening, when many, the multitude, they which went before, would have invited that cry for help be silent as an unwarrantable intrusion and interruption, if not a needless and meaningless application. But only all the louder and more earnest rose the cry, as the blind felt that they might forever be robbed of the opportunity that was slipping past. And He, Who listens to every cry of distress, heard this. He stood still, and commanded the blind to be called. Then it was that the sympathy of sudden hope seized the multitude the wonder about to be performed fell, so to speak, in its heavenly influences upon them, as they comforted the blind in the agony of rising despair with the words, He calls you. As so often, we are indebted to Mark for the vivid sketch of what passed. We can almost see Bartimaeus as, on receiving Christ's summons, he tosses aside his upper garment and hastily comes. That question: what would he that Jesus should do to him, must have been meant for those around more than for the blind. The cry to the son of David had been only for mercy. It might have been for alms, though, as the address, so the gift bestowed in answer, would be right royal, after the order of David. But our general cry for mercy must ever become detailed when we come into the Presence of the Christ. And the faith of the blind rose to the full height of the Divine possibilities opened before them. Their inward eyes had received capacity for The Light, before that of earth lit up their long darkness. In the language of Matthew, Jesus had compassion on them and touched their eyes. This is one aspect of it. The other is that given by Mark and Luke, in recording the words with which He accompanied the healing: Your faith has saved you.

And these two results came of it: all the people, when they saw it gave praise to God; and, as for Bartimaeus, though Jesus had invited him go your way, yet, immediately he received his sight, he followed Jesus in the way, glorifying God. And this is Divine disobedience, or rather the obedience of the spirit as against the observance of the letter.

The arrival of the Paschal band from Galilee and Perea was not in advance of many others. In truth, most pilgrims from a distance would probably come to the Holy City some days before the Feast, for the sake of purification in the Temple, since those who for any reason needed such, and there would be few families that did not require it, generally deferred it until the festive season brought them to Jerusalem. We owe this notice, and that which follows, to John, and in this again recognize the Jewish writer of the Fourth Gospel. It was only natural that these pilgrims should have sought for Jesus, and, when they did not find Him, discuss among themselves the probability of His coming to the Feast. His absence would, after the work which He had done these three years, the claim which He made, and the defiant denial of it by the priesthood and the Sanhedrin, have been regarded as a virtual surrender to the enemy. There was a time when He need not have appeared at the Feast, when, as we see it, it was better He should not come. But that time was past. The chief priests and the Pharisees also knew it, and they had given commandment that, if anyone knew where He was, he would show it, that they might take Him. It would be better to ascertain where He lodged, and to seize Him before He appeared in public, in the Temple.

But it was not as they had imagined. Without concealment Christ came to Bethany, where Lazarus lived, whom He had raised from the dead. He came there six days before the Passover, and yet His coming was such that they could not take Him. They might as well take Him in the Temple; more easily. For, the moment His stay in Bethany became known, many people of the Jews came out, not only for His sake, but to see that Lazarus whom He had raised from the dead. And, of those who so came, many went away believing. And how, could it be otherwise? Thus one of their plans was frustrated, and the evil seemed only to grow worse. The Sanhedrin could perhaps not be moved to such flagrant outrage of all Jewish Law, but the chief priests, who had no such scruples, consulted how they might put Lazarus also to death.

Yet, not until His hour had come could man do anything whatever against Christ or His disciples. And, in contrast to such scheming, haste and search, we mark the majestic calm and quiet of Him Who knew what was before Him. Jesus had arrived at Bethany six days before the Passover, that is, on a Friday. The day after was the Sabbath, and they made Him a supper. It was the special festive meal of the Sabbath. The words of John seem to indicate that the meal was a public one, as if the people of Bethany had combined to do Him this honor, and so share the privilege of attending the feast. In point of fact, we know from Matthew and Mark that it took place in the house of Simon the Leper, not an actual leper, but one who had been such. Perhaps his guest chamber was the largest in Bethany; perhaps the house was nearest to the Synagogue; or there may have been other reasons for it, unknown to us, least likely is the suggestion that Simon was the husband of Martha, or else her father. But all is in character. Among the guests is Lazarus: and, prominent in service, Martha; and Mary (the unnamed woman of the other two Gospels, which do not mention that household by name), is also true to her character. She had an alabaster of genuine spikenard, which was very precious. It held a litra which was a Roman pound, and its value could not have been less than nearly 9l. Remembering the price of Nard, as given by Pliny, and that the Syrian was only next in value to the Indian, which Pliny regarded as the best ointment of genuine Nard, unadulterated and unmixed with any other balsam (as the less expensive kinds were), such a price (300 dinars = nearly 9l.) would be by no means excessive; indeed, much lower than at Rome. But, viewed in another light, the sum spent was very large, remembering that 200 dinars (about 6l.) nearly sufficed to provide bread for 5,000 men with their families, and that the ordinary wages of a laborer amounted to only one dinar a day.

We can here offer only conjectures. But it is, at least, not unreasonable to suppose, remembering the fondness of Jewish women for such perfumes, that Mary may have had that alabaster of very costly ointment for a long time, before she had learned to serve Christ. Then, when she came to know Him, and must have learned how constantly that death, of which He ever spoke, was before His Mind, she may have put it aside, kept it, for the day of His burying. And now the decisive hour had come. Jesus may have told her, as He had told the disciples, what was before Him in Jerusalem at the Feast, and she would be far more quick to understand, even as she must have known far better than they, how great was the danger from the Sanhedrin. And it is this believing apprehension of the mystery of His death on her part, and this preparation of deepest love for it, this mixture of sorrow, faith, and devotion, which made her deed so precious, that, wherever in the future the Gospel would be preached, this also that she had done would be recorded for a memorial of her. And the more we think of it, the better can we understand, how at that last feast of fellowship, when all the other guests did not realize, no, not even His disciples, how near the end was, she would come beforehand to anoint His Body for the burying. Her faith made it a twofold anointing: that of the best Guest at the last feast, and that of preparation for that Burial which, of all others, she apprehended as so terribly near. And deepest humility now offered, what most earnest love had provided, and intense faith, in view of what was coming, applied. And so she poured the precious ointment over His Head, over His Feet, then, stooping over them, wiped them with her hair, as if, not only in evidence of service and love, but in fellowship of His death. And the house was filled and to all time His House, the Church, is filled, with the odor of the ointment.

It is ever the light which throws the shadows of objects, and this deed of faith and love now cast the features of Judas in gigantic dark outlines against the scene. He knew the nearness of Christ's Betrayal, and hated the more; she knew of the nearness of His precious death, and loved the more. It was not that he cared for the poor, when, taking the mask of charity, he simulated anger that such costly ointment had not been sold, and the price given to the poor. For he was essentially dishonest, a thief, and covetousness was the underlying master passion of his soul. The money, claimed for the poor, would only have been used by himself. Yet such was his pretence of righteousness, such his influence as a man of prudence among the disciples, and such their sad weakness, that they, or at least some, expressed indignation among themselves and against her who had done the deed of love, which, when viewed in the magnificentness of a faith, that accepted and prepared for the death of a Savior Whom she so loved, and to Whom this last, the best service she could, was to be devoted, would forever cause her to be though of as an example of loving. There is something inexpressibly sad, yet so patient, gentle, and tender in Christ's Let her alone. Surely, never could there be waste in ministry of love to Him! There is unspeakable pathos in what He says of His near burying, as if He would still their souls in view of it. That He, Who was ever of the poor and with them, Who for our sakes became poor, that through His poverty we might be made rich, should have to plead for a last service of love to Himself, and for Mary, and as against a Judas, seems indeed, the depth of self abasement. Yet, even so, has this falsely spoken plea for the poor become a real plea, since He has left us this, as it were, as His last charge, and that by His own death, that we have the poor always with us.

And so do even the words of covetous dishonesty become, when passing across Him, transformed into the command of charity, and the breath of hell is changed into the summer warmth of the Church's constant service to Christ in the ministry to His poor.

End Notes:

[93] The word here used is katalo, and the hostelry at Bethlehem (Luke 2:7) was katluma.

[94] Literally, if I have politically flattered any man anything. It should be remarked, as making this restoration by Zaccheus the more intelligible, that to a penitent Jew this would immediately occur. In the Talmud there is a long discussion as to restoration by penitents in cases where the misappropriation was open to question, when the Talmud lays down the principle, that if anyone wishes to escape the Divine punishment, he must restore even that which, according to strict justice, he might not be obliged to give up (Baba Mez. 37 a).

[95] These alabasters, for the flask itself obtained that name from the stone used, had at the top the form of a cylinder, and are likened by Pliny to a closed rose bud.

[96] John. There is manifestly neither contradiction nor divergence here between the Evangelists. Mary first poured the nard over the Head, and then over His Feet (Godet sees this implied in the katcheen ato of Mark). John notices the anointing of the Feet, not only as the act of greatest humility and the mark of deepest veneration, but from its unusual character, while anointing of the head was not so uncommon. We recall the ideal picture of Aaron when anointed to the priesthood, Psalm 133:2, to mark here the fulfillment of the type when the Great High Priest was anointed for His Sacrifice. She who had so often sat at His feet, now anoints them, and for love, reverence, and fellowship of His sufferings, will not wipe them but with her hair.

Book 5

THE CROSS AND THE CROWN

Chapter 1

Palm Sunday and the Royal Entry Into Jerusalem

At length the time of the end had come. Jesus was about to make Entry into Jerusalem as King: King of the Jews, as Heir of David's royal line, with all of symbolic, typic, and prophetic import attaching to it. Yet not as Israel after the flesh expected its Messiah was the Son of David to make triumphal entrance, but as deeply and significantly expressive of His Mission and Work, and as of old the absorbed seer had seen far off the outlined picture of the Messiah King: not in the proud triumph of war conquests, but in the meek rule of peace.

It is surely one of the strangest mistakes of modern criticism to regard this Entry of Christ into Jerusalem as implying that, fired by enthusiasm, He had for the moment expected that the people would receive Him as the Messiah. And it seems little, if at all better, when this Entry is described as an apparent concession to the fevered expectations of His disciples and the multitude . . . the grave, sad accommodation to thoughts other than His own to which the Teacher of new truths must often have recourse when He finds Himself misinterpreted by those who stand together on a lower level. Apologies are the weakness of Apologetics, and any accommodation theory can have no place in the history of the Christ. On the contrary, we regard His Royal Entry into the Jerusalem of Prophecy and of the Crucifixion as an integral part of the history of Christ, which would not be complete, nor thoroughly consistent, without it. It was necessary for Him to so enter Jerusalem, because He was a King; and as King to enter it in such manner, because He was such a King, and both the one and the other were in accordance with the prophecy of old.

It was a bright day in early spring of the year 29, when the festive procession set out from the home at Bethany. There can be no reasonable doubt as to the locality of that hamlet (the modern El Azariye, of Lazarus), perched on a broken rocky plateau on the other side of Olivet. More difficulty attaches to the identification of Bethphage, which is associated with it, the place not being mentioned in the Old Testament, though repeatedly in Jewish writings. But, even so, there is a curious contradiction, since Bethphage is sometimes spoken of as distinct from Jerusalem, while at others it is described as, for ecclesiastical purposes, part of the City itself. Perhaps the name Bethphage, house of figs, was given to that district generally, and to a little village close to Jerusalem where the district began. And this may explain the peculiar reference, in the Synoptic Gospels, to Bethphage (Matthew), and again to Bethphage and Bethany. For, Matthew and Mark relate Christ's brief stay at Bethany and His anointing by Mary not in chronological order, but introduce it at a later period, as it were, in contrast to the betrayal of Judas. Accordingly, they pass from the Miracles at Jericho immediately to the Royal Entry into Jerusalem, from Jericho to Bethphage, or, more exactly, to Bethphage and Bethany, leaving for the present unnoticed what had occurred in the latter hamlet.

Although all the four Evangelists relate Christ's Entry into Jerusalem, they seem to do so from different standpoints. The Synoptists accompany Him from Bethany, while John, in accordance with the general scheme of his narrative, seems to follow from Jerusalem that multitude which, on news of His approach, hurried to meet Him. Even this circumstance, as also the scantiness of events recorded on that day, proves that it could not have been at early morning that Jesus left Bethany. Remembering, that it was the last morning of rest before the great contest, we may reverently think of much that may have passed in the Soul of Jesus and in the home of Bethany. And now He has left that peaceful resting place. It was probably soon after His outset, that He sent the two disciples, possibly Peter and John, into the village over against them, presumably Bethphage. There they would find by the side of the road a donkey colt tied, whereon never man had sat. We mark the significant symbolism of the latter, in connection with the general conditions of consecration to Jehovah—and note in it, as also in the Mission of the Apostles, that this was intended by Christ to be His Royal and Messianic Entry. This colt they were to loose and to bring to Him.

The disciples found all as He had said. When they reached Bethphage, they saw, by a doorway where two roads met, the colt tied by its mother. As they loosed it, the owners and certain of them that stood by asked their purpose, to which, as directed by Jesus, they answered: The Lord [the Master, Christ] has need of him, when, as predicted, no further hindrance was offered. In explanation of this we need not resort to the theory of a miraculous influence, nor even suppose that the owners of the colt were themselves disciples. Their challenge to the two, and the little more than permission which they gave, seem to forbid this idea. Nor is such explanation required. From the pilgrim band which had accompanied Jesus from Galilee and Perea, and preceded Him to Jerusalem, from the guests at the Sabbath feast in Bethany, and from the people who had gone out to see both Jesus and Lazarus, the news of the nearness of Jesus and of His approaching arrival must have spread in the City. Perhaps that very morning some had come from Bethany, and told it in the Temple, among the festive bands, especially among his own Galileans, and generally in Jerusalem, that on that very day, in a few hours, Jesus might be expected to enter the City. Such, must have been the case, since, from John's account, a great multitude went forth to meet Him. The latter, we can have little doubt, must have mostly consisted, not of citizens of Jerusalem, whose hostility to Christ was settled, but of those that had come to the Feast. With these went also a number of Pharisees, their hearts filled with bitterest thoughts of jealousy and hatred. And, as we shall now see, it is of great importance to keep in mind this composition of the multitude.

If such were the circumstances, all is natural. We can understand, how eager questioners would gather about the owners of the colt (Mark), there at the cross roads at Bethphage, just outside Jerusalem; and how, so soon as from the bearing and the peculiar words of the disciples they understood their purpose, the owners of the donkey and colt would grant its use for the solemn Entry into the City of the Teacher of Nazareth, Whom the multitude was so eagerly expecting; and, lastly, how, as from the gates of Jerusalem news spread of what had passed in Bethphage, the multitude would stream forth to meet Jesus.

In the meantime Christ and those who followed Him from Bethany had slowly entered on the well known caravan road from Jericho to Jerusalem. It is the most southern of three, which converge close to the City, perhaps at the very place where the colt had stood tied. The road soon loses sight of Bethany. It is now a rough, but still broad and well defined mountain track, winding over rock and loose stones; a steep descent on the left; the sloping shoulder of Olivet above on the right; fig trees below and above, here and there growing out of the rocky soil. Somewhere here the disciples who brought the colt must have met Him. They were accompanied by many, and immediately followed by more. For, as already stated, Bethphage, we presume the village, formed almost part of Jerusalem, and during Easter week must have been crowded by pilgrims, who could not find accommodation within the City walls. And the announcement, that disciples of Jesus had just fetched the beast of burden on which Jesus was about to enter Jerusalem, must have quickly spread among the crowds which thronged the Temple and the City.

As the two disciples, accompanied, or immediately followed by the multitude, brought the colt to Christ, two streams of people met, the one coming from the City, the other from Bethany. The impression left on our minds is, that what followed was unexpected by those who accompanied Christ, that it took them by surprise. The disciples, who did not understand, until the light of the Resurrection glory had been poured on their minds, the significance of these things, even after they had occurred, seem not even to have guessed, that it was of set purpose that Jesus was about to make His Royal Entry into Jerusalem. Their enthusiasm seems only to have been kindled when they saw the procession from the town come to meet Jesus with palm branches, cut down by the way, and greeting Him with Hosanna shouts of welcome. Then they spread their garments on the colt, and set Jesus thereon, unwrapped their loose cloaks from their shoulders and stretched them along the rough path, to form a momentary carpet as He approached. Then also in their turn they cut down branches from the trees and gardens through which they passed, or braided and twisted palm branches, and strewed them as a crude matting in His way, while they joined in, and soon raised to a much higher pitch the Hosanna of welcoming praise. Nor need we wonder at their ignorance at first of the meaning of that, in which themselves were chief actors. We are too apt to judge them from our standpoint, eighteen centuries later, and after full apprehension of the significance of the event. These men walked in the procession almost as in a dream, or as dazzled by a brilliant light all around, as if impelled by a necessity, and carried from event to event, which came upon them in a succession of but partially understood surprises.

They had now arranged themselves: the multitude which had come from the City preceding, that which had come with Him from Bethany following the triumphant progress of Israel's King, meek, and sitting upon a donkey, and a colt the foal of a donkey. Gradually the long procession swept up and over the ridge where first begins "the descent of the Mount of Olives" towards Jerusalem. At this point the first view is caught of the southeastern corner of the City. The Temple and the more northern portions are hid by the slope of Olivet on the right; what is seen is only Mount Zion, now for the most part a rough field. But at that time it rose, terrace upon terrace, from the Palace of the Maccabees and that of the High Priest, a very city of palaces, until the eye rested in the summit on that castle, city, and palace, with its frowning towers and magnificent gardens, the royal abode of Herod, supposed to occupy the very site of the Palace of David. They had been greeting Him with Hosannas! But enthusiasm, especially in such a cause, is infectious. They were mostly stranger pilgrims that had come from the City, chiefly because they had heard of the raising of Lazarus. And now they must have questioned them which came from Bethany, who in turn related that of which themselves had been eyewitnesses. We can imagine it all, how the fire would leap from heart to heart. So He was the promised Son of David, and the Kingdom was at hand! It may have been just as the precise point of the road was reached, where the City of David first suddenly emerges into view, at the descent of the Mount of Olives, that the whole multitude of the disciples began to rejoice and praise God with a loud voice for all the mighty works that they had seen. As the burning words of joy and praise, the record of what they had seen, passed from mouth to mouth, and they caught their first sight of the City of David, adorned as a bride to welcome her King, Davidic praise to David's Greater Son awakened the echoes of old Davidic Psalms in the morning light of their fulfillment. Hosanna to the Son of David! Blessed is He that comes in the Name of the Lord . . . . Blessed the Kingdom that comes, the Kingdom of our father David . . . Blessed is He that comes in the Name of the Lord . . . . Hosanna . . . Hosanna in the highest . . . Peace in heaven, and glory in the highest.

They were but broken utterances, partly based upon Psalm 118, partly taken from it, the Hosanna, or Save now, and the Blessed be He that comes in the Name of the Lord, forming part of the responses by the people with which this Psalm was chanted on certain of the most solemn festivals. Most truly did they thus interpret and apply the Psalm, old and new Davidic praise mingling in their acclamations. At the same time it must be remembered that, according to Jewish tradition, Psalm 116:25-28, was also chanted antiphonally by the people of Jerusalem, as they went to welcome the festive pilgrims on their arrival, the latter always responding in the second clause of each verse, until the last verse of the Psalm, 25-28, was reached, which was sung by both parties in unison, Psalm 103:17 being added by way of conclusion. But as the shout rang through the long narrow gorge, carrying evidence far and wide, that, so far from condemning and forsaking, more than the ordinary pilgrim welcome had been given to Jesus, the Pharisees, who had mingled with the crowd, turned to one another with angry frowns: Look [see intently], how you prevail nothing! See, the world is gone after Him! It is always so, that, in the disappointment of malice, men turn in impotent rage against each other with taunts and reproaches. Then, psychologically true in this also, they made a desperate appeal to the Master Himself, Whom they so bitterly hated, to check and rebuke the honest zeal of His disciples. He had been silent up to this point—alone unmoved, or only deeply moved inwardly, amid this enthusiastic crowd. He could be silent no longer, but, with a touch of quick and righteous indignation, pointed to the rocks and stones, telling those leaders of Israel, that, if the people held their peace, the very stones would cry out. It would have been so in that day of Christ's Entry into Jerusalem. And it has been so ever since. Silence has fallen these many centuries upon Israel; but the very stones of Jerusalem's ruin and desolateness have cried out that He, Whom in their silence they rejected, has come as King in the Name of the Lord.

Again the procession advanced. The road descends a slight decline, and the glimpse of the City is again withdrawn behind the intervening ridge of Olivet. A few moments and the path mounts again, it climbs a rugged ascent, it reaches a ledge of smooth rock, and in an instance the whole City bursts into view. As now the dome of the Mosque El Aksa rises like a Ghost from the earth before the traveler stands on the ledge, so then must have risen the Temple tower; as now the vast enclosure of the Mussulman sanctuary, so then must have spread the Temple courts; as now the grey town on its broken hills, so then the magnificent City, with its background, long since vanished away, of gardens and suburbs on the western plateau behind. Immediately before was the Valley of the Kedron, here seen in its greatest depth as it joins the Valley of Hinnom, and thus giving full effect to the great peculiarity of Jerusalem, seen only on its eastern side, its situation as of a City rising out of a deep abyss. It is hardly possible to doubt that this rise and turn of the road, this rocky ledge, was the exact point where the multitude paused again, and "He, when He beheld the City, wept over it." Not with still weeping (dkrusen), as at the grave of Lazarus, but with loud and deep lamentation (klausen). The contrast was, terrible between the Jerusalem that rose before Him in all its beauty, glory, and security, and the Jerusalem which He saw in vision dimly rising on the sky, with the camp of the enemy around about it on every side, hugging it closer and closer in deadly embrace, and the very stockade which the Roman Legions raised around it; then, another scene in the shifting panorama, and the city laid with the ground, and the gory bodies of her children among her ruins; and yet another scene: the silence and desolateness of death by the Hand of God, not one stone left upon another! We know only too well how literally this vision has become reality; and yet, though uttered as prophecy by Christ, and its reason so clearly stated, Israel to this day does not know the things which belong to its peace, and the upturned scattered stones of its dispersion are crying out in testimony against it. But to this day, also do the tears of Christ plead with the Church on Israel's behalf, and His words bear within them precious seed of promise.

We turn once more to the scene just described. For, it was no common pageantry; and Christ's public Entry into Jerusalem seems so altogether different from, we had almost said, inconsistent with, His previous mode of appearance. Evidently, the time for the silence so long enjoined had passed, and that for public declaration had come. And such, this Entry was. From the moment of His sending forth the two disciples to His acceptance of the homage of the multitude, and His rebuke of the Pharisees attempt to arrest it, all must be regarded as designed or approved by Him: not only a public assertion of His Messiahship, but a claim to its national acknowledgment. And yet, even so, it was not to be the Messiah of Israel's conception, but He of prophetic picture: just and having salvation; lowly, and riding upon a donkey. It is foreign to our present purpose to discuss any general questions about this prophecy, or even to vindicate its application to the Messiah. But, when we brush aside all the trafficking and bargaining over words, that constitutes so much of modern criticism, which in its care over the lesson so often loses the spirit, there can, at least, be no question that this prophecy was intended to introduce, in contrast to earthly warfare and kingly triumph, another Kingdom, of which the just King would be the Prince of Peace, Who was meek and lowly in His Advent, Who would speak peace to the pagan, and Whose sway would yet extend to earth's utmost bounds. Thus much may be said, that if there ever was true picture of the Messiah King and His Kingdom, it is this, and that, if ever Israel was to have a Messiah or the world a Savior, He must be such as described in this Prophecy, not merely in the letter, but in the spirit of it. And as so often indicated, it was not the letter but the spirit of prophecy, and of all prophecy, which the ancient Synagogue, and that rightly, saw fulfilled in the Messiah and His Kingdom. Accordingly, with singular unanimity the Talmud and the ancient Rabbinic authorities have applied this prophecy to the Christ. Nor was it quoted by Matthew and John in the stiffness and deadness of the letter. On the contrary (as so often in Jewish writings, two prophets, Isaiah 62:11, and Zechariah 9:9, are made to shed their blended light upon this Entry of Christ, as exhibiting the reality, of which the prophetic vision had been the real Exodus. Nor yet are the words of the Prophets given literally, as modern criticism would have them weighed out in the critical balances, either from the Hebrew text, or form the LXX rendering; but their real meaning is given, and they are Targumed by the sacred writers. according to their habit. Yet who that sets the prophetic picture by the side of the reality, the description by the side of Christ's Entry into Jerusalem, can fail to recognize in the one the real fulfillment of the other?

Another point seems to require comment. We have seen reasons to regard the bearing of the disciples as one of surprise, and that, all through these last scenes, they seem to have been hurried from event to event. But the enthusiasm of the people, their royal welcome of Christ, how is it to be explained, and how reconciled with the speedy and terrible reaction of His Betrayal and Crucifixion? Yet it is not so difficult to understand it; and, if we only keep clear of unconscious exaggeration, we shall gain in truth and reasonableness what we lose in dramatic effect. It has already been suggested, that the multitude which went to meet Jesus must have consisted chiefly of pilgrim strangers. The overwhelming majority of the citizens of Jerusalem were bitterly and determinately hostile to Christ. But we know that, even so, the Pharisees dreaded to take the final steps against Christ during the presence of these pilgrims at the Feast, apprehending a movement in His favor. It proved, otherwise; for these country people were but ill informed; they dared not resist the combined authority of their own Sanhedrin and of the Romans. Besides, the prejudices of the populace, and especially of an Eastern populace, are easily raised, and they readily sway from one extreme to the opposite. Lastly, the very suddenness and completeness of the blow, which the Jewish authorities delivered, would have stunned even those who had deeper knowledge, more cohesion, and greater independence than most of them who, on that Palm Sunday, had gone forth from the City.

Again, as regards their welcome of Christ, deeply significant as it was, we must not attach to it deeper meaning than it possessed. Modern writers have mostly seen in it the demonstrations of the Feast of Tabernacles, as if the homage of its services had been offered to Christ. It would, have been symbolic of much about Israel if they had thus confounded the Second with the First Advent of Christ, the Sacrifice of the Passover with the joy of the Feast of Ingathering. But, in reality, their conduct does not bear that interpretation. It is true that these responses from Psalm 118, which formed part of what was known as the (Egyptian) Hallel, were chanted by the people on the Feast of Tabernacles also, but the Hallel was equally sung with responses during the offering of the Passover, at the Paschal Supper, and on the Feasts of Pentecost and of the Dedication of the Temple. The waving of the palm branches was the welcome of visitors or kings, and not distinctive of the Feast of Tabernacles. At the latter, the worshippers carried, not simple palm branches, but the Lulabh, which consisted of palm, myrtle, and willow branches intertwined. Lastly, the words of welcome from Psalm 116:were (as already stated) those with which on solemn occasions the people also greeted the arrival of festive pilgrims, although, as being offered to Christ alone, and as accompanied by such demonstrations, they may have implied that they hailed Him as the promised King, and have converted His Entry into a triumph in which the people did homage. And, if proof were required of the more sober, and, may we not add, rational view here advocated, it would be found in this, that not until after His Resurrection did even His own disciples understand the significance of the whole scene which they had witnessed, and in which they had borne such a part.

The anger and jealousy of the Pharisees understood it better, and watched for the opportunity of revenge. But, for the present, on that bright spring day, the weak, excitable, fickle populace streamed before Him through the City gates, through the narrow streets, up the Temple mount. Everywhere the tramp of their feet, and the shout of their acclamations brought men, women, and children into the streets and on the housetops. The City was moved, and from mouth to mouth the question passed among the eager crowd of curious onlookers: Who is He? And the multitude answered, not, this is Israel's Messiah King, but: This is Jesus the Prophet of Nazareth of Galilee. And so up into the Temple!

He alone was silent and sad among this excited multitude, the marks of the tears He had wept over Jerusalem still on His cheek. It is not so, that an earthly King enters His City in triumph; not so, that the Messiah of Israel's expectation would have gone into His Temple. He did not speak, but only looked round about on all things, as if to view the field on which He was to suffer and die. And now the shadows of evening were creeping up; and, weary and sad, He once more returned with the twelve disciples to the shelter and rest of Bethany.

End Notes:

[1] The expression: stones bearing witness when sin has been committed, is not uncommon in Jewish writings. See Taan. 11 a; Chag. 16 a.

[2] Such were, and even now are, common demonstrations in the East, to welcome a king, a conqueror, or a deliverer. For a large number of pagan and Jewish instances of the same time, comp. Wetstein, ad loc. (1: pp. 460, 461).

[3] I am aware, that so great an authority as Professor Delitzsch calls this in question (Zeitschr. fuer Luther. Theol. for 1855, p. 653). But the testimony of the Midrash is against him. Delitzsch regards it as the shout of the Feast of Tabernacles. But how should that have been raised before the Feast of Passover? Again, it does not seem reasonable to suppose, that the multitude had with full consciousness proclaimed Jesus as the Messiah, and intended to celebrate there and then the fulfillment of the typical meaning of the Feast of Tabernacles.

Chapter 2

Second Day and the Cleansing
of the Temple

How the King of Israel spent the night after the triumphal Entry into His City and Temple, we may venture reverently to infer. His royal banquet would be fellowship with the disciples. We know how often His nights had been spent in lonely prayer, and surely it is not too bold to associate such thoughts with the first night in Passion week. Thus, also, we can most readily account for that exhaustion and faintness of hunger, which next morning made Him seek fruit on the fig tree on His way to the City.

It was very early on the morning of the second day in Passion week (Monday), when Jesus, with his disciples, left Bethany. In the fresh, crisp, spring air, after the exhaustion of that night, He hungered. By the roadside, as so often in the East, a solitary tree grew in the rocky soil. It must have stood on an eminence, where it caught the sunshine and warmth, for He saw it far off, and though spring had but lately wooed nature into life, it stood out, with its wide spreading mantle of green, against the sky. It was not the season of figs, but the tree, covered with leaves, attached His attention. It might have been, that they hid some of the fruit which hung through the winter, or else the springing fruits of the new crop. For it is a well known fact, that in Palestine the fruit appears before the leaves, and that this fig tree, whether from its exposure or soil, was promising, is evident from the fact that it was in leaf, which is quite unusual at that season on the Mount of Olives. The old fruit would have been edible, and in regard to the unripe fruit we have the distinct evidence of the Mishnah, confirmed by the Talmud, that the unripe fruit was eaten, so soon as it began to assume a red color, as it is expressed, in the field, with bread, or, as we understand it, by those whom hunger overtook in the fields, whether working or traveling. But in the present case there was neither old nor new fruit, but leaves only. It was evidently a barren fig tree, cumbering the ground, and to be cut down. Our mind almost instinctively reverts to the Parable of the Barren Fig tree, which He had so lately spoken. To Him, Who but yesterday had wept over the Jerusalem that did not know the day of its visitation, and over which the sharp axe of judgment was already lifted, this fig tree, with its luxuriant mantle of leaves, must have recalled, with pictorial vividness, the scene of the previous day. Israel was that barren fig tree; and the leaves only covered their nakedness, as formerly they had that of our first parents after their Fall. And the judgment, symbolically spoken in the Parable, must be symbolically executed in this leafy fig tree, barren when searched for fruit by the Master. It seems almost an inward necessity, not only symbolically but really also, that Christ's Word should have laid it low. We cannot conceive that any other should have eaten of it after the hungering Christ had in vain sought fruit thereon. We cannot conceive that anything should resist Christ, and not be swept away. We cannot conceive, that the reality of what He had taught should not, when occasion came, be visibly placed before the eyes of the disciples. Lastly, we seem to feel (with Bengel) that, as always, the manifestation of His true Humanity, in hunger, should be accompanied by that of His Divinity, in the power of His Word of judgment.

With Matthew, who, for the sake of continuity, relates this incident after the events of that day (the Monday) and immediately before those of the next, we anticipate what was only witnessed on the morrow. As Matthew has it: on Christ's Word the fig tree immediately withered away. But according to the more detailed account of Mark, it was only next morning, when they again passed by, that they noticed the fig tree had withered from its very roots. The spectacle attracted their attention, and vividly recalled the Words of Christ, to which, on the previous day, they had, perhaps, scarcely attached sufficient importance. And it was the suddenness and completeness of the judgment that had been denounced, which now struck Peter, rather than its symbolic meaning. It was rather the Miracle than its moral and spiritual significance, the storm and earthquake rather than the still small Voice, which impressed the disciples. Besides, the words of Peter are at least capable of this interpretation, that the fig tree had withered in consequence of, rather than by the Word of Christ. But He ever leads His own from mere wonderment at the Miraculous up to that which is higher.

His answer now combined all that they needed to learn. It pointed to the typical lesson of what had taken place: the need of realizing, simple faith, the absence of which was the cause of Israel's leafy barrenness, and which, if present and active, could accomplish all, however impossible it might seem by outward means. And yet it was only to have faith in God; such faith as becomes those who know God; a faith in God, which seeks not and has not its foundation in anything outward, but rests on Him alone. To one who shall not doubt in his heart, but shall believe that what he saith comes to pass, it shall be to him. And this general principle of the Kingdom, which to the devout and reverent believer needs neither explanation nor limitation, received its further application, especially to the Apostles in their coming need: Therefore I say to you, what ever things, praying, you ask for, believe that you have received them [not, in the counsel of God, but actually, in answer to the prayer of faith], and it shall be to you.

These two things follow: faith gives absolute power in prayer, but it is also its moral condition. None other than this is faith; and none other than faith, absolute, simple, trustful, gives glory to God, or has the promise. This is, so to speak, the New Testament application of the first Table of the Law, summed up in the You shall love the Lord your God. But there is yet another moral condition of prayer closely connected with the first, a New Testament application of the second Table of the Law, summed up in the You shall love your neighbor as yourself. If the first moral condition was God ward, the second is man-ward; if the first bound us to faith, the second binds us to charity, while hope, the expectancy of answered prayer, is the link connecting the two. Prayer, unlimited in its possibilities, stands midway between heaven and earth; with one hand it reaches up to heaven, with the other down to earth; in it, faith prepares to receive, what charity is ready to dispense. He who so prays believes in God and loves man; such prayer is not selfish, self seeking, self conscious; least of all, is it compatible with mindfulness of wrongs, or an unforgiving spirit. This, then, is the second condition of prayer, and not only of such all prevailing prayer, but even of personal acceptance in prayer. We can, therefore, have no doubt that Mark correctly reports in this connection this as the condition which Jesus attaches to acceptance, that we previously put away all uncharitableness. We remember, that the promise had a special application to the Apostles and early disciples; we also remember, how difficult to them was the thought of full forgiveness of offenders and persecutors; and again, how great the temptation to avenge wrongs and to wield miraculous power in the vindication of their authority. In these circumstances Peter and his fellow disciples, when assured of the unlimited power of the prayer of faith, required all the more to be both reminded and warned of this as its second moral condition: the need of hearty forgiveness, if they had anything whatever against any.

From this digression we return to the events of that second day in Passion week (the Monday), which began with the symbolic judgment on the leafy, barren fig tree. The same symbolism of judgment was to be immediately set forth still more clearly, and that in the Temple itself. On the previous afternoon, when Christ had come to it, the services were probably over, and the Sanctuary comparatively empty of worshippers and of those who there carried on their traffic. When treating of the first cleansing of the Temple, at the beginning of Christ's Ministry, sufficient has been said to explain the character and mode of that reprehensible traffic, the profits of which went to the leaders of the priesthood, as also how popular indignation was roused against this trade and the traders. We need not here recall the words of Christ; Jewish authorities sufficiently describe, in even stronger terms, this transformation of the House of Prayer into a den of robbers. If, when beginning to do the business of His Father, and for the first time publicly presenting Himself with Messianic claim, it was fitting He should take such authority, and first cleanse the Temple of the wicked intruders who, under the guise of being God's chief priests, made His House one of traffic, much more was this appropriate now, at the close of His Work, when, as King, He had entered His City, and publicly claimed authority. At the first it had been for teaching and warning, now it was in symbolic judgment; what and as He then began, that and so He now finished. Accordingly, as we compare the words, and even some of the acts, of the first cleansing with those accompanying and explaining the second, we find the latter, we shall not say, much more severe, but bearing a different character, that of final judicial sentence.

Nor did the Temple authorities now, as on the former occasion, seek to raise the populace against Him, or challenge His authority by demanding the warrant of a sign. The contest had reached quite another stage. They heard what He said in their condemnation, and with bitter hatred in their hearts sought for some means to destroy Him. But fear of the people restrained their violence. For, marvelous indeed was the power which He wielded. With absorbed attention the people hung entranced on his lips, astonished at those new and blessed truths which dropped from them. All was so other than it had been! By His authority the Temple was cleansed of the unholy, thievish traffic which a corrupt priesthood carried on, and so, for the time, restored to the solemn Service of God; and that purified House now became the scene of Christ's teaching, when He spoke those words of blessed truth and of comfort concerning the Father, thus truly realizing the prophetic promise of a House of Prayer for all the nations. And as those traffickers were driven from the Temple, and He spoke, there flocked in from porches and Temple Mount the poor sufferers, the blind and the lame, to get healing to body and soul. It was truly spring time in that Temple, and the boys that gathered about their fathers and looked in turn from their faces of absorbed wonderment and enthusiasm to the Godlike Face of the Christ, and then on those healed sufferers, took up the echoes of the welcome at His entrance into Jerusalem, in their simplicity understanding and applying them better, as they burst into Hosanna to the Son of David.

It rang through the courts and porches of the Temple, this Children's Hosanna. They heard it, whom the wonders He had spoken and done, so far from leading to repentance and faith, had only filled with indignation. Once more in their impotent anger they sought, as the Pharisees had done on the day of His Entry, by a hypocritical appeal to His reverence for God, not only to mislead, and so to use His very love of the truth against the truth, but to betray Him into silencing those Children's Voices. But the undimmed mirror of His soul only reflected the light. These Children's Voices were Angels Echoes, echoes of the far off praises of heaven, which children's souls had caught and children's lips welled forth. Not from the great, the wise, nor the learned, but out of the mouth of babes and sucklings has He perfected praise. And this, also, is the Music of the Gospel.

End Notes:

[4]   We remind the reader, that the expression rooting up mountains is in common Rabbinic use as a hyperbole for doing the impossible or the incredible. For the former, see Babha B. 3 b ; for the latter Ber. 64 a; Sanh. 24 a; Horay. 14 a.

[5]   The grounds on which this second has to be distinguished from the first cleansing of the Temple, which is recorded only by John (2:13-23) have been explained on a previous occasion. They are stated in most commentaries, though perhaps not always satisfactorily. But intelligent readers can have no difficulty in gathering them for themselves. The difficulty lies not in the two purifications, nor yet in the silence of the Synoptists as to the first, since the early Jerusalem Ministry lay not within the scope of their

narratives, but in the silence of the Fourth Gospel in regard to the second purification. But here we would remark that, less than any of the others, is the Fourth Gospel a history or successive narration; but, if we may so say, historical dogmatics, the Logos in the historical manifestation of His Person and Work. If so, the first included the second purification of the Temple. Again, to have introduced it, or the cursing of the fig tree, would have been to break up the course, and mar the symmetry of the narrative (John 12), which presents in successive and deepening shading the attestation of the Christ: at the Supper of Bethany, on His Entry into Jerusalem, before the Greeks in the Temple, by the Voice from Heaven before His opposers, and to his disciples.

[6]   We may here note, once for all, that the manner of answering used by Christ, that of answering a question by putting another in which the answer appeared with irresistible force. was very common among the Jews. Another mode was by an allegory, whether of word or action.

[7]   So in the LXX, rightly giving the sense; in the original strength. It is perhaps one of the grandest of the grand contrasts in the Psalms: God opposing and appeasing His enemies, not by a display of power, as they understand it, but by the mouth of young boys [such is the proper rendering] and sucklings. The Eternal of Hosts has these for His armor bearers, and needs none other. The ancient Synagogue, somewhat realistically, yet with a basis of higher truth, declared (in the Haggadah), that at the Red Sea little children, even the babes in the womb, had joined in Israel's song of triumph, so fulfilling this saying of the Psalmist.

Chapter 3

The Third Day and Disputes
with Religious Rulers

The record of this third day is so crowded, the actors introduced on the scene are so many, the occurrences so varied, and the transitions so rapid, that it is even more than usually difficult to arrange all in chronological order. Nor need we wonder at this, when we remember that this was, so to speak, Christ's last working day, the last, of His public Mission to Israel, so far as its active part was concerned; the last day in the Temple; the last, of teaching and warning to Pharisees and Sadducees; the last, of his call to national repentance.

That what follows must be included in one day, appears from the circumstance that its beginning is expressly mentioned by Mark in connection with the notice of the withering of the fig tree, while its close is not only indicated in the last words of Christ's discourses, as reported by the Synoptists, but the beginning of another day is afterwards equally clearly marked.

Considering the multiplicity of occurrences, it will be better to group them together, rather than follow the exact order of their succession. Accordingly, this chapter will be devoted to the events of the third day in Passion Week.

1. As usually, the day commenced with teaching in the Temple. We gather this from the expression: as He was walking, namely, in one of the Porches, where, as we know considerable freedom of meeting, conversing, or even teaching, was allowed. It will be remembered, that

on the previous day the authorities had been afraid to interfere with Him. In silence they had witnessed, with impotent rage, the expulsion of their traffic mongers; in silence they had listened to His teaching, and seen His miracles. Not until the Hosanna of the little boys, perhaps those children of the Levites who acted as choristers in the Temple, awakened them from the stupor of their fears, had they ventured on a feeble protest, in the forlorn hope that He might be induced to appease them. But with the night and morning other counsels had come. Besides, the circumstances were somewhat different. It was early morning, the hearers were new, and the wondrous influence of His Words had not yet bent them to His Will. From the formal manner in which the chief priests, the scribes, and the elders are introduced, and from the circumstance that they so met Christ immediately on His entry into the Temple, we can scarcely doubt that a meeting, although informal, of the authorities had been held to concert measures against the growing danger. Yet, even so, cowardice as well as cunning marked their procedure. They dared not directly oppose Him, but endeavored, by attacking Him on the one point where he seemed to lay Himself open to it, to appropriate to themselves the appearance of strict legality, and so to turn popular feeling against Him.

For, there was no principle more firmly established by universal consent than that authoritative teaching required previous authorization. This logically followed from the principle of Rabbinism. All teaching must be authoritative, since it was traditional, approved by authority, and handed down from teacher to disciple. The highest honor of a scholar was, that he was like a well plastered cistern, from which not a drop had leaked of what had been poured into it. The ultimate appeal in cases of discussion was always to some great authority, whether an individual Teacher or a Decree by the Sanhedrin. In this manner had the great Hillel first vindicated his claim to be the Teacher of his time and to decide the disputes then pending. And, to decide differently from authority, was either the mark of ignorant assumption or the outcome of daring rebellion, in either case to be visited with the ban. And this was at least one aspect of the controversy as between the chief authorities and Jesus. No one would have thought of interfering with a mere Haggadist, a popular expositor, preacher, or teller of legends. But authoritatively to teach, required other warrant. In fact there was regular ordination (Semikhah) to the office of Rabbi, Elder, and Judge, for the three functions were combined in one. According to the Mishnah, the disciples sat before the Sanhedrin in three rows, the members of the Sanhedrin being recruited successively from the front rank of the Scholars. At first the practice is said to have been for every Rabbi to accredit his own disciples. But afterwards this right was transferred to the Sanhedrin, with the proviso that this body might not ordain without the consent of its Chief, though the latter might do so without consent of the Sanhedrin. But this privilege was afterwards withdrawn on account of abuses. Although we have not any description of the earliest mode of ordination, the very name, Semikhah, implies the imposition of hands. Again, in the oldest record, reaching up, no doubt, to the time of Christ, the presence of at least three ordained persons was required for ordination. At a later period, the presence of an ordained Rabbi, with the assessorship of two others, even if unordained, was deemed sufficient. In the course of time certain formalities were added. The person to be ordained had to deliver a discourse; hymns and poems were recited; the title Rabbi was formally bestowed on the candidate, and authority given him to teach and to act as Judge [to bind and loose, to declare guilty or free]. There seem to have been even different orders, according to the authority bestowed on the person ordained. The formula in bestowing full orders was: Let him teach; let him teach; let him judge; let him decide on questions of first born; let him decide; let him judge! At one time it was held that ordination could only take place in the Holy Land. Those who went abroad took with them their letters of orders.

At whatever periods some of these practices may have been introduced, it is at least certain that, at the time of Jesus, no one would have ventured authoritatively to teach without proper Rabbinic authorization. The question, therefore, with which the Jewish authorities met Christ, while teaching, was one which had a very real meaning, and appealed to the habits and feelings of the people who listened to Jesus. Otherwise, also, it was cunningly framed. For, it did not merely challenge Him for teaching, but also asked for His authority in what He did, referring not only to His Work generally, but, perhaps, especially to what had happened on the previous day. They were not there to oppose Him; but, when a man did as He had done in the Temple, it was their duty to verify his credentials. Finally, the alternative question reported by Mark: or, if You have not proper Rabbinic commission, who gave You this authority to do these things? seems clearly to point to their contention, that the power which Jesus wielded was delegated to Him by none other than Beelzebul.

The point in Jesus' reply seems to have been strangely overlooked by commentators. As His words are generally understood, they would have amounted only to silencing His questioners, and that, in a manner which would, under ordinary circumstances, be scarcely regarded as either fair or ingenuous. It would have been simply to turn the question against themselves, and so in turn to raise popular prejudice. But Jesus' words meant quite other. He answered their question, though He also exposed the cunning and cowardice which prompted it. To the challenge for His authority, and the dark hint about Satanic agency, He replied by an appeal to the Baptist. He had borne full witness to the Mission of Christ from the Father, and all men counted John, that he was a prophet indeed. Were they satisfied? What was their view of the Baptism in preparation for the Coming of Christ? No? They would not, or could not answer! If they said the Baptist was a prophet, this implied not only the authorization of the Mission of Jesus, but the call to believe on Him. On the other hand, they were afraid publicly to disown John! And so their cunning and cowardice stood out self condemned, when they pleaded ignorance, a plea so grossly and manifestly dishonest, that Christ, having given what all must have felt to be a complete answer, could refuse further discussion with them on this point.

2. Foiled in their endeavor to involve Him with the ecclesiastical, they next attempted the much more dangerous device of bringing Him into collision with the civil authorities. Remembering the ever watchful jealousy of Rome, the reckless tyranny of Pilate, and the low deceptions of Herod, who was at that time in Jerusalem, we instinctively feel, how even the slightest compromise on the part of Jesus in regard to the authority of Caesar would have been absolutely fatal. If it could have been proved, on undeniable testimony, that Jesus had declared Himself on the side of, or even encouraged, the so called Nationalist party, He would quickly perished, like Judas of Galilee. The Jewish leaders would thus have readily accomplished their object, and its unpopularity have recoiled only on the hated Roman power. How great the danger was which threatened Jesus, may be gathered from this, that, despite His clear answer, the charge that He prevented the nation, forbidding to give tribute to Caesar, was actually among those brought against Him before Pilate.

The plot, for such it was, was most cunningly concocted. The object was to spy out His inmost thoughts, and, if possible, entangle Him in His talk. For this purpose it was not the old Pharisees, whom He knew and would have distrusted, who came, but some of their disciples, apparently fresh, earnest, zealous, conscientious men. With them had combined certain of the Herodians, of course, not a sect nor religious school, but a political party at the time. We know comparatively little of the deeper political movements in Judea, only so much as it has suited Josephus to record. But we cannot be greatly mistaken in regarding the Herodians as a party which honestly accepted the House of Herod as occupants of the Jewish throne. Differing from the extreme section of the Pharisees, who hated Herod, and from the Nationalists, it might have been a middle or moderate Jewish party, semi-Roman and semi-Nationalist. We know that it was the ambition of Herod Antipas again to unite under his sway of the whole of Palestine; but we do not know what intrigues may have been carried on for that purpose, with the Pharisees and the Romans. Nor is it the first time in this history, that we find the Pharisees and the Herodians combined. Herod may, have been unwilling to incur the unpopularity of personally proceeding against the Great Prophet of Nazareth, especially as he must have had so keen a remembrance of what the murder of John had cost him. Perhaps he would gladly, if he could, have made use of Him, and played Him off as the popular Messiah against the popular leaders. But, as matters had gone, he must have been anxious to rid himself of what might be a formidable rival, while, at the same time, his party would be glad to join with the Pharisees in what would secure their gratitude and allegiance. Such, or similar, may have been the motives which brought about this strange alliance of Pharisees and Herodians.

Pretending themselves to be just men, they now came to Jesus with honeyed words, intended to disarm His suspicions, but, by an appeal to His fearlessness and singleness of moral purpose, to induce Him to commit Himself without reserve. Was it lawful for them to give tribute to Caesar, or not? were they to pay the pole tax of one drachm, or to refuse it? We know how later Judaism would have answered such a question. It lays down the principle, that the right of coinage implies the authority of levying taxes, and indeed constitutes such evidence of de facto government as to make it duty absolutely to submit to it. So much was this felt, that the Maccabees, and, in the last Jewish war, Bar Kokhabh, the false Messiah, issued a coinage dating from the liberation of Jerusalem. We cannot therefore doubt, that this principle about coinage, taxation, and government was generally accepted in Judea. On the other hand, there was a strong party in the land; with which, not only politically but religiously, many of the noblest

spirits would sympathize, which maintained, that to pay the tribute money
to Caesar was virtually to own his royal authority, and so to disown that
of Jehovah, Who alone was Israel's King. They would argue, that all the
miseries of the land and people were due to this national unfaithfulness.
This was the fundamental principle of the Nationalist movement. History
has recorded many similar movements, in which strong political feelings
have been strangely blended with religious fanaticism, and which have
numbered in their ranks, together with unscrupulous partisans, not a few
who were sincere patriots or earnest religionists. It has been suggested in
a former part of this book, that the Nationalist movement may have had
an important preparatory bearing on some of the earlier followers of Jesus,
perhaps at the beginning of their inquiries, just as, in the West, Alexandrian
philosophy moved to many a preparation for Christianity. At any rate,
the scruple expressed by these men would, if genuine, have called forth
sympathy. But what was the alternative here presented to Christ? To have
said No, would have been to command rebellion; to have said simply Yes,
would have been to give a painful shock to keep feeling, and, in a sense,
in the eyes of the people, the lie to His own claim of being Israel's Messiah
King!

But Jesus escaped from this temptation, because, being true, it was
no real temptation to Him. Their trickery and hypocrisy He immediately
perceived and exposed, in this also responding to their appeal of being
true. Once more and emphatically must we disclaim the idea that Christ's
was rather an evasion of the question than a reply. It was a very real rather,
when pointing to the image and inscription on the coin, for which He
had called, He said, What is Caesar's render to Caesar, and what is God's
to God. It did far more than rebuke their hypocrisy and presumption; it
answered not only that question of theirs to all earnest men of that time,
as it would present itself to their minds, but it settles to all time and for all
circumstances the principle underlying it. Christ's Kingdom is not of this
world; a true Theocracy is not inconsistent with submission to the secular
power in things that are really its own; politics and religion neither include,
nor yet exclude, each other; they are, side by side, in different domains.
The State is Divinely sanctioned, and religion is Divinely sanctioned, and
both are equally the ordinance of God. On this principle did Apostolic
authority regulate the relations between Church and State, even when
the latter was pagan. The question about the limits of either province has
been hotly discussed by sectarians on either side, who have claimed the
saying of Christ in support of one or the opposite extreme which they

have advocated. And yet, to the simple searcher after duty, it seems not so difficult to see the distinction, if only we succeed in purging ourselves of logical refinements and strained references.

It was an answer not only most truthful, but of marvelous beauty and depth. It elevated the controversy into quite another sphere, where there was no conflict between what was due to God and to man no conflict at all, but Divine harmony and peace. Nor did it speak harshly of the Nationalist aspirations, nor yet plead the cause of Rome. It said not whether the rule of Rome was right or should be permanent, but only what all must have felt to be Divine. And so they, who had come to entangle Him, went away, not convinced nor converted, but marveling exceedingly.

3. Passing for the present from the hair splitting of the Sadducees and the controdiction of the Scribes, we come unexpectedly on one of those sweet pictures, a historical miniature, as it is presented to us, which affords real relief to the eye amid the glare all around. From the bitter malice of His enemies and the predicted judgment upon them, we turn to the silent worship of she who gave her all, and to the words with which Jesus owned it, all unknown to her. It comes to us the more welcome, that it exhibits in deed what Christ had said to those hypocrites who had discussed it, whether the tribute given to Caesar was not robbing God of what was His. Truly here was one, who, in the simplicity of her humble worship, gave to the Lord what was His!

Weary with the contention, Jesus had left those to whom He had spoken in the Porches, and, while the crowd wrangled about His Words or His Person, had ascended the flight of steps which led from the Terrace into the Temple building. From these steps, whether those leading up to the Beautiful Gate, or one of the side gates, He could gain full view into The Court of the Women, into which they opened. On these steps, or within the gate (for in no other place was it lawful), He sat Him down, watching the multitude. The time of Sacrifice was past, and those who still lingered had remained for private devotion, for private sacrifices, or to pay their vows and offerings. Although the topography of the Temple, especially of this part of it, is not without its difficulties, we know that under the colonnades, which surrounded the Court of the Women, but still left in the middle room for more than 15,000 worshippers, provision was made for receiving religious and charitable shaped boxes (Shopharoth); somewhere here also we must locate two chambers: that of the silent, for gifts to be distributed in secret to the children of the pious poor, and that where votive vessels were deposited. Perhaps there was here also a special chamber for offerings. These trumpets bore each inscriptions, marking the objects of contribution, whether to make up for past neglect, to pay for certain sacrifices, to provide incense, wood, or for other gifts.

As they passed to this or that treasury box, it must have been a study of deep interest, especially on that day, to watch the givers. Some might come with appearance of self righteousness, some even with showiness, some as cheerfully performing a happy duty. Many that were rich cast in much, yes, very much, for such was the tendency that (as already stated) a law had to be enacted, forbidding the gift of the Temple of more than a certain proportion of ones possessions. And the amount of such contributions may be inferred by recalling the circumstances, that, at the time of Pompey and Crassus, the Temple Treasury, after having lavishly defrayed every possible expenditure, contained in money nearly half a million, and precious vessels to the value of nearly two millions sterling.

And as Jesus so sat on these steps, looking out on the ever shifting panorama, His gaze was riveted by a solitary figure. The simple words of Mark sketch a story of singular sadness. It was one pauper widow. We can see her coming alone, as if ashamed to mingle with the crowd of rich givers; ashamed to have her offering seen; ashamed, perhaps, to bring it; a widow, in the garb of a desolate mourner; her condition, appearance, and bearing that of a pauper. He observed her closely and read her truly. She held in her hand only the smallest coins, two Perutahs, and it should be known that it was not lawful to contribute a less amount. Together these two Perutahs made a guadrans, which was the ninety sixth part of a denar, itself of the value of about seven pence. But it was all her living (bos), perhaps all that she had been able to save out of her scanty housekeeping; more probably, all that she had to live upon for that day and until she worked for more. And of this she now made humble offering to God. He spoke not to her words of encouragement, for she walked by faith; He offered not promise of return, for her reward was in heaven. She did not know that anyone had seen it, for the knowledge of eyes turned on her, even His, would have flushed with shame the pure cheek of her love; and any word, conscious notice, or promise would have married and turned aside the rising incense of her sacrifice. But for all time has it remained in the Church, like the perfume of Mary's alabaster that filled the house, this deed of self denying sacrifice. More, far more, than the great gifts of their overabundance, which the rich cast in, was, and is to all time, the gift of absolute self surrender and sacrifice, tremblingly offered by the solitary mourner. And though He spoke not to her, yet the sunshine of his words must have fallen into the dark desolateness of her heart; and, though perhaps she did not know why, it must have been a happy day, a day of rich feast in the heart, that when she gave up her whole living to God. And so, perhaps, is every sacrifice for God all the more blessed, when we do not know of its blessedness.

Would that to all time its lesson had been cherished, not theoretically, but practically, by the Church! How much richer would have been her treasury: twice blessed in gift and givers. But so is not legend written. If it had been a story invented for a purpose or adorned with the tinsel of embellishment, Jesus and the widow would not have so parted, to meet and to speak not on earth, but in heaven. She would have worshipped, and He spoken or done some great thing. Their silence was a meeting for heaven.

4. One other event of solemn joyous import remains to be recorded on that day. But so closely is it connected with what Jesus afterwards spoke, that the two cannot be separated. It is narrated only by John, who, as before explained, tells it as one of a series of progressive manifestations of the Christ: first in His Entry into the City, and then in the Temple, successively, to the Greeks, by the Voice from Heaven, and before the people.

Precious as each part and verse here is, when taken by itself, there is some difficulty in combining them, and in showing their connection, and its meaning. But here we ought not to forget, that we have, in the Gospel narrative, only the briefest account, as it were, headings, summaries, outlines, rather than a report. Nor do we know the surrounding circumstances. The words which Christ spoke after the request of the Greeks to be admitted to His Presence may bear some special reference also to the state of the disciples, and their unreadiness to enter into and share His predicted sufferings. And this may again be connected with Christ's prediction and discourse about the last things. For the position of the narrative in John's Gospel seems to imply that it was the last event of the day the conclusion of Christ's public Ministry. If this be so, words and admonitions, otherwise somewhat mysterious in their connection, would acquire a new meaning.

It was then, as we suppose, the evening of a long weary day of teaching. As the sun had been hastening towards its setting in red, He had spoken of that other sun setting, with the sky all aglow in judgment, and of the darkness that was to follow, but also of the better Light would arise in it. And in those Temple porches they had been hearing Him, seeing Him in His wonder working yesterday, hearing Him in His wonder speaking that day, those men of other tongues. They were Proselytes, Greeks by birth, who had groped their way to the porch of Judaism, just as the first streaks of light were falling within upon his altar. They must have been stirred in their inmost being; felt, that it was just for such as they, and to them that He spoke; that this was what in the Old Testament they had guessed, anticipated, dimly hoped for, if they had not seen it, its grand faith, its grander hope, its grandest reality. Not one by one, and almost by stealth, were they from then on to come to the gate; but the portals were to be flung wide open, and as the golden light streamed out upon the way, He stood there, that bright Divine Personality, Who was not only the Son of David, but the Son of Man, to bid them the Father's welcome of good pleasure to the Kingdom.

And so, as the lengthening shadows gathered around the Temple court and porches, they would gladly have seen Him, not far off, but near: spoken to Him. They had became Proselytes of Righteousness; they would become disciples of the Lord our Righteousness; as Proselytes they had come to Jerusalem to worship, and they would learn to praise. Yet, in the simple self unconscious modesty of their religious childhood, they dared not go to Jesus directly, but came with their request to Philip of Bethsaida. We do not know why to him: whether from family connections, or that his education, or previous circumstances, connected Philip with these Greeks, or whether anything in his position in the Apostolic circle, or something that had just occurred, influenced their choice. And he also, such was the ignorance of the Apostles of the inmost meaning of their Master, dared not go directly to Jesus, but went to his own townsman, who had been his early friend and fellow disciple, and now stood so close to the Person of Jesus, Andrew, the brother of Simon Peter. Together the two came to Jesus, Andrew apparently foremost. The answer of Jesus implies what, at any rate, we would have expected, that the request of these Gentile converts was granted, though this is not expressly stated, and it is extremely difficult to determine whether, and what portion of what He spoke was addressed to the Greeks, and what to the disciples. Perhaps we should regard the opening words as bearing reference to the request of the Greeks, and therefore as primarily addressed to the disciples, but also as serving as introduction of the words that follow, which were spoken primarily the Greeks, but secondarily also to the disciples, and which bear on that terrible, very near, mystery of His death, and their Baptism into it.

As we see these Greeks approaching, the beginning of Christ's History seems re-enacted at its close. Not now in the stable of Bethlehem, but in the Temple, are the wise men, the representatives of the Gentile world, offering their homage to the Messiah. But the life which had then begun was now all behind Him, and yet, in a sense, before Him. The hour of decision was about to strike. Not merely as the Messiah of Israel, but in His world wide bearing as the Son of Man, was He about to be glorified by receiving the homage of the Gentile world, of which the symbol and the first fruits were now before Him. But only in one way could He thus be glorified: by dying for the salvation of the world, and so opening the Kingdom of Heaven to all believers. On a thousand hills was the glorious harvest to tremble in the golden sunlight; but the grain of wheat falling into the ground, must, as it falls, die, burst its envelope, and so spring into a very manifoldedness of life. Otherwise would it have remained alone. This is the great paradox of the Kingdom of God, a paradox which has its symbol and analogy in nature, and which has also almost become the law of progress in history: that life which has not sprung of death abides alone, and is really death, and that death is life. A paradox this, which has its ultimate reason in this, that sin has entered into the world.

And as to Jesus, the Prince of Life, so to the disciples, as bearing forth the life. If, in this world of sin, He must fall as the seed grain into the ground and die, that many may spring of Him, so must they also hate their life, that they may keep it to life eternal. Thus serving, they must follow Him, that where He is they may also be, for the Father will honor them that honor the Son.

It is now sufficiently clear to us, that Jesus spoke primarily to these Greeks, and secondarily to His disciples, of the meaning of His impending death, of the necessity of faithfulness to Him in it, and of the blessing attaching thereto. Yet was not unconscious of the awful realities which this involved. He was true, Man, and His Human Soul was troubled in view of it: True Man, therefore He felt it; True Man, therefore He spoke it, and so also sympathized with them in their coming struggle. Truly Man, but also truly more than Man, and therefore both the expressed desire, and at the same time the victory over that desire: What shall I say? "Father, save Me from this hour? But for this cause I came to this hour!" And the seeming discord is resolved, as both the Human and the Divine in the Son, faith and sight, join in glorious accord; Father, glorify Your Name!

Such appeal and prayer, made in such circumstances, could not have remained unacknowledged, if He was the Messiah, Son of God. As at His Baptism, so at this Baptism of self humiliation and absolute submission to suffering, came the Voice from Heaven, audible to all, but its words intelligible only to Him: I both glorified it, and will again glorify it! Words these, which carried the Divine seal of confirmation to all Christ's past work, and assured it for that which was to come. The words of confirmation could only be for Himself; the Voice was for all. What did it matter, that some spoke of it as thunder on a spring evening, while others, with more reason, thought of Angel Voices? To him it bore the assurance, which had all along been the ground of His claims, as it was the comfort in His Sufferings, that, as God had in the past glorified Himself in the Son, so would it be in the future in the perfecting of the work given Him to do. And this He now spoke, as, looking on those Greeks as the emblem and first fruits of the work finished in His Passion, He saw of the travail of His Soul, and was satisfied. Of both He spoke in the prophetic present. To His view judgment had already come to this world, as it lay in the power of the Evil One, since the Prince of it was cast out from his present rule. And, in place of it, the Crucified Christ, lifted up out of the earth, in the twofold sense, was, as the result of His Work, drawing, with sovereign, conquering power, all to Him, and up with Him.

The Jews who heard it, so far understood Him, that His words referred to His removal from earth, or His death, since this was a common Jewish mode of expression. But they failed to understand His special reference to the manner of it. And yet, in view of the peculiarly shameful death to the cross, it was most important that He should ever point to it also. But, even in what they understood, they had a difficulty. They understood Him to imply that He would be taken from earth; and yet they had always been taught from the Scriptures that the Messiah was, when fully manifested, to stand for forever, or, as the Rabbis put it, that His Reign was to be followed by the Resurrection. Or did He refer to any other One by the expression, Son of Man? Into the controversial part of the question Jesus did not enter; nor would it have been fitting to have so in that hour. But to their inquiry He fully replied, and that with such earnest, loving admonition as became His last address in the Temple. Yes; it was so! But a little while would the Light be among them. Let them hurry to avail themselves of it, for fear that darkness overtake them, and he that walked in darkness did not know where he went. Oh, that His love could have arrested them! While they still had the Light, would that they might learn to believe in the Light, that so they might become the children of Light!

They were His last words of appeal to them, before He withdrew to spend His Sabbath of soul before the Great Contest. And the writer of the Fourth Gospel gathers up, by way of epilogue, the great contrast between Israel and Christ. Although He had shown so many miracles, they did not believe on Him, and thus their willful unbelief was the fulfillment of Esaias prophecy of old concerning the Messiah. On the other hand, their willful unbelief was also the judgment of God in accordance with prophecy. Those who have followed the course of this history must have learned this above all, that the rejection of Christ by the Jews was not an isolated act, but the outcome and direct result of their whole previous religious development. In face of the clearest evidence, they did not believe, because they could not believe. The long course of their resistance to the prophetic message, and their perversion of it, was itself a hardening of their hearts, although at the same time a God decreed sentence on their resistance. Because they would not believe, through this their mental doubtfulness, which came upon them in Divine judgment, although in the natural course of their self chosen religious development, therefore, despite all evidence, they did not believe, when He came and did such miracles before them. And all this in accordance with prophecy, when Isaiah saw in far off vision the bright glory of Messiah, and spoke of Him. Thus far Israel as a nation. And though, even among their chief rulers, there were many who believed on him, yet dared they not make confession, from fear that the Pharisees would put them out of the Synagogues, with all the terrible consequences which this implied. For such surrender of all were they not prepared, whose intellect might be convinced, but whose heart was not converted, who loved the glory of men more than the glory of God.

Such was Israel. On the other hand, what was the summary of the Christ's activity? His testimony now rose so loud, as to be within hearing of all (Jesus cried). From first to last that testimony had pointed from Himself up to the Father. Its substance was the reality and the realization of that which the Old Testimony had pointed from Himself up to the Father. Its substance was the reality and the realization of that which the Old Testament had infolded and gradually unfolded to Israel, and through Israel to the world: the Fatherhood of God. To believe on him was really not faith in him, but faith in him that sent Him. A step higher: To regard Christ was to regard Him that had sent Him. To combine these two: Christ had come a light into the world, God had sent Him as the Sun of Righteousness, that by believing on him as the God sent, men might attain moral vision, no longer live in darkness, but in the bright spiritual light that and risen. But as for the others, there were those who heard and did not keep His words; and, again, who rejected, Him, and did not receive His words. Neither in one nor the other case was the controversy as between His sayings and men. As regarded the one class, He had come into the world with the Word of salvation, not with the sword of judgment. As regarded His open enemies, He left the issue until the evidence of His word should appear in the terrible judgment of the last Day.

Once more, and more emphatic than ever, was the final appeal to His Mission by the Father. From first to last it had not been His own work: what He should say, and what He should speak, the Father Himself had given Him commandment. This commandment, and what He spoke in it, was not mere teaching, nor Law: it was Life everlasting. And so it is, and ever shall be, eternal thanks to the love of Him Who sent, and the grace of Him Who came: that the things which He spoke, He spoke as the Father said to Him.

These two things, then, are the final summary by the Apostle of the History of the Christ in His public activity. On the one hand, he shows us how Israel, hardened in the self chosen course of its religious development, could not, and, despite the clearest evidence, did not, believe. And, on the other hand, he sets before us the Christ absolutely surrendering Himself to do the Will and Work of the Father; witnessed by the Father; revealing the Father; coming as the Light of the world to chase away its moral darkness; speaking to all men, bringing to them salvation, not judgment, and leaving the vindication of His Word to its manifestation in the Last Day; and finally, as the Christ, Whose every message is commanded of God, and Whose every commandment is life everlasting, and therefore and so speaking it, as the Father said to Him.

These two things: concerning the history of Israel and their necessary unbelief, and concerning the Christ as God sent, God witnessed, God revealing, bringing light and life as the Father's gift and command, the Christ as absolutely surrendering Himself to this Mission and embodying it, are the sum of the Gospel narratives. They explain their meaning, and set forth their object and lessons.

End Notes:

[8]   Some might have even religious scruples about handling a coin of Caesar. Such an instance is mentioned in Ab. Zar. 6 b, where a Rabbi is advised to throw it into the water, and pretend it had accidentally dropped from his hand, but probably that instance refers to the avoidance of all possibility of being regarded as sharing in idol festivities.

[9]   By a strange concurrence the coin, which on Christ's demand was handed to Him, bore the image of the Emperor. It must, therefore, have been either a foreign one (Roman), or else one of the Tetrarch Philip, who exceptionally had the image of Tiberius on his coins (comp. Schuerer, N.T. Zeitgesch. p. 231). Neither Herod nor Herod Antipas had any image on their coins, but only the usual devices of the Maccabean period. And the coins, which the Roman emperors had struck especially for Palestine, bore until the time of Vespasian, in accommodation to Jewish prejudices, no image of any kind.

[10]   Jewish tradition, though it ever had painfully thrusts forward the reward, has some beautiful legends, allegories, and sayings about the gifts of the poor. One quotation must here suffice (Bemidb. R. 14). It is to the effect, that, if one who is poor, does charity, God says of him: This one is preventing Me. He has kept My commandments before they have come to him. I must recompense him. In Vayyikra R. 3, we read of a woman, whose offering of a handful of flour the priest despised, when God admonished him in a dream to value the gifts as highly as if she had offered herself. Yet another quotation from the Mishnah. The tractate Menachoth closes with these words: As regards burnt offerings of beasts and those of fowls (those of the poor) and the meat offering, we find the expression "for a sweet savor," to teach us, that to offer much or to offer little is the same, provided only that a person direct mind and heart towards God.

[11]   We mark here that only proselytes of righteousness, who had submitted to circumcision, would be allowed fellowship in the regular worship.

Chapter 4

The Third Day and the Eight Woes

(Matthew 22:23-33; Mark 12:18-27; Luke 20:27-39; Matthew 22:34-40; Mark 12:28-34; Matthew 22:41-46; Mark 12:35-40; Luke 20:40-47; Matthew 23)

The last day in the Temple was not to pass without other temptations than that of the Priests when they questioned His authority, or of the Pharisees when they cunningly sought to entangle Him in His speech. Indeed, Christ had on this occasion taken a different position; He had claimed supreme authority, and thus challenged the leaders of Israel. For this reason, and because at the last we expect assaults from all His enemies, we are prepared for the controversies of that day.

We remember that, during the whole previous history, Christ had only on one occasion come into public conflict with the Sadducees, when, characteristically, they had asked Him for a sign from heaven. Their Rationalism would lead them to treat the whole movement as beneath serious notice, the outcome of ignorant fanaticism. Nevertheless, when Jesus assumed such a position in the Temple, and was evidently to such extent swaying the people, it compelled them, if only to guard their position, no longer to stand by. Possibly, the discomfiture and powerlessness of the Pharisees may also have had their influence. At any rate, the impression left is, that those of them who now went to Christ were delegates, and that the question which they put had been well planned.

Their object was certainly not serious argument, but to use the much more dangerous weapon of ridicule. Persecution the populace might have resented; for open opposition all would have been prepared; but to come with icy politeness and philosophic calm, and by a well turned question to reduce the renowned Galilean Teacher to silence, and show the absurdity of His teaching, would have been to inflict on His cause the most damaging blow. To this day such appeals to rough and ready common sense are the main stock-in-trade of that coarse infidelity, which, ignoring the demands of higher thinking and the facts of history, appeals, so often, unfortunately effectually, to the untrained intellect of the multitude, and, shall we not say it?, to the coarse and lower in us all. Besides, had the Sadducees succeeded, they would at the same time have gained a signal triumph for their tenets, and defeated, together with the Galilean Teacher, their own Pharisaic opponents. The subject of attack was to be the Resurrection, the same which is still the favorite topic for the appeals of the coarser forms of infidelity to the common sense of the masses. Making allowance for difference of circumstances, we might almost imagine we were listening to one of our modern orators of materialism. And in those days the defense of belief in the Resurrection labored under twofold difficulty. It was as yet a matter of hope, not of faith: something to look forward to, not to look back upon. The isolated events recorded in the Old Testament, and the miracles of Christ, granting that they were admitted, were rather instances of resuscitation than of Resurrection. The grand fact of history, than which none is better attested, the Resurrection of Christ, had not yet taken place, and was not even clearly in view of anyone. Besides the utterances of the Old Testament on the subject of the hereafter were, as became that stage of revelation and the understanding of those to whom it was addressed, far from clear. In the light of the New Testament it stands out in the sharpest proportions, although as an Alpine height far off; but then that Light had not yet risen upon it.

Besides, the Sadducees would allow no appeal to the highly poetic language of the Prophets, to whom, at any rate, they attached less authority, but demanded proof from that clear and precise letter of the Law, every tittle and iota of which the Pharisees exploited for their doctrinal inferences, and from which alone they derived them. Here, also, it was the Nemesis of Pharisaism, that the claims of their system laid it open to attack. In vain would the Pharisees appeal to Isaiah, Ezekiel, Daniel, or the Psalms. To such an argument as from the words, this people will rise up, the Sadducees would rightly reply, that the context prohibitted the application to the Resurrection; to the quotation of Isaiah 25:19, they would answer that that promise must be understood spiritually, like the vision of the dry bones in Ezekiel; while such a reference as to this, causing the lips of those that are asleep to speak, would scarcely require serious refutation. Of similar character would be the argument from the use of a special word, such as return in Genesis 3:19, or that from the twofold mention of the word cut off in the original of Numbers 15:31, as implying punishment in the present and in the future dispensation. Scarcely more convincing would be the appeal to such passages as Deuteronomy 32:39: I kill and make alive, or the statement that, whenever a promise occurs in the form which in Hebrew represents the future tense, it indicates a reference to the Resurrection. Perhaps more satisfactory, although not convincing to a Sadducee, whose special contention it was to insist on proof from the Law, might be an appeal to such passages as Daniel 12:2, 13, or to the restoration of life by certain of the prophets, with the superadded canon, that God had in part prefiguratively performed by His prophets whatever He would fully restore in the future.

If Pharisaic argumentation had failed to convince the Sadducees on Biblical grounds, it would be difficult to imagine that, even in the then state of scientific knowledge, any enquiring person could have really believed that there was a small bone in the spine which was indestructible, and from which the new man would spring; or that there existed even now a species of mice, or else of snails, which gradually and visibly developed out of the earth. Many clever sayings of the Pharisees are, here recorded in their controversies, as on most subjects, and by which a Jewish opponent might have been silenced. But here, especially, must it have been felt that a reply was not always an answer, and that the silencing of an opponent was not identical with proof of ones own assertion. And the additions with which the Pharisees had encumbered the doctrine of the Resurrection would not only surround it with fresh difficulties, but deprive the simple fact of its grand majesty. Thus, it was a point in discussion, whether a person would rise in his clothes, which one Rabbi tried to establish by a reference to the grain of wheat, which was buried naked, but rose clothed. Indeed, some Rabbis held, that a man would rise in exactly the same clothes in which he had been buried, while others denied this. On the other hand, it was beautifully argued that body and soul must be finally judged together, so that, in their contention to which of them the sins of man had been due, justice might be meted out to each, or rather to the two in their combination, as in their combination they had sinned. Again, it was inferred from the apparition of Samuel that the risen would look exactly as in life, have even the same bodily defects, such as lameness, blindness, or deafness. It is argued, that they were only afterwards to be healed, for fear that enemies might say that

God had not healed them when they were alive, but that He did so when they were dead, and that they were perhaps not the same persons. In some respects even more strange was the contention that, in order to secure that all the pious of Israel should rise on the sacred soil of Palestine, there were cavities underground in which the body would roll until it reached the Holy Land, there to rise to newness of life.

But all the more, that it was so keenly controverted by pagans, Sadducees, and heretics, as appears from many reports in the Talmud, and that it was so encumbered with realistic legends, should we admire the tenacity with which the Pharisees clung to this doctrine. The hope of the Resurrection world appears in almost every religious utterance of Israel. It is the spring bud on the tree, stripped by the long winter of disappointment and persecution. This hope pours its morning carol into the prayer which every Jew is bound to say on awakening; it sheds its warm breath over the oldest of the daily prayers which date from before the time of Jesus; in the formula from age to age, world without end, it forms, so to speak, the rear guard to every prayer, defending it from Sadducean assault; it is one of the few dogma denials of which involves, according to the Mishnah, the loss of eternal life, the Talmud explaining, almost in the words of Christ, that in the retribution of God this is only measure according to measure; it is venerable even in its exaggeration, that only our ignorance fails to perceive it in every section of the Bible, and to hear it in every commandment of the Law.

But in the view of Christ the Resurrection would necessarily occupy a place different from all this. It was the innermost shrine in the Sanctuary of His Mission, towards which He steadily tended; it was also, at the same time, the living corner stone of that Church which he had built, and its spire, which, as with uplifted finger, ever pointed all men heavenwards. But of such thoughts connected with His Resurrection Jesus could not have spoken to the Sadducees; they would have been unintelligible at that time even to His own disciples. He met the hair splitting of the Sadducees majestically, seriously, and solemnly, with words most lofty and spiritual, yet such as they could understand, and which, if they had received them, would have led them onwards and upwards far beyond the standpoint of the Pharisees. A lesson this to us in our controversies.

The story under which the Sadducees conveyed their sneer was also intended covertly to strike at their Pharisaic opponents. The ancient ordinance of marrying a brother's childless widow had more and more fallen into discredit, as its original motive ceased to have influence. A large array of limitations narrowed the number of those on whom this obligation now devolved. Then the Mishnah laid it down that, in ancient times, when the ordinance of such marriage was obeyed in the spirit of the Law, its obligation took precedence of the permission of dispensation, but that afterwards this relationship became reversed. Later authorities went further. Some declared every such union, if for beauty, wealth, or any other than religious motives, as incestuous, while one Rabbi absolutely prohibited it, although opinions continued divided on the subject. But what here most interests us is, that what are called in the Talmud the Samaritans, but, as we judge, the Sadducees, held the opinion that the command to marry a brothers widow only applied to a betrothed wife, not to one that had actually been wedded. This gives point to the controversial question, as addressed to Jesus.

A case such as they told, of a woman who had successively been married to seven brothers, might, according to Jewish Law, have really happened. Their sneering question now was, whose wife she was to be in the Resurrection. This on the assumption of the grossly materialistic views of the Pharisees. In this the Sadducean hair splitting was, in a sense, anticipating certain objections of modern materialism. It proceeded on the assumption that the relations of time would apply to eternity, and the conditions of the things seen hold true in regard to those that are unseen. But perchance it is otherwise; and the future may reveal what in the present we do not see. The reasoning as such may be faultless; but, perchance, something in the future may have to be inserted in the major or the minor, which will make the conclusion quite other! All such hair splitting we would meet with the twofold appeal of Christ to the Word and to the Power of God, how God has manifested, and how He will manifest Himself, the one flowing from the other.

In His argument against the Sadducees Christ first appealed to the power of God. What God would work was quite other than they imagined: not a mere re-awakening, but a transformation. The world to come was not to be a reproduction of that which had passed away, or else why should it have passed away, but a regeneration and renovation; and the body with which we were to be clothed would be like that which Angels bear. What, therefore, in our present relations is of the earth, and of our present body of sin and corruption, will cease; what is eternal in them will continue. But the power of God will transform all, the present terrestrial into the future heavenly, the body of humiliation into one of exaltation. This will be the perfecting of all things by that Almighty Power by which He shall subdue all things to Himself in the Day of His Power, when death shall be swallowed up in victory. And herein also consists the dignity of man, in virtue of the Redemption introduced, and, so to speak, begun at his Fall, that man is capable of such renovation and perfection, and herein, also, is the power of God, that He has quickened us together with Christ, so that here already the Church receives in Baptism into Christ the germ of the Resurrection, which is afterwards to be nourished and fed by faith, through the believers participation in the Sacrament of fellowship with His body and Blood. Nor ought questions here to rise, like dark clouds, such as of the eternity of those relations which on earth are not only so precious to us, but so holy. Assuredly, they will endure, as all that is of God and good; only what in them is earthly will cease, or rather be transformed with the body. And we shall also recognize each other, not only by the fellowship of the soul; but as, even now, the mind impresses its stamp on the features, so then, when all shall be quite true, shall the soul, so to speak, body itself forth, fully impress itself on the outward appearance, and for the first time shall we then fully recognize those whom we shall now fully know, with all of earth that was in them left behind, and all of God and good fully developed and ripened into perfectness of beauty.

But it was not enough to brush aside the flimsy hair splitting, which had only meaning on the supposition of grossly materialistic views of the Resurrection. Our Lord would not merely reply, He would answer the Sadducees; and more grand or noble evidence of the Resurrection has never been offered than that which He gave. Of course as speaking to the Sadducees, He remained on the ground of the Pentateuch; and yet it was not only to the Law but to the whole Bible that He appealed to that which underlay Revelation itself: the relation between God and man. Not this nor that isolated passage only proved the Resurrection: He Who, not only historically but in the fullest sense, calls Himself the God of Abraham, of Isaac, and of Jacob, cannot leave them dead. Revelation implies, not merely a fact of the past, as is the notion which traditionalism attaches to it, a dead letter; it means a living relationship. He is not the God of the dead, but of the living, for all live to Him.

The Sadducees were silenced, the multitude was astonished, and even from some of the Scribes the admission was involuntarily wrung: Teacher, You have beautifully said. One point, however, still claims our attention. It is curious that, as regards both these arguments of Christ, Rabbinism offers statements closely similar. Thus, it is recorded as one of the frequent sayings of a later Rabbi, that in the world to come there would be neither eating nor drinking, fruitfulness nor increase, business nor envy, hatred nor strife, but that the just would sit with crowns on their heads, and feast on the splendor of the Shechinah. This reads like a Rabbinic adaptation of the saying of Christ. As regards the other point, the Talmud reports a discussion on the Resurrection between Sadducees, or perhaps Jewish heretics (Jewish-Christian heretics), in which Rabbi Gamaliel II at last silences his opponents by an appeal to the promise that you may prolong your days in the land which the Lord swore to your father to give to them, to them, emphasizes the Rabbi, not to you. Although this almost entirely misses the spiritual meaning conveyed in the reasoning of Christ, it is impossible to mistake its Christian origin. Gamaliel II lived after Christ, but at a period when there was lively intercourse between Jews and Jewish Christians; while, lastly, we have abundant evidence that the Rabbi was acquainted with the sayings of Christ, and took part in the controversy with the Church. On the other hand, Christians in his day—unless heretical sects, neither denied that Resurrection, nor would they have so argued with the Jewish Patriarch; while the Sadducees no longer existed as a party engaging in active controversy. But we can easily perceive, that intercourse would be more likely between Jews and such heretical Jewish Christians as might maintain that the Resurrection was past, and only spiritual. The point is deeply interesting. It opens such further questions as these: In the constant intercourse between Jewish Christians and Jews, what did the latter learn? and may there not be much in the Talmud which is only an appropriation and adaptation of what had been derived from the New Testament?

2. The answer of Jesus was not without its further results. As we conceive it, among those who listened to the brief but decisive passage between Jesus and the Sadducees were some Scribes, Sopherim, or, as they are also designated, lawyers, teachers of the Law, experts, expounders, practitioners of the Jewish Law. One of them, perhaps he who exclaimed: Beautifully said, Teacher! hurried to the knot of Pharisees, whom it requires no stretch of the imagination to picture gathered in the Temple on that day, and watching, with restless, ever foiled malice, Jesus' every movement. As the Scribe came up to them, he would relate how Jesus had literally gagged and muzzled the Sadducees, just as, according to the will of God, we are by well doing to gag the lack or knowledge of senseless men. There can be little doubt that the report would give rise to mingled feelings, in which that prevailing would

be, that, although Jesus might thus have embarrassed the Sadducees, He would be unable to cope with other questions, if only properly put forward by Pharisaic learning. And so we can understand how one of the number, perhaps the same Scribe, would volunteer to undertake the office; and how his question was, as Matthew reports, in a sense really intended to tempt Jesus.

We dismiss here the well known Rabbinic distinctions of heavy and light commandments, because Rabbinism declared the light to be as binding as the heavy, those of the Scribes more heavy (or binding) than those of Scripture, and that one commandment was not to be considered to carry greater reward, and to be therefore more carefully observed, than another. That such thoughts were not in the mind of the questioner, but rather the grand general problem, however himself might have answered it, appears even from the form of his inquiry: Which [qualis] is the great, the first, commandment in the Law? So challenged, Jesus could have no hesitation in replying. Not to silence him, but to speak the absolute truth, He quoted the well remembered words which every Jew was bound to repeat in his devotions, and which were ever to be on his lips, living or dying, as the inmost expression of his faith: Hear, O Israel, the Lord our God is one Lord. And then continuing, He repeated the command concerning love to God which is the outcome of that profession. But to have stopped here would have been to offer a theoretic abstraction without concrete reality, a mere Pharisaic worship of the letter. As God is love, His Nature so manifesting itself, so is love to God also love to man. And so this second is like the first and great commandment. It was a full answer to the Scribe when He said: There is none other commandment greater than these.

But it was more than an answer, even deepest teaching, when, as Matthew reports, He added: on these two commandments hang all the law and the prophets. It little matters for our present purpose how the Jews at the time understood and interpreted these two commandments. They would know what it meant that the Law and the Prophets hung on them, for it was a Jewish expression. He taught them, not that anyone commandment was greater or smaller, heavier or lighter, than another, might be set aside or neglected, but that all sprang from these two as their root and principle, and stood in living connection with them. It was teaching similar to that concerning the Resurrection; that, as concerning the promises, so concerning the commandments, all Revelation was one connected whole; not disjointed ordinances of which the letter was to be weighed, but a life springing from love to God and love to man. So noble was the answer, that for the moment the generous enthusiasm of the Scribe, who had previously been favorably impressed by Christ's answer to the Sadducees, was kindled. For the moment, at least, traditionalism lost its sway; and, as Christ pointed to it, he saw the exceeding moral beauty of the Law. He was not far from the Kingdom of God. Whether or not he ever actually entered it, is written on the yet unread page of its history.

3.   The Scribe had originally come to put his question with mixed motives, partially inclined towards Him from His answer to the Sadducees, and yet intending to subject Him to the Rabbinic test. The effect now performed in him, and the silence which from that moment fell on all His would be questioners, induced Christ to follow up the impression that had been made. Without addressing anyone in particular, He set before them all, what perhaps was the most familiar subject in their theology, that of the descent of Messiah. Whose Son was He? And when they replied: The Son of David, He referred them to the opening words of Psalm 110, in which David called the Messiah Lord. The argument proceeded on the two fold supposition that the Psalm was Davidic and that it was Messianic. Neither of these statements would have been questioned by the ancient Synagogue. But we could not rest satisfied with the explanation that this sufficed for the purpose of Christ's argument, if the foundation on which it rested could be seriously called in question. Such, however, is not the case. To apply Psalm 110, verse by verse and consistently, to anyone of the Maccabees, was to undertake a critical task which only a series of unnatural explanations of the language could render possible. Strange, also, that such an interpretation of what at the time of Christ would have been a comparatively young composition, should have been wholly unknown to Sadducee and Pharisee. For our own part, we are content to rest the Messianic interpretation on the obvious and natural meaning of the words taken in connection with the general teaching of the Old Testament about the Messiah, on the undoubted interpretation of the ancient Jewish Synagogue, on the authority of Christ, and on the testimony of History.

Compared with this, the other question as to the authorship of the Psalm is of secondary importance. The character of infinite Divine, superiority to any earthly Ruler, and of course to David, which the Psalm sets forth in regard to the Messiah, would sufficiently support the argument of Christ. But, besides, what does it matter, whether the Psalm was composed by David, or only put into the mouth of David (David's or Davidic), which, on the supposition of Messianic application, is the only rational alternative?

But we should greatly err if we thought that, in calling the attention of His hearers to this apparent contradiction about the Christ, Jesus only intended to show the utter incompetence of the Pharisees to teach the higher truths of the Old Testament. Such, was the case, and they felt it in His Presence. But far beyond this, as in the proof which He gave for the Resurrection, and in the view which He presented of the great commandment, Jesus would point to the grand harmonious unity of Revelation. Viewed separately, the two statements, that Messiah was David's Son, and that David owned Him as Lord, would seem incompatible. But in their combination in the Person of the Christ, how harmonious and how full of teaching, to Israel of old, and to all men, concerning the nature of Christ's Kingdom and of His Work!

It was but one step from this demonstration of the incompetence of Israel's teachers for the position they claimed to a solemn warning on this subject. And this appropriately constitutes Christ's Farewell to the Temple, to its authorities, and to Israel. As might have been expected, we have the report of it in Matthew's Gospel. Much of this had been said before, but in quite other connection, and therefore with different application. We notice this, when comparing this discourse with the Sermon on the Mount, and, still more, with what Christ had said when at the meal in the house of the Pharisee in Perea. But here Matthew presents a regular series of charges against the representatives of Judaism, formulated in logical manner, taking up successively one point after the other, and closing with the expression of deepest compassion and longing for that Jerusalem, whose children He would gladly have gathered under His sheltering wings from the storm of Divine judgment.

To begin with, Christ would have them understand, that, in warning them of the incompetence of Israel's teachers for the position which they occupied, He neither wished for Himself nor His disciples the place of authority which they claimed, nor yet sought to incite the people to resistance thereto. On the contrary, so long as they held the place of authority they were to be regarded, in the language of the Mishnah, as if instituted by Moses himself, as sitting in Moses seat, and were to be obeyed, so far as merely outward observances were concerned. We regard this direction, not as of merely temporary application, but as involving as important principle.

But we also recall that the ordinances to which Christ made reference were those of the Jewish canon law, and did not involve anything which could really affect the conscience, except that of the ancient, or of our modern Pharisees. But while they thus obeyed their outward directions, they were equally to have nothing to do with the spirit which characterized their observances. In this respect of twofold charge is laid against them: of lack of spiritual earnestness and love, and of more externalism, vanity, and self seeking. And here Christ interrupted His discourse to warn His disciples against the first beginnings of what had led to such fearful consequences, and to point them to the better way.

This constitutes the first part of Christ's charge. Before proceeding to those which follow, we may give a few illustrative explanations. Of the opening accusation about the binding (truly in bondage: desmeo) of heavy burdens and grievous to be borne, and laying them on men's shoulders, proof can scarcely be required. As frequently shown, Rabbinism placed the ordinances of tradition above those of the Law, and this by a necessity of the system, since they were professedly the authoritative exposition and the supplement of the written Law. And although it was a general rule, that no ordinance should be directed heavier that the congregation could bear, yet (as previously stated) it was admitted, that whereas the words of the Law contained what lightened and what made heavy, the words of the Scribes contained only what made heavy. Again, it was another principle, that was an aggravation or increase of the burden had once been introduced, it must continue to be observed. Thus the burdens became intolerable. And the blame rested equally on both the great Rabbinic Schools. For, although the School of Hillel was supposed in general to make the yoke lighter, and that of Shammai heavier, yet not only did they agree on many points, but the School of Hillel was not infrequently even more strict than that of his rival. In truth, their differences seem too often only prompted by a spirit of opposition, so that the serious business of religion became in their hands one of rival authority and mere wrangling.

It is not so easy to understand the second part of Christ's accusation. There were, many hypocrites among them, who might, in the language of the Talmud, alleviate for themselves and make heavy for others. Yet the charge of not moving them with the finger could scarcely apply to the Pharisees as a party, not even in this sense, that Rabbinic ingenuity mostly found some means of evading what was unpleasant. But, as previously explained, we would understand the word rendered move as meaning to set in motion, or move away, in the sense that they did not alleviate where they might have done so, or else with reference to their admitted principle, that their ordinances always made heavier, never lighter, always imposed grievous burdens, but never, not even with the finger, moved them away.

With this charge of unreality and lack of love, those of externalism, vanity, and self seeking are closely connected. Here we can only make selection from the abundant evidence in our support of it. By a merely external interpretation of Exodus 13:9, 16, and Deuteronomy 6:8; 10:18, practice of wearing Phylacteries or, as they were called, Tephillin, prayer fillets, was introduced. These, as will be remembered, were square capsules, covered with leather, containing on small scrolls of parchment, these four sections of the law: Exodus 13:1-10; 11-16: Deuteronomy 6:4-9; 10:13-21. The Phylacteries were fastened by long leather straps to the forehead, and around the left arm, near the heart. Most superstitious reverence was attached to them, and in later times they were even used as amulets. Nevertheless, the Talmud itself gives confirmation that the practice of constantly wearing phylacteries, or, it might be, making them broad, and enlarging the borders of the garments, we intended for to be seen of men. Thus we are told of a certain man who had done so, in order to cover his dishonest practices in appropriating what had been entrusted to his keeping. The Rabbis had in so many words to lay it down as a principle, than the Phylacteries were not to be worn for show.

Detailed proof is scarcely required of the charge of vanity and self seeking in claiming marked outward honors, such as the upper-most places at feasts and in the Synagogue, respectful salutations in the market, the ostentatious repetition of the title Rabbi, or Abba, Father, or Master, or the distinction of being acknowledged as greatest. The very earnestness with which the Talmud sometimes warns against such motives for study or for piety sufficiently establishes it. But, Rabbinic writings lay down elaborate directions, what place is to be assigned to the Rabbis, according to their rank, and to their disciples, and how in the College the most learned, but at feast the most aged, among the Rabbis, are to occupy the upper seats. So weighty was the duty of respectful salutation by the title Rabbi, that to neglect it would involve the heaviest punishment. Two great Rabbis are described as literally complaining, that they must have lost the very appearance of learning, since in the market place they only had been greeted with May your peace be great, without the addition My masters.

A few further illustrations of the claims which Rabbinism preferred may throw light on the words of Christ. It reads like a wretched imitation from the New Testament, when the pagan Governor of Caesarea is represented as rising up before Rabbis because he beheld the faces as it were of Angels; or like an adaptation of the well known story about Constantine the Great when the Governor of Antioch is described as vindicating a similar mark of respect to the Rabbis by this, that he had seen their faces and by them conquered in battle. From another Rabbi rays of light are said to have visibly proceeded. According to some, they were Epicuraeans, who had no part in the world to come, who referred slightingly to these Rabbis. To supply a learned man with the means of gaining money in trade, would procure a high place in heaven. It was said that, according to Proverbs 8:15, the sages were to be saluted as kings; in some respects, they were higher, for, as between a sage and a king, it would be duty to give the former priority in redemption from captivity, since every Israelite was fit to be a king, but the loss of a Rabbi could not easily be made up. But even this is not all. The curse of a Rabbi, even if uncaused, would surely come to pass. It would be too painful to repeat some of the miracles pretended to have been done by them or for them, occasionally in protection of a lie; or to record their disputes which among them was greatest, or how they established their respective claims. Their self assertion extended beyond this life, and a Rabbi went so far as to order that he should be buried in white garments, to show that he was worthy of appearing before his Maker. But perhaps the climax of blasphemous self assertion is reached in the story, that, in a discussion in heaven between God and the heavenly Academy on a Halakhic question about purity, a certain Rabbi, deemed that most learned on the subject, was summoned to decide the point! As his soul passed from the body he exclaimed: Pure, pure, which the Voice from Heaven applied to the state of the Rabbis soul; and immediately afterwards a letter had fallen from heaven to inform the sages of the purpose of which the Rabbi had been summoned to the heavenly assembly, and afterwards another commands a weeks universal mourning for him on pain of excommunication.

Such daring profanities must have crushed out all spiritual religion, and reduced it to a mere intellectual display, in which the Rabbi was always chief, here and hereafter. Repulsive as such legends are, they will at least help us to understand what otherwise might seem harsh in Jesus' denunciations of Rabbinism. In view of all this, we need not discuss the Rabbinic warnings against pride and self seeking when connected with study, nor their admonitions to humility. For, the question here is, what Rabbinism regarded as pride, and what as humility, in its teachers? Nor is it maintained that all were equally guilty in this matter; and what passed around may well have led more earnest to energetic admonitions to humility and unselfishness, but no ingenuity can explain away the facts as above stated, and, when such views prevailed, it would have been almost superhuman wholly to avoid what Jesus denounced as characteristic of Pharisaism. And in this sense, not with Pharisaic painful literalism, but as opposed to Rabbinic bearing, are we to understand Jesus' warning to His own not to claim among brethren to be Rabbi, or Abba, or guide. The Law of the Kingdom, as repeatedly taught, was the opposite. As regarded aims, they were to seek the greatness of service; and as regarded that acknowledgment which would come from God, it would be the exaltation of humiliation.

It was not a break in the discourse, rather an intensification of it, when Christ now turned to make final denunciation of Pharisaism in its sin and hypocrisy. Corresponding to the eight Beatitudes in the Sermon on the Mount with which His public Ministry began, He now closed it with eight denunciations of judgment. These are the pouring forth of His holy wrath, the last and fullest testimony against those whose guilt would involve Jerusalem in common sin and common judgment. Step by step, with logical sequence and intensified sorrow of energy, is each charge advanced, and with it the Judgment of Divine wrath announced.

The first Judgment against Pharisaism was on their shutting the Kingdom of God against men by their opposition to the Christ. All knew how exclusive were their pretensions in confining piety to the possession of knowledge, and that they declared it impossible for an ignorant person to be pious. Had they taught men the Scriptures, and shown them the right way, they would have been true to their office; but judgment to them who, in their positions as leaders, had themselves stood back with their backs to the door of the Kingdom, and prevented the entrance of others.

The second Judgment was on their covetousness and hypocrisy. They made long prayers, but how often did it only cover the vilest selfishness, even to the devouring of widows houses. We can scarcely expect the Talmud here to furnish us with illustrative instances, and yet at least one such is recorded; and we recall how often broad phylacteries covered fraudulent minds.

The third Judgment was on their proselytism, which issued only in making their converts twofold more the children of hell than themselves. Against this charge, rightly understood, Judaism has in vain sought to defend itself. It is, true that, in its pride and exclusiveness, Judaism seemed to denounce proselytism, laid down strict rules to test the sincerity of converts, and spoke of them in general contempt as a plague of leprosy.

Yet the bitter complaint of classical writers, the statements of Josephus, the frequent allusions in the New Testament and even the admissions of the Rabbis, prove their zeal for making proselytes, which, but for its moral sequences, would neither have deserted nor drawn down the denunciation of a judgment. Thus the Midrash, commenting on the words: the souls that they had gotten in Haran, refers it to the converts which Abraham had made, adding that every proselyte was to be regarded as if a soul had been created. To this we may add the pride with which Judaism looked back upon the 150,000 Gibeonite converts said to have been made when David avenged the sin of Saul; the satisfaction with which it looked forward to the times of Messiah as those of spontaneous conversion to the Synagogue; and not the infrequent instances in which a spirit favorable to proselytism is exhibited in Jewish writings, as, also, such a saying as this, that when Israel is obedient to the will of God, He brings in as converts to Judaism all the just of the nations, such as Jethro, Rahab, Ruth, etc. But after all, may Jesus not have referred, not to conversion to Judaism in general, but to proselytism to the sect of the Pharisees, which was undoubtedly sought to the compassing of sea and land?

The fourth Judgment is denounced on the moral blindness of these guides rather than on their hypocrisy. From the nature of things it is not easy to understand the precise allusion of Christ. It is true that the Talmud makes the strangest distinction between an oath or adjuration, such as by heaven or by earth, which is not supposed to be binding; and that by any of the letters of which Divine Being, when the oath is supposed to be binding. But it seems more likely that Jesus refers to oaths or adjurations in connection with vows, where the dishonest deception was of the most complicated kind. In general, Jesus here condemns the arbitrariness of all such Jewish distinctions, which, by attaching excessive value to the letter of an oath or vow, really tended to diminish its sanctity. All such distinctions argued folly and more blindness.

The fifth Judgment referred to one of the best known and strangest Jewish ordinances, which extended the mosaic law of tithing, in most burdensome minuteness, even to the smallest products of the soil that were edible and could be preserved, such as anise. Of these, according to some, not only the seeds, but, in certain cases, even the leaves and stalks, had to be tithed. And this, together with grievous omission of the weightier matters of the Law: judgment, mercy, and faith. Truly, this was to strain out the gnat, and swallow the camel! We remember that this conscientiousness in tithing constituted one of the characteristics of the Pharisees; but we could scarcely be prepared for such an instance of it, as when the Talmud gravely assures us that the donkey of a certain Rabbi had been so well trained as to refuse grain of which the tithes had not been taken! And experience, not only in the past but in the present, has only too plainly shown, that a religious zeal which expends itself on trifles has not room nor strength left for the weightier matters of the Law.

From tithing to purification the transition was natural. It constituted the second grand characteristic of Pharisaic piety. We have seen with what punctiliousness questions of outward purity of vessels were discussed. But judgment to the hypocrisy which, caring for the outside, did not take note of whether that which filled the cup and platter had been procured by extortion or was used for excess. And, unfortunately for the blindness which did not perceive, that internal purity was the real condition of that which was outward!

Judgment similarly to another species of hypocrisy, of which, the preceding were but the outcome: that of outward appearance of righteousness, while heart and mind were full of iniquity, just as those annually whited tombs of theirs seemed so fair outwardly, but within were full of dead men's bones and all uncleanness. Judgment, lastly, to that hypocrisy which built and decorated tombs of prophets and righteous men, and by so doing sought to shelter itself from share in the guilt of those who had killed them. It was not spiritual repentance, but national pride, which actuated them in this, the same spirit of self sufficiency, pride, and impenitence which had led their fathers to commit the murders. And were they not about to stain their hands in the blood of Him to Whom all the prophets had pointed? Fast were they in the Divine judgment filling up the measure of their fathers.

And thicker and heavier than ever before fell the hailstorm of His denunciations, as He foretold the certain doom which awaited their national impenitence. Prophets, wise men, and scribes would be sent them of Him; and only murder, sufferings, and persecutions would await them, not reception of their message and warnings. And so would they become heirs of all the blood of martyred saints, from that of him whom Scripture records as the first one murdered, down to that last martyr of Jewish unbelief of whom tradition spoke in such terms, Zechariah, stoned by the kings command in the Court of the Temple, whose blood, as legend had it, did not dry up those two centuries and a half, but still bubbled on the pavement, when Nebuzaradan entered the Temple, and at last avenged it.

And yet it would not have been Jesus, if, while denouncing certain judgment on them who, by continuance and completion of the crimes of their fathers, through the same unbelief, had served themselves heirs to all their guilt, He had not also added to it the passionate lament of a love which, even when spurned, lingered with regretful longing over the lost. They all knew the common illustration of the hen gathering her young brood for shelter, and they knew also what of Divine protection, blessing, and rest it implied, when they spoke of being gathered under the wings of the Shechinah. Gladly and often would Jesus have given to Israel, His people, that shelter, rest, protection, and blessing, but they would not. Looking around on those Temple buildings, that House, it shall be left to them desolate! And he left its courts with these words, that they of Israel should not see Him again until, the night of their unbelief past, they would welcome His return with a better Hosanna than that which greeted His Royal Entry three days before. And this was the Farewell and the parting of Israel's Messiah from Israel and its temple. Yet a Farewell which promised a coming again; and a parting which implied a welcome in the future from a believing people to a gracious, pardoning King!

End Notes:

[12]   Jeremiah Yebam. 6 b, relates what I regard as a legendary story of a man who was thus induced to wed the twelve widows of his twelve brothers, each widow promising to pay for the expenses of one month, and the directing Rabbi for those of the 13th (intercalatory) month. But to his horror, after three years the women returned, laden with thirty six children, to claim the fulfillment of the Rabbis promise! On the other hand it was, however, also laid down that, if a woman had lost two husbands, she should not marry a third, according to others, if she had married three, not a fourth, as there might be some fate connected with her (Yeb. 64 b). On the question of the Levirate, from the modern Jewish standpoint, see an interesting article by Gutmann in Geigers Wiss. Zeitschr. f. Jued. Theol. vol. iv. (1839), pp. 61-87.

[13]   The reproach You err, not knowing the Scriptures, occurs in almost the same form in the discussions on the Resurrection between the Pharisees and the Sadducees which are recorded in the Talmud.

[14]   Through the Resurrection of Christ resurrection has become the gift of universal humanity. But, beyond this general gift to humanity, we believe that we receive in Baptism, as becoming connected with Christ, the inner

germ of the glorious Resurrection body. Its nourishment (or otherwise) depends on our personal relationship to Christ by faith, and is carried on through the Sacrament of His Body and Blood.

[15] We also recall that Gamaliel II was the brother-in-law of that Eliezer b. Hyrcanos, who was rightly suspected of leanings towards Christianity. This might open up a most interesting field of inquiry.

[16] Meyer rightly remarks on the use of gapseis here, implying moral high estimation and corresponding conduct, and not philen, which refers to love as an affection. The latter could not have been commanded, although such phila of the world is forbidden (James 4:4) while the philen of ones own psuch (John 12:25) and the m philen tn krio (1 Corinthians 15:22) are stigmatized.

[17] Keim, with keen insight, characterizes the Woes which contrasts their proselytizing with their resistance to the progress of the Kingdom; then, the third and fourth which denounce their false teaching, the fifth, and sixth their false attempts at purity, while the last sets forth their relations to those forerunners of Christ, whose graves they built.

[18] We need scarcely remind the reader that this Zechariah was the son of Jehoiada. The difference in the text of Matthew may either be due to family circumstances, unknown to us, which might admit of his designation as the son of Barachias (the reading is undoubtedly correct), or an error may have crept into the text, how, we do not know, and it is of little moment. There can be no question that the reference is to this Zecharias. It seems scarcely necessary to refer to the strange notion that the notice in Matthew 23: 35 has been derived from the account of the murder of Zacharias, the son of Baruch, in the Temple during the last siege (Jos. War. 4:5. 4). To this there are the following four objections: (1) Baruch (as in Jos.) and Barachias (as in Matthew) are quite different names, in Greek as in Hebrew, blessed, Baroch, and Jehovah will bless, Barachas. Comp. for Exodus LXX, Nehemiah 3:20 with 3:30. (2) Because the place of their slaughter was different, that of the one between the porch and the altar, that of the other in the midst of the Temple, either the court of the women, or that of the Israelites. (3) Because the murder of the Zacharias referred to by Matthew stood out as the crowning national crime, and as such is repeatedly referred to in Jewish legend (see references in margin), and dwelt upon with many miraculous embellishments (4) Because the clumsiest forger would scarcely have put into the mouth of Jesus an event connected with the last siege of Jerusalem and derived from Josephus. In general, we take this opportunity strongly to assert that only unacquaintance with the whole subject could

lead anyone to look to Josephus for the source of any part of the evangelic narrative. To these remarks we have to add that precisely the same error (if such it be) as in our text of Matthew occurs in the Targum on Lament. 2:20, where this Zechariah is designated the son (= grandson) of Iddo, comp. Ezra 5:1, and Zechariah 1:1, 7. For the correct reading (son of Jehoiada) in the Gospel of the Hebrews, comp. Nicholson, p. 59.

Chapter 5

The Third Day, Parables in the Temple

Although it may not be possible to mark their exact succession, it will be convenient here to group together the last series of Parables. Most, if not all of them, were spoken on that third day in Passion week: the first four to a more general audience; the last three (to be treated in another chapter) to the disciples, when, on the evening of that third day, on the Mount of Olives, He told them of the Last Things. They are the Parables of Judgment, and in one form or another treat of the End.

1.   The Parable of the Laborers in the Vineyard. As treating of the End, this Parable evidently belongs to the last series, although it may have been spoken previously to Passion Week, perhaps on that Mission journey in Perea, in connection with which it is recorded by Matthew. At any rate, it stands in internal relation with what passed on that occasion, and must therefore be studied with reference to it.

We remember, that on the occasion of the rich young rulers failure to enter the Kingdom, to which he was so near, Christ had uttered an earnest warning on the danger of riches. In the low spiritual stage which the Apostles had as yet attained, it was, perhaps only natural that Peter should, as spokesman of the rest, have, in a kind of spiritual covetousness, clutched at the promised reward, and that in a tone of self righteousness he should have reminded Christ of the yet part of what He, the Lord. had always to bear, and bore so patiently and lovingly, from their ignorance and failure to understand Him and His work. And this lack of true sympathy, this constant contending with the moral dullness even of those nearest to Him, must have been part of His great humiliation and sorrow, one element in the terrible solitariness of His Life, which made Him feel that, in the truest sense, the Son of Man had not where to lay His Head. And yet we also mark the wondrous Divine generosity which, even in moments of such great disappointment, would not let Him take for nothing what should have been freely offered in the joyfully service of grateful love. Only there was here deep danger to the disciples: danger of lapsing into feelings kindred to those with which the Pharisees viewed the pardoned Publicans, or the elder son in the Parable his younger brother; danger of misunderstanding the right relations, and with it the very character of the Kingdom, and of work in and for it. It is to this that the Parable of the Laborers in the Vineyard refers.

The principle which Christ lays down is, that, while nothing done for Him shall lose its reward, yet, from one reason or another, no forecast can be made, no inferences of self righteousness may be drawn. It does not by any means follow, that most work done, at least, to our seeing and judging, shall entail a greater reward. On the contrary, many that are first shall be last; and the last shall be first. Not all, not yet always and necessarily, but many. And in such cases no wrong has been done; there exists no claim, even in view of the promises of due acknowledgement of work. Spiritual pride and self assertion can only be the outcome either of misunderstanding God's relation to us, or else of a wrong state of mind towards others, that is, it betokens mental or moral unfitness.

Of this the Parable of the Laborers is an illustration. It teaches nothing beyond this. But, while illustrating how it may come that some who were first are last, and how utterly mistaken or wrong is the thought that they must necessarily receive more than others, who, seemingly, have done more, how, in short, work for Christ is not a ponderable quantity, so much for so much, nor yet we the judges of when and why a worker has come, it also conveys much that is new, and, in many respects, most comforting.

We mark, first, the bearing of the householder, who went out immediately, at earliest morn (ma pro), to hire laborers into his vineyard. That he did not send his steward, but went himself, and with the dawn of morning, shows both that there was much work to do, and the householders anxiety to have it done. That householder is God, and the vineyard His Kingdom; the laborers, whom with earliest morning He seeks in the market place of busy life, are His Servants. With these he agreed for a denarius a day, which was the ordinary wages for a days labor, and so sent them into the vineyard; in other words, He told them He would pay the reward promised to laborers. So passed the early hours of the morning. About the third hour (the Jewish working day being reckoned from sunrise to sunset), that is, probably as it was drawing towards a close, he went out again, and, as he saw others standing idle in the market place, he said to them, Go you also into the vineyard. There was more than enough to do in that vineyard; enough and more to employ them. And when he came, they had stood in the marketplace ready and waiting to go to work, yet idle, unemployed as yet. It might not have been precisely their blame that they had not gone before; they were others than those in the market place when the master had first come, and they had not been there at that time. Only as he now sent them, he made no definite promise. They felt that in their special circumstances they had no claim; he told them, that what ever was right he would give them; and they implicitly trusted to his word, to his justice and goodness. And so happened it yet again, both at the sixth and at the ninth hour of the day. We repeat, that in none of these instances was it the guilt of the laborers, in the sense of being due to their unwillingness or refusal, that they had not before gone into the vineyard. For some reason, perhaps by their fault, perhaps not, they had not been earlier in the market place. But as soon as they were there and called, they went, although the loss of time, however caused, implied loss of work. Neither did Jesus in any case make, nor they ask for, other promise than that implied in his word and character.

These four things, then, stand out clearly in the Parable: the abundance of work to be done in the vineyard; the anxiety of the householder to secure all available laborers; the circumstance that, not from unwillingness or refusal, but because they had not been there and available, the laborers had come at later hours; and that, when they had so come, they were ready to go into the vineyard without promise of definite reward, simply trusting to the truth and goodness of him whom they went to serve. We think here of those last, the Gentiles from the east, west, north, and south; of the converted publicans and sinners; of those, a great part of whose lives has, unfortunately been spent somewhere else, and who have only come at a late hour into the market place; of them also whose opportunities, capacity, strength, or time have been very limited, and we thank God for the teaching of this Parable. And if doubt should still exist, it must be removed by the concluding sentences of this part of the Parable, in which the householder is represented as going out at the last hour, when, finding others standing he asks them why they stood there all the day idle, to which they reply, that no man had hired them. These also are, in turn, sent into the vineyard, though apparently without any expressed promise at all. It thus appears, that in proportion to the lateness of their work was the felt absence of any claim on the part of the laborers, and their simple reliance on their employer.

And now it is evening. The time for working is past, and the Lord of the vineyard bids His Steward [here the Christ] pay His laborers. But here the first surprise awaits them. The order of payment is the inverse of that of labor: beginning from the last to the first. This is almost a necessary part of the Parable. For, if the first laborers had been paid first, they would either have gone away without knowing what was done to the last, or, if they had remained, their objection could not have been urged, except on the ground of manifest malevolence towards their neighbors. After having received their wages, they could not have objected that they had not received enough, but only that the others had received too much. But it was not the scope of the Parable to charge with conscious malevolence those who sought a higher reward or deemed themselves entitled to it. Again, we notice, as indicating the disposition of the later laborers, that those of the third hour did not murmur, because they had not got more than they of the eleventh hour. This is in accordance with their not having made any bargain at the first, but trusted entirely to the householder. But they of the first hour had their selfishness excited. Seeing what the others had received, they expected. to have more than their due. When they like wise received every man a denarius, they murmured, as if injustice had been done them. And, as mostly in like circumstances, truth and fairness seemed on their side. For, selecting the extreme case of the eleventh hour laborers, had not the Householder made those who had performed only one hour equal to them who had borne the burden of the day and the heat? Yet, however fair their reasoning might seem, they had no claim in truth or equity, for had they not agreed for one denarius with him? And it had not even been in the general terms of a days wages, but they had made the express bargain of one denarius. They had gone to work with a stipulated sum as their hire distinctly in view. They now appealed to justice; but from first to last they had had justice. This as regards the so much for so much principle of claim, law, work, and pay.

But there was yet another aspect than that of mere justice. Those other laborers, who had felt that, owning to the lateness of their appearance, they had no claim, and, unfortunately which of us must not feel how late we have been in coming, and therefore how little we can have performed, had made no bargain, but trusted to the Master. And as they had believed, so was it to them. Not because they made or had any claim, I will, however, to give to this last, even as to you, the word I will (thlo) being emphatically put first to mark the good pleasure of His grace as the ground of action. Such a Master could not have given less to those who had come when called, trusting to His goodness, and not in their deserts. The reward was now reckoned, not of work nor of debt, but of grace. In passing we also mark, as against complainers, the profound accord between what negative critics would call the true Judaic Gospel of Matthew, and what constitutes the very essence of the anti-Judaic teaching of Paul, and we ask our opponents to reconcile on their theory what can only be explained on the ground that Paul, like Matthew, was the true disciple of the true Teacher, Jesus Christ.

But if all is to be placed on the new ground of grace, with which, the whole bearing of the later laborers accords, then (as Paul also shows) the laborers who murmured were guilty either of ignorance in failing to perceive the sovereignty of grace, that it is within His power to do with His own as He wills, or else of wickedness, when, instead of with grateful joy, they looked on with an evil eye, and this in proportion as the Householder was good. But such a state of mind may be equally that of the Jews, and of the Gentiles. And so, in this illustrative case of the Parable, the first shall be last, and the last first. And in other instances also, though not in all, many shall be last that are first; and first that are last. But He is the God, Sovereign in grace, in Whose Vineyard there is work to do for all, however limited their time, power, or opportunity; Whose laborers we are, if His Children; Who, in His desire for the work, and condescension and patience towards the workers, goes out into the market place even to the eleventh hour, and, with only gentlest rebuke for not having earlier come there and thus lost our day in idleness, still, even to the last, bids us come; Who promises what is right, and gives far more than is due to them who simply trust Him: the God not of the Jews nor of the Gentiles only, but our Father; the God Who not only pays, but freely gives of His own, and in Whose Wisdom and by Whose Grace it may be, that, even as the first shall be last, so the last shall be first.

Another point still remains to do not advantage. If anywhere, we expect in these Parables, addressed to the people, forms of teaching and speaking with which they were familiar, in other words, Jewish parallels. But we equally expect that the teaching of Christ, while conveyed under illustrations with which the Jews were familiar, would be entirely different in spirit. And such we find it notably in the present instances. To begin with, according to Jewish Law, if a man engaged a laborer without any definite bargain, but on the statement that he would be paid as one or another of the laborers in the place, he was, according to some, only bound to pay the lowest wages in the place; but, according to the majority, the average between the lowest and the highest. Again, as regards the letter of the Parable itself, we have a remarkable parallel in a funeral oration on a Rabbi, who died at the early age of twenty eight. The text chosen was: The sleep of a laboring man is sweet, and this was illustrated by a Parable of a king who had a vineyard, and engaged many laborers to work in it. One of them was distinguished above the rest by his ability. So the king took him by the hand, and walked up and down with him. At evening, when the laborers were paid, this one received the same wages as the others, just as if he had performed the whole day. Upon this the others murmured, because he who had performed only two hours had received the same as they who had labored the whole day, when the king replied: Why murmur you? This laborer has by his skill performed as much in two hours as you during the whole day. This in reference to the great merits of the deceased young Rabbi.

But it will be observed that, with all its similarity of form, the moral of the Jewish Parable is in exactly the opposite direction from the teaching of Christ. The same spirit of work and pay breathes in another Parable, which is intended to illustrate the idea that God had not revealed the reward attaching to each commandment, in order that men might not neglect those which brought less return. A king, so the Parable runs, had a garden, for which he hired laborers without telling them what their wages would be. In the evening he called them, and, having ascertained from each under what tree he had been working, he paid them according to the value of the trees on which they had been engaged. And when they said that he ought to have told them, which trees would bring the laborers most pay, the king replied that thereby a great part of his garden would have been neglected. So had God in like manner only revealed the reward of the greatest of the commandments, that to honor father and mother, and that of the least, about letting the mother bird fly away, attaching to both precisely the same reward.

To these, if need were, might be added other illustrations of that painful reckoning about work, or else sufferings, and reward, which characterizes Jewish theology, as it did those laborers in the Parable.

2. The second Parable in this series, or perhaps rather illustration, was spoken within the Temple. The Savior had been answering the question

of the Pharisees as to His authority by an appeal to the testimony of the Baptist. This led Him to refer to the twofold reception of that testimony, on the one hand, by the Publicans and harlots, and, on the other, by the Pharisees.

The Parable, which now follows, introduces a man who has two sons. He goes to the first, and in language of affection (tknon) bids him go and work in his vineyard. The son curtly and rudely refuses; but afterwards he changes his mind and goes. Meantime the father, when refused by the one, has gone to his other son on the same errand. The contrast here is marked. The tone is most polite, and the answer of the son contains not only a promise, and we almost see him going: Yes sir!, and he did not go. The application was easy. The first son represented the Publicans and harlots, whose curt and rude refusal of the Father's call was implied in their life of reckless sin. But afterwards they changed their mind, and went into the Father's vineyard. The other Son, with his politeness of tone and ready promise, but utter neglect of obligations undertaken, represented the Pharisees with their hypocritical and empty professions. And Christ obliged them to make application of the Parable. When challenged by Jesus, which of the two had done the will of his father, they could not avoid the answer. Then it was that, in language equally stern and true. He pointed the moral. The Baptist had come preaching righteousness, and, while the self righteous Pharisees had not believed him, those sinners had. And yet, even when the Pharisees saw the effect on these former sinners, they did not change their minds that they might believe. Therefore the Publicans and harlots would and did go into the Kingdom before them.

3. Closely connected with the two preceding Parables, and, with the whole tenor of Christ's sayings at that time, is that about the Evil Husbandmen in the Vineyard. As in the Parable about the Laborers sought by the Householder at different times, the object here is to set forth the patience and goodness of the owner, even towards the evil. And as, in the Parable of the Two Son's, reference is made to the practical rejection of the testimony of the Baptist by the Jews, and their consequent self exclusion from the Kingdom, so in this there is allusion to John as greater than the prophets, to the exclusion of Israel as a people from their position in the Kingdom, and to their punishment as individuals. Only we mark here a terrible progression. The neglect and non-belief which had appeared in the former Parable have now

ripened into rebellion, deliberate, aggravated, and carried to its utmost consequences in the murder of the Kings only and loved Son. Similarly, what formerly appeared as their loss, in that sinners went into the Kingdom of God before them, is now presented as their guilt and their judgment, both national and individual.

The Parable opens, like that in Isaiah 5, with a description of the complete arrangements made by the Owner of the Vineyard, to show how everything had been done to ensure a good yield of fruit, and what right the Owner had to expect at least a share in it. In the Parable, as in the prophecy, the Vineyard represents the Theocracy, although in the Old Testament, necessary, as identified with the nation of Israel, while in the Parable the two are distinguished, and the nation is represented by the laborers to whom the Vineyard was let out. The whole structure of the Parable shows, that the husbandmen are Israel as a nation, although they are addressed and dealt with in the persons of their representatives and leaders. And so it was spoken to the people, and yet the chief priests and Pharisees rightly perceived that He spoke of them.

This vineyard the owner had let out to husbandmen, while he himself traveled away [abroad], as Luke adds, for a long time. From the language it is evident, that the husbandmen had the full management of the vineyard. We remember, that there were three modes of dealing with land. According to one of these (Arisuth), the laborers employed received a certain portion of the fruits, say, a third or fourth of the produce. In such cases it seems, at least sometimes, to have been the practice, besides giving them a proportion of the produce, to provide also the seed (for a field) and to pay wages to the laborers. The other two modes of letting land were, either that the tenant paid a money rent to the proprietor, or else that he agreed to give the owner a definite amount of produce, whether the harvest had been good or bad. Such leases were given by the year or for life: sometimes the lease was even hereditary, passing from father to son. There can scarcely be a doubt that it is the latter kind of lease (Chakhranutha, from) which is referred to in the Parable, the lessees being bound to give the owner a certain amount of fruits in their season.

Accordingly, when the time of the fruits drew near, he sent his servants to the husbandmen to receive his fruits, the part of them belonging to him, or, as Mark and Luke express it, of the fruits of the vineyard. We gather, that it was a succession of servants, who received increasingly ill treatment from them evil husbandmen. We might have expected that the owner would now have taken severe measures; but instead of this he sent, in his patience and goodness, other servants, not more, which would scarcely have any meaning, but greater than the first, no doubt, with the idea that their greater authority would command respect. And when these also received the same treatment, we must regard it as involving, not only additional, but increased guilt on the part of the husbandmen. Once more, and with deepening force, does the question arise, what measures the owner would now take. But once more we have only a fresh and still greater display of his patience and unwillingness to believe that these husbandmen were so evil. As Mark pathetically put it, indicating not only the owners goodness, but the spirit of determined rebellion and the wickedness of the husbandmen: He had yet one, a beloved son, he sent him last to them, on the supposition that they would reverence him. The result was different. The appearance of the legal heir made them apprehensive of their tenure. Practically, the vineyard was already theirs; by killing the heir, the only claimant to it would be put out of the way, and so the vineyard become in every respect their own. For, the husbandmen proceeded on the idea, that as the owner was abroad for a long time, he would not personally interfere—an impression strengthened by the circumstance that he had not avenged the former ill usage of his servants, but only sent others in the hope of influencing them by gentleness. So the laborers. taking him [the son], cast him forth out of the vineyard, and killed him, the first action indicating that by violence they thrust him out of his possession, before they wickedly slew him.

The meaning of the Parable is sufficiently plain. The owner of the vineyard, God, had let out His Vineyard, the Theocracy, to His people of old. The covenant having been instituted, He withdrew, as it were, the former direct communication between Him and Israel ceased. Then in due season He sent His Servants, the prophets, to gather His fruits, they had had theirs in all the temporal and spiritual advantages of the covenant. But, instead of returning the fruits meet to repentance, they only ill treated His messengers, and that increasingly, even to death. In His longsuffering He next sent on the same errand greater than them, John the Baptist. And when he also received the same treatment, He sent last His own Son, Jesus Christ. His appearance made them feel, that it was now a decisive struggle for the Vineyard—and so, in order to gain its possession for themselves, they cast the rightful heir out of His own possession, and then killed Him!

And they must have understood the meaning of the Parable, who had served themselves heirs to their fathers in the murder of all the prophets, who had just been convicted of the rejection of the Baptist's message, and

whose hearts were even then full of murderous thoughts against the rightful
Heir of the Vineyard. But, even so, they must speak their own judgment.
In answer to His challenge, what in their view the owner of the vineyard
would do to these husbandmen, the chief priests and Pharisees could only
reply: As evil men evilly will he destroy them. And the vineyard will He
let out to other husbandmen, which shall render Him the fruits in their
season.

The application was obvious, and it was made by Christ, first, as always,
by a reference to the prophetic testimony, showing not only the unity of all
God's teaching, but also the continuity of the Israel of the present with that
of old in their resistance and rejection of God's counsel and messengers.
The quotation, than which none more applicable could be imagined, was
from Psalm 116:22, 23, and is made in the (Greek) Gospel of Matthew,
not necessarily by Christ, from the LXX Version. The only, almost verbal,
difference between it and the original is, that, whereas in the latter the
adoption of the stone rejected by the builders as head of the corner (this,
hoc,) is ascribed to Jehovah, in the LXX its original designation (ate) as
head of the corner (previous to the action of the builders), is traced to
the Lord. And then followed, in plain and unmistakable language, the
terrible prediction, first, nationally, that the Kingdom of God would be
taken from them, and given to a nation bringing forth the fruits thereof;
and then individually, that whoever stumbled at that stone and fell over it,
in personal offence or hostility, should be broken in pieces, but whoever
stood in the way of, or resisted its progress, and on whom therefore it fell,
it would scatter Him as dust.

Once more was their wrath roused, but also their fears. They knew that
He spoke of them, and would gladly have laid hands on Him; but they
feared the people, who in those days regarded Him as a prophet. And so
for the present they left Him, and went their way.

4. If Rabbinic writings offer scarcely any parallel to the preceding Parable,
    that of the Marriage Feast of the King's Son and the Wedding Garment
    seems almost reproduced in Jewish tradition. In its oldest form it is
    ascribed to Jochanan ben Zakkai, who flourished about the time of
    the composition of the Gospel of Matthew. It appears with variety
    of, or with additional details in Jewish commentaries. But while the
    Parable of Jesus only consists of two parts, forming one whole and
    having one lesson, the Talmud divides it into two separate Parables,
    of which the one is intended to show the necessity of being prepared

for the next world, to stand in readiness for the King's feast; while the other is meant to teach that we ought to be able to present our soul to God at the last in the same state of purity in which we had (according to Rabbinic notions) originally received it. Even this shows the infinite difference between Jesus' and the Rabbinic use of the Parable. In the Jewish Parable a King is represented as inviting to a feast, without, however, fixing the exact time for it. The wise adorn themselves in time, and are seated at the door of the palace, so as to be in readiness, since, as they argue, no elaborate preparation for a feast can be needed in a palace; while the foolish go away to their work, arguing there must be time enough, since there can be no feast without preparation. (The Midrash has it, that, when inviting the guests, the King had told them to wash, anoint, and array themselves in their festive garments; and that the foolish, arguing that, from the preparation of the food and the arranging of the seats, they would learn when the feast was to begin, had gone, the mason to his cask of lime, the potter to his clay, the smith to his furnace, the fuller to his bleaching ground.) But suddenly comes the King's summons to the feast, when the wise appear festively adorned, and the King rejoices over them, and they are made to sit down, eat and drink; while he is angry with the foolish, who appear squalid, and are ordered to stand by and look on in anguish, hunger and thirst.

The other Jewish Parable is of a king who committed to his servants the royal robes. The wise among them carefully laid them by while the foolish put them on when they did their work. After a time the king asked back the robes, when the wise could restore them clean, while the foolish had them soiled. Then the king rejoiced over the wise, and, while the robes were laid up in the treasury, they were invited go home in peace. But to the foolish he commanded that the robes should be handed over to the fuller, and that they themselves should be cast into prison. We readily see that the meaning of this Parable was, that a man might preserve His soul perfectly pure, and so enter into peace, while the careless, who had lost their original purity (no original sin here), would, in the next world, by suffering, both atone for their guilt and purify their souls.

When, from these Rabbinic perversions, we turn to the Parable of Jesus, its meaning is not difficult to understand. The King made a marriage for his Son, when he sent his Servants to call them that were invited to the wedding. Evidently, as in the Jewish Parable, and as before in that of the guests invited to the Great Supper, a preliminary general invitation had preceded the announcement that all was ready. Indeed, in the Midrash on Lamentations 4:2, it is expressly mentioned among other distinctions of the inhabitants of Jerusalem, that none of them went to a feast until the invitation had been given and repeated. But in the Parable those invited would not come. It reminds us both of the Parable of the laborers for the Vineyard, sought at different times, and of the repeated sending of messengers to those Evil Husbandmen for the fruits that were due, when we are next told that the king sent forth other servants to tell them to come, for he had made ready his early meal (not dinner, as in the KJV and Revised Version), and that, no doubt with a view to the later meal, the oxen and fatlings were killed. These repeated endeavors to call, to admonish, and to invite, form a characteristic feature of these Parables, showing that it was one of the central objects of Jesus' teaching to exhibit the longsuffering and goodness of God. Instead of giving heed to these repeated and pressing calls, in the words of the Parable: but they (the one class) made light of it, and went away, the one to his own land, the other to his own merchandise.

So the one class; the other made not light of it, but acted even worse than the first. But the rest laid hands on his servants, entreated them shamefully, and killed them. By this we are to understand, that, when the servants came with the second and more pressing message, the one class showed their contempt for the king, the wedding of his son, and the feast, and their preference for and preoccupation with their own possessions or acquisitions, their property or their trading, their enjoyments or their aims and desires. And, when these had gone, and probably the servants still remained to plead the message of their Lord, the rest evil entreated, and then killed them, proceeding beyond mere contempt, lack of interest, and preoccupation with their own affairs, to hatred and murder. The sin was the more aggravated that he was their king, and the messengers had invited them to a feast, and that one in which every loyal subject should have rejoiced to take part. Theirs was, therefore, not only murder, but also rebellion against their sovereign. On this the King, in his wrath sent forth his armies, which, and here the narrative in point of time anticipates the event, destroyed the murderers, and burnt their city.

But the deserved punishment of these rebels forms only part of the Parable. For it still leaves the wedding unprovided with guests, to sympathize with the joy of the king, and partake of his feast. And so the narrative continues: Then, after the king had given commandment for his armies to go forth, he said to his servants, The wedding indeed is ready, but they that were invited were not worthy. Go you therefore into the partings of the highways (where a number of roads meet and cross), and, as many as you shall find, invite to the marriage. We remember that the Parable here runs parallel to that other, when first the outcasts from the city lanes, and then the wanderers on the world's highway, were brought in to fill the place of the invited guests. At first sight it seems as if there were no connection between the declaration that those who had been invited had proved themselves unworthy, and the direction to go into the crossroads and gather any whom they might find, since the latter might naturally be regarded as less likely to prove worthy. Yet this is one of the main points in the Parable. The first invitation had been sent to selected guests, to the Jews, who might have been expected to be worthy, but had proved themselves unworthy; the next was to be given, not to the chosen city or nation, but to all that traveled in whatever direction on the world's highway, reaching them where the roads of life meet and part.

We have already in part anticipated the interpretation of this Parable. The Kingdom is here, as so often in the Old and in the New Testament, likened to a feast, and more specifically to a marriage feast. But we mark as distinctive, that the King makes it for His Son, Thus Christ, as Son and Heir of the Kingdom, forms the central Figure in the Parable. This is the first point set before us. The next is, that the chosen, invited guests were the ancient Covenant People, Israel. To them God had sent first under the Old Testament. And, although they had not given heed to His call, yet a second class of messengers was sent to them under the New Testament. And the message of the latter was, that the early meal was ready (Christ's first coming), and that all preparations had been made for the great evening meal (Christ's Reign). Another prominent truth is set forth in the repeated message of the King, which points to the goodness and longsuffering of God. Next, our attention is drawn to the refusal of Israel, which appears in the contemptuous neglect and preoccupation with their things of one party, and the hatred, resistance, and murder by the other. Then follow in quick succession the command of judgment on the nation, and the burning of their city, God's army being, in this instance, the Romans, and, finally, the direction to go into the crossways to invite all men, Jews and Gentiles.

With verse 10 begins the second part of the Parable. The Servants, that is, the New Testament messengers, had fulfilled their commission; they had brought in as many as they found, both bad and good: that is, without respect to their previous history, or their moral and religious state up the time of their call; and the wedding was filled with guests, that is, the table at the marriage feast was filled with those who as guests lay around it (nakeimnon). But, if ever we are to learn that we must not expect on earth, not even at the King's marriage table, a pure Church, it is, surely, from what now follows. The King entered to see His guests, and among them he described one of who had not on a wedding garment. Manifestly, the quickness of the invitation and the previous unpreparedness. As the guests had been travelers, and as the feast was in the King's palace, we cannot be mistaken in supposing that such garments were supplied in the palace itself to all those who sought them. And with this agrees the circumstance, that the man so addressed was speechless [literally, gagged, or muzzled]. His conduct argued utter insensibility as regarded that to which he had been called, ignorance of what was due to the King, and what became such a feast. For, although no previous state of preparedness was required of the invited guests, all being invited, whether good or bad, yet the fact remained that, if they were to take part in the feast, they must put on a garment suited to the occasion. All are invited to the Gospel feast; but they who will partake of it must put on the King's wedding garment of Evangelical holiness. And whereas it is said in the Parable, that only one was described without this garment, this is intended to teach, that the King will only generally view His guests, but that each will be separately examined, and that no one, no, not a single individual, will be able to escape discovery amid the mass of guests, if he has not the wedding garment. In short, in that day of trial, it is not a scrutiny of Churches, but of individuals in the Church. And so the King called the servants, diaknois, not the same who had previously carried the invitation (dolois), but others, evidently here the Angels, His ministers, to bind him hand and foot, and to cast him out into the darkness, the outer, that is, unable to offer resistance and as a punished captive, he was to be cast out into that darkness which is outside the brilliantly lighted guest chamber of the King. And, still further to mark that darkness outside, it is added that this is the well known place of suffering and anguish: There shall be the weeping and the gnashing of teeth.

And here the Parable closes with the general statement, applicable to the first part of the Parable, to the first invited guests, Israel, and to the second, the guests from all the world: For (this is the meaning of the whole Parable) many are called, but few chosen. For the understanding of these words we have to keep in view that, logically, the two clauses must be supplemented by the same words. Thus, the verse would read: Many are called out of the world by God to partake of the Gospel feast, but few out of the world, not, out of the called, are chosen by God to partake of it. The call to the feast and the choice for the feast are not identical. The call comes to all; but it may outwardly accepted, and a man may sit down to the feast, and yet he may not be chosen to partake of the feast, because he has not the wedding garment of converting, sanctifying grace. And so one may be thrust from the marriage board into the darkness without, with its sorrow and anguish.

Thus, side by side, yet wide apart, are these two, God's call and God's choice. The connecting link between them is the taking of the wedding garment, freely given in the Palace. Yet, we must seek it, ask it, put it on. And so here also, we have, side by side, God's gift and man's activity. And still, to all time, and to all men, in its warning, teaching, and blessing, it is true: Many are called, but few are chosen!

End Notes:

[19]   Instead of discussing the explanations of others, I prefer simply to expound that which I have to propose. The difficulties of the usual interpretations are so great that a fresh study seemed requisite. Our interpretation turns on this, that the Parable is only an illustration of what is said in Matthew 19:30.

[20]   The word is not the same as that for repent in Matthew 3:2. The latter refers to a change of heart, and means something spiritual. The word used in the text means only a change of mind and purpose. It occurs besides in Matthew 25:3; 2 Corinthians 5:8; Hebrews 5:21.

[21]   In the Talmud he invites his servants; in the Midrash, others.

Chapter 6

Third Day Evening Discourses
to the Disciples

The last and most solemn denunciation of Jerusalem had been uttered, the last and most terrible prediction of judgment upon the Temple spoken, and Jesus was suiting the action to the word. It was as if He had cast the dust of His Shoes against the House that was to be left desolate. And so He left forever the Temple and them that held office in it.

They had left the Sanctuary and the City, had crossed black Kidron, and were slowly climbing the Mount of Olives. A sudden turn in the road, and the Sacred Building was once more in full view. Just then the western sun was pouring its golden beams on tops of marble cloister and on the terraced courts, and glittering on the golden spikes on the roof of the Holy Place. In the setting, even more than in the rising sun, must the vast proportions, the symmetry, and the sparkling sheen of this mass of snowy marble and gold have stood out gloriously. And across the black valley, and up the slopes of Olivet, lay the dark shadows of these gigantic walls built of massive stones, some of them nearly twenty four feet long. Even the Rabbis, despite their hatred of Herod, grow enthusiastic, and dream that the very Temple walls would have been covered with gold, had not the multicolored marble, resembling the waves of the sea, seemed more beautiful. It was probably as they now gazed on all this grandeur and strength, that they broke the silence imposed on them by gloomy thoughts of the near desolateness of that House, which Jesus had predicted. One and another pointed out to Him those massive stones and splendid buildings, or speak of the rich offerings with which the Temple was adorned. It was but natural that the contrast between this and the predicted desolation should have impressed them; natural, also, that they should refer to it, not as matter of doubt, but rather as of question. Then Jesus, probably turning to one, perhaps to the first, or else the principal, of His questioners, spoke fully of that terrible contrast between the present and the near future, when, as fulfilled with almost incredible literality, not one stone would be left upon another that was not upturned.

In silence they pursued their way. Upon the Mount of Olives they sat down, right over against the Temple. Whether or not the others had gone farther, or Christ had sat apart with these four, Peter and James and John and Andrew are named as those who now asked Him further of what must have weighed so heavily on their hearts. It was not idle curiosity, although inquiry on such as subject, even merely for the sake of information, could scarcely have been blamed in a Jew. But it did concern them personally, for had not Jesus connected the desolateness of that House with His own absence? He had explained the former as meaning the ruin of the City and the utter destruction of the Temple. But to His prediction of it had been added these words: You shall not see Me from then on, until you shall say, Blessed is He that comes in the Name of the Lord. In their view, this could only refer to His Second Coming, and to the End of the world as connected with it. This explains the twofold question which the four now addressed to Christ: Tell us, when shall these things be? and what shall be the sign of your Coming, and of the consummation of the age?

Irrespective of other sayings, in which a distinction between these two events is made, we can scarcely believe that the disciple could have connected the desolation of the Temple with the immediate Advent of Christ and the end of the world. For, in the saying which gave rise to their question, Christ had placed an indefinite period between the two. Between the desolation of the House and their new welcome to Him, would intervene a period of indefinite length, during which they would not see Him again. The disciples could not have overlooked this; and therefore neither their question, nor yet the discourse of Jesus, have been intended to conjoin the two. It is necessary to keep this in view when studying the words of Christ; and any different impression must be due to the exceeding compression in the language of Matthew, and to this, that Christ would purposely leave indefinite the interval between the desolation of the house and His own Return.

Another point of considerable importance remains to no advantage. When Jesus, on leaving the Temple, Said: You shall not see Me from then on, He must have referred to Israel in their national capacity, to the Jewish polity in Church and State. If so, the promise in the text of visible reappearance must also apply to the Jewish Commonwealth, to Israel in their national capacity. Accordingly, it is suggested that in the present passage Christ refers to His Advent, not from the general cosmic viewpoint of universal, but from the Jewish standpoint of Jewish, history, in which the destruction of Jerusalem and the appearance of false Christ's are the last events of national history, to be followed by the dreary blank and silence of the many centuries of the Gentile dispensation, broken and silence of the events that usher in His Coming.

Keeping in mind, then, that the disciples could not have connected the desolation of the Temple with the immediate Advent of Christ into His Kingdom and the end of the world, their question to Christ was twofold: When would these things be? and, What would be the signs of His Royal Advent and the consummation of the Age? On the former Jesus gave no information; to the latter His discourse on the Mount of Olives was directed. On one point the statement of Jesus had been so novel as almost to account for their question. Jewish writings speak very frequently of the so called sorrows of the Messiah (Chebhley shel Mashiach.) These were partly those of the Messiah, and partly, perhaps chiefly, those coming of the Messiah. There can be no purpose in describing them in detail, since the particulars mentioned vary so much, and the descriptions are so fanciful. But they may generally be characterized as marking a period of internal corruption and of outward distress, especially of famine and war, of which land of Palestine was to be the scene, and in which Israel was to be the chief sufferers. As the Rabbinic notices which we possess all date from after the destruction of Jerusalem, it is impossible to make any absolute assertion on the point; but, as a matter of fact, none of them refers to desolation of the City and Temple as one of the signs or sorrows of the Messiah. It is true that isolated voices proclaimed that fate of the Sanctuary, but not in any connection with the triumphant Advent of Messiah; and, if we are to judge from the hope entertained by the fanatics during the last siege of Jerusalem, they rather expected a Divine, not doubt Messianic, interjection to save the City and Temple, even at the last moment. When Christ, therefore, proclaimed the desolation of the house, and even placed it in indirect connection with His Advent, He taught that which must have been new and unexpected.

This may be the most suitable place for explaining the Jewish expectation connected with the Advent of the Messiah. Here we have first to dismiss, as belonging to a later period, the Rabbinic fiction of two Messiahs: the one, the primary and reigning, the Son of David; the other, the secondary and warfaring Messiah, the Son of Ephraim or of Manasseh. The earliest Talmudic reference to this second Messiah dates from the third century of our era, and contains the strange and almost blasphemous notices that the prophecy of Zechariah, concerning the mourning for Him Whom they had pierced, referred to Messiah the Son of Joseph, Who would be killed in the war of Gog and Magog; and that, when Messiah the Son of David saw it, He asked life of God, who gave it to Him, as it is written in Psalm 2: Ask of Me, and I will give You, upon which God informed the Messiah that His father David had already asked and obtained this for Him, according to Psalm 20:4. Generally the Messiah, Son of Joseph, is connected with the gathering and restoration of the ten tribes. Later Rabbinic writings connect all the sufferings of the Messiah for sin with this Son of Joseph. The war in which the Son of Joseph succumbed would finally be brought to a victorious termination by the Son of David, when the supremacy of Israel would be restored, and all nations walk in His Light.

It is scarcely matter for surprise, that the various notices about the Messiah, Son of Joseph, are confused and sometimes inconsistent, considering the circumstances in which this dogma originated. Its primary reason was, no doubt, controversial. When hardly pressed by Christian argument about the Old Testament prophecies of the sufferings of the Messiah, the fiction about the Son of Joseph as distinct from the Son of David would offer a welcome means of escape. Besides, when in the Jewish rebellion under the false Messiah Bar Kokhba (the Son of a Star) the latter succumbed to the Romans and was killed, the Synagogue deemed it necessary to rekindle Israel's hope, that had been quenched in blood, by the picture to two Messiahs, of whom the first should fall in warfare, while the second, the Son of David, would carry the contest to a triumphant issue.

In general, we must here remember that there is a difference between three terms used in Jewish writings to designate that which is to succeed the present dispensation or world (Olam hazzeh), although the distinction is not always consistently carried out. This happy period would begin with the days of the Messiah. These would stretch into the coming age (Athid labho), and end with the world to come (Olam habba), although the latter is sometimes made to include the whole of that period. The most divergent opinions are expressed of the duration of the Messianic period. It seems like a round number when we are told that it would last for three generations. In the fullness discussion on the subject, the opinions of different Rabbis are mentioned, who variously fix the period at from forty to one, two, and even seven thousands years, according to fanciful analogies.

Where statements rest on such fanciful considerations, we can scarcely attach serious value to them, nor expect agreement. This remark holds equally true in regard to most of the other points involved. Suffice it to say, that, according to general opinion, the Birth of the Messiah would be unknown to His contemporaries; that He would appear, carry on His work, then disappear, probably for forty five days; then reappear again, and destroy the hostile powers of the world, notably Edom, Armilos, the Roman Power, the fourth and last world empire (sometimes it is said: through Ishmael). Ransomed Israel would now be miraculously gathered from the ends of the earth, and brought back to their own land, the ten tribes sharing in their restoration, but this only on condition of their having repented of their former sins. According to the Midrash, all circumcised Israel would then be released from Gehenna, and the dead be raised, according to some authorities, by the Messiah, to Whom God would give the Key of the Resurrection of the Dead. This Resurrection would take place in the land of Israel, and those of Israel who had been buried elsewhere would have to roll under ground, not without suffering pain, until they reach the sacred soil. Probably the reason of this strange idea, which was supported by an appeal to the direction of Jacob and Joseph as to their last resting place, was to induce the Jews, after the final desolation of their land, not to quit Palestine. This Resurrection, which is variously supposed to take place at the beginning or during the course of the Messianic manifestation, would be announced by the blowing of the great trumpet. It would be difficult to say how many of these strange and confused views prevailed at the time of Christ; which of them were universally entertained as real dogmas; or from what source they had been originally derived. Probably many of them were popularly entertained, and afterwards further developed, as we believe, with elements distorted from Christian teaching.

We have now reached the period of the coming age (the Athid labho, or saeculum futurum). All the resistance to God would be concentrated in the great war of Gog and Magog, and with it the prevalence of all the wickedness be connected. And terrible would be the straits of Israel. Three times would the enemy seek to storm the Holy City. But each time would the assault be repelled, at the last with complete destruction of the enemy. The sacred City would now be wholly rebuilt and inhabited. But oh, how different from of old! Its Sabbath boundaries would be strewed with pearls and precious gems. The City itself would be lifted to a height of some nine miles with realistic application of Isaiah 49:20, it would reach up to the throne of God, while it would extend from Joppa as far as the gates of Damascus! For, Jerusalem was to be the dwelling place of Israel, and the resort of all nations. But more glorious in Jerusalem would be the new Temple which the Messiah was to rear, and to which those five things were to be restored which had been lacking in the former Sanctuary; the Golden Candlestick, the Ark, and Heaven lit fire on the Altar, the Holy Spirit, and the Cherubim. And the land of Israel would then be as wide as it had been sketched in the promise which God had given to Abraham, and which had never before been fulfilled, since the largest extent of Israel's rule had only been over seven nations, whereas the Divine promise extended it over ten, if not over the whole earth.

Strangely realistic and exaggerated by Eastern imagination as these hopes sound, there is connected with them, a point of deepest interest on which, as explained in another place, remarkable divergence of opinion prevailed. It concerns the Services of the rebuilt Temple, and the observance of The Law in Messianic days. One party here insisted on the restoration of all the ancient Services, and the strict observance of the Mosiac and Rabbinic Law on its full imposition on the Gentile nation. But this view must have been at least modified by the expectation, that the Messiah would give a new Law. But was this new Law to apply only to the Gentiles, or also to Israel? Here again there is divergence of opinions. According to some, this Law would be binding on Israel, but not on the Gentiles, or else the latter would have a modified or condensed series of ordinances (at most thirty commandments). But the most liberal view, and, as we may suppose, that most acceptable to the enlightened, was, that in the future only these two festive seasons would be observed: The Day of Atonement, and the Feast of Esther (or else that of Tabernacles), and that of all the sacrifices only thank offerings would be continued. Opinion went even further, and many held that in Messianic days the distinctions of pure and impure, lawful and unlawful, as regarded food, would be abolished. There can be little doubt that these different views were entertained even in the days of Jesus and in Apostolic times, and they account for the exceeding bitterness with which the extreme Pharisaic party in the Church at Jerusalem contended, that the Gentile converts must be circumcised, and the full weight of the yoke of the Law laid on their necks. And with a view to this new Law, which God would give to his world through the Messiah, the Rabbis divided all time into three periods: the primitive, that under the Law, and that of the Messiah.

It only remains briefly to describe the beatitude of Israel, both physical and moral, in those days, the state of the nations, and, lastly, the end of that age and its merging into the world to come (Olam habba). Morally, this would be a period of holiness, of forgiveness, and of peace. Without, there would be no longer enemies nor oppressors. And within the City and Land a more than Paradisiacal state would prevail, which is depicted in even more than the usual realistic Eastern language. For that vast new Jerusalem (not in heaven, but in the literal Palestine) Angels were to cut gems 45 feet long and broad (30 cubits), and place them in its gates; the windows and gates were to be of precious stones, the walls of silver, gold, and gems, while all kinds of jewels would be strewed about, of which every Israelite was at liberty to take. Jerusalem would be as large as, at present, all Palestine, and Palestine as all the world. Corresponding to this miraculous extension would be a miraculous elevation of Jerusalem into the air. And it is one of the strangest mixtures of self righteousness and realism with deeper and more spiritual thoughts, when the Rabbis prove by references to the prophetic Scriptures, that every event and miracle in the history of Israel would find its counterpart, or rather larger fulfillment, in Messianic days. Thus, what was recorded of Abraham would, on account of his merit, find, clause by clause, its counterpart in the future: Let a little water be fetched, in what is predicted in Zechariah 14:8; wash your feet, in what is predicted in Isaiah 4:5; rest yourselves under the tree, in what is said in Isaiah 4:4; and I will fetch a morsel of bread, in the promise of Psalm 72:16.

But by the side of this we find much coarse realism. The land would spontaneously produce the best dresses and the finest cakes; the wheat would grow as high as palm trees as the mountains, while the wind would miraculously convert the grain into flour, and cast it into the valleys. Every tree would become fruit bearing; they were to break forth, and to bear fruit every day; daily was every woman to bear child, so that ultimately every Israelite family would number as many as all Israel at the time of the Exodus. All sickness and disease, and all that could hurt, would pass away. As regarded death, the promise of its final abolition was, with characteristic ingenuity, applied to Israel, while the statement that the child should die an hundred years old was understood as referring to the Gentiles, and as teaching that, although they would die, yet their age would be greatly prolonged, so that a centenarian would be regarded as only a child. Lastly, such physical and outward loss as Rabbinism regarded as the consequence of the Fall, would be again restored to man.

It would be easy to multiply quotations even more realistic than these, if such could serve any good purpose. The same literalism prevails in regard to the reign of King Messiah over the nations of the world. Not only is the figurative language of the prophets applied in the most external manner, but illustrative details of the same character are added. Jerusalem would, as the residence of the Messiah, become the capital of the world, and Israel take the place of the (fourth) world monarchy, the Roman Empire. After the Roman Empire none other was to rise, for it was to be immediately followed by the reign of Messiah. But that day, or rather that of the fall of the (ten) Gentile nations, which would inaugurate the Empire of Messiah, was among the seven things unknown to man. God had directed Israel not to communicate to the Gentiles the mystery of the calculation of the times. But the very origin of the wicked world Empire had been caused by Israel's sin. It had been (ideally) founded when Solomon contracted alliance with the daughter of Pharaoh, while Romulus and Remus rose when Jeroboam set up the worship of the two calves. Thus, what would have become the universal Davidic Rule had, through Israel's sin, been changed into subjection to the Gentiles. Whether or not these Gentiles would in the Messianic future become proselytes, seems a moot question. Sometimes it is affirmed; at others it is stated that no proselytes would then be received, and for this good reason, that in the final war and rebellion those proselytes would, from fear, cast off the yoke of Judaism and join the enemies.

That war, which seems a continuation of that Gog and Magog, would close the Messianic era. The nations, who had up to this point given tribute to Messiah, would rebel against Him, when He would destroy them by the breath of His mouth, so that Israel alone would be left on the face of the earth. The duration of that period of rebellion is stated to be seven years. It seems, at least, a doubtful point, whether a second or general Resurrection was expected, the more probable view being, that there was only one Resurrection, and that of Israel alone, or, at any rate, only of the studious and the pious, and that this was to take place at the beginning of the Messianic reign. If the Gentiles rose at all, it would only be immediately again to die.

Then the final Judgment would commence. We must here once more make distinction between Israel and the Gentiles, with whom as more punishable than they, certain notorious sinners, heretics, and all apostates, were to be ranked. Whereas to Israel the Gehenna, to which all but the perfectly righteous had been consigned at death, had proved a kind of purgatory, from which they were all ultimately delivered by Abraham, or, according to some of the later Midrashim, by the Messiah, no such deliverance was in prospect for the pagan nor for sinners of Israel. The question whether the fiery torments suffered (which are very realistically described) would at last end in annihilation, is one which at different times received different answers, as fully explained in another place. At the time of Christ the punishment of the wicked was certainly regarded as of eternal duration. Rabbi Jose, a teacher of the second century, and a representative of the more rationalistic school, says expressly, The fire of Gehinnom is never quenched. And even the passage, so often (although only partially) quoted, to the effect, that the final torments of Gehenna would last for twelve months, after which body and soul would be annihilated, excepts from this a number of Jewish sinners, especially mentioned, such as heretics, Epicureans, apostates, and persecutors, who are designated as children of Gehenna (ledorey doroth, to ages of ages). And with this other statements agree, so that at most it would follow that, while annihilation would await the less guilty, the most guilty were to be reserved for eternal punishment.

Such, then, was the final Judgment, to be held in the valley of Jehoshaphat by God, at the head of the Heavenly Sanhedrin, composed of the elders of Israel. Realistic as its description is, even this is terribly surpassed by a passage in which the supposed pleas for mercy by the various nations are cited and refuted, when, after an unseemly contention between God and the Gentiles, equally shocking to good taste and blasphemous, about the partiality that had been shown to Israel, the Gentiles would be consigned to punishment. All this in a manner revolting to all reverent feeling. And the contrast between the Jewish picture of the last Judgment and that outlined in the Gospel is so striking, as alone to vindicate (were such necessary) the eschatological parts of the New Testament, and to prove what infinite distance there is between the Teaching of Christ and the Theology of the Synagogue.

After the final judgment we must look for the renewal of heaven and earth. In the latter neither physical nor moral darkness would any longer prevail, since the Yetser ha Ra, or Evil impulse, would be destroyed. And renewed earth would bring forth all without blemish and in Paradisiacal perfection, while physical and moral evil had ceased. Then began the Olam habba, or world to come. The question, whether any functions or enjoyments of the body would continue, is variously answered. The reply of Jesus to the question of the Sadducees about marriage in the other world seems to imply, that materialistic views on the subject were entertained at the time. Many Rabbinic passages, such as about the great feast upon Leviathan and

Behemoth prepared for the righteous in the latter days, confirm only too painfully the impression of grossly materialistic expectations. On the other hand, passages may be quoted in which the utterly unmaterial character of the world to come is insisted upon in most emphatic language. In truth, the same fundamental divergences here exist as on other points, such as the abode of the beatified, the visible or else invisible glory which they would enjoy, and even the new Jerusalem. And in regard to the latter, as indeed to all those references to the beatitudes of the world to come, it seems at least doubtful, whether the Rabbis may not have intended to describe rather the Messianic days than the final winding up of all things.

To complete this sketch of Jewish opinions, it is necessary, however briefly, to refer to the Pseudepigraphic Writings, which, as will be remembered, expressed the Apocalyptic expectancies of the Jews before the time of Christ. But here we have always to keep in mind this twofold difficulty: that the language used in works of this kind is of a highly figurative character, and must therefore not be literally pressed; and that more than one of them, notably IV Esdras, dates from post-Christian times, and was, in important respects, admittedly influenced by Christian teaching. But in the main the picture of Messianic times in these writings is the same as the presented by the Rabbis. Briefly, the Pseudepigraphic view may be thus sketched. Of the so called Wars of the Messiah there had been already a kind of prefigurement in the days of Antiochus Epiphanes, when armed soldiery had been seen to carry on warfare in the air. This sign is mentioned in the Sibylline Books as marking the coming end, together with the sight of swords in the starlit sky at night, the falling of dust from heaven, the extinction of the sunlight and appearance of the moon by day, and the dropping of blood from the rocks. A somewhat similar, though even more realistic, picture is presented in connection with the blast of the third trumpet in IV (II) Esdras. Only that there the element of moral judgment is more clearly introduced. This appears still more fully in another passage of the same book, in which, apparently in connection with the Judgment, the influence of Christian teaching, although in an externalized form, may be clearly traced. A perhaps even more detailed description of the wickedness, distress, and physical desolation upon earth at that time, is given in the Book of Jubilees.

At last, when these distresses have reached their final height, when signs are in the sky, ruin upon earth, and the unburied bodies that cover the ground are devoured by birds and wild beasts, or else swallowed up by the earth, would God send the King, Who would put an end to unrighteousness. Then would follow the last war against Jerusalem, in which God would fight from heaven with the nations, when they would submit to, and own Him. But while in the Book of Enoch and in another work of the same class the judgment is ascribed to God, and the Messiah represented as appearing only afterwards, in the majority of these works the judgment or its execution is assigned to the Messiah.

In the land thus restored to Israel, and under the rule of King Messiah, the new Jerusalem would be the capital, purified from the pagan, enlarged quite transformed. This Jerusalem had been shown to Adam before his Fall, but after that both it and Paradise had been withdrawn from him. It had again been shown to Abraham, to Moses, and to Ezra. The splendor of this new Jerusalem is described in most glowing language. Of the glorious Kingdom thus instituted, the Messiah would be King, although under the supremacy of God. His reign would extend over the pagan nations. The character of their submission was differently viewed, according to the more or less Judaic standpoint of the writers. Thus, in the Book of Jubilees the seed of Jacob are promised possession of the whole earth; they would rule over all nations according to their pleasure; and after that draw the whole earth to themselves, and inherit it forever. In the Assumption of Moses this ascendency of Israel seems to be connected with the idea of vengeance upon Rome, although the language employed is highly figurative. On the other hand, in the Sibylline Books the nations are represented as, in view of the blessings enjoyed by Israel, themselves turning to acknowledge God, when perfect mental enlightenment and absolute righteousness, as well as physical well being, would prevail under the rule and judgeship (whether literal or figurative) of the Prophets. The most Grecian view of the Kingdom, is that expressed by Philo. He anticipates, that the happy moral condition of man would ultimately affect the wild beasts, which, relinquishing their solitary habits, would first become gregarious; then, imitating the domestic animals, gradually come to respect man as their master become as affectionate and cheerful as Maltese dogs. Among men, the pious and virtuous would bear rule, their dignity inspiring respect, their terror fear, and their beneficence good will. Probably intermediate between this extreme Grecian and the Judaic conception of the Millennium, are such utterances as ascribe the universal acknowledgment of the Messiah to the recognition, that God had invested Him with glory and power, and that His Reign was that of blessing.

It must have been remarked, that the differences between the Apocalyptic teaching of the Pseudepigrapha and that of the New Testament are as marked as those between the latter and that of the Rabbis. Another point of divergence is, that the Pseudepigrapha uniformly represent the Messianic reign as eternal, not broken up by any further apostasy or rebellion. Then would the earth be renewed, and this would be followed, lastly, by the Resurrection. In the Apocalypse of Baruch, as by the Rabbis, it is set forth that men would rise in exactly the same condition which they had borne in life, so that, by being recognized, the reality of the Resurrection would be attested, while in the re-union of body and soul each would receive its due punishment for the sins committed in their state of combination while upon earth. But after that a transformation would take place: of the just into the Angelic splendor of their glory, while, on view of this, the wicked would correspondingly fade away. Josephus states that the Pharisees taught only a Resurrection of the Just. As we know that such was not the case, we must regard this as one of the many assertions made by that writer for purposes of his own, probably to present to outsiders the Pharisaic doctrine in the most attractive and rational light of which it was capable. Similarly, the modern contention, that some of the Pseudepigraphic Writings propound the same view of only a Resurrection of the Just, is contrary to evidence. There can be no question that, according to the Pseudepigrapha, in the general Judgment, which was to follow the universal Resurrection, the reward and punishment assigned are represented as of eternal duration, although it may be open to question, as in regard to Rabbinic teaching, which of those who had been sinners would suffer final and endless torment.

The many and persistent attempts, despite the gross inconsistencies involved, to represent the teaching of Christ concerning the Last Things as only the reflection of contemporary Jewish opinion, have rendered detailed evidence necessary. When, with the information just summarized, we again turn to the questions addressed to Him by the disciples, we recall that (as previously shown) they could not have connected, or rather confounded, the when of these things, that is, of the destruction of Jerusalem and the Temple, with the when of His Second Coming and the end of the Age. We also recall the suggestion, that Christ referred to His Advent, as to His disappearance, from the Jewish standpoint of Jewish, rather than from the general cosmic view point of universal, history.

As regards the answer of Jesus to the two questions of His disciples, it may be said that the first part of His discourse is intended to supply information on the two facts of the future: the destruction of the Temple, and His Second Advent and the end of the Age, by setting before them the signs indicating the approach or beginning of these events. But even here the exact period of each is not defined, and the teaching given intended for purely practical purposes. In the second part of His discourse Jesus distinctly tells them, what they are not to know, and why; and how all that was communicated to them was only to prepare them for that constant watchfulness, which has been to the Church at all times the proper outcome of Christ's teaching on the subject. This, then we may take as a guide in our study: that the words of Christ contain nothing beyond what was necessary for the warning and teaching of the disciples and of the Church.

The first Part of Christ's discourse consists of four Sections, of which the first describes the beginning of the birth woes of the new Age about to appear. The expression: The End is not yet clearly indicates, that it marks only the earliest period of the beginning, the farthest terminus a quo of the birth woes. Another general consideration, which seems of importance, is, that the Synoptic Gospels report this part of Jesus' discourse in almost identical language. If the inference from this seems that their accounts were derived from a common source, say, the report of Peter, yet this close and unvarying repetition also conveys an impression, that the Evangelists themselves may not have fully understood the meaning of what they recorded. This may account for the rapid and unconnected transitions from subject to subject. At the same time it imposes on us the duty of studying the language anew, and without regard to any scheme of interpretation. This only may be said, that the obvious difficulties of negative criticism are here equally great, whether we suppose the narratives to have been written before or after the destruction of Jerusalem.

1. The purely practical character of the discourse appears from its opening words. They contain a warning, addressed to the disciples in their individual, not in their corporate, capacity, against being led astray. This, more particularly in regard to Judaic seductions leading them after false Christ's. Though in the multitude of impostors, who, in the troubled times between the rule of Pilate and the destruction of Jerusalem, promised Messianic deliverance to Israel, few names and claims of this kind have been especially recorded, yet the hints in the New Testament, and the references, however guarded, by the Jewish historian, imply the appearance of many such seducers. And their influence, not only upon Jews, but on Jewish Christians, might be the more dangerous, that the latter would naturally regard the woes, which were the occasion of their pretensions, as the judgments which would usher in the Advent of their Lord. Against such seduction they

must be peculiarly on their guard. So far for the things connected with the destruction of Jerusalem and the overthrow of the Jewish commonwealth. But, taking a wider and cosmic view, they might also be misled by either rumors of war at a distance, or by actual warfare, so as to believe that the dissolution of the Roman Empire, and with it the Advent of Christ, was at hand. This also would be a Misapprehension, grievously misleading, and to be carefully guarded against.

Although primarily applying to them, yet the peculiarly Judaic, or, it might be even Christian, and the general cosmic sources of misapprehension as to the near Advent of Christ, must not be limited to the times of the Apostles. They rather indicate these twofold grounds of misapprehension which in all ages have misled Christians into an erroneous expectancy of the immediate Advent of Christ: the seductions of false Messiahs, or, it may be, teachers, and violent disturbances in the political world. So far as Israel was concerned, these attained their climax in the great rebellion against Rome under the false Messiah, Bar Kokhba, in the time of Hadrian, although echoes of similar false claims, or hope of them, have again and again roused Israel during the night of these many centuries into brief, startled waking. And, as regards the more general cosmic signs, have not Christians, in the early ages watched, not only the wars on the boundaries of the Empire, but the condition of the state in the age of Nero the risings, turmoils, and threatenings; and so onwards, those of later generations, even down to the commotions of our own period, as if they betokened the immediate Advent of Christ, instead of marking in them only the beginning of the birth woes of the new Age?

2. From the warning to Christians as individuals, Jesus next turns to give admonition to the Church in her corporate capacity. Here we mark, that the events now described must not be regarded as following, with strict chronological precision, those referred to in the previous verses. Rather is it intended to indicate a general connection and partly after, those formerly predicted. They form, in fact, the continuation of the birth woes. This appears even from the language used. Thus, while Matthew writes: Then (at that time) shall they deliver you up, Luke places the persecutions before all these things; while Mark, who reports this part of the discourse most fully, omits every note of time, and only emphasizes the admonition which the fact conveys. As regards the admonition itself, expressed in this part of Jesus' discourse, we notice

that, as formerly to individuals, so now to the Church, two sources of danger are pointed out: internal from heresies (false prophets) and the decay of faith, and external, from persecutions, whether Judaic and from their own kindred, or from the secular powers throughout the world. But, along with these two dangers, two consoling facts are also pointed out. As regards the persecutions in prospect, full Divine aid is promised to Christians, to individuals and to the Church. Thus all care and fear may be dismissed: their testimony shall neither be silenced, nor shall the Church be suppressed or extinguished; but inward joyousness, outward perseverance, and final triumph, are secured by the Presence of the Risen Savior with, and the felt indwelling of the Holy Spirit in His Church. And, as for the other and equally consoling fact: despite the persecution of Jews and Gentiles, before the End comes this the Gospel of the Kingdom shall be preached in all the inhabited earth for a testimony to all the nations. This, then, is really the only sign of the End of the present Age.

3. From these general predictions, Jesus proceeds, in the third part of this discourse, to advertise the Disciples of the great historic fact immediately before them, and of the dangers which might spring from it. In truth, we have here His answer to their question, When shall these things be? not, as regards the when, but the what of them. And with this He conjoins the present application of His general warning regarding false Christ's, given in the first part of this discourse. The fact of which He now, in this third part of His discourse, advertises them, is the destruction of Jerusalem. Its twofold dangers would be, outwardly, the difficulties and perils which at that time would necessarily come upon men, and especially the members of the infant Church; and, religiously, the pretensions and claims of false Christ's or prophets at a period when all Jewish thinking and expectancy would lead men to anticipate the near Advent of the Messiah. There can be no question, that from both these dangers the warning of Jesus delivered the Church. As directed by him, the members of the Christian Church fled at an early period of the siege. Of Jerusalem to Pella, while the words in which He had told that His Coming would not be in secret, but with the brightness of that lightning which shot across the sky, prevented not only their being deceived, but perhaps even the record, if not the rise of many who otherwise would have deceived them. As for Jerusalem, the prophetic vision initially fulfilled in the days of Antiochus would once more, and now fully, become reality, and the abomination of desolation stand in

the Holy Place. This, together with tribulation to Israel, unparalleled in the terrible past of its history, and unequalled even in its bloody future. So dreadful would be the persecution, that, if Divine mercy had not interposed for the sake of the followers of Christ, the whole Jewish race that inhabited the land would have been swept away. But on the morrow of that day no new Maccabee would arise, no Christ come, as Israel fondly hoped; but over that carcass would the vultures gather; and so through all the Age of the Gentiles, until converted Israel should raise the welcoming shout: Blessed be He that comes in the Name of the Lord!

4. The Age of the Gentiles, the end of the Age, and with it the new allegiance of His now penitent people Israel; the sign of the Son of Man in heaven, perceived by them; the conversion of all the world, the Coming of Christ, the last Trumpet, the Resurrection of the dead, such, in most rapid sketch, is the outline which Jesus draws of His Coming and the End of the world.

It will be remembered that this had been the second question of the disciples. We again recall, that the disciples did not, could not have connected, as immediately subsequent events, the destruction of Jerusalem and His Second Coming, since he had expressly placed between them the period, apparently protracted, of His Absence, with the many events that were to happen in it, notably, the preaching of the Gospel over the whole inhabited earth. To this point Jesus had, in His discourse, dwelt in detail only on those events which would be fulfilled before this generation should pass. It had been for admonition and warning that He had spoken, not for the gratification of curiosity. It had been prediction of the immediate future for practical purposes, with such dim and general indication of the more distant future of the Church as was absolutely necessary to mark her position in the world as one of persecution, with promise, however, of His Presence and Help; with indication also of her work in the world, to its terminus ad quem, the preaching of the Gospel of the Kingdom to all nations on earth.

More than this concerning the future of the Church could not have been told without defeating the very object of the admonition and warning which Christ had exclusively in view, when answering the question of the disciples. Accordingly, what follows in ver. 29, describes the history, not of the Church, far less any visible physical signs in the literal heavens, but, in prophetic imagery, the history of the hostile powers of the world, with its lessons. A constant succession of empires and dynasties would characterize politically, and it is only the political aspect with which we are here concerned, the whole period after the extinction of the Jewish State. Immediately after that would follow the appearance to Israel of the Sign of the Son of Man in heaven, and with it the conversion of all nations (as previously predicted), the Coming of Christ, and, finally, the blast of the last Trumpet and the Resurrection.

5. From this rapid outline of the future Jesus once more turned to make present application to the disciples; application, also, to all times. From the fig tree, under which, on that spring afternoon, they may have rested on the Mount of Olives, they were to learn a parable. We can picture Christ taking one of its twigs, just as its softening tips were bursting into young leaf. Surely, this meant that summer was near, not that it had actually come. The distinction is important. For, it seems to prove that all these things, which were to indicate to them that it was near, even at the doors, and which were to be fulfilled before this generation had passed away, could not have referred, to the last signs connected with the immediate Advent of Christ, but must apply to the previous prediction of the destruction of Jerusalem and of the Jewish Commonwealth. At the same time we again admit, that the language of the Synoptists seems to indicate, that they had not clearly understood the words of Jesus which they reported, and that in their own minds they had associated the last signs and the Advent of Christ with the fall of the City. Thus may they have come to expect that Blessed Advent even in their own days.

II. It is at least a question, whether Jesus, while distinctly indicating these facts, and intended to remove the doubt and uncertainty of their succession from the minds of His disciples. To have done so would have necessitated that which, in the opening sentence of the Second Division of this discourse, He had expressly declared to lie beyond their understanding. The when, the day and the hour of His Coming, was to remain hidden from men and Angels. Even the Son Himself, as they viewed Him and as He spoke to them, knew it not. It formed no part of His present Messianic Mission, nor subject for His Messianic Teaching. Had it done so, all the teaching that follows concerning the need of constant watchfulness, and the pressing duty of working for Christ in faith, hope, and love, with purity, self denial, and endurance, would have been lost. The peculiar attitude of the Church: with loins prepared for work, since the time was short, and the Lord might come at any moment; with her hands busy; her mind faithful; her face upturned towards the Sun that was so soon to rise; and her ear straining to catch the first notes of heavens song of triumph, all this would have been lost! What has sustained the Church during the night of sorrow these many centuries; what has nerved her courage for the battle, with steadfastness to bear, with love to work, with patience and joy in disappointments, would all have been lost! The Church would not have been that of the New Testament, had she known the mystery of that day and hour, and not ever waited as for the immediate Coming of her Lord and Bridegroom.

And what the Church of the New Testament has been, and is, that her Lord and Master made her, and by no agency more effectually than by leaving undetermined the precise time of His return. To the world this would indeed become the occasion for utter carelessness and practical disbelief of the coming Judgment. As in the days of Noah the long delay of threatened judgment had led to absorption in the ordinary engagements of life, to the entire disbelief of what Noah had preached, so would it be in the future. But that day would come certainly and unexpectedly, to the sudden separation of those who were engaged in the same daily business of life, of whom one might be taken up (paralambnetai, received), the other left to the destruction of the coming Judgment.

But this very mixture of the Church with the world in the ordinary avocations of life indicated a greater danger. As in all such, the remedy which the Lord would set before us is not negative in the avoidance of certain things, but positive. We shall best succeed, not by going out of the world, but by being watchful in it, and keeping fresh on our hearts, as well as our minds, the fact that he is Jesus, and that we are, and always most lovingly, to look and long for His Return. Otherwise twofold damage might come to us. Not expecting the arrival of the Lord in the night time (which is the most unlikely for His Coming), we might go to sleep, and the Enemy, taking advantage or it, rob us of our peculiar treasure. Thus the Church, not expecting her lord, might become as poor as the world. This would be loss. But there might be even worse. According to Jesus' appointment, each one had, during Christ's absence, his work for Him, and the reward of grace, or else the punishment of neglect, were in assured prospect. The faithful steward, to whom the Master had entrusted the care of His household, to supply His found faithful, be rewarded by advancement to far larger and more responsible work. On the other hand, belief on the delay of Jesus' Return would lead to neglect to Jesus' work, to unfaithfulness, tyranny, self indulgence and sin. And when the Lord suddenly came, as certainly he would come, there would not be only loss, but damage, hurt, and the punishment awarded to the hypocrites. Therefore, let the Church be ever on her watch, let her ever be in readiness! And how terribly the moral consequences of unreadiness, and the punishment threatened, have ensued, the history of the Church during these eighteen centuries has only too often and too sadly shown.

End Notes:

[22]   According to Josephus (War 5:1. 1) the city was so upheaved and dug up, that it was difficult to believe it had ever been inhabited. At a later period Turnus Rufus had the ploughshare drawn over it. And in regard to the Temple walls, notwithstanding the massiveness of the stones, with the exception of some corner or portion of wall, left almost to show how great had been the ruin and desolation, there is, certainly, nothing now in place.

[23]   40 years = "the" wilderness wanderings: 1000 years = one day, Psalm 90:4; 2000 years of salvation = the day of vengeance and the year of salvation (Isaiah 63:4); 7000 years = the marriage week (Isaiah 62:5), a day being = 1000 years.

[24]   On the Resurrection body, the bone Luz, the dress worn, and the reappearance of the former bodily defects, see previous remarks, pp. 398, 399.

[25]   They are the following six: His splendor, the continuance of life, his original more than gigantic stature, the fruits of the ground, and of trees, and the brightness of the heavenly lights.

[26]   At the same time, many quotations by Christian writers intended to show the materialism of Jewish views are grossly unfair. Thus, for example, Ber. 57 b, quoted by Weber certainly does not express the grossly carnal expectancy imputed to it. On the other hand, it is certainly grossly materialistic, when we read how the skin of slaughtered Leviathan is to be made into tents, girdles, necklets, or armlets for the blessed, according to their varying merits. Altogether the account of the nature and hunt of this Leviathan, of the feast held, the various dishes served, and the wine drunk on the occasion (Targ. Pseudo-Jon. on Genesis 25:25; Targ. on Song of Solomon

8:2; on Ecclesiastes 9:7), are too coarsely materialistic for quotation. But what a contrast to the description of the Last Things by Jesus and His Apostles! This alone would furnish sufficient presumptive evidence in favor of the New Testament. I have tried to touch this very painful matter as delicately as I could, rather by allusions than by descriptions, which could only raise prejudices.

[27] This is the Jerusalem built of sapphire, which is to descend from heaven, and in the central sanctuary of which (unlike the worship of the Book of Revelation) Aaron is to officiate and to receive the priestly gifts (Taan. 5 a; Baba B. 75 b).

[28] Generally, these are regarded as the birth woes of the end. But this not only implies a logical impossibility (the birth woes of the end), but it must be remembered that these travail pains are the judgments on Jerusalem, or else on the world, which are to usher in the new, to precede its birth.

[29] We know how persistently Nero has been identified with Anti-Christ, and how the Church then expected the immediate return of Christ; in all ages, the End has been associated with troubles in the Roman Empire.

[30] So Eusebius (Hist. Ecclesiastes 3:5) relates that the Christians of Judea fled to Pella, on the northern boundary of Perea in 68 AD Comp. also Jos. War iv. 9. 1, v. 10. 1.

Chapter 7

Third Day Evening Parables
of the Last Days

1. As might have been expected, the Parables concerning the Last
Things are closely connected with the discourse of the Last Things,
which Christ had just spoken to His Disciples. In fact, that of the Ten
Virgins, which seems the fullest in many sided meaning, is, in its main
object, only an illustration of the last part of Christ's discourse. Its great
practical lessons had been: the unexpectedness of Jesus' Coming; the
consequences to be apprehend from its delay; and the need of personal
and constant preparedness. Similarly, the Parable of the Ten Virgins
may, in its great outlines, be thus summarized: Be you personally
prepared; be you prepared for any length of time; be you prepared to
go to Him directly.

Before proceeding, we mark that this Parable also is connected
with those that had preceded. But we notice not only connection, but
progression. Indeed, it would be deeply interesting, historically and for
the better understanding of Christ's teaching, but especially as showing
its internal unity and development, and the credibility of the Gospel
narratives, generally to trace this connection and progress. And this, not
merely in the three series of parables which mark the three stages of His
History, the Parables of the Founding of the Kingdom, of its Character,
and of its Consummation, but as regards the parables themselves, that
so the first might be joined to the last as a string of heavenly pearls. But
this lies beyond our task. Not so, to mark the connection between the

Parable of the Ten Virgins and that of the Man without the Wedding Garment.

Like the Parable of the Ten Virgins, it had pointed to the future. If the exclusion and punishment of the Unprepared Guest did not primarily refer to the Last Day, or to the Return of Christ, but perhaps rather to what would happen in death, it pointed, at least secondarily, to the final consummation. On the other hand, in the Parable of the Ten Virgins this final consummation is the primary point. So far, then, there is both connection and advance. Again, from the appearance and the fate of the Unprepared Guest we learned, that not everyone who, following the Gospel call, comes to the Gospel feast, will be allowed to partake of it; but that God will search and try each one individually. There is, a society of guests, the Church; but we must not expect either that the Church will, while on earth, be wholly pure, or that its purification will be achieved by man. Each guest may, come to the banqueting hall, but the final judgment as to his worthiness belongs to God. Lastly, the Parable also taught the no less important opposite lesson, that each individual is personally responsible; that we cannot shelter ourselves in the community of the Church, but that to partake of the feast requires personal and individual preparation. To express it in modern terminology: It taught Churchism as against one sided individualism, and spiritual individualism as against dead Churchism. All these important lessons are carried forward in the Parable of the Ten Virgins. If the union of the Ten Virgins for the purpose of meeting the Bridegroom, and their `a priori claims to enter in with Him, which are, so to speak, the historical data and necessary premises in the Parable, point to the Church, the main lessons of the Parade are the need of individual, personal, and spiritual preparation. Only such will endure the trial of the long delay of Christ's Coming; only such will stand that of an immediate summons to meet the Christ.

It is late at even, the world's long day seems past, and the Coming of the Bridegroom must be near. The day and the hour we do not know, for the bridegroom has been far away. Only this we know, that it is the Evening of the Marriage which the Bridegroom had fixed, and that his word of promise may be relied upon. Therefore all has been made ready within the bridal house, and is in waiting there; and therefore the Virgins prepare to go forth to meet Him on His Arrival. The Parable proceeds on the assumption that the Bridegroom is not in the town, but somewhere far away; so that it cannot be known at what precise hour He may arrive. But it is known that He will come that night; and the Virgins who are to meet

Him have gathered, presumably in the house where the Marriage is to take place, waiting for the summons to go forth and welcome the Bridegroom. The common mistake, that the Virgins are represented in verse 1 as having gone forth on the road to meet the Bridegroom, is not only irrational, since it is scarcely credible that they would all have fallen asleep by the wayside, and with lamps in their hands, but incompatible with the circumstance, that at midnight the cry is suddenly raised to go forth and meet Him. In these circumstances, no precise parallel can be derived from the ordinary Jewish marriage processions, where the bridegroom, accompanied by his groomsmen and friends, went to the bride's house, and from there conducted the bride, with her attendant maidens and friends, into his own or his parent's home. But in the Parable, the Bridegroom comes from a distance and goes to the bridal house. Accordingly, the bridal procession is to meet Him on His Arrival, and escort Him to the bridal place. No mention is made of the Bride, either in this Parable of in that or the Marriage of the King's Son. This, for reasons connected with their application: since in the one case the Wedding Guests, in the other the Virgins, occupy the place of the Bride. And here we must remind ourselves of the general canon, that, in the interpretation of a Parable, details must not be too closely pressed. The Parables illustrate the Sayings of Christ, as the Miracles His Doings; and the Parables and the Miracles present only one or another, not all the aspects of the truth.

Another archaeological inquiry will, perhaps, be more helpful to our understanding of this Parable. The lamps, not torches, which the Ten Virgins carried, were of well known construction. They bear in Talmudic writings commonly the name Lappid, but the Aramaised from the Greek word in the New Testament also occurs as Lampad and Lampadas. The lamp consisted of a round receptacle for pitch or oil for the wick. This was placed in a hollow cup or deep saucer, the Beth Shiqqua, which was fastened by a pointed end into a long wooden pole, on which it was borne in the air. According to Jewish authorities, it was the custom in the East to carry in a bridal procession about ten such lamps. We have the less reason to doubt that such was also the case in Palestine, since, according to rubric, ten was the number required to be present at any office or ceremony, such as at the benedictions accompanying the marriage ceremonies. And, in the peculiar circumstances supposed in the Parable, Ten Virgins are represented as going forth to meet the Bridegroom, each bearing her lamp.

The first point which we mark is, that the Ten Virgins brought, presumably to the bridal house, their own lamps. Emphasis must be laid on this. Thus much was there of personal preparation on the part of all. But while the five that were wise brought also oil in the vessels [presumably the hollow receptacles in which the lamp proper stood], the five foolish Virgins neglected to do so, no doubt expecting that their lamps would be filled out of some common stock in the house. In the text the foolish Virgins are mentioned before the wise, because the Parable turns to this. We cannot be at a loss to interpret the meaning of it. The Bridegroom far away is Christ, Who is come for the Marriage Feast from the far country, the Home above, certainly on that night, but we do not know at what hour of it. The ten appointed bridal companions who are to go forth to meet Him are His professed disciples, and they gather in the bridal house in readiness to welcome His arrival. It is night, and a marriage procession: therefore, they must go forth with their lamps. All of them have brought their own lamps, they all have the Christian, or say, the Church profession: the lamp, in the hollow cup on the top of the pole. But only the wise Virgins have more than this, the oil in the vessels, without which the lamps cannot give their light. The Christian or Church profession is but an empty vessel on the top of a pole, without the oil in the vessels. We here remember the words of Christ: Let your light so shine before men, that they may see your good works, and glorify your Father Which is in heaven. The foolishness of the Virgins, which consisted in this that they had omitted to bring their oil, is thus indicated in the text: All they which [atines] were foolish, when they brought their own lamps, brought not with them oil: they brought their own lamps, but not their own oil. This (as already explained), probably, not from forgetfulness, for they could scarcely have forgotten the need of oil, but from the willful neglect, in the belief that there would be a common stock in the house, out of which they would be supplied, or that there would be sufficient time for the supply of their need after the announcement that the Bridegroom was coming. They had no conception either of any personal obligation in this matter, nor that the call would come so suddenly, nor yet that there would be so little interval between the arrival of the Bridegroom and the closing of the door. And so they deemed it not necessary to undertake what must have involved both trouble and carefulness, the bringing their own oil in the hollow vessels in which the lamps were fixed.

We have proceeded on the supposition that the oil was not carried in separate vessels, but in those attached to the lamps. It seems scarcely likely that these lamps had been lighted while waiting in the bridal house, where the Virgins assembled, and which, no doubt, was festively illuminated:

Many practical objections to this view will readily occur. The foolishness of the five Virgins therefore consisted, not (as is commonly supposed) in their lack of perseverance, as if the oil had been consumed before the Bridegroom came, and they had only not provided themselves with a sufficient extra supply, but in the entire absence of personal preparation, having brought no oil of their own in their lamps. This corresponds to their conducts, who, belonging to the Church, having the profession, being bridal companions provided with lamps, ready to go forth, and expecting to share in the wedding feast, neglect the preparation of grace, personal conversation and holiness, trusting that in the hour of need the oil may be supplied out of the common stock. But they do not know, or else do not heed, that everyone must be personally prepared for meeting the Bridegroom, that the call will be sudden, that the stock of oil is not common, and that the time between His arrival and the shutting of the door will be awfully brief.

For, and here begins the second scene in the Parable, the interval between the gathering of the Virgins in readiness to meet Him, and the arrival of the Bridegroom is much longer than had been anticipated. And so it came, that both the wise and the foolish Virgins slumbered and slept. Manifestly, this is but a secondary trait in the Parable, chiefly intended to accentuate the surprise of the sudden announcement of the Bridegroom. The foolish Virgins did not ultimately fail because of their sleep, nor yet were the wise reproved of it. True, it was evidence of their weakness, but then it was night; all the world was asleep; and their own drowsiness might be in proportion to their former excitement. What follows is intended to bring into prominence the startling suddenness of the Bridegrooms Coming. It is midnight—when sleep is deepest, when suddenly there was a cry, Look, the Bridegroom comes! Come out to the meeting of Him. Then all those Virgins awoke, and prepared (trimmed) their lamps. This, not in the sense of heightening the low flame in their lamps, but in that of hastily drawing up the wick and lighting it, when, as there was no oil in the vessels, the flame immediately died out. Then the foolish said to the wise, Give us of your oil; for our lamps are going out. But the wise answered, saying: Not at all, it will never suffice for us and you! Go rather to the sellers, and buy for your own selves.

This advice must not be regarded as given in irony. This trait is introduced to point out the proper source of supply, to emphasize that the oil must be their own, and also to prepare for what follows. But while they were going to buy, the Bridegroom came; and the ready ones [they that were ready] went in with Him to the Marriage Feast, and the door was shut, The sudden cry at midnight: The Bridegroom comes! Had come with startling surprise both to the wise and the foolish Virgins; to the one class it had come only unexpectedly, but to the other also unpreparedly. Their hope of sharing or borrowing the oil of the wise Virgins being disappointed, the foolish were unable to meet the Bridegroom. And while they hurried to the sellers of oil, those that had been ready not only met; but entered with the Bridegroom into the bridal house, and the door was shut. It is of no importance here, whether or not the foolish Virgins finally succeeded in obtaining oil, although this seems unlikely at that time of night, since it could no longer be of any possible use, as its object was to serve in the festive procession, which was now past. Nevertheless, and when the door was shut, those foolish Virgins came, calling on the Bridegroom to open to them. But they had failed in that which could alone give them a claim to admission. Professing to be bridesmaids, they had not been in the bridal procession, and so, in truth and righteousness, He could only answer from within: Truly I say to you, I know you not. This, not only in punishment, but in the right order of things.

The personal application of this Parable to the disciples, which Jesus makes, follows almost of necessity. Watch therefore, for you do not know the day, nor the hour. Not enough to be in waiting with the Church; His Coming will be far on in the night; it will be sudden; it will be rapid: be prepared therefore, be ever and personally prepared! Christ will come when least expected, at midnight, and when the Church, having become accustomed to His long delay, has gone to sleep. So sudden will be His Coming, that after the cry of announcement there will not be time for anything but to go forth to meet Him; and so rapid will be the end, that, before the foolish Virgins can return, the door has been forever closed. To present all this in the most striking manner, the Parable takes the form of a dialogue, first between the foolish and the wise Virgins, in which the latter only state the bare truth when saying, that each has only sufficient oil for what is necessary. Lastly, we are to learn from the dialogue between the foolish Virgins and the Bridegroom, that it is impossible in the day of Christ's Coming to make up for neglect of previous preparation, and that those who have failed to meet Him, even though the bridal Virgins, shall be finally excluded as being strangers to the Bridegroom.

2. The Parable of the Talents, their use and misuse—follows closely on the admonition to watch, in view of the sudden and certain Return of Christ, and the reward or punishment which will then be meted out.

Only that, whereas in the Parable of the Ten Virgins the reference was to the personal state, in that of the Talents it is to the personal work of the Disciples. In the former instance, they are portrayed as the bridal maidens who are to welcome His Return; in the latter, as the servants who are to give an account of their stewardship.

From its close connection with what precedes, the Parable opens almost abruptly with the words: For [it is] like a Man going abroad, [who] called His own servants, and delivered to them His goods. The emphasis rests on this, that they were His own servants, and to act for His interest. His property was handed over to them, not for safe custody, but that they might do with it as best they could in the interest of their Master. This appears from what immediately follows: and so to one He gave five talents (about 1,170l.), but to one two (about 468l.), and to one (=6,000 denarii, about 234l.), to each according to his own capability, that is, He gave to each according to his capacity, in proportion as He deemed severally qualified for larger or smaller administration. And He journeyed abroad without delay. Having entrusted the management of His affairs to His servants, according to their capacity, He at once went away.

Thus far we can have no difficulty in understanding the meaning of the Parable. Our Lord, Who has left us for the Father's Home, is He Who has gone on the journey abroad, and to His own servants has He entrusted, not for custody, but to use for Him in the time between His departure and His return, what He claims as His own goods. We must not limit this to the administration of His Word, nor to the Holy Ministry, although these may have been pre-eminently in view. It refers generally to all that a man has, with which to serve Christ; for, all that the Christian has, his time, money, opportunities, talents, or learning (and not only the Word), is Christ's, and is entrusted to us, not for custody, but to trade withal for the absent Master, to further the progress of His Kingdom. And to each of us He gives according to our capacity for working, mental, moral, and even physical, to one five, to another two, and to another one talent. This capacity for work lies not within our own power; but it is in our power to use for Christ whatever we may have.

And here the characteristic difference appears. He that received the five talents went and traded with them, and made other five talents. In like manner he that had received the two gained other two. As each had received according to his ability, so each worked according to his power, as good and faithful servants of their Lord. If the outward result was different, their labor, devotion, and faithfulness were equal. It was otherwise with him who had least to do for his Master, since only one talent had been entrusted to him. He went away, dug up earth, and hid the money of his Lord. The prominent fact here is, that he did not employ it for the Master, as a good servant, but shunned the labor and the responsibility, and acted as if it had been some strangers, and not his Lord's property. In so doing he was not only unfaithful to his trust, but practically disowned that he was a servant who had received much, two others are introduced in the Parable, who had both received comparatively little, one of whom was faithful, while the other in idle selfishness hid the money, not accounting it as his Lord's. Thus, while the second servant, although less had been entrusted to him was as faithful and conscientious as he to whom much had been given, and while both had, by their gain, increased the possessions of their Master, the third had by his conduct rendered the money of his Lord a dead, useless, buried thing.

And now the second scene opens. But after a long time comes the Lord of those servants, and makes reckoning with them. The notice of the long absence of the Master not only connects this with the Parable of the Ten Virgins, but is intended to show that the delay might have rendered the servants who traded more careless, while it also increased the guilt of him, who all this time had not done anything with his Masters money. And now the first of the servants, without speaking of his labor in trading, or his merit in making money, answers with simple joyousness: Lord, five talents delivered You to me. See, another five talents have I gained besides. We can almost see his honest face beaming with delight, as he points to his Masters increased possession. His approval was all that the faithful servant had looked for, for which he had toiled during that long absence. And we can understand, how the Master welcomed and owned that servant, and assigned to him appropriate reward. The latter was twofold. Having proved his faithfulness and capacity in a comparatively limited sphere, one much greater would be assigned to him. For, to do the work, and increase the wealth of his Master, had evidently been his joy and privilege, as well as his duty. Therefore also the second part of his reward, that of entering into the joy of his Lord, must not be confined to sharing in the festive meal at His return, still less to advancement from the position of a servant to that of a friend who shares his Masters lordship. It implies far more than this: even satisfied heart sympathy with the aims and gains of his Master, and participation in them, with all that thus conveys.

A similar result followed on the reckoning with the servant to whom two talents had been entrusted. We mark that, although he could only speak of two talents gained, he met his Master with the same frank joyness as he who had made five. For he had been as faithful, and labored as earnestly as he to whom more had been entrusted. And what is more important, the former difference between the two servants, dependent on greater or less capacity for work, now ceased, and the second servant received precisely the same welcome and exactly the same reward, and in the same terms, as the first. And yet a deeper, and in some sense mysterious, truth comes to us in connection with the words: You have been faithful over a few things, I will set you over many things. Surely, then, if not after death, yet in that other dispensation, there must be work to do for Christ, for which the preparation is in this life by faithful application for Him of what He has entrusted to us, be it much or little. This gives quite a new and blessed meaning to the life that now is, as most truly and in all its aspects part of that into which it is to unfold. No; not the smallest share of talents, if only faithfully used for Christ, can be lost, not merely as regards His acknowledgement, but also their further and wider employment. And may we not suggest, that this may, if not explain, yet cast the halo of His purpose and Presence around what so often seems mysterious in the removal of those who had just attained to opening, or to full usefulness, or even of those who are taken from us in the early morning of youth and loveliness. The Lord may have need of them, where or how we do not know, and beyond this working day and working world there are many things over which the faithful servant in little may be set, that he may still do, and with greatly enlarged opportunities and powers, the work for Christ which he had loved so well, while at the same time he also shares the joy of his Lord.

It only remains to refer to the third servant, whose sad unfaithfulness and failure of service we already, in some measure, understand. Summoned to his account, he returned the talent entrusted to him with this explanation, that, knowing his Master to be a hard man, reaping where he did not sow, and gathering (the grain) where He did not winnow, he had been afraid of incurring responsibility, and therefore hid in the earth the talent which he now restored. It needs no comment to show that his own words, however honest and self righteous they might sound, admitted dereliction of his work and duty as a servant, and entire misunderstanding as well as heart alienation from his Master. He served Him not, and he knew Him not; he loved Him not, and he sympathized not with Him. But, besides, his answer was also an insult and a untruthful pretext. He had been idle and unwilling to work for his Master. If he worked it would be for himself. He would not incur the difficulties, the self denial, perhaps the reproach, connected with his Masters work. We recognize here those who, although His servants, yet, from self indulgence and worldliness, will not do work for Christ with the one talent entrusted to them, that is, even though the responsibility and claim upon them be the smallest; and who deem it sufficient to hide it in the ground, not to lose it, or to preserve it, as they imagine, from being used for evil, without using it to trade for Christ. The falseness of the excuse, that he was afraid to do anything with it, an excuse too often repeated in our days, for fear that, for the possibility, he might do more harm than good, was now fully exposed by the Master. Confessedly, it proceeded from a lack of knowledge of Him, as if He were a hard, exacting Master, not One Who reckons even the least service as done to Himself; from misunderstanding also of what work for Christ is, in which nothing can ever fail or be lost; and, lastly, from lack of joyous sympathy with it. And so the Master put aside the flimsy pretext. Addressing him as a wicked and slothful servant, He pointed out that, even on his own showing, if he had been afraid to incur responsibility, he might have tossed (a word intended to mark the absence of labor) the money to the bankers, when, at His return, He would have received His own, with interest. Thus he might, without incurring responsibility, or much labor, have been, at least in a limited sense, faithful to his duty and trust as a servant.

The reference to the practice of lodging money, at interest, with the bankers, raises questions too numerous and lengthy for full discussion in this place. The Jewish Law distinguished between interest and increase (neshekh and tarbith), and entered into many and intricate details on the subject. Such transactions were forbidden with Israelites, but allowed with Gentiles. As in Rome, the business of money changers (argentarii, nummularii) and that of bankers (collectarii, mensularii) seem to have run into each other. The Jewish bankers bear precisely the same name (Shulchani, mensularius, trapeztes). In Rome very high interest seems to have been charged in early times; by and by it was lowered, until it was fixed, first at 8 1/2, and then at 4 1/6, per cent. But these laws were not of permanent duration. Practically, usury was unlimited. It soon became the custom to charge monthly interest at the rate of 1 percent a month. Yet there were prosperous times, as at the close of the Republic, when the rate of interest was so low as 4 percent; during the early Empire it stood at 8 per cent. This in what we may call fair business transactions. Beyond them, in the almost incredible extravagance, luxury, and indebtedness of even some of the chief historical personages, most usurious transactions took place (especially in the provinces), and that by people in high position (Brutus in Cyprus, and Seneca in Britain). Money was lent at 12, 24, and even 48 percent; the bills bore a larger sum than that actually received; and the interest was added to the capital, so that debt and interest grew. In Greece there were regular State banks, while in Rome such provision was only made under exceptional circumstances. Not infrequently the twofold business of money changing and banking was combined. Such bankers undertook to make payments, to collect moneys and accounts, to place out money at interest, in short, all the ordinary business of this kind. There can be no question that the Jewish bankers of Palestine and elsewhere were engaged in the same undertakings, while the dispersion of their race over the world would render it more easy to have trusted correspondents in every city. Thus, we find that Herod Agrippa borrowed from the Jewish Alabarch at Alexandria the sum of 20,000 drachms, which was paid him in Italy, the commission and interest on it amounting to no less than 8 1/2 per cent. (2,500 drachms).

We can thus understand the allusion to the bankers, with whom the wicked and unfaithful servant might have lodged his lord's money, if there had been truth in his excuse. To unmask its hollowness is the chief object of this part of the Parable. Accordingly, it must not be too closely pressed; but it would be in the spirit of the Parable to apply the expression to the indirect employment of money in the service of Christ, as by charitable contributions, etc. But the great lesson intended is, that every good and faithful servant of Christ must, whatever his circumstances, personally and directly use such talent as he may have to make gain for Christ. Tried by this test, how few seem to have understood their relation to Christ, and how cold has the love of the Church grown in the long absence of her Lord!

But as regards the unprofitable servant in the Parable, the well known punishment of him that had come to the Marriage Feast without the wedding garment shall await him, while the talent, which he had failed to employ for his master, shall be entrusted to him who had shown himself most capable of working. We need not seek an elaborate interpretation for this. It points to the principle, equally true in every administration of God, that to everyone that has shall be given, and he shall be placed in abundance; but as to him that has not, also what he has shall be away from him. Not a cynical rule this, such as the world, in its selfishness or worship of success, caricatures it; nor yet the worship of superior force; but this, that faithful use for God of every capacity will ever open fresh opportunities, in proportion as the old ones have been used, while spiritual unprofitableness must end in utter loss even of that which, however humble, might have been used, at one time or another, for God and for good.

3. To these Parables, that of the King who on his return makes reckoning with His servants and His enemies may be regarded as supplemental. It is recorded only by Luke, and placed by him in somewhat loose connection with the conversion of Zacchaeus. The most superficial perusal will show such unmistakable similarity with the Parable of The Talents, that their identity will naturally suggest itself to the reader. On the other hand, there are remarkable divergences in detail, some of which seem to imply a different standpoint from which the same truth is viewed. We have also now the additional feature of the message of hatred on the part of the citizens, and their fate in consequence of it. It may have been that Christ spoke the two Parables on the two different occasions mentioned respectively by Luke and Matthew, the one on the journey to Jerusalem, the other on the Mount of Olives. And yet it seems difficult to believe that He would, with a few days of telling the Parable recorded by Luke, have repeated it in almost the same words to the disciples, who must have heard it in Jericho. This objection would not be so serious, if the Parable addressed, in the first instance, to the disciples (that of the Talents) had been afterwards repeated (in the record of Luke) in a wider circle, and not, as according to the Synoptists, the opposite. If, however, we are to regard the two Parables of the Talents and of the Pieces of Money as substantially the same, we would be disposed to consider the revision by Matthew as the original, being the more homogeneous and compact, while that of Luke would seem to combine with this another Parable, that of the rebellious citizens. Perhaps it is safest to assume, that, on His way to Jerusalem, when his adherents (not merely the disciples) would naturally expect that He would inaugurate His Messianic Kingdom, Christ may have spoken the latter Parable, to teach them that the relation in which Jerusalem stood towards Him, and its fate, were quite different form what they imagined, and that His Entrance into the City and the Advent of His Kingdom would be separated by a long distance of time. Therefore the prospect before them was that of working, not of reigning; after that would the reckoning come, when the faithful worker would become the trusted ruler. These points were closely connected with the lessons of the Parable of the Talents, and, with the view of presenting the

subject as a whole, Luke may have borrowed details from that Parable, and supplemented its teaching by presenting another aspect of it.

It must be admitted, that if Luke had really these two Parables in view (that of the King and of the Talents), and wished to combine them into new teaching, he has most admirably welded them together. For, as the Nobleman Who is about to entrust money to His servants, is going abroad to receive a Kingdom, it was possible to represent Him in relation to rebellious citizens and to His own servants, and to connect their reward with His Kingdom. And so the two Parables are joined by deriving the illustration from political instead of social life. It has been commonly supposed, that the Parable contains an allusion to what had happened after the death of Herod the Great, when his son Archelaus hurried to Rome to obtain confirmation of his father's will, while a Jewish deputation followed to oppose his appointment, an act of rebellion which Archelaus afterwards avenged in the blood of his enemies. The circumstance must have been still fresh in popular remembrance, although more than thirty years had elapsed. But if otherwise, applications to Rome for installation to the government, and popular opposition thereto, were of such frequent occurrence amid the quarrels and intrigues of the Herodians, that no difficulty could have been felt in understanding the allusions of the Parable.

A brief analysis will suffice to point out the special lessons of this Parable. It introduces a certain Nobleman, Who has claims to the throne, but has not yet received the formal appointment from the sovereign power. As He is going away to receive it, He deals as yet only with His servants. His object, apparently, is to try their aptitude, devotion, and faithfulness: and so He hands, not to each according to his capacity, but to all equally, a sum, not large (such as talents), but small, to each a mina, equal to 100 drachms, or about 3l. 5s. of our money. To trade with so small a sum would be much more difficult, and success would imply greater ability, even as it would require more constant labor. Here we have some traits in which this differs from the Parable of the Talents. The same small sum is supposed to have been entrusted to all, in order to show which of them was most able and most earnest, and therefore who should be called to largest employment, and with it to greatest honor in the Kingdom. While the Nobleman was at the court of His sovereign, a deputation of His fellow citizens arrived to urge this resolution of theirs: We do not want this One to reign over us. It was simply an expression of hatred; it stated no reason, and only urged personal opposition, even if such were in the face of the personal wish of the sovereign who appointed him king.

In the last scene, the King, now duly appointed, has returned to His country. He first reckons with His servants, when it is found that all but one have been faithful to their trust, though with varying success (the mina of the one having grown into ten; that of another into five, and so on). In strict accordance with that success is now their further appointment to rule, work here corresponding to rule there, which, however, as we know from the Parable of the Talents, is also work for Christ: a rule that is work, and work that is rule. At the same time, the acknowledgment is the same to all the faithful servants. Similarly, the motives, the reasoning, and the fate of the unfaithful servant are the same as in the Parable of the Talents. But as regards His enemies, that would not have Him reign over them, manifestly, Jerusalem and the people of Israel, who, even after He had gone to receive the Kingdom, continued the personal hostility of their We will not that this One shall reign over us, the ashes of the Temple, the ruins of the City, the blood of the fathers, and the homeless wanderings of their children, with the Cain curse branded on their brow and visible to all men, attest, that the King has many ministers to execute that judgment which obstinate rebellion must surely bring, if His Authority is to be vindicated, and His Rule to secure submission.

Chapter 8

Fourth Day and the Betrayal

From the record of Christ's Sayings and Doings, furnished by Matthew, we turn once more to that of public events, as, from one or another aspect they are related by all the Evangelists. With the discourses in the Temple the public Teaching of Christ had come to an end; with that spoken on the Mount of Olives, and its application in the Parables of the Virgins and the Talents, the instruction of the disciples had been concluded. What follows in His intercourse with His own is persuasive, rather than teaching, exhortation, advice, and consolation: rather, perhaps, all these combined.

The three busy days of Passion Week were past. The day before that on which the Paschal Lamb was to be slain, with all that was to follow, would be one of rest, a Sabbath to His Soul before its Great Agony. He would refresh Himself, gather Himself up for the terrible conflict before Him. And He did so as the Lamb of God, meekly submitting Himself to the Will and Hand of His Father, and so fulfilling all types, from that of Isaac's sacrifice on Mount Moriah to the Paschal Lamb in the Temple; and bringing the reality of all prophecy, from that of the Woman's Seed that would crush the Serpent's head to that of the Kingdom of God in its fullness, when its golden gates would be flung open to all men, and Heaven's own light flow out to them as they sought its way of peace. Only two days more, as the Jews reckoned them, that Wednesday and Thursday, and at its Evening the Paschal supper! And Jesus knew it well, and He passed that day of rest and preparation in quiet retirement with His disciples, perhaps in some hollow of the Mount of Olives, near the home of Bethany, speaking to them of His Crucifixion on the near Passover. They sorely needed His words; they, rather than He, needed to be prepared for what was coming. But what

Divine calm, what willing obedience, and also what outgoing of love to them, with full consciousness of what was before Him, to think and speak of this only on that day! So would not a Messiah of Jewish conception have acted; He would not have been placed in such circumstances. So would not a Messiah of ambitious aims or of Jewish Nationalist aspirations have acted; He would have done what the Sanhedrin feared, and raised a tumult of the people, prepared for it as the multitude was, which had so lately raised the Hosanna cry in street and Temple. So would a disillusioned enthusiast not have acted; he would have withdrawn from the impending fate. But Jesus knew it all, far more the agony of shame and suffering, even the unfathomable agony of soul. And the while He thought only of them in it all. Such thinking and speaking is not that of Man, it is that of the Incarnate Son of God, the Christ of the Gospels.

He had, before that, sought gradually to prepare them for what was to happen on the morrow's night. He had pointed to it in dim figure at the very opening of His Ministry, on the first occasion that he had taught in the Temple, as well as to Nicodemus. He had hinted it, when He spoke of the deep sorrow when the Bridegroom would be taken from them, of the need of taking up His cross, of the fulfillment in Him of the Jonah type, of His Flesh which He would give for the life of the world, as well as in what might have seemed the Parabolic teaching about the Good Shepherd, Who laid down His life for the Sheep, and the Heir Whom the evil husbandmen threw out and killed. But He had also spoken of it quite directly, and this, let us especially notice, always when some highpoint in His History had been reached, and the disciples might have been carried away into Messianic expectations of an exaltation without humiliation, a triumph not a sacrifice. We remember, that the first occasion on which He spoke thus clearly was immediately after that confession of Peter, which laid the foundation of the Church, against which the gates of hell should not prevail; the next, after descending from the Mount of Transfiguration; the last, on preparing to make His triumphal Messianic Entry into Jerusalem. The darker hints and Parabolic sayings might have been misunderstood. Even as regarded the clear prediction of His death, preconceived ideas could find no room for such a fact. Deep veneration, which could not associate it with His Person, and love which could not bear the thought of it, might, after the first shock of the words was past, and their immediate fulfillment did not follow, suggest some other possible explanation of the prediction. But on that Wednesday it was impossible to misunderstand; it could scarcely have been possible to doubt what Jesus said of His near Crucifixion. If illusions had still existed, the last two days must have rudely dispelled them. The triumphal Hosannas of His Entry into the City, and the acclamations in the Temple, had given place to the hair splitting of Pharisees, Sadducees, and Scribes, and with a Judgment upon it Jesus had taken His last departure from Israel's sanctuary. And better far than those rulers, whom conscience made cowards, did the disciples know how little reliance could be placed on the adherence of the multitude. And now the Master was telling it to them in plain words; was calmly contemplating it, and that not as in the dim future, but in the immediate present, at that very Passover, from which scarcely two days separated them. Much as we wonder at their brief scattering on His arrest and condemnation, those humble disciples must have loved Him much to sit around Him in mournful silence as He thus spoke, and to follow Him to His Dying.

But to one of them, in whose heart the darkness had long been gathering, this was the decisive moment. The prediction of Christ, which Judas as well as the others must have felt to be true, extinguished the last glimmering of such light of Christ as his soul had been capable of receiving. In its place flared up the lurid flame of hell. By the open door out of which he had thrust the dying Christ Satan entered into Judas. Yet, even so, not permanently. It may, be doubted, whether, since God is in Christ, such can ever be the case in any human soul, at least on this side eternity. Since our world's night has been lit up by the promise from Paradise, the rosy hue of its morning has lain on the edge of the horizon, deepening into gold, brightening into day, growing into midday strength and evening glory. Since God's Voice awakened earth by its early Christmas Hymn, it has never been quite night there, nor can it ever be quite night in any human soul.

But it is a terrible night study, that of Judas. We seem to tread our way over loose stones of hot molten lava, as we climb to the edge of the crater, and shudderingly look down its depths. And yet there, near there, have stood not only Peter in the night of his denial, but mostly all of us, save they whose Angels have always looked up into the Face of our Father in heaven. And yet, in our weakness, we have even wept over them! There, near there, have we stood, not in the hours of our weakness, but in those of our great temptation, when the blast of doubt had almost quenched the flickering light, or the storm of passion or self will broken the bruised reed. But He prayed for us, and through the night came over desolate moor and stony height the Light of His Presence, and above the wild storm rose the Voice of Him, Who has come to seek and to save that which was lost. Yet near to us, close to us, was the dark abyss; and we can never more forget out last, almost sliding, foothold as we left its edge.

A terrible night study this of Judas, and best to make it here, at once, from its beginning to its end. We shall indeed, catch sudden glimpse of him again, as the light of the torches flashes on the traitor face in Gethsemane; and once more hear his voice in the assembly of the proud, sneering councilors of Israel, when his footfall on the marble pavement of the Temple halls; and the clink of those thirty accursed pieces of silver shall awaken the echoes, awaken also the dirge of despair in his soul, and he shall flee from the night of his soul into the night that forever closes around him. But all this as rapidly as we may pass from it, after this present brief study of his character and history.

We remember, that Judas, the man of Kerioth, was, so far as we know, the only disciple of Jesus from the province of Judea. This circumstance; that he carried the bag, i.e. was treasurer and administrator of the small common stock of Christ and His disciples; and that he was both a hypocrite and a thief, this is all that we know for certain of his history. From the circumstance that he was appointed to such office of trust in the Apostolic community, we infer that he must have been looked up to by the others as an able and prudent man, a good administrator. And there is probably no reason to doubt, that he possessed the natural gift of administration or of government (kubrnesis). The question, why Jesus left him the bag after he knew him to be a thief, which, as we believe, he was not at the beginning, and only became in the course of time and in the progress of disappointment, is best answered by this other: Why He originally allowed it to be entrusted to Judas? It was not only because he was best fitted, probably, absolutely fitted, for such work, but also in mercy to him, in view of his character. To engage in that for which a man is naturally fitted is the most likely means of keeping him from brooding, dissatisfaction, alienation, and eventual apostasy. On the other hand, it must be admitted that, as mostly all our life temptations come to us from that for which we have most aptitude, when Judas was alienated and unfaithful in heart, this very thing became also his greatest temptation, and, hurried him to his ruin. But only after he had first failed inwardly. And so, as ever in like circumstances, the very things which might have been most of blessing become most of curse, and the judgment of hardening fulfills itself by that which in itself is good. Nor could the bag have been afterwards taken from him without both exposing him to the others, and precipitating his moral destruction. And so he had to be left to the process of inward ripening, until all was ready for the sickle.

This very gift of government in Judas may also help us to understand how he may have been first attracted to Jesus, and through what process, when alienated, he came to end in that terrible sin which had cast its snare about him. The gift of government would, in its active aspect, imply the desire for it. From there to ambition in its worst, or selfish, aspect, there is only a step, scarcely that: rather, only different moral premises. Judas was drawn to Jesus as the Jewish Messiah, and he believed in Him as such, possibly both earnestly and ardently; but he expected that His would be the success, the result, and the triumphs of the Jewish Messiah, and he also expected personally and fully to share in them. How deep rooted were such feelings even in the best, purest, and most unselfish of Jesus disciples, we gather from the request of the mother of John and James for her sons, and from Peter's question: What shall we have? it must have been sorrow, the misery of moral loneliness, and humiliation, to Him Who was Unselfishness Incarnate, Who lived to die and was full to empty Himself, to be associated with such as even His most intimate disciples, who in this sense also could not watch with Him even one hour, and in whom, at the end of His Ministry, such heaviness was mentally and morally the outcrop, if not the outcome. And in Judas all this must have been an hundredfold more than in them who were in heart true to Christ.

He had, from such conviction as we have described, joined the movement at its very beginning. Then, multitudes in Galilee followed His Footsteps, and watched for His every appearance; they hung entranced on His lips in the Synagogue or on the Mount; they flocked to Him from every town, village, and hamlet; they bore the sick and dying to His Feet, and witnessed, awestruck, how conquered devils gave their testimony to His Divine Power. It was the spring time of the movement, and all was full of promise, land, people, and disciples. The Baptist, who had bowed before Him and testified to Him, was still lifting his voice to proclaim the near Kingdom. But the people had turned after Jesus, and He swayed them. And, oh! what power was there in His Face and Word, and His look and deed. And Judas, also, had been one of them who, on their early Mission, had temporarily had power given Him, so that the very devils had been subject to them. But, step by step, had come the disappointment. John was beheaded, and not avenged; on the contrary, Jesus withdrew Himself. This constant withdrawing, whether from enemies or from success, almost amounting to flight, even when they would have made Him a King; this refusal to show Himself openly, either at Jerusalem, as His own brethren had taunted Him, or, anywhere else; this uniform preaching of discouragement to them, when they came to Him elated and hopeful at some success; this gathering hostility of Israel's leaders, and His marked avoidance of, or, as some might have put it, His failure in taking up the repeated public challenge of the Pharisees to show a sign from heaven; last, and chief of all, this constant and growing reference to shame, disaster, and death, what did it all mean, if not disappointment of all those hopes and expectations which had made Judas at the first a disciple of Jesus?

He that so knew Jesus, not only in His Words and Deeds, but in His inmost Thoughts, even to His night long communing with God on the hill side, could not have seriously believed in the coarse Pharisaic charge of Satanic agency as the explanation of all. Yet, from the then Jewish standpoint, he could scarcely have found it impossible to suggest some other explanation of His miraculous power. But, as increasingly the moral and spiritual aspect of Christ's Kingdom must have become apparent to even the dullest intellect, the bitter disappointment of his Messianic thoughts and hopes must have gone on, increasing in proportion as, side by side with it, the process of moral alienation, unavoidably connected with his resistance to such spiritual manifestation, continued and increased. And so the mental and the moral alienation went on together, affected by and affecting each other. As if we were pressed to name a definite moment when the process of disintegration, at least sensibly, began, we would point to that Sabbath morning at Capernaum, when Christ had preached about His Flesh as the Food of the World, and so many of His adherents ceased to follow after Him; when the leaven so worked even in His disciples, that He turned to them with the searching question, intended to show them the full import of the crisis, whether they also would leave Him? Peter conquered by grasping the moral element, because it was germane to him and to the other true disciples: To whom shall we go? You have the words of eternal life. But this moral element was the very cliff on which Judas made shipwreck. After this, all was wrong, and increasingly so. We see disappointment in his face when not climbing the Mount of Transfiguration, and disappointment in the failure to heal the demonized child. In the disputes by the way, in the quarrels who was greatest among them, in all the pettiness of misunderstandings and realistic folly of their questions or answers, we seem to hear the echo of his voice, to see the result of his influence, the leaven of his presence. And in it all we mark the downward hastening of his course, even to the moment when, in contrast to the deep love of a Mary, he first stands before us unmasked, as heartless, hypocritical, full of hatred, disappointed ambition having broken down into selfishness, and selfishness slid into covetousness, even to the crime of stealing that which was destined for the poor.

For, when an ambition which rests only on selfishness gives way there lies close by it the coarse lust of covetousness, as the kindred passion and lower expression of that other form of selfishness. When the Messianic faith of Judas gave place to utter disappointment, the moral and spiritual character of Christ's Teaching would affect him, not sympathetically but contrarily. Thus, that which should have opened the door of his heart, only closed and double barred it. His attachment to the Person of Jesus would give place to actual hatred, though only of a temporary character; and the wild intenseness of his Eastern nature would set it all in flame. Thus, when Judas had lost his slender foothold, or, rather, when it had slipped from under him, he fell down, down the eternal abyss. The only hold to which he could cling was the passion of his soul. As he laid hands on it, it gave way, and fell with him into fathomless depths. We, each of us, have also some master passion; and if, which God forbid! we should lose our foothold, we also would grasp this master passion, and it would give way, and carry us with it into the eternal dark and deep.

On that spring day, in the restfulness of Bethany, when the Master was taking His sad and solemn Farewell of sky and earth, of friends and disciples, and told them what was to happen only two days later at the Passover, it was all settled in the soul of Judas. Satan entered it. Christ would be crucified; this was quite certain. In the general cataclysm let Judas have at least something. And so, on that sunny afternoon, he left them out there, to seek speech of them that were gathered, not in their ordinary meeting place, but in the High Priests Palace. Even this indicates that it was an informal meeting, consultative rather than judicial. For, it was one of the principles of Jewish Law that, in criminal cases, sentence must be spoken in the regular meeting place of the Sanhedrin. The same inference is conveyed by the circumstance, that the captain of the Temple guard and his immediate subordinates seem to have been taken into the council, no doubt to coordinate the measures for the actual arrest of Jesus. There had previously been a similar gathering and consultation, when the report of the raising of Lazarus reached the authorities of Jerusalem. The practical resolution adopted at that meeting had apparently been, that a strict watch should from then on be kept on Christ's movements, and that everyone of them, as well as the names of His friends, and the places of His secret retirement, should be communicated to the authorities, with the view to His arrest at the proper moment.

It was probably in professed obedience to this direction, that the traitor presented himself that afternoon in the Palace of the High Priest Caiaphas. Those assembled there were the chiefs of the Priesthood, no doubt, the Temple officials, heads of the course of Priests, and connections of the High Priestly family, who constituted what both Josephus and the Talmud designate as the Priestly Council. All connected with the Temple, its ritual, administration, order, and laws, would be in their hands. Moreover, it was but natural, that the High Priest and his council should be the regular official medium between the Roman authorities and the people. In matters which concerned, not ordinary misdemeanors, but political crimes (such as it was wished to represent the movement of Jesus), or which affected the status of the established religion, the official chiefs of the Priesthood would be the persons to appeal, in conjunction with the Sanhedrists, to the secular authorities. This, irrespective of the question, to which reference will be made in the sequel, what place the Chief Priests held in the Sanhedrin. But in that meeting in the Palace of Caiaphas, besides these Priestly Chiefs, the leading Sanhedrists (Scribes and Elders) were also gathered. They were deliberating how Jesus might be taken by subtlety and killed. Probably they had not yet fixed on any definite plan. Only at this conclusion had they arrived, probably in consequence of the popular acclamations at His Entry into Jerusalem, and of what had since happened—that nothing must be done during the Feast, for fear of some popular tumult. They knew only too well the character of Pilate, and how in any such tumult all parties, the leaders as well as the led, might experience terrible vengeance.

It must have been intense relief when, in their perplexity, the traitor now presented himself before them with his proposals. Yet his reception was not such as he may have looked for. He probably expected to be hailed and treated as a most important ally. They were, glad, and covenanted to give him money, even as he promised to dog His steps, and watch for the opportunity which they sought. In truth, the offer of the betrayer changed the whole aspect of matters. What formerly they dreaded to attempt seemed now both safe and easy. They could not allow such an opportunity to slip; it was one that might never occur again. Might it not even seem, from the defection of Judas, as if dissatisfaction and disbelief had begun to spread in the innermost circle of Christ's disciples?

Yet, withal, they treated Judas not as an honored associate, but as a common informer, and a contemptible betrayer. This was not only natural but, in the circumstances, the wisest policy, in order to save their own dignity, and to keep most secure hold on the betrayer. And, after all, it might be said, so as to minimize his services, that Judas could really not do much for them, only show them how they might seize Him at unawares in the absence of the multitude, to avoid the possible tumult of an open arrest. So little did they understand Christ! And Judas had at last to speak it out barefacedly, so selling himself as well as the Master: What will you give me? It was in literal fulfillment of prophecy, that they weighed out to him from the very Temple treasury those thirty pieces of silver (about 3l. 15s.). And here we mark, that there is always terrible literality about the prophecies of judgment, while those of blessing far exceed the words of prediction. And yet it was surely as much in contempt of the seller as of Him Whom he sold, that they paid the legal price of a slave. Or did they mean some kind of legal fiction, such as to buy the Person of Jesus at the legal price of a slave, so as to hand it afterwards over to the secular authorities? Such fictions, to save the conscience by a logical quibble, are not so uncommon, and the case of the Inquisitors handing over the condemned heretic to the secular authorities will recur to the mind. But, in truth, Judas could not now have escaped their toils. They might have offered him ten or five pieces of silver, and he must still have stuck to his bargain. Yet none the less do we mark the deep symbolic significance of it all, in that Jesus was, so to speak, paid for out of the Temple money which was destined for the purchase of sacrifices, and that He, Who took on Him the form of a servant, was sold and bought at the legal price of a slave.

And yet Satan must once more enter the heart of Judas at that Supper, before he can finally do the deed. But, even so, we believe it was only temporarily, not for always, for, he was still a human being, such as on this side eternity we all are, and he had still a conscience working in him. With this element he had not reckoned in his bargain in the High Priests Palace. On the morrow of His condemnation would it exact a terrible account. That night in Gethsemane never more passed from his soul. In the thickening and encircling gloom all around, he must have ever seen only the torch light glare as it fell on the pallid Face of the Divine Sufferer. In the terrible stillness before the storm, he must have ever heard only these words: Do you betray the Son of Man with a kiss? He did not hate Jesus then, he hated nothing; he hated everything. He was utterly desolate, as the storm of despair swept over his disenchanted soul, and swept him before it. No one in heaven or on earth to appeal to; no one, Angel or man, to stand by him. Not the priests, who had paid him the price of blood, would have anything whatever of him, not even the thirty pieces of silver, the blood money of his Master and of his own soul, even as the modern

Synagogue, which approves of what has been done, but not of the deed, will have none of him! With their See you to it! they sent him reeling back into his darkness. Not so could conscience be stilled. And, louder than the ring of the thirty silver pieces as they fell on the marble pavement of the Temple, rang it ever in his soul, I have betrayed innocent blood! Even if Judas possessed that which on earth sticks closest and longest to us, a woman's love, it could not have residence in him. It would have turned into madness and fled; or it would have withered, struck by the lightning flash of that night of terrors.

Deeper, farther out into the night! to its farthest bounds, where rises and falls the dark flood of death. The wild howl of the storm has lashed the dark waters into fury: they toss and break in wild billows at his feet. One narrow rift in the cloud curtain over head, and, in the pale, deathlike light lies the Figure of the Christ, so calm and placid, untouched and unharmed, on the storm tossed waters, as it had been that night lying on the Lake of Galilee, when Judas had seen Him come to them over the surging billows, and then bid them be peace. Peace! What peace to him now, in earth or heaven? It was the same Christ, but thorn crowned, with nail prints in His Hands and Feet. And this Judas had done to the Master! Only for one moment did it seem to lie there; then it was sucked up by the dark waters beneath. And again the cloud curtain is drawn, only more closely; the darkness is thicker, and the storm wilder than before. Out into that darkness, with one wild plunge, there, where the Figure of the Dead Christ had lain on the waters! And the dark waters have closed around him in eternal silence.

In the lurid morning that broke on the other shore where the flood cast him up, did he meet those searching, loving Eyes of Jesus, Whose gaze he knew so well, when he came to answer for the deeds done in the flesh? And, can there be a store in the Eternal Compassion for the Betrayer of Christ?

End Notes:

[31] On the relation between ambition and covetousness, generally, and in the case of Judas, see p. 77.

[32] The shekel of the Sanctuary = 4 dinars. The Jerusalem shekel is found, on an average, to be worth about 2s. 6d.

Chapter 9

Fifth Day and Readying for Passover

When the traitor returned from Jerusalem on the Wednesday afternoon, the Passover, in the popular and canonical, though not in the Biblical sense, was close at hand. It began on the 14th Nisan, that is, from the appearance of the first three stars on Wednesday evening [the evening of what had been the 13th], and ended with the first three stars on Thursday evening [the evening of what had been the 14th day of Nisan]. As this is an exceedingly important point, it is well here to quote the precise language of the Jerusalem Talmud: What means: On the Pesach? On the 14th [Nisan]. And so Josephus describes the Feast as one of eight days, evidently reckoning its beginning on the 14th, and its close at the end of the 21st Nisan. The absence of the traitor so close upon the Feast would therefore, be the less noticed by the others. Necessary preparations might have to be made, even though they were to be guests in some house, they did not know which. These would devolve on Judas. Besides, from previous conversations, they may also have judged that the man of Kerioth would gladly escape what Jesus had all that day been telling them about, and which was now filling their minds and hearts.

Everyone in Israel was thinking about the Feast. For the previous month it had been the subject of discussion in the Academies, and, for the last two Sabbaths at least, that of discourse in the Synagogues. Everyone was going to Jerusalem, or had those near and dear to them there, or at least watched the festive processions to the Metropolis of Judaism. It was a gathering of universal Israel, that of the memorial of the birth night of the nation, and of its Exodus, when friends from far would meet, and new friends be made; when offerings long due would be brought, and purification long needed be obtained, and all worship in that grand and glorious Temple, with its gorgeous ritual. National and religious feelings were stirred in what reached far back to the first, and pointed far forward to the final Deliverance. On that day a Jew might well glory in being a Jew. But we must not dwell on such thoughts, nor attempt a general description of the Feast. Rather shall we try to follow closely the footsteps of Christ and His disciples, and see or know only what on that day they saw and did.

For ecclesiastical purposes Bethphage and Bethany seem to have been included in Jerusalem. But Jesus must keep the Feast in the City itself, although, if His purpose had not been interrupted, He would have spent the night outside its walls. The first preparations for the Feast would commence shortly after the return of the traitor. For, on the evening [of the 13th] commenced the 14th of Nisan, when a solemn search was made with lighted candle throughout each house for any leaven that might be hidden, or have fallen aside by accident. Such was put by in a safe place, and afterwards destroyed with the rest. In Galilee it was the usage to abstain wholly from work; in Judea the day was divided, and actual work ceased only at noon, though nothing new was taken in hand even in the morning. This division of the day for festive purposes was a Rabbinic addition; and, by way of a hedge around it, an hour before midday was fixed after which nothing leavened might be eaten. The more strict abstained from it even an hour earlier (at ten o'clock), for fear that the eleventh hour might insensibly run into the forbidden midday. But there could be little real danger of this, since, by way of public notification, two desecrated thank offering cakes were laid on a bench in the Temple, the removal of one of which indicated that the time for eating what was leavened had passed; the removal of the other, that the time for destroying all leaven had come.

It was probably after the early meal, and when the eating of leaven had ceased, that Jesus began preparations for the Paschal Supper. John, who, in view of the details in the other Gospels, summarizes, and, in some sense, almost passes over, the outward events, so that their narration may not divert attention from those all important teachings which he alone records, simply tells by way of preface and explanation, of the Last Supper and of what followed, that Jesus, knowing that His hour was come that He should depart out of this world to the Father . . . having loved His own which were in the world, He loved them to the end. But Luke's account of what actually happened, being in some points the most explicit, requires to be carefully studied, and that without thought of any possible consequences in regard to the harmony of the Gospels. It is almost impossible to imagine anything more evident, than that he wishes us to understand that Jesus was about to celebrate the ordinary Jewish Paschal Supper. And the Day of Unleavened Bread came, on which the Passover must be sacrificed. The designation is exactly that of the beginning of the Pascha, which, as we have seen, was the 14th Nisan, and the description that of the slaying of the Paschal Lamb. What follows is in exact accordance with it: And He sent Peter and John, saying, Go and make ready for us the Pascha, that we may eat it. Then occur these three notices in the same account: And . . . they made ready the Pascha; and when the hour was come, He reclined [as usual at the Paschal Supper], and the Apostles with Him; and, finally, these words of His: With desire I have desired to eat this Pascha with you. And with this fully agrees the language of the other two Synoptists, Matthew 25:17-20, and Mark 14:12-17. No ingenuity can explain away these facts. The suggestion, that in that year the Sanhedrin had postponed the Paschal Supper form Thursday evening (the 14th-15th Nisan) to Friday evening (15-16th Nisan), so as to avoid the Sabbath following on the first day of the feast, and that the Paschal Lamb was therefore in that year eaten on Friday, the evening of the day on which Jesus was crucified, is an assumption void of all support in history or Jewish tradition. Equally untenable is it, that Christ had held the Paschal Supper a day in advance of that observed by the rest of the Jewish world, a supposition not only inconsistent with the plain language of the Synoptists, but impossible, since the Paschal Lamb could not have been offered in the Temple, and, therefore, no Paschal Supper held, out of the regular time. But, perhaps, the strangest attempt to reconcile the statement of the Synoptists with what is supposed inconsistent with it in the narration of John is, that while the rest of Jerusalem, including Christ and His Apostles, partook of the Paschal Supper, the chief priests had been interrupted in, or rather prevented from it by their proceedings against Jesus, that, in fact, they had not touched it when they feared to enter Pilates Judgment Hall; and that, after that, they went back to eat it, turning the Supper into a breakfast. Among the various objections to this extraordinary hypothesis, this one will be sufficient, that such would have been absolutely contrary to one of the plainest rubrical directions, which has it: The Pascha is not eaten but during the night, nor yet later than the middle of the night.

It was, therefore, with the view of preparing the ordinary Paschal Supper that Jesus now sent Peter and John. For the first time we see them here joined together by Jesus, these two, who from then on were to be so closely connected: he of deepest feeling with him of quickest action.

And their question, where He would have the Paschal Meal prepared, gives us a momentary glimpse of the mutual relation between the Master and His Disciples; how He was still the Master, even in their most intimate converse, and would only tell them what to do just when it needed to be done; and how they presumed not to ask beforehand (far less to propose, or to interfere), but had simple confidence and absolute submission as regarded all things. The direction which Jesus gave, while once more evidencing to them, as it does to us, the Divine foreknowledge of Christ, had also its deep human meaning. Evidently, neither the house where the Passover was to be kept, nor its owner, was to be named beforehand within hearing of Judas. That last Meal with its Institution of the Holy Supper, was not to be interrupted, nor their last retreat betrayed, until all had been said and done, even to the last prayer of Agony in Gethsemane. We can scarcely err in seeing in this combination of foreknowledge with prudence the expression of the Divine and the Human: the two Natures in One Person. The sign which Jesus gave the two Apostles reminds us of that by which Samuel of old had conveyed assurance and direction to Saul. On their entrance into Jerusalem they would meet a man, manifestly a servant, carrying a pitcher of water. Without accosting, they were to follow him, and, when they reached the house, to deliver to its owner this message: The Master saith, My time is at hand, with you [i.e. in your house the emphasis is on this] I hold the Passover with My disciples. Where is My hostelry [or hall], where I shall eat the Passover with My disciples?

Two things here deserve marked attention. The disciples were not invited to the chief or Upper Chamber, but for what we have rendered, for lack of better, by hostelry, or hall, katluma, the place in the house where, as in an open Khan, the beasts of burden were unloaded, shoes and staff, or dusty garment and burdens put down, if an apartment, at least a common one, certain not the best. Except in this place, the word only occurs as the designation of the inn or hostelry in Bethlehem, where the Virgin Mother brought forth her first born Son, and laid Him in a manger. He Who was born in a hostelry, Katalyma, was content to ask for His last Meal in a Katalyma. Only, and this we mark secondly, it must be His own: My Katalyma. It was a common practice, that more than one company partook of the Paschal Supper in the same apartment. In the multitude of those who would sit down to the Paschal Supper this was unavoidable, for all partook of, including women and children, only excepting those who were Levitically unclean. And, though each company might not consist of less than ten, it was not to be larger than that each should be able to partake of at least a small portion of the Paschal Lamb, and we know how small lambs are in the East. But, while He only asked for His last Meal in the Katalyma, some hall opening on the open court, Christ would have it His own, to Himself, to eat the Passover alone with His Apostles. Not even a company of disciples, such as the owner of the house unquestionably was, nor yet, be it marked, even the Virgin Mother, might be present; witness what passed, hear what He said, or be at the first Institution of His Holy Supper. To us at least this also recalls the words of Paul: I have received of the Lord that which I also delivered to you.

There can be no reasonable doubt that, as already hinted, the owner of the house was a disciple, although at festive seasons unbounded hospitality was extended to strangers generally, and no man in Jerusalem considered his house as strictly his own, far less would let it out for hire. But no mere stranger would, in answer to so mysterious a message, have given up, without further questioning, his best room. Had he known Peter and John; or recognized Him Who sent the message by the announcement that it was The Master; or by the words to which His Teaching had attached such meaning: that His time had come; or even by the peculiar emphasis of His command: With you I hold the Pascha with My disciples? It matters little which it was, and, in fact, the impression on the mind almost is, that the owner of the house had not, expected, but held himself ready for such a call. It was the last request of the dying Master, and could he have refused it? But he would do more than immediately and unquestioningly comply. The Master would only ask for the hall: as He was born in a Katalyma, so He would have been content to eat there His last Meal—at the same time meal, feast, sacrifice, and institution. But the unnamed disciple would assign to Him, not the Hall, but the best and chief, the upper chamber, or Aliyah, at the same time the most honorable and the most retired place, where from the outside stairs entrance and departure might be had without passing through the house. And the upper room was large, furnished and ready. From Jewish authorities we know, that the average dining apartment was computed at fifteen feet square; the expression furnished, no doubt, refers to the arrangement of couches all around the Table, except at its end, since it was a canon, that the very poorest must partake of that Supper in a reclining attitude, to indicate rest, safety, and liberty; while the term ready seems to point to the ready provision of all that was required for the Feast. In that case, all that the disciples would have to make ready would be the Paschal Lamb, and perhaps that first Chagigah, or festive Sacrifice, which, if the Paschal Lamb itself would not suffice for Supper, was added to it. And here it must be remembered, that it was of religion to fast until the Paschal Supper, as the Jerusalem Talmud explains, in order the better to relish the Supper.

Perhaps it is not wise to attempt lifting the veil which rests on the unnamed such a one, whose was the privilege of being the last Host of the Lord and the first Host of His Church, gathered within the new bond of the fellowship of His Body and Blood. And yet we can scarcely abstain from speculating. To us at least it seems most likely, that it was the house of Mark's father (then still alive), a large one, as we gather from Acts 12:13. For, the most obvious explanation of the introduction by Mark alone of such an incident as that about the young man who was accompanying Christ as He was led away captive, and who, on fleeing from those that would have laid hold on him, left in their hands the inner garment which he had loosely cast about him, as, roused from sleep, he had rushed into Gethsemane, is, that he was none other than Mark himself. If so, we can understand it all: how the traitor may have first brought the Temple guards, who had come to seize Christ, to the house of Mark's father, where the Supper had been held, and that, finding Him gone, they had followed to Gethsemane, for Judas knew the place, for Jesus often times resorted there with His disciples, and how Mark, startled from his sleep by the appearance of the armed men, would hastily cast about him his loose tunic and run after them; then, after the flight of the disciples, accompany Christ, but escape intended arrest by leaving his tunic in the hands of his would be captors.

If the view formerly expressed is correct, that the owner of the house had provided all that was needed for the Supper, Peter and John would find there the Wine for the four Cups, the cakes of unleavened Bread, and probably also the bitter herbs. Of the latter five kinds are mentioned, which were to be dipped once in salt water, or vinegar, and another time in a mixture called Charoseth (a compound made of nuts, raisins, apples almonds, etc.), although this Charoseth was not obligatory. The wine was the ordinary one of the country, only red; it was mixed with water, generally in the proportion of one part to two of water. The quantity for each of the four Cups is stated by one authority as five sixteenths of a log, which may be roughly computed at half a tumbler, of course mixed with water. The Paschal Cup is described (according to the rubrical measure, which of course would not always be observed) as two fingers long by two fingers broad, and its height as a finger, half a finger, and one third of a finger. All things being, as we presume, ready in the furnished upper room, it would only remain for Peter and John to see to the Paschal Lamb, and anything else required for the Supper, possibly also to what was to be offered as Chagigah, or festive sacrifice, and afterwards eaten at the Supper. If the latter were to be brought, the disciples would have to attend earlier in the Temple. The cost of the Lamb, which had to be provided, was very small. So low a sum as about three pence of our money is mentioned for such a sacrifice. But this must refer to a hypothetical case rather than to the ordinary cost, and we prefer the more reasonable computation, from one Sela to three Selaim, i.e. from 2s. 6d. to 7s. 6d. of our money.

If we mistake not, these purchases had, however, already been made on the previous afternoon by Judas. It is not likely that they would have been left to the last; nor that He Who had so lately condemned the traffic in the Courts of the Temple would have sent His two disciples there to purchase the Paschal Lamb, which would have been necessary to secure an animal that had passed Levitical inspection, since on the Passover day there would have been no time to subject it to such scrutiny. On the other hand, if Judas had made this purchase, we perceive not only on what pretext he may have gone to Jerusalem on the previous afternoon, but also how, on his way from the Sheep market to the Temple, to have his lamb inspected, he may have learned that the Chief Priests and Sanhedrists were just then in session in the Palace of the High Priest close by.

On the supposition just made, the task of Peter and John would, have been simple. They left the house of Mark with wondering but saddened hearts. Once more had they had evidence, how Jesus' Divine glance searched the further in all its details. They had met the servant with the pitcher of water; they had delivered their message to the master of the house; and they had seen the large Upper Room furnished and ready. But this prescience of Christ afforded only further evidence, that what He had told of His impending Crucifixion would also come true. And now it would be time for the ordinary Evening Service and Sacrifice. Ordinarily this began about 2.30 PM, the daily Evening Sacrifice being actually offered up about an hour later; but on this occasion, on account of the Feast, the Service was an hour earlier. As at about half past one of our time the two Apostles ascended the Temple Mount, following a dense, motley crowd of joyous, chatting pilgrims, they must have felt terribly lonely among them. In all that crowd how few to sympathize with them; how many enemies! The Temple Courts were thronged to the utmost by worshippers from all countries and from all parts of the land. The Priests Court was filled with white robed Priests and Levites, for on that day all the twenty four Courses were on duty, and all their services would be called for, although only the Course for that week would that afternoon engage in the ordinary service, which preceded that of the Feast. Almost mechanically would they witness the various parts of the well remembered ceremonial. There must have been a peculiar meaning to them, a mournful significance, in the language of Psalm 81, as the Levites chanted it that afternoon in three sections, broken three times by the threefold blast from the silver trumpets of the Priests.

Before the incense was burnt for the Evening Sacrifice, or yet the lamps in the Golden Candlestick were trimmed for the night, the Paschal Lambs were slain. The worshippers were admitted in three divisions within the Court of the Priests. When the first company had entered, the massive Nicanor Gates, which led from the Court of the Women to that of Israel, and the other side gates into the Court of the Priests, were closed. A threefold blast from the Priests trumpets intimated that the Lambs were being slain. This each Israelite did for himself. We can scarcely be mistaken in supposing that Peter and John would be in the first of the three companies into which the offerers were divided; for they must have been anxious to be gone, and to meet the Master and their brethren in that Upper Room. Peter and John had slain the Lamb. In two rows the officiating Priest stood, up to the great Altar of Burnt offering. As one caught up the blood from the dying Lamb in a golden bowl, he handed it to his colleague, receiving in return an empty bowl; and so the blood was passed on to the Great Altar, where it was sprayed in one jet at the base of the Altar. While this was going on, the Hallel was being chanted by the Levites. We remember that only the first line of every Psalm was repeated by the worshippers; while to every other line they responded by a Halleluyah, until Psalm 116: was reached, when, besides the first, these three lines were also repeated:

> Save now, I beseech You, Lord;
> O Lord, I beseech You, send now prosperity.
> Blessed be He that comes in the Name of the Lord.

As Peter and John repeated them on that afternoon, the words must have sounded most deeply significant. But their minds must have also reverted to that triumphal Entry into the City a few days before, when Israel had greeted with these words the Advent of their King. And now, was it not, as if it had only been an anticipation of the Hymn, when the blood of the Paschal Lamb was being shed?

Little more remained to be done. The sacrifice was laid on staffs which rested on the shoulders of Peter and John, flayed, cleansed, and the parts which were to be burnt on the Altar removed and prepared for burning. The second company of offerers could not have proceeded far in the service, when the Apostles, bearing their Lamb, were finding their way back to the home of Mark, there to make final preparations for the Supper. The Lamb would be roasted on a pomegranate spit that passed right through it from mouth to vent, special care being taken that, in roasting, the Lamb did not touch the oven. Everything else, also, would be made ready: the Chagigah for supper (if such was used); the unleavened cakes, the bitter herbs, the dish with vinegar, and that with Charoseth would be placed on a table which could be carried in and moved at will; finally, the festive lamps would be prepared.

It was probably as the sun was beginning to decline in the horizon that Jesus and the other ten disciples descended once more over the Mount of Olives into the Holy City. Before them lay Jerusalem in her festive attire. All around, pilgrims were hastening towards it. White tents dotted the grassy turf, gay with the bright flowers of early spring, or peered out from the gardens or the darker foliage of the olive plantations. From the gorgeous Temple buildings, dazzling in their snow white marble and gold, on which the slanting rays of the sun were reflected, rose the smoke of the Altar of Burnt offering. These courts were now crowded with eager worshippers, offering for the last time, in the real sense, their Paschal Lambs. The streets must have been thronged with strangers, and the flat roofs covered with eager gazers, who either feasted their eyes with a first sight of the sacred City for which they had so often longed, or else once more rejoiced in view of the well known localities. It was the last day view which Jesus could take, free and unhindered, of the Holy City until His Resurrection. Once more, in the approaching night of His Betrayal, would He look upon it in the pale light of the full moon. He was going forward to accomplish His death in Jerusalem; to fulfill type and prophecy, and to offer Himself up as the true Passover Lamb, "the Lamb of God, Which takes away the sin of the world." They who followed Him were busy with many thoughts. They knew that terrible events awaited them, and they had only shortly before been told that these glorious Temple buildings, to which, with a national pride not unnatural, they had directed the attention of their Master, were to become desolate, not one stone being left upon the other. Among them, revolving his dark plans, and goaded on by the great Enemy, moved the betrayer. And now they were within the City. Its Temple, its royal bridge, its splendid palaces, its busy marts, its streets filled with festive pilgrims, were well known to them, as they made their way to the house where the guest chamber had been prepared. Meanwhile, the crowd came down from the Temple Mount, each bearing on his shoulders the sacrificial Lamb, to make ready for the Paschal Supper.

End Notes:

[33] The Jerusalem Talmud gives the most minute details of the places in which search is to be made. One Rabbi proposed that the search should be repeated at three different times! If it had been omitted on the evening of the 13th, it would be made on the forenoon of the 14th Nisan.

[34] These phrases occur frequently in Jewish writings for dying: the hour has come to depart out of this world. Thus, in Targum on Song of Solomon 1:7, when the hour had come that Moses should depart out of the world; Shem. R. 33, what hour the time came for our father Jacob that he should depart out of the world.

[35] The words may also be rendered to the uttermost. But it seems more natural to understand the having loved as referring to all Christ's previous sayings and doings, as it were, the summing up of the whole past, like Matthew 25:1: when Jesus had finished all these sayings, and the other clause (He loved them to the end) as referring to the final and greatest manifestation of His love; the one being the terminus a quo, the other the terminus ad quem.

[36] According to the Targum Pseudo-Jon., each company was not to consist of less than ten persons; according to Josephus (War 6:9. 3), of not more than twenty.

[37] The Talmud puts it that slaves were habit to take their meals standing, and that this reclining best indicated how Israel had passed from bondage into liberty.

[38] The contention that it was unfermented wine is not worth serious discussion, although in modern practice (for reasons needless to mention) its use is allowed.

[39] The whole rubric is found in Jeremiah Pes. 37 c. The log = to the contents of six eggs. Herzfeld (Handelsgesch. p. 184) makes 1/32 of a log = a dessert spoon. 12 log = 1 hin.

[40] But it may have been otherwise; perhaps the lamb was even procured by the owner of the Upper Chamber, since it might be offered for another. At the same time the account in the text seems to accord best with the Gospel narrative.

[41] Although, so far as we know, not of practical importance here, we should perhaps bear in mind that John was a priest.

[42]   If we may suppose that there was a double row of priests to hand up the blood, and several to sprinkle it, or else that the blood from one row of sacrifices was handed to the priests in the opposite row, there could be no difficulty in the offering of lambs sufficient for all the companies, which consisted of from ten to twenty persons.

Chapter 10

The Lord's Supper

The period designated as between the two evenings, when the Paschal Lamb was to be slain, was past. There can be no question that, in the time of Christ, it was understood to refer to the interval between the beginning of the sun's decline and what was reckoned as the hour of its final disappearance (about 6 PM). The first three stars had become visible, and the threefold blast of the Silver Trumpets from the Temple Mount rang it out to Jerusalem and far away, that the Pascha had once more commenced. In the festively lit Upper Chamber of Mark's house the Master and the Twelve were now gathered. Was this place of Christ's last, also that of the Church's first, entertainment; that, where the Holy Supper was instituted with the Apostles, also that, where it was afterwards first partaken of by the Church; the Chamber where He last waited with them before His death, that in which He first appeared to them after His Resurrection; that, also, in which the Holy Spirit was poured out, even as (if the Last Supper was in the house of Mark) it undoubtedly was that in which the Church was at first habit to gather for common prayer? We do not know, and can only venture to suggest, deeply soul stirring as such thoughts and associations are.

So far as appears, or we have reason to infer, this Passover was the only sacrifice ever offered by Jesus Himself. We remember indeed, the first sacrifice of the Virgin Mother at her Purification. But that was hers. If Christ was in Jerusalem at any Passover before His Public Ministry began, He would have been a guest at some table, not the Head of a Company (which must consist of at least ten persons). Therefore, He would not have been the offerer of the Paschal lamb. And of the three Passovers since His

Public Ministry had begun, at the first His Twelve Apostles had not been gathered, so that He could not have appeared as the Head of a Company; while at the second He was not in Jerusalem but in the utmost parts of Galilee, in the borderland of Tyre and Sidon, where no sacrifice could be brought. Thus, the first, the last, the only sacrifice which Jesus offered was that in which, symbolically, He offered Himself. Again, the only sacrifice which He brought is that connected with the Institution of His Holy Supper; even as the only purification to which He submitted was when, in His Baptism, He sanctified water to the mystical washing away of sin. But what additional meaning does this give to the words which He spoke to the Twelve as He sat down with them to the Supper: With desire have I desired to eat this Pascha with you before I suffer.

And, in truth, as we think of it, we can understand not only why Jesus could not have offered any other Sacrifice, but that it was most fitting He should have offered this one Pascha, partaken of its commemorative Supper, and connected His own New Institution with that to which this Supper pointed. This joining of the Old with the New, the one symbolic Sacrifice which He offered with the One Real Sacrifice, the feast on the sacrifice with that other Feast upon the One Sacrifice, seems to cast light on the words with which He followed the expression of His longing to eat that one Pascha with them: I say to you, I will not eat any more thereof, until it is fulfilled in the Kingdom of God. And has it not been so, that this His last Pascha is connected with that another Feast in which He is ever present with His Church, not only as its Food but as its Host, as both the Pascha and He Who dispenses it? With a Sacrament did Jesus begin His Ministry: it was that of separation and consecration in Baptism. With a second Sacrament did He close His Ministry: it was that of gathering together and fellowship in the Lord's Supper. Both were into His death: yet not as something that had power over Him, but as a death that has been followed by the Resurrection. For, if in Baptism we are buried with Him, we also rise with Him; and if in the Holy Supper we remember His death, it is as that of Him Who is risen again, and if we show forth that death, it is until He come again. And so this Supper, also, points forward to the Great Supper at the final consummation of His Kingdom.

Only one Sacrifice did the Lord offer. We are not thinking now of the significant Jewish legend, which connected almost every great event and deliverance in Israel with the Night of the Passover. But the Pascha was, a Sacrifice, yet one distinct from all others. It was not of the Law, for it was instituted before the Law had been given or the Covenant ratified by blood; in a sense it was the cause and the foundation of all the Levitical Sacrifices and of the Covenant itself. And it could not be classed with either one or the other of the various kinds of sacrifices, but rather combined them all, and yet differed from them all. Just as the Priesthood of Christ was real, yet not after the order of Aaron, so was the Sacrifice of Christ real, yet not after the order of Levitical sacrifices but after that of the Passover. And as in the Paschal Supper all Israel were gathered around the Paschal Lamb in commemoration of the past, in celebration of the present, in anticipation of the future, and in fellowship in the Lamb, so has the Church been ever since gathered together around its better fulfillment in the Kingdom of God.

It is difficult to decide how much, not only of the present ceremonial, but even of the Rubric for the Paschal Supper, as contained in the oldest Jewish Documents, may have been obligatory at the time of Christ. Ceremonialism rapidly develops, too often in proportion to the absence of spiritual life. Probably in the earlier days, even as the ceremonies were simpler, so more latitude may have been left in their observance, provided that the main points in the ritual were kept in view. We may take it, that, as prescribed, all would appear at the Paschal Supper in festive array. We also know, that, as the Jewish Law directed, they reclined on pillows around a low table, each resting on his left hand, so as to leave the right free. But ancient Jewish usage casts a strange light on the painful scene with which the Supper opened. Sadly humiliating as it reads, and almost incredible as it seems, the Supper began with a contention among them, which of them should be accounted to be greatest. We can have no doubt that its occasion was the order in which they should occupy places at the table. We know that this was subject of contention among the Pharisees, and that they claimed to be seated according to their rank. A similar feeling now appeared, unfortunately in the circle of the disciples and at the Last Supper of the Lord. Even if we had not further indications of it, we should instinctively associate such a strife with the presence of Judas. John seems to refer to it, at least indirectly, when he opens his narrative with this notice: And during supper, the devil having already cast it into his heart, that Judas Iscariot, the son of Simon, shall betray Him. For, although the words form a general introduction to what follows, and refer to the entrance of Satan into the heart of Judas on the previous afternoon, when he sold his Master to the Sanhedrists, they are not without special significance as place in connection with the Supper. But we are not left to general conjecture in regard to the influence of Judas in this strife. There is, we believe, ample evidence that he not only claimed, but actually obtained, the chief seat at the table next to Jesus. This, as previously explained, was not, as is generally believed, at the right, but at the left of Christ, not below, but above Him, on the couches or pillows on which they reclined.

From the Gospel narratives we infer, that John must have reclined next to Jesus, on His Right Hand, since otherwise he could not have leaned back on His Bosom. This, as we shall now show, would be at one end, the head of the table, or, to be more precise, at one end of the couches. For, dismissing all conventional ideas, we must think of it as a low Eastern table. In the Talmud, the table of the disciples of the sages is described as two parts covered with a cloth, the other third being left bare for the dishes to stand on. There is evidence that this part of the table was outside the circle of those who were ranged around it. Occasionally a ring was fixed in it, by which the table was suspended above the ground, so as to preserve it from any possible Levitical defilement. During the Paschal Supper, it was the custom to remove the table at one part of the service; or, if this be deemed a later arrangement, the dishes at least would be taken off and put on again. This would render it necessary that the end of the table should protrude beyond the line of guests who reclined around it. For, as already repeatedly stated, it was the custom to recline at table, lying on the left side and leaning on the left hand, the feet stretching back towards the ground, and each guest occupying a separate divan or pillow. It would, therefore, have been impossible to place or remove anything from the table from behind the guests. Therefore, as a matter of necessity, the free end of the table, which was not covered with a cloth, would protrude beyond the line of those who reclined around it. We can now form a picture of the arrangement. Around a low Eastern table, oval or rather elongated, two parts covered with a cloth, and standing or else suspended, the single divans or pillows are arranged in the form of an elongated horseshoe, leaving free one end of the table, somewhat as in the accompanying woodcut.

So far for the arrangement of the table. Jewish documents are equally explicit as to that of the guests. It seems to have been quite an established rule that, in a company of more than two, say of three, the chief personage or Head, in this instance Christ, reclined on the middle divan. We know from the Gospel narrative that John occupied the place on His right, at that end of the divans, as we may call it, at the head of the table. But the chief place next to the Master would be that to His left, or above Him. In the strife of the disciples, which should be accounted the greatest, this had been claimed, and we believe it to have been actually occupied, by Judas.

This explains how, Christ whispered to John by what sign to recognize the traitor, none of the other disciples heard it. It also explains, how Christ would first hand to Judas the sop, which formed part of the Paschal ritual, beginning with him as the chief guest at the table, without thereby exciting special notice. Lastly, it accounts for the circumstance that, when Judas, desirous of ascertaining whether his treachery was known, dared to ask whether it was he, and received the affirmative answer, no one at table knew what had passed. But this could not have been the case, unless Judas had occupied the place next to Christ; in this case, necessarily that at His left, or the post of chief honor. As regards Peter, we can quite understand how, when Jesus with such loving words rebuked their self seeking and taught them of the greatness of Christian humility, he should, in his consciousness of shame, have rushed to take the lowest place at the other end of the table. Finally, we can now understand how Peter could beckon to John, who sat at the opposite end of the table, over against him, and ask him across the table, who the traitor was. The rest of the disciples would occupy such places as were most convenient, or suited their fellowship with one another.

The words which the Master spoke as He appeased their unseemly strife must, have touched them to the quick. First, He showed them, not so much in the language of even gentlest reproof as in that of teaching, the difference between worldly honor and distinction in the Church of Christ. In the world kingship lay in supremacy and lordship, and the title of Benefactor accompanied the sway of power. But in the Church the greater would not exercise lordship, but become as the less and the younger [the latter referring to the circumstance, that age next to learning was regarded among the Jews as a claim to distinction and the chief seats]; while, instead of him that had authority being called Benefactor, the relationship would be reversed, and he that served would be chief. Self forgetful humility instead of worldly glory, service instead of rule: such was to be the title to greatness and to authority in the Church. Having thus shown them the character and title to that greatness in the Kingdom, which was in prospect for them, He pointed them in this respect also to Himself as their example. The reference here is not to the act of symbolic foot washing, which Luke does not relate, although, as immediately following on the words of Christ, it would illustrate them, but to the tenor of His whole Life and the object of His Mission, as of One Who served, not was served. Lastly, He woke them to the higher consciousness of their own calling. Assuredly, they would not lose their reward; but not here, nor yet now. They had shared,

and would share His trials, His being set at nothing, despised, persecuted;
but they would also share His glory. As the Father had covenanted to Him,
so He covenanted and bequeathed to them a Kingdom, in order, or so that,
in it they might have festive fellowship of rest and of joy with Him. What
to them must have been temptations, and in that respect also to Christ,
they had endured: instead of Messianic glory, such as they may at first have
thought of, they had witnessed only contradiction, denial, and shame, and
they had continued with Him. But the Kingdom was also coming. When
His glory was manifested, their acknowledgement would also come. Here
Israel had rejected the King and His Messengers, but then would that same
Israel be judged by their word. A Royal dignity this, but one of service; a
full Royal acknowledgement, but one of work. In that sense were Israel's
Messianic hopes to be understood by them. Whether or not something
beyond this may also be implied, and, in that day when He again gathers
the outcasts of Israel, some special Rule and Judgment may be given to His
faithful Apostles, we venture not to determine. Sufficient for us the words
of Christ in their primary meaning.

So speaking, Jesus commenced that Supper, which in itself was symbol
and pledge of what He had just said and promised. The Paschal Supper
began, as always, by the Head of the Company taking the first cup, and
speaking over it the thanksgiving. The form now in use consists really of
two benedictions, the first over the wine, the second for the return of this
Feast day with all that it implies, and for being preserved once more to
witness it. Turning to the Gospels, the words which follow the record of
the benediction on the part of Christ seem to imply, that Jesus had, at any
rate, so far made use of the ordinary thanksgiving as to speak both these
benedictions. We know, that they were in use before His time, since it
was in dispute between the Schools of Hillel and Shammai, whether that
over the wine or that over the day should take precedence. That over the
wine was quite simple: Blessed are You, Jehovah our God, Who has created
the fruit of the Vine! The formula was so often used in blessing the cup,
and is so simple, that we need not doubt that these were the very words
spoken by Jesus. It is otherwise as regards the benediction over the day,
which is not only more compound, but contains words expressive of Israel's
national pride and self righteousness, such as we cannot think would have
been uttered by Jesus. With this exception, however, they were no doubt
identical in contents with the present formula. This we infer from what
Jesus added, as He passed the cup around the circle of the disciples. No
more, so He told them, would He speak the benediction over the fruit

of the vine, not again utter the thanks over the day that they had been preserved alive, sustained, and brought to this season. Another Wine, and at another Feast, now awaited Him, that in the future, when the Kingdom would come. It was to be the last of the old Paschas; the first, or rather the symbol and promise, of the new. And so, for the first and last time, did He speak the twofold benediction at the beginning of the Supper.

The cup, in which, according to express Rabbinic testimony, the wine had been mixed with water before it was blessed, had passed around. The next part of the ceremonial was for the Head of the Company to rise and wash hands. It is this part of the ritual of which John records the adaptation and transformation on the part of Christ. The washing of the disciples feet is evidently connected with the ritual of hand washing. Now this was done twice during the Paschal Supper: the first time by the Head of the Company alone, immediately after the first cup; the second time by all present, at a much later part of the service, immediately before the actual meal (on the Lamb, etc.). If the foot washing had taken place on the latter occasion, it is natural to suppose that, when Jesus rose, all the disciples would have followed His example, and so the washing of their feet would have been impossible. Again, the foot washing, which was intended both as a lesson and as an example of humility and service, was evidently connected with the dispute which of them should be accounted to be greatest. If so, the symbolical act of Jesus must have followed close on the strife of the disciples, and on Jesus' teaching what in the Church constituted rule and greatness. Therefore the act must have been connected with the first hand washing, that by the Head of the Company, immediately after the first cup, and not with that at a later period, when much else had intervened.

All else fits in with this. For clearness sake, the account given by John may here be repeated. The opening words concerning the love of Christ to His own to the end form the general introduction. Then follows the account of what happened during Supper, the Supper itself being left undescribed, beginning, by way of explanation of what is to be told about Judas, with this: The Devil having already cast into his (Judas) heart, that Judas Iscariot, the son of Simon, shall betray Him. General as this notice is, it contains much that requires special attention. Thankfully we feel, that the heart of man was not capable of originating the Betrayal of Christ; humanity had fallen, but not so low. It was the Devil who had cast it into Judas heart, with force and overwhelming power. Next, we mark the full description of the name and parentage of the traitor. It reads like the wording of a formal indictment. And, although it seems only an introductory explanation, it also points to the contrast with the love of Christ which persevered to the end, even when hell itself opened its mouth to swallow Him up; the contrast, also, between what Jesus and what Judas were about to do, and between the wild storm of evil that raged in the heart of the traitor and the calm majesty of love and peace which reigned in that of Jesus.

If what Satan had cast into the heart of Judas explains his conduct so does the knowledge which Jesus possessed account for that He was about to do. Many as are the thoughts suggested by the words, Knowing that the Father had given all things into His Hands, and that He came forth from God, and goes to God, yet, from evident connection, they must in the first instance be applied to the foot washing, of which they are, so to speak, the logical predecessor. It was His greatest act of humiliation and service, and yet He never lost in it for one moment anything whatever of the majesty or consciousness of His Divine dignity; for He did it with the full knowledge and assertion that all things were in His Hands, and that He came forth from and was going to God, and He could do it, because He knew this. Here, not side by side, but in combination, are the Humiliation and Exaltation of the God Man. And so, during Supper, which had begun with the first cup, He got up from Supper. The disciples would scarcely marvel, except that He should conform to that practice of hand washing, which, as He had often explained, was, as a ceremonial observance, unavailing for those who were not inwardly clean, and needless and unmeaning in them whose heart and life had been purified. But they must have wondered as they saw Him put off His upper garment, wrap Himself with a towel, and pour water into a basin, like a slave who was about to perform the most common service.

From the position which, as we have shown, Peter occupied at the end of the table, it was natural that Jesus should begin with him the act of foot washing. Besides, had He first turned to others, Peter must either have protested before, or else his later challenge would have been tardy, and an act either of self righteousness or of needless voluntary humility. As it was, the surprise with which he and the others had witnessed the preparation of the Lord burst into characteristic language when Jesus approached him to wash his feet. Lord, You, of me wash the feet! It was the utterance of deepest reverence for the Master, and yet of utter misunderstanding of the meaning of His action, perhaps even of His Work. Jesus was now doing what before He had spoken. The act of externalism and self righteousness represented by the washing of hands, and by which the Head of the Company was to be distinguished from all others and consecrated, He changed into a foot washing, in which the Lord and Master was to be distinguished, from the others, but by the humblest service of love, and in which He showed by His example what characterized greatness in the Kingdom, and that service was evidence of rule. And, as mostly in every symbol, there was the real also in this act of Jesus. For, by sympathetically sharing in this act of love and service on the part of Jesus, they who had been bathed, who had previously become clean in heart and spirit, now received also that cleansing of the feet, of active and daily walk, which comes from true heart humility, in opposition to pride, and consists in the service which love is willing to render even to the uttermost.

But Peter had understood none of these things. He only felt the incongruousness of their relative positions. And so Jesus, partly also wishing thereby to lead his impulsiveness to the absolute submission of faith, and partly to indicate the deeper truth he was to learn in the future, only told him, that though he knew it not now, he would understand hereafter what Jesus was doing. Yes, hereafter, when, after that night of terrible fall, he would learn by the Lake of Galilee what it really meant to feed the lambs and to tend the sheep of Christ; yes, hereafter, when no longer, as when he had been young, he would wrap around himself and walk where he would. But, even so, Peter could not content himself with the prediction that in the future he would understand and enter into what Christ was doing in washing their feet. Never, he declared, could he allow it. The same feelings, which had prompted him to attempt withdrawing Jesus from the path of humiliation and suffering, now asserted themselves again. It was personal affection, but it was also unwillingness to submit to the humiliation of the Cross. And so Jesus told him, that if He washed him not, he had no part with Him. Not that the bare act of washing gave him part in Christ, but that the refusal to submit to it would have deprived him of it; and that, to share in this washing, was, as it were, the way to have part in Christ's service of love, to enter into it, and to share it.

Still, Peter did not understand. But as, on that morning by the Lake of Galilee, it appeared that, when he had lost all else, he had retained love, so did love to the Christ now give him the victory, and, once more with characteristic impulsiveness, he would have offered not only his feet to be washed, but his hands and head. Yet here, also, was there misunderstanding. There was deep symbolical meaning, not only in that Christ did it, but also in what He did. Submission to His doing it meant symbolically share and part with Him, part in His Work. What He did, meant His work and service of love; the constant cleansing of ones walk and life in the love of

Christ, and in the service of that love. It was not a meaningless ceremony of humiliation on the part of Christ, not yet one where submission to the utmost was required; but the action was symbolic, and meant that the disciple, who was already bathed and made clean in heart and spirit, required only this, to wash his feet in spiritual consecration to the service of love which Christ had here shown forth in symbolic act. And so His Words referred not, as is so often supposed, to the forgiveness of our daily sins, the introduction of which would have been wholly abrupt and unconnected with the context, but, in contrast to all self seeking, to the daily consecration of our life to the service of love after the example of Christ.

And still do all these words come to us in manifold and ever varied application. In the misunderstanding of our love to Him, we too often imagine that Christ cannot will or do what seems to us incongruous on His part, or rather, incongruous with what we think about Him. We know it not now, but we shall understand it hereafter. And still we persist in our resistance, until it comes to us that so we would even lose our part in and with Him. Yet not much, not very much, does He ask, Who gives so much. He that has washed us wholly would only have us cleanse our feet for the service of love, as He gave us the example.

They were clean, these disciples, but not all. For He knew that there was among them he that was betraying Him. He knew it, but not with the knowledge of an inevitable fate impending far less of an absolute decree, but with that knowledge which would again and again speak out the warning, if by any means he might be saved. What would have come, if Judas had repented, is as idle a question as this: What would have come if Israel, as a nation, had repented and accepted Christ? For, from our human standpoint, we can only view the human aspect of things, that earthwards; and here every action is not isolated, but ever the outcome of a previous development and history, so that a man always freely acts, yet always in consequence of an inward necessity.

The solemn service of Christ now went on in the silence of reverent awe. None dared ask Him nor resist. It was ended, and He had resumed His upper garment, and again taken His place at the Table. It was His now to follow the symbolic deed by illustrative words, and to explain the practical application of what had just been done. Let it not be misunderstood. They were habit to call Him by the two highest names of Teacher and Lord, and these designations were rightly His. For the first time He fully accepted and owned the highest homage. How much more, then, must His Service of love, Who was their Teacher and Lord, serve as example of what was due by each to his fellow disciple and fellow servant! He, Who really was Lord and Master, had rendered this lowest service to them as an example that, as He had done, so should they do. No principle better known, almost proverbial in Israel, than that a servant was not to claim greater honor than his master, nor yet he that was sent than he who had sent him. They knew this, and now also the meaning of the symbolic act of foot washing; and if they acted it out, then theirs would be the promised Beatitude.

This reference to what were familiar expressions among the Jews, especially noteworthy in John's Gospel, leads us to supplement a few illustrative notes from the same source. The Greek word for the towel, with which Jesus wrapped around Himself, occurs also in Rabbinic writings, to denote the towel used in washing and at baths (Luntith and Aluntith). Such wrapping around was the common mark of a slave, by whom the service of foot washing was ordinarily performed. And, in a very interesting passage, the Midrash contrasts what, in this respect, is the way of man with what God had done for Israel. For, He had been described by the prophet as performing for them the service of washing, and others usually rendered by slaves. Again, the combination of these two designations, Rabbi and Lord, or Rabbi, Father, and Lord, were among those most common on the part of disciples. The idea, that if a man knows (for example, the Law) and does not do it, it was better for him not to have been created, is not infrequently expressed. But the most interesting reference is in regard to the relation between the sender and the sent, and a servant and his master. In regard to the former, it is proverbially said, that while he that is sent stands on the same footing as he who sent him, yet he must expect less honor. And as regards Christ's statement that the servant is not greater than his Master, there is a passage in which we read this, in connection with the sufferings of the Messiah: It is enough for the servant that he be like his Master.

But to return. The foot washing on the part of Christ, in which Judas had shared, together with the explanatory words that followed, almost required, in truthfulness, this limitation: I speak not of you all. For it would be a night of terrible moral sifting to them all. A solemn warning was needed by all the disciples. But, besides, the treachery of one of their own number might have led them to doubt whether Christ had really Divine knowledge. On the other hand, this clear prediction of it would not only confirm their faith in Him, but show that there was some deeper meaning in the presence of a Judas among them. We come here upon these words of deepest mysteriousness: I know those I chose; but that the Scripture may be fulfilled, He that eats My Bread lifts up his heel against Me! It was almost impossible to believe, even if not forbidden by the context, that this knowledge of which Christ spoke, referred to an eternal foreknowledge; still more, that it meant Judas had been chosen with such foreknowledge in order that this terrible Scripture might be fulfilled in him. Such foreknowledge and foreordination would be to sin, and it would involve thoughts such as only the harshness of our human logic in its fatal system making could induce anyone to entertain. Rather must we understand it as meaning that Jesus had, from the first, known the inmost thoughts of those He had chosen to be His Apostles; but that by this treachery of one of their number, the terrible prediction of the worst hostility, that of ingratitude, true in all ages of the Church, would receive its complete fulfillment. The word that, that the Scripture may be fulfilled, does not mean in order that, or for the purpose of; it never means this in that connection; and it would be altogether irrational to suppose that an event happened in order that a special prediction might be fulfilled. Rather does it indicate the higher internal connection in the succession of events, when an event had taken place in the free determination of its agents, by which, all unknown to them and unthought of by others, that unexpectedly came to pass which had been Divinely foretold. And herein appears the Divine character of prophecy, which is always at the same time announcement and forewarning, that is, has besides its predictive a moral element: that, while man is left to act freely, each development tends to the goal Divinely foreseen and foreordained. Thus the word that marks not the connection between causation and effect, but between the Divine predecessor and the human subsequent.

There is, behind this a much deeper question, to which brief reference has already formerly been made. Did Christ know from the beginning that Judas would betray Him, and yet, so knowing, did He choose him to be one of the Twelve? Here we can only answer by indicating this as a canon in studying the Life on earth of the God Man, that it was part of His Self examination, of that emptying Himself, and taking upon Him the form of a Servant, voluntarily to forego His Divine knowledge in the choice of His Human actions. So only could He, as perfect Man, have perfectly obeyed the Divine Law. For, if the Divine had determined Him in the choice of His Actions, there could have been no merit attaching to His Obedience, nor could He be said to have, as perfect Man, taken our place, and to have obeyed the Law in our stead and as our Representative, nor yet be our Example. But if His Divine knowledge did not guide Him in the choice of His actions, we can see, and have already indicated, reasons why the discipleship and service of Judas should have been accepted, if it had been only as that of a Judean, a man in many respects well fitted for such an office, and the representative of one of the various directions which tended towards the reception of the Messiah.

We are not in circumstances to judge whether or not Christ spoke all these things continuously, after He had sat down, having washed the disciples feet. More probably it was at different parts of the meal. This would also account for the seeming abruptness of this concluding sentence: He that receives whom ever I send receives Me. And yet the internal connection of thought seems clear. The apostasy and loss of one of the Apostles was known to Christ. Would it finally dissolve the bond that bound together the College of Apostles, and so invalidate their Divine Mission (the Apostolate) and its authority? The words of Christ conveyed an assurance which would be most comforting in the future, that any such break would not be lasting, only transitory, and that in this respect also the foundation of God stands.

In the meantime the Paschal Supper was proceeding. We mark this important note of time in the words of Matthew: as they were eating, or, as Mark expresses it, as they reclined and were eating. According to the Rubric, after the washing the dishes were immediately to be brought on the table. Then the Head of the Company would dip some of the bitter herbs into the salt water or vinegar, speak a blessing, and partake of them, then hand them to each in the company. Next, he would break one of the unleavened cakes (according to the present ritual the middle of the three), of which half was put aside for after supper. This is called the Aphiqomon, or after dish, and as we believe that the bread of the Holy Eucharist was the Aphiqomon, some particulars may here be of interest. The dish in which the broken cake lies (not the Aphiqomon), is elevated, and these words are spoken: This is the bread of misery which our fathers ate in the land of Egypt. All that are hungry, come and eat; all that are needy, come, keep the Pascha. In the more modern ritual the words are added: This year here, next year in the land of Israel; this year bondsmen, next year free! On this the second cup is filled, and the youngest in the company is instructed to make formal inquiry as to the meaning of all the observances of that night, when the Liturgy proceeds to give full answers as regards the festival, its occasion, and ritual. The Talmud adds that the table is to be previously removed, so as to excite the greater curiosity. We do not suppose that even the earlier ritual represents the exact observances at the time of Christ, or that, even if it does so, they were exactly followed at that Paschal Table of the Lord. But so much stress is laid in Jewish writings on the duty of fully rehearsing at the Paschal Supper the circumstances of the first Passover and the deliverance connected with it, that we can scarcely doubt that what the Mishnah declares as so essential formed part of the services of that night. And as we think of Jesus' comment on the Passover and Israel's deliverance, the words spoken when the unleavened cake was broken come back to us, and with deeper meaning attaching to them.

After this the cup is elevated, and then the service proceeds somewhat lengthily, the cup being raised a second time and certain prayers spoken. This part of the service concludes with the two first Psalms in the series called the Hallel, when the cup is raised a third time, a prayer spoken, and the cup drunk. This ends the first part of the service. And now the Paschal meal begins by all washing their hands, a part of the ritual which we scarcely think Christ observed. It was, we believe, during this lengthened exposition and service that the trouble in spirit of which John speaks passed over the soul of the God Man. Almost presumptuous as it seems to inquire into its immediate cause, we can scarcely doubt that it concerned not so much Himself as them. His Soul could not, but have been troubled, as, with full consciousness of all that it would be to Him, infinitely more than merely human suffering, He looked down into the abyss which was about to open at His Feet. But He saw more than even this. He saw Judas about to take the last fatal step, and His Soul yearned in pity over him. The very sop which He would so soon hand to him, although a sign of recognition to John, was a last appeal to all that was human in Judas. And, besides all this, Jesus also saw, how, all unknown to them, the terrible tempest of fierce temptation would that night sweep over them; how it would lay low and almost uproot one of them, and scatter all. It was the beginning of the hour of Christ's utmost loneliness, of which the climax was reached in Gethsemane. And in the trouble of His Spirit did He solemnly testify to them of the near Betrayal. We wonder not, that they all became exceeding sorrowful, and each asked, Lord, is it I? This question on the part of the eleven disciples, who were conscious of innocence of any purpose of betrayal, and conscious also of deep love to the Master, affords one of the clearest glimpses into the inner history of that Night of Terror, in which, so to speak, Israel became Egypt. We can now better understand their heavy sleep in Gethsemane, their forsaking Him and fleeing, even Peter's denial. Everything must have seemed to these men to give way; all to be enveloped in outer darkness, when each man could ask whether he was to be the Betrayer.

The answer of Christ left the special person undetermined, while it again repeated the awful prediction, shall we not add, the most solemn warning, that it was one of those who took part in the Supper. It is at this point that John resumes the thread of the narrative. As he describes it, the disciples were looking one on another, doubting of whom He spoke. In this agonizing suspense Peter motioned from across the table to John, whose head, instead of leaning on his hand, rested, in the absolute surrender of love and intimacy born of sorrow, on the bosom of the Master. Peter would have John ask of whom Jesus spoke. And to the whispered question of John, leaning back as he was on Jesus breast, the Lord gave the sign, that it was he to whom He would give the sop when He had dipped it. Even this perhaps was not clear to John, since each one in turn received the sop.

At present, the Supper itself began by eating, first, a piece of the unleavened cake, then of the bitter herbs dipped in Charoseth, and lastly two small pieces of the unleavened cake, between which a piece of bitter radish has been placed. But we have direct testimony, that, about the time of Christ, the sop which was handed around consisted of these things wrapped together: meat of the Paschal Lamb, a piece of unleavened bread, and bitter herbs. This, we believe, was the sop, which Jesus, having dipped it for him in the dish, handed first to Judas, as occupying the first and chief place at Table. But before He did so, probably while He dipped it in the dish, Judas, who could not but fear that his purpose might be known, reclining at Christ's left hand, whispered into Jesus' ear, Is it I, Rabbi? It must have been whispered, for no one at the Table could have heard either the question of Judas or the affirmative answer of Christ. It was the last outgoing of the pitying love of Christ after the traitor. Coming after the terrible warning and judgment on the Betrayer, it must be regarded as the final warning and also the final attempt at rescue on the part of Jesus. It was with full knowledge of all, even of this that his treachery was known, though he may have attributed the information not to Divine insight but to some secret human communication, that Judas went on his way to destruction. We are too apt to attribute crimes to madness; but surely there is normal, as well as mental mania; and it must have been in a convulsion of that, when all feeling was turned to stone, and mental self delusion was combined with moral perversion, that Judas took from the Hand of Jesus the sop. It was to descend alive into the grave, and with a heavy sound the gravestone fell and closed over the mouth of the pit. That moment Satan entered again into his heart. But the deed was virtually done; and Jesus, longing for the quiet fellowship of His own with all that was to follow, called him do quickly that he did.

But even so there are questions connected with the human motives that actuated Judas, to which, however, we can only give the answer of some suggestions. Did Judas regard Christ's denunciation of judgment on the Betrayer not as a prediction, but as intended to be deterrent, perhaps in language Orientally exaggerated, or if he regarded it as a prediction, did he not believe in it? Again, when after the plain intimation of Christ and His Words to do quickly what he was about to do, Judas still went to the betrayal, could he have had an idea, rather, sought to deceive himself, that Jesus felt that He could not escape His enemies, and that He rather wished it to be all over? Or had all his former feelings towards Jesus turned, although temporarily, into actual hatred which every Word and Warning of Christ only intensified? But above all and in all we have, first and foremost, to think of the peculiarly Judaic character of his first adherence to Christ; of the gradual and at last final and fatal disenchantment of his hopes; of his utter moral, consequent upon his spiritual, failure; of the change of all that had in it the possibility of good into the actuality of evil; and, on the other hand, of the direct agency of Satan in the heart of Judas, which his moral and spiritual shipwreck rendered possible.

From the meal scarcely begun Judas rushed into the dark night. Even this has its symbolic significance. None there knew why this strange haste, unless from obedience to something that the Master had invited him. Even John could scarcely have understood the sign which Christ had given of the traitor. Some of them thought, he had been directed by the words of Christ to purchase what was needful for the feast: others, that he was invited go and give something to the poor. Unwarranted objection has been raised, as if this indicated that, according to the Fourth Gospel, this meal had not taken place on the Paschal night, since, after the beginning of the Feast (on the 15th Nisan), it would be unlawful to make purchases. But this certainly was not the case. Sufficient here to state, that the provision and preparation of the needful food, and indeed of all that was needful for the Feast, was allowed on the 15th Nisan. And this must have been especially necessary when, as in this instance, the first festive day, or 15th Nisan, was to be followed by a Sabbath, on which no such work was permitted. On the other hand, the mention of these two suggestions by the disciples seems almost necessarily to involve, that the writer of the Fourth Gospel had placed this meal in the Paschal Night. Had it been on the evening before, no one could have imagined that Judas had gone out during the night to buy provisions, when there was the whole next day for it, nor would it have been likely that a man should on any ordinary day go at such an hour to seek out the poor. But in the Paschal Night, when the great Temple gates were opened at midnight to begin early preparations for the offering of the Chagigah, or festive sacrifice, which was not voluntary but of due, and the remainder of which was afterwards eaten at a festive meal, such preparations would be quite natural. And equally so, that the poor, who gathered around the Temple, might then seek to obtain the help of the charitable.

The departure of the betrayer seemed to clear the atmosphere. He was gone to do his work; but let it not be thought that it was the necessity of that betrayal which was the cause of Christ's suffering of soul. He offered Himself willingly, and though it was brought about through the treachery of Judas, yet it was Jesus Himself Who freely brought Himself a Sacrifice, in fulfillment of the work which the Father had given Him. And all the more did He realize and express this on the departure of Judas. So long as he was there, pitying love still sought to keep him from the fatal step. But when the traitor was at last gone, the other side of His own work clearly emerged into Christ's view. And this voluntary sacrificial aspect is further clearly indicated by His selection of the terms Son of Man and God instead of Son and Father. Now is glorified the Son of Man, and God is glorified in Him. And God shall glorify Him in Himself, and without delay shall He glorify Him. If the first of these sentences expressed the meaning of what was about to take place, as exhibiting the utmost glory of the Son of Man in the triumph of the obedience of His Voluntary Sacrifice, the second sentence pointed out its acknowledgment by God: the exaltation which followed the humiliation, the reward as the necessary sequel of the work, the Crown after the Cross.

Thus far for one aspect of what was about to be enacted. As for the other, that which concerned the disciples: only a little while would He still be with them. Then would come the time of sad and great perplexity, when they would seek Him, but could not come where He had gone, during the terrible hours between His Crucifixion and His manifested Resurrection. With reference to that period especially, but in general to the whole time of His Separation from the Church on earth, the great commandment, the bond which alone would hold them together, was that of love one to another, and such love as that which He had shown towards them. And this, shame on us, as we write it!, was to be the mark to all men of their discipleship. As recorded by John, the words of Jesus were succeeded by a question of Peter, indicating perplexity as to the primary and direct meaning of Christ's going away. On this followed Christ's reply about the impossibility of Peter's now sharing his Lord's way of Passion, and, in answer to the disciples impetuous assurance of his readiness to follow the Master not only into peril, but to lay down his Life for Him, Jesus' indication of Peter's present unpreparedness and the prediction of His impending denial. It may have been, that all this occurred in the Supper Chamber and at the time indicated by John. But it is also recorded by the Synoptists as on the way to Gethsemane, and in, what we may term, a more natural connection. Its consideration will therefore be best reserved until we reach that stage of the history.

We now approach the most solemn part of that night: The Institution of the Lord's Supper. It would manifestly be beyond the object, as assuredly it would necessarily stretch beyond the limits, of the present work, to discuss the many questions and controversies which, unfortunately have gathered around the Words of the Institution. On the other hand, it would not be truthful wholly to pass them by. On certain points, we need have no hesitation. The Institution of the Lord's Supper is recorded by the Synoptists, although without reference to those parts of the Paschal Supper and its Services with which one or another of its acts must be connected. In fact, while the historical connection with the Paschal Supper is evident, it almost seems as if the Evangelists had intended, by their studied silence in regard to the Jewish Feast, to indicate that with this Celebration and the new Institution the Jewish Passover had forever ceased. On the other hand, the Fourth Gospel does not record the new Institution, it may have been, because it was so fully recorded by the others; or for reasons connected with the structure of that Gospel; or it may be accounted for on other grounds. But whatever way we may account for it, the silence of the Fourth Gospel must be a great difficulty to those who regard it as an Ephesian product of symbolico sacramentarian tendency, dating from the second century.

The absence of a record by John is compensated by the narrative of Paul in 1 Corinthians 10:23-26, to which must be added as supplementary the reference in 1 Corinthians 10:16 to the Cup of Blessing which we bless as fellowship of the Blood of Christ, and the Bread which we broke as fellowship of the Body of Christ. We have thus four accounts, which may be divided into two groups: Matthew and Mark, and Luke and Paul. None of these give us the very words of Christ, since these were spoken in Aramaic. In the renderings which we have of them one series may be described as the more rugged and literal, the other as the more free and roundabout. The differences between them are, exceedingly minute; but they exist. As regards the text which underlies the rendering in our KJV, the difference suggested are not of any practical importance, with the exception of two points. First, the connecting link is [This is My Body, This is My Blood] was certainly not spoken by Jesus in the Aramaic, just as it does not occur in the Jewish formula in the breaking of bread at the beginning of the Paschal Supper. Secondly, the words: Body which is given, or, in 1 Corinthians 10:24, broken, and Blood which is shed, should be more correctly rendered: is being given, broken, shed.

If we now ask ourselves at what part of the Paschal Supper the new Institution was made, we cannot doubt that it was before the Supper was completely ended. We have seen, that Judas had left the Table at the beginning of the Supper. The meal continued to its end, amid such conversation as has already been noted. According to the Jewish ritual, the third Cup was filled at the close of the Supper. This was called, as by Paul, the Cup of Blessing, partly, because a special blessing was pronounced over it. It is described as one of the ten essential rites in the Paschal Supper. Next, grace after meat was spoken. But on this we need not dwell, nor yet on the washing of hands that followed. The latter would not be observed by Jesus as a religious ceremony; while, in regard to the former, the composite character of this part of the Paschal Liturgy affords internal evidence that it could not have been in use at the time of Christ. But we can have little doubt, that the Institution of the Cup was in connection with this third Cup of Blessing. If we are asked, what part of the Paschal Service corresponds to the Breaking of Bread, we answer, that this being really the last Pascha, and the cessation of it, Jesus anticipated the later rite, introduced when, with the destruction of the Temple, the Paschal as all other Sacrifices ceased. While the Paschal Lamb was still offered, it was the Law that, after partaking of its flesh, nothing else should be eaten. But since the Paschal Lamb had ceased, it is the custom after the meal to break and partake as Aphikomon, or after dish, of that half of the unleavened cake, which, as will be remembered, had been broken and put aside at the beginning of the Supper. The Paschal Sacrifice having now really ceased, and consciously so to all the disciples of Christ, He anticipated this, and connected with the breaking of the Unleavened Cake at the close of the Meal the institution of the breaking of Bread in the Holy Eucharist.

What did the Institution really mean, and what does it mean to us? We cannot believe that it was intended as merely a sign for remembrance of His death. Such remembrance is often equally vivid in ordinary acts of faith or prayer; and it seems difficult, if no more than this had been intended, to account for the Institution of a special Sacrament, and that with such solemnity, and as the second great rite of the Church, that for its nourishment. Again, if it were a mere token of remembrance, why the Cup as well as the Bread? Nor can we believe, that the connecting link is, which, did not occur in the words spoken by Christ Himself, can be equivalent to signifies. As little can it refer to any change of substance, be it in what is called Transubstantiation or Consubstantiation. If we may venture an explanation, it would be that this, received in the Holy Eucharist, conveys to the soul as regards the Body and Blood of the Lord, the same effect as the Bread and the Wine to the body, receiving of the Bread and the Cup in the Holy Communion is, really, though spiritually, to the Soul what the outward elements are to the Body: that they are both the symbol and the vehicle of true, inward, spiritual feeding on the Very Body and Blood of Christ. So is this Cup which we bless fellowship of His Blood, and the Bread we break of His Body, fellowship with Him Who died for us, and in His dying; fellowship also in Him with one another, who are joined together in this, that for us this Body was given, and for the remission of our sins this precious Blood was shed.

Most mysterious words these, yet most blessed mystery this of feeding on Christ spiritually and in faith. Most mysterious, yet he who takes from us our mystery takes from us our Sacrament. And ever since has this blessed Institution lain as the golden morning light far out even in the Church's darkest night, not only the seal of His Presence and its pledge, but also the promise of the bright Day at His Coming. For as often as we eat this Bread and drink this Cup, we do show forth the death of the Lord, for the life of the world, to be assuredly yet manifested, until He comes. Even so, Lord Jesus, come quickly!

End Notes:

[43]   Not temptation, i.e. not assaults from within, but assaults from without.

[44]   The sitting down with Him at the feast is evidently a promise of joy, reward, and fellowship. The sitting on thrones and judging Israel must be taken as in contrast to the temptation of the contradiction of Christ and of their Apostolic message, as their vindication against Israel's present controdiction.

[45]   I have often expressed my conviction that in the ancient Services there was considerable elasticity and liberty left to the individual. At present a cup is filled for each individual, but Christ seems to have passed the one

cup round among the Disciples. Whether such was sometimes done, or the alteration was designedly, and as we readily see, significantly, made by Christ, cannot now be determined.

[46] The contrast is the more marked as the same verb (bllein) is used both of Satan casting it into the heart of Judas, and of Christ throwing into the basin the water for the foot washing.

[47] podeigma. The distinctive meaning of the word is best gathered from the other passages in the New Testament in which it occurs, namely Hebrews 4:11; 8:5; 9:23; James 5:10; 2 Peter 2:6. For the literal outward imitation of this deed of Christ in the ceremony of foot washing, still common in the Roman Catholic Church, see Bingham, Antiq. 12:4, 10.

[48] There is a terrible literality about this prophetic reference to one who ate his bread, when we remember that Judas, like the rest, lived of what was supplied to Christ, and at that very moment sat at His Table. On Psalm 41: see the Commentaries.

[49] To a Jew it might seem that with the sop, containing as it did a piece of the Paschal Lamb, the chief part in the Paschal Supper was over.

[50] Though most widely differing from what is an attempt to trace an analogy between the Ritual of the Roman Mass and the Paschal Liturgy of the Jews, the article on it by the learned Professor Bickell, of Innsbruck, possesses a curious interest. See Zeitsch. Fur Kathol. Theol. for 1880, pp. 90-112.

Chapter 11

Last Discourses of Jesus

The new Institution of the Lord's Supper did not finally close what passed at that Paschal Table. According to the Jewish Ritual, the Cup is filled a fourth time, and the remaining part of the Hallel repeated. Then follow, besides Psalm 136, a number of prayers and hymns, of which the comparatively late origin is not doubtful. The same remark applies even more strongly to what follows after the fourth Cup. But, so far as we can judge, the Institution of the Holy Supper was followed by the discourse recorded in John 14. Then the concluding Psalms of the Hallel were sung, after which the Master left the Upper Chamber. The discourse of Christ recorded in John 16, and His prayer, were certainly uttered after they had risen from the Supper, and before they crossed the brook Kidron. In all probability they were, however, spoken before Jesus left the house. We can scarcely imagine such a discourse, and still less such a Prayer, to have been uttered while traversing the narrow streets of Jerusalem on the way to Kidron.

1. In any case there cannot be doubt, that the first discourse was spoken while still at the Supper Table. It connects itself closely with that statement which had caused them so much sorrow and perplexity, that, where He was going, they could not come. If so, the discourse itself may be arranged under these four particulars: explanatory and corrective; explanatory and teaching; exhortation and promissory; promissory and consolatory. Thus there is constant and connected progress, the two great elements in the discourse being: teaching and comfort.

At the outset we ought, perhaps, to remember the very common Jewish idea, that those in glory occupied different abodes, corresponding to their ranks. If the words of Christ, about the place where they could not follow Him, had awakened any such thoughts, the explanation which He now gave must effectually have dispelled them. Let not their hearts, then, be troubled at the prospect. As they believed in God, so let them also have trust in Him. It was His Father's House of which they were thinking, and although there were many mansions, or rather stations, in it, and the choice of this word may teach us something, yet they were all in that one House. Could they not trust Him in this? Surely, if it had been otherwise, He would have told them, and not left them to be bitterly disappointed in the end. The object of His going was the opposite of what they feared: it was to prepare by His death and Resurrection a place for them. Nor let them think that His going away would imply permanent separation, because He had said they could not follow Him there. Rather did His going, not away, but to prepare a place for them, imply His Coming again, primarily as regarded individuals at death, and secondarily as regarded the Church, that He might receive them to Himself, there to be with Him. Not final separation, then, but ultimate gathering to Himself, did His present going away mean. And where I go, you know the way.

Jesus had referred to His going to the Father's House, and implied that they knew the way which would bring them there also. But His Words had only the more perplexed, at least some of them. If, when speaking of their not being able to go where He went, He had not referred to a separation between them in that land far away, where was He going? And, in their ignorance of this, how could they find their way there? If any Jewish ideas of the disappearance and the final manifestation of the Messiah lurked beneath the question of Thomas, the answer of Jesus placed the matter in the clearest light. He had spoken of the Father's House of many stations, but only one road led there. They must all know it: it was that of personal apprehension of Christ in the life, the mind, and the heart. The way to the Father was Christ; the full manifestation of all spiritual truth, and the spring of the true inner life were equally in Him. Except through Him, no man could consciously come to the Father. Thomas had put his twofold question thus: What was the goal? and, what was the way to it? In His answer Christ significantly reversed this order, and told them first what was the way, Himself; and then what was the goal. If they had spiritually known Him as the way, they would also have known the goal, the Father, and now, by having the way clearly pointed out, they must also know the goal, God; He was, so to speak, visibly before them, and, gazing on Him, they saw the shining track up to heaven, the Jacob's ladder at the top of which was the Father.

But once more appeared in the words of Philip that carnal literalizing, which would take the words of Christ in only an external sense. Sayings like these help us to perceive the absolute need of another Teacher, the Holy Spirit. Philip understood the words of Christ as if He held out the possibility of an actual sight of the Father; and this, as they imagined, would forever have put an end to all their doubts and fears. We also, too often, would gladly have such solution of our doubts, if not by actual vision, yet by direct communication from on high. In His reply Jesus once more and emphatically returned to this truth, that the vision, which was that of faith alone, was spiritual, and in no way external; and that this manifestation had been, and was fully, though spiritually and to faith, in Him. Or did Philip not believe that the Father was really manifested in Christ, because he did not actually seen Him? Those words which had drawn them and made them feel that heaven was so near, they were not His own, but the message which He had brought them from the Father; those works which He had done, they were the manifestation of the Father's dwelling in Him. Let them then believe this vital union between the Father and Him, and, if their faith could not absolutely rise to that height, let it at least rest on the lower level of the evidence of His works. And so would He still lead us upwards, from the experience of what He does to the knowledge of what He is. Yes, and if they were ever tempted to doubt His works, faith might have evidence of them in personal experience. Primarily, no doubt, the words about the greater works which they who believed in Him would do, because He went to the Father, refer to the Apostolic preaching and working in its greater results after the outpouring of the Holy Spirit. To this also must primarily refer the promise of unlimited answer to prayer in His Name. But in a secondary, yet most true and blessed, sense, both these promises have, ever since the Ascension of Christ, also applied both to the Church and to all individual Christians.

A twofold promise, so wide as this, required, it must be felt, not indeed limitation, but qualification, let us say, definition, so far as concerns the indication of its necessary conditions. Unlimited power of working by faith and of praying in faith is qualified by obedience to His Commandments, such as is the outcome of personal love to Him. And for such faith, which compasses all things in the obedience of love to Christ, and can obtain all by the prayer of faith in His Name, there will be a need of Divine Presence ever with them. While He had been with them, they had had one Paraclete, or Advocate, Who had pleaded with them the cause of God, explained and advocated the truth, and guarded and guided them. Now that His outward Presence was to be withdrawn from earth, and He was to be their Paraclete or Advocate in Heaven with the Father, He would, as His first act of advocacy, pray the Father, Who would send them another Paraclete, or Advocate, who would continue with them forever. To the guidance and pleadings of that Advocate they could implicitly trust themselves, for He was the Spirit of Truth. The world, would not listen to His pleadings, nor accept Him as their Guide, for the only evidence by which they judged was that of outward sight and material results. But theirs would be other ones guided by experience: and experience not outward, but inward and spiritual. They would know the reality of His Existence and the truth of His pleadings by the continual Presence with them as a body of this Paraclete, and by His dwelling in them individually.

Here (as Bengel justly remarks) begins the essential difference between believers and the world. The Son was sent into the world; not so the Holy Spirit. Again, the world receives not the Holy Spirit, because it knows Him not; the disciples know Him, because they possess Him. Therefore to have known and to have are so connected, that not to have known is the cause of not having, and to have is the cause of knowing. In view of this promised Advent of the other Advocate, Christ could tell the disciples that He would not leave them orphans in this world. In this Advocate Christ Himself came to them. True, the world, which only saw and knew what fell within the range of its sensuous and outward vision (ver. 17), would not behold Him, but they would behold Him, because He lived, and they also would live, and therefore there was fellowship of spiritual life between them. On that day of the Advent of His Holy Spirit would they have full knowledge, because experience, of the Christ's Return to the Father, and of their own being in Christ, and of His being in them. And, as regarded this threefold relationship, this must be ever kept in view: to be in Christ meant to love Him, and this was: to have and to keep His commandments; Christ's being in the Father implied, that they who were in Christ or loved Him would be loved also of His Father; and, lastly, Christ's being in them implied, that He would love them and manifest Himself to them.

One outstanding novel fact here arrested the attention of the disciples. It was contrary to all their Jewish ideas about the future manifestation of the Messiah, and it led to the question of one of their number, Judas, not Iscariot: Lord, what has happened, that to us You will manifest Yourself, and not to the world? Again they thought of an outward, while He spoke of a spiritual and inward manifestation. It was of this coming of the Son and the Father for the purpose of making station with them that He spoke, of which the condition was love to Christ, manifested in the keeping of His Word, and which secured the love of the Father also. On the other hand, not to keep His Word was not to love Him, with all that it involved, not only as regarded the Son, but also the Father, since the Word which they heard was the Father's.

Thus far then for this inward manifestation, springing from life fellowship with Christ, rich in the unbounded spiritual power of faith, and fragrant with the obedience of love. All this He could say to them now in the Father's Name, as the first Representative, Pleader, and Advocate, or Paraclete. But what, when He was no longer present with them? For that He had provided another Paraclete, Advocate, or Pleader. This Paraclete, the Holy Spirit, Whom the Father will send in My Name, that same will teach you all things, and bring to your remembrance all things that I said to you. It is quite evident, that the interpretation of the term Paraclete as the Comforter will not meet the description here given of His twofold function as teaching all, and recalling all, that Christ Himself had said. Nor will the other interpretation of Advocate meet the requirements, if we regard the Advocate as one who pleads for us. But if we regard the Paraclete or Advocate as the Representative of Christ, and pleading, as it were, for Him, the cause of Christ, all seems harmonious. Christ came in the Name of the Father, as the first Paraclete, as His Representative; the Holy Spirit comes in the Name of Christ, as the second Paraclete, the Representative of Christ, Who is in the Father. As such the second Paraclete is sent by the Father in Name of the first Paraclete, and He would both complete in them, and recall to them, His Cause.

And so at the end of this discourse Jesus returned again, and now with fuller meaning, to its beginning. Then He had said: Let not your heart be troubled; you believe in God, believe also in Me. Now, after the fuller communication of His purpose, and of their relation to Him. He could convey to them the assurance of peace, even His Own peace, as His gift in the present, and His legacy for the future. In their hearing, the fact of His going away, which had filled them with such sorrow and fear, had now been connected with that of His Coming to them. Yes, as He had explained it, His departure to the Father was the necessary predecessor and condition of His Coming to them in the permanent Presence of the other Paraclete, the Holy Spirit. That Paraclete, however, would, in the economy of grace, be sent by the Father alone. In the dispensation of grace, the final source from which all comes, Who sends both the Son and the Holy Spirit, is God the Father. The Son is sent by the Father, and the Holy Spirit also, though proceeding from the Father and the Son, is sent by the Father in Christ's Name. In the economy of grace, then, the Father is greater than the Son. And the return of the Son to the Father marks the completion of Christ's work, and its perfection, in the Mission of the Holy Spirit, with all that His Advent implies. Therefore, if, discarding thoughts of themselves, they had only given room to feelings of true love to Him, instead of mourning they would have rejoiced because He went to the Father, with all that this implied, not only of rest and triumph to Him, but of the perfecting of His Work, since this was the condition of that Mission of the Holy Spirit by the Father, Who sent both the Son and the Holy Spirit. And in this sense also should they have rejoiced, because, through the presence of the Holy Spirit in them, as sent by the Father in His greater work, they would, instead of the present selfish enjoyment of Christ's Personal Presence, have the more power of showing their love to Him in apprehending His Truth, obeying His Commandments, doing His Works, and participating in His Life. Not that Christ expected them to understand the full meaning of all these words. But afterwards, when it had all come to pass, they would believe.

With the meaning and the issue of the great contest on which He was about to enter thus clearly before Him, did He now go forth to meet the last assault of the Prince of this World. But why that fierce struggle, since in Christ he has nothing? To exhibit to the world the perfect love which He had to the Father; how even to the utmost of self examination, obedience, submission, and suffering He was doing as the Father had given Him commandment, when He sent Him for the redemption of the world. In the execution of this Mission He would endure the last sifting assault and contest on the part of the Enemy, and, enduring, conquer for us. And so might the world be won from its Prince by the full manifestation of Christ, in His infinite obedience and righteousness, doing the Will of the Father and the Work which He had given Him, and in His infinite love doing the work of our salvation.

2. The work of our salvation! To this aspect of the subject Christ now addressed Himself, as He rose from the Supper Table. If in the discourse recorded in the fourteenth chapter of John's Gospel the Godward aspect of Christ's impending departure was explained, in that of the fifteenth chapter the new relation is set forth which was to exist between Him

and His Church. And this, although pithy sayings are so often untrue, may be summarized in these three words: Union, Communion, Disunion. The Union between Christ and His Church is corporate, vital, and effective, as regards results and blessings. This Union issues in Communion, of Christ with His disciples, of His disciples with Him, and of His disciples among themselves. The principle of all these is love: the love of Christ to the disciples, the love of the disciples to Christ, and the love in Christ of the disciples to one another. Lastly, this Union and Communion has for its necessary counterpart Disunion, separation from the world. The world repudiates them for their union with Christ and their communion. But, for all that, there is something that must keep them from going out of the world. They have a Mission in it, initiated by, and carried on in the power of, the Holy Spirit, that of uplifting the testimony of Christ.

As regards the relation of the Church to the Christ Who is about to depart to the Father, and to come to them in the Holy Spirit as His Representative, it is to be one of Union, corporate, vital, and effective. In the nature of it, such a truth could only be set forth by illustration. When Christ said: I am the Vine, the true one, and My Father is the Husbandman; or again, You are the branches, bearing in mind that, as He spoke it in Aramaic, the linking verb am, is, and are, would be omitted, He did not mean that He signified the Vine or was its sign, nor the Father that of the Husbandman, nor yet the disciples that of the branches. What He meant was, that He, the Father, and the disciples, stood in exactly the same relationship as the Vine, the Husbandman, and the branches. That relationship was of corporate union of the branches with the Vine for the production of fruit to the Husbandman, Who for that purpose pruned the branches. Nor can we forget in this connection, that, in the old Testament, and partially in Jewish thought, the Vine was the symbol of Israel, not in their national but in their Church capacity. Christ, with His disciples as the branches, is the Vine, the true One, the reality of all types, the fulfillment of all promises. They are many branches, yet a grand unity in that Vine; there is one Church of which He is the Head, the Root, the Sustenance, the Life. And in that Vine will the object of its planting of old be realized: to bring forth fruit to God.

Yet, though it be one Vine, the Church must bear fruit not only in her corporate capacity, but individually in each of the branches. It seems remarkable that we read of branches in Him that bear not fruit. This must apparently refer to those who have by Baptism been inserted into the Vine, but remain fruitless, since a merely outward profession of Christ could scarcely be described as a branch in Him. On the other hand, every fruit bearing branch the Husbandman cleanses, not necessarily nor exclusively by pruning, but in whatever manner may be requisite, so that it may produce the largest possible amount of fruit. As for them, the process of cleansing had already been accomplished through, or because of [the meaning is much the same], the Word which He had spoken to them. If that condition of fruit bearing now existed in them in consequence of the impression of His Word, it followed as a related condition that they must abide in Him, and He would abide in them. This was a vital condition of fruit bearing, arising from the fundamental fact that He was the Vine and they the branches. The proper, normal condition of every branch in that Vine was to bear much fruit in proportion to its size and vigor. But, both figuratively and really, the condition of this was to abide in Him, since apart from Him they could do nothing. It was not like a force once set in motion that would afterwards continue by itself. It was a life, and the condition of its permanence was continued union with Christ, from Whom alone it could spring.

And now as regarded the two alternatives: he that did not abide in Him was the branch cast outside and withering, which, when ready for it, men would cast into the fire, with all of symbolic meaning as regards the gathers and the burning that the illustration implies. On the other hand, if the corporate and vital union was effective, if they abode in Him, and in consequence, His Words resided in them, then: What ever you will you shall ask, and it shall be done to you. It is very noteworthy that the unlimitedness of prayer is limited, or, rather, conditioned, by our abiding in Christ and His Words in us, just as in John 14:12-14 it is conditioned by fellowship with Him, and in John 15:16 by permanent fruitfulness. For, it were the most dangerous fanaticism, and entirely opposed to the teaching of Christ, to imagine that the promise of Christ implies such absolute power, as if prayer were magic, that a person might ask for anything, no matter what it was, in the assurance of obtaining his request. In all moral relations, duties and privileges are correlative ideas, and in our relation to Christ conscious immanence in Him and of His Word in us, union and communion with Him, and the obedience of love, are the indispensable conditions of our privileges. The believer may, ask for anything, because he may always and absolutely go to God; but the certainty of special answers to prayer is proportionate to the degree of union and communion with

Christ. And such unlimited liberty of prayer is connected with our bearing much fruit, because thereby the Father is glorified and our discipleship evidenced.

This union, being inward and moral, necessarily unfolds into communion, of which the principle is love. Like as the Father loved Me, even so loved I you. Abide in My love. If you keep My commandments, you shall abide in the love that is Mine. We mark the continuity in the scale of love: the Father towards the Son, and the Son towards us; and its kindredness of forth going. And now all that the disciples had to do was to abide in it. This is connected, not with sentiment nor even with faith, but with obedience. Fresh supplies are drawn by faith, but continuance in the love of Christ is the manifestation and the result of obedience. It was so even with the Master Himself in His relation to the Father. And Jesus immediately explained what His object was in saying this. In this, also, were they to have communion with Him: communion in that joy which was His in consequence of His perfect obedience. These things have I spoken to you, in order that the joy that is Mine may be in you, and your joy may be fulfilled [completed].

But what of those commandments to which such importance attached? Clean as they now were through the Words which He had spoken, one great commandment stood forth as especially His Own, consecrated by His Example and to be measured by His observance of it. From whatever point we view it, whether as especially demanded by the pressing necessities of the Church; or as, from its contrast to what Paganism exhibited, affording such striking evidence of the power of Christianity; or, on the other hand, as so in agreement to all the fundamental thoughts of the Kingdom: the love of the Father in sending His Son for man, the work of the Son in seeking and saving the lost at the price of His Own Life, and the new bond which in Christ bound them all in the fellowship of a common calling, common mission, and common interests and hopes, love of the brethren was the one outstanding Farewell Command of Christ. And to keep His commandments was to be His friend. And they were His friends. No longer did He call them servants, for the servant did not know what his lord did. He had now given them a new name, and with good reason: You have I called friends, because all things which I heard of My Father I made known to you. And yet deeper did He descend, in pointing them to the example and measure of His love as the standard of theirs towards one another. And with this teaching He combined what He had said before, of bearing fruit and of the privilege of fellowship with Himself. They were His friends; He had proved it by treating them as such in now opening up before them the whole counsel of God. And that friendship: Not you did choose Me, but I did choose you, the object of His choosing [that to which they were appointed] being, that, as they went forth into the world, they should bear fruit, that their fruit should be permanent, and that they should possess the full privilege of that unlimited power to pray of which He had previously spoken. All these things were bound up with obedience to His commands, of which the outstanding one was to love one another.

But this very choice on His part, and their union of love in Him and to one another, also implied not only separation from, but repudiation by, the world. For this they must be prepared. It had come to Him, and it would be evidence of their choice to discipleship. The hatred of the world showed the essential difference and antagonism between the life principle of the world and theirs. For evil or for good, they must expect the same treatment as their Master. Was it not their privilege to realize, that all this came upon them for His sake? And should they not also remember, that the ultimate ground of the world's hatred was ignorance of Him Who had sent Christ? And yet, though this should banish all thoughts of personal resentment, their guilt who rejected Him was truly terrible. Speaking to, and in, Israel, there was no excuse for their sin, the most awful that could be conceived; since, most truly: He that hates Me, hates My Father also. For, Christ was the Sent of God, and God manifest. It was a terrible charge this to bring against God's ancient people Israel. And yet there was, besides the evidence of His Words, that of His Works. If they could not apprehend the former, yet, in regard to the latter, they could see by comparison with the works of other men that they were unique. They saw it, but only hated Him and His Father, ascribing it all to the power and agency of Beelzebul. And so the ancient prophecy had now been fulfilled: They hated Me without cause. But all was not yet at an end: neither His Work through the other Advocate, nor yet theirs in the world. When the Advocate is come, Whom I will send to you from the Father, the Spirit of the Truth, Who proceeds from the Father [goes forth on His Mission as sent by the Father], this Same will bear witness about Me. And you also bear witness, because you are with Me from the beginning.

3. The last of the parting discourses of Christ, in the sixteenth chapter of John, was, interrupted by questions from the disciples. But these, being germane to the subject, carry it only forward. In general, the subjects treated in it are: the new relations arising from the departure of Christ

and the coming of the other Advocate. Thus the last point needed would be supplied, Chapter 14 giving the comfort and teaching in view of His departure; Chapter 15 describing the personal relations of the disciples towards Christ, one another, and the world; and Chapter 15: fixing the new relations to be established.

The chapter appropriately opens by reflecting on the predicted hostility of the world. Christ had so clearly foretold it, for fear that this should prove a stumbling block to them. Best, to know distinctly that they would not only be put out of the Synagogue, but that everyone who killed them would deem it to offer a religious service to God. So, no doubt, Saul of Tarsus once felt, and so did many others who, unfortunately never became Christians. Indeed, according to Jewish Law, a zealot might have slain without formal trial those caught in flagrant rebellion against God, or in what might be regarded as such, and the Synagogue would have deemed the deed as meritorious as that of Phinehas. It was a sorrow, and yet also a comfort, to know that this spirit of hostility arose from ignorance of the Father and Christ. Although they had in a general way been prepared for it before, yet He had not told it all so definitely and connectedly from the beginning, because He was still there. But now that He was going away, it was absolutely necessary to do so. For even the mention of it had thrown them into such confusion of personal sorrow, that the main point, where Christ was going, had not even emerged into their view. Personal feelings had quite engrossed them, to the forgetfulness of their own higher interests. He was going to the Father, and this was the condition, as well as the predecessor of His sending the Paraclete.

But the Advent of the Advocate would mark a new era, as regarded the Church and the world. It was their Mission to go forth into the world and to preach Christ. That other Advocate, as the Representative of Christ, would go into the world and convict on the three cardinal points on which their preaching turned. These three points on which all Missioning proceeds, are, Sin, Righteousness, and Judgment. And on these would the New Advocate convict the world. Bearing in mind that the term convict is uniformly used in the Gospels for clearly establishing or carrying home guilt, we have here three separate facts presented to us. As the Representative of Christ, the Holy Spirit will carry home to the world, establish the fact of its guilt in regard to sin, on the ground that the world believes not in Christ. Again, as the Representative of Christ, He will carry home to the world the fact of its guilt in regard to righteousness, on the ground that

Christ has ascended to the Father, and therefore is removed from the sight of man. Lastly, as the Representative of Christ, He will establish the fact of the world's guilt, because of this: that its Prince, Satan, has already been judged by Christ, a judgment established in His sitting at the Right Hand of God, and which will be vindicated at His Second Coming. Taking, then, the three great facts in the History of the Christ: His First Coming to salvation, His Resurrection and Ascension, and His Sitting at the Right Hand of God, of which His Second Coming to Judgment is the final issue, this Advocate of Christ will in each case convict the world of guilt; in regard to the first, concerning sin, because it believes not on Him Whom God has sent; in regard to the second, concerning righteousness, because Christ is at the Father's Right Hand; and, in regard to the third, concerning judgment, because that Prince whom the world still owns has already been judged by Christ's Session at the Right Hand of God, and by His Reign, which is to be completed in His Second Coming to Earth.

Such was the cause of Christ which the Holy Spirit as the Advocate would plead to the world, working conviction as in a hostile guilty party. Quite other was that cause of Christ which, as His Advocate, He would plead with the disciples, and quite other in their case the effect of His advocacy. We have, even on the present occasion, marked how often Jesus was hindered, as well as grieved, by the misunderstanding and unbelief of man. Now it was the self imposed law of His Mission, the outcome of His Victory in the Temptation in the Wilderness, that He would not achieve His Mission in the exercise of Divine Power, but by treading the ordinary path of humanity. This was the limitation which He set to Himself, one aspect of His Self examination. But from this His constant sorrow must also have flowed, in view of the unbelief of even those nearest to Him. It was, therefore, not only expedient, but even necessary for them, since at present they could not bear more, that Christ's Presence should be withdrawn, and His Representative take His place, and open up His Cause to them. And this was to be His special work to the Church. As Advocate, not speaking from Himself, but speaking what ever He shall hear, as it were, according to His heavenly brief, He would guide them into all truth. And here His first declaration would be of the things that are coming. A whole new order of things was before the Apostles, the abolition of the Jewish, the establishment of the Christian Dispensation, and the relation of the New to the Old, together with many kindred questions. As Christ's Representative, and speaking not from Himself, the Holy Spirit would be with them, not suffer them to go astray into error or wrong, but be their way leader into all truth. Further, as the Son glorified the Father, so would the Spirit glorify the Son, and in analogous manner, because He shall take of His and declare it to them. This would be the second line, as it were, in the declarations of the Advocate, Representative of Christ. And this work of the Holy Spirit, sent by the Father, in His declaration about Christ, was explained by the circumstance of the union and communication between the Father and Christ. And so, to sum up, in one brief Farewell, all that He had said to them, there would be a little while in which they would not behold Him (okti theoret me), and again a little while and they would see Him (psesth me), though in quite different manner, as even the wording shows.

If we had entertained any doubt of the truth of Jesus' previous words, that in their absorbedness in the present the disciples had not thought of where Christ was going, and that it was needful for them that He should depart and the other Advocate come, this conviction would be forced upon us by their perplexed questioning among themselves as to the meaning of the twofold little while, and of all that He had said about, and connected with, His going to the Father. They would gladly have asked, yet dared not. But He knew their thoughts, and answered them. That first little while comprised those terrible days of His death and Entombment, when they would weep and lament, but the world rejoice. Yet their brief sorrow would be turned into joy. It was like the short sorrow of childbearing, afterwards no more remembered in the joy that a human being had been born into the world. Thus would it be when their present sorrow would be changed into the Resurrection joy, a joy which no man could ever afterwards take from them. On that day of joy would He have them dwell in thought during their present night of sorrow. That would be, a day of brightness, in which there would be no need of their making further inquiry of Him. All would then be clear in the new light of the Resurrection. A day this, when the promise would become true, and what ever they asked the Father (atsete), He would give it to them in Christ's Name. To this point they had not yet asked in His Name; let them ask: they would receive, and so their joy be completed. Ah! that day of brightness. To this point He had only been able to speak to them, as it were, in parables and allegory, but then would He declare to them in all plainness about the Father. And, as He would be able to speak to them directly and plainly about the Father, so would they then be able to speak directly to the Father, as the Epistle to the Hebrews expresses it, come with plainness or directness to the throne of grace. They would ask directly in the Name of Christ; and no longer would it be needful, as at present, first to come to Him that He may inquire of the Father about them. For, God loved them as lovers of Christ, and as recognizing that He had come forth from God. And so it was, He had come forth from out of the Father when He came into the world, and, now that He was leaving it, He was going to the Father.

The disciples imagined that they understood this at least. Christ had read their thoughts, and there was no need for anyone to express questions. He knew all things, and by this they believed, it afforded them evidence, that He came forth from God. But how little did they know their own hearts! The hour had even come when they would be scattered, every man to his own home, and leave Him alone, yet, truly, He would not be alone, because the Father would be with Him. Yet, even so, His latest as His first thought was of them; and through the night of scattering and of sorrow did He invite them to look to the morning of joy. For, the battle was not theirs, nor yet the victory doubtful: I [emphatically] have overcome [it is accomplished] the world.

We now enter most reverently what may be called the innermost Sanctuary. For the first time we are allowed to listen to what was really the Lord's Prayer, and, as we hear, we humbly worship. That Prayer was the great preparation for His Agony, Cross, and Passion; and, also, the outlook on the Crown beyond. In its three parts it seems almost to look back on the teaching of the three previous chapters, and convert them into prayer. We see the great High Priest first solemnly offering up Himself, and then consecrating and interceding for His Church and for her work.

The first part of that Prayer is the consecration of Himself by the Great High Priest. The final hour had come. In praying that the Father would glorify the Son, He was really not asking anything for Himself, but that the Son might glorify the Father. For, the glorifying of the Son, His support, and then His Resurrection, was really the completion of the work which the Father had given Him to do, as well as its evidence. It was really in accordance (even as) with the power or authority which the Father gave Him over all flesh, when He put all things under His Feet as the Messiah, the object of this Messianic Rule being, that the totality (the all) that You have given Him, He should give to them eternal life. The climax in His Messianic appointment, the object of His Rule over all flesh, was the Father's gift to Christ of the Church as a totality and a unity; and in that Church Christ gives to each individually eternal life. What follows seems an inserted sentence, as shown even by the use of the particle and, with which the all important definition of what is eternal life is introduced, and by the last words in the verse. But although embodying, so to speak, as regards the form, the record which John had made of Christ's Words, we must remember that, as regards the substance, we have here Christ's own Prayer for that eternal life to each of His own people. And what constitutes the eternal life? Not what we so often think, who confound with the thing its effects or else its results. It refers not to the future, but to the present. It is the realization of what Christ had told them in these words: You believe in God, believe also in Me. It is the pure sunlight on the soul, resulting in, or reflecting the knowledge of Jehovah; the Personal, Living, True God, and of Him Whom He did send, Jesus Christ. These two branches of knowledge must not so much be considered as co-ordinate, but rather as inseparable. Returning from this explanation of the eternal life which they who are bathed in the Light possess even now and here, the Great High Priest first offered up to the Father that part of His work which was on earth and which He had completed. And then, both as the consummation and the sequel of it, He claimed what was at the end of His Mission: His return to that fellowship of essential glory, which He possessed together with the Father before the world was.

The gift of His consecration could not have been laid on more glorious Altar. Such Cross must have been followed by such Crown. And now again His first thought was of them for whose sake He had consecrated Himself. These He now solemnly presented to the Father. He introduced them as those (the individuals) whom the Father had especially given to him out of the world. As such they were really the Father's, and given over the Christ, and He now presented them as having kept the Word of the Father. Now they knew that all things whatever the Father had given the Son were of the Father. This was the outcome, then, of all His teaching, and the sum of all their learning, perfect confidence in the Person of Christ, as in His Life, Teaching, and Work sent not only of God, but of the Father. Neither less nor yet more did their knowledge represent. All else that sprang out of it they had yet to learn. But it was enough, for it implied everything; chiefly these three things, that they received the words which He gave them as from the Father; that they knew truly that Christ had come out from the Father; and that they believed that the Father had sent Him. And, reception of Christ's Word, knowledge of His Essential Nature, and faith in His Mission: such seem the three essential characteristics of those who are Christ's.

And now He brought them in prayer before the Father. He was interceding, not for the world that was His by right of His Messiahship, but for them whom the Father had especially given Him. They were the Father's in the special sense of covenant mercy, and all that in that sense was the Father's was the Son's, and all that was the Son's was the Father's. Therefore, although all the world was the Son's, He prayed not now for it; and although all in earth and heaven were in the Father's Hand, He sought not now His blessing on them, but on those whom, while He was in the world, He had shielded and guided. They were to be left behind in a world of sin, evil, temptation, and sorrow, and He was going to the Father. And this was His prayer: Holy Father, keep them in Your Name which You have given Me, that so (in order that) they may be one (a unity), as We are. The peculiar address, Holy Father, shows that Jesus once more referred to the keeping in holiness, and what is of equal importance, that the unity of the Church sought for was to be primarily one of spiritual character, and not a merely outward combination. Unity in holiness and of nature, as was that of the Father and Son, such was the great object sought, although such union would, if properly carried out, also issue in outward unity. But while moral union rather than outward unity was in His view, our present unhappy divisions, arising so often from willfulness and unreadiness to bear slight differences among ourselves, each others burdens, are so entirely contrary not only to the Christian, but even to the Jewish, spirit, that we can only trace them to the pagan element in the Church.

While He was with them, He kept them in the Father's Name. Them whom the Father had given Him, by the effective drawing of His grace within them, He guarded (phlaxa) and none from among them was lost, except the son of perdition, and this, according to prophecy. But before He went to the Father, He prayed thus for them, that in this realized unity of holiness the joy that was His, might be completed in them. And there was the more need of this, since they were left behind with nothing but His Word in a world that hated them, because, as Christ, so they also were not of it [from it]. Nor yet did Christ ask with a view to their being taken out of the world, but with this that [in order that] the Father should keep them [preserve, terss] from the Evil One. And this the more emphatically, because, even as He was not, so were they not out of the world, which lay in the Evil One. And the preservative which He sought for them was not outward but inward, the same in kind as while He had been with them, only coming now directly from the Father. It was sanctification in the truth, with this significant addition: The word that is Yours is truth.

In its last part this intercessory Prayer of the Great High Priest bore on the work of the disciples and its fruits. As the Father had sent the Son, so did the Son send the disciples into the world, in the same manner, and on the same Mission. And for their sakes He now solemnly offered Himself, consecrated or sanctified Himself, that they might in truth, truly, be consecrated. And in view of this their work, to which they were consecrated, did Christ pray not for them alone, but also for those who, through their word, would believe in Him, in order, or that so, all may be one, form a unity. Christ, as sent by the Father, gathered out the original unity; they, as sent by Him, and consecrated by His consecration, were to gather others, but all were to form one great unity, through the common spiritual communication. As You in Me, and I also in You, so that [in order that] they also may be in Us, so that [in order that] the world may believe that You did send Me. And the glory that You have given Me, referring to His Mission in the world, and His setting apart and authorization for it, I have given to them, so that [in order that] [in this respect also] they may be one, even as We are One [a unity]. I in them, and You in Me, so that they may be perfected into One, the ideal unity and real character of the Church, this, so that the world may know that You did send Me, and loved them as You loved Me.

After this unspeakably magnificent consecration of His Church, and communication to her of His glory as well as of His Work, we cannot marvel at what follows and concludes the Lord's Prayer. We remember the unity of the Church, a unity in Him, and as that between the Father and the Son, as we listen to this: That which You have given Me, I will that, where I am, they also may be with Me, so that they may gaze [behold] on the glory that is Mine, which You have given Me [be sharers in the Messianic glory]: because You loved Me before the foundation of the world.

And we all would gladly place ourselves in the shadow of this final consecration of Himself and of His Church by the Great High Priest, which is final appeal, claim, and prayer: O Righteous Father, the world knew You not, but I know You, and these know that You sent Me. And I made known to them Your Name, and will make it known, so that [in order that] the love with what You loved Me may be in them, and I in them. This is the charter of the Church: her possession and her joy; her faith, her hope also, and love; and in this she stands, prays, and works.

End Notes:

[51] As this chapter is really in the nature of a commentation on John 14, 15, 16, 17, the reader is requested to peruse it with the Bible text beside him. Without this it could scarcely be intelligently followed.

[52] Without entering on the discussion of what has engaged so much attention, I must content myself here with indicating the result at which I have arrived. This is simply to abide by the real and natural meaning of the word, in the Greek and in Rabbinic usage. This is: not Comforter but Advocate, or, it may be, according to circumstances, Defender, Representative, Counselor, and Pleader.

[53] The great difficulty in understanding the last part of ver. 28 lies not in anyone of the clauses nor in the combination of two, but in that of three of them. We could understand that if they loved Him, they would rejoice that He went to the Father, as marking the completion of His work; and again, that they should rejoice in His going to the Father, Who was greater, and would send the Holy Spirit, as implying benefit to themselves. But the difficulty of combining all these, so that love to Christ should induce a wish that He should go to the Father, because He was greater, seems one, of which I can only see the natural solution in the interpretation which I have ventured to suggest.

[54] There the two could with difficulty be separated. Therefore the vine the symbol of Israel, the sages being the ripe grapes, Chull. 92 a.

[55] Some, to me at least, horrible instances of this supposed absolute license of prayer have appeared in a certain class of American religious literature which of late has found too wide circulation among us.

[56] The question of Thomas (John 14:5) bore as to the way, rather than the goal; that of Peter (13:36) seemed founded either on the Jewish idea that the Messiah was to disappear, or else referred to Christ's going among enemies and into danger, where Peter thought he would follow Him. But none of the questions contemplated the Messianic Return of the Son to the Father with a view to the Mission of the Holy Spirit.

[57] The same word (paesa) is used of Christ's plainly declaring the Father (ver. 25), and of our liberty in prayer in Hebrews 4:16; comp. also 10:19. For the Johannine use of the word, comp. John 5:4, 13, 26; 10:24; 10:14, 54; 15:25, 29; 16:20; 1 John 2:28; 3:21; 4:17; 5:14.

[58] According to the better reading: k to patrs. Surely, if words have any meaning, these teach the unity of Essence of the Son and the Father.

[59]   I cannot agree with Canon Westcott that these last discourses and this Prayer were spoken in the Temple. It is, true, that on that night the Temple was thrown open at midnight, and speedily thronged. But if Jesus had come before that time, He would have found its gates closed; if after that time, He could not have found a place of retirement and quiet, where it is conceivable that could have been said and prayed which is recorded in John 14, 15, 16, 17.

[60]   It need scarcely be said that by the term unity we refer not to unity of Person, but of Nature, Character, and Work.

Chapter 12

Gethsemane

We turn once more to follow the steps of Christ, now among the last He walked upon earth. The hymn, with which the Paschal Supper ended, had been sung. Probably we are to understand this of the second portion of the Hallel, sung some time after the third Cup, or else of Psalm 136, which, in the present Ritual, stands near the end of the service. The last discourses had been spoken, the last Prayer, that of Consecration, had been offered, and Jesus prepared to go forth out of the City, to the Mount of Olives. The streets could scarcely be said to be deserted, for, from many a house shone the festive lamp, and many a company may still have been gathered; and everywhere was the bustle of preparation for going up to the Temple, the gates of which were thrown open at midnight.

Passing out by the gate north of the Temple, we descend into a lonely part of the valley of black Kidron, at that season swelled into a winter torrent. Crossing it, we turn somewhat to the left, where the road leads towards Olivet. Not many steps farther (beyond, and on the other side of the present Church of the Sepulcher of the Virgin) we turn aside from the road to the right, and reach what tradition has since earliest times, and probably correctly, pointed out as Gethsemane, the Oil press. It was a small property enclosed (choron), a garden in the Eastern sense, where probably, amid a variety of fruit trees and flowering shrubs, was a lowly, quiet summer retreat, connected with, or near by, the Olive press. The present Gethsemane is only some seventy steps square, and though its old gnarled olives cannot be those (if such there were) of the time of Jesus, since all trees in that valley, those also which stretched their shadows over Jesus, were hewn down in the Roman siege, they may have sprung from the old roots, or from the odd kernels. But we love to think of this Garden as the place where Jesus often, not merely on this occasion, but perhaps on previous visits to Jerusalem, gathered with His disciples. It was a quiet resting place, for retirement, prayer, perhaps sleep, and a meeting place also where not only the Twelve, but others also, may have been habit to meet the Master. And as such it was known to Judas, and there he led the armed band, when they found the Upper Chamber no longer occupied by Jesus and His disciples. Whether it had been intended that He should spend part of the night there, before returning to the Temple, and whose that enclosed garden was, the other Eden, in which the Second Adam, the Lord from heaven, bore the penalty of the first, and in obeying gained life, we do not know, and perhaps ought not to inquire. It may have belonged to Mark's father. But if otherwise, Jesus had loving disciples even in Jerusalem, and, we rejoice to think, not only a home at Bethany, and an Upper Chamber furnished in the City, but a quiet retreat and meeting place for His own under the bosom of Olivet, in the shadow of the garden of the Oil press.

The sickly light of the moon was falling full on them as they were crossing Kidron. It was here, we imagine, after they had left the City behind them, that Jesus addressed Himself first to the disciples generally. We can scarcely call it either prediction or warning. Rather, as we think of that last Supper, of Christ passing through the streets of the City for the last time into that Garden, and especially of what was now immediately before Him, does what He spoke seem natural, even necessary. To them, yes, to them all, He would that night be even a stumbling block. And so had it been foretold of old, that the Shepherd would be struck, and the sheep scattered. Did this prophecy of His suffering, in its grand outlines, fill the mind of Jesus as He went forth on His Passion? Such Old Testament thoughts were at any rate present with Him, when, not unconsciously nor of necessity, but as the Lamb of God, He went to the slaughter. A peculiar significance also attaches to His prediction that, after He was risen, He would go before them into Galilee. For, with their scattering upon His death, it seems to us, the Apostolic circle or College, as such, was for a time broken up. They continued, to meet together as individual disciples, but the Apostolic bond was temporarily dissolved. This explains many things: the absence of Thomas on the first, and his peculiar position on the second Sunday; the uncertainty of the disciples, as evidenced by the words of those on the way to Emmaus; as well as the seemingly strange movements of the Apostles, all which are quite changed when the Apostolic bond is restored. Similarly, we mark, that only seven of them seem to have been together by the Lake of Galilee, and that only afterwards the Eleven met Him on the mountain to which He had directed them. It was here that the Apostolic circle or College was once more re-formed, and the Apostolic commission renewed, and from there they returned to Jerusalem, once more sent forth from Galilee, to wait the final events of His Ascension, and the Coming of the Holy Spirit.

But in that night they understood none of these things. While all were staggering under the blow of their predicted scattering, Jesus seems to have turned to Peter individually. What he said, and how He put it, equally demand our attention: Simon, Simon, using His old name when referring to the old man in him, Satan has obtained [out asked, xtsato] you, for the purpose of sifting like as wheat. But I have made request for you, that your faith fail not. The words admit us into two mysteries of heaven. This night seems to have been the power of darkness, when, left of God, Christ had to meet by himself the whole assault of hell, and to conquer in His own strength as Man's Substitute and Representative. It is a great mystery: but quite consistent with itself. We do not, as others, here see any analogy to the permission given to Satan in the opening chapter of the Book of Job, always supposing that this embodies a real, not an allegorical story. But in that night the fierce wind of hell was allowed to sweep unbroken over Jesus, and even to expend its fury upon those that stood behind in His Shelter. Satan had out asked, obtained it, yet not to destroy, nor to cast down, but to sift, like as wheat is shaken in a sieve to cast out of it what is not grain. To this point, and no farther, had Satan obtained it. In that night of Christ's Agony and loneliness, of the utmost conflict between Christ and Satan, this seems almost a necessary element.

This, then, was the first mystery that had passed. And this sifting would affect Peter more than the others. Judas, who loved not Jesus at all, has already fallen; Peter, who loved Him, perhaps not most intensely, but, if the expression be allowed, most extensely, stood next to Judas in danger. In truth, though most widely apart in their direction, the springs of their inner life rose in close proximity. There was the same readiness to kindle into enthusiasm, the same desire to have public opinion with him, the same shrinking from the Cross, the same moral inability or unwillingness to stand alone, in the one as in the other. Peter had abundant courage to venture out, but not to stand out. Viewed in its primal elements (not in its development), Peter's character was, among the disciples, the most like that of Judas. If this shows what Judas might have become, it also explains how Peter was most in danger that night; and, the husks of him were cast out of the sieve in his denial of the Christ. But what distinguished Peter from Judas was his faith of spirit, soul, and heart, of spirit, when he apprehended the spiritual element in Christ; of soul, when he confessed Him as the Christ; and of heart, when he could ask Him to sound the depths of his inner being, to find there real, personal love to Jesus.

The second mystery of that night was Christ's prayer for Peter. We dare not say, as the High Priest, and we do not know when and where it was offered. But the expression is very strong, as of one who has need of a thing. And that for which He made such supplication was, that Peter's faith should not fail. This, and not that something new might be given him, or the trial removed from Peter. We mark, how Divine grace presupposes, not supersedes, human liberty. And this also explains why Jesus had so prayed for Peter, not for Judas. In the former case there was faith, which only required to be strengthened against failure, an eventuality which, without the intercession of Christ, was possible. To these words of His, Christ added this significant commission: And you, when you have turned again, confirm your brethren. And how fully he did this, both in the Apostolic circle and in the Church, history has chronicled. Thus, although such may come in the regular moral order of things, Satan has not even power to sift without permission from God; and thus does the Father watch in such terrible sifting over them for whom Christ has prayed. This is the first fulfillment of Christ's Prayer, that the Father would keep them from the Evil One. Not by any process from without, but by the preservation of their faith. And thus also may we learn, to our great and unspeakable comfort, that not every sin, not even conscious and willful sin, implies the failure of our faith, very closely though it lead to it; still less, our final rejection. On the contrary, as the fall of Simon was the outcome of the natural elements in him, so would it lead to their being brought to light and removed, thus fitting him the better for confirming his brethren. And so would light come out of darkness. From our human standpoint we might call such teaching needful: in the Divine arrangement it is only the Divine successor to the human predecessor.

We can understand the vehement earnestness and sincerity with which Peter protested against of any failure on his part. We mostly deem those sins farthest which are nearest to us; else, much of the power of their temptation would be gone, and temptation changed into conflict. The things which we least anticipate are our falls. In all honesty, and not necessarily with self elevation over the others, he said, that even if all should be offended in Christ, he never could be, but was ready to go with Him into prison and death. And when, to enforce the warning, Christ predicted that before the repeated crowing of the rooster ushered in the morning, Peter would three times deny that he knew Him, Peter not only persisted in his claims, but was joined in them by the rest. Yet, and this seems the meaning and object of the words of Christ which follow, they were not aware of how terribly changed the former relations had become, and what they would have to suffer in consequence. When formerly He had sent forth, both without provision and defense, had they lacked anything? No! But now no helping hand would be extended to them; what seemingly they would need even more than anything else would be a sword, defense against attacks, for at the close of His history He was reckoned with transgressors. The Master a crucified criminal, what could His followers expect? But once more they understood Him in a grossly realistic manner. These Galileans, after the custom of their countrymen, had provided themselves with short swords, which they concealed under their upper garment. It was natural for men of their disposition, so imperfectly understanding their Masters teaching, to have taken what might seem to them only a needful precaution in coming to Jerusalem. At least two of them, among them Peter, now produced swords. But this was not the time of reason with them, and Jesus simply put it aside. Events would only too soon teach them.

They had now reached the entrance of Gethsemane. It may have been that it led through the building with the oil press, and that the eight Apostles, who were not to come nearer to the Bush burning, but not consumed, were left there. Or they may have been taken within the entrance of the Garden, and left there, while, pointing forward with a gesture of the Hand, He went over there and prayed According to Luke, He added the parting warning to pray that they might not enter into temptation.

Eight did He leave there. The other three, Peter, James and John, companions before of His glory, both when He raised the daughter of Jairus and on the Mount of Transfiguration, He took with Him farther. If in that last contest His Human Soul craved for the presence of those who stood nearest Him and loved Him best, or if He would have them baptized with His Baptism, and drink of His Cup, these were the three of all others to be chosen. And now of a sudden the cold flood broke over Him. Within these few moments He had passed from the calm of assured victory into the anguish of the contest. Increasingly, with every step forward, He became sorrowful, full of sorrow, great amazed, and desolate. He told them of the deep sorrow of His Soul (psuch) even to death, and called them to wait there to watch with Him. Himself went forward to enter the contest with prayer. Only the first attitude of the wrestling Savior saw they, only the first words in that Hour of Agony did they hear. For, as in our present state not uncommonly in the deepest emotions of the soul, and as had been the case on the Mount of Transfiguration, irresistible sleep crept over their frame. But what, we may reverently ask, was the cause of this sorrow to death of the Lord Jesus Christ? Not fear, either of bodily or mental suffering: but death. Man's nature, created of God immortal, shrinks (by the law of its nature) from the dissolution of the bond that binds body to soul. Yet to fallen man death is not by any means fully death, for he is born with the taste of it in his soul. Not so Christ. It was the Unfallen Man dying; it was He, Who had no experience of it, tasting death, and that not for Himself but for every man, emptying the cup to its bitter dregs. It was the Christ undergoing death by man and for man; the Incarnate God, the God Man, submitting Himself vicariously to the deepest humiliation, and paying the utmost penalty: death, all death. No one as He could know what death was (not dying, which men dread, but Christ dreaded not); no one could taste its bitterness as He. His going into death was His final conflict with Satan for man, and on his behalf. By submitting to it He took away the power of death; He disarmed death by burying his shaft in His own Heart. And beyond this lies the deep, unutterable mystery of Christ bearing the penalty due to our sin, bearing our death, bearing the penalty of the broken Law, the accumulated guilt of humanity, and the holy wrath of the Righteous Judge upon them. And in view of this mystery the heaviness of sleep seems to steal over our apprehension.

Alone, as in His first conflict with the Evil One in the Temptation in the wilderness, must Jesus enter on the last contest. With what agony of soul He took upon Him now and there the sins of the world, and in taking atoned for them, we may learn from this account of what passed, when, with strong crying and tears to Him that was able to save Him from death, He offered up prayers and supplications. And, we anticipate it already, with these results: that He was heard; that He learned obedience by the things which He suffered; that He was made perfect; and that He became: to us the Author of Eternal Salvation, and before God, a High Priest after the order of Melchizedek. Alone, and yet even this being parted from them (pespsthe), implied sorrow. And now, on His knees, prostrate on the ground, prostrate on His Face, began His Agony. His very address bears witness to it. It is the only time, so far as recorded in the Gospels, when He addressed God with the personal pronoun: My Father. The object of the prayer was, that, if it was possible, the hour might pass away from Him. The subject of the prayer (as recorded by the three Gospels) was, that the Cup itself might pass away, yet always with the limitation, that not His Will but the Father's might be done. The petition of Christ, therefore, was subject not only to the Will of the Father, but to His own Will that the Father's Will might be done. We are here in full view of the deepest mystery of our faith: the two Natures in One Person. Both Natures spoke here, and the if it be possible of Matthew and Mark is in Luke if You be willing. In any case, the possibility is not physical, for with God all things are possible, but moral: that of inward fitness. Was there, then, any thought or view of a possibility, that Christ's work could be accomplished without that hour and Cup? Or did it only mark the utmost limit of His endurance and submission? We dare not answer; we only reverently follow what is recorded.

It was in this extreme Agony of Soul almost to death, that the Angel appeared (as in the Temptation in the wilderness) to strengthen and support His Body and Soul. And so the conflict went on, with increasing earnestness of prayer, all that terrible hour. For, the appearance of the Angel must have intimated to Him, that the Cup could not pass away. And at the close of that hour, as we infer from the fact that the disciples must still have seen on His Brow the marks of the Bloody Sweat, His Sweat, mingled with Blood, fell in great drops on the ground. And when Jesus with this mark of His Agony on His Brow returned to the three, He found that deep sleep held them. While He lay in prayer, they lay in sleep; and yet where soul agony leads not to the one, it often induces the other. His words, primarily addressed to Simon, roused them, yet not sufficiently to fully carry to their hearts either the loving reproach, the admonition to Watch and pray in view of the coming temptation, or the most seasonable warning about the weakness of the flesh, even where the spirit was willing, ready and ardent (prthumon).

The conflict had been virtually, though not finally, decided, when Jesus went back to the three sleeping disciples. He now returned to complete it, though both the attitude in which He prayed (no longer prostrate) and the wording of His Prayer, only slightly altered as it was, indicate how near it was to perfect victory. And once more, on His return to them, He found that sleep had weighted their eyes, and they scarcely knew what answer to make to Him. Yet a third time He left them to pray as before. And now He returned victorious. After three assaults had the Tempter left Him in the wilderness; after the threefold conflict in the Garden he was vanquished. Christ came forth triumphant. No longer did He ask His disciples watch. They might, they should, sleep and take rest, before the near terrible events of His Betrayal, for, the hour had come when the Son of Man was to be betrayed into the hands of sinners.

A very brief period of rest this, soon broken by the call of Jesus to rise and go to where the other eight had been left, at the entrance of the Garden, to go forward and meet the band which was coming under the guidance of the Betrayer. And while He was speaking, the heavy tramp of many men and the light of lanterns and torches indicated the approach of Judas and his band. During the hours that had passed all had been prepared. When, according to arrangement, he appeared at the High Priestly Palace, or more probably at that of Annas, who seems to have had the direction of affairs, the Jewish leaders first communicated with the Roman garrison. By their own admission they possessed no longer (for forty years before the destruction of Jerusalem) the power of pronouncing capital sentence. It is difficult to understand how, in view of this fact (so fully confirmed in the New Testament), it could have been imagined (as so generally) that the Sanhedrin had, in regular session, sought formally to pronounce on Jesus what, admittedly, they had not the power to execute. Nor, did they, when appealing to Pilate, plead that they had pronounced sentence of death, but only that they had a law by which Jesus should die. It was otherwise as regarded civil causes, or even minor offences. The Sanhedrin, not possessing the power of the sword, had neither soldiery, nor regularly armed band at command. The Temple guard under their officers served merely for purposes of police, and, were neither regularly armed nor trained. Nor would the Romans have tolerated a regular armed Jewish force in Jerusalem.

We can now understand the progress of events. In the fortress of Antonia, close to the Temple and connected with it by two stairs, lay the Roman garrison. But during the Feast the Temple itself was guarded by an armed Cohort, consisting of from 400 to 600 men, so as to prevent or quell any tumult among the numerous pilgrims. It would be to the captain of this Cohort that the Chief Priests and leaders of the Pharisees would, in the first place, apply for an armed guard to effect the arrest of Jesus, on the ground that it might lead to some popular tumult. This, without necessarily having to state the charge that was to be brought against Him, which might have led to other complications. Although John speaks of the band by a word (spera) which always designates a Cohort, in this case the Cohort, the definite article marking it as that of the Temple, yet there is no reason for believing that the whole Cohort was sent. Still, its commander would scarcely have sent a strong detachment out of the Temple, and on what might lead to a riot, without having first referred to the Procurator, Pontius Pilate. And if further evidence were required, it would be in the fact that the band was led not by a Centurion, but by a Chiliarch, which, as there were no intermediate grades in the Roman army, must represent one of the six tribunes attached to each legion. This also explains not only the apparent preparedness of Pilate to sit in judgment early next morning, but also how Pilates wife may have been disposed for those dreams about Jesus which so frightened her.

This Roman detachment, armed with swords and clubs, with the latter of which Pilate on other occasions also directed his soldiers to attack them who raised a tumult, was accompanied by servants from the High Priest's Palace, and other Jewish officers, to direct the arrest of Jesus. They bore torches and lamps placed on the top of poles, so as to prevent any possible concealment.

Whether or not this was the great multitude mentioned by Matthew and Mark, or the band was swelled by volunteers or curious onlookers, is a matter of no importance. Having received this band, Judas proceeded on his errand. As we believe, their first move was to the house where the Supper had been celebrated. Learning that Jesus had left it with His disciples, perhaps two or three hours before, Judas next directed the band to the spot he knew so well: to Gethsemane. A signal by which to recognize Jesus seemed almost necessary with so large a band, and where escape or resistance might be apprehended. It was, terrible to say, none other than a kiss. As soon as he had so marked Him, the guard were to seize, and lead Him safely away.

Combining the notices in the four Gospels, we thus picture to ourselves the succession of events. As the band reached the Garden, Judas went somewhat in advance of them, and reached Jesus just as He had roused the three and was preparing to go and meet His captors. He saluted Him, Hail, Rabbi, so as to be heard by the rest, and not only kissed but covered Him with kisses, kissed Him repeatedly, loudly, effusively (katephilesen). The Savior submitted to the indignity, not stopping, but only saying as He passed on: Friend, that for which you are here; and then, perhaps in answer to his questioning gesture: Judas, with a kiss deliver you up the Son of Man? If Judas had wished, by thus going in advance of the band and saluting the Master with a kiss, even now to act the hypocrite and deceive Jesus and the disciples, as if he had not come with the armed men, perhaps only to warn Him of their approach, what Jesus said must have reached his inmost being. Indeed, it was the first mortal shaft in the soul of Judas. The only time we again see him, until he goes on what ends in his self destruction, is as he stands, as it were sheltering himself, with the armed men.

It is at this point, as we suppose, that the notices from John's Gospel come in. Leaving the traitor, and ignoring the signal which he had given them, Jesus advanced to the band, and asked them: Whom seek you? To the brief spoken, perhaps somewhat contemptuous, Jesus the Nazarene, He replied with infinite calmness and majesty: I am He. The immediate effect of these words was, we shall not say magical, but Divine. They had no doubt been prepared for quite other: either compromise, fear, or resistance. But the appearance and majesty of that calm Christ, heaven in His look and peace on His lips, was too overpowering in its effects on that untutored pagan soldiery, who perhaps cherished in their hearts secret misgivings of the work they had in hand. The foremost of them went backward, and they fell to the ground. But Christ's hour had come. And once more He now asked them the same question as before, and, on repeating their former answer, He said: I told you that I am He; if therefore you seek Me, let these go their way, the Evangelist seeing in this watchful care over His own the initial fulfillment of the words which Jesus had previously spoken concerning their safe preservation, not only in the sense of their outward preservation, but in that of their being guarded from such temptations as, in their then state, they could not have endured.

The words of Christ about those that were with Him seem to have recalled the leaders of the guard to full consciousness, perhaps awakened in them fears of a possible rising at the incitement of His adherents. Accordingly, it is here that we insert the notice of Matthew, and of Mark, that they laid hands on Jesus and took Him. Then it was that Peter, seeing what was coming, drew the sword which he carried, and putting the question to Jesus, but without awaiting His answer, struck at Malchus, the servant of the High Priest, perhaps the Jewish leader of the band, cutting off his ear. But Jesus immediately restrained all such violence, and rebuked all self vindication by outward violence (the taking of the sword that had not been received) with it all merely outward zeal, pointing to the fact how easily He might, as against this cohort, have commanded Angelic legions. He had in wrestling Agony received from His Father that Cup to drink, and the Scriptures must in that wise be fulfilled. And so saying, He touched the ear of Malchus, and healed him.

But this faint appearance of resistance was enough for the guard. Their leaders now bound Jesus. It was to this last, most underserved and uncalled for indignity that Jesus replied by asking them, why they had come against

Him as against a robber, one of those wild, murderous outlaws: Had He not been all that week daily in the Temple, teaching? Why not then seize Him? But this hour of theirs that had come, and the power of darkness, this also had been foretold in Scripture!

And as the ranks of the armed men now closed around the bound Christ, none dared to stay with Him, for fear that they also should be bound as resisting authority. So they all forsook Him and fled. But there was one there who joined not in the flight, but remained, a deeply interested onlooker. When the soldiers had come to seek Jesus in the Upper Chamber of his home, Mark, roused from sleep, had hastily cast about him the loose linen garment or wrapper that lay by his bedside, and followed the armed band to see what would come of it. He now lingered in the rear, and followed as they led away Jesus, never imagining that they would attempt to lay hold on him, since he had not been with the disciples nor yet in the Garden. But they, perhaps the Jewish servants of the High Priest, had noticed him. They attempted to lay hold on him, when, disengaging himself from their grasp, he left his upper garment in their hands, and fled. So ended the first scene in the terrible drama of that night.

End Notes:

[61] Curiously enough, Roman Catholic writers see in the prediction of his fall by implication a assertion of Peter's supremacy. This, because they regard Peter as the representative and head of the others.

[62] This crowing of the rooster has given rise to a curious controversy, since, according to Rabbinic law, it was forbidden to keep fowls in Jerusalem, on account of possible Levitical defilements through them (Baba K. 5:7). Reland has written a special dissertation on the subject, of which Schoettgen has given a brief abstract. We need not reproduce the arguments, but Reland urges that, even if that ordinance was really in force at the time of Christ (of which there is grave doubt), Peter might have heard the rooster crow from Fort Antonia, occupied by the Romans, or else that it might have reached thus far in the still night air from outside the walls of Jerusalem. But there is more than doubt as to the existence of this ordinance at the time. There is repeated mention of rooster crow in connection with the Temple watches, and if the expression be regarded as not literal, but simple a designation of time, we have in Jeremiah Erub. 10:1 (p. 26 a, about middle) a story in which a rooster caused the death of a child at Jerusalem, proving that fowls must have been kept there.

[63] Matthew speaks of this night, Mark and Luke of this day, proving, if such were needed, that the day was reckoned from evening to evening.

[64] The objection has been raised, that, according to the Mishnah (Shabb. 6:4), it was not lawful to carry swords on the Sabbath. But even this Mishnah seems to indicate that there was divergence of opinion on the subject, even as regarded the Sabbath, much more a feast day.

[65] We mark a climax. The last word (demonen) used both by Matthew and Mark seems to indicate utter loneliness, desertion, and desolateness.

[66] Observe that we place an interval of time, however brief, between Matthew 25:45 (and similarly Mark 14:41) and the following verse. So already Augustine.

[67] The number varied. See Marquardt, Roem. Alterthumsk. vol. v. 2, pp. 359, 386, 441. Canon Westcott suggests that it might have been, not a cohort, but a manipulus (of about 200 men); but, as himself points out, the expression as used in the N.T. seems always to indicate a cohort.

[68] The name Malchus, which occurs also in Josephus (Ant. 1:15. 1.; 14:5.2; 11. 4; War 1:8. 3), must not be derived, as is generally done, from a king. Its Hebrew equivalent, apparently, is Malluch, Counselor, a name which occurs both in the Old Testament and in the LXX (1 Chronicles 6:44; Nehemiah 10:4, etc.), and as a later Jewish name in the Talmud. But both Frankel (Einl. in d. Jeremiah Talm. p. 114) and Freudenthal (Hell. Stud. p. 131) maintain that it was not a Jewish name, while it was common among Syrians, Phoenicians, Arabians, and Samaritans. The suggestion therefore lies near, that Malchus was either a Syrian or a Phoenician by birth.

[69] The definite article here marks that he was, in a special sense, the servant of the High Priest, his body servant.

[70] A legion had ten cohorts.

[71] This reference to the cup which the Father had given Him to drink by John, implies the whole history of the Agony in Gethsemane, which is not recorded in the Fourth Gospel. And this is, on many grounds, very instructive.

[72] sindn. This, no doubt, corresponds to the Sadin or Sedina which, in Rabbinic writings, means a linen cloth, or a loose linen wrapper, though, possibly, it may also mean a night dress (see Levy, ad voc.).

Chapter 13

Thursday Night before Annas and Caiaphas

It was not a long way that they led the bound Christ. Probably through the same gate by which He had gone forth with His disciples after the Paschal Supper, up to where, on the slope between the Upper City and the Tyropeon, stood the well known Palace of Annas. There were no idle strollers in the streets of Jerusalem at that late hour, and the tramp of the Roman guard must have been too often heard to startle sleepers, or to lead to the inquiry why that glare of lamps and torches, and Who was the Prisoner, guarded on that holy night by both Roman soldiers and servants of the High Priest.

If every incident in that night were not of such supreme interest, we might dismiss the question as almost idle, why they brought Jesus to the house of Annas, since he was not at that time the actual High Priest. That office now devolved on Caiaphas, his son-in-law, who, as the Evangelist significantly reminds us, had been the first to enunciate in plain words what seemed to him the political necessity for the judicial murder of Christ. There had been no pretence on his part of religious motives or zeal for God; he had cynically put it in a way to override the scruples of those old Sanhedrists by raising their fears. What was the use of discussing about forms of Law or about that Man? it must in any case be done; even the friends of Jesus in the Council, as well as the conscientious observers of Law, must regard His death as the less of two evils. He spoke as the bold, unscrupulous, determined man that he was; Sadducee in heart rather than by conviction; a worthy son-in-law of Annas.

No figure is better known in contemporary Jewish history than that of Annas; no person deemed more fortunate or successful, but none also more generally detested than the late High Priest. He had held the Pontificate for only six or seven years; but it was filled by not fewer than five of his sons, by his son-in-law Caiaphas, and by a grandson. And in those days it was, at least for one of Annas disposition, much better to have been than to be High Priest. He enjoyed all the dignity of the office, and all its influence also, since he was able to promote to it those most closely connected with him. And, while they acted publicly, he really directed affairs, without either the responsibility or the restraints which the office imposed. His influence with the Romans he owned to the religious views which he professed, to his open partisanship of the foreigner, and to his enormous wealth. The Sadducean Annas was an eminently safe Churchman, not troubled with any special convictions nor with Jewish fanaticism, a pleasant and a useful man also who was able to furnish his friends in the Praetorium with large sums of money. We have seen what immense revenues the family of Annas must have derived from the Temple booths, and how reprehensible and unpopular was the traffic. The names of those bold, licentious, unscrupulous, degenerate sons of Aaron were spoken with whispered curses. Without referring to Christ's interference with that Temple traffic, which, if His authority had prevailed, would, have been fatal to it, we can understand how antithetic in every respect a Messiah, and such a Messiah as Jesus, must have been to Annas. He was as resolutely bent on His death as his son-in-law, though with his characteristic cunning and coolness, not in the hasty, bluff manner of Caiaphas. It was probably from a desire that Annas might have the conduct of the business, or from the active, leading part which Annas took in the matter; perhaps for even more ordinary and practical reasons, such as that the Palace of Annas was nearer to the place of Jesus capture, and that it was desirable to dismiss the Roman soldiery as quickly as possible, that Christ was first brought to Annas, and not to the actual High Priest.

In any case, the arrangement was most in agreement, whether as regards the character of Annas, or the official position of Caiaphas. The Roman soldiers had evidently orders to bring Jesus to the late High Priest. This appears from their proceeding directly to him, and from this, that apparently they returned to quarters immediately on delivering up their prisoner. And we cannot ascribe this to any official position of Annas in the Sanhedrin, first, because the text implies that it had not been due to this cause, and, secondly, because, as will now appear, the proceedings against Christ were not those of the ordinary and regular meetings of the Sanhedrin.

No account is given of what passed before Annas. Even the fact of Christ's being first brought to him is only mentioned in the Fourth Gospel. As the disciples had all forsaken Him and fled, we can understand that they were in ignorance of what actually passed, until they had again rallied, at least so far, that Peter and another disciple, evidently John, followed Him into the Palace of the High priest, that is, into the Palace of Caiaphas, not of Annas. For as, according to the three Synoptic Gospels, the Palace of the High Priest Caiaphas was the scene of Peter's denial, the account of it in the Fourth Gospel must refer to the same locality, and not to the Palace of Annas, while the suggestion that Annas and Caiaphas occupied the same dwelling is not only very unlikely in itself, but seems incompatible with the obvious meaning of the notice, Now Annas sent Him bound to Caiaphas the High Priest. But if Peter's denial, as recorded by John, is the same as that described by the Synoptists, and took place in the house of Caiaphas, then the account of the examination by the High Priest, which follows the notice about Peter, must also refer to that by Caiaphas, not Annas. We thus know absolutely nothing of what passed in the house of Annas, if, anything passed, except that Annas sent Jesus bound to Caiaphas.

Of what occurred in the Palace of Caiaphas we have two accounts. That of John seems to refer to a more private interview between the High Priest and Christ, at which, apparently, only some personal attendants of Caiaphas were present, from one of whom the Apostle may have derived his information. The second account is that of the Synoptists, and refers to the examination of Jesus at dawn of day by the leading Sanhedrists, who had been hastily summoned for the purpose.

It sounds almost like presumption to say, that in His first interview with Caiaphas Jesus bore Himself with the majesty of the Son of God, Who knew all that was before Him, and passed through it as on the way to the accomplishment of His Mission. The questions of Caiaphas bore on two points: the disciples of Jesus, and His teaching, the former to incriminate Christ's followers, the latter to incriminate the Master. To the first inquiry it was only natural that He should not have condescended to return an answer. The reply to the second was characterized by that openness which He claimed for all that He had said. If there was to do not be unprejudiced, but even fair inquiry, let Caiaphas not try to extort confessions to which he had no legal right, nor to ensnare Him when the purpose was evidently murderous. If he really wanted information, there could be no difficulty in procuring witnesses to speak to His doctrine: all Jewry knew it. His was no secret doctrine (in secret I spoke nothing). He always spoke in Synagogue and in the Temple, where all the Jews gather together. If the inquiry were a fair one, let the judge act judicially, and ask not Him, but those who had heard Him.

It must be admitted, that the answer sounds not like that of one accused, who seeks either to make apology, or even greatly cares to defend himself. And there was in it that tone of superiority which even injured human innocence would have a right to assume before a wicked judge, who sought to ensnare a victim, not to elicit the truth. It was this which emboldened one of those servile attendants, with the brutality of an Eastern in such circumstances, to inflict on the Lord that terrible blow. Let us hope that it was a pagan, not a Jew, who so lifted his hand. We are almost thankful that the text leaves it in doubt, whether it was with the palm of the hand, or the lesser indignity, with a rod. Humanity itself seems to reel and stagger under this blow. In pursuance of His Human submission, the Divine Sufferer, without murmuring or complaining, or without asserting His Divine Power, only answered in such tone of patient challenge as must have convicted the man of his wrong, or at least have left him speechless. May it have been that these words and the look of Christ had gone to his heart, and that the now strangely silenced criminal became the confessing narrator of this scene to the Apostle John?

2. That Apostle was, at any rate, no stranger in the Palace of Caiaphas. We have already seen that, after the first panic of Christ's sudden capture and their own flight, two of them at least, Peter and John, seem speedily to have rallied. Combining the notices of the Synoptists with the fuller details, in this respect, of the Fourth Gospel, we derive the impression that Peter, so far true to his word, had been the first to stop in his flight and to follow far off. If he reached the Palace of Annas in time, he certainly did not enter it, but probably waited outside during the brief space which preceded the transference of Jesus to Caiaphas. He had now been joined by John, and the two followed the glum procession which escorted Jesus to the High Priest. John seems to have entered the court along with the guard, while Peter remained outside until his fellow Apostle, who apparently was well known in the High Priests house, had spoken to the maid who kept the door, the male servants being probably all gathered in the court, and so procured his admission.

Remembering that the High Priest's Palace was built on the slope of the hill, and that there was an outer court, from which a door led into the inner court, we can, in some measure, realize the scene. As previously stated, Peter had followed as far as that inner door, while John had entered with the guard. When he missed his fellow disciple, who was left outside this inner door, John went out, and, having probably told the waiting maid that this was a friend of his, procured his admission. While John now hurried up to be in the Palace, and as near Christ as he might, Peter advanced into the middle of the court, where, in the chill spring night, a coal fire had been lighted. The glow of the charcoal, around which occasionally a blue flame played, threw a peculiar sheen on the bearded faces of the men as they crowded around it, and talked of the events of that night, describing, with Eastern fluency, to those who had not been there what had passed in the Garden, and exchanging, as is the manner of such serving men and officials, opinions and exaggerated denunciations concerning Him Who had been captured with such unexpected ease, and was now their master's safe Prisoner. As the red light glowed and flickered, it threw the long shadows of these men across the inner court, up the walls towards the gallery that ran round, up there, where the lamps and lights within, or as they moved along apartments and corridors, revealed other faces: there, where, in an inner audience chamber, the Prisoner was confronted by His enemy, accuser, and judge.

What a contrast it all seemed between the Purification of the Temple only a few days before, when the same Jesus had overturned the trafficking tables of the High Priest, and as He now stood, a bound Prisoner before him, at the mercy of every menial who might carry favor by wantonly insulting Him? It was a chill night when Peter, down beneath, looked up to the lighted windows. There, among the serving men in the court, he was in every sense without. He approached the group around the fire. He would hear what they had to say; besides, it was not safe to stand apart; he might be recognized as one of those who had only escaped capture in the Garden by hasty flight. And then it was chill, and not only to the body, the chill had struck to his soul. Was he right in having come there at all? Commentators have discussed it as involving neglect of Christ's warning. As if the love of anyone who was, and felt, as Peter, could have credited the possibility of what he had been warned of; and, if he had credited it, would, in the first moments of returning flood after the panic of his flight, have remembered that warning, or with cool calculation acted up to the full measure of it! To have fled to his home and shut the door behind him, by way of rendering it impossible to deny that he knew Christ, would not have been Peter nor any true disciple. It would itself have been a worse and more cowardly denial than that of which he was actually guilty. Peter followed far off, thinking of nothing else but his imprisoned Master, and that he would see the end, whatever it might be. But now it was chill, very chill, to body and soul, and Peter remembered it all; not, the warning, but that of which he had been warned. What good could his confession do? perhaps much possible harm; and why was he there?

Peter was very restless, and yet he must seem very quiet. He sat down among the servants, then he stood up among them. It was this restlessness of attempted indifference which attracted the attention of the maid who had at the first admitted him. As in the uncertain light she scanned the features of the mysterious stranger, she boldly charged him, though still in a questioning tone, with being one of the disciples of the Man Who stood incriminated up there before the High Priest. And in the chattering of his souls fever, into which the chill had struck, Peter vehemently denied all knowledge of Him to Whom the woman referred of the very meaning of what she said. He had said too much not to bring soon another charge upon himself. We need not inquire which of the slightly varying reports in the Gospels represents the actual words of the woman or the actual answer of Peter. Perhaps neither; perhaps all, certainly, she said all this, and, certainly, he answered all that, though neither of them would confine their words to the short sentences reported by each of the Evangelists.

What had he to do there? And why should he incriminate himself, or perhaps Christ, by a needless confession to those who had neither the moral nor the legal right to exact it? That was all he now remembered and thought; nothing about any denial of Christ. And so, as they were still chatting together, perhaps bandying words, Peter withdrew. We cannot judge how long time had passed, but this we gather, that the words of the woman had either not made any impression on those around the fire, or that the bold denial of Peter had satisfied them. Now we find Peter walking away down the porch, which ran round and opened into the outer court. He was not thinking of anything else now than how chilly it felt, and how right he had been in not being entrapped by that woman. And so he heeded it not, while his footfall sounded along the marble paved porch, that just at this moment a rooster crowed. But there was no sleep that night in the High Priests Palace. As he walked down the porch towards the outer court, first one maid met him; and then, as he returned from the outer court, he once more encountered his old accuser, the door keeper; and as he crossed the inner court to mingle again with the group around the fire, where he had formerly found safety, he was first accosted by one man, and then they all around the fire turned upon him, and each and all had the same thing to say, the same charge, that he was also one of the disciples of Jesus of Nazareth. But Peter's resolve was taken; he was quite sure it was right; and to each separately, and to all together, he gave the same denial, more brief now, for he was collected and determined, but more emphatic, even with an oath. And once more he silenced suspicion for a time. Or, perhaps, attention was now otherwise directed.

3. For, already, hasty footsteps were heard along the porches and corridors, and the maid who that night opened the gate at the High Priest's Palace was busy at her post. They were the leading Priests, Elders, and Sanhedrists, who had been hastily summoned to the High Priest's Palace, and who were hurrying up just as the first faint streaks of gray light were lying on the sky. The private examination by Caiaphas we place (as in the Gospel of John) between the first and second denial of Peter; the first arrival of Sanhedrists immediately after his second denial. The private inquiry of Caiaphas had elicited nothing; and, it was only preliminary. The leading Sanhedrists must have been warned that the capture of Jesus would be attempted that night, and to hold themselves in readiness when summoned to the High Priest. This is not only quite in accordance with all the previous and after circumstances in the narrative, but nothing short of a procedure of such supreme importance would have warranted the presence for such a purpose of these religious leaders on that holy Passover night.

But whatever view be taken, thus much at least is certain, that it was no formal, regular meeting of the Sanhedrin. We put aside, as `a priori reasoning, such considerations as that protesting voices would have been raised, not only from among the friends of Jesus, but from others whom (with all their Jewish hatred of Christ) we cannot but regard as incapable of such gross violation of justice and law. But all Jewish order and law would have been grossly infringed in almost every particular, if this had been a formal meeting of the Sanhedrin. We know what their forms were, although many of them (as so much in Rabbinic accounts) may represent rather the ideal than the real, what the Rabbis imagined should be, rather than what was; or else what may date from later times. According to Rabbinic testimony, there were three tribunals. In towns numbering less than 120 (or, according to one authority, 230) male inhabitants, there was only the lowest tribunal, that consisting of three Judges. Their jurisdiction was limited, and notably did not extend to capital causes. The authority of the tribunal of next instance, that of twenty three, was also limited, although capital causes lay within its competence. The highest tribunal was that of seventy one, or the Great Sanhedrin, which met first in one of the Temple Chambers, the so called Lishkath ha Gazith, or Chamber of Hewn Stones, and at the time of which we write in the booths of the sons of Annas. The Judges of all these Courts were equally set apart by ordination (Semikhah), originally that of the laying on of hands. Ordination was conferred by three, of whom one at least must have been himself ordained, and able to trace up his ordination through Joshua to Moses. This, on the theory that there had been a regular succession of ordained Teachers, not only up to Ezra, but beyond him to Joshua and Moses. The members of the tribunals of twenty three were appointed by the Great Sanhedrin. The members of the tribunals of three were likewise appointed by the Great Sanhedrin, which entrusted to men, especially accredited and worthy, the duty of traveling through the towns of Palestine and appointing and ordaining in them the men best fitted for the office. The qualifications mentioned for the office remind us of those which Paul indicates as requisite for the Christian eldership.

Some inferences seem here of importance, as throwing light on early Apostolic arrangements, believing, as we do, that the outward form of the Church was in great measure derived from the Synagogue. First, we notice that there was regular ordination, and, at first at least, by the laying on of hands. Further, this ordination was not requisite either for delivering addresses or conducting the liturgy in the Synagogue, but for authoritative teaching, and especially for judicial functions, to which would correspond in the Christian Church the power of the Keys, the administration of discipline and of the Sacraments as admitting into, and continuing in the fellowship of the Church. Next, ordination could only be conferred by those who had themselves been rightly ordained, and who could, therefore, through those previously ordained, trace their ordination upwards. Again, each of these Colleges of Presbyters had its Chief or President. Lastly, men entrusted with supreme (Apostolic) authority were sent to the various towns to appoint elders in every city.

The appointment to the highest tribunal, or Great Sanhedrin, was made by that tribunal itself, either by promoting a member of the inferior tribunals or one from the foremost of the three rows, in which the disciples or students sat facing the Judges. The latter sat in a semicircle, under the presidency of the Nasi (prince) and the vice presidency of the Ab beth din (father of the Court of Law). At least twenty three members were required to form a quorum. We have such minute details of the whole arrangements and proceedings of this Court as greatly confirms our impression of the chiefly ideal character of some of the Rabbinic notices. Facing the semicircle of Judges, we are told, there were two shorthand writers, to note down, respectively, the speeches in favor and against the accused. Each of the students knew, and sat in his own place. In capital causes the arguments in defense of and afterwards those incriminating the accused, were stated. If one had spoken in favor, he might not again speak against the panel. Students might speak for, not against him. He might be pronounced not guilty on the same day on which the case was tried; but a sentence of guilty might only be pronounced on the day following that of the trial. It seems, however, at least doubtful, whether in case of profanation of the Divine Name (Chillul haShem), judgment was not immediately executed. Lastly, the voting began with the youngest, so that juniors might not be influenced by the seniors; and a bare majority was not sufficient for condemnation.

These are only some of the regulations laid down in Rabbinic writings. It is of greater importance to enquire, how far they were carried out under the iron rule of Herod and that of the Roman Procurators. Here we are in great measure left to conjecture. We can well believe that neither Herod nor the Procurators would wish to abolish the Sanhedrin, but would leave to them the administration of justice, especially in all that might in any way be connected with purely religious questions. Equally we can understand, that both would deprive them of the power of the sword and of decision on all matters of political or supreme importance. Herod would reserve to himself the final disposal in all cases, if he saw fit to interfere, and so would the Procurators, who especially would not have tolerated any attempt at jurisdiction over a Roman citizen. In short, the Sanhedrin would be accorded full jurisdiction in inferior and in religious matters, with the greatest show, but with the least amount, of real rule or of supreme authority. Lastly, as both Herod and the Procurators treated the High Priest, who was their own creature, as the real head and representative of the Jews; and as it would be their policy to curtail the power of the independent and fanatical Rabbis, we can understand how, in great criminal causes or in important investigations, the High Priest would always preside, the presidency of the Nasi being reserved for legal and ritual questions and discussions. And with this the notices in the New Testament and in Josephus accord.

Even this brief summary about the Sanhedrin would be needless, if it were a question of applying its rules of procedure to the arraignment of

Jesus. For, Jewish and Christian evidence establish the fact, that Jesus was not formally tried and condemned by the Sanhedrin. It is admitted on all hands, that forty years before the destruction of the Temple the Sanhedrin ceased to pronounce capital sentences. This alone would be sufficient. But, besides, the trial and sentence of Jesus in the Palace of Caiaphas would (as already stated) have outraged every principle of Jewish criminal law and procedure. Such causes could only be tried, and capital sentence pronounced, in the regular meeting place of the Sanhedrin, not, as here, in the High Priest's Palace; no process, least of all such a one, might be begun in the night, not even in the afternoon, although if the discussion had gone on all day, sentence might be pronounced at night. Again, no process could take place on Sabbaths or Feast days, or even on the eves of them, although this would not have nullified proceedings, and it might be argued on the other side, that a process against one who had seduced the people should preferably by carried on, and sentence executed, at the great public Feasts, for the warning of all. Lastly, in capital causes there was a very elaborate system of warning and cautioning witnesses, while it may safely be affirmed, that at a regular trial Jewish Judges, however prejudiced, would not have acted as the Sanhedrists and Caiaphas did on this occasion.

But as we examine it more closely, we perceive that the Gospel narratives do not speak of a formal trial and sentence by the Sanhedrin. Such references as to the Sanhedrin (council), or to all the Sanhedrin, must be taken in the wider sense, which will now be explained. On the other hand, the four Gospels equally indicate that the whole proceedings of that night were carried on in the Palace of Caiaphas, and that during that night no formal sentence of death was pronounced. John, does not report the proceedings at all; Matthew only records the question of Caiaphas and the answer of the Sanhedrists; and even the language of Mark does not convey the idea of a formal sentence. And when in the morning, in consequence of a fresh consultation, also in the Palace of Caiaphas, they led Jesus to the Praetorium, it was not as a prisoner condemned to death of whom they asked the execution, but as one against whom they laid certain accusations worthy of death, while, when Pilate called them judge Jesus according to Jewish Law, they replied, not: that they had done so already, but, that they had no competence to try capital causes.

4.   But although Christ was not tried and sentenced in a formal meeting of the Sanhedrin, there can, unfortunately be no question that His Condemnation and death were the work, if not of the Sanhedrin, yet of

the Sanhedrists, of the whole body of them (all the council), in the sense of expressing what was the judgment and purpose of all the Supreme Council and Leaders of Israel, with only very few exceptions. We bear in mind, that the resolution to sacrifice Christ had for some time been taken. Terrible as the proceedings of that night were, they even seem a sort of concession, as if the Sanhedrists would gladly have found some legal and moral justification for what they had determined to do. They first sought witness, or as Matthew rightly designates it, false witness against Christ. Since this was throughout a private investigation, this witness could only have been sought from their own creatures. Hatred, fanaticism, and unscrupulous Eastern exaggeration would readily misrepresent and distort certain sayings of Christ, or falsely impute others to Him. But it was altogether too hasty and excited a assemblage, and the witnesses contradicted themselves so grossly, or their testimony so notoriously broke down, that for very shame such trumped up charges had to be abandoned. And to this result the majestic calm of Christ's silence must have greatly contributed. On directly false and contradictory testimony it must be best not to cross examine at all, not to interpose, but to leave the false witness to destroy itself.

Abandoning this line of testimony, the Priests next brought forward probably some of their own order, who on the first purging of the Temple had been present when Jesus, in answer to the challenge for a sign in evidence of His authority, had given them that mysterious sign of the destruction and upraising of the Temple of His Body. They had quite misunderstood it at the time, and its reproduction now as the ground of a criminal charge against Jesus must have been directly due to Caiaphas and Annas. We remember, that this had been the first time that Jesus had come into collision, not only with the Temple authorities, but with the greed of the family of Annas. We can imagine how the incensed High Priest would have challenged the conduct of the Temple officials, and how, in reply, he would have been told what they had attempted, and how Jesus had met them. Perhaps it was the only real inquiry which a man like Caiaphas would care to institute about what Jesus said. And here, in its grossly distorted form, and with more than Eastern exaggeration of partisanship it was actually brought forward as a criminal charge!

Dexterously manipulated, the testimony of these witnesses might lead up to two charges. It would show that Christ was a dangerous seducer of the people, Whose claims might have led those who believed them to lay violent hands on the Temple, while the supposed assertion, that He would or was able to build the Temple again within three days, might be made to imply Divine or magical pretensions. A certain class of writers have ridiculed this part of the Sanhedrist plot against Jesus. It is, true, that, viewed as a Jewish charge, it might have been difficult, if not impossible, to construe a capital crime out of such charges, although, to say the least, a strong popular prejudice might thus have been raised against Jesus, and this, no doubt, was one of the objects which Caiaphas had in view. But it has been strangely forgotten that the purpose of the High Priest was not to formulate a capital charge in Jewish Law, since the assembled Sanhedrists had no intention so to try Jesus, but to formulate a charge which would tell before the Roman Procurator. And here none other could be so effective as that of being a fanatical seducer of the ignorant populace, who might lead them on to wild tumultuous acts. Two similar instances, in which the Romans quenched Jewish fanaticism in the blood of the pretenders and their deluded followers, will readily recur to the mind. In any case, Caiaphas would naturally seek to ground his accusation of Jesus before Pilate on anything rather than His claims to Messiahship and the inheritance of David. It would be a cruel irony if a Jewish High Priest had to expose the loftiest and holiest hope of Israel to the mockery of a Pilate; and it might prove a dangerous proceeding, whether as regarded the Roman Governor or the feelings of the Jewish people.

But this charge of being a seducer of the people also broke down, through the disagreement of the two witnesses whom the Mosaic Law required, and who, according to Rabbinic ordinance, had to be separately questioned. But the divergence of their testimony does not exactly appear in the differences in the accounts of Matthew and of Mark. If it be deemed necessary to harmonize these two narratives, it would be better to regard both as relating the testimony of these two witnesses. What Mark reported may have been followed by what Matthew records, or vice versa, the one being, so to speak, the basis of the other. But all this time Jesus preserved the same majestic silence as before, nor could the impatience of Caiaphas, who sprang from his seat to confront, and, if possible, browbeat his Prisoner, extract from Him any reply.

Only one thing now remained. Jesus knew it well, and so did Caiaphas. It was to put the question, which Jesus could not refuse to answer, and which, once answered, must lead either to His acknowledgement or to His condemnation. In the brief historical summary which Luke furnishes, there is an inversion of the sequence of events, by which it might seem as if what he records had taken place at the meeting of the Sanhedrists on the next morning. But a careful consideration of what passed there obliges us to regard the report of Luke as referring to the night meeting described by Matthew and Mark. The motive for Luke's inversion of the sequence of events may have been, that he wished to group in a continuous narrative Peter's threefold denial, the third of which occurred after the night sitting of the Sanhedrin, at which the final adjuration of Caiaphas elicited the reply which Luke records, as well as the other two Evangelists. Be this as it may, we owe to Luke another trait in the drama of that night. As we suppose, the simple question was first addressed to Jesus, whether He was the Messiah? to which He replied by referring to the needlessness of such an enquiry, since they had predetermined not to credit His claims had only a few days before in the Temple refused to discuss them. It was upon this that the High Priest, in the most solemn manner, adjured the True One by the Living God, Whose Son He was, to say it, whether He were the Messiah and Divine, the two being so joined together, not in Jewish belief, but to express the claims of Jesus. No doubt or hesitation could here exist. Solemn, emphatic, calm, majestic, as before had been His silence, was now His speech. And His assertion of what He was, was connected with that of what God would show Him to be, in His Resurrection and Sitting at the Right Hand of the Father, and of what they also would see, when He would come in those clouds of heaven that would break over their city and polity in the final storm of judgment.

They all heard it, and, as the Law directed when blasphemy was spoken, the High Priest rent both his outer and inner garment, with a rent that might never be repaired. But the object was attained. Christ would neither explain, modify, nor retract His claims. They had all heard it; what use was there of witnesses, He had spoken Giddupha, blaspheming. Then, turning to those assembled, he put to them the usual question which preceded the formal sentence of death. As given in the Rabbinical original, it is: What think you gentlemen? And they answered, if for life, "For life!" and if for death, "For death." But the formal sentence of death, which, if it had been a regular meeting of the Sanhedrin, must now have been spoken by the President, was not pronounced.

There is a curious Jewish conceit, that on the Day of Atonement the golden band on the High Priests miter, with the graven words, Holiness to Jehovah, atoned for those who had blasphemed. It stands out in terrible contrast to the figure of Caiaphas on that awful night. Or did the unseen miter on the True and Eternal High Priest's Brow, marking the consecration of His Humiliation to Jehovah, plead for them who in that night were gathered there, the blind leaders of the blind? Yet amid so many most solemn thoughts, some press prominently forward. On that night of terror, when all the hostility of man and the power of hell were unchained, even the falsehood of wickedness could not lay any crime to His charge, nor yet any accusation be brought against him other than the misrepresentation of His symbolic Words. What testimony to Him this solitary false and ill according witness! Again: They all condemned Him to be worthy of death. Judaism itself would not now re-echo this sentence of the Sanhedrists. And yet is it not after all true, that He was either the Christ, the Son of God, or a blasphemer? This Man, alone so calm and majestic among those impassioned false judges and false witnesses; majestic in His silence, majestic in His speech; unmoved by threats to speak, undaunted by threats when He spoke; Who saw it all, the end from the beginning; the Judge among His judges, the Witness before His witnesses: which was He, the Christ or a blaspheming impostor? Let history decide; let the heart and conscience of mankind give answer. If He had been what Israel said, He deserved the death of the Cross; if He is what the Christmas bells of the Church, and the chimes of the Resurrection morning ring out, then do we rightly worship Him as the Son of the Living God, the Christ, the Savior of men.

5. It was after this meeting of the Sanhedrists had broken up, that, as we learn from the Gospel of Luke, the revolting insults and injuries were perpetrated on Him by the guards and servants of Caiaphas. All now rose in combined rebellion against the Perfect Man: the abject servility of the East, which delighted in insults on One Whom it could never have vanquished, and had not even dared to attack; that innate vulgarity, which loves to trample on fallen greatness, and to deck out in its own manner a triumph where no victory has been won; the brutality of the worse than animal in man (since in him it is not under the guidance of Divine instinct), and which, when unchained, seems to intensify in coarseness and ferocity; and the profanity and devilry which are habit to apply the wretched witticisms of what is misnamed common sense and the blows of tyrannical usurping of power to all that is higher and better, to what these men cannot grasp and dare not look up to, and before the shadows of which, when cast by superstition, they cower and tremble in abject fear! And yet these insults, taunts, and blows which fell upon that lonely Sufferer, not defenseless, but undefending, not

vanquished, but uncontending, not helpless, but majestic in voluntary self submission for the highest purpose of love, have not only exhibited the curse of humanity, but also removed it by letting it descend on Him, the Perfect Man, the Christ, the Son of God. And ever since has every noble hearted sufferer been able on the strangely clouded day to look up, and follow what, as it touches earth, is the black misty shadow, to where, illumined by light from behind, it passes into the golden light, a mantle of darkness as it enwraps us, merging in light up there where its folds seem held together by the Hand from heaven.

This is our Sufferer, the Christ or a blasphemer; and in that alternative which of us would not choose the part of the Accused rather than of His judges? So far as recorded, not a word escaped His Lips; not a complaint, nor murmur; nor utterance of indignant rebuke, nor sharp cry of deeply sensitive, pained nature. He was drinking, slowly, with the consciousness of willing self surrender, the Cup which His Father had given Him. And still His Father, and this also especially in His Messianic relationship to man.

We have seen that, when Caiaphas and the Sanhedrists left the audience chamber, Jesus was left to the unrestrained license of the attendants. Even the Jewish Law had it, that no prolonged death (Mithah Arikhta) might be inflicted, and that he who was condemned to death was not to be previously scourged. At last they were weary of insult and smiting, and the Sufferer was left alone, perhaps in the covered gallery, or at one of the windows that overlooked the court below. About one hour had passed since Peter's second denial had, so to speak, been interrupted by the arrival of the Sanhedrists. Since then the excitement of the mock trial, with witnesses coming and going, and, no doubt, in Eastern fashion repeating what had passed to those gathered in the court around the fire; then the departure of the Sanhedrists, and again the insults and blows inflicted on the Sufferer, had diverted attention from Peter. Now it turned once more upon him; and, in the circumstances, naturally more intensely than before. The chattering of Peter, whom conscience and consciousness made nervously talkative, betrayed him. This one also was with Jesus the Nazarene; truly, he was of them, for he was also a Galilean! So spoke the bystanders; while, according to John, a fellow servant and kinsman of that Malchus, whose ear Peter, in his zeal, had cut off in Gethsemane, asserted that he actually recognized him. To one and all these declarations Peter returned only a more vehement denial, accompanying it this time with oaths to God and curses on himself.

The echo of his words had scarcely died out, their inflammation of words had scarcely returned them with gurgling noise upon his conscience, when loud and shrill the second rooster crowing was heard. There was that in its harsh persistence of sound that also awakened his memory. He now remembered the words of warning prediction which Jesus had spoken. He looked up; and as he looked, he saw, how up there, just at that moment; Jesus turned around and looked upon him, yes, in all that assembly, upon Peter! His eyes spoke His Words; much more; they searched down to the innermost depths of Peter's heart, and broke them open. They had pierced through all self delusion, false shame, and fear: they had reached the man, the disciple, the lover of Jesus. Forth they burst, the waters of conviction, of true shame, of heart sorrow, of the agonies of self condemnation; and, bitterly weeping, he rushed from under those suns that had melted the ice of death and burnt into his heart, out from that cursed place of betrayal by Israel, by its High Priest, and even by the representative Disciple.

Out he rushed into the night. Yet a night lit up by the stars of promise, chief among them this, that the Christ up there, the conquering Sufferer, had prayed for him. God grant us in the night of our conscious self condemnation the same star light of His Promises, the same assurance of the intercession of the Christ, that so, as Luther puts it, the particularness of the account of Peter's denial, as compared with the briefness of that of Christ's Passion, may carry to our hearts this lesson: The fruit and use of the sufferings of Christ is this, that in them we have the forgiveness of our sins.

End Notes:

[73] In this argument we lay little stress on the designation, High Priest, which John (ver. 19) gives to the examiner of Christ, although it is noteworthy that he carefully distinguishes between Annas and Caiaphas, marking the latter as the High Priest (vv. 13, 24).

[74] Canon Westcott supposes that the Apostle himself was present in the audience chamber. But, although we readily admit that John went into the house, and was as near as possible to Christ, many reasons suggest themselves why we can scarcely imagine John to have been present, when Caiaphas inquired about the disciples and teaching of Jesus.

[75] Christ proves that He had had no secret doctrine, about which He might be questioned, by three facts: 1. He had spoken parresa without reserve; 2. He had spoken t ksmo to everybody, without confining Himself to a select

audience; 3. He had taught in the most public places, in Synagogue and in the Temple, where all Jews resorted.

[76] The circumstance that Josephus (Ant. 5:2. 1) on the ground of 2 Samuel 4:6 (LXX) speaks of a female porter, and that Rhoda opened the door in the house of the widowed mother of John Mark (Acts 12:13), does not convince me, that in the Palace of the High Priest a female servant regularly discharged that office.

[77] The expression all the council must evidently be taken in a general, not literal sense. No one would believe, for example, that either Nicodemus or Gamaliel was present. I would not, however, attach any great importance to this. The reference to the Elders (in Matthew) is spurious.

[78] The late Dr. Jost (Gesch. d. Judenth. 1: pp. 402-409) designates it a private murder (Privat-Mord), committed by burning enemies, not the sentence of a regularly constituted Sanhedrin. The most prominent men who represented the Law, such as Gamaliel, Jochanan b. Zakkai, and others, were not present.

[79] Various modern writers have of late denied the existence of tribunals of three. But the whole weight of evidence is against them. A number of passages might here be quoted, but the reader may be generally referred to the treatment of the subject in Selden, de Synedriis, 2: c. 5, and especially to Maimonides, Hilkh. Sanh.

[80] In the case of a Mumcheh or admitted authority, even one Judge could in certain civil cases pronounce sentence (Sanh. 2 b; 3 a).

[81] In Jerusalem there were said to have been two such tribunals; one whose locale was at the entrance to the Temple Court, the other at that to the inner or Priest Court.

[82] It is a mistake to identify these with the four shops on the Mount of Olives. They were the Temple shops previously described.

[83] There is truly not a tittle of evidence for the assumption of commentators, that Christ was led from the Palace of Caiaphas into the Council Chamber. The whole proceedings took place in the former, and from it Christ was brought to Pilate (John 16:28).

[84] The ordinary Court hours were from after morning service until the time of the meal (Sabb. 10 a).

[85] In civil cases at least no process was carried on in the months of Nisan and Tishri (comp. Bloch, Civil Process Ordnung).

[86] The details on these points are given in most commentaries. (Comp. the Tractate Sanhedrin and the Gemara on it.) In a capital cause not only would the formal and very solemn warning charge against false testimony

have been addressed to the witnesses, but the latter would be tested by the threefold process known as Chaqiroth, Derishoth, and Bediqoth; the former two referring to questions on the main points, the third or secondary points in the evidence.

[87]   The Pharisaic Law of witness was very peculiar. Witnesses who contradicted each other were not considered in Rabbinic Law as false witnesses, in the sense of being punishable. Nor would they be so, even if an alibi of the accused were proved, only if the alibi of the witnesses themselves were proved (comp. Baehr, Gesetz u. Falsche Zeug., pp. 29).

[88]   Critically also this is of interest. The first purging of the Temple is not related by the Synoptists, but they here confirm John's account of it. On the other hand, John's account of the Temple purgation confirms that of the Temple purgation which John does not relate. And the evidence is the stronger, that the two sets of accounts are manifestly independent of each other, and that of the Fourth Gospel younger than that of the Synoptists.

[89]   At the same time neither this, nor even the later charge of blasphemy, would have made Jesus what was technically called either a Massith, or a Maddiach. The former is described as an individual who privately seduces private individuals into idolatry (Sanh. 5:10; Jeremiah Yeb. 15 d), it being added that he speaks with a loud voice (in praise of some false god) and uses the Holy (Hebrew) language (Jeremiah Sanh. 25 d). On the other hand, the Maddiach is one who publicly seduces the people to idolatry, using, as it is added, the language spoken commonly by the people. The two Talmudic stories, that witnesses had lain in wait to hear and report the utterances of Christ (Sanh. 67 a), and that forty days before His execution heralds had summoned any evidence in His favor (Sanh. 43 a), may be dismissed without comment.

[90]   Besides other movements, we refer here especially to that under Theudas, who led out some 400 persons under promise of dividing Jordan, when both he and his adherents were cut down by the Romans (Jos. Ant. 20:5. 1). At a later time an Egyptian Jew gathered 3,000 or 4,000 on the Mount of Olives, promising to cast down the walls of Jerusalem by the breath of his mouth (u. s. 20:8, 6). Another impostor of that kind was Simon of Cyprus (u. s. 20:7. 2), and Bar Kokhabh.

[91]   There is not any indication in the text that, as Commentators suppose, Christ was at that moment led bound across the Court; nor, that until the morning He was at all removed from near the place where He had been examined.

Chapter 14

The Morning of Good Friday

The pale grey light had passed into that of early morning, when the Sanhedrists once more assembled in the Palace of Caiaphas. A comparison with the terms in which they who had formed the gathering of the previous night are described will convey the impression, that the number of those present was now increased, and that they who now came belonged to the wisest and most influential of the Council. It is not unreasonable to suppose, that some who would not take part in deliberations which were virtually a judicial murder might, once the resolution was taken, feel in Jewish dishonest deception absolved from guilt in advising how the informal sentence might best be carried into effect. It was this, and not the question of Christ's guilt, which formed the subject of deliberation on that early morning. The result of it was to bind Jesus and hand Him over as a criminal to Pilate, with the resolve, if possible, not to frame any definite charge; but, if this became necessary, to lay all the emphasis on the purely political, not the religious aspect of the claims of Jesus.

To us it may seem strange, that they who, in the lowest view of it, had committed so grossly unrighteous, and were now coming on so cruel and bloody a deed, should have been prevented by religious scruples from entering the Praetorium. And yet the student of Jewish dishonest deception will understand it; sadly, history and even common observation furnish only too many parallel instances of unscrupulous scrupulosity and unrighteous conscientiousness. Conscience and religiousness are only moral tendencies natural to man; where they tend, must be decided by considerations outside of them: by enlightenment and truth. The Praetorium, to which the Jewish leaders, or at least those of them who represented the leaders, for neither

Annas nor Caiaphas seems to have been personally present, brought the bound Christ, was (as always in the provinces) the quarters occupied by the Roman Governor. In Caesarea this was the Palace of Herod, and there Paul was afterwards a prisoner. But in Jerusalem there were two such quarters: the fortress Antonia, and the magnificent Palace of Herod at the northwestern angle of the Upper City. Although it is impossible to speak with certainty, the balance of probability is entirely in favor of the view that, when Pilate was in Jerusalem with his wife, he occupied the truly royal residence of Herod, and not the fortified barracks of Antonia. From the slope at the eastern angle, opposite the Temple Mount, where the Palace of Caiaphas stood, up the narrow streets of the Upper City, the sad procession wound to the portals of the grand Palace of Herod. It is recorded, that they who brought Him would not themselves enter the portals of the Palace, that they might not be defiled, but might eat the Passover.

Few expressions have given rise to more earnest controversy than this. On two things at least we can speak with certainty. Entrance into a pagan house did Levitically render impure for that day, that is, until the evening. The fact of such defilement is clearly attested both in the New Testament and in the Mishnah, though its reasons might be various. A person who had so become Levitically unclean was technically called Tebhul Yom (bathed of the day). The other point is, that, to have so become impure for the day, would not have disqualified for eating the Paschal Lamb, since the meal was partaken of after the evening, and when a new day had begun. In fact, it is distinctly laid down that the bathed of the day, that is, he who had been impure for the day and had bathed in the evening, did partake of the Paschal Supper, and an instance is related, when some soldiers who had guarded the gates of Jerusalem immersed, and ate the Paschal Lamb. It follows that those Sanhedrists could not have abstained from entering the Palace of Pilate because by so doing they would have been disqualified for the Paschal Supper.

The point is of importance, because many writers have interpreted the expression the Passover as referring to the Paschal Supper, and have argued that, according to the Fourth Gospel, Jesus did not on the previous evening partake of the Paschal Lamb, or else that in this respect the account of the Fourth Gospel does not accord with that of the Synoptists. But as, for the reason just stated, it is impossible to refer the expression Passover to the Paschal Supper, we have only to inquire whether the term is not also applied to other offerings. And here both the Old Testament and Jewish writings show, that the term Pesach, or Passover, was applied not only to the Paschal Lamb, but to all the Passover sacrifices, especially to what was called the Chagigah, or festive offering (from Chag, or Chagag, to bring the festive sacrifice usual at each of the three Great Feasts). According to the express rule (Chag. 1:3) the Chagigah was brought on the first festive Paschal Day. It was offered immediately after the morning service, and eaten on that day, probably some time before the evening, when, as we shall by and by see, another ceremony claimed public attention. We can therefore quite understand that, not on the eve of the Passover but on the first Paschal day, the Sanhedrists would avoid incurring a defilement which, lasting until the evening, would not only have involved them in the inconvenience of Levitical defilement on the first festive day, but have actually prevented their offering on that day the Passover, festive sacrifice, or Chagigah. For, we have these two express rules: that a person could not in Levitical defilement offer the Chagigah; and that the Chagigah could not be offered for a person by someone else who took his place (Jeremiah Chag. 76 a, lines 16 to 14 from bottom). These considerations and canons seem decisive as regards the views above expressed. There would have been no reason to fear defilement on the morning of the Paschal Sacrifice; but entrance into the Praetorium on the morning of the first Passover day would have rendered it impossible for them to offer the Chagigah, which is also designated by the term Pesach.

It may have been about seven in the morning, probably even earlier, when Pilate went out to those who summoned him to dispense justice. The question which he addressed to them seems to have startled and disconcerted them. Their procedure had been private; it was of the very essence of proceedings at Roman Law that they were in public. Again, the procedure before the Sanhedrists had been in the form of a criminal investigation, while it was of the essence of Roman procedure to enter only on definite accusations. Accordingly, the first question of Pilate was, what accusation they brought against Jesus. The question would come upon them the more unexpectedly, that Pilate must, on the previous evening, have given his consent to the employment of the Roman guard which effected the arrest of Jesus. Their answer displays humiliation, ill humor, and an attempt at evasion. If He had not been a criminal, they would not have delivered Him up! On this vague charge Pilate, in whom we mark throughout a strange reluctance to proceed, perhaps from unwillingness to please the Jews, perhaps from a desire to wound their feelings on the tenderest point, perhaps because restrained by a Higher Hand, refused to proceed. He proposed that the Sanhedrists should try Jesus according to the Jewish Law. This is another important trait, as apparently implying that Pilate had been previously aware both of the peculiar claims of Jesus, and that the action of the Jewish authorities had been determined by envy. But, under ordinary circumstances, Pilate would not have wished to hand over a person accused of so grave a charge as that of setting up Messianic claims to the Jewish authorities, to try the case as a merely religious question. Taking this in connection with the other fact, apparently inconsistent with it, that on the previous evening the Governor had given a Roman guard for the arrest of the prisoner, and with this other fact of the dream and warning of Pilate's wife, a peculiar impression is conveyed to us. We can understand it all, if, on the previous evening, after the Roman guard had been granted, Pilate had spoken of it to his wife, whether because he knew her to be, or because she might be interested in the matter. Tradition has given her the name Procula; while an Apocryphal Gospel describes her as a convert to Judaism; while the Greek Church has actually placed her in the Catalogue of Saints. What if the truth lay between these statements, and Procula had not only been a proselyte, like the wife of a previous Roman Governor, but known about Jesus and spoken of Him to Pilate on that evening? This would best explain his reluctance to condemn Jesus, as well as her dream of Him.

As the Jewish authorities had to decline the Governor's offer to proceed against Jesus before their own tribunal, on the avowed ground that they had not power to pronounce capital sentence, it now compelled them to formulate a capital charge. This is recorded by Luke alone. It was, that Jesus had said, He Himself was Christ a King. It will hide, that in so saying they falsely imputed to Jesus their own political expectations concerning the Messiah. But even this is not all. They prefaced it by this, that He perverted the nation and prohibitted to give tribute to Caesar. The latter charge was so grossly unfounded, that we can only regard it as in their mind a necessary inference from the premise that He claimed to be King. And, as telling most against Him, they put this first and foremost, treating the inference as if it were a fact, a practice this only too common in controversies, political, religious, or private.

This charge of the Sanhedrists explains what, according to all the Evangelists, passed within the Praetorium. We presume that Christ was within, probably in charge of some guards. The words of the Sanhedrists brought peculiar thoughts of Pilate. He now called Jesus and asked Him: You are the King of the Jews? There is that mixture of contempt for all that was Jewish, and of that general cynicism which could not believe in the existence of anything higher, we mark a feeling of awe in regard to Christ, even though the feeling may partly have been of superstition. Out of all that the Sanhedrists had said, Pilate took only this, that Jesus claimed to be a King. Christ, Who had not heard the charge of His accusers, now ignored it, in His desire to stretch out salvation even to a Pilate. Not heeding the implied irony, He first put it to Pilate, whether the question, be it criminal charge or inquiry, was his own, or merely the repetition of what His Jewish accusers had told Pilate of Him. The Governor quickly disowned any personal inquiry. How could he raise any such question? he was not a Jew, and the subject had no general interest. Jesus own nation and its leader had handed Him over as a criminal: what had He done?

The answer of Pilate left nothing else for Him Who, even in that supreme hour, thought only of others, not of Himself. but to bring before the Roman directly that truth for which his words had given the opening. It was not, as Pilate had implied, a Jewish question: it was one of absolute truth; it concerned all men. The Kingdom of Christ was not of this world at all, either Jewish or Gentile. Had it been otherwise, He would have led His followers to a contest for His claims and aims, and not have become a prisoner of the Jews. One word only in all this struck Pilate. So then a King are You! He was incapable of apprehending the higher thought and truth. We mark in his words the same mixture of scoffing and misgiving. Pilate was now in no doubt as to the nature of the Kingdom; his exclamation and question applied to the Kingship. That fact Christ would now emphasize in the glory of His Humiliation. He accepted what Pilate said; He adopted his words. But He added to them an appeal, or rather an explanation of His claims, such as a pagan, and a Pilate, could understand. His Kingdom was not of this world, but of that other world which He had come to reveal, and to open to all believers. Here was the truth! His Birth or Incarnation, as the Sent of the Father, and His own voluntary Coming into this world, for both are referred to in His words, had it for their object to testify of the truth concerning that other world, of which was His Kingdom. This was no Jewish Messianic Kingdom, but one that appealed to all men. And all who had moral affinity to the truth would listen to His testimony, and so come to own Him as King.

But these words struck only a hollow void, as they fell on Pilate. It was not merely cynicism, but utter despair of all that is higher, a moral suicide, which appears in his question: What is truth? He had understood Christ, but it was not in him to respond to His appeal. He, whose heart and life had so little kinship to the truth, could not sympathize with, though he dimly perceived, the grand aim of Jesus' Life and Work. But even the question of Pilate seems an admission, an implied homage to Christ. Assuredly, he would not have so opened his inner being to one of the priestly accusers of Jesus.

That man was no rebel, no criminal! They who brought Him were moved by the lowest passions. And so he told them, as he went out, that he found no fault in Him. Then came from the assembled Sanhedrists a perfect hailstorm of accusations. As we picture it to ourselves, all this while the Christ stood near, perhaps behind Pilate, just within the portals of the Praetorium. And to all this clamor of charges He made no reply. It was as if the surging of the wild waves broke far beneath against the base of the rock, which, untouched, reared its head far aloft to the heavens. But as He stood in the calm silence of Majesty, Pilate greatly wondered. Did this Man not even fear death; was He so conscious of innocence, so infinitely superior to those around and against Him, or had He so far conquered death, that He would not condescend to their words? And why then had He spoken to him of His Kingdom and of that truth?

Gladly would he have withdrawn from it all; not that he was moved for absolute truth or by the personal innocence of the Sufferer, but that there was that in the Christ which, perhaps for the first time in his life, had made him reluctant to be unrighteous and unjust. And so, when, amid these confused cries, he caught the name Galilee as the scene of Jesus labors, he gladly seized on what offered the prospect of devolving the responsibility on another. Jesus was a Galilean, and therefore belonged to the jurisdiction of King Herod. To Herod, therefore, who had come for the Feast to Jerusalem, and there occupied the old Maccabean Palace, close to that of the High Priest, Jesus was now sent.

To Luke alone we owe the account of what passed there, as, of so many traits in this last scene of the terrible drama. The opportunity now offered was welcome to Herod. It was a mark of reconciliation (or might be viewed as such) between himself and the Roman, and in a manner flattering to himself, since the first step had been taken by the Governor, and that, by an almost ostentatious acknowledgement of the rights of the Tetrarch, on which possibly their former feud may have turned. Besides, Herod had long wished to see Jesus, of Whom he had heard so many things. In that hour coarse curiosity, a hope of seeing some magic performances, was the only feeling that moved the Tetrarch. But in vain did he ply Christ with questions. He was as silent to him as formerly against the virulent charges of the Sanhedrists. But a Christ Who would or could do no signs, nor even kindle into the same denunciations as the Baptist, was, to the coarse realism of Antipas, only a helpless figure that might be insulted and scoffed at, as did the Tetrarch and his men of war. And so Jesus was once more sent back to the Praetorium.

It is in the interval during which Jesus was before Herod, or probably soon afterwards, that we place the last weird scene in the life of Judas, recorded by Matthew. We infer this from the circumstance, that, on the return of Jesus from Herod, the Sanhedrists do not seem to have been present, since Pilate had to call them together, presumably from the Temple. And here we recall that the Temple was close to the Maccabean Palace. Lastly, the impression left on our minds is, that from then on the principal part before Pilate was sustained by the people, the Priests and Scribes rather instigating them than conducting the case against Jesus. It may therefore well have been, that, when the Sanhedrists went from the Maccabean Palace into the Temple, as might be expected on that day, only a part of them returned to the Praetorium on the summons of Pilate.

But, however that may have been, sufficient had already passed to convince Judas what the end would be. Indeed, it is difficult to believe that he could have deceived himself on this point from the first, however he had failed to realize the fact in its terrible import until after his deed. The words which Jesus had spoken to him in the Garden must have burnt into his soul. He was among the soldiery that fell back at His look. Since then Jesus had been led bound to Annas, to Caiaphas, to the Praetorium, to Herod. Even if Judas had not been present at any of these occasions, and we do not suppose that his conscience had allowed this, all Jerusalem must by that time have been full of the report, probably in even exaggerated form. One thing he saw: that Jesus was condemned. Judas did not repent in the Scriptural sense; but a change of mind and feeling came over him. Even had Jesus been an ordinary man, and the relation to Him of Judas been the ordinary one, we could understand his feelings, especially considering his ardent temperament. The instant before and after sin represents the difference of feeling as portrayed in the history of the Fall of our first parents. With the commission of sin, all the bewitching, intoxicating influence, which incited to it, has passed away, and only the naked fact remains. All the glamour has been dispelled; all the reality abides. If we knew it, probably scarcely one out of many criminals but would give all he has life itself, if he could recall the deed done, or awake from it to find it only an evil dream. But it cannot be; and the increasingly terrible is, that it is done, and done forever. Yet this is not repentance, or, at least, God alone knows whether it is such; it may be, and in the case of Judas it only was, change of mind and feeling towards Jesus. Whether this might have passed into repentance, whether, if he had cast himself at the Feet of Jesus, as undoubtedly he might have done, this would have been so, we need not here ask. The mind and feelings of Judas, as regarded the deed he had done, and as regarded Jesus, were now quite other; they became increasingly so with ever growing intensity. The road, the streets, the peoples faces, all seemed now to bear witness against him and for Jesus. He read it everywhere; he felt it always; he imagined it, until his whole being was on flame. What had been; what was; what would be! Heaven and earth receded from him; there were voices in the air, and pangs in the soul, and no escape, help, counsel, or hope anywhere.

It was despair, and his a desperate resolve. He must get rid of these thirty pieces of silver, which, like thirty serpents, coiled round his soul with terrible hissing of death. Then at least his deed would have nothing of the selfish in it: only a terrible error, a mistake, to which he had been incited by these Sanhedrists. Back to them with the money, and let them have it again! And so forward he pressed amid the wondering crowd, which would give way before that haggard face with the wild eyes, that crime had made old in those few hours, until he came upon that knot of priests and Sanhedrists, perhaps at that very moment speaking of it all. A most unwelcome sight and intrusion on them, this necessary but odious figure in the drama, belonging to its past, and who should rest in its obscurity. But he would be heard; his words would cast the burden on them to share it with him, as with hoarse cry he broke into this: I have sinned, in that I have betrayed, innocent blood! They turned from him with impatience, in contempt, as so often the seducer turns from the seduced, and, God help such, with the same fiendish guilt of hell: What is that to us? See you to it! And now they were again deep in conversation or consultation. For a moment he stared wildly before him, the very thirty pieces of silver that had been weighed to him, and which he had now brought back, and would gladly have given them, still clutched in his hand. For a moment only, and then he wildly rushed forward, towards the Sanctuary itself, probably to where the Court of Israel bounded on that of the Priests, where generally the penitents stood in waiting, while in the Priests Court the sacrifice was offered for them. He bent forward, and with all his might hurled from him those thirty pieces of silver, so that each resounded as it fell on the marble pavement.

Out he rushed from the Temple, out of Jerusalem, into solitude. Where shall it be? Down into the horrible solitude of the Valley of Hinnom, the

Tophet of old, with its ghastly memories, the Gehenna of the future, with its ghostly associations. But it was not solitude, for it seemed now peopled with figures, faces, sounds. Across the Valley, and up the steep sides of the mountain! We are now on the potters field of Jeremiah, somewhat to the west above where the Kidron and Hinnom valleys merge. It is cold, soft clay soil, where the footsteps slip, or are held in clammy bonds. Here jagged rocks rise perpendicularly: perhaps there was some gnarled, bent, stunted tree. Up there climbed to the top of that rock. Now slowly and deliberately he unwound the long girdle that held his garment. It was the girdle in which he had carried those thirty pieces of silver. He was now quite calm and collected. With that girdle he will hang himself on that tree close by, and when he has fastened it, he will throw himself off from that jagged rock.

It is done; but as, unconscious, not yet dead perhaps, he swung heavily on that branch, under the unusual burden the girdle gave way, or perhaps the knot, which his trembling hands had made, unloosed, and he fell heavily forward among the jagged rocks beneath, and perished in the manner of which Peter reminded his fellow disciples in the days before Pentecost. But in the Temple the priests did not know what to do with these thirty pieces of money. Their unscrupulous scrupulosity came again upon them. It was not lawful to take into the Temple treasury, for the purchase of sacred things, money that had been unlawfully gained. In such cases the Jewish Law provided that the money was to be restored to the donor, and, if he insisted on giving it, that he should be induced to spend it for something for the public use. This explains the apparent discrepancy between the accounts in the Book of Acts and by Matthew. By a fiction of law the money was still considered to be Judas, and to have been applied by him in the purchase of the well known potters field, for the charitable purpose of burying in it strangers. But from then on the old name of potters field, became popularly changed into that of field of blood (Haqal Dema). And yet it was the act of Israel through its leaders: they took the thirty pieces of silver, the price of him that was valued, whom they of the children of Israel did value, and gave them for the potters field! It was all theirs, though they would have gladly made it all Judas: the valuing, the selling, and the purchasing. And the potters field, the very spot on which Jeremiah had been Divinely directed to prophesy against Jerusalem and against Israel: how was it now all fulfilled in the light of the completed sin and apostasy of the people, as prophetically described by Zechariah! This Tophet of Jeremiah, now that they had valued and sold at thirty shekel Israel's Messiah Shepherd, truly a

Tophet, and become a field of blood! Surely, not an accidental coincidence this, that it should be the place of Jeremiah's announcement of judgment: not accidental, but veritably a fulfillment of his prophecy! And so Matthew, targuming this prophecy in form as in its spirit, and in true Jewish manner stringing to it the prophetic description furnished by Zechariah, sets the event before us as the fulfillment of Jeremiah's prophecy.

We are once more outside the Praetorium, to which Pilate had summoned from the Temple Sanhedrists and people. The crowd was momentarily increasing from the town. It was not only to see what was about to happen, but to witness another spectacle, that of the release of a prisoner. For it seems to have been the custom, that at the Passover the Roman Governor released to the Jewish populace some notorious prisoner who lay condemned to death. A very significant custom of release this, for which they now began to clamor. It may have been, that to this also they were incited by the Sanhedrist who mingled among them. For if the stream of popular sympathy might be diverted to Bar Abbas, the doom of Jesus would be the more securely fixed. On the present occasion it might be the more easy to influence the people, since Bar Abbas belonged to that class, not uncommon at the time, which, under the colorable pretence of political aspirations, committed robbery and other crimes. But these movements had deeply struck root in popular sympathy. A strange name and figure, Bar Abbas. That could scarcely have been his real name. It means Son of the Father. Was he a political Anti-Christ? And why, if there had not been some conjunction between them, should Pilate have proposed the alternative of Jesus or Bar Abbas, and not rather that of one of the two criminals who were actually crucified with Jesus?

But when the Governor, hoping to enlist some popular sympathy, put this alternative to them urged it, on the ground that neither he nor yet Herod had found any crime in Him, and would even have appeased their thirst for vengeance by offering to submit Jesus to the cruel punishment of scourging, it was in vain. It was now that Pilate sat down on the judgment seat. But before he could proceed, came that message from his wife about her dream, and the warning entreaty to have nothing to do with that righteous man. An omen such as a dream, and an appeal connected with it, especially in the circumstances of that trial, would powerfully impress a Roman. And for a few moments it seemed as if the appeal to popular feeling on behalf of Jesus might have been successful. But once more the Sanhedrists prevailed. Apparently, all who had been followers of Jesus had been scattered. None of them seem to have been there; and if one or another feeble voice might have been raised for Him, it was hushed in fear of the Sanhedrists. It was Bar Abbas for whom, incited by the priesthood, the populace now clamored with increasing vehemence. To the question, half bitter, half mocking, what they wished him to do with Him Whom their own leaders had in their accusation called King of the Jews, surged back, louder and louder, the terrible cry: Crucify him! That such a cry should have been raised, and raised by Jews, and before the Roman, and against Jesus, are in themselves almost inconceivable facts, to which the history of these eighteen centuries has made terrible echo. In vain Pilate protested, reasoned, appealed. Popular frenzy only grew as it was opposed.

All reasoning having failed, Pilate had recourse to one more expedient, which, under ordinary circumstances, would have been effective. When a Judge, after having declared the innocence of the accused, actually rises from the judgment seat, and by a symbolic act pronounces the execution of the accused a judicial murder, from all participation in which he wishes solemnly to clear himself, surely no jury would persist in demanding sentence of death. But in the present instance there was even more. Although we find allusions to some such custom among the pagan, that which here took place was an essentially Jewish rite, which must have appealed the more forcibly to the Jews that it was done by Pilate. And, not only the rite, but the very words were Jewish. They recall not merely the rite prescribed in Deuteronomy 20:6, etc., to mark the freedom from guilt of the elders of a city where untracked murder had been committed, but the very words of such Old Testament expressions as in 2 Samuel 3:28, and Psalm 25:6, 73:13, and, in later times, in Sus. ver. 46. The Mishnah bears witness that this rite was continued. As administering justice in Israel, Pilate must have been aware of this rite. It does not affect the question, whether or not a judge could, especially in the circumstances recorded, free himself from guilt. Certainly, he could not; but such conduct on the part of a Pilate appears so utterly unusual, as, his whole bearing towards Christ, that we can only account for it by the deep impression which Jesus had made upon him. All the more terrible would be the guilt of Jewish resistance. There is something overawing in Pilate's, See you to it, a reply to the Sanhedrists See you to it, to Judas, and in the same words. It almost seems, as if the scene of mutual imputation of guilt in the Garden of Eden were being reenacted. The Mishnah tells us, that, after the solemn washing of hands of the elders and their disclaimer of guilt, priest responded with this prayer: Forgive it to Your people Israel, whom You have redeemed, O Lord, and lay not innocent blood upon Your people Israel! But here, in answer to

Pilate's words, came back that deep, hoarse cry: His Blood be upon us, and, God help us!, on our children! Some thirty years later, and on that very spot, was judgment pronounced against some of the best in Jerusalem; and among the 3,600 victims of the Governor's fury, of whom not a few were scourged and crucified right over against the Praetorium, were many of the noblest of the citizens of Jerusalem. A few years more, and hundreds of crosses bore Jewish mangled bodies within sight of Jerusalem. And still have these wanderers seemed to bear, from century to century, and from land to land, that burden of blood; and still does it seem to weigh on us and our children.

The Evangelists have passed as rapidly as possible over the last scenes of indignity and horror, and we are too thankful to follow their example. Bar Abbas was at once released. Jesus was handed over to the soldiery to be scourged and crucified, although final and formal judgment had not yet been pronounced. Indeed, Pilate seems to have hoped that the horrors of the scourging might still move the people to desist from the ferocious cry for the Cross. For the same reason we may also hope, that the scourging was not inflicted with the same ferocity as in the case of Christian martyrs, when, with the object of eliciting the incrimination of others, or else recantation, the scourge of leather thongs was loaded with lead, or armed with spikes and bones, which lacerated back, and chest, and face, until the victim sometimes fell down before the judge a bleeding mass of torn flesh. But, however modified, and without repeating the harrowing realism of a Cicero, scourging was the terrible introduction to crucifixion, the intermediate death. Stripped of His clothes, His hands tied and back bent, the Victim would be bound to a column or stake, in front of the Praetorium. The scourging ended, the soldiery would hastily cast upon Him His upper garments, and lead Him back into the Praetorium. Here they called the whole cohort together, and the silent, faint Sufferer became the object of their coarse jesting. From His bleeding Body they tore the clothes, and in mockery arrayed Him in scarlet or purple. For crown they wound together thorns, and for scepter they placed in His Hand a reed. Then alternately, in mock proclamation they hailed Him King, or worshipped Him as God, and smote Him or heaped on Him other indignities.

Such a spectacle might well have disarmed hostility, and forever allayed worldly fears. And so Pilate had hoped, when, at his inviting, Jesus came forth from the Praetorium, arrayed as a mock king, and the Governor presented Him to the populace in words which the Church has ever since treasured: Look, the Man! But, so far from appeasing, the sight only incited to fury the chief priests and their subordinates. This Man before them was the occasion, that on this Paschal Day a pagan dared in Jerusalem itself insult their deepest feeling, mock their most cherished Messianic hopes! Crucify! Crucify! Resounded from all sides. Once more Pilate appealed to them, when, unwittingly and unwillingly, it elicited this from the people, that Jesus had claimed to be the Son of God.

If nothing else, what light it casts on the mode in which Jesus had borne Himself amid those tortures and insults, that this statement of the Jews filled Pilate with fear, and led him to seek again converse with Jesus within the Praetorium. The impression which had been made at the first, and been deepened all along, had now passed into the terror of superstition. His first question to Jesus was, from where He was? And when, as was most fitting, since he could not have understood it, Jesus returned no answer, the feelings of the Romans became only the more intense. Would he not speak; did He not know that he had absolute power to release or to crucify Him? Not absolute power, all power came from above; but the guilt in the abuse of power was far greater on the part of apostate Israel and its leaders, who knew from where power came, and to Whom they were responsible for its exercise.

So spoke not an impostor; so spoke not an ordinary man, after such sufferings and in such circumstances, to one who, from what so ever place derived, had the power of life or death over Him. And Pilate felt it, the more keenly, for his cynicism and disbelief of all that was higher. And the more earnestly did he now seek to release Him. But, proportionately, the louder and fiercer was the cry of the Jews for His Blood, until they threatened to implicate in the charge of rebellion against Caesar the Governor himself, if he persisted in uncharacteristic mercy.

Such danger a Pilate would never encounter. He sat down once more in the judgment seat, outside the Praetorium, in the place called Pavement, and, from its outlook over the City, Gabbatha, the rounded height. So solemn is the transaction that the Evangelist pauses to note once more the day the very hour, when the process had commenced. It had been the Friday in Passover week, and between six and seven in the morning. And at the close Pilate once more in mockery presented to them Jesus: Look, your King! Once more they called for His Crucifixion, and, when again challenged, the chief priests burst into the cry, which preceded Pilate's final sentence, to be now executed: We have no king but Caesar!

With this cry Judaism was, in the person of its representatives, guilty of denial of God, of blasphemy, of apostasy. It committed suicide; and, ever since, has its dead body been carried in show from land to land, and from century to century: to be dead, and to remain dead, until He comes a second time, Who is the Resurrection and the Life!

End Notes:

[92]   The Palace of Herod undoubtedly became (as all royal residences) the property of the State, and as we have distinct evidence that Roman Procurators resided there, and took their seat in front of that Palace on a raised pavement to pronounce judgment (Jos. War 2:14. 8; comp. Philo, ad Caj. S: 38), the inference is obvious, that Pilate, especially as he was accompanied by his wife, resided there also.

[93]   The apparently strange statement, John 16:32, affords another undesigned confirmation of the Jewish authorship of the Fourth Gospel. It seems to imply, that the Sanhedrin might have found a mode of putting Jesus to death in the same informal manner in which Stephen was killed and they sought to destroy Paul. The Jewish law recognized a form of procedure, or rather a lack of procedure, when a person caught in flagrante delicto of blasphemy might be done to death without further inquiry.

[94]   It is impossible to say, whether the gorgeous apparel in which Herod arrayed Christ was purple, or white. Certainly it was not, as Bishop Haneberg suggests (Relig. Alterth. p. 554), an old high priestly garment of the Maccabees.

[95]   The verb designating Scriptural repentance is metanoo; that here used is metamlomai, as in Matthew 20:29, as in Matthew 20:29, 32; 2 Corinthians 5:8; Hebrews 5:21.

[96]   The expression nas is always used in the N.T. of the Sanctuary itself, and not of the outer courts; but it would include the Court of the Priests, where the sacrifices were offered.

[97]   There was no idea that his death would expiate for his sin. No such idea attached to suicide among the Jews.

[98]   According to the better reading of Mark 15:8 the multitude was going up.

[99]   How can they who regard the Johannine account as implying that Christ was crucified on the morning before the Passover, explain the words of John, You have a custom, that I should release to you one at the Passover?

[100]   The Sagum, or short woolen military cloak, scarlet or purple (the two colors are often confounded, comp. Wetstein ad loc.), fastened by a clasp on the right shoulder. It was also worn by Roman generals, and sometimes (in more costly form and material) presented to foreign kings.

[101] Origen already marks in this a notable breach of military discipline. Keim (Jesu von Naz. 3:2, pp. 393, etc.) gives a terribly graphic and realistic account of the whole scene. The soldiers were, as mostly in the provinces, chiefly provincials, in this case, probably Syrians. They were all the more bitterly hostile to the Jews (Jos. Ant. 19:9. 1; War 2:12, 1. 2; 5:11, 1, there also derision at execution). A strange illustration of the scene is afforded by what happened only a few years afterwards at Alexandria, when the people in derision of King Agrippa I, arrayed a well known maniac (Karabas) in a common door mat, put a papyrus crown on his head, and a reed in his hand, and saluted him Maris, lord (Philo, In Flacc. ed. Mang. 2:522; Wetstein, N.T, 1: p. 535). On all the classical illustrations and corroborations of the whole proceedings in every detail, the reader should consult Wetstein, ad loc.

[102] Gabbath or Gabbetha means a rounded height. It occurs also as the name of a town (Jeremiah Taan. 69 b).

[103] The hour (about the sixth) could only refer to when the process was taken in hand.

Chapter 15

Crucifixion and Burial

It matters little as regards their guilt, whether, pressing the language of John, we are to understand that Pilate delivered Jesus to the Jews to be crucified, or, as we rather infer, to his own soldiers. This was the common practice, and it accords both with the Governor's former taunt to the Jews, and with the after notice of the Synoptists. They, to whom He was delivered, led Him away to be crucified: and they who so led Him forth compelled the Cyrenian Simon to bear the Cross. We can scarcely imagine, that the Jews, still less the Sanhedrists, would have done this. But whether formally or not, the terrible crime of slaying, with wicked hands, their Messiah King rests, sadly, on Israel.

Once more was He unrobed and robed. The purple robe was torn from His Wounded Body, the crown of thorns from His Bleeding Brow. Arrayed again in His own, now blood stained, garments, He was led forth to execution. Only about two hours and a half had passed since the time that He had first stood before Pilate (about 6:30 AM), when the sad procession reached Golgotha (at 9 AM). In Rome an interval, ordinarily of two days, intervened between a sentence and its execution; but the rule does not seem to have applied to the provinces, if, in this case the formal rules of Roman procedure were at all observed.

The terrible preparations were soon made: the hammer, the nails, the Cross, the very food for the soldiers who were to watch under each Cross. Four soldiers would be detailed for each Cross, the whole being under the command of a centurion. As always, the Cross was borne to the execution by Him Who was to suffer on it, perhaps His Arms bound to it with cords. But there is happily no evidence, rather, every indication to the contrary, that, according to ancient custom, the neck of the Sufferer was fastened within the patibulum, two horizontal pieces of wood, fastened at the end, to which the hands were bound. Ordinarily, the procession was headed by the centurion, or rather, preceded by one who proclaimed the nature of the crime, and carried a white, wooden board, on which it was written. Commonly, also, it took the longest road to the place of execution, and through the most crowded streets, so as to attract most public attention. But we would suggest, that this long circuit and the proclamation of the herald were, in the present instance, dispensed with. They are not hinted at in the text, and seem incongruous to the festive season, and the other circumstances of the history.

Discarding all later legendary embellishments, as only disturbing, we shall try to realize the scene as described in the Gospels. Under the leadership of the centurion, whether or not attended by one who bore the board with the inscription, or only surrounded by the four soldiers, of whom one might carry this tablet, Jesus came forth bearing His Cross. He was followed by two criminals—robbers, probably of the class then so numerous, that covered its crimes by pretensions of political motives. These two, also, would bear each his cross, and probably be attended each by four soldiers. Crucifixion was not a Jewish mode of punishment, although the Maccabee King Jannaeus had so far forgotten the claims of both humanity and religion as on one occasion to crucify not less than 800 persons in Jerusalem itself. But even Herod, with all cruelty, did not resort to this mode of execution. Nor was it employed by the Romans until after the time of Caesar, when, with the fast increasing cruelty of punishments, it became fearfully common in the provinces. Especially does it seem to characterize the domination of Rome in Judea under every Governor. During the last siege of Jerusalem hundreds of crosses daily arose, until there seemed not sufficient room nor wood for them, and the soldiery diversified their horrible amusement by new modes of crucifixion. So did the Jewish appeal to Rome for the Crucifixion of Israel's King come back in hundredfold echoes. But, better than such retribution, the Cross of the God Man has put an end to the punishment of the cross, and instead, made the Cross the symbol of humanity, civilization, progress, peace, and love.

As mostly all abominations of the ancient world, whether in religion or life, crucifixion was of Phoenician origin, although Rome adopted, and improved on it. The modes of execution among the Jews were: strangulation, beheading, burning, and stoning. In all ordinary circumstances the Rabbis were most reluctant to pronounce sentence of death. This appears even from the injunction that the Judges were to fast on the day of such a sentence. Two of the leading Rabbis record it, that no such sentence would ever have been pronounced in a Sanhedrin of which they had been members. The indignity of hanging, and this only after the criminal had been otherwise executed, was reserved for the crimes of idolatry and blasphemy. The place where criminals were stoned (Beth haSeqilah) was on an elevation about eleven feet high, from which the criminal was thrown down by the first witness. If he had not died by the fall, the second witness would throw a large stone on his heart as he lay. If not yet lifeless, the whole people would stone him. At a distance of six feet from the place of execution the criminal was undressed, only the covering absolutely necessary for decency being left. In the case of Jesus we have reason to think that, while the mode of punishment to which He was subjected was un-Jewish, every concession would be made to Jewish custom, and therefore we thankfully believe that on the Cross He was spared the indignity of exposure. Such would have been truly un-Jewish.

Three kinds of Cross were in use: the so called Andrews Cross (x, the Crux decussata), the Cross in the form of a T (Crux Commissa), and the ordinary Latin Cross (+, Crux immissa). We believe that Jesus bore the last of these. This would also most readily admit of affixing the board with the threefold inscription, which we know His Cross bore. Besides, the universal testimony of those who lived nearest the time (Justin Martyr, Irenaeus, and others), and who, unfortunately had only too much occasion to learn what crucifixion meant, is in favor of this view. This Cross, as John expressly states, Jesus Himself bore at the outset. And so the procession moved on towards Golgotha. Not only the location, but even the name of that which appeals so strongly to every Christian heart, is matter of controversy. The name cannot have been derived from the skulls which lay about, since such exposure would have been unlawful, and therefore must have been due to the skull-like shape and appearance of the place. Accordingly, the name is commonly explained as the Greek form of the Aramaic Gulgalta, or the Hebrew Gulgoleth, which means a skull.

Such a description would fully correspond, not only to the requirements of the narrative, but to the appearance of the place which, so far as we can judge, represents Golgotha. We cannot here explain the various reasons for which the traditional site must be abandoned. Certain it is, that Golgotha was outside the gate, and near the City. In all likelihood it was the usual place of execution. Lastly, we know that it was situated near gardens, where there were tombs, and close to the highway. The three last conditions point to the north of Jerusalem. It must be remembered that the third wall, which afterwards surrounded Jerusalem, was not built until several years after the Crucifixion. The new suburb of Bezetha extended at that time outside the second wall. Here the great highway passed northwards; close by, were villas and gardens; and here also rock hewn tombs have been discovered, which date from that period. But this is not all. The present Damascus Gate in the north of the city seems, in most ancient tradition, to have borne the name of Stephen's Gate, because the Proto Martyr was believed to have passed through it to his stoning. Close by, then, must have been the place of execution. And at least one Jewish tradition fixes upon this very spot, close by what is known as the Grotto of Jeremiah, as the ancient place of stoning (Beth haSeqilah). And the description of the locality answers all requirements. It is a weird, dreary place, two or three minutes aside from the high road, with a high, rounded, skull-like rocky plateau, and a sudden depression or hollow beneath, as if the jaws of the skull had opened. Whether or not the tomb of the Herodian period in the rocky knoll to the west of Jeremiah's Grotto was the most sacred spot upon earth, the Sepulcher in the Garden, we dare not positively assert, though every probability attaches to it.

To there, then, did that sad procession wind, between 8 and 9 AM on that Friday in Passover week. From the ancient Palace of Herod it descended, and probably passed through the gate in the first wall, and so into the busy quarter of Acra. As it proceeded, the numbers who followed from the Temple, from the dense business quarter through which it moved, increased. Shops, bazaars, and markets were, closed on the holy feast day. But quite a crowd of people would come out to line the streets and to follow; and, especially, women, leaving their festive preparations, raised loud laments, not in spiritual recognition of Christ's claims, but in pity and sympathy. And who could have looked unmoved on such a spectacle, unless fanatical hatred had burnt out of his bosom all that was human? Since the Paschal Supper Jesus had not tasted either food or drink. After the deep emotion of that Feast, with all of holiest institution which it included; after the anticipated betrayal of Judas, and after the farewell to His disciples, He had passed into Gethsemane. There for hours, alone, since His nearest disciples could not watch with Him even one hour, the deep waters had rolled up to His soul. He had drunk of them, immersed, almost perished in them. There had he agonized in mortal conflict, until the great drops of blood forced themselves on His Brow. There had He been delivered up, while they all had fled. To Annas, to Caiaphas, to Pilate, to Herod, and again to Pilate; from indignity to indignity, from torture to torture, had He been hurried all that livelong night, all that morning. All throughout He had borne Himself with a Divine Majesty, which had awakened the deeper feelings of Pilate and the infuriated hatred of the Jews. But if His Divinity gave its true meaning to His Humanity, that Humanity gave its true meaning to His voluntary Sacrifice. So, far, then, from seeking to hide its manifestations, the Evangelists, not indeed needlessly but unhesitatingly, put them forward. Unrefreshed by food or sleep, after the terrible events of that night and morning, while His pallid Face bore the blood marks from the crown of thorns, His mangled Body was unable to bear the weight of the Cross. No wonder the pity of the women of Jerusalem was stirred. But ours is not pity, it is worship at the sight. For, underlying His Human Weakness was the Divine Strength which led Him to this voluntary self surrender and self examination. It was the Divine strength of His pity and love which issued in His Human weakness.

Up to that last Gate which led from the Suburb towards the place of execution did Jesus bear His Cross. Then, as we infer, His strength gave way under it. A man was coming from the opposite direction, one from that large colony of Jews which, as we know, had settled in Cyrene. He would be especially noticed; for, few would at that hour, on the festive day, come out of the country, although such was not contrary to the Law. So much has been made of this, that it ought to be distinctly known that traveling, which was forbidden on Sabbaths, was not prohibited on feast days. Besides, the place from which he came, perhaps his home, might have been within the ecclesiastical boundary of Jerusalem. At any rate, he seems to have been well known, at least afterwards, in the Church, and his sons Alexander and Rufus even better than he. Thus much only can we say with certainty; to identify them with persons of the same name mentioned in other parts of the New Testament can only be matter of speculation. But we can scarcely repress the thought that Simon the Cyrenian had not before that day been a disciple; had only learned to follow Christ, when, on that day, as he came in by the Gate, the soldiery laid hold on him, and against his will forced him to bear the Cross after Christ. Yet another indication of the need of such help comes to us from Mark, who uses an expression which conveys, though not necessarily that Jesus had to be borne, yet that He had to be supported to Golgotha from the place where they met Simon.

Here, where, if Jesus did not actually sink under His burden, it yet required to be transferred to the Cyrenian, while Himself from then on needed bodily support, we place the next incident in this history. While the

Cross was laid on the unwilling Simon, the women who had followed with the populace closed around the Sufferer, raising their lamentations. At His Entrance into Jerusalem, Jesus had wept over the daughters of Jerusalem; as He left it for the last time, they wept over Him. But far different were the reasons for His tears from theirs of mere pity. And, if proof were required of His Divine strength, even in the utmost depth of His Human weakness, how, conquered, He was Conqueror, it would surely be found in the words in which He called them turn their thoughts of pity where pity would be called for, even to themselves and their children in the near judgment upon Jerusalem. The time would come, when the Old Testament curse of barrenness would be coveted as a blessing. To show the fulfillment of this prophetic lament of Jesus, it is not necessary to recall the harrowing details recorded by Josephus, when a frenzied mother roasted her own child, and in the mockery of desperateness reserved the half of the horrible meal for those murderers who daily broke in upon her to rob her of what scanty food had been left her; nor yet other of those incidents, too revolting for needless repetition, which the historian of the last siege of Jerusalem chronicles. But how often, these many centuries, must Israel's women have felt that terrible longing for childlessness, and how often must the prayer of despair for the quick death of falling mountains and burying hills rather than prolonged torture have risen to the lips of Israel's sufferers! And yet, even so, these words were also prophetic of a still more terrible future! For, if Israel had put such flame to its green tree how terribly would the Divine judgment burn among the dry wood of an apostate and rebellious people, that had so delivered up its Divine King, and pronounced sentence upon itself by pronouncing it upon Him!

And yet natural, and, in some respects, genuine, as were the tears of the daughters of Jerusalem, mere sympathy with Christ almost involves guilt, since it implies a view of Him which is essentially the opposite of that which His claims demand. These tears were the emblem of that modern sentiment about the Christ which, in its effusiveness, offers insult rather than homage, and implies rejection rather than acknowledgment of Him. We shrink with horror from the assumption of a higher standpoint, implied in so much of the modern so called criticism about the Christ. But even beyond this, all mere sentimentalism is here the outcome of unconsciousness of our real condition. When a sense of sin has been awakened in us, we shall mourn, not for what Christ has suffered, but for what He suffered for us. The effusiveness of mere sentiment is impertinence or folly: impertinence, if He was the Son of God; folly, if He was merely Man. And, even from quite another point of view, there is here a lesson to learn. It is the peculiarity of Roman Catholicism ever to present the Christ in His Human weakness. It is that of an extreme section on the opposite side, to view Him only in His Divinity. Be it ours ever to keep before us, and to worship as we remember it, that the Christ is the Savior God Man.

It was 9 AM when the sad procession reached Golgotha, and the yet more sad preparations for the Crucifixion commenced. Avowedly, the punishment was invented to make death as painful and as lingering as the power of human endurance. First, the upright wood was planted in the ground. It was not high, and probably the Feet of the Sufferer were not above one or two feet from the ground. Thus could the communication described in the Gospels take place between Him and others; thus, also, might His Sacred Lips be moistened with the sponge attached to a short stalk of hyssop. Next, the transverse wood (antenna) was placed on the ground, and the Sufferer laid on it, when His Arms were extended, drawn up, and bound to it. Then (this not in Egypt, but in Carthage and in Rome) a strong, sharp nail was driven, first into the Right, then into the Left Hand (the clavi trabales). Next, the Sufferer was drawn up by means of ropes, perhaps ladders; the transverse either bound or nailed to the upright, and a rest or support for the Body (the cornu or sedile) fastened on it. Lastly, the Feet were extended, and either one nail hammered into each, or a larger piece of iron through the two. We have already expressed our belief that the indignity of exposure was not offered at such a Jewish execution. And so might the crucified hang for hours, even days, in the unutterable anguish of suffering, until consciousness at last failed.

It was a merciful Jewish practice to give to those led to execution a drink of strong wine mixed with myrrh so as to deaden consciousness. This charitable office was performed at the cost of, if not by, an association of women in Jerusalem. That drink was offered to Jesus when He reached Golgatha. But having tasted it, and ascertained its character and object, He would not drink it. It was like His former refusal of the pity of the daughters of Jerusalem. No man could take His Life from Him; He had power to lay it down, and to take it up again. Nor would He here yield to the ordinary weakness of our human nature; nor suffer and die as if it had been a necessity, not a voluntary self surrender. He would meet death, even in his sternest and fiercest mood, and conquer by submitting to the full. A lesson this also, though one difficult, to the Christian sufferer.

And so was He nailed to His Cross, which was placed between, probably somewhat higher than, those of the two criminals crucified with Him. One thing only still remained: to affix to His Cross the so called title (titulus), on which was inscribed the charge on which He had been condemned. As already stated, it was customary to carry this board before the prisoner, and there is no reason for supposing any exception in this respect. Indeed, it seems implied in the circumstance, that the title had evidently been drawn up under the direction of Pilate. It was, as might have been expected, and yet most significantly, trilingual: in Latin, Greek, and Aramaic. We imagine, that it was written in that order, and that the words were those recorded by the Evangelists (excepting Luke, who seems to give a modification of the original, or Aramaic, text). The inscription given by Matthew exactly corresponds with that which Eusebius records as the Latin titulus on the cross of one of the early martyrs. We therefore conclude, that it represents the Latin words. Again, it seems only natural, that the fullest, and to the Jews most offensive, description should have been in Aramaic, which all could read. Very significantly this is given by John. It follows, that the inscription given by Mark must represent that in Greek. Although much less comprehensive, it had the same number of words, and precisely the same number of letters, as that in Aramaic, given by John.

It seems probable, that the Sanhedrists had heard from someone, who had watched the procession on its way to Golgotha, of the inscription which Pilate had written on the titulus, partly to avenge himself on, and partly to deride, the Jews. It is not likely that they would have asked Pilate to take it down after it had been affixed to the Cross; and it seems scarcely credible, that they would have waited outside the Praetorium until the sad procession commenced its march. We suppose that, after the condemnation of Jesus, the Sanhedrists had gone from the Praetorium into the Temple, to take part in its services. When informed of the offensive tablet, they hurried once more to the Praetorium, to induce Pilate not to allow it to be put up. This explains the inversion in the order of the account in the Gospel of John, or rather, its location in that narrative in immediate connection with the notice, that the Sanhedrists were afraid the Jews who passed by might be influenced by the inscription. We imagine, that the Sanhedrists had originally no intention of doing anything so un-Jewish as not only to gaze at the sufferings of the Crucified, but to even deride Him in His Agony, that, in fact, they had not intended going to Golgotha at all. But when they found that Pilate would not yield to their objections, some of them hurried to the place of Crucifixion, and, mingling with the crowd, sought to incite their jeers, so as to prevent any deeper impression which the significant words of the inscription might have produced.

Before nailing Him to the Cross, the soldiers parted among them the poor worldly inheritance of His clothing. On this point there are slight seeming differences between the notices of the Synoptists and the more detailed account of the Fourth Gospel. Such differences, if real, would afford only fresh evidence of the general trustworthiness of the narrative. For, we bear in mind that, of all the disciples, only John witnessed the last scenes, and that therefore the other accounts of it circulating in the early Church must have been derived, so to speak, from second sources. This explains, why perhaps the largest number of seeming discrepancies in the Gospels occurs in the narrative of the closing hours in the Life of Christ, and how, contrary to what otherwise we might have expected, the most detailed as well as precise account of them comes to us from John. In the present instance these slight seeming differences may be explained in the following manner. There was, as John states, first a division into four parts, one to each of the soldiers, of such garments of the Lord as were of nearly the same value. The head gear, the outer cloak like garment, the girdle, and the sandals, would differ little in cost. But the question, which of them was to belong to each of the soldiers, would naturally be decided, as the Synoptists inform us, by lot.

But, besides these four articles of dress, there was the seamless woven inner garment, by far the most valuable of all, and for which, as it could not be partitioned without being destroyed, they would especially cast lots (as John reports). Nothing in this world can be accidental, since God is not far from any of us. But in the History of the Christ the Divine purpose, which forms the subject of all prophecy, must have been constantly realized; this must have forced itself on the mind of the observer, and the more irresistibly when, as in the present instance, the outward circumstances were in such sharp contrast to the higher reality. To John, the loving and loved disciple, greater contrast could scarcely exist than between this rough partition by lot among the soldiery, and the character and claims of Him Whose garments they were thus apportioning, as if He had been a helpless Victim in their hands. Only one explanation could here suggest itself: that there was a special Divine meaning in the permission of such an event, that it was in fulfillment of ancient prophecy. As he gazed on the terrible scene, the words of the Psalm which portrayed the desertion, the sufferings, and the contempt even to death of the Servant of the Lord, stood out in the red light of the Sun setting in Blood. They flashed upon his mind, for the first time he understood them; and the flames which played around the Sufferer were seen to be the sacrificial fire that consumed the Sacrifice which He offered. That this quotation is made in the Fourth Gospel alone, proves that its writer was an eyewitness; that it was made in the Fourth Gospel at all, that he was a Jew, deeply imbued with Jewish modes of religious thinking. And the evidence of both is the stronger, as we recall the comparative rareness, and the peculiarly Judaic character of the Old Testament quotations in the Fourth Gospel.

It was when they thus nailed Him to the Cross, and parted His clothing, that He spoke the first of the so called Seven Words: Father, forgive them, for they do not know what they do. Even the reference in this prayer to what they do (not in the past, nor future) points to the soldiers as the primary, though certainly not the sole object of Jesus' prayer. But higher thoughts also come to us. In the moment of the deepest abasement of Christ's Human Nature, the Divine bursts forth most brightly. It is, as if Jesus would discard all that is merely human in His Sufferings, just as before He had discarded the Cup of stupefying wine. These soldiers were but the unconscious instruments: the form was nothing; the contest was between the Kingdom of God and that of darkness, between the Christ and Satan, and these sufferings were but the necessary path of obedience, and to victory and glory. When He is most human (in the moment of His being nailed to the Cross), then is He most Divine, in the utter discarding of the human elements of human instrumentality and of human suffering. Then also in the utter self forgetfulness of the God Man, which is one of the aspects of the Incarnation, does He only remember Divine mercy, and pray for them who crucify Him; and thus also does the Conquered truly conquer His conquerors by asking for them what their deed had forfeited. And lastly, in this, that the first and the last of His Utterances begin with Father, does He show by the unbrokenness of His faith and fellowship the real spiritual victory which He has won. And He has won it, not only for the martyrs, who have learned from Him to pray as He did, but for everyone who, in the midst of all that seems most opposed to it, can rise, beyond mere forgetfulness of what is around, to realizing faith and fellowship with God as the Father, who through the dark curtain of cloud can discern the bright sky, and can feel the unshaken confidence, if not the unbroken joy, of absolute trust.

This was His first Utterance on the Cross, as regarded them; as regarded Himself; and as regarded God. So, surely, suffered not Man. Has this prayer of Christ been answered? We dare not doubt it; we perceive it in some measure in those drops of blessing which have fallen upon pagan men, and have left to Israel also, even in its ignorance, a remnant according to the election of grace.

And now began the real agonies of the Cross, physical, mental, and spiritual. It was the weary, unrelieved waiting, as thickening darkness gradually gathered around. Before sitting down to their sad watch over the Crucified, the soldiers would refresh themselves, after their exertion in nailing Jesus to the Cross, lifting it up, and fixing it, by drinks of the cheap wine of the country. As they drank it heartily, they drank to Him in their coarse brutality, and mockingly came to Him, asking Him to pledge them in response. Their jests were, chiefly directed not against Jesus personally, but in His Representative capacity, and so against the hated, despised Jews, whose King they now derisively challenged to save Himself. Yet even so, it seems to us of deepest significance, that He was so treated and derided in His Representative Capacity and as the King of the Jews. It is the undesigned testimony of history, as regarded the character of Jesus and the future of Israel. But what from almost any point of view we find so difficult to understand is, the unutterable abasement of the Leaders of Israel, their moral suicide as regarded Israel's hope and spiritual existence. There, on that Cross, hung He, Who at least embodied that grand hope of the nation; Who, even on their own showing, suffered to the extreme for that idea, and yet renounced it not, but clung fast to it in unshaken confidence; One, to Whose Life or even Teaching no objection could be offered, save that of this grand idea. And yet, when it came to them in the lewd mockery of this pagan soldiery, it evoked no other or higher thoughts in them; and they had the indescribable baseness of joining in the jeer at Israel's great hope, and of leading the popular chorus in it!

For, we cannot doubt, that, perhaps also by way of turning aside the point of the jeer from Israel, they took it up, and tried to direct it against Jesus; and that they led the ignorant mob in the piteous attempts at derision. And did none of those who so reviled Him in all the chief aspects of His Work feel, that, as Judas had sold the Master for nothing and committed suicide, so they were doing in regard to their Messianic hope? For, their jeers cast contempt on the four great facts in the Life and Work of Jesus, which were also the underlying ideas of the Messianic Kingdom: the new relationship to Israel's religion and the Temple (You that destroy the Temple, and build it in three days); the new relationship to the Father through the Messiah, the Son of God (if You are the Son of God); the new all sufficient help brought to body and soul in salvation (He saved others); and, finally, the new relationship to Israel in the fulfillment and perfecting of its Mission through its King (if He is the King of Israel). On all these, the taunting challenge of the Sanhedrists, to come down from the Cross, and save Himself, if he would claim the allegiance of their faith, cast what Matthew and Mark characterize as the blaspheming of doubt. We compare with theirs the account of Luke and John. That of Luke reads like the report of what had passed, given by one who throughout had been quite close by, perhaps taken part in the Crucifixion, one might almost venture to suggest, that it had been furnished by the Centurion. The narrative of John reads markedly like that of an eyewitness, and he a Judean. And as we compare both the general Judean cast and Old Testament quotations in this with the other parts of the Fourth Gospel, we feel as if (as so often), under the influence of the strongest emotions, the later development and peculiar thinking of so many years afterwards had for the time been effaced from the mind of John, or rather given place to the Jewish modes of conception and speech, familiar to him in earlier days. Lastly, the account of Matthew seems as if written from the priestly point of view, as if it had been furnished by one of the Priests or Sanhedrist party, present at the time.

Yet other inferences come to us. First, there is a remarkable relationship between what Luke quotes as spoken by the soldiers: If You are the King of the Jews, save Yourself, and the report of the words in Matthew: He saved others, Himself He cannot save. He is the King of Israel! Let Him now come down from the Cross, and we will believe on Him! These are the words of the Sanhedrists, and they seem to respond to those of the soldiers, as reported by Luke, and to carry them further. The if of the soldiers: If You are the King of the Jews, now becomes a direct blasphemous challenge. As we think of it, they seem to re-echo, and now with the laughter of hellish triumph, the former Jewish challenge for an outward, infallible sign to demonstrate His Messiahship. But they also take up, and re-echo, what Satan had set before Jesus in the Temptation of the wilderness. At the beginning of His Work, the Tempter had suggested that the Christ should achieve absolute victory by an act of presumptuous self assertion, utterly opposed to the spirit of the Christ, but which Satan represented as an act of trust in God, such as He would assuredly own. And now, at the close of His Messianic Work, the Tempter suggested, in the challenge of the Sanhedrists, that Jesus had suffered absolute defeat, and that God had publicly disowned the trust which the Christ had put in Him. He trusts in God: let Him deliver Him now, if He will have Him. Here, as in the Temptation of the Wilderness, the words misapplied were those of Scripture, in the present instance those of Psalm 22:8.

And the quotation, as made by the Sanhedrists, is the more remarkable, that, contrary to what is generally asserted by writers, this Psalm was Messianically applied by the ancient Synagogue. More especially was this verse, which precedes the mocking quotation of the Sanhedrists, expressly applied to the sufferings and the derision which Messiah was to undergo from His enemies: All they that see Me laugh Me to scorn: they shoot out the lip, they shake the head.

The derision of the Sanhedrists under the Cross was, as previously stated, not entirely spontaneous, but had a special motive. The place of Crucifixion was close to the great road which led from the North to Jerusalem. On that Feast day, when, as there was no law to limit, as on the weekly day of rest, locomotion to a Sabbath day's journey, many would pass in and out of the City, and the crowd would naturally be arrested by the spectacle of the three Crosses. Equally naturally would they have been impressed by the titulus over the Cross of Christ. The words, describing the Sufferer as the King of the Jews, might, when taken in connection with what was known of Jesus, have raised most dangerous questions. And this the presence of the Sanhedrists was intended to prevent, by turning the popular mind in a totally different direction. It was just such a taunt and argumentation as would appeal to that coarse realism of the common people, which is too often misnamed common sense. Luke significantly ascribes the derision of Jesus only to the Rulers, and we repeat, that that of the passers by, recorded by Matthew and Mark, was excited by them. Thus here also the main guilt rested on the leaders of the people.

One other trait comes to us from Luke, confirming our impression that his account was derived from one who had stood quite close to the Cross, probably taken official part in the Crucifixion. Matthew and Mark merely remark in general, that the derision of the Sanhedrists and people was joined in by the thieves on the Cross. A trait this, which we feel to not be only psychologically true, but the more likely of occurrence, that any sympathy or possible alleviation of their sufferings might best be secured by joining in the scorn of the leaders, and concentrating popular indignation upon Jesus. But Luke also records a vital difference between the two robbers on the Cross. The impenitent thief takes up the jeer of the Sanhedrists: Are You not the Christ? Save Yourself and us! The words are the more significant, in their bearing on the majestic calm and pitying love of the Savior on the Cross, and on the utterance of the penitent thief, that, strange as it may sound, it seems to have been a terrible phenomenon, noted by historians, that those on the cross were habit to utter insults and imprecations on the onlookers, goaded nature perhaps seeking relief in such outbursts. Not so when the heart was touched in true repentance.

If a more close study of the words of the penitent thief may seem to diminish the fullness of meaning which the traditional view attaches to them, they gain all the more as we perceive their historic reality. His first words were of reproof to his comrade. In that terrible hour, amid the tortures of a slow death, did not the fear of God creep over him, at least so far as to prevent his joining in the vile jeers of those who insulted the dying agonies of the Sufferer? And this all the more, in the peculiar circumstances. They were all three sufferers; but they two justly, while He Whom he insulted had done nothing amiss. From this basis of fact, the penitent rapidly rose to the height of faith. This is not uncommon, when a mind is learning the lessons of truth in the school of grace. Only, it stands out here the more sharply, because of the dark background against which it is traced in such broad and brightly shining outlines. The hour of the deepest abasement of the Christ was, as all the moments of His greatest Humiliation, to be marked by a manifestation of His Glory and Divine Character, as it were, by God's testimony to Him in history, if not by the Voice of God from heaven. And, as regarded the penitent himself, we notice the progression in his soul. No one could have been ignorant, least of all those who were led forth with Him to crucifixion, that Jesus did not suffer for any crime, nor for any political movement, but because He professed to embody the great hope of Israel, and was rejected by its leaders. And, if any had been ignorant, the title over the Cross and the bitter hostility of the Sanhedrists, which followed Him with jeers and jibes, where even ordinary humanity, and still more Jewish feeling, would have enjoined silence, if not pity, must have shown what had been the motives of the condemnation of Jesus. But, once the mind was opened to perceive all these facts, the progress would be rapid. In hours of extremity a man may deceive himself and fatally mistake fear for the fear of God, and the remembrance of certain external knowledge for spiritual experience. But, if a man really learns in such seasons, the teaching of years may be compressed into moments, and the dying thief on the Cross might outdistance the knowledge gained by Apostles in their years of following Christ.

One thing stood out before the mind of the penitent thief, who in that hour did fear God. Jesus had done nothing amiss. And this surrounded with a halo of moral glory the inscription on the Cross, long before its words acquired a new meaning. But how did this Innocent One bear Himself in suffering? Right royally, not in an earthly sense, but in that in which alone He claimed the Kingdom. He had so spoken to the women who had lamented Him, as His faint form could no longer bear the burden of the Cross; and He had so refused the drink that would have deadened consciousness and sensibility. Then, as the three were stretched on the transverse beam, and, in the first and sharpest agony of pain, the nails were driven with cruel stroke of hammer through the quivering flesh, and, in the nameless agony that followed the first moments of the Crucifixion, only a prayer for those who in ignorance, were the instruments of His torture, had passed His lips. And yet He was innocent, Who so cruelly suffered. All that followed must have only deepened the impression. With what calm of endurance and majesty of silence He had borne the insult and jeers of those who, even to the spiritually unenlightened eye, must have seemed so infinitely far beneath Him! This man did feel the fear of God, who now learned the new lesson in which the fear of God was truly the beginning of wisdom. And, once he gave place to the moral element, when under the fear of God he reproved his comrade, this new moral decision became to him, as so often, the beginning of spiritual life. Rapidly he now passed into the light, and onwards and upwards: Lord, remember me, when You come in Your Kingdom!

The familiar words of our KJV, When You come into Your Kingdom, convey the idea of what we might call a more spiritual meaning of the petition. But we can scarcely believe, that at that moment it implied either that Christ was then going into His Kingdom, or that the penitent thief looked to Christ for admission into the Heavenly Kingdom. The words are true to the Jewish point of vision of the man. He recognized and owned Jesus as the Messiah, and he did so, by a wonderful forth going of faith, even in the utmost Humiliation of Christ. And this immediately passed beyond the Jewish standpoint, for he expected Jesus soon to come back in His Kingly might and power, when he asked to be remembered by Him in mercy. And here we have again to bear in mind that, during the Life of Christ upon earth, and, before the outpouring of the Holy Spirit, men always first learned to believe in the Person of the Christ, and then to know His teaching and His Mission in the forgiveness of sins. It was so in this case also. If the penitent thief had learned to know the Christ, and to ask for gracious recognition in His coming Kingdom, the answering assurance of Jesus conveyed not only the comfort that his prayer was answered, but the teaching of spiritual things which he did not know yet, and so much needed to know. The penitent had spoken of the future, Christ spoke of today; the penitent had prayed about that

Messianic Kingdom which was to come, Christ assured him in regard to the state of the disembodied spirits, and conveyed to him the promise that he would be there in the abode of the blessed, Paradise, and that through means of Himself as the Messiah: Amen, I say to you, Today with Me shall you be in the Paradise. Thus Christ gave him that spiritual knowledge which he did not yet possess, the teaching concerning the today, the need of gracious admission into Paradise, and that with and through Himself, in other words, concerning the forgiveness of sins and the opening of the Kingdom of Heaven to all believers. This, as the first and foundation creed of the soul, was the first and foundation fact concerning the Messiah.

This was the Second Utterance from the Cross. The first had been of utter self forgetfulness; the second of deepest, wisest, most gracious spiritual teaching. And, had He spoken none other than these, He would have been proved to be the Son of God.

Nothing more would require to be said to the penitent on the Cross. The events which followed, and the words which Jesus would still speak, would teach him more fully than could otherwise have been done. Some hours, probably two, had passed since Jesus had been nailed to the Cross. We wonder how it came that John, who tells us some of the incidents with such exceeding particularity, and relates all with the vivid realization of a most deeply interested eyewitness, should have been silent as to others, especially as to those hours of derision, as well as to the conversion of the penitent thief. His silence seems to us to have been due to absence from the scene. We part company with him after his detailed account of the last scene before Pilate. The final sentence pronounced, we suppose him to have hurried into the City, and to have acquainted such of the disciples as he might find, but especially those faithful women and the Virgin Mother, with the terrible scenes that had passed since the previous evening. From there he returned to Golgotha, just in time to witness the Crucifixion, which he again describes with peculiar fullness of details. When Jesus was nailed to the Cross, John seems once more to have returned to the City, this time, to bring back with him those women, in company of whom we now find him standing close to the Cross. A more delicate, tender, loving service could not have been rendered than this. Alone, of all the disciples, he is there, not afraid to be near Christ, in the Palace of the High Priest, before Pilate, and now under the Cross. And alone he renders to Christ this tender service of bringing the women and Mary to the Cross, and to them the protection of his guidance and company. He loved Jesus best; and it was fitting that to his manliness and affection should be entrusted the unspeakable privilege of Christ's dangerous inheritance.

The narrative leaves the impression that with the beloved disciple these four women were standing close to the Cross: the Mother of Jesus, the Sister of His Mother, Mary the wife of Clopas, and Mary of Magdala. A comparison with what is related by Matthew and Mark supplies further important particulars. We read there of only three women, the name of the Mother of Jesus being omitted. But then it must be remembered that this refers to a later period in the history of the Crucifixion. It seems as if John had fulfilled to the letter Jesus' command: Look upon your mother, and literally from that very hour taken her to his own home. If we are right in this supposition, then, in the absence of John, who led away the Virgin Mother from that scene of horror, the other three women would withdraw to a distance, where we find them at the end, not by the Cross, as in John 19:25, but watching from far, and now joined by others also, who had loved and followed Christ.

We further notice that, the name of the Virgin Mother being omitted, the other three are the same as mentioned by John; only, Mary of Clopas is now described as the mother of James and Jose, and Christ's Mother's Sister as Solome and the mother of Zebedee's children. Thus Salome, the wife of Zebedee and John's mother, was the sister of the Virgin, and the beloved disciple the cousin (on the mother's side) of Jesus, and the nephew of the Virgin. This also helps to explain why the care of the Mother had been entrusted to him. Nor was Mary the wife of Clopas unconnected with Jesus. What we have every reason to regard as a trustworthy account describes Clopas as the brother of Joseph, the husband of the Virgin. Thus, not only Salome as the sister of the Virgin, but Mary also as the wife of Clopas, would, in a certain sense, have been His aunt, and her son's His cousins. And so we notice among the twelve Apostles five cousins of Jesus: the two sons of Salome and Zebedee, and the three sons of Alphaeus or Clopas and Mary: James, Judas surnamed Lebbaeus and Thaddaeus, and Simon surnamed Zelotes or Cananean.

We can now in some measure realize events. When John had seen Jesus nailed to the Cross, he had gone to the City and brought with him for a last mournful farewell the Virgin, accompanied by those who, as most nearly connected with her, would naturally be with her: her own sister Salome, the sister-in-law of Joseph and wife (or more probably widow) of Clopas, and her who of all others had experienced most of His blessed power to save, Mary of Magdala. Once more we reverently mark His Divine calm of utter self forgetfulness and His human thoughtfulness for others. As they stood under the Cross, He committed His Mother to the disciple whom He loved, and established a new human relationship between him and her who was nearest to Himself. And calmly, earnestly, and immediately did that disciple undertake the sacred charge, and bring her, whose soul the sword had pierced, away from the scene of unutterable judgment to the shelter of his home. And this temporary absence of John from the Cross may account for the lack of all detail in his narrative until quite the closing scene.

Now at last all that concerned the earthward aspect of His Mission, so far as it had to be done on the Cross, was ended. He had prayed for those who had nailed Him to it, in ignorance of what they did; He had given the comfort of assurance to the penitent, who had owned His Glory in His Humiliation; and He had made the last provision of love in regard to those nearest to Him. So to speak, the relations of His Humanity, that which touched His Human Nature in any direction, had been fully met. He had done with the Human aspect of His Work and with earth. And, appropriately, Nature seemed now to take sad farewell of Him, and mourned its departing Lord, Who, by His Personal connection with it, had once more lifted it from the abasement of the Fall into the region of the Divine, making it the dwelling place, the vehicle for the manifestation, and the obedient messenger of the Divine.

For three hours had Jesus hung on the Cross. It was midday. And now the Sun was craped in darkness from the sixth to the ninth hour. No purpose can be served by attempting to trace the source of this darkness. It could not have been an eclipse, since it was the time of full moon; nor can we place reliance on the later reports on this subject of ecclesiastical writers. It seems only in accordance with the Evangelic narrative to regard the occurrence of the event as supernatural, while the event itself might have been brought about by natural causes; and among these we must call special attention to the earthquake in which this darkness terminated. For, it is a well known phenomenon that such darkness not infrequently precedes earthquakes. On the other hand, it must be freely admitted, that the language of the Evangelists seems to imply that this darkness extended, not only over the land of Israel, but over the inhabited earth. The expression must not be pressed to its full literality, but explained as meaning that it extended far beyond Judea and to other lands. No reasonable objection can be raised from the circumstance, that neither the earthquake nor the preceding darkness are mentioned by any profane writer whose works have been preserved, since it would surely not be maintained that an historical record must have been preserved of every earthquake that occurred, and of every darkness that may have preceded it. But the most unfair argument is that, which tries to establish the unhistorical character of this narrative by an appeal to what are described as Jewish sayings expressive of similar expectancy. It is quite true that in old Testament prophecy, whether figuratively or really, the darkening, though not only of the sun, but also of the moon and stars, is sometimes connected, not with the Coming of Messiah, still less with His death, but with the final Judgment. But Jewish tradition never speaks of such an event in connection with Messiah, or even with the Messianic judgments, and the quotations from Rabbinic writings made by negative critics must be characterized as not only inapplicable but even unfair.

But to return from this painful digression. The three hours darkness was such not only to Nature; Jesus, also, entered into darkness: Body, Soul, and Spirit. It was now, not as before, a contest, but suffering. Into this, to us, fathomless depth of the mystery of His Sufferings, we dare not, as indeed we cannot, enter. It was of the Body; yet not of the Body only, but of physical life. And it was of the Soul and Spirit; yet not of them alone, but in their conscious relation to man and to God. And it was not of the Human only in Christ, but in its indissoluble connection with the Divine: of the Human, where it reached the utmost verge of humiliation to body, soul, and spirit, and in it of the Divine, to utmost self examination. The increasing, nameless agonies of the Crucifixion were deepening into the bitterness of death. All nature shrinks from death, and there is a physical horror of the separation between body and soul which, as a purely natural phenomenon, is in every instance only overcome, and that only by a higher principle. And we conceive that the purer the being the greater the violence of the tearing asunder of the bond with which God Almighty originally bound together body and soul. In the Perfect Man this must have reached the highest degree. So, also, had in those dark hours the sense of man forsakenness and His own isolation from man; so, also, had the intense silence of God, the withdrawal of God, the sense of His God forsakenness and absolute loneliness. We dare not here speak of punitive suffering, but of forsakenness and loneliness. And yet as we ask ourselves how this forsakenness can be thought of as so complete in view of His Divine consciousness, which at least could not have been wholly extinguished by His Self examination, we feel that yet another element must be taken into account. Christ on the Cross suffered for man; He offered Himself a sacrifice; He died for our sins, that, as death was the wages of sin, so He died as the Representative of man, for man and in room of man; He obtained for man eternal redemption, having given His Life a ransom, for many. For, men were redeemed with the precious Blood of Christ, as of a Lamb without blemish and without spot; and Christ gave Himself for us, that He might "redeem" us from all iniquity; He gave Himself "a ransom" for all; Christ died for all; Him, Who knew no sin, God made sin for us; Christ redeemed us from the curse of the Law, having become a curse for us, and this, with express reference to the Crucifixion. This sacrifice, vicarious, expiatory, and redemptive character of His death, if it does not explain to us, yet helps us to understand, Christ's sense of God forsakenness in the supreme moment of the Cross; if one might so word it, the passive character of His activeness through the active character of His passiveness.

It was this combination of the Old Testament idea of sacrifice, and of the Old Testament ideal of willing suffering as the Servant of Jehovah, now fulfilled in Christ, which found its fullest expression in the language of the twenty second Psalm. It was fitting, rather, it was true, that the willing suffering of the true Sacrifice should now find vent in its opening words: My God, My God, why have You forsaken Me?, Eli, Eli, lema sabachthanei? These words, cried with a loud voice at the close of the period of extreme agony, marked the climax and the end of this suffering of Christ, of which the utmost compass was the withdrawal of God and the felt loneliness of the Sufferer. But they that stood by the Cross, misinterpreting the meaning, and mistaking the opening words for the name Elijah, imagined that the Sufferer had called for Elijah. We can scarcely doubt, that these were the soldiers who stood by the Cross. They were not necessarily Romans; on the contrary, as we have seen, these Legions were generally recruited from Provincials. On the other hand, no Jew would have mistaken Eli for the name of Elijah, not yet misinterpreted a quotation of Psalm 22:1 as a call for that prophet. And it must be remembered, that the words were not whispered, but cried with a loud voice. But all entirely accords with the misunderstanding of non-Jewish soldiers, who, as the whole history shows, had learned from His accusers and the infuriated mob snatches of a distorted story of the Christ.

And now the Sufferer emerged on the other side. It can scarcely have been a minute or two from the time that the cry from the twenty second Psalm marked the high point of His Agony, when the words I thirst seem to indicate, by the prevalence of the merely human aspect of the suffering, that the other and more terrible aspect of sin bearing and God forsakenness was past. To us, therefore, this seems the beginning, if not of Victory, yet of Rest, of the End. John alone records this Utterance, prefacing it with this distinctive statement, that Jesus so surrendered Himself to the human feeling, seeking the bodily relief by expressing His thirst: knowing that all things were now finished, that the Scripture might be fulfilled. In other words, the climax of The human Suffering in His feeling of God forsakenness, which had led to the utterance of Psalm 22:1, was now, to His consciousness, the end of all which in accordance with Scripture prediction He had to bear. He now could and did yield Himself to the mere physical wants of His Body.

It seems as if John, having perhaps just returned to the scene, and standing with the women far off, beholding these things, had hurried forward on the cry from Psalm 22, and heard Him express the feeling of thirst, which immediately followed. And so John alone supplies the link between that cry and the movement on the part of the soldiers, which Matthew and Mark, as well as John, report. For, it would be impossible to understand why, on what the soldiers regarded as a call for Elijah, one of them should have hurried to relieve His thirst, but for the Utterance recorded in the Fourth Gospel. But we can quite understand it, if the Utterance, I thirst, followed immediately on the previous cry.

One of the soldiers, may we not be allowed to believe, one who either had already learned from that Cross, or was about to learn, to own Him Lord, moved by sympathy, now ran to offer some slight refreshment to the Sufferer by filling a sponge with the rough wine of the soldiers and putting it to His lips, having first fastened it to the stem (reed) of the caper (hyssop), which is said to grow to the height of even two or three feet. But, even so, this act of humanity was not allowed to pass unchallenged by the coarse jibes of the others who would bid him leave the relief of the Sufferer to the agency of Elijah, which in their opinion He had invoked. Nor should we perhaps wonder at the weakness of that soldier himself, who, though he would not be hindered in his good deed, yet averted the opposition of the others by apparently joining in their mockery.

By accepting the physical refreshment offered Him, Jesus once more indicated the completion of the work of His Passion. For, as He would not enter on it with His senses and physical consciousness lulled by narcotized wine, so He would not pass out of it with senses and physical consciousness dulled by the absolute failure of life power. Therefore He took what for the moment restored the physical balance, needful for thought and word. And so He immediately passed on to taste death for every man. For, the two last sayings of Jesus now followed in rapid succession: first, that with a loud voice, which expressed it, that the work given Him to do, as far as concerned His Passion, was finished; and then, that in the words of Psalm 30:5, in which He commended His Spirit into the Hands of the Father. Attempts at comment could only weaken the solemn thoughts which the words awaken. Yet some points should be helpful for our teaching. His last cry with a loud voice was not like that of one dying. Mark notes, that this made such deep impression on the Centurion. In the language of the early Christian hymn, it was not death which approached Christ, but Christ death: He died without death. Christ encountered death, not as conquered, but as the Conqueror. And this also was part of His work, and for us: now the beginning of His Triumph. And with this agrees the peculiar language of John, that He bowed the Head, and gave up the Spirit.

Nor should we fail to mark the peculiarities of His last Utterance. The My God of the fourth Utterance had again passed into the Father of conscious fellowship. And yet neither in the Hebrew original of this Psalm, nor in its Greek rendering by the LXX, does the word Father occur. Again, in the LXX translation of the Hebrew text this word expressive of entrustment, the commending, is in the future tense; on the lips of Jesus it is in the present tense. And the word, in its New Testament sense, means not merely commending: it is to deposit, to commit for safe keeping. That in dying, or rather meeting and overcoming death, He chose and adapted these words, is matter for deepest thankfulness to the Church. He spoke them for His people in a twofold sense: on their behalf, that they might be able to speak them; and for them, that from then on they might speak them after Him. How many thousands have pillowed their heads on them when going to rest! They were the last words of a Polycarp, a Bernard, Huss, Luther, and Melanchthon. And to us also they may be the fittest and the softest lullaby. And in the Spirit which He had committed to God did He now descend into Hades, and preached to the spirits in prison. But behind this great mystery have closed the two leaved gates of brass, which only the Hand of the Conqueror could burst open.

And now a shudder ran through Nature, as its Sun had set. We dare not do more than follow the rapid outlines of the Evangelic narrative. As the first token, it records the rending of the Temple Veil in two from the top downward to the bottom; as the second, the quaking of the earth, the rending of the rocks and the opening of the graves. Although most writers have regarded this as indicating the strictly chronological succession, there is nothing in the text to bind us to such a conclusion. Thus, while the rending of the Veil is recorded first, as being the most significant token to Israel, it may have been connected with the earthquake, although this alone might scarcely account for the tearing of so heavy a Veil from the top to the bottom. Even the latter circumstance has its significance. That some great catastrophe, betokening the impending destruction of the Temple, had occurred in the Sanctuary about this very time, is confirmed by not less than four mutually independent testimonies: those of Tacitus, of Josephus, of the Talmud, and of earliest Christian tradition. The most important of these are, the Talmud and Josephus. The latter speaks of the mysterious extinction of the middle and chief light in the Golden Candlestick, forty years before the destruction of the Temple; and both he and the Talmud refer to a supernatural opening by themselves of the great Temple gates that had been previously closed, which was regarded as a portent of the coming destruction of the Temple. We can scarcely doubt, that some historical fact must underlie so peculiar and widespread a tradition, and we cannot help feeling that it may be a distorted version of the occurrence of the rending of the Temple Veil (or of its report) at the Crucifixion of Christ.

But even if the rending of the Temple Veil had commenced with the earthquake, and, according to the Gospel to the Hebrews, with the breaking of the great lintel over the entrance, it could not be wholly accounted for in this manner. According to Jewish tradition, there were, two Veils before the entrance to the Most Holy Place. The Talmud explains this on the ground that it was not known, whether in the former Temple the Veil had hung inside or outside the entrance and whether the partition wall had stood in the Holy or Most Holy Place. Therefore (according to Maimonides) there was not any wall between the Holy and Most Holy Place, but the space of one cubit, assigned to it in the former Temple, was left unoccupied, and one Veil hung on the side of the Holy, the other on that of the Most Holy Place. According to an account dating from Temple times, there were altogether thirteen Veils used in various parts of the Temple, two new ones being made every year. The Veils before the Most Holy Place were 40 cubits (60 feet) long, and 20 (30 feet) wide, of the thickness of the palm of the hand, and consisting of 72 squares, which were joined together; and these Veils were so heavy, that, in the exaggerated language of the time, it needed 3000 priests to manipulate each. If the Veil was at all such as is described in the Talmud, it could not have been torn in two by a mere earthquake or the fall of the lintel, although its composition in squares fastened together might explain, how the tear might be as described in the Gospel.

Indeed, everything seems to indicate that, although the earthquake might furnish the physical basis, the tear of the Temple Veil was, with reverence be it said, really made by the Hand of God. As we compute, it may just have been the time when, at the Evening Sacrifice, the officiating Priesthood entered the Holy Place, either to burn the incense or to do other sacred service there. To see before them, not as the aged Zacharias at the beginning of this history the Angel Gabriel, but the Veil of the Holy Place torn from top to bottom, that beyond it they could scarcely have seen, and hanging in two parts from its fastenings above and at the side, was, a terrible portent, which would soon become generally known, and must, in some form or other, have been preserved in tradition. And they all must have understood, that it meant that God's Own Hand had torn the Veil, and forever deserted and thrown open that Most Holy Place where He had so long dwelt in the mysterious gloom, only lit up once a year by the glow of the censer of him, who made atonement for the sins of the people.

Other tokens were not lacking. In the earthquake the rocks were split, and their tombs opened. This, as Christ descended into Hades. And when He ascended on the third day, it was with victorious saints who had left those open graves. To many in the Holy City on that ever memorable first day, and in the week that followed, appeared the bodies of many of those saints who had fallen on sleep in the sweet hope of that which had now become reality.

But on those who stood under the Cross, and near it, did all that was witnessed make the deepest and most lasting impression. Among them we especially mark the Centurion under whose command the soldiers had been. Many a scene of horror must he have witnessed in those sad times of the Crucifixion, but none like this. Only one conclusion could force itself on his mind. It was that which, we cannot doubt, had made its impression on his heart and conscience. Jesus was not what the Jews, His infuriated enemies, had described Him. He was what He professed to be, what His bearing on the Cross and His death attested Him to be: righteous, and therefore, the Son of God. From this there was only a step to personal allegiance to Him, and, as previously suggested, we may possibly owe to him some of those details which Luke alone has preserved.

The brief spring day was verging towards the evening of the Sabbath. In general, the Law ordered that the body of a criminal should not be left hanging unburied over night. Perhaps in ordinary circumstances the Jews might not have appealed so confidently to Pilate as actually to ask him to shorten the sufferings of those on the Cross, since the punishment of crucifixion often lasted not only for hours but days, before death ensued. But here was a special occasion. The Sabbath about to open was a high day, it was both a Sabbath and the second Paschal Day, which was regarded as in every respect equally sacred with the first more so, since the so called Wave sheaf was then offered to the Lord. And what the Jews now proposed to Pilate was, a shortening, but not in any sense a mitigation, of the punishment. Sometimes there was added to the punishment of crucifixion that of breaking the bones (crurifragium, skelokopa) by means of a club or hammer. This would not itself bring death, but the breaking of the bones was always followed by a coup de grace, by sword, lance, or stroke (the perforatio or percussio sub sadly), which immediately put an end to what remained of life. Thus the breaking of the bones was a sort of increase of punishment, by way of compensation for its shortening by the final stroke that followed.

It were unjust to suppose, that in their anxiety to fulfill the letter of the Law as to burial on the eve of that high Sabbath, the Jews had sought to intensify the sufferings of Jesus. The text gives no indication of this; and they could not have asked for the final stroke to be inflicted without the breaking of the bones, which always preceded it. The irony of this punctilious care for the letter of the Law about burial and high Sabbath by those who had betrayed and crucified their Messiah on the first Passover day is sufficiently great, and, let us add, terrible, without importing ficticious elements. John, who, perhaps, immediately on the death of Christ, left the Cross, alone reports circumstance. Perhaps it was when he concerted with Joseph of Arimathea, with Nicodemus, or the two Marys, measures for the burying of Christ, that he learned of the Jewish deputation to Pilate, followed it to Praetorium, and then watched how it was all carried out on Golgotha. He records, how Pilate agreed to the Jewish demand, and gave directions for the crurifragium, and permission for the after removal of the dead bodies, which otherwise might have been left to hang, until decomposition or birds of prey had destroyed them. But John also tells us what he evidently regards as so great a wonder that he especially vouches for it, pledging his own trueness, as an eyewitness, and grounding on it an appeal to the faith of those to whom his Gospel is addressed. It is, that certain things came to pass [not as in our Authorized Version, were done] that the Scripture should be fulfilled, or, to put it otherwise, by which the Scripture was fulfilled. These things were two, to which a third phenomenon, not less remarkable, must be added. For, first, when, in the crurifragium, the soldiers had broken the bones of two criminals, and then came to the Cross of Jesus, they found that He was dead already, and so a bone of Him was not broken. Had it been otherwise, the Scripture concerning the Paschal Lamb, as well that concerning the Righteous Suffering Servant of Jehovah, would have been broken. In Christ alone these two ideas of the Paschal Lamb and the Righteous Suffering Servant of Jehovah are combined into a unity and fulfilled in their highest meaning. And when, by a strange concurrence of circumstances, it came to pass that, contrary to what might have been expected, a bone of Him was not broken this outward fact served as the finger to point to the predictions which were fulfilled of Him.

Not less remarkable is the second fact. If, on the Cross of Christ, these two fundamental ideas in the prophetic description of the work of the Messiah had been set forth: the fulfillment of the Paschal Sacrifice, which, as that of the Covenant, underlie all sacrifices, and the fulfillment of the ideal of the Righteous Servant of God, suffering in a world that hated God, and yet proclaimed and realizing His Kingdom, a third truth remained to be exhibited. It was not in regard to the character, but the effects, of the Work of Christ, its reception, in the present and in the future. This had been indicated in the prophecies of Zechariah, which foretold how, in the day of Israel's final deliverance and national conversion, God would pour out the spirit of grace and of supplication, and as they shall look on Him Whom they pierced, the spirit of true repentance would be granted them, nationally and individually. The application of this to Christ is the more striking, that even the Talmud refers the prophecy to the Messiah. And as these two things really applied to Christ, in His rejection and in His future return, so did the strange historical occurrence at His Crucifixion once more point to it as the fulfillment of Scripture prophecy. For, although the soldiers, on finding Jesus dead, broke not one of His Bones, yet, as it was necessary to make sure of His death, one of them, with a lance, pierced His Side, with a wound so deep, that Thomas might afterwards have thrust his hand into His Side.

And with these two, as fulfilling Holy Scripture, yet a third phenomenon was associated, symbolic of both. As the soldier pierced the side of the Dead Christ, immediately came out from there Blood and Water. It has been thought by some, that there was physical cause for this, that Christ had literally died of a broken heart, and that, when the lance pierced first the lung filled with blood and then the pericardium filled with serous fluid, there flowed from the wound this double stream. In such cases, the lesson would be that reproach had literally broken His Heart. But we can scarcely believe that John could have wished to convey this without clearly setting it forth, thus assuming on the part of his readers knowledge of an obscure, and, it must be added, a scientifically doubtful phenomenon. Accordingly, we rather believe that to John, as to most of us, the significance of the fact lay in this, that out of the Body of One dead had flowed Blood and Water, that corruption had not fastened on Him. Then, there would be the symbolic meaning conveyed by the Water (from the pericardium) and the Blood (from the heart)—a symbolism most true, if corruption had no power nor hold on Him, if in death He was not dead, if He vanquished death and Corruption, and in this respect also fulfilled the prophetic ideal of not seeing corruption. To this symbolic bearing of the flowing of Water and Blood from His pierced side, on which the Evangelist dwells in his Epistle, and to its external expression in the symbolism of the two Sacraments, we can only point the thoughtful Christian. For, the two Sacraments mean that Christ had come; that over Him, Who was crucified for us and loved us to death with His broken heart, death and Corruption had no power; and that He lives for us with the pardoning and cleansing power of His offered Sacrifice.

Yet one other scene remains to be recorded. Whether before, or, more probably, after the Jewish deputation to the Roman Governor, another and a strange application came to Pilate. It was from one apparently well known, a man not only of wealth and standing, whose noble bearing corresponded to his social condition, and who was known as a just and a good man. Joseph of Arimathea was a Sanhedrist, but he had not consented either to the counsel or the deed of his colleagues. It must have been generally known that he was one of those which waited for the Kingdom of God. But he had advanced beyond what that expression implies. Although secretly, for fear of the Jews, he was a disciple of Jesus. It is in strange contrast to this fear, that Mark tells us, that, having dared, he went in to Pilate and asked for the Body of Jesus. Thus, under circumstances the most unlikely and unfavorable, were his fears converted into boldness, and he, whom fear of the Jews had restrained from making open declaration of discipleship during the life time of Jesus, not only professed such of the Crucified Christ, but took the most bold and decided step before Jews and Gentiles in connection with it. So does trial elicit faith, and the wind, which quenches the feeble flame that plays around the outside, fan into brightness the fire that burns deep within, though for a time unseen. Joseph of Arimathea, now no longer a secret disciple, but bold in the declaration of his reverent love, would show to the Dead Body of his Master all veneration. And the Divinely ordered concurrence of circumstances not only helped his pious purpose, but invested all with deepest symbolic significance. It was Friday afternoon, and the Sabbath was drawing near. No time therefore was to be lost, if due honor were to be paid to the Sacred Body. Pilate give it to Joseph of Arimathea. Such was within his power, and a favor not infrequently accorded in like circumstances. But two things must have powerfully impressed the Roman Governor, and deepened his former thoughts about Jesus: first, that the death on the Cross had taken place so rapidly, a circumstance on which he personally questioned the Centurion, and then the bold appearance and request of such a man as Joseph of Arimathea. Or did the Centurion express to the Governor also some such feeling as that which had found utterance under the Cross in the words: Truly this Man was the Son of God?

The proximity of the holy Sabbath, and the consequent need of haste, may have suggested or determined the proposal of Joseph to lay the Body of Jesus in his own rock hewn new tomb, wherein no one had yet been laid. The symbolic significance of this is the more marked, that the symbolism was undersigned. These rock hewn tombs, and the mode of laying the dead in them, have been very fully described in connection with the burying of Lazarus. We may therefore wholly surrender over selves to the sacred thoughts that gather around us. The Cross was lowered and laid on the ground; the cruel nails drawn out, and the ropes unloosed. Joseph, with those who attended him, wrapped the Sacred Body in a clean linen cloth, and rapidly carried It to the rock hewn tomb in the garden close by. Such a rock hewn tomb or cave (Meartha) had niches (Kukhin), where the dead were laid. It will be remembered, that at the entrance to the tomb, and within the rock, there was a court, nine feet square, where ordinarily the bier was deposited, and its bearers gathered to do the last offices for the Dead. To there we suppose Joseph to have carried the Sacred Body, and then the last scene to have taken place. For now another, kindered to Joseph in spirit, history, and position, had come. The same spiritual Law, which had brought Joseph to open confession, also constrained the profession of that other Sanhedrist, Nicodemus. We remember, how at the first he had, from fear of detection, come to Jesus by night, and with what bated breath he had pleaded with his colleagues not so much the cause of Christ, as on His behalf that of law and justice. He now came, bringing a roll of myrrh and aloes, in the fragrant mixture well known to the Jews for purposes of anointing or burying.

It was in the court of the tomb that the hasty embalmment, if such it may be called, took place. None of Christ's former disciples seem to have taken part in the burying. John may have withdrawn to bring news to, and to comfort the Virgin Mother; the others also, that had stood after off, watching, appear to have left. Only a few faithful ones, notably among them Mary Magdalene and the other Mary, the mother of Joses, stood over against the tomb, watching at some distance where and how the Body of Jesus was laid. It would scarcely have been in accordance with Jewish manners, if these women had mingled more closely with the two Sanhedrists and their attendants. From where they stood they could only have had a dim view of what passed within the court, and this may explain how, on their return, they prepared spices and ointments for the more full honors which they hoped to pay the Dead after the Sabbath was past. For, it is of the greatest importance to remember, that haste characterized all that was done. It seems as if the clean linen cloth in which the Body had been wrapped, was now torn into cloths or swathes, into which the Body, limb by limb, was now bound, no doubt, between layers of myrrh and aloes, the Head being wrapped in a napkin. And so they laid Him to rest in the niche of the rock hewn new tomb. And as they went out, they rolled, as was the custom, a great stone, the Golel, to close the entrance to the tomb, probably leaning against it for support, as was the practice, a smaller stone, the so called Dopheq. It would be where the one stone was laid against the other, that on the next day, Sabbath though it was, the Jewish authorities would have affixed the seal, so that the slightest disturbance might become apparent.

It was probably about the same time, that a noisy throng prepared to follow delegates from the Sanhedrin to the ceremony of cutting the Passover sheaf. The Law had it, "he shall bring a sheaf [literally, the Omer] with the first fruits of your harvest, to the priest; and he shall wave the Omer before Jehovah, to be accepted for you." This Passover sheaf was reaped in public the evening before it was offered, and it was to witness this ceremony that the crowd had gathered around the elders. Already on the 14th Nisan the spot from which the first sheaf was to be reaped had been marked out, by tying together in bundles, while still standing, the barley that was to be cut down, according to custom, in the sheltered Ashes Valley across Kidron. When the time for cutting the sheaf had arrived, that is, on the evening of the 15th Nisan, even though it was a Sabbath, just as the sun went down, three men, each with a sickle and basket, set to work. Clearly to bring out what was distinctive in the ceremony, they first asked of the bystanders three times each of these questions: "Has the sun gone down?" "With this sickle?" "Into this basket?" "On this Sabbath? (or first Passover day)", and, lastly, "shall I reap?" Having each time been answered in the affirmative, they cut down barley to the amount of one ephah, or about three pecks and three pints of our English measure. This is not the place to follow the ceremony farther, how the grain was threshed out, parched, ground, and one omer of the flour, mixed with oil and frankincense, waved before the Lord in the Temple on the second Paschal day (or 16th of Nisan). But, as this festive procession started, amid loud demonstrations, a small band of mourners turned from having laid their dead Master in His resting place. The contrast is as sad as it is suggestive. And yet, not in the Temple, nor by the priest, but in the silence of that garden tomb, was the first Omer of the new Paschal flour to be waved before the Lord.

Now on the morrow, which is after the preparation [the Friday], the chief priests and the Pharisees were gathered together to Pilate, saying, Sir, we remember that that deceiver said, when He was yet alive, After three days I will rise again. Command, therefore, that the tomb be made sure until the third day, for fear that by chance His disciples come and steal Him away, and say to the people, He is risen from the dead: so the last error shall be worse than the first. Pilate said to them, Take a guard, go your way, make it as sure as you can. So they went, and made the tomb sure, sealing the stone, the guard being with them.

But was there really need for it? Did they, who had spent what remained of daylight to prepare spices with which to anoint the Dead Christ, expect His Body to be removed, or did they expect, perhaps in their sorrow even think of His word: I will rise again? But on that holy Sabbath, when the Sanhedrists were thinking of how to make sure of the Dead Christ, what were the thoughts of Joseph of Arimathea and Nicodemus, of Peter and John, of the other disciples, and especially of the loving women who only waited for the first streak of Easter light to do their last service of love? What were their thoughts of God, what of Christ, what of the Words He had spoken, the Deeds He had performed, the salvation He had come to bring, and the Kingdom of Heaven which He was to open to all believers? Behind Him had closed the gates of Hades; but upon them rather than upon Him had fallen the shadows of death. Yet they still loved Him, and stronger than death was love.

End Notes:

[104] This was the Jewish practice also (Sanh. 6:2). At the same time it must be remembered, that this was chiefly to elicit testimony in favor of the criminal, when the execution would be immediately arrested; and also that,

as the Sanhedrin had, for centuries before the editing of the Mishnah, been deprived of the power of life and death, such descriptions read very like ideal arrangements. But the practice seems also to have been Roman (per praeconem pronunciati). This explains how the witnesses at the stoning of Stephen laid down their garments at the feet of Paul.

[105] According to the Rabbis, when we read in Scripture generally of the punishment of death, this refers to the strangulation (Sanh. 52 b). Another mode of execution reads like something between shutting up alive and starvation (Sanh. 81 b), something like the manner in which in the Middle Ages people were starved to death.

[106] For the description of Jeremiahs Grotto, Baeedeker Socin, u. s. p. 126. Of course, proof is in the nature of things impossible; yet to me this seems the most sacred and precious locality in Jerusalem.

[107] A person would scarcely return from labor in the field at 9 AM (Mark 15:25). But Nebe denies the use of ladders, and, in general, tries to prove by numerous quotations that the whole Cross was first erected, and then the Sufferer lifted up to it, and, only after that, the nails fastened into His Arms and Feet. Strange though it may seem, the question cannot be absolutely decided.

[108] The two alleged discrepancies, between Matthew and Mark, though, even if they did exist, scarcely worth mention, may be thus explained: 1. If Matthew wrote vinegar (although the best manuscripts read wine), he, no doubt, so translated literally the word Chomets which, though literally, vinegar, refers to an inferior kind of wine which was often mixed (comp. Pes. 42 b). 2. If our Greek text of Matthew speaks of wormwood (as in the LXX), not gall, and Mark of myrrh, we must remember, that both may have been regarded as stupefying, perhaps both used, and that possibly the mistake may have arisen from the similarity of words and their writing, Lebhonah, myrrh, Laanah, wormwood, when may have passed into, the into.

[109] Sepp, vol. v1: p. 336, recalls the execution of Savonarola between Fra Silvestro and Fra Domenico, and the taunt of his enemies: Now, brother!

[110] Professor Westcott beautifully remarks: These three languages gathered up the result of the religious, the social, the intellectual. Probably it would read Jeshu han Notsri malka dihudaey. Both have four words and, in all, twenty letters. The Latin inscription (Matthew) would be, Hic est Jesus Rex Judaeorum, five words and twenty two letters. It will be seen how each would fill a line of about the same length. The notice of the three languages in Luke is spurious. We retain the textus receptus of John 19:19, as in any case it seems most unlikely that Pilate would have placed the Latin in the middle and not at the top. The Aramaic would stand last.

[111] Thus, the notice in John 19:21, 22, would be parenthetic, chronologically belonging to an earlier part, and inserted here for the sake of historical connection.

[112] It is deeply significant that the dress of the priests was not sewed but woven (Zehbach. 88 a), and especially so that of the High Priest (Yoma 72 b). According to tradition, during the seven days of consecration, Moses ministered in a seamless white dress, woven throughout. (Taan. 11 b.)

[113] The various modes of casting the lot are described by Adam, Roman Antiq. pp. 397-399. Possibly, however, it was much more simple and rough than any of these.

[114] Strauss calls Psalm 22: the program of the Passion of Christ. We may accept the description, though not in his sense.

[115] It would be presumptuous to seek to determine how far that prayer extended. Generally, I agree with Nebe, to all (Gentiles and Jews) who, in their participation in the sufferings inflicted on Jesus, acted in ignorance.

[116] The question why Christ did not Himself forgive, but appeal for it to the Father, is best answered by the consideration, that it was really a crimen laesae majestatis against the Father, and that the vindication of the Son lay with God the Father.

[117] There is no evidence, that the Centurion was still present when the soldier came to pierce Jesus' side (John 19:31-37).

[118] The objection, that the Sanhedrists could not have quoted this verse, as it would have branded them as the wicked persons described in Psalm 22, has no force when we remember the loose way in which the Jews were in the habit of quoting the Old Testament.

[119] Mark introduces the mocking speeches (15:29) by the particle o (Ah) which occurs only here in the N.T. It is evidently the Latin Vah, an exclamation of ironical admiration. (See Bengel and Nebe, ad loc.) The words literally were: Ha! the down breaker of the sanctuary and upbuilding it in three days, save Yourself. Except the introductory particle and the order of the words, the words are the same in Matthew.

[120] The language of Matthew and Mark is quite general, and refers to the thieves; that of Luke is precise and detailed. But I cannot agree with those who, for the sake of harmony, represent the penitent thief as joining in his comrades blasphemy before turning to Christ. I do not deny, that such a sudden change might have taken place; but there is no evidence for it in the text, and the supposition of the penitent thief first blaspheming gives rise to many incongruities, and does not seem to fit into the text.

[121]   Tradition names the impenitent thief Gestas, which Keim identifies with
        stegans, silenced, hardened, although the derivation seems to me forced.
        The penitent thief is called Dysmas, which I would propose to derive from
        dusm in the sense of the setting, viz, of the sun: he who turns to the setting
        sun. Do you not even fear God, seeing you are in the same condemnation?
        Condemnation here means that to which one is condemned: the sufferings
        of the cross; and the challenge is: Suffering as you are like Him and me,
        can you join in the jeers of the crowd? Do you not even fear God, should
        not fear of Him now creep over your soul, or at least prevent you from
        insulting the dying Sufferer? And this all the more, since the circumstances
        are as immediately afterwards described.

[122]   Fully to understand it, we ought to realize what would be the Jewish ideas
        of the penitent thief, and what his understanding of the words of Christ.
        Broadly, one would say, that as a Jew he would expect that his death would
        be punishment for his sins. Thoughts of need of forgiveness through the
        Messiah would not therefore come to him. But the words of Christ must
        have supplied all this. Again when Christ spoke of Paradise, His hearer
        would naturally understand that part of Hades in which the spirits of the
        righteous dwell until the Resurrection. On both these points there are so
        many passages in Rabbinic writings that it is needless to quote (see for
        Exodus Westein, ad loc., and our remarks on the Parable of Lazarus and
        Dives). The prayer: let my death be the punishment for my sins, is still in
        the Jewish office for the dying, and the underlying dogma is firmly rooted
        in Rabbinic belief. The words of Jesus, so far from encouraging this belief,
        would teach him that admission to Paradise was to be granted by Christ. It
        is scarcely necessary to add, that Christ's words in no way encouraged the
        realistic conceptions which Judaism attached to Paradise. In Biblical Hebrew
        the word is used for a choice garden: in Ecclesiastes 2:5; Song of Solomon
        4:13; Nehemiah 2:8. But in the LXX and the Apocr. the word is already used
        in our sense of Paradise. Lastly, nothing which Jesus had said to the penitent
        thief about being today with Him in Paradise, is in any way inconsistent
        with, rather confirms, the doctrine of the Descent into Hades.

[123]   The first impression left is that the brothers of Jesus were not yet, at least in
        the full sense, believers. But this does not by any means necessarily follow,
        since both the presence of John under the Cross, and even his outward
        circumstances, might point him out as the most fit custodian of the Virgin
        Mother. At the same time it seems the more likely supposition, that the
        brothers of Jesus were converted by the appearance to James of the Risen
        One (1 Corinthians 15:7).

[124] There is the difficulty that Judas (Lebbaeus) and Simon Zelotes are not here mentioned as her sons. But they may have been her stepsons, or there may have other reasons for the omission. Judas of James could scarcely have been the son of James, and Simon is expressly mentioned by Hegesippus as the son of Clopas.

[125] Alphaeus and Clopas are the same name. The first occurs in the Babylon Talmud as Ilphai, or Ilpha, as in R. haSh. 17 b, and often; the other in the Jerusalem Talmud as Chilphai, as for Exodus in Jeremiah B. Kama 7 a.

[126] I regard the Simon Zelotes of the list of Apostles as the Simon son of Clopas, or Alphaeus, of Hegesippus, first, because of his position in the lists of the Apostles along with the two other sons of Alphaeus; secondly, because, as there were only two prominent Simons in the N.T. (the brother of Jesus, and Zelotes), and Hegesippus mentions him as the son of Clopas, it follows that the Simon son of Clopas was Simon Zelotes. Levi Matthew was, also a son of Alphaeus, but we regard this as another Clopas than the husband of Mary.

[127] There are frequent notices in classical writers of eclipses preceding disastrous events or the death of great men, such as of Caesar (Nebe, u. s. p. 300). But these were, if correctly related, eclipses in the true sense, and, as such, natural events, having in no way a supernatural bearing, and therefore in no sense analogous to this darkness at the Crucifixion.

[128] To be quite fair, I will refer to all the passages quoted in connection with the darkening of the sun as a token of mourning. The first (quoted by Wetstein) is from the Midrash on Lament. 3:28 (ed. Warsh. p. 72 a). But the passage, evidently a highly figurative one, refers to the destruction of Jerusalem and the dispersion of Israel, and, besides the darkening of the sun, moon, and stars (not the sun only), refers to a realistic fulfillment of Nahum 1:3 and Lamentations 3:28 in God's walking in dust and keeping silence. The second quotation of Wetstein, that when a great Rabbi dies it is as portentous as if the sun went down at midday, has manifestly no bearing whatever on the matter in hand (though Strauss adduces it). The last and only quotation really worth mention is from Sukk. 29 a. In a somewhat lengthened statement there, the meaning of an obscuration of the sun or moon is discussed. I have here to remark (1) that these phenomena are regarded as signs in the sense of betokening coming judgments, such as war, famine, etc., and that these are supposed to affect various nations according as the eclipse is towards the rising or setting of the sun. The passage therefore can have no possible connection with such a phenomenon as the death of Messiah. (2) This is further confirmed by the enumeration of certain sins for

which heavenly luminaries are eclipsed. Some are not fit for mention, while others are such as false witness bearing, the needless cutting down of fruit trees, etc. (3) But the unfairness, as well as the inaptitude, of the quotation appears from this, that only the beginning of the passage is quoted (Strauss and Keim): At a time when the sun is obscured, it is an evil sign to all the world, while what follows is omitted: When the sun is obscured, it is an evil sign to the nations of the world; when the moon is obscured, it is an evil sign to Israel, because Israel reckons according to the moon, the nations of the world according to the sun. And yet Wuensche (Erlauter. pp. 355, 356) quotes both that which precedes and that which follows this passage, but leaves out this passage itself. (Comp. Mechilta, p. 3 b.)

[129] So in Matthew, according to the best reading. In Mark, Eloi, Eloi [apparently the Syriac form], lema sabachthanei? Might it be that Matthew represents the current Judean or Galilean dialect, and Mark the Syrian, and that this casts light on the dialects in Palestine at the time of Christ, and even, to some extent, on the composition of the Gospels, and the land in which they were written? The Targum renders Psalm 22:2: Eli, Eli, metul mah shebhaqtani? (On account of what have You forsaken me?).

[130] So in the Gospel according to the Hebrews, from which Jerome quotes (in Matthew 25:51, and in a letter to Hedibia) to the effect, that the huge lintel of the Temple was broken and splintered, and fell. Jerome connects the rending of the Veil with this, and it would seem an obvious inference to connect again this breaking of the lintel with an earthquake.

[131] A story is told in Jewish tradition (Gitt, 56 b, about the middle; Ber. R. 10; Vayyik. R. 22, and in other places) to the effect that, among other vilenesses, Titus the wicked had penetrated into the Sanctuary, and cut through the Veil of the Most Holy Place with his sword, when blood dropped down. I mention the legend to express my emphatic protest against the manner in which Dr. Joel (Blicke in d. Religionsgesch. 1: pp. 7, 8, treating of the passage in the Midr. On Lamentations 2:17) has made use of it. He represents it, as if the Veil had been torn (Zerreissen des Vorhanges bei d. Tempelzerstoerung), not cut through by Titus, and on the basis of this misrepresentation has the boldness to set a legend about Titus side by side with the Evangelic account of the rending of the Temple Veil! I write thus strongly because I am sorry to say that this is by no means the only instance in which Jewish writers adapt their quotations to controversial purposes. Joel refers to Dr. Sachs, Beitr. 1: p. 29, but that learned writer draws no such inference from the passage in question. May this phenomenon account for the early conversion of so many priests recorded in Acts 6:7?

[132] I dare not express myself dogmatically on the precise import of Matthew 25:52, 53. Does it mean that they were actually clothed with the Resurrection body, or with the body which they had formerly borne, or that many saints from out Hades appeared to those who loved them, and with them had waited for the Kingdom, in the forms which they had known? We know too little of the connection between the other world and this, and the mode in which the departed may communicate with those here, to venture on any decided statement, especially as we take into account the unique circumstances of the occasion.

[133] But certainly not through a separation of the serum and the cruor, which is the mark of beginning putrefaction.

[134] The Arimathea of Joseph is probably the modern Er Ram, two hours north of Jerusalem, on a conical hill, somewhat east of the road that leads from Jerusalem to Nablus (Jos. Ant. 8:12. 3), the Armathaim of the LXX. It is one of the undesigned evidences of the accuracy of Luke, that he described it as belonging to Judea. For, whereas Ramah in Mount Ephraim originally belonged to Samaria, it was afterwards separated from the latter and joined to the province of Judea (comp. 1 Maccabees 10:38; 10:28, 34).

[135] John computes it at about 100 litras. As in all likelihood this would refer to Roman pounds, of about twelve ounces each, the amount is large, but not such as to warrant any reasonable objection. A servant could easily carry it, and it is not said that it was all used in the burying. If it were possible to find any similar use of the expression (ltras), one might be tempted to regard the litras as indicating not the weight, but a coin. In that sense the word litra is used, sometimes as = 100 denars, in which case 100 litras would be = about 250 l., but more frequently as = 4 drachms, in which case 100 litras would be=about 12l. (comp. Herzfeld. Handelsgesch. p. 181). But the linguistic difficulty seems very great, while any possible objection to the weight of the spices is really inconsiderable. For the kind of spices used in the burying, see Book IV, Chapter 20: (as the burying of Lazarus). In later times there was a regular rubric and prayers with Kabbalistic symbolism (see Perles, Leichenfeierlichk. p. 11, Note 12). No doubt, the wounds in the Sacred Body of Jesus had been washed from their gore.

[136] The Synopsists record, that the Body of Jesus was wrapped in a linen cloth; John tells us that it was bound with the aloes and myrrh by Nicodemus into swathes or cloths, even as they were found afterwards in the empty tomb, and by their side the napkin, or soudarion, for the head. I have tried to combine the account of the Synopsists and that of John into a continuous narrative.

Chapter 16

The Resurrection

The history of the Life of Christ upon earth closes with a Miracle as great as that of its inception. It may be said that the one casts light upon the other. If He was what the Gospels represent Him, He must have been born of a pure Virgin, without sin, and He must have risen from the Dead. If the story of His Birth is true, we can believe that of His Resurrection; if that of His Resurrection is true, we can believe that of His Birth. In the nature of things, the latter was incapable of strict historical proof; and, in the nature of things, His Resurrection demanded and was capable of the fullest historical evidence. If such exists, the keystone is given to the arch; the miraculous Birth becomes almost a necessary claim, and Jesus is the Christ in the full sense of the Gospels. And yet we mark, as another parallel point between the account of the miraculous Birth and that of the Resurrection, the utter absence of details as regards these events themselves. If this circumstance may be taken as indirect evidence that they were not legendary, it also imposes on us the duty of observing the reverent silence so well befitting the case, and not intruding beyond the path which the Evangelic narrative has opened to us.

That path is sufficiently narrow, and in some respects difficult; not, as to the great event itself, nor as to its leading features, but as to the more minute details. And here, again, our difficulties arise, not so much from any actual disagreement, as from the absence of actual identity. Much of this is owning to the great compression in the various narratives, due partly to the character of the event narrated, partly to the incomplete information possessed by the narrators, of whom only one was strictly an eyewitness, but chiefly to this, that to the different narrators the central point of interest lay in one or the other aspect of the circumstances connected with the Resurrection. Not only Matthew, but also Luke, so compresses the narrative that the distinction of points of time is almost effaced. Luke seems to crowd into the Easter Evening what himself tells us occupied forty days. His is, so to speak, the pre-eminently Jerusalem account of the evidence of the Resurrection; that of Matthew the pre-eminently Galilean account of it. Yet each implies and corroborates the facts of the other. In general we ought to remember, that the Evangelists, and afterwards Paul, are not so much concerned to narrate the whole history of the Resurrection as to furnish the evidence for it. And here what is distinctive in each is also characteristic of his special view point. Matthew describes the impression of the full evidence of that Easter morning on friend and foe, and then hurries us from the Jerusalem stained with Christ's Blood back to the sweet Lake and the blessed Mount where first He spoke. It is, as if he longed to realize the Risen Christ in the scenes where he had learned to know Him. Mark, who is much more brief, gives not only a mere summary, but, if one might use the expression, tells it as from the bosom of the Jerusalem family, from the house of his mother Mary. Luke seems to have made most full inquiry as to all the facts of the Resurrection, and his narrative might almost be inscribed: Easter Day in Jerusalem. John paints such scenes, during the whole forty days, whether in Jerusalem or Galilee, as were most significant and teachful of this threefold lesson of his Gospels: that Jesus was the Christ, that He was the Son of God, and that, believing, we have life in His Name. Lastly, Paul, as one born out of due time, produces the testimony of the principal witnesses to the fact, in a kind of ascending climax. And this the more effectively, that he is evidently aware of the difficulties and the import of the question, and has taken pains to make himself acquainted with all the facts of the case.

The question is of such importance, in itself and as regards this whole history, that a discussion, however brief and even imperfect, preliminary to the consideration of the Evangelic narrations, seems necessary.

What thoughts concerning the Dead Christ filled the minds of Joseph of Arimathea, of Nicodemus, and of the other disciples of Jesus, as well as of the Apostles and of the pious women? They believed Him to be dead, and they did not expect Him to rise again from the dead, at least, in our accepted sense of it. Of this there is abundant evidence from the moment of His death, in the burial spices brought by Nicodemus, in those prepared by the women (both of which were intended as against corruption), in the sorrow of the women at the empty tomb, in their supposition that the Body had been removed, in the perplexity and bearing of the Apostle, in the doubts of so many, and indeed in the express statement: For as yet they did not know the Scripture, that He must rise again from the dead. And the notice in Matthew's Gospel, that the Sanhedrists had taken precautions against His Body being stolen, so as to give the appearance of fulfillment to His prediction that He would rise again after three days, that, therefore, they knew of such a prediction, and took it in the literal sense, would give only more emphasis to the opposite bearing of the disciples and their manifest non-expectancy of a literal Resurrection. What the disciples expected, perhaps wished, was not Christ's return in glorified corporeity, but His Second Coming in glory into His Kingdom.

But if they regarded Him as really dead and not to rise again in the literal sense, this had evidently no practical effect, not only on their former feelings towards Him, but even on their faith in Him as the promised Messiah. This appears from the conduct of Joseph and Nicodemus, from the language of the women, and from the whole bearing of the Apostles and disciples. All this must have been very different, if they had regarded the death of Christ, even on the Cross, as having given the lie to His Messianic Claims. On the contrary, the impression left on our minds is, that, although they deeply grieved over the loss of their Master, and the seeming triumph of His foes, yet His death came to them not unexpectedly, but rather as of internal necessity and as the fulfillment of His often repeated prediction. Nor can we wonder at this, since He had, ever since the Transfiguration, labored, against all their resistance and reluctance, to impress on them the act of His Betrayal and death. He had although by no means so frequently or clearly, also referred to His Resurrection. But of this they might, according to their Jewish ideas, form a very different conception from that of a literal Resurrection of that Crucified Body in a glorified state, and yet capable of such terrestrial intercourse as the Risen Christ held with them. And if it be objected that, in such case, Christ must have clearly taught them all this, it is sufficient to answer, that there was no need for such clear teaching on the point at that time; that the event itself would soon and best teach them; that it would have been impossible really to teach it, except by the event; and that any attempt at it would have involved a far fuller communication on this mysterious subject than, to judge from what is told us in Scripture, it was the purpose of Christ to impart in our present state of faith and expectancy. Accordingly, from their point of view, the prediction of Christ might have referred to the continuance of His Work, to his Vindication, or to some apparition of Him, whether from heaven or on earth, such as that of the saints in Jerusalem after the Resurrection, or that of Elijah in Jewish belief, but especially to His return in glory; certainly, not to the Resurrection as it actually took place. The fact itself would be quite foreign to Jewish ideas, which embraced the continuance of the soul after death and the final resurrection of the body, but not a state of spiritual corporeity, far less, under conditions such as those described in the Gospels. Elijah, who is so constantly introduced in Jewish tradition, is never represented as sharing in meals or offering his body for touch; the Angels who visited Abraham are represented as only making show of, not really, eating. Clearly, the Apostles had not learned the Resurrection of Christ either from the Scriptures, and this proves that the narrative of it was not intended as a fulfillment of previous expectancy, nor yet from the predictions of Christ to that effect; although without the one, and especially without the other, the empty grave would scarcely have performed in them the assured conviction of the Resurrection of Christ.

This brings us to the real question in hand. Since the Apostles and others evidently believed Him to be dead, and expected not His Resurrection, and since the fact of His death was not to them a formidable, if any, objection to His Messianic Character, such as might have induced them to invent or imagine a Resurrection, how are we to account for the history of the Resurrection with all its details in all the four Gospels and by Paul? The details, or signs are clearly intended as evidences to all of the reality of the Resurrection, without which it would not have been believed; and their multiplication and variety must, therefore, be considered as indicating what otherwise would have been not only numerous but insurmountable difficulties. similarly, the language of Paul implies a careful and searching inquiry on his part; the more rational, that, besides intrinsic difficulties and Jewish preconceptions against it, the objections to the fact must have been so often and coarsely pushed forth on him, whether in disputation or by the jibes of the Greek scholars and students who derided his preaching.

Therefore, the question to be faced is this: Considering their previous state of mind and the absence of any motive, how are we to account for the change of mind on the part of the disciples in regard to the Resurrection? There can at least be no question, that they came to believe, and with the most absolute certitude, in the Resurrection as an historical fact; nor yet, that it formed the basis and substances of all their preaching of the Kingdom; nor yet, that Paul, up to his conversion a bitter enemy of Christ, was fully persuaded of it; nor, to go a step back, that Jesus Himself expected it. The world would not have been converted to a dead Jewish Christ, however

His intimate disciples might have continued to love His memory. But they preached everywhere, first and foremost, the Resurrection from the dead! In the language of Paul: If Christ has not been raised, then is our preaching vain, your faith also is vain. Yes, and we are found false witnesses of God . . . you are yet in your sins. We must here dismiss what probably underlies the chief objection to the Resurrection: its miraculous character. The objection to Miracles, as such, proceeds on that false Supernaturalism, which traces a Miracle to the immediate fiat of the Almighty without any intervening links; and, as already shown, it involves a vicious fallacy in reasoning. But, after all, the Miraculous is only to us unprecedented and uncognisable, a very narrow basis on which to refuse historical investigation. And the historian has to account for the undoubted fact, that the Resurrection was the fundamental personal conviction of the

Apostles and disciples, the basis of their preaching, and the final support of their martyrdom. What explanation then can be offered of it?

1. We may here put aside two hypotheses, now universally discarded even in Germany, and which probably have never been seriously entertained in this country. They are that of gross fraud on the part of the disciples, who had stolen the Body of Jesus, as to which even Strauss remarks, that such a falsehood is wholly incompatible with their after life, heroism, and martyrdom; and again this, that Christ had not been really dead when taken from the Cross, and that He gradually revived again. Not to speak of the many absurdities which this theory involves, it really shifts, if we acquit the disciples of complicity, the fraud upon Christ Himself.

2. The only other explanation, worthy of attention, is the so called Vision hypothesis: that the Apostles really believed in the Resurrection, but the mere visions of Christ had performed in them this belief. The hypothesis has been variously modified. According to some, these visions were the outcome of an excited imagination, of a morbid state of the nervous system. To this there is the preliminary objection, that such visions presuppose a previous expectancy of the event, which, as we know, is the opposite of the fact. Again, such a Vision hypothesis in no way agrees with the many details and circumstances narrated in connection with Risen One, Who is described as having appeared not only to one or another in the retirement of the chamber, but to many, and in a manner and circumstances which render the idea of a mere vision impossible. Besides, the visions of an excited imagination would

not have endured and led to such results; most probably they would soon have given place to corresponding depression.

The Vision hypothesis is not much improved, if we regard the supposed vision as the result of reflection, that the disciples, convinced that the Messiah could not remain dead (and this again is contrary to fact) had performed themselves first into a persuasion that He must rise, and then into visions of the Risen One. Nor yet would it commend itself more to our mind, if were to assume that these visions had been directly sent from God Himself, to attest the fact that Christ lived. For, we have here to deal with a series of facts that cannot be so explained, such as the showing them His Sacred Wounds; the offer touch them; the command to handle Him, so as to convince themselves of His real corporeity; the eating with the disciples; the appearance by the Lake of Galilee, and others. Besides, the Vision hypothesis has to account for the events of the Easter morning, and especially for the empty tomb from which the great stone had been rolled, and in which the very graveclothes of death were seen by those who entered it. In fact, such a narrative as that recorded by Luke seems almost designed to render the Vision hypothesis impossible. We are expressly told, that the appearance of the Risen Christ, so far from meeting their anticipations, had frightened them, and that they had thought it supernatural, on which Christ had reassured them, and invited them handle Him, for a spirit has not flesh and bones, as you behold Me having. Lastly, who removed the Body of Christ from the tomb? Six weeks afterwards, Peter preached the Resurrection of Christ in Jerusalem. If Christ's enemies had removed the Body, they could easily have silenced Peter; if His friends, they would have been guilty of such fraud, as not even Strauss deems possible in the circumstances. The theories of deception, delusion, and vision being thus impossible, and the 'a priori objection to the fact, as involving a Miracle, being a fallacy in reasoning, the historical student is shut up to the simple acceptance of the narrative. To this conclusion the unpreparedness of the disciples, their previous opinions, their new testimony to martyrdom, the foundation of the Christian Church, the testimony of so many, singly and in company, and the series of recorded manifestations during forty days, and in such different circumstances, where mistake was impossible, had already pointed with unerring certainty. And even if slight discrepancies some not strictly historical details, which might have been the outcome of earliest tradition in the Apostolic Church, could be shown in those accounts which were not of eyewitnesses, it would assuredly not invalidate the great fact itself, which may unhesitatingly be pronounced that best established in history. At the same time we would carefully guard ourselves against the admission that those hypothetical flaws really exist in the narratives. On the contrary, we believe them capable of the most satisfactory arrangement, unless under the strain of hypercriticism.

The importance of all this cannot be adequately expressed in words. A dead Christ might have been a Teacher and Wonder worker, and remembered and loved as such. But only a Risen and Living Christ could be the Savior, the Life, and the Life Giver, and as such preached to all men. And of this most blessed truth we have the fullest and most unquestionable evidence. We can, therefore, implicitly yield ourselves to the impression of these narratives, and, still more, to the realization of that most sacred and blessed fact. This is the foundation of the Church, the inscription on the banner of her armies, the strength and comfort of every Christian heart, and the grand hope of humanity: The Lord is risen indeed.

End Notes:

[137] The reader who is desirous of further studying this point is referred to the admirable analysis by Canon Westcott in his notes prefatory to John 20: At the same time I must respectfully express dissent from his arrangement of some of the events connected with the Resurrection (u.s., p. 288 a).

[138] I may here state that I accept the genuineness of the concluding portion of Mark (15:9-20). If, on internal grounds, it must be admitted that it reads like a postscript; on the other hand, without it the section would read like a mutilated document. This is not the place to discuss the grounds on which I have finally accepted the genuineness of these verses. The reader may here be referred to Canon Cooks Revised Version of the first three Gospels, pp. 120-125, but especially to the masterly and exhaustive work by Dean Burgon on The last twelve verses of the Gospel according to Mark. At the same time I would venture to say, that Dean Burgon has not attached sufficient importance to the adverse impression made by the verses in question on the ground of internal evidence (see his chapter on the subject, pp. 136-190). And it must be confessed, that, whichever view we may ultimately adopt, the subject is plagued with considerable difficulties.

[139] But even if a belief in His Resurrection had been a requirement in their faith, as Keim rightly remarks, such realistic demonstration of it would not have been looked for. Herod Antipas did not search the tomb of the Baptist when he believed him risen from the dead, how much more should

the disciples of Christ have been satisfied with evidence far less realistic and frequent than that described in the Gospels. This consideration shows that there was no motive for inventing the details connected with the history of the Resurrection.

[140] How with pierced Feet He could have gone to Emmaus.

[141] This argument might be variously elaborated, and the account in the Gospels represents as the form which it afterwards took in the belief of the Church. But (a) the whole Vision hypothesis is shadowy and unreal, and the sacred writers themselves show that they knew the distinction between visions and real appearances; (b) it is impossible to reconcile it with such occurrences as that in Luke 24:38-43 and John 20:13, and, if possible, even more so, to set aside all these details as the outcome of later tradition, for which there was no other basis than the desire of vindicating a vision; (c) it is incompatible with the careful inquiry of Paul, who, as on so many other occasion, is here a most important witness. (d) The theory involves the most arbitrary handling of the Gospel narratives, such as that the Apostles had at once returned to Galilee, where the sight of the familiar scenes had kindled in them this enthusiasm; that all the notices about the third day are to be rejected, etc. (e). What was so fundamental a belief as that of the Resurrection could not have had its origin in a delusive vision. This, as Keim has shown, would be incompatible with the calm clearness of conviction and strong purpose of action which were its outcome. Besides, are we to believe that the enthusiasm had first seized the women, then the Apostle, and so on? But how, in that case, about the 500 of whom Paul speaks? They could scarcely all have been seized with the same mania. (f) A mere vision is unthinkable under such circumstances as the walk to Emmaus, the conversation with Thomas, with Peter, etc. Besides, it is incompatible with the giving of such definite promises by the Risen Christ as that of the Holy Spirit, and of such detailed directions as that of Evangelizing the world. (g) Lastly, as Keim points out, it is incompatible with the fact that these manifestations ceased with the Ascension. We have eight or at most nine such manifestations in the course of six weeks, and then they suddenly and permanently cease! This would not accord with the theory of visions on the part of excited enthusiasts. But were the Apostles such? Does not the perusal of the Gospel narratives leave on the impartial reader exactly the opposite impression?

[142] These two modes of accounting for the narrative of the Resurrection: by fraud, and that Christ's was not real death, were already attempted by Celsus, 1700 years ago, and the first, by the Jews long before that. Keim

has subjected them, as modified by different advocates, to a searching criticism, and, with keen irony, exhibited their utter absurdity. In regard to the supposition of fraud he says: it shows that not even the faintest idea of the holy conviction of the Apostles and first Christians has penetrated hardened spirits. The objection that the Risen One had only manifested Himself to friends, not before enemies, is also as old as Celsus. It ignores that, throughout, the revelation of Christ does not supersede, but imply faith; that there is no such thing in Christianity as forcing conviction, instead of eliciting faith; and that the purpose of the manifestations of the Risen Christ was to confirm, to comfort, and to teach His disciples. As for His enemies, Jesus had expressly declared that they would not see Him again until the judgment.

[143] The most deeply painful, but also interesting study is that of the conclusion at which Keim ultimately arrives (Gesch. Jesu v. Naz. 3: pp. 600-605). It has already been stated with what merciless irony he exposes the fraud and the non-death theory, as well as the arguments of Strauss. The Vision hypothesis he seems at first to advocate with considerable ingenuity and rhetorical power. And he succeeds in this the more easily, that, sadly, he surrenders, although most arbitrarily, almost every historical detail in the narrative of the Resurrection! And yet what is the result at which he ultimately arrives? He shows, perhaps more conclusively than anyone else, that the vision hypothesis is also impossible! having done so, he virtually admits that he cannot offer any explanation as to the mysterious exit of the life of Jesus. Probably the visions of the Risen Christ were granted directly by God Himself and by the glorified Christ (p. 602). Even the bodily appearance itself may be conceded to those who without it fear to lose all (p. 603). But from this there is but a very small step to the teaching of the Church. At any rate, the greatest of negative critics have, by the admission of his inability to explain the Resurrection in a natural manner, given the fullest confirmation to the fundamental article of our Christian faith.

[144] Reuss (HiEvang. p. 698) well remarks, that if this fundamental dogma of the Church had been the outcome of invention, care would have been taken that the accounts of it should be in the strictest and most literal agreement.

[145] Godet aptly concludes his able discussion of the subject by observing that, if Strauss admits that the Church would have never arisen if the Apostles had not had unshaken faith in the reality of Christ's Resurrection, we may add, that this faith of the Apostles would have never arisen unless the Resurrection had been a true historical fact.

Chapter 17

The Resurrection and Ascension

Grey dawn was streaking the sky, when they who had so lovingly watched Him to His Burying were making their lonely way to the rock hewn Tomb in the Garden. Considerable as are the difficulties of exactly harmonizing the details in the various narratives, if, importance attaches to such attempts, we are thankful to know that any hesitation only attaches to the arrangement of minute particulars, and not to the great facts of the case. And even these minute details would, as we shall have occasion to show, be harmonious, if only we knew all the circumstances.

The difference, if such it may be called, in the names of the women, who at early morning went to the Tomb, scarce requires elaborate discussion. It may have been, that there were two parties, starting from different places to meet at the Tomb, and that this also accounts for the slight difference in the details of what they saw and heard at the Grave. At any rate, the mention of the two Marys and Joanna is supplemented in Luke by that of the other women with them, while, if John speaks only of Mary Magdalene, her report to Peter and John: We do not know where they have laid Him, implies, that she had not gone alone to the Tomb. It was the first day of the week, according to Jewish reckoning the third day from His death. The narrative leaves the impression that the Sabbath's rest had delayed their visit to the Tomb; but it is at least a curious coincidence that the relatives and friends of the deceased were in the habit of going to the grave up to the third day (when presumably corruption was supposed to begin), so as to make sure that those laid there were really dead. Commenting on this, that Abraham described Mount Moriah on the third day, the Rabbis insist on the importance of the third day in various events connected with Israel, and especially speak of it in connection with the resurrection of the dead, referring in proof to Hosea 6:2. In another place, appealing to the same prophetic saying, they infer from Genesis 42:7, that God never leaves the just more than three days in anguish. In mourning also the third day formed a sort of period, because it was thought that the soul hovered around the body until the third day, when it finally parted from its tabernacle.

Although these things are here mentioned, we need scarcely say that no such thoughts were present with the holy mourners who, in the grey of that Sunday morning, went to the Tomb. Whether or not there were two groups of women who started from different places to meet at the Tomb, the most prominent figure among them was Mary Magdalene, as prominent among the pious women as Peter was among the Apostles. She seems to have reached the Grave, and, seeing the great stone that had covered its entrance rolled away, hastily judged that the Body of Jesus had been removed. Without waiting for further inquiry, she ran back to inform Peter and John of the fact. The Evangelist here explains, that there had been a great earthquake, and that the Angel of the Lord, to human sight as lightning and in brilliant white garment, had rolled back the stone, and sat upon it, when the guard, frightened by what they heard and saw, and especially by the look and attitude of heavenly power in the Angel, had been seized with mortal faintness. Remembering the events connected with the Crucifixion, which had no doubt been talked about among the soldiery, and bearing in mind the impression of such a sight on such minds, we could readily understand the effect on the two sentries who that long night had kept guard over the solitary Tomb. The event itself (we mean: as regards the rolling away of the stone), we suppose to have taken place after the Resurrection of Christ, in the early dawn, while the holy women were on their way to the Tomb. The earthquake cannot have been one in the ordinary sense, but a shaking of the place, when the Lord of Life burst the gates of Hades to re-tenant His Glorified Body, and the lightning-like Angel descended from heaven to roll away the stone. To have left it there, when the Tomb was empty, would have implied what was no longer true. But there is a magnificent irony in the contrast between man's elaborate precautions and the ease with which the Divine Hand can sweep them aside, and which, as throughout the history of Christ and of His Church, recalls the prophetic declaration: He that sits in the heavens shall laugh at them.

While the Magdalene hurried, probably by another road, to the quarters of Peter and John, the other women also had reached the

Tomb, either in one party, or, it may be, in two companies. They had wondered and feared how they could accomplish their pious purpose, for, who would roll away the stone for them? But, as often, the difficulty apprehended no longer existed. Perhaps they thought that the now absent Mary Magdalene had obtained help for this. At any rate, they now entered the vestibule of the Sepulcher. Here the appearance of the Angel filled them with fear. But the heavenly Messenger called them to dismiss apprehension; he told them that Christ was not there, nor yet any longer dead, but risen, as indeed, He had foretold in Galilee to His disciples; finally, he called them to hurry with the announcements to the disciples, and with this message, that, as Christ had directed them before, they were to meet Him in Galilee. It was not only that this connected, so to speak, the wondrous present with the familiar past, and helped them to realize that it was their very Master; nor yet that in the retirement, quiet, and security of Galilee, there would be best opportunity for fullest manifestation, as to the five hundred, and for final conversation and instruction. But the main reason, and that which explains the otherwise strange, almost exclusive, prominence given at such a moment to the direction to meet Him in Galilee, has already been indicated in a previous chapter. With the scattering of the Eleven in Gethsemane on the night of Christ's betrayal, the Apostolic College was temporarily broken up. They continued, still to meet together as individual disciples, but the bond of the Apostolate was for the moment, dissolved. And the Apostolic circle was to be reformed, and the Apostolic Commission renewed and enlarged, in Galilee; not, by its Lake, where only seven of the Eleven seem to have been present, but on the mountain where He had directed them to meet Him. Thus was the end to be like the beginning. Where He had first called, and directed them for their work, there would He again call them, give fullest directions, and bestow new and most ample powers. His appearances in Jerusalem were intended to prepare them for all this, to assure them completely and joyously of the fact of His Resurrection, the full teaching of which would be given in Galilee. And when the women, perplexed and scarcely conscious, obeyed the command to go in and examine for themselves the now empty niche in the Tomb, they saw two Angels, probably as the Magdalene afterwards saw them, one at the head, the other at the feet, where the Body of Jesus had lain. They waited no longer, but hurried, without speaking to anyone, to carry to the disciples the news of which they could not even yet grasp the full import.

2. But whatever unclearness of detail may rest on the narratives of the Synoptists, owing to their great compression, all is distinct when we follow the steps of the Magdalene, as these traced in the Fourth Gospel. Hurrying from the Tomb, she ran to the lodging of Peter and to that of John, the repetition of the preposition to probably marking, that the two occupied different, although perhaps closely adjoining, quarters. Her startling news induced them to go at once, and they went towards the tomb. But they began to run, the two together, probably so soon as they were outside the town and near the Garden. John, as the younger, outran Peter. Reaching the Sepulcher first, and stooping down, he saw (blpei) the linen clothes, but, from his position, not the napkin which lay apart by itself. If reverence and awe prevented John from entering the Sepulcher, his impulsive companion, who arrived immediately after him, thought of nothing else than the immediate and full clearing up of the mystery. As he entered the tomb, he steadfastly (intently) sees (theore) in one place the linen swathes that had bound about His Head. There was no sign of haste, but all was orderly, leaving the impression of One Who had leisurely divested Himself of what no longer befitted Him. Soon the other disciples followed Peter. The effect of what he saw was, that he now believed in his heart that the Master was risen, for until then they had not yet derived from Holy Scripture the knowledge that He must rise again. And this also is most instructive. It was not the belief previously derived from Scripture, that the Christ was to rise from the Dead, which led to expectancy of it, but the evidence that He had risen which led them to the knowledge of what Scripture taught on the subject.

3. Yet whatever light had risen in the inmost sanctuary of John's heart, he spoke not his thoughts to the Magdalene, whether she had reached the Sepulcher before the two left it, or met them by the way. The two Apostles returned to their home, either feeling that nothing more could be learned at the Tomb, or to wait for further teaching and guidance. Or it might even have been partly due to a desire not to draw needless attention to the empty Tomb. But the love of the Magdalene could not rest satisfied, while doubt hung over the fate of His Sacred Body. It must be remembered that she knew only of the empty Tomb. For a time she gave away the agony of her sorrow; then, as she wiped away her tears, she stopped to take one more look into the Tomb, which she thought empty, when, as she intently gazed (theore), the Tomb seemed no longer empty. At the head and feet, where the Sacred

Body had lain, were seated two Angels in white. Their question, so deeply true from their knowledge that Christ had risen: Woman, why do you weep? Seems to have come upon the Magdalene with such overpowering suddenness, that, without being able to realize, perhaps in the semi-gloom, who it was that had asked it, she spoke, bent only on obtaining the information she sought: Because they have taken away my Lord, and I do not know where they have laid Him. So is it often with us, that, weeping, we ask the question of doubt or fear, which, if we only knew, would never have risen to our lips; that heaven's own Why? fails to impress us, even when the Voice of its Messengers would gently recall us from the error of our impatience.

But already another was to given to the Magdalene. As she spoke, she became conscious of another Presence close to her. Quickly turning round, she gazed (theore) on One Whom she recognized not, but regarded as the gardener, from His presence there and from His question: Woman, why do you weep? Whom do you seek? The hope, that she might now learn what she sought, gave wings to her words, intensity and pathos. If the supposed gardener had borne to another place the Sacred Body, she would take It away, if she only knew where It was laid. This depth and agony of love, which made the Magdalene forget even the restraints of a Jewish woman's interaction with a stranger, was the key that opened the Lips of Jesus. A moments pause, and He spoke her name in those well remembered accents, that had first unbound her from sevenfold demoniac power and called her into a new life. It was as another unbinding, another call into a new life. She had not known His appearance, just as the others did not know at first, so unlike, and yet so like, was the glorified Body to that which they had known. But she could not mistake the Voice, especially when It spoke to her, and spoke her name. So do we also often fail to recognize the Lord when He comes to us in another form than we had known. But we cannot fail to recognize Him when He speaks to us and speaks our name.

Perhaps we may here be allowed to pause, and, from the non-recognition of the Risen Lord until He spoke, ask this question: With what body shall we rise? Like or unlike the past? Assuredly, most like. Our bodies will then be true; for the soul will body itself forth according to its past history, not only impress itself, as now on the features, but express itself, so that a man may be known by what he is, and as what he is. Thus, in this respect also, has the Resurrection a moral aspect, and is the completion of the history of mankind and of each man. And the Christ also must have borne in His glorified Body all that He was, all that even His most intimate disciples had not known nor understood while He was with them, which they now failed to recognize, but knew at once when He spoke to them.

It was precisely this which now prompted the action of the Magdalene, prompted also, and explains, the answer of Jesus. As in her name she recognized His Name, the rush of old feeling came over her, and with the familiar Rabboni!, my Master, she would gladly have grasped Him. Was it the unconscious impulse to take hold on the precious treasure which she had thought forever lost; the unconscious attempt to make sure that it was not merely an apparition of Jesus from heaven, but the real Christ in His corporeity on earth; or a gesture of generation, the beginning of such acts of worship as her heart prompted? Probably all these; and yet probably she was not at the moment distinctly conscious of either or of any of these feelings. But to them all there was one answer, and in it a higher direction, given by the words of the Lord: Touch Me not, for I am not yet ascended to the Father. Not the Jesus appearing from heaven, for He had not yet ascended to the Father; not the former interaction, not the former homage and worship. There was yet a future of completion before Him in the Ascension, of which Mary did not know. Between that future of completion and the past of work, the present was a gap, belonging partly to the past and partly to the future. The past could not be recalled, the future could not be anticipated. The present was of reassurance, of consolation, of preparation, of teaching. Let the Magdalene go and tell His brethren of the Ascension. So would she best and most truly tell them that she had seen Him; so also would they best learn how the Resurrection linked the past of His Work of love for them to the future: I ascend to My Father, and your Father, and to my God, and your God. Thus, the fullest teaching of the past, the clearest manifestation of the present, and the brightest teaching of the future, all as gathered up in the Resurrection, came to the Apostles through the mouth of love of her out of whom He had cast seven devils.

4. Yet another scene on that Easter morning does Matthew relate, in explanation of how the well known Jewish slander had arisen that the disciples had stolen away the Body of Jesus. He tells, how the guard had reported to the chief priests what had happened, and how they had in turn bribed the guard to spread this rumor, at the same time promising that if the fictitious account of their having slept while the disciples robbed the Sepulcher should reach Pilate, they would intercede on their behalf. Whatever else may be said, we know that from the time of

Justin Martyr this has been the Jewish explanation. Of late, however, it has, among thoughtful Jewish writers, given place to the so called Vision hypothesis, to which full reference has already been made.

5. It was the early afternoon of that spring day perhaps soon after the early meal, when two men from that circle of disciples left the City. Their narrative affords deeply interesting glimpses into the circle of the Church in those first days. The impression conveyed to us is of utter bewilderment, in which only some things stood out unshaken and firm: love to the Person of Jesus; love among the brethren; mutual confidence and fellowship; together with a dim hope of something yet to come, if not Christ in His Kingdom, yet some manifestation of, or approach to it. The Apostolic College seems broken up into units; even the two chief Apostles, Peter and John, are only certain of them that were with us. And no wonder; for they are no longer Apostles, sent out. Who is to send them forth? Not a dead Christ! And what would be their commission, and to whom and where? And above all rested a cloud of utter uncertainty and perplexity. Jesus was a Prophet mighty in word and deed before God and all the people. But their rulers had crucified Him. What was to be their new relation to Jesus; what to their rulers? And what of the great hope of the Kingdom, which they had connected with Him?

Thus they were unclear on that very Easter Day even as to His Mission and Work: unclear as to the past, the present, and the future. What need for the Resurrection, and for the teaching which the Risen One alone could bring! These two men had on that very day been in communication with Peter and John. And it leaves on us the impression, that, amid the general confusion, all had brought such news as they, or had come to hear them, and had tried but failed, to put it all into order or to see light around it. The women had come to tell of the empty Tomb and of their vision of Angels, who said that He was alive. But as yet the Apostles had no explanation to offer. Peter and John had gone to see for themselves. They had brought back confirmation of the report that the Tomb was empty, but they had seen neither Angels nor Him Whom they were said to have declared alive. And, although the two had evidently left the circle of the disciples, if not Jerusalem, before the Magdalene came, yet we know that even her account did not carry conviction to the minds of those that heard it.

Of the two, who on that early spring afternoon left the City in company, we know that one bore the name of Cleopas. The other, unnamed, has for that very reason, and because the narrative of that work bears in its vividness the character of personal recollection, been identified with Luke himself. If so, then, as has been finely remarked, each of the Gospels would, like a picture, bear in some dim corner the indication of its author: the first, that of the publican; that by Mark, that of the young man, who, in the night of the Betrayal, had fled from his captors; that of Luke in the Companion of Cleopas; and that of John, in the disciple whom Jesus loved. Uncertainty, almost equal to that about the second traveler to Emmaus, rests on the identification of that place. But such great probability attaches, if not to the exact spot, yet to the locality, or rather the valley, that we may in imagination follow the two companies on their road.

We have leave the City by the Western Gate. A rapid progress for about twenty five minutes, and we have reached the edge of the plateau. The blood strained City, and the cloud and gloom capped trying place of the followers of Jesus, are behind us; and with every step forward and upward the air seems fresher and freer, as if we felt in it the scent of mountains, or even the far off breezes of the sea. Other twenty five or thirty minutes, perhaps a little more, passing here and there country houses, and we pause to look back, now on the wide prospect far as Bethlehem. Again we pursue our way. We are now getting beyond the dreary, rocky region, and are entering on a valley. To our right is the pleasant spot that marks the ancient Nephtoah, on the border of Judah, now occupied by the village of Lifta. A short quarter of an hour more, and we have left the well paved Roman road and are heading up a lovely valley. The path gently climbs in a northwesterly direction, with the height on which Emmaus stands prominently before us. About equidistant are, on the right Lifta, on the left Kolonieh. The roads from these two, describing almost a semicircle (the one to the northwest, the other to the northeast), meet about a quarter of a mile to the south of Emmaus (Hammoza, Beit Mizza). What an oasis this in a region of hills! Among the course of the stream, which babbles down, and low in the valley is crossed by a bridge, are scented orange and lemon gardens, olive groves, luscious fruit trees, pleasant enclosures, shady nooks, bright dwellings, and on the height lovely Emmaus. A sweet spot to which to wander on that spring afternoon; a most suitable place where to meet such companionship, and to find such teaching, as on that Easter Day.

It may have been where the two roads from Lifta and Kolonieh meet, that the mysterious Stranger, Whom they did not know, their eyes being occupied, joined the two friends. Yet all these six or seven miles their conversation had been of Him, and even now their flushed faces bore the marks of sadness on account of those events of which they had been speaking, disappointed hopes, all the more bitter for the perplexing news about the empty Tomb and the absent Body of the Christ. So is Christ often near to us when our eyes are occupied, and we know Him not; and so do ignorance and unbelief often fill our hearts with sadness, even when truest joy would most become us. To the question of the Stranger about the topics of a conversation which had so visibly affected them, they replied in language which shows that they were so absorbed by it themselves, as scarcely to understand how even a festive pilgrim and stranger in Jerusalem could have failed to know it, or perceive its supreme importance. Yet, strangely unsympathetic as from His question He might seem, there was that in His Appearance which unlocked their inmost hearts. They told Him their thoughts about this Jesus; how He had showed Himself a prophet mighty in deed and word before God and all the people; then, how their rulers had crucified Him; and, lastly, how fresh perplexity had come to them from the news which the women had brought, and which Peter and John had so far confirmed, but were unable to explain. Their words were almost childlike in their simplicity, deeply truthful, and with a pathos and earnest craving for guidance and comfort that goes straight to the heart. To such souls it was, that the Risen Savior would give His first teaching. The very rebuke with which He opened it must have brought its comfort. We also, in our weakness, are sometimes great distressed when we hear what, at the moment, seem to us overwhelming difficulties raised to any of the great of our holy faith; and, in perhaps equal weakness, feel comforted and strengthened, when some great one turns them aside, or avows himself in face of them a believing disciple of Christ. As if man's puny height could reach up to heaven's mysteries, or any big infant's strength was needed to steady the building which God has reared on that great Cornerstone! But Christ's rebuke was not of such kind. Their sorrow arose from their folly in looking only at the things seen, and this, from their slowness to believe what the prophets had spoken. Had they attended to this, instead of allowing it all. Did not the Scriptures with one voice teach this twofold truth about the Messiah, that He was to suffer and to enter into His glory? Then why wonder, why not rather expect, that He had suffered, and that Angels had proclaimed Him alive again?

He spoke it, and fresh hope sprang up in their hearts, new thoughts rose in their minds. Their eager gaze was fastened on Him as He now opened up, one by one, the Scriptures, from Moses and all the prophets, and in each well remembered passage interpreted to them the things concerning

Himself. Oh, that we had been there to hear, though in silence of our hearts also, if only we crave for it, and if we walk with Him, He sometimes so opens from the Scriptures from all the Scriptures, that which does not come to us by critical study: the things concerning Himself. All too quickly fled the moments. The brief space was traversed, and the Stranger seemed about to pass on from Emmaus, not the feigning it, but really: for, the Christ will only abide with us if our longing and loving constrain Him. But they could not part with Him. They constrained Him. Love made them ingenious. It was toward evening; the day was far spent; He must even abide with them. What rush of thought and feeling comes to us, as we think of it all, and try to realize time, scenes, circumstances in our experience, that are blessedly akin to it.

The Master allowed Himself to be held back. He went in to be their guest, as they thought, for the night. The simple evening meal was spread. He sat down with them to the frugal table. And now He was no longer the Stranger; He was the Master. No one asked, or questioned, as He took the bread and spoke the words of blessing, then, breaking, gave it to them. But that moment it was, as if an unfelt Hand had been taken from their eyelids, as if suddenly the film had been cleared from their sight. And as they knew Him, He vanished from their view, for, that which He had come to do had been done. They were unspeakably rich and happy now. But, amid it all, one thing forced itself ever anew upon them, that, even while their eyes had yet been occupied, their hearts had burned within them, while He spoke to them and opened to them the Scriptures. So, then, they had learned to full the Resurrection lesson, not only that He was risen indeed, but that it needed not His seen Bodily Presence, if only He opened up to the heart and mind all the Scriptures concerning Himself. And this, concerning those other words about holding and touching Him, about having conversation and fellowship with Him as the Risen One, had been also the lesson taught the Magdalene, when He would not suffer her loving, worshipful touch, pointing her to the Ascension before Him. This is the great lesson concerning the Risen One, which the Church fully learned in the Day of Pentecost.

6. That same afternoon, in circumstances and manner to us unknown, Jesus had appeared to Peter. We may perhaps suggest, that it was after His manifestation at Emmaus. This would complete the cycle of mercy: first, to the loving sorrow of the woman; next, to the loving perplexity of the disciples; then, to the anxious heart of the stricken Peter, last, in

the circle of the Apostles, which was again drawing together around the assured fact of His Resurrection.

7. These two in Emmaus could not have kept the good news to themselves. Even if they had not remembered the sorrow and perplexity in which they had left their fellow disciples in Jerusalem that forenoon, they could not have kept it to themselves, could not have remained in Emmaus, but must have gone to their brethren in the City. So they left the uneaten meal, and hurried back the road they had traveled with the now well known Stranger, but, ah, with what lighter hearts and steps!

They knew well the meeting place where to find the Twelve not the Twelve now, but the Eleven, and even thus their circle was not complete, for, as already stated, it was broken up, and at least Thomas was not with the others on that Easter Evening of the first Lord's Day. But, as Luke is careful to inform us, with the others who then associated with them. This is of extreme importance, as marking that the words which the Risen Christ spoke on that occasion were addressed not to the Apostles as such, a thought forbidden also by the absence of Thomas, but to the Church, although it may be as personified and represented by such of the Twelve, or rather Eleven, as were present on the occasion.

When the two from Emmanus arrived, they found the little band as sheep sheltering within the fold from the storm. Whether they apprehended persecution simply as disciples, or because the news of the empty Tomb, which had reached the authorities, would stir the fears of the Sanhedrists, special precautions had been taken. The outer and inner doors were shut, to conceal their gathering and to prevent surprise. But those assembled were now sure of at least one thing. Christ was risen. And when they from Emmanus told their wondrous story, the others could antiphonally reply by relating how He had appeared, not only to the Magdalene, but also to Peter. And still they seem not yet to have understood His Resurrection; to have regarded it as rather an Ascension to Heaven, from which He had made manifestation, that as the reappearance of His real, though glorified Corporeity.

They were sitting at supper, if we may infer from the notice of Mark, and from what happened immediately afterwards, discussing, not without considerable doubt and misgiving, the real import of these appearances of Christ. That to the Magdalene seems to have been put aside, at least, it is not mentioned, and, even in regard to the others, they seem to have been considered, at any rate by some, rather as what we might call supernatural appearances. But all at once He stood in the midst of them. The common salutation, on His Lips not common, but a reality, fell on their hearts at first with terror rather than joy. They had spoken of supernatural appearances, and now they believed they were gazing (theoren) on a spirit. This the Savior first, and once for all, corrected, by the exhibition of the glorified marks of His Sacred Wounds, and by inviting them handle Him to convince themselves, that His was a real Body, and what they saw not a disembodied spirit. The unbelief of doubt now gave place to the not daring to believe all that it meant, for very gladness, and for wondering whether there could now be any longer fellowship or bond between this Risen Christ and them in their bodies. It was to remove this also, which, though from another aspect, was equally unbelief, that Jesus now partook before them of their supper of broiled fish, thus holding with them true human fellowship as of old.

It was this lesson of His continuity, in the strictest sense, with the past, which was required in order that the Church might be, so to speak, reconstituted now in the Name, Power, and Spirit of the Risen One Who had lived and died. Once more He spoke the Peace be to you! and now it was to them not occasion of doubt or fear, but the well known salutation of their old Lord and Master. It was followed by the regathering and constituting of the Church as that of Jesus Christ, the Risen One. The Church of the Risen One was to be the Ambassador of Christ, as He had been the Delegate of the Father. The Apostles were [say rather, the Church was] commissioned to carry on Christ's work, and not to begin a new one. As the Father has sent Me [in the past, for His Mission was completed], even so send I you [in the constant, present, until His coming again]. This marks the threefold relation of the Church to the Son, to the Father, and to the world, and her position in it. In the same manner, for the same purpose so far as possible, with the same qualification and the same authority as the Father had sent Christ, does He commission His Church. And so it was that He made it a very real commission when He breathed on them, not individually but as a assembly, and said: Take you the Holy Spirit; and this, manifestly not in the absolute sense, since the Holy Spirit was not yet given, but as the connecting link with, and the qualification for, the authority bestowed on the Church. Or, to set forth another aspect of it by somewhat inverting the order of the words: The Mission of the Church and her authority to forgive or retain sins are connected with a personal qualification: Take you the Holy Spirit;, in which the word take should also be marked. This is the authority which the Church possesses, not ex opere operato, but as not connected with the taking and the indwelling of the Holy Spirit in the Church.

It still remains to explain, so far as we can, these two points: in what this power of forgiving and retaining sins consists, and in what manner it resides in the Church. In regard to the former we must first inquire what idea it would convey to those to whom Christ spoke the words. It has already been explained, that the power of loosing and binding referred to the legislative authority claimed by, and conceded to, the Rabbinic College. Similarly, as previously stated, that here referred to applied to their juridical or judicial power, according to which they pronounced a person either, Zakkai, innocent or free; absolved, Patur; or else liable, guilty, Chayyabh (whether liable to punishment or sacrifice.) In the true sense, therefore, this is rather administrative, disciplinary power, the power of the keys, such as Paul would have had the Corinthian Church put in force, the power of admission and exclusion, of the authoritative declaration of the forgiveness of sins, in the exercise of which power (as it seems to the present writer) the authority for the administration of the Holy Sacraments is also involved. And yet it is not, as is sometimes represented, absolution from sin, which belongs only to God and to Christ as Head of the Church, but absolution of the sinner, which He has delegated to His Church: Who ever sins you forgive, they are forgiven. These words also teach us, that the Rabbis claimed in virtue of their office, that the Lord bestowed on His Church in virtue of her receiving, and of the indwelling of, the Holy Spirit.

In answering the second question proposed, we must bear in mind one important point. The power of binding and loosing had been primarily committed to the Apostles, and exercised by them in connection with the Church. On the other hand, that of forgiving and retaining sins, in the sense explained, was primarily bestowed on the Church, and exercised by her through her representatives, the Apostles, and those to whom they committed rule. Although, therefore, the Lord on that night committed this power to His Church, it was in the person of her representatives and rulers. The Apostles alone could exercise legislative function, but the Church, has to the end of time the power of the keys.

8. There had been absent from the circle of disciples on that Easter Evening one of the Apostles, Thomas. Even when told of the marvelous events at that gathering, he refused to believe, unless he had personal and sensous evidence of the truth of the report. It can scarcely have been, that Thomas did not believe in the fact that Christ's Body had left the Tomb, or that He had really appeared. But he held fast by what we may term the Vision hypothesis, or, in this case, rather the supernatural

theory. But until this Apostle also had come to conviction of the Resurrection in the only real sense, of the identical though glorified Corporeity of the Lord, and therefore of the continuity of the past with the present and future, it was impossible to reform the Apostolic Circle, or to renew the Apostolic commission, since its primal message was testimony concerning the Risen One. This, if we may so suggest, seems the reason why the Apostles still remain in Jerusalem, instead of hastening, as directed, to meet the Master in Galilee.

A quiet week had passed, during which, and this also may be for our twofold learning, the Apostles excluded not Thomas, nor yet Thomas withdrew from the Apostles. Once more the day of days had come, the Octave of the Feast. From that Easter Day onwards the Church must, even without special institution, have celebrated the weekly recurring memorial of His Resurrection, as that when He breathed on the Church the breath of a new life, and consecrated it to be His Representative. Thus, it was not only the memorial of His Resurrection, but the birthday of the Church, even as Pentecost was her baptism day. On that Octave, then, the disciples were again gathered, under circumstances precisely similar to those of Easter, but now Thomas was also with them. Once more, and it is again especially marked: the doors being shut, the Risen Savior appeared in the midst of the disciples with the well known salutation. He now offered to Thomas the demanded evidence; but it was no longer either needed or sought. With a full rush of feeling he yielded himself to the blessed conviction, which once formed, must immediately have passed into act of adoration: My Lord and my God! The fullest confession this up to this point made, and which truly embraced the whole outcome of the new conviction concerning the reality of Christ's Resurrection. We remember how, under similar circumstances, Nathnael had been the first to utter fullest confession. We also remember the analogous reply of Jesus. As then, so now, He pointed to the higher: to a faith which was not the outcome of sight, and therefore limited and bounded by sight, whether of the sense or of perception by the intellect. As one has finely remarked: This last and greatest of the Beatitudes is the peculiar heritage of the later Church, and thus most aptly comes as the consecration gift of that Church.

9.   The next scene presented to us is once again by the Lake of Galilee. The manifestation to Thomas, and, with it, the restoration of unity in the Apostalic Circle, had originally concluded the Gospel of John. But the

report which had spread in the early Church, that Disciple whom Jesus loved was not to die, led him to add to his Gospel, by way of Appendix, and account of the events with which this expectancy had connected itself. It is most instructive to the critic, when challenged at every step to explain why one or another fact is not mentioned or mentioned only in one Gospel, to find that, but for the correction of a possible misapprehension in regard to the aged Apostle, the Fourth Gospel would have contained no reference to the manifestation of Christ in Galilee to the presence of the disciples there before the Ascension. Yet, for all that John had it in his mind. And should we not learn from this, that what appear to us strange omissions, which, when held by the side of the other Gospel narratives, seem to involve discrepancies, may be capable of the most satisfactory explanation, if we only knew all the circumstance?

The history itself sparkles like a gem in its own peculiar setting. It is of green Galilee, and of the blue Lake, and recalls the early days and scenes of this history. As Matthew has it, the eleven disciples went away into Galilee, probably immediately after that Octave of the Easter. It can scarcely be doubted, that they made known not only the fact of the Resurrection, but the meeting which the Risen One had given them, perhaps at that Mountain where He had spoken His first Sermon. And so it was, that some doubted, and that He afterwards appeared to the five hundred at once. But on that morning there were by the Lake of Tiberias only seven of the disciples. Five of them only are named. They are those who most closely kept in company with Him, perhaps also they who lived nearest the Lake.

The scene is introduced by Peter's proposal to go fishing. It seems as if the old habits had come back to them with the old associations. Peter's companions naturally proposed to join him. All that still, clear night they were on the Lake, but caught nothing. Did not this recall to them for former event, when James and John, and Peter and Andrew were called to be Apostles, and did it not especially recall to Peter the searching and sounding of his heart on the morning that followed? But so utterly self unconscious were they, and, let us add, so far is this history from any trace of legendary design, that not the slightest indication of this appears. Early morning was breaking, and under the rosy glow above the cool shadows were still lying on the pebbly beach. There stood the Figure of One Whom they recognized not not even when He spoke. Yet His Words were intended to bring them this knowledge. The direction to cast the net to the right side of the ship brought them, as He had said, the haul for which they had toiled all night in vain. And more than this: such a multitude of fish, enough for the disciple whom Jesus loved, and whose heart may previously have misgiven him. He whispered it to Peter: It is the Lord, and Simon, only reverently gathering about him his fishers upper garment, threw himself into the sea. Yet even so, except to be sooner by the side of Christ, Peter seems to have gained nothing by his haste. The others, leaving the ship, and transferring themselves to a small boat, which must have been attached to it followed, rowing the short distance of about one hundred yards, and dragging after them the net, weighted with the fish.

They stepped on the beach, hallowed by His Presence, in silence, as if they had entered Church or Temple. They dared not even dispose of the net full of fish which they had dragged on shore, until He directed them what to do. This only they notice, that some unseen hand had prepared the morning meal, which, when asked by the Master, they had admitted they had not of their own. And now Jesus directed them to bring the fish they had caught. When Peter dragged up the weight net, it was found full of great fish, not less than a hundred and fifty three in number. There is no need to attach any symbolic import to that number, as the Fathers and later writers have done. We can quite understand it seems almost natural, that, in the peculiar circumstances, they should have counted the large fish in that miraculous catch that still left the net unbroken. It may have been, that they were told to count the fish, partly, also, to show the reality of what had taken place. But on the fire the coals there seems to have been only one fish, and beside it only one bread. To this meal He now called them, for they seem still to have hung back in reverent awe, nor dared they ask him, Who He was, well knowing it was the Lord. This, as John notes, was the third appearance of Christ to the disciples as a body.

10. And still this morning of blessing was not ended. The frugal meal was past, with all its significant teaching of just sufficient provision for His servants, and abundant supply in the unbroken net beside them. But some special teaching was needed, more even that that to Thomas, for him whose work was to be so prominent among the Apostles, whose love was so ardent, and yet in its very ardor so full of danger to himself. For, our dangers spring not only from deficiency, but it may be from excess of feeling, when that feeling is not commensurate with inward strength. Had Peter not confessed, quite honestly, yet,

as the event proved, mistakenly, that his love to Christ would endure even an ordeal that would disperse all the others? And had he not, almost immediately afterwards, and though prophetically warned of it, three times denied his Lord? Jesus had, since then appeared especially to Peter as the Risen One. But this threefold denial still, stood, as it were, uncancelled before the other disciples before Peter himself. It was to this that the threefold question to the Risen Lord now referred. Turning to Peter, with pointed though most gentle allusion to be danger of self confidence, a confidence springing from only a sense of personal affection, even though genuine, He asked: Simon, son of Jona, as it were with fullest reference to what he was naturally, do you love Me more than these? Peter understood it all. No longer with confidence in self, avoiding the former reference to the others, and even with marked choice of a different word to express his affection from that which Jesus had used, he replied, appealing rather to his Lord's, than to his own consciousness: Yes, Lord, You know that I love You. And even here the answer of Christ is characteristic. it was to set him first the humblest work, that which needed most tender care and patience: Feed [provide with food] My Lambs.

Yet a second time came the same question, although now without the reference to the others, and, with the same answer by Peter, the now varied and enlarged commission: Feed [shepherd, pomaine] My Sheep. Yet a third time did Jesus repeat the same question, now adopting in it the very word which Peter had used to express his affection. Peter was grieved at this threefold repetition. It recalled only too bitterly his threefold denial. And yet Jesus was not doubtful of Peter's love, for each time He followed up His question with a fresh Apostle commission; but now that He put it for the third time, Peter would have the Lord send down the sounding line quite into the lowest deep of this heart: Lord, You know all things, You perceive that I love You! And now Jesus spoke it: Feed [provide food for] My sheep. His Lamb, His Sheep, to be provided for, to be tended as such! And only love can do such service.

Yes, and Peter did love the Lord Jesus. He had loved Him when he said it, only too confident in the strength of his feelings, that he would follow the Master even to death. And Jesus saw it all, yes, and how this love of the ardent temperament which had once made him rove at wild liberty, would give place to patient work of love, and be crowned with that martyrdom which, when the beloved disciple wrote, was already matter of the past. And the very manner of death by which he was to glorify God was indicated in the words of Jesus.

As He spoke them, He joined the symbolic action to His Follow Me. This command, and the encouragement of being in death literally made like Him, following Him, was Peter's best strength. He obeyed; but as he turned to do so, he saw another following. As John himself puts it, it seems almost to convey that he had longed to share Peter's call, with all that it implied. For, John speaks of himself as the disciple whom Jesus loves, and he reminds us that in that night of betrayal he had been especially a sharer with Peter had spoken what the other had silently asked of him. Was it impatience, was it a touch of the old Peter, or was it a simple inquiry of brotherly interest which prompted the question, as he pointed to John: Lord, and this man, what? Whatever had been the motive, to him, as to us all, when perplexed about those who seem to follow Christ, we ask it, sometimes in bigoted narrowness, sometimes in ignorance, folly, or jealousy, is this answer: What is that to you? follow you Me. For John also had his life work for Christ. It was to wait while He was coming, to wait those many years in patient labor, while Christ was coming.

But what did it mean? The saying went aboard among the brethren that John was not to die, but to wait until Jesus came again to reign, when death would be swallowed up in victory. But Jesus had not so said, only: If I will that he wait while I am coming. What that Coming was, Jesus had not said, and John did not know. So, then, there are things, and connected with His Coming, on which Jesus has left the veil, only to be lifted by His own Hand, which He means us not to know at present, and which we should be content to leave as He has left them.

11. Beyond this narrative we have only briefest notices: by Paul, of Christ manifesting Himself to James, which probably finally decided him for Christ, and the Eleven meeting Him at the mountain, where He had appointed them; by Luke, of the teaching in the Scriptures during the forty days of communication between the Risen Christ and the disciples.

But this twofold testimony comes to us from Matthew and Mark, that then the worshipping disciples were once more formed into the Apostolic Circle, Apostles, now, of the Risen Christ. And this was the warrant of their new commission: All power (authority) has been given to Me in heaven and on earth. And this was their new commission: Go you, therefore, and make disciples of all the nations, baptizing them into the Name of the Father, and of the Son, and of the Holy Spirit. And this was their work: Teaching them to observe all things whatever I commanded you. And this is His final and sure promise: And look, I am with you always, even to the end of the world.

12. We are once more in Jerusalem, where He had invited them go to wait for the fulfillment of the great promise. The Pentecost was drawing near. And on that last day, the day of His Ascension, He led them forth to the well remembered Bethany. From where He had made His last triumphal Entry into Jerusalem before His Crucifixion, would He make His triumphant Entry visibly into Heaven. Once more would they have asked Him about that which seemed to them the final consummation, the restoration of the Kingdom to Israel. But such questions became them not. Theirs was to be work, not rest; suffering, not triumph. The great promise before them was of spiritual, not outward, power: of the Holy Spirit, and their call not yet to reign with Him, but to bear witness for Him. And, as He so spoke, He lifted His Hands in blessing upon them, and, as He was visibly taken up, a cloud received Him. And still they gazed, with upturned faces, on that luminous cloud which had received Him, and two Angels spoke to them this last message from him, that He should so come in like manner, as they had beheld Him going into heaven.

And so their last question to Him, before He had parted from them, was also answered, and with blessed assurance. Reverently they worshipped Him; then, with great joy, returned to Jerusalem. So it was all true, all real, and Christ sat down at the Right Hand of God! From here on, neither doubting, ashamed, nor yet afraid, they were continually in the Temple, blessing God, And they went forth and preached everywhere, the Lord working with them, and confirming the word by the signs that followed. Amen.

Amen! It is so. Ring out the bells of heaven; sing forth the Angelic welcome of worship; carry it to the utmost bound of earth! Shine forth from Bethany, You Sun of Righteousness, and chase away earth's mist and darkness, for Heaven's golden day has broken!

Easter Morning, 1883. Our task is ended, and we also worship and look up. And we go back from this sight into a hostile world, to love, and to live, and to work for Risen Christ. But as earth's day is growing dim, and, with earth's gathering darkness, breaks over it heavens storm, we ring out, as of old they were habit, from church tower, to the mariners that hugged a rock bound coast, our Easter bells to guide them who are overdue, over the storm tossed sea, beyond the breakers, into the desired shelter. Ring out, earth, all your Easter chimes; bring you offerings, all you people; worship in faith, for This Jesus, When was received up from you into heaven, shall so come, in like manner as you saw Him going into heaven. Even so, Lord Jesus, come quickly!

End Notes:

[146] The accounts imply, that the women did not know of the sealing of the stone and of the guard set over the Tomb. This may be held as evidence, that Matthew could have not meant that the two Marys had visited the grave on the previous evening (106:1). In such case they must have seen the guard. Nor could the women in that case have wondered who roll away the stone for them.

[147] I cannot believe that Matthew 26:1 refers to a visit of the two Marys on the Saturday evening, nor Mark 15:1 to a purchasing at that time of spices.

[148] It may, however, have been that the appearance of the one Angel was to one company of women, that of two Angels to another.

[149] While I would speak very hesitantly on the subject, it seems to me as if the Evangelist has compressed the whole of that mornings event into one narrative: The Women at the Sepulcher. It is this compression which gives the appearance of more events than really took place, owing to the appearance of being divided into scenes, and the circumstance that the different writers give prominence to different persons or else to different details in what is really one scene. I am disposed, though again with great hesitancy, to regard the appearance of Jesus to the women (Matthew 26:9) as the same with that to Mary Magdalene, recorded in John 20:11-17, and referred to in Mark 15:9, the more so as the words in Matthew 26:9 as they went to tell His disciples are spurious, being probably intended for harmonious purposes. But, while suggesting this view, I would by no means maintain it as one certain to my own mind, although it would simplify details otherwise very intricate.

[150] It may be regarded as a specimen of what one might designate as the imputation of sinister motives to the Evangelists, when the most advanced negative criticism describes this legend as implying the contest between Jewish and Gentile Christianity (Peter and John) in which the younger

gains the race! Similarly, we are informed that the penitent on the Cross is intended to indicate the Gentiles, the impenitent the Jews! But no language can be to strong to repudiate the imputation, that so many parts of the Gospels were intended as covert attacks by certain tendencies in the early Church against others, the Petrine and Jacobine against the Johannine and Pauline directions.

[151] When Meyer contends that the plural in John 20:2, We do not know where they have laid Him, does not refer to the presence of other women with the Magdalene, but is a general expression for: We, all His followers, have no knowledge of it, he must have overlooked that, when alone, she repeats the same words in ver. 13, but markedly uses the singular number: I do not know.

[152] This may represent the Galilean form of the expression, and, if so, would be all the more evidential. Not less than four localities have been identified with Emmaus. But some preliminary difficulties must be cleared. The name Emmaus is spelt in different ways in the Tulmud (comp. Neubauer, Geogr. d. Talm. p. 100, Note 3). Josephus (War 4:1. 3; Ant. 16:2. 3) explains the meaning of the name as warm baths, or thermal springs. We will not complicate the question by discussing the derivation of Emmaus. In another place (War 5:6. 6) Josephus speaks of Vespasian having settled in an Emmaus, sixty furlongs from Jerusalem, a colony of soldiers. There can be little doubt that the Emmaus of Luke and that of Josephus are identical. Lastly, we read in Mishnah (Sukk. 4:5) of a Motsa from which they fetched the willow branches with which the altar was decorated at the Feast of Tabernacles, and the Talmud explains this Moza as Kolonieh, which again is identified by Christian writers with Vespasians colony of Roman soldiers (Caspari, Chronol Geogr. Einl. p. 207; Quart. Rep. of the Pal Explor. Fund, July 1881, p. 237 [not without some slight inaccuracies]). But an examination of the passage in the Mishanah must lead us to dismiss this part of the theory. No one could imagine that the worshippers would walk sixty stadia (seven or eight miles) for willow branches to decorate the altar, while the Mishah, besides, describes this Moza as below, or south of Jerusalem, whereas the modern Kolonieh (which is identified with the Colonia of Josephus) is northwest of Jerusalem. No doubt, the Talmud, knowing that there was an Emmaus which was Colonia, blunderingly identified with it the Moza of the willow branches. This, however, it seems lawful to infer from it, that the Emmaus of Josephus bore popularly the name of Kolonieh. We can now examine the four proposed identifications of Emmaus. The oldest and the youngest of these may be briefly dismissed.

The most common, perhaps the earliest identification, was with the ancient Nicopolis, the modern Amwas, which in Rabbinic writings also bears the name of Emmaus (Neubauer, u.s.). But this is impossible, as Nicopolis is twenty miles from Jerusalem. The latest proposed identification is that with Urtas, to the south of Bethlehem (Mrs. Finn, Quart. Rep. of Pal. Exlor. Fund, Jan. 1883, p. 53). It is impossible here to enter into the various reasons urged by the talented and accomplished proposer of this identification. Suffice it, in refutation, to note, that, admittedly, there were no natural hot baths,or thermal springs, here, only artificial Roman baths, such as, no doubt, in many other places, and that this Emmaus was Emmaus only at the particular period when they (Luke and Josephus) were writing (u.s. p. 62). There now only remain two localities, the modern Kolonieh and Kubeibeh, for the strange proposed identification by Lieut. Conder in the Quarterly Rep. of the Pal. Explor. Fund, Oct. 1876 (pp. 172-175) seems now abandoned even by its author. Kolonieh would, represent the Colonia of Josephus, according to the Talmud = Emmaus. But this is only 45 furlongs from Jerusalem. But at the head of the same valley, in the Wady Buwai, and at a distance of about three miles north, is Kubeibeh, the Emmaus of the Crusaders, just sixty furlongs from Jerusalem. Between these places is Beit Mizza, or Hammoza, which I regard as the real Emmaus. It would be nearly 55 or about 60 furlongs (Luke), sufficiently near to Kolonieh (Colonia) to account for the name, since the colony would extend up the valley, and sufficiently near to Kubeibeh to account for the tradition. The Palestine Exploration Fund has now apparently fixed on Kubeibeh as the site (see Q. Report, July, 1881, p. 237, and their N. T. map.

[153] Even to this day seems a favorite resort of the inhabitants of Jerusalem for an afternoon (comp. Conders Tent Work in Palestine, i. pp. 25-27).

[154] 60 furlongs about = 7 1/2 miles.

[155] I cannot persuade myself that the right reading of the close of ver. 17 (Luke 24) can be And they stood still, looking sad. Every reader will mark this as an incongruous, jejune break up in the vivid narrative, quite unlike the rest. We can understand the question as in our KJV, but scarcely the standing still and looking sad on the question as in the R. V.

[156] Such seems to me the meaning of His eating; any attempt at explaining, we willingly forego in our ignorance of the conditions of a glorified body, just as we refuse to discuss the manner in which He suddenly appeared in the room while the doors were shut. But I at least cannot believe, that His body was then in a transition state, not perfected not quite glorified until

His Ascension. The words in the two clauses are different in regard to the sending of Christ (pstalkn me) and in regard to the Church (pmpo ms). No doubt, there must be deeper meaning in this distinction, yet both are used of Christ and of the disciples. It may be as Cremer seems to hint (Bibl. Theol. L Exodus of the N.T. p. 529) that postllo, from which apostle and apostolate are derived, refers to a mission with a definite commission, or rather for a definite purpose, while pmpo is sending in a general sense. See the learned and ingenious Note of Canon Westcott (Comm. on John, p. 298).]

[157] It must, however, be remembered that Thomas did not deny that Christ was risen, except as in the peculiar sense of the Resurrection. Had he denied the other, he would scarcely have continued in the company of the Apostles.

[158] Significantly, the expression for fear of the Jews no longer occurs. That apprehension had for the present passed away. The account of Luke (24:44-48) is a condensed narrative, without distinction of time or place, of what occurred during all the forty days.

[159] Canon Westcott gives, from Augustine, the points of difference between this and the miraculous catch of fish on the former occasion (Luke 5). These are very interesting. Not so the fanciful speculations of the Fathers about the symbolic meaning of the number 153.

[160] So Canon Westcott renders the meaning. The coming might refer to the second Coming, to the destruction of Jerusalem, or even to the firm establishment of the Church. The tradition that John only slept in the grave at Ephesus is mentioned even by Augustine.

Appendices

Appendix 1

Pseudepigraphic Writings

I. The Book of Enoch., As the contents and the literature of this remarkable book, which is quoted by Jude (vv. 14, 15), have been fully described in Dr. Smiths and Waces Dictionary of Christian Biography (Volume 2: pp. 124-128), we may here refer to it the more shortly.

It comes to us from Palestine, but has only been preserved in an Ethiopic translation (published by Archbishop Laurence [Oxford, 1838; in English transl. 3rd ed. 1821-1838; German transl. by A. G. Hoffmann], then from five different manuscripts. by Professor Dillmann [Leipzig, 1851; in German transl. Leipzig, 1853]). But even the Ethiopic translation is not from the original Hebrew or Aramaic, but from a Greek version, of which a small fragment has been discovered (Chapter 89:42-49; published by Cardinal Mai: Comp. also Gildemeister, Zeitschr. d. D. Morg. Ges. for 1855, pp. 621-624, and Gebhardt, Merx Arch. 2:1872, p. 243).

As regards the contents of the work: An Introduction of five brief chapters, and the book (which, however, contains not a few spurious passages) consists of five parts, followed by a suitable Epilogue. The most interesting portions are those which tell of the Fall of the Angels and its consequences, of Enochs absorbed journeys through heaven and earth, and of what he saw and heard (Chapter 6-26); the Apocalyptic portions about the Kingdom of Heaven and the Advent of the Messiah (83-91); and, lastly, the exhortation discourses (91-105). When we add, that it is pervaded by a tone of intense faith and earnestness about the Messiah, the last things, and other doctrines especially brought out in the New Testament, its importance will be understood. Altogether the Book of Enoch contains 108 chapters.

From a literary point of view, it has been arranged (by Schuerer and others) into three parts: 1. The Original Work (Grundschrift), Chapter 1-36; 72-105. This portion is supposed to date from about 175 BC. 2. The Parables, Chapter 37-54:6; 55:3-59; 61-64; 69:26-70. This part also dates previous to the Birth of Christ, perhaps from the time of Herod the Great. 3. The so called Noachian Sections, Chapter 54:7-55:2; 60; 65-69:25. To these must be added Chapter 104, and the later conclusion in Chapter 105:3. On the dates of all these portions it is impossible to speak definitely.

II. Even greater, though a different interest, attaches to the Sibylline Oracles, written in Greek hexameters. In their present form they consist of twelve books, together with several fragments. Passing over two large fragments, which seem to have originally formed the chief part of the introduction to Book III, we have (1) the two first Books. These contain part of an older and Hellenist Jewish Sibyl, as well as of a poem by the Jewish Pseudo-Phocylides, in which pagan myths concerning the first ages of man are curiously welded with Old Testament views. The rest of these two books was composed, and the whole put together, not earlier than the close of the second century, perhaps by a Jewish Christian. (2) The third Book is by far the most interesting. Besides the fragments already referred to, vv. 97-807 are the work of a Hellenist Jew, deeply imbued with the Messianic hope. This part dates from about 160 BC, while vv. 49-96 seem to belong to the year 31 BC. The rest (vv. 1-45, 818-828) dates from a later period. We must here confine our attention to the most ancient portion of the work. For our present purpose, we may arrange it into three parts. In the first, the ancient pagan theogony is recast in a Jewish mold, Uranus becomes Noah; Shem, Ham, and Japheth are Saturn, Titan, and Japetus, while the building of the Tower of Babylon is the rebellion of the Titans. Then the history of the world is told, the Kingdom of Israel and of David forming the center of all. What we have called the second is the most curious part of the work. It embodies ancient pagan oracles, so to speak, in a Jewish edit, and interwoven with Jewish elements. The third part may be generally described as anti-pagan, polemical, and Apocalyptic. The Sibyl is thoroughly Hellenistic in spirit. She is loud and earnest in her appeals, bold and defiant in the tone of her Jewish pride, self conscious and triumphant in her anticipations. But the most remarkable circumstance is, that this Judaizing and Jewish Sibyl seems to have passed, though possibly only in parts, as the oracles of the ancient Erythrean Sibyl, which had predicted to the Greeks the fall of Troy, and those of the Sibyl of Cumae, which, in the infancy of Rome, Tarquinius Superbus had deposited in the Capitol, and that as such it is quoted from by Virgil (in his 4th Eclogue) in his description of the Golden Age.

Of the other Sibylline Books little need be said. The 4th, 5th, 9th, and 12th Books were written by Egyptian Jews at dates varying from the year 80 AD to the third century AD. Book VI is of Christian origin, the work of a Judaizing Christian, about the second half of the second century. Book VIII, which embodies Jewish portions, is also of Christian authorship, as are Books X and XI.

III. The collection of eighteen hymns, which in their Greek version bear the name of the Psalter of Solomon, must originally have been written in Hebrew, and dates from more than half a century BC. They are the outcome of a soul intensely earnest, although we not infrequently meet expressions of Pharisaic self religiousness. It is a time of national sorrow in which the poet sings, and it almost seems as if these Psalms had been intended to take up one or another of the leading thoughts in the corresponding Davidic Psalms, and to make, as it were, application of them to the existing circumstances. Though somewhat Hellenistic in its cast, the collection breathes ardent Messianic expectancy, and firm faith in the resurrection, and eternal reward and punishment (3:16; 13:9, 10; 14:2, 6, 7; 15:11 to the end).

IV. Another work of that class, Little Genesis, or The Book of Jubilees, has been preserved to us in its Ethiopic translation (though a Latin version of part of it has lately been discovered) and is a Haggadic Commentary on Genesis. Professing to be a revelation to Moses during the forty days on Mount Sinai, it seeks to fill a gap in the sacred history, especially in reference to its chronology. Its character is exhortation and warning, and it breathes a strong anti-Roman spirit. It was written by a Palestinian in Hebrew, or rather Aramean, probably about the time of Christ. The name, Book of Jubilees, is derived from the circumstance that the Scripture chronology is arranged according to Jubilee periods of forty nine years, fifty of these (or 2,450 years) being counted from the Creation to the entrance into Canaan.

V. Among the Pseudepigraphic Writings we also include the 4th Book of Esdras, which appears among our Apocrypha as 2 Esdras Chapter 3-14 (the two first and the two last chapters being spurious additions). The work, originally written in Greek, has only been preserved in translation into five different languages (Latin, Arabic, Syriac, Ethiopic, and Armenian). It was composed probably about the end of the first century AD. From this circumstance, and the influence of Christianity on the mind of the writer, who, however, is an earnest Jew, its interest and importance can be scarcely exaggerated. The name of Ezra was probably assumed, because the writer wished to treat mainly of the mystery of Israel's fall and restoration.

The other Pseudepigraphic Writings are:

VI. The Ascension (Chapter 1-5) and Vision (Chapter 6-11) of Isaiah, which describes the martyrdom of the prophet (with a Christian interpretative influence [Chapter 3:14-4:22] ascribing his death to prophecy of Christ, and containing Apocalyptic portions), and then what he saw in heaven. The book is probably based on an older Jewish account, but is chiefly of Christian heretical authorship. It exists only in translations, of which that in Ethiopic (with Latin and English versions) has been edited by Archbishop Laurence.

VII. The Assumption of Moses (probably quoted in Jude ver. 9) also exists only in translation, and is really a fragment. It consists of twelve chapters. After an Introduction (Chapter 1), containing an address of Moses to Joshua, the former, professedly, opens to Joshua the future of Israel to the time of Varus. This is followed by an Apocalyptic portion, beginning at Chapter 5: and ending with Chapter 10. The two concluding chapters are dialogues between Joshua and Moses. The book dates probably from about the year 2 BC, or shortly afterwards. Besides the Apocalyptic portions the interest lies chiefly in the fact that the writer seems to belong to the Nationalist party, and that we gain some glimpses of the Apocalyptic views and hopes, the highest spiritual tendency, of that deeply interesting movement. Most markedly, this Book at least is strongly anti-Pharisaic, especially in its opposition to their purifications (Chapter 7). We would here especially note a remarkable resemblance between 2 Timothy 3:1-5 and this in Assump. Mos. 5:3-10. It is very significant, that instead of the denunciation of the Pharisees in vv. 9, 10 of the Assumptio, we have in 2 Timothy 3:5 the words having the form of godliness, but denying the power thereof.

VIII. The Apocalypse of Baruch., This also exists only in Syriac translation, and is apparently fragmentary, since the vision promised in Chapter 75:3 is not reported, while the Epistle of Baruch to the two and a half tribes in Babylon, referred to in 75:19, is also missing. The book had been divided into seven sections (1-12; 13-20; 21-34; 35-46; 47-52; 53-76; 77-87). The whole is in a form of revelation to Baruch, and of his replies, and questions, or of notices about his bearing, fast, prayers, etc. The most interesting parts are in sections 5 and 6: In the former we mark (Chapter 48:31-41) the reference to the consequence of the sin of our first parents (ver. 42; comp. also 15:3; 23:4; 54:15, 19), and in Chapter 49 the discussion and information; with what body and in what form the dead shall rise, which is answered, not as by Paul in 1 Corinthians 15, though the question raised (1 Corinthians 15:35) is precisely the same, but in the strictly Rabbinic manner, described by us in Vol. 2: pp. 398, 399. In section 6: we especially mark (Chapter 69-74) the Apocalyptic descriptions of the Last Days, and of the Reign and Judgment of Messiah. In general, the figurative language in that Book is instructive in regard to the phraseology used in the Apocalyptic portions of the New Testament. Lastly, we mark that the views on the consequences of the Fall are much more limited than those expressed in 4 Esdras. They do not go beyond physical death as the consequence of the sin of our first parents (see especially 54:19). At the same time, it seems to use, as if perhaps the reasoning rather than the language of the writer indicated hesitation on his part (4:14-19; comp. also first clause of 48:43). It almost seems as if 54:14-19 were intended as against the reasoning of Paul, Rom. 5:12 to the end. In this respect the passage in Baruch is most interesting, not only in itself (see for Exodus ver. 16), but in reference to the teaching of 4 Esdras which, as regards original sin, takes another direction than Baruch. But I have little doubt that both allude to the, to them, novel teaching of Paul on that doctrine. Lastly, as regards the question when this remarkable work was written, we would place its composition after the destruction of Jerusalem. Most writers date it before the publication of 4 Esdras, Even the appearance of a Pseudo-Baruch and Pseudo-Esdras are significant of the political circumstances and the religious hopes of the nation.

Appendix 2

Philo of Alexandria and Rabbinic Theology

In comparing the allegorical Canons of Philo with those of Jewish traditionalism, we think first of all of the seven exegetical canons which are ascribed to Hillel. These bear chiefly the character of logical deductions, and as such were largely applied in the Halakhah. These seven canons were next expanded by R. Ishmael (in the first century) into thirteen, by the analysis of one of them (the 5th) into six, and the addition of this sound exegetical rule, that where two verses seem to be contradictory, their conciliation must be sought in a third passage. The real rules for the Haggadah, if such there were, were the thirty two canons of R. Jose the Galilean (in the second century). It is here that we meet so much that is kindred in form to the allegorical canons of Philo. Only they are not rationalizing, and far more brilliant in their application. Most taking results, at least to a certain class of minds, might be reached by finding in each consistent of a word the initial letter of another (Notariqon). Thus, the word MiSBeaCH (altar) was resolved into these four words, beginning respectively with M, S, B, CH: Forgiveness, Merit, Blessing, Life. Then there was Gematria, by which every letter in a word was resolved into its arithmetical equivalent. Thus, the two words Gog and Magog = 70, which was the supposed number of all the pagan nations. Again, in Athbash the letters of the Hebrew alphabet were transposed (the first for the last of the alphabet, and so on), so that SHeSHaKH(Jeremiah 25:26; 11:41) became BaBeL, while in Albam, the twenty two Hebrew letters were divided into two rows, which might be exchanged (L for A, M for B, etc.).

1. In other respects also the Palestinian had the advantage of the Alexandrian mode of interpretation. There was at least ingenuity, if not always truth,

in explaining a word by resolving it into two others, or in discussing the import of exclusive particles (such as only, but, from,), and inclusives (such as also, with, all,) or in discovering shades of meaning from the derivation of a word, as in the eight synonyms for poor, of which one (Ani), indicated simply the poor; another (Ebhyon, from abhah), one who felt both need and desire; a third (misken), one humiliated; a fourth (rash from rush), one who had been emptied of his property; a fifth (dal), one who property had become exhausted; a sixth (dakh), one who felt broken down; a seventh (makh), one who had come down; and the eighth (chelekh), one who was wretched, or in discussing such differences as between amar, to speak gently, and dabhar, to speak strongly, and many others. Here intimate knowledge of the language and tradition might be of real use. At other times striking thoughts were suggested, as when it was pointed out that all mankind was made to spring from one man, in order to show the power of God, since all coins struck from the same machine were precisely the same, while in man, whatever the resemblance, there was still a difference in each.

2. The distinction between the unapproachable God and God as manifest and manifesting Himself, which lies at the foundation of so much in the theology of Philo in regard to the intermediary beings, Potencies, and the Logos, occurs equally in Rabbinic theology, though there it is probably derived from a different source. Indeed, we regard this as explaining the marked and striking avoidance of all anthropomorphisms in the Targumim. It also accounts for the designation of God by two classes of terms, of which in our view, the first expresses the idea of God as revealed, the other that of God as revealing Himself; or, to put it otherwise, which indicate, the one a state, the other an act on the part of God. The first of these classes of designations embraces two terms: Yeqara, the excellent glory, and Shechinah, or Shechinah, the abiding Presence. On the other hand, God, as in the act of revealing himself, is described by the term Memra, the Logos, the word. A distinction of ideas also obtains between the terms Yeqara and Shechinah. The former indicates, as we think, the inward and upward, the latter the outward and downward, aspect of the revealed God. This distinction will appear by comparing the use of the two words in the Targumim, and even by the consideration of passages in which the two are placed side by side (as for Exodus, in the Targum Onkelos on Exodus 15:16; Numbers 14:14; in Pseudo-Jonathan, Genesis 15:13, 14; in the Jerusalem Targum, Exodus 19:18; and in the Targum Jonathan, Isaiah

6:1, 3; Hagg. 1:8). Thus, also, the allusion in 2 Peter 1:17, to the voice from the excellent glory must have been the Yeqara. The varied use of the terms Shechinah and Yeqara, and then Memra, in the Targum of Isaiah 6, is very remarkable. In ver. 1 it is the Yeqara, and its train, the heavenward glory, which fills the Heavenly Temple. In ver. 3 we hear the Trishagion in connection with the dwelling of His Shechinah, while the splendor (Ziv) of His Yeqara fills the earth, as it were, falls down to it. In ver. 5 the prophet dreads, because he had seen the Yeqara of the Shechinah, while in ver. 6 the coal is taken from before the Shechinah (which is) upon the throne of the Yeqara (a remarkable expression, which occurs often; so especially in 9, 15:16). Finally, in ver. 8, the prophet hears the voice of the Memra of Jehovah speaking the words of vv. 9, 10. It is intensely interesting to notice that in John 12:40, these words are prophetically applied in connection with Christ. Thus John applies to the Logos what the Targum understands of the Memra of Jehovah.

But, theologically, by far the most interesting and important point, with reference not only to the Logos of Philo, but to the term Logos as employed in the Fourth Gospel, is to ascertain the precise import of the equivalent expression Memra in the Targumim. As stated in the text of this book (Volume 1: p. 47), the term Memra as applied to God, occurs 176 times in the Targum Onkelos, 99 times in the Jerusalem Targum, and 321 times in the Targum Pseudo-Jonathan. We append the list of these passages, arranged in three classes. Those in Class I mark where the term does not apply to this, or where it is at least doubtful; those in Class II where the fair interpretation of a passage shows; and Class III where it is undoubted and unquestionable, that the expression Memra refers to God as revealing Himself, that is the Logos.

Only one illustration of Philo's peculiar method of interpreting the Old Testament can here be given. It will at the same time show how he found confirmation for his philosophical speculations in the Old Testament, and further illustrate his system of moral theology in its most interesting, but also most difficult, point. The question is, how the soul was to pass from its state of sensuousness and sin to one of devotion to reason, which was religion and righteousness. It will be remarked that the change from the one state to the other is said to be accomplished in one of three ways: by study, by practice, or through a good natural disposition (mthesis, skesis, ephua) exactly as Aristotle put it. But Philo found a symbol for each, and for a preparatory state in each, in Scripture. The three Patriarchs represented this threefold mode of reaching the supersensuous: Abraham, study; Jacob, practice; Isaac, a good disposition; while Enos, Enoch, and Noah, represented the respective preparatory stages. Enos (hope), the first real ancestor of our race, represented the mind awakening to the existence of a better life. Abraham (study) received command to leave the land (sensuousness). But all study was threefold. It was, first, physical, Abram in the land of Ur, contemplating the starry sky, but not knowing God. Next to the physical was that intermediate (mse) study, which embraced the ordinary cycle of knowledge (nkklios paidea). This was Abram after he left Haran, and that knowledge was symbolized by his union with Hagar, who waited (intermediately) between Kadesh and Bered. But this stage also was insufficient, and the soul must reach the third and highest stage, that of Divine philosophy (truly, the love of wisdom, philosopha) where eternal truth was the subject of contemplation. Accordingly, Abram left Lot, he became Abraham, and he was truly united to Sarah, no longer Sarai: Onwards and ever upwards would the soul now rise to the knowledge of virtue, of heavenly realities, of the nature of God Himself.

But there was yet another method than study, by which the soul might rise, that of askesis, discipline, practice, of which Scripture speaks in Enoch and Jacob. Enoch, whom God took, and he was not (Genesis 5:24), meant the soul turning from the lower to the higher, so that it was no longer found in its former place of evil. From Enoch, as the preparatory stage, we advance to Jacob, first merely fleeing from sensuous entanglements (from Laban), then contending with the affections, ridding himself of five of the seventy five souls with which he had entered Egypt (Deuteronomy 10:22, comp. with Genesis 46:27), often nearly misled by the Sophists (Dinah and Hamor), often nearly failing and faint in the conflict (Jacob's wrestling), but helped by God, and finally victorious, when Jacob became Israel.

But the highest of all was the spiritual life which came neither from study nor discipline, but through a good disposition. Here we have, first of all, Noah, who symbolizes only the beginning of virtue, since we read not of any special virtue in him. Rather is he rest—as the name implies, good, relatively to those around. It was otherwise with Isaac, who was perfect before his birth (and therefore chosen), even as Rebekah meant constancy in virtue. In that state the soul enjoyed true rest (the Sabbath, Jerusalem) and joy, which Isaac's name implied. But true virtue, which was also true wisdom, was Paradise, from which issued the one stream (goodness), which again divided into four branches (the four Stoic virtues):, Pison, prudence (phrnesis); Gihon, fortitude (ndra); Tigris, desire (pithuma), and Euphrates, justice (dikaiosne). And yet, though these were the Stoic virtues, they all spring from Paradise, the Garden of God, and all that is good, and all help to it, comes to us ultimately from God Himself, and is in God.

End Notes:

[1]   Besides the designations of God to which reference is made in the text, Philo also applies to Him that of topos, place, in precisely the same manner as the later Rabbis (and especially the Kabbalah) use the word. To Philo it implies that God is extramundane. He sees this taught in Genesis 22:3, 4, where Abraham came to the place of which God had told him; but, when he lifted up his eyes, saw the place far off. Similarly, the Rabbis when commenting on Genesis 28:11, assign this as the reason why God is designated that He is extramundane; the discussion being whether God is the place of His Word or the reverse, and the decision in favor of the former, Genesis 28:11 being explained by Exodus 33:21, and Deut 33:27 by Psalm 90:1 (Ber. R. 68, ed. Warsh. p 125 b).

[2]   I think it is Koester (Trinitaetslehre vor Christo) who distinguishes the two as God's Presence within and without the congregation. With much learning and not a little ingenuity he tries to prove by a detailed analysis, that the three terms Memra, Shechinah, and Yeqara have not the meaning above explained.

Appendix 3

Rabbinic Views as to the Lawfulness Of Images, Pictorial Representations on Coins, Etc.

On this point, especially as regarded images, statues, and coins, the views of the Rabbis underwent (as stated in the text) changes and modifications according to the outward circumstances of the people. The earlier and strictest opinions, which absolutely prohibited any representation, were relaxed in the Mishnah, and still further in the Talmud.

In tracing this development, we mark as a first stage that a distinction was made between having such pictorial representations and making use of them, in the sense of selling or bartering them; and again between making and finding them. The Mishnah forbids only such representations of human beings as carry in their hand some symbol of power, such as a staff, bird, globe, or as the Talmud adds, a sword, or even a signet ring (Ab. Z. 3:1). The Commentaries explain that this must refer to the making use of them, since their possession was, at any rate, prohibited. The Talmud adds (Ab. Z. 40 b, 41 a) that these were generally representations of kings, that they were used for purposes of worship, and that their prohibition applied only to villages, not to towns, where they were used for ornament. Similarly the Mishnah directs that everything bearing a representation of sun or moon, or of a dragon, was to be thrown into the Dead Sea (Ab. Z. iii. 3). On the other hand, the Talmud quotes (Ab. Z. 42 b) a proposition, to the effect that all representations of the planets were allowed, except those of the sun and moon, likewise all statues except those of man, and all

557

pictures except those of a dragon, the discussion leading to the conclusion that in two, if not in all the cases mentioned, the Talmudic directions refer to finding, not making such. So stringent was the law as regarded signet rings, that it was forbidden to have raised work on them, and only such figures were allowed as were sunk beneath the surface, although even then they were not to be used for sealing (Ab. Z. 43 b). But this already marks a concession, accorded apparently to a celebrated Rabbi, who had such a ring. Still further in the same direction is the excuse, framed at a later period, for the Rabbis who worshipped in a Synagogue that had a statue of a king to the effect that they could not be suspected of idolatry, since the place, and therefore their conduct, was under the inspection of all men. This more liberal tendency had appeared at a much earlier period, in the case of the Nasi Gamaliel II, who made use of a public bath at Acco in which there was a statue of Aphrodite. The Mishnah (Ab. Z. 3:4) puts this twofold plea into his mouth, that he had not gone into the domain of the idol, but the idol came into his, and that the statue was there for ornament, not for worship. The Talmud endorses these arguments, but in a manner showing that the conduct of the great Gamaliel was not really approved of (Ab. Z. 44 b). But a statue used for idolatrous purposes was not only to be pulverized, but the dust cast to the winds or into the sea, for fear that it might possible serve as manure to the soul! (Ab. Z. 3:3.) This may explain how Josephus ventured even to blame King Solomon for the figures on the Brazen sea and on his throne (Ant. v3:7. 5), and how he could excite a fanatical rabble at Tiberias, to destroy the palace of Herod Antipas because it contained figures of living creatures (Life 12).

End Notes

[3]   The Nasi R. Gamaliel made use of representations of the moon in questioning ignorant witnesses with a view of fixing (by the new moon) the beginning of the month. But this must be regarded as a necessary exception to the rule.

[4]   Following the insufficient reasoning of Ewald (Gesch. d. Volkes Isr. Volume v. p. 83), Schuerer represents the non-issue of coins with the image of Herod as a concession to Jewish prejudices, and argues that the coins of the Emperors struck in Palestine bore no effigy. The assertion is, however, unsupported, and Matthew 22:20 proves that coins with an image of Caesar were in general circulation. Wieseler (Beitr. pp. 83-87 had shown that the

absence of Herod's effigy on coins proves his inferior position relatively to Rome, and as this has an important bearing on the question of a Roman census during his reign, it was scarcely fair to simply ignore it. The Talmud (Baba K. 97 b) speaks of coins bearing on one side David and Solomon (was it their effigies or their names), and on the other Jerusalem, the holy City. But if it be doubtful whether these coins had respectively the effigies of David or of Solomon, there can be no doubt about the coins ascribed in Ber. R. (Par. 39, ed. Warshau, p. 71 b) to Abraham, Joshua, David, and Mordecai, that of Abraham being described as bearing on one side the figures of an old man and an old woman (Abraham and Sarah), and on the other those of a young man and a young woman (Isaac and Rebekah). The coins of Joshua are stated to have borne on one side a bullock, on the other a ram, according to Deuteronomy 33:17. There could, therefore, have been no such abhorrence of such coins, and if there had been Herod was scarcely the man to be deterred by it. On these supposed coins of David, etc., see the very curious remarks of Wagenseil, Sota, pp. 574, and following. The fullest and most accurate information on all connected with the coins of the Jews is contained in the large and learned work of Mr. Madden, Coins of the Jews (Volume 2: of The International Numismata Orientalia, 1881). Comp. also the Review of this book in the Journal of the Royal Archaeological Infor 1882 Volume 39, pp. 203-206.

Appendix 4

History from Alexander the Great to Herod

The political connection of the Grecian world, and, with it, the conflict with Hellenism, may be said to have connected with the victorious progress of Alexander the Great through the then known world (333 BC). It was not only that his destruction of the Persian empire put an end to the easy and peaceful allegiance which Judea had owned to it for about two centuries, but that the establishment of such a vast Hellenic empire, as was the aim of Alexander, introduced a new element into the world of Asia. Everywhere the old civilization gave way before the new. So early as the beginning of the second century before Christ, Palestine was already surrounded, north, east, and west, with a girdle of Hellenic cities, while in the interior of the land itself Grecianism had its foothold in Galilee and was dominant in Samaria. But this is not all. After continuing the frequent object of contention between the rulers of Egypt and Syria, Palestine ultimately passed from Egyptian to Syrian domination during the reign of Seleucus IV (187-175 BC). His successor was that Antiochus IV, Epiphanes (175-164), whose reckless determination to exterminate Judaism, and in its place to substitute Hellenism, led to the Maccabean rising. Mad as this attempt seems, it could scarcely have been made had there not been in Palestine itself a party to favor his plans. In truth, Grecianism, in its worst form, had long before made its way, slowly but surely, into the highest quarters. For the proper understanding of this history its progress must be briefly indicated.

After the death of Alexander, Palestine passed first under Egyptian domination. Although the Ptolemies were generally favorable to the Jews (at least of their own country), those of Palestine at times felt the heavy hand of the conqueror (Jos. Ant. 12:1. 1). Then followed the contests between Syria and Egypt for its possession, in which the county must have severely suffered. As Josephus aptly remarks (Ant. 12:3. 3), whichever partly gained, Palestine was like a ship in a storm which is tossed by the waves on both sides. Otherwise it was a happy time, because one of the comparative independence. The secular and spiritual power was vested in the hereditary High Priests, who paid for their appointment (probably annually) the sum of twenty (presumably Syrian) talents, amounting to five ordinary talents, or rather less than 1,200l (year 1865 British Pounds). Besides this personal, the country paid a general tribute, its revenues being let to the highest bidder. The sum levied on Judea itself has computed at 81,900l. (350 ordinary talents). Although this tribute appears by no means excessive, bearing in mind that in later times the dues from the balsam district around Jericho were reckoned at upwards of 46,800l. (200 talents), the hardship lay in the mode of levying it by strangers, often unjustly, and always harshly, and in the charges connected with its collection. This cause of complaint was indeed, removed in the course of time, but only by that which led to far more serious evils.

The succession of the High Priests, as given in Nehem. 12:10, 11, 22, furnishes the following names: Jeshua. Joiakin, Eliashib, Joiada, Johanan, Jonathan, and Jaddua, who was the contemporary of Alexander the Great. After the death of Jaddua, we have the following list: Onias I. (Jos. Ant. 11, 8. 7), Simon I. the Just (Ant. 12:2. 5), Eleazar, Manasseh (Ant. 12:4. 1), Onias II., Simon II. (Ant. 12:4. 10), Onias III., Jason (Ant. 12:5. 1), Menelaus, and Alcimus (Ant. 12:9. 7), with whom the series of the Pontiffs is brought down to the Maccabees. Internal peace and happiness ceased after the death of Simon the Just (in the beginning of the third century BC), one of the last links in that somewhat mysterious chain of personages, to which tradition has given the name of the Great Assemblage, or Great Synagogue.

Jewish legend has much that is miraculous to tell of Simon the Just, and connects him with events both long anterior and long posterior to his Pontificate. Many of these traditions read like the outcome of loving, longing remembrance of a happy past which was never to return. Such a venerable form would never again be seen in the Sanctuary (Ecclus. 1. 1-4), nor would such miraculous attestation be given to any other ministrations (Yoma 39 a and b; Jeremiah Yoma 5:2; 6:3). All this seems to point to the close of a period when the High Priesthood was purely Jewish in spirit, just as the hints about dissensions among his sons (Jeremiah Yoma 43 d, at top) sound like faint reminiscences of the family, and public troubles which followed. In point of fact he was succeeded not by his Onias who was under age, but by his brother Eleazar, and he, after a Ponficate of twenty years, by his brother Manasseh. It was only twenty seven years later, after the death of Manasseh, that Onias II became High Priest. If Eleazar, and especially Manasseh, owned their position, or at least strengthened it, by courting the favor of the ruler of Egypt, it was almost natural that Onias should have taken the opposite or Syrian part. His refusal to pay the High Priestly tribute to Egypt could scarcely have been wholly due to avarice, as Josephus suggests. The anger and threats of the king were appeased by the High Priests nephew Joseph, who claimed descent from the line of David. He knew how to ingratiate himself at the court of Alexandria, and obtained the lease of the taxes of Coele Syria (which included Judea), by offering for it double sum previously paid. The removal of the foreign tax gatherer was very grateful to the Jews, but the authority obtained by Joseph became a new source of danger, especially in the hands of his ambitious son, Hyrcanus. Thus we already mark the existence of three parties: the Egyptian, the Syrian, and that of the sons of Tobias (Ant. 12:5. 1), as the adherents of Joseph were called, after his father. If the Egyptian party ceased when Palestine passed under Syrian rule in the reign of Antiochis III the Great (223-187 BC), and ultimately became wholly subject to it under Seleucus IV (187-173), the Syrian, and especially the Tobias party, had already become Grecianized. In truth, the contest now became one for power and wealth in which each sought to outbid the other by bribery and subserviency to the foreigner. As the submission of the people could only be secured by the virtual extinction of Judaism, this aim was steadily kept in view by the degenerate priesthood.

The storm did not break under the Pontificate of Simon II, the son and successor of Onias II, but the times were becoming more and more troublous. Although the Syrian rulers occasionally showed favor to the Jews, Palestine was now covered with a network of Syrian officials, into whose hands the temporal power mainly passed. The taxation also sensibly increased, and, besides crown money, consisted of a poll tax, the third of the field crops, the half of the produce of trees, a royal monopoly of salt and of the forests, and even a tax on the Levitical tithes and on all revenues of the Temple. Matters became much more worse under the Pontificate of Onias II, the son and successor of Simon II. A dispute between him and one Simon, a priest, and captain of the temple guard, apparently provoked by the unprincipled covetousness of the latter, induced Simon to appeal to the greed of the Syrians by referring to the untold treasures which he described as deposited in the Temple. His motive may have been partly a desire for revenge, partly the hope of attaining the office of Onias. It was ascribed to a super-natural apparition, but probably it was only superstition which arrested the Syrian general at that time. But a dangerous lesson had been learned by Jew and Gentile.

Seleucus IV was succeeded by his brother Antiochus IV, Epiphanes (175-164 BC). Whatever psychological explanation may be offered of his bearing, whether his conduct was that of a madman, or of a despot intoxicated to absolute forgetfulness of every consideration beyond his own caprice by the fancied possession of power uncontrolled and unlimited, cruelty and recklessness of tyranny were as prominently his characteristics as revengefulness and unbounded devotion to superstition. Under such a reign the precedent which Simon, the Captain of the Temple, had set, was successfully followed up by no less a person than the brother of the High Priest himself. The promise of a yearly increase of 360 talents in the taxes of the country, besides a payment of 80 talents from another revenue (2 Maccabees 6:8, 9), purchased the deposition of Onias III, the first event of that kind recorded in Jewish history, and the substitution of his brother Joshua, Jesus, or Jason (as he loved to Grecianize his name), in the

Pontificate. But this was not all. The necessities, if not the inclinations, of the new High Priest, and his relations to the Syrian king, prescribed a Grecian policy at home. It seems almost incredible, and yet it is quite in accordance with the circumstances, that Jason should have actually paid to Antiochus a sum of 150 talents for permission to erect a Gymnasium in Jerusalem, that he entered citizens of Antioch on the registers of Jerusalem, and that on one occasion he went so far as to send a deputation to attend the games at Tyre, with money for purchasing offerings to Heracles! And in Jerusalem, and throughout the land, there was a strong and increasing party to support Jason in his plans, and to follow his lead (2 Maccabees 4:9, 19). Thus far had Grecianism already swept over the country, as not only to threaten the introduction of views, manners, and institutions wholly incompatible with the religion of the Old Testament, but even the abolition of the bodily mark which distinguished its professors (1 Maccabees 1:15; Jos. Ant. 12:5. 1).

But the favor which Antiochus showed Jason was not of long duration. One even more unscrupulous than he, Menelaus (or, according to his Jewish name, Onias), the brother of that Simon who had first excited the Syrian greed about the Temple treasure, out bid Jason with Antichus by a promise of 300 talents in addition to the tribute which Jason had paid. Accordingly, Menelaus was appointed High Priest. In the expressive language of the time: he came, bringing nothing worthy of the High Priesthood, but having the fury of a cruel tyrant and the rage of a savage beast (2 Maccabees 4:25). In the conflict for the Pontificate, which now ensued, Menelaus conquered by the help of the Syrians. A terrible period of internal misrule and external troubles followed. Menelaus and his associates cast off every restraint, and even plundered the Temple of some of its precious vessels. Antiochus, who had regarded the resistance to his nominee as rebellion against himself, took fearful vengeance by slaughter of the inhabitants of Jerusalem and pillage of the Temple. But this was not all. When checked in his advance against Egypt, by the peremptory mandate of Rome, Antiochus made up for his disappointment by an expedition against Judea, of which the avowed object was to crush the people and to sweep away Judaism. The horrors which now ensued are equally recorded in the Books of the Maccabees, by Josephus, and in Jewish tradition. All sacrifices, the service of the Temple, and the observance of the Sabbath and of feast days were prohibited; the Temple at Jerusalem was dedicated to Jupiter Olympius; the Holy Scriptures were searched for and destroyed; the Jews forced to take part in pagan rites; a small pagan altar was reared on the great altar of burnt offering—in short, every insult was heaped on the religion of the Jews, and its every trace was to be swept away. The date of the final profanation of the Temple was the 25th Chislev (corresponding to our December)—the same on which, after its purification by Judas Maccabee, its services were restored, the same on which the Christian Church celebrates the dedication of a better Temple, that of the Holy Spirit in the Incarnation of Jesus Christ.

But the relentless persecution, which searched for its victims in every part of the land, also called forth a deliverer in the person of Mattathias. The story of the glorious rising and final deliverance of the country under the Maccabees or Asmoneans, as they are always called in Jewish writings, is sufficiently known. Only the briefest outline of it can here be attempted. Mattathias died before it came to any actual engagement with the Syrians, but victory after victory attended the arms of his son, Judas the Maccabee, until at last the Temple could be purified and its services restored, exactly three years after its desecration (25 Chislev, 165 BC). The rule of the Jewish hero lasted another five years, which can scarcely be described as equally successful with the beginning of his administration. The first two years were occupied in fortifying strong positions and chastising those hostile pagan border tribes which harassed Judea. Towards the close of the year 164 BC Antiochus Epiphanes died. But his successor, or rather Lysias, who administered the kingdom during his minority, was not content to surrender Palestine without a further contest. No deeds of heroism, however great, could compensate for the inferiority of the forces under Judas command. The prospect was becoming hopeless, when troubles at home recalled the Syrian army, and led to a treaty of peace in which the Jews acknowledged Syrian supremacy, but were secured liberty of conscience and worship.

But the truce was of short duration. As we have seen there were already in Palestine two parties, that which, from its character and aims, may generally be designated as the Grecian, and the Chasidim (Assideans). There can be little doubt that the latter name originally in the designation Chasidim, applied to the pious in Israel in such passages as Psalm 30:4; 30:24; 35:28). Jewish tradition distinguishes between the earlier and the later Chasidim (Ber. 5:1 and 32 b; Men. 40 b). The descriptions of the former are of so late a date, that the characteristics of the party are given in accordance with views and practices which belong to a much further development of Rabbinical piety. Their fundamental views may, however, be gathered from the four opening sentences of the Mishnic Tractate Abhoth, of which the last are ascribed to Jose the son of Joezer, and Jose the son of Jochanan, who, as we know, still belonged to the earlier Chasidim. These flourished about 140 BC, and later. This date throws considerable light upon the relation between the earlier and later Chasidim, and the origin of the sects of the Pharisees and Sadducees. Comparing the sentences of the earlier Chasidim (Ab. 1:2-4) with those which follow, we notice a marked simplicity about them, while the others either indicate a rapid development of Rabbinism, or are echoes of the political relations subsisting, or else seems to allude to present difficulties or controversies. We infer that the earlier Chasidim represented the pious in Israel, of course, according to the then standpoint, who, in opposition to the Grecian party, rallied around Judas Maccabee and his successor, Jonathan. The assumption of the High Priestly dignity by Jonathan the Maccabee, on the nomination of the Syrian king (about 152 BC), was a step which the ultraorthodox party never forgave the Asmoneans. From that period, therefore, we date the alienation of the Chasidim, or rather the cessation of the earlier Chasidim. From here on, the party, as such, degenerated, or, to speak more correctly, ran into extreme religious views, which made them the most advanced section of the Pharisees. The latter and the Sadducees from then on represented the people in its twofold religious direction. With this view agrees the statement of Josephus (Ant.

13:5. 9), who first mentions the existence of Pharisees and Sadducees in the time of Jonathan, and even the confused notice in Aboth de Rabbi Nathan 5, which ascribes the origin of the Sadducees to the first or second generation of Zadoks disciples, himself a disciple of Antigonus of Socho, which would bring the date to nearly the same time as Josephus.

From this digression, necessary for the proper understanding of the internal relations in Judea, we return to the political history. There was another change on the throne of Syria. Demetrius, the new king readily listened to the complaints of a Jewish deputation, and appointed their leader, Alcimus (Jakim or Eljakim) High Priest. At first the Chasidin were disposed to support him, as having formerly filled a high post in the priesthood, and as the nephew of Jose the son of Jazer, one of their leaders. But they suffered terribly for their rashness. Aided by the Syrians, Alcimus seized the Pontificate. But Judas once more raised the national standard against the intruder and the allies. At first victory seemed to incline to the national side, and the day of the final defeat and slaughter of the Syrian army and of Nicanor their general was enrolled in the Jewish Calendar as one on which fasting and mourning were prohibited (the 13th Adar, or March). Still, the prospect was far from reassuring, the more so as division had already appeared in the ranks of the Jews. In these circumstances Judas directed his eyes towards the new Western power which was beginning to overshadow the East. It was a fatal step, the beginning of all future troubles, and, even politically, a grave mistake, to enter into a defensive and offensive alliance with Rome. But before even more temporary advantage could be derived from this measure, Judas the Maccabee had already succumbed to superior numbers, and heroically fallen in battle against the Syrians.

The war of liberation had lasted seven years, and yet when the small remnant of the Asmonean party chose Jonathan, the youngest brother of Judas, as his successor, their cause seemed more hopeless than almost at any previous period. The Grecian party was dominant in Judea, the Syrian host occupied the land and Jonathan and his adherents were obliged to retire to the other side Jordan. The only hope, if such it may be called, lay in the circumstances that after the death of Alcimus the Pontificate was not filled by another Syrian nominee, but remained vacant for two years. During this time the nationalists must have gained strength, since the Grecian party now once more sought and obtained Syrian help against them. But the almost passive resistance which Jonathan successfully offered wearied out the Syrian general and led to a treaty of peace (1 Maccabees 9:58-73). In the period which followed, the Asmonean party steadily increased, so that when a rival king claimed the Syrian crown, both pretenders vied for the support of Jonathan. He took the side of the new monarch, Alexander Balas, who sent him a crown of gold and a purple mantle, and appointed him High Priest, a dignity which Jonathan at once accepted. The Jewish Pontiff was faithful to his patron even against a new claimant to the crown of Syria. And such was his influence, that the latter, on gaining possession of the throne, not only forgave the resistance of Jonathan, but confirmed him in the Pontificate, and even remitted the taxation of Palestine on a tribute (probably annual) of 300 talents. But the faithlessness and ingratitude of the Syrian king led Jonathan soon afterwards to take the side of another Syrian pretender, an infant, whose claims were ostensibly defended by his general Trypho. In the end, however, Jonathans resistance to Trypho's schemes for obtaining the crown for himself led to the murder of the Jewish High Priest by treachery.

The government of Judea could not, in these difficult times, have developed upon one more fitted for it than Simon, an elder brother of Judas Maccabee. His father had, when making his dying disposition, already designated him as the man of counsel among his sons (1 Maccabees 2:65). Simon's policy lay chiefly in turning to good account the disputes in Syria, and in consolidating such rule as he had acquired (143-135 BC). After the murder of his brother by Trypho, he took part of the Syrian claimant (Demetrius) to whom Trypho was opposed. Demetrius was glad to purchase his support by a remission of all taxation for all time to come. This was the first great success, and the Jews perpetuated its memory by enrolling its anniversary (the 27th Iyar, or May) in their Calendar. An even more important date, in the Calendar (Meg. Taan. Per. 2) and in Jewish history (1 Maccabees 13:51), was the 23rd Iyar, when the work of clearing the country of the foreigner was completed by the Syrian party. The next measures of Simon were directed to the suppression of the Grecian party in Judea, and the establishments of peace and security to his own adherents. To the popular mind this Golden Age described in glowing language in 1 Maccabees 14:8-14, seemed to culminate in an event by which the national vanity was gratified and the future safety of their country apparently ensured. This was the arrival of a Roman embassy in Judea to renew the league which had already been made both by Judas Maccabee and by Jonathan. Simon replied by sending a Jewish embassy to Rome, which brought a valuable shield of gold in token of gratitude. In their intoxication the Jews passed a decree, and engraved it on tables of brass, making Simon their High Priest and a Governor forever, until there should arise a faithful prophet; in other words, appointing him to the twofold office of spiritual and secular chief, and declaring it hereditary (1 Maccabees 14:41-45). The fact that he should have been appointed to dignities which both he and his predecessor had already held, and that offices which in themselves were hereditary should now be declared such in the family of Simon, as well as the significant limitation: until there should arise a faithful prophet, sufficiently indicate that there were dissensions among the people and opposition to the Asmoneans. In truth, as the Chasidim had already had been alienated, so there was a growing party among the Pharisees, their successors, whose hostility to the Asmoneans increased until it developed into positive hatred. This antagonism was, however, not grounded on their possession of the secular power, but on their occupancy of the Pontificate, perhaps on their combination of the two offices. How far their hostility went, will appear in the sequel. For a time it was repressed by the critical state of affairs. For, the contest with the Syrians had to be once more renewed, and although Simon, or rather his sons, obtained the victory, the aged High Priest and two of his sons, Mattathias and Judas, fell by the treachery of Ptolomaeus, Simons son-in-law.

The Pontificate and the government now developed upon the only one of Simons sons still left, known as John Hyranus I (Jochanan Horkenos, Jannai), 135-105 BC. His first desire naturally was to set free his mother, who was still in the power of Ptolomaeus, and to chastise him for his crimes. But in this he failed. Ptolemy purchased immunity by threatening to kill his captive, and afterwards treacherously slew her. Soon after this a Syrian army besieged Jerusalem. The City was reduced to great straits. But when at the Feast of Tabernacles the Syrian king not only granted a truce to the besieged, but actually provided them with what was needed for the services of the Temple, Hyrcanus sought and obtained peace, although the Syrian councilors urged their king to use the opportunity for exterminating Jerusalem. The conditions, though hard, were not unreasonable in the circumstances. But fresh troubles in Syria gave a more favorable turn to affairs in Judea. First, Hyrcanus subjected Samaria, and then conquered Idumea, whose inhabitants he made proselytes by giving them the alternative of circumcision or exile. Next, the treaty with the Romans was renewed, and finally Hyrcanus availed himself of the rapid decay of the Syrian monarchy to throw off his allegiance to the foreigner. Jewish exclusiveness was further gratified by the utter destruction of Samaria, of which the memorial day (the 25th Marcheshvan, November) was inserted in the festive Calendar

(Meg. Taan. Per. 8). This was not the only date which his successors added to the calendar of national feasts.

But his reign is of the deepest importance in our history as marking the first public contest between the great parties, the Pharisees and the Sadducees, and also as the turning point in the history of the Maccabees. Even the coins of that period are instructive. They bear the inscription: Jochanan, the High Priest, and the Chebher of the Jews; or else, Jochanan the High Priest, Chief, and the Chebher of the Jews. The term Chebher, which on the coins occurs only in connection with High Priest, unquestionably refers, not to the Jewish people generally, but to them in their ecclesiastical organization, and points therefore to the acknowledgment of an Eldership, or representative body, which presided over affairs along with and under the High Priest as Chief. In this respect the presence or absence of the word Chebher, or even mention of the Jews, might afford hints as to the relationship of a Maccabee chief to the ecclesiastical leaders of the people. It has already been explained that the Chasidim, viewed as the National party, had ceased, and that the leaders were now divided into Pharisees and Sadducees. By tradition and necessity Hyrcanus belonged to the former, by tendency and, probably, inclination to the later. His interference in religious affairs was by no means to the liking of the Pharisees, still less to that of their extreme sectaries, the Chasidim. Tradition ascribes to Hyrcanus no less than nine innovations, of which only five were afterwards continued as legal ordinances. First, the payment of tithes (both of the Levitical and the so called poors tithe) was declared no longer obligatory on a seller, if he were one of the Am ha Arets, or country people, but on the buyer. Complaints had long been made that this heavy impost was not paid by the majority of the common people, and it was deemed better to devote the responsibility on the buyer, unless the seller were what was called neeman, trusted; i.e., one who had solemnly bound himself to pay tithes. In connection with this, secondly, the declaration ordered in Deuteronomy 26:3-10 was abolished as no longer applicable. Thirdly, all work that caused noise was forbidden during the days intermediate between the first and the last great festive days of the Passover and of the Feast of Tabernacles. Fourthly, the formula: Awake, why sleep You, O Lord (Psalm 44:23), with which, since the Syrian persecution, the morning service in the Temple had commenced, was abolished. Fifthly, the cruel custom of wounding the sacrificial animals on the head was prohibited and rings fastened in the pavement to which the animals were attached (Jeremiah Maas. Sh. 5:9; Jeremiah Sot. 9:11; Tos. Sot. 13; Sotah 48 a). The four ordinances of Hyrcanus which were abolished referred to the introduction in official documents, after the title of the High Priest, of the expression El Elyon, the Most High God; to the attempt to declare the Syrian and Samaritan towns liable to tithes (implying their virtual incorporation) while according to an old principle, this obligation only applied when a place could be reached from Judea without passing over pagan soil; to the abrogation by Hyrcanus of a former enactment by Jose ben Joezer, which discouraged emigration by declaring all pagan soil defiled, and which rendered social intercourse with Gentiles impossible by declaring vessels of glass capable of contracting Levitical defilement (Jeremiah Shabb. 1. 4; Shabb.14 b), and which was re-enacted; and, lastly, to the easy terms on which the King had admitted the Idumeans into the Jewish community.

From all this it is not difficult to from an idea of the relations between Hyrcanus and the Pharisees. If Hyrcanus had not otherwise known of the growing aversion of the Pharisees, a Sadducean friend and councilor kept him informed, and turned it to account for his party. The story of the public breach between Hyrcanus and the Pharisees is told by Josephus (Ant. 13:10. 5, 6), and in the Talmud (Kidd. 66 a), with only variations of names and details. Whether from a challenge thrown out to the Pharisees (according to the Talmud), or in answer to a somewhat strange request by Hyrcanus, to point out any part of his conduct which was not in accordance with the law (so Josephus), one of the extreme section of the Pharisees, at a feast given to the party, called upon Hyrcanus to be content with secular power, and to resign the Pontificate, on the ground that he was disqualified for it, because his mother had been a captive of war. Even the Talmud admits that this report was slanderous, while it offered a gratuitous insult to the memory of a really noble heroic woman, all the more unwarrantable that the Pontificate had, by public decree, been made the case if the charge now brought had been other than a pretext to cover the hostility of the Chasidim. The rash declaration was avenged on the whole party. In the opinion of Hyrcanus they all proved themselves accomplishes, when, on being questioned, they declared the offender only guilty of stripes and bonds. Hyrcanus now joined the Sadducees, and although the statement of the Talmud about the slaughter of the leading Pharisees is incorrect, there can be no doubt that they were removed from power and exposed to persecution. The Talmud adds this, which, although chronologically incorrect, is significant, Jochanan the High Priest served in the Pontificate eighty years, and at the end of them he became a Sadducee. But this was only the beginning of troubles to the Pharisaic party, which revenged itself by most bitter hatred, the beginning, also of the decline of the Maccabees.

Hycranus left five sons. To the oldest of them, Aristobulus (in Hebrew Jehudah), he bequeathed the Pontificate, but appointed his own widow to succeed him in the secular government. But Aristobulus cast his mother into prison, where she soon afterwards perished, as the story went, by hunger. The only one of his brothers whom he had left at large, and who was his favorite, soon fell also a victim to his jealous suspicions. Happily his reign lasted only one year (105-104 BC). He is described as openly favoring the Grecian party, although, on conquering Iturea, a district east of Lake of Galilee, he obliged its inhabitants to submit to circumcision.

On the death of Aristobulus I, his widow, Alexandra Salome, released his brothers from prison, and apparently married the eldest of them, Alexander Janneus (or in Hebrew Jonathan), who succeeded both to the Pontificate and the secular government. The three periods of his reign (104-78 BC) seem indicated in the varying inscriptions on his coins. The first period, which lasted eight or ten years, was that in which Jannai was engaged in those wars of conquest, which added the cities on the maritime coast to his possessions. During the time Salome seems to have managed internal affairs. As she was devoted to the Pharisaic party, indeed one of their leaders, Simeon ben Shetach, is said to have been her brother (Ber.18 a), this was the time of their ascendency. Accordingly, the coins of that period bear the inscription, Jonathan the High Priest and the Chebher of the Jews. But on his return to Jerusalem he found the arrogance of the Pharisaic party at odds with his own views and tastes. The king now joined the Sadducees, and Simeon ben Shetach had to seek safety in flight (Jeremiah Ber. 5:2 p. 11 b). But others of his party met a worse fate. A terrible tragedy was enacted in the Temple itself. At the Feast of Tabernacles Jannai, officiating as High Priest, set the Pharisaic custom at open defiance by pouring the water out of the sacred vessel on the ground instead of upon the altar. Such a high handed breach of what was regarded as most sacred, excited the feelings of the worshippers to the highest pitch of frenzy. They pelted him with the festive Ethrogs (citrons), which they carried in their hands, and loudly reproached him with his descent from a captive. The king called in his foreign mercenaries, and no fewer than 6,000 of the people fell under their swords. This was an injury which could neither be forgiven nor atoned for by conquests. One insurrection followed after the other, and 5,000 of the people are said to have fallen in these contests. Weary of the strife, Jannai asked the Pharisaic party to name their conditions of peace, to which they caustically replied, Your death (Jos. Ant. 13:13. 5). Indeed, such was the embitterment that they actually called in, and joined the Syrians against him. But the success of the foreigner produced a popular revulsion in his favor, of which Jannai profited to take terrible vengeance of his opponents. No fewer than 800 of them were nailed to the cross, their sufferings being intensified by seeing their wives and children butchered before their eyes, while the degenerate Pontiff lay feasting with abandoned women. A general flight of the Pharisees ensued. This closes the second period of his reign, marked on the coin by the significant absence of the words Chebher of the Jews, the words being on one side in Hebrew, Jonathan the king, and on the other in Greek, Alexander the King.

The third period is marked by coins which bear the inscription Jehonathan the High Priest and the Jews. It was a period of outward military success, and of reconciliation with the Pharisees, or at least of their recall, notable of Simeon ben Shetach, and then of his friends, probably at the instigation of the queen (Ber. 48 a; Jeremiah 5:2). Jannai died in his fiftieth year, after a reign of twenty seven years, bequeathing the government to his wife Salome. On his death bed he is said to have advised her to promote the Pharisees, or rather such of them as made not their religiousness a mere pretext intrigue: Be not afraid of the Pharisees, nor of those of Zimri, and seek the reward of Phinehas (Sot. 22 b). But of chief interest to us is, that this period of the recall of the Pharisees marks a great internal change, indicated even in the coins. For the first time we now meet the designation Sanhedrin. The Chebher, or eldership, had ceased as a ruling power, and become transformed into a Sanhedrin, or ecclesiastical authority although the latter endeavored, with more or less success, to claim to itself civil jurisdiction, at least in ecclesiastical matters.

The nine years of Queen Alexandras (in Hebrew Salome) reign were the Golden Age of the Pharisees, when heaven itself smiled on a land that was wholly subject to their religious sway. In the extravagant language of the Talmud (Tann. 23 a, second line from top): In the days of Simeon ben Shetach, the rains came down in the nights of fourth days, and on those of the Sabbaths, so that the grains of grain became like kidneys, those of barley the stones of olives, and lentils like gold dinars, and they preserved a specimen (dogma) of them for future generations to show them what disastrous result may follow upon sin. That period of miraculous blessing was compared to the equally miraculous dispensation of heaven during the time that the Temple of Herod was building, when rain only fell at night, while the morning wind and heat dried all, so that the builders could continue their work without delay. Queen Salome had appointed her eldest son, Hyrcanus II, a weak prince, to the Poltificate. But, as Josephus puts it (Am. 13:16. 2), although Salome had the title, the Pharisees held the real rule of the country, and they administered it with the harshness, insolence, and recklessness of a fanatical religious party which suddenly obtains unlimited power. The lead was taken by Simeon ben Shetach, whom even the Talmud characterizes as having hot hands (Jeremiah Sanh. 6:5, p. 23 b). First, all who were suspected of Sadducean leaning were removed by intrigue or violence from the Sanhedrin. Next, previous ordinances differing from Pharisaical views were abolished, and others breathing their spirit substituted. So sweeping and thorough was the change produced, that the Sadducees never recovered from the blow, and whatever they might teach, yet those in office were obligated in all time coming to conform to Pharisaic practice (Jos. Ant. 16:1.4; Tos Yoma 1:8).

But the Pharisaic party was not content with dogmatical victories, even though they celebrated each of them by the insertion in the Calendar of a commemorative feast day. Partly, to discourage the Sadducees, partly from the supposed necessities of the time, and to teach others (to make an example; Siphre on Deuteronomy), they carried their principles even beyond their utmost inferences, and were guilty of such injustice and cruelty, that, according to tradition, Simeon even condemned his own innocent son to death, for the sake of logical consistency. On the other hand, the Pharisaic party knew how to flatter the queen, by introducing a series of ordinances which protected the rights of married women and rendered divorce more difficult. The only ordinance of Simeon ben Shetach, which deserves permanent record, is that which enjoined regular school attendance by all children, although it may have been primarily intended to place the education of the country in the hands of the Pharisees. The general discontent caused by the tyranny of the Pharisees must have rallied most of the higher classes to the party of the Sadducees. It led at last to a protest with the queen, and was probably the first occasion of that revolt of Aristobulus, the younger son of Salome, which darkened the last days of her reign.

Salome died (in the beginning of 69 BC) before the measures proposed against Aristobulus could be carried out. Although Hyrcanus II, now united the royal office with the Pontificate, his claims were disputed by his brother Aristobulus II, who conquered, and obliged his brother to abdicate in his favor his twofold dignity. To cement their reconciliation, Alexander the son of Arisobulus married Alexandra the daughter of Hycranus. They little thought how ill fated that union would prove. For already another power was intriguing to interject in Jewish affairs, with which it was from then on to be identified. Alexander Hannai had appointed one Antipas, or Antipater, of whose origin the most divergent accounts are given, to the governorship of Idumea. He was succeeded by a son of the same name. The dissension between the two Asmoneans seemed to offer the opportunity for realizing his ambitious schemes. Of course, he took the part of the weak Hyrcanus as against the warlike Aristobulus, and persuaded the former that he was in danger of his life. Ultimately he prevailed on him to flee to Aretas, King of Arabia, who, in consideration of liberal promises, undertook to reinstate Hycranus in the government. The Arab army proved successful, and was joined by a large proportion of the troops of Aristobulus, who was not shut up within the fortified Temple buildings. To add to the horrors of war, a long famine desolated the land. It was during its prevalence that Onias, reputed for his omnipotence in prayer, achieved what procured for him the designation hammeaggel, the circle drawer. When his prayer for rain remained unanswered, he drew a circle around him, declaring his determination not to leave it until the Almighty had granted rain, and that not in drops, nor yet in desolating floods (which successively happened), but in copious, refreshing showers. It could serve no good purpose to reproduce the realistic manner in which this supposed power of the Rabbi with God is described (Taan. 23 a). But it was difficult to say whether this is more repugnant to feelings of reverence, or the reported reproof of Simeon ben Shetach, who refrained to pronounce the ban upon him because he was like a spoiled child who might ask anything of his father, and would obtain it. But this supposed power ultimately proved fatal to Onias during the siege of Jerusalem by Hyrcanus and Aretas. Refusing to intercede either for one or the other of the rival brothers, he was stoned to death (Ant. 14:2. 1).

But already another power had appeared on the scene. Pompey was on his victorious march through Asia when both parties appeal to him for help. Scaurus, whom Pompey detached to Syria, was bought by Aristobulus, and Aretas was ordered to raise the siege of Jerusalem. But Pompey quickly discovered that Hycranus might, under the tutelage of the cunning Idumean, Antipater, prove an instrument more likely to serve his ulterior purposes than Aristobulus. Three deputations appeared before Pompey at Damascus, those of the two brothers, and one independent of both, which craved the abolition of the Asmonean rule and the restoration of the former mode of government, as we understand it, by the Chebher or

Eldership under the presidency of the High Priest. It need scarcely be said that such a demand would find no response. The consideration of the rival claims of the Asmonean's Pompey postponed. The conduct of Aristobulus not only confirmed the unfavorable impression which the insolent bearing of his deputies had made on Pompey, but sealed his own fate and that of the Jewish people. Pompey laid siege to Jerusalem. The adherents of Hyrcanus surrendered the City, but those of Aristobulus retired into the Temple. At last the sacred precincts were taken by storm amid fearful carnage. The priests, who were engaged in their sacred functions, and who continued them during this terrible scene, were cut down at the altar. No fewer than 12,000 Jews are said to have perished.

With the taking of Jerusalem by Pompey (63 BC) the history of the Maccabees as a reigning family, and that of the real independence of Palestine, came to an end. So truly did Jewish tradition realize this, that it has left us not a single notice either of this capture of Jerusalem or of all the subsequent sad events to the time of Herod. It is as if their silence meant that for them Judea, in its then state, had no further history. Still, the Roman conqueror had as yet dealt gently with his prostrate victim. Pompey had penetrated into the most Holy Place in contemptuous outrage of the most sacred feelings of Israel; but he left the treasure of the Temple untouched, and even made provision for the continuance of its services. Those who had caused the resistance of Jerusalem were executed, and the country made tributary to Rome. But Judea not only became subject to the Roman Governor of Syria, its boundaries were also narrowed. All the Grecian cities had their independence restored; Samaria was freed from Jewish supremacy; and the districts comprised within the so called Decapolis (or ten cities) again obtained self government. It was a sadly curtailed land over which Hyrcanus II, as High Priest, was left Governor, without being allowed to wear the diadem (Ant. 20:10). Aristobulus II had to adorn as captive the triumphal entry of the conqueror into Rome.

The civil rule of Hycranus as Ethnarch must from the first have been very limited. It was still more contracted when, during the Proconsulate of Ganinius (57-55 BC), Alexander, a son of Aristobulus, who had escaped from captivity, tried to possess himself of the government of Judea (Ant. 14:5. 2-4). The office of Hyrcanus was now limited to the Temple, and the Jewish territory, divided into five districts, was apportioned among five principal cities, ruled by a council of local notables (ristoi). Thus, for a short time, monarchical gave place to aristocratic government in Palestine. The renewed attempts of Aristobulus or of his family to recover power only led to fresh troubles, which were sadly diversified by the greediness and severity of the Romans. The Triumvir Crassus, who succeeded Gabinius (55-53 BC), plundered the Temple not only of its treasures but of its precious vessels. A new but not much happier era began with Julius Caesar. If Aristobulus and his son Alexander had not fallen victims to the party of Pompey, the prospects of Hyrcanus and Antipater might now have been very unpromising. But their death and that of Pompey (whom they had supported) changed the aspect of matters. Antipater not only espoused the cause of the victor of Pharsalus, but made himself eminently useful to Caesar. In reward, Hyrcanus was confirmed as Pontiff and Ethnarch of Judea, while Antipater was made a Roman citizen and nominated Epitrophos, or (Roman) administrator of the country. Of course, the real power was in the hands of the Idumean, who continued to hold it, despite the attempts of Antigonus, the only surviving son of Aristobulus. And from then on Caesar made it part of his policy to favor the Jews (comp. the decrees in their favor, Ant. 14:10).

Meantime Antipater had, in pursuance of his ambitious plans, appointed his son Phasael Governor of Jerusalem, and Herod Governor of Galilee. The latter, although only twenty five years of age, soon displayed the vigor and sternness which characterized his after career. He quelled what probably was a nationalist rising in Galilee, in the blood of Ezekias, its leader, and of his chief associates. This indeed secured him the favor of Sextus Caesar, the Governor of Syria, a relative of the great Imperator. But in Jerusalem, and among the extreme Pharisaic party, it excited the utmost indignation. They foresaw the advent of a foe most dangerous to their interests and liberty, and vainly sought to rid themselves of him. It was argued that the government of the country was in the hands of the High Priest, and that Herod, as Governor of Galilee, appointed by a foreign administrator, had no right to pronounce capital punishment without a sentence of the Sanhedrin. Hycranus yielded to the clamor; but Herod appeared before the Sanhedrin, not as a criminal, but arrayed in purple, surrounded by a body guard, and supported by the express command of Sextus Caesar to acquit him. The story which is related, though in different version, and with different names, in the Talmud (Sanh. 19 a), and by Josephus (Ant. 14:9. 3-5), presents a vivid picture of what passed in the Sanhedrin. The appearance of Herod had so terrified that learned body that none ventured to speak, until their president, Shemajah (Sameas), by his bold speech, rallied their courage. Most truly did he foretell the fate which overtook them ten years later, when Herod ruled in the Holy City.

But Hyrcanus adjourned the meeting of the Sanhedrin, and persuaded Herod to withdraw from Jerusalem. His was, however, only a temporary humiliation. Sextus Caesar named Herod Governor of Coele Syria, and he soon appeared with an army before Jerusalem, to take vengeance on Hycranus and the Sanhedrin. The entreaties of his father and brother induced him to desist for the time, but ten years later Hyrcanus and the members of the Sanhedrin fell victims to his revenge.

Another turn of affairs seemed imminent when Caesar fell under the daggers of the conspirators (15 March, 44BC), and Cassius occupied Syria. But Antipater and Herod proved as willing and able to serve him as formerly Caesar. Antipater perished through a court—or perhaps a Nationalist plot, but his murderers soon experienced the same fate at the hands of those whom Herod had hired for the purpose. And still the star of Herod seemed in the rising. Not only did he repel attempted inroads by Antigonus, but when Antonius and Octavianus (in 42 BC) took the place of Brutus and Cassius, he succeeded once more in ingratiating himself with the former, on whom the government of Asis devolved. The accusations made by Jewish deputation had no influence on Antony. Indeed, he went beyond his predecessors in appointing Phasael and Herod tetrarchs of Judea. Thus the civil power was now nominally as well as really in their hands. But the restless Antigonus was determined not to forego his claim. When the power of Antony was fast waning, in consequence of his reckless indulgences, Antigonus seized the opportunity of the incursion of the Parthians into Asia Minor to attend the great object of his ambition. In Jerusalem the adherents of the two parties were engaged in daily conflicts, when a Parthian division appeared. By treachery Phasael and Hycranus were lured into the Parthian camp, and finally handed over to Antigonus. Herod, warned in time, had escaped from Jerusalem with his family and armed adherents. Of his other opponents Antigonus made sure. To unfit Hyrcanus for the Pontificate his ears were cut off, while Phasael destroyed himself in prison. Antigonus was now undisputed High Priest and king. His brief reign of three years (40-37 BC) is marked by coins which bear in Hebrew the device: Matthatjah the High Priest, and in Greek: King Antigonus.

The only hope of Herod lay in Roman help. He found Antony in Rome. What difficulties there were, were removed by gold, and when Octavian gave his consent, a decree of the Senate declared Antigonus the enemy of Rome, and at the same time appointed Herod King of Judea (40 BC). Early in the year 39 BC Herod was in Palestine to conquer his new kingdom by help of the Romans. But their aid was at first tardy and reluctant, and it was 38 BC, or more probably 37 BC, before Herod could gain possession of Jerusalem itself. Before that he had wed the beautiful and unhappy Mariamme, the daughter of Alexander and granddaughter of Hyrcanus, to whom he had been betrothed five years before. His conquered capital was desolate indeed, and its people impoverished by taxations. But Herod had reached the goal of his ambition. All opposition was put down, all rivalry rendered impossible. Antigonus was beheaded, as Herod had wished; the feeble and aged Hyrcanus was permanently disqualified for the Pontificate; and any youthful descendants of the Maccabees left were absolutely in the conquerors power. The long struggle for power had ended, and the Asmonean family was virtually destroyed. Their sway had lasted about 130 years.

Looking back on the rapid rise and decline of the Maccabees, on their speedy degeneration, on the deeds of cruelty with which their history soon became stained, on the selfishness and reckless ambition which characterized them, and especially on the profoundly anti-nationalist and anti-Pharisaic, we had almost said anti-Jewish, tendency which marked their sway, we can understand the bitter hatred with which Jewish tradition had followed their memory. The mention of them is of the scantiest. No universal acclamation glorifies even the deeds of Judas the Maccabee; no Talmudic tractate is devoted to that feast of the dedication which celebrated the purging of the Temple and the restoration of Jewish worship. In fact such was the feeling, that the priestly course of Joiarib, to which the Asmoneans belonged, is said to have been on service when the first and the second Temple were destroyed, because guilt was to be punished on the guilty. More than that, R. Levi said: Yehoyaribh ["Jehovah will contend"], the man [the name of the man or family]; Meron ["rebellion," evidently a play upon Modin, the birthplace of the Maccabees], the town; Mesarbey ["the rebels," evidently a play upon Makkabey], (masar beitha) He has given up the Temple to the enemies. Rabbi Berachjah said: Yah heribh [Jehoiarib], God contended with His children, because they revolted and rebelled against Him (Jeremiah Taan. 4:8, p. 68 d, line 35 from bottom). The shameful designation of rebellion, and Sarbaney El, rebels against God, became in course of time so identified with the Maccabees that it was used when its meaning was no longer understood. Thus Origen (Euseb. HiEcclesiastes 6:25) speaks of the (Apocryphal) books of the Maccabees as inscribed Sarbeth Sarbane El (=), the disobedience, or rebellion (resistance) of the disobedient, or rebels, against God. So thoroughly had these terms become identified in popular parlance, that even the tyranny and cruelty of a Herod could not procure a milder judgment on the sway of the Asmoneans.

End Notes:

[5]   Some Christian and all Jewish writers assign the designation of The Just to Simon II. This is directly contrary to the express statement of Josephus.

[6]   The designation Maccabee was originally given to Judas (1 Maccabees 2:4, 66; 3:1; v. 24, 34). The name was probably derived from, or in Chaldee, a hammer.

[7]   The Syrian force is said to have amounted to 100,000 footmen, 20,000 horsemen, and 32 war elephants (1 Maccabees 6:30).

[8]   According to Jeremiah Soath ix. 13, and Sot. 33 a, a Bath Qol, or Heavenly Voice, issuing from the Most Holy Place, had announced to Hyrcanus, while officiating in the Temple, the victory of his sons at Samaria. Josephus (Ant. 13:10. 7), assigns on this ground to Hyrcanus the prophetic, as well as the priestly and royal, title.

[9]   Jewish tradition vindicates a much earlier origin for the Sanhedrin, and assumes its existence not only in the time of Moses, David, and Solomon, but even in that of Mordecai.

[10]   The words are, in one sense, most significant, since these fertilizing rains, descending on these two nights when it was especially forbidden to go out, since on them innumerable demons haunted on the air (Pes. 112 b, line 10 from the bottom), indicated an exceptional blessing. The reason why these two nights are singled out as dangerous is, that Chanina b. Dosa, of whom Rabbinic tradition has so many miracles to relate, conceded them to the hurtful sway of Agrath bath Machlath and her 18 myriads of Angels. See App. x3:In view of this, M. Derenbourgs explanatory note would seem to require to be modified. But, in general, rain even on the night before the Sabbath was regarded as a curse (Vayy. R. 35), and it has been ingeniously suggested that the in the Midrash must be taken in the sense in which that word is explained in Taan. 6 a, namely as the ordinary time of rain. Why the night before Wednesday and Friday night are represented as left in the power of hurtful demons might open an interesting field for speculation.

[11]   The captives brought to Rome and sold as slaves became the nucleus of the Jewish community in the imperial city.

Appendix 5

Rabbinic Theology and Literature

1. The Traditional Law., The brief account given in Volume 1 of the character and authority claimed for the traditional law may here be supplemented by a chronological arrangement of the Halakhoth in the order of their supposed introduction or promulgation.

In the first class, or Halakhoth of Moses from Sinai, tradition enumerates fifty five, which may be thus designated: religio-agrarian, four; ritual, including questions about clean and unclean, twenty three; concerning women and intercourse between the sexes, three; concerning formalities to be observed in the copying, fastening, etc., of the Law and the phylacteries, eighteen; exegetical, four; purely superstitious, one; not otherwise included, two. Eighteen ordinances are ascribed to Joshua, of which only one is ritual, the other seventeen being agrarian and police regulations. The other traditions can only be briefly noted. Boaz, or else the tribunal of Samuel, fixed, that Deuteronomy 23:3 did not apply to alliances with Ammonite and Moabite women. Two ordinances are ascribed to David, two to Solomon, one to Jehoshaphat, and one to Jehoida. The period of Isaiah and of Hezekiah is described as of immense Rabbinic activity. To the prophets at Jerusalem three ritual ordinances are ascribed. Daniel is represented as having prohibited the bread, wine and oil of the pagan (Daniel 1:5). Two ritual determinations are ascribed to the prophets of the Exile.

After the return from Babylon traditionalism rapidly expanded, and its peculiar character more and more clearly developed. No fewer than twelve traditions are traced back to the three prophets who flourished at that period, while four other important legal determinations are attributed to the prophet Haggai individually. It will readily be understood that Ezra occupied a high place in tradition. Fifteen ordinances are ascribed to him, of which some are nominal. Three of his supposed ordinances have a general interest. They enjoin the general education of children, and the exclusion of Samaritans from admission into the Synagogue and from social intercourse. If only one legal determination is assigned to Nehemiah, the men of the great Synagogue are credited with fifteen, of which six bear on important critical and exegetical points connected with the text of the Scriptures, the others chiefly on questions connected with ritual and worship. Among the pairs (Zugoth) which succeeded the Great Synagogue, three alleviating ordinances (of a very thorough character) are ascribed to Jose, the son of Joezer, and two, intended render all contact with pagans impossible, to him and his colleague. Under the Maccabees the feast of the dedication of the Temple was introduced. To Joshua the son of Perachya, one thorough legal determination is ascribed. Of the decrees of the Maccabean High Priest Jochanan we have already spoken in another place; similarly, of those of Simon the son of Shetach and of his learned colleague. Four legal determinations of their successors Shemayah and Abhtalion are mentioned. Next in order comes the prohibition of Greek during the war between the Maccabean brothers Hyrcanus and Aristobulus. This brings us to the time of Hillel and Shammai, that is, to the period of Jesus, to which further reference will have to be made in another place.

2. The Canon of Scripture., Reference has been made in the text (Volume 1) to the position taken by Traditionalism in reference to the written as compared with what was regarded as the oral Revelation. Still, nominally, the Scriptures were appealed to by the Palestinians as of supreme authority. The views which Josephus expresses in this respect, although in a popular and Grecianized form, were substantially those entertained by the Rabbis and by his countrymen generally (comp. Ag. Apion, 1:7, 8). A sharp distinction was made between canonical and non-canonical books. The test of the former was inspiration, which had ceased in the time of Artaxerxes, that is, with the prophet Malachi: Accordingly, the work of the elder Jesus the son of Sirach (Jeshua ben Sira, ben Eliezer) was excluded from the Canon, although it is not infrequently referred to by Rabbinic authorities in terms with which ordinarily only Biblical quotations are introduced. According to the view propounded by Josephus, not only were the very words inspired

in which a prediction was uttered, but the prophets were unconscious and passive vehicles of the Divine message (Ant. 4:6. 5, comp generally, Ant 2:8. 1; vl:8, 2; 8:13, 3; 9:3, 2, 8, 6; 10:2, 2; 4, 3). Although pre-eminence in this respect was assigned to Moses (Ant. 4:8, 49), yet Divine authority equally attached to the sayings of the prophets, and even, though perhaps in a still inferior degree, to the Hymns, as the Hagiographa generally were called from the circumstance that the Psalter stood at the head of them (Luke 24: 44). Thus the division of the Bible into three sections, the Law, the Prophets, and the other Writings, which already occurs in the prologue to the work of Jesus the son of Sirach, seems to have been current at the time. And here it is of great interest, in connection with modern controversies, that Josephus seems to attach special importance to the prophecies of Daniel as still awaiting fulfillment (Ant. 20:4; 11. 7).

That the Rabbis entertained the same views of inspiration, appears not only from the distinctive name of Holy Writings given to the Scriptures, but also from the directions that their touch defiled the hands, and that it was duty on the Sabbath to save them from fire, and to gather them up if accidentally scattered, and that it was not lawful for heirs to make division of a sacred roll (Comp. Shabb. 15:1; Erub. 10:3; Kel. 15:6; Yad. 3:2-5; 4:5 [where special reference is made to Daniel 6]). From what we know of the state of feeling, we might have inferred, even if direct evidence had not existed that a distinctive and superior place would be ascribed to the Books of Moses. In point of fact, the other books of Scripture, the Prophets and the Hagiographa, are only designated as Qabbalah (received, handed down, tradition), which is also the name given to oral tradition. It was said that the Torah was given to Moses (Jeremiah Sheq. 6:1) in (letters of) white fire graven upon black fire, although it was matter of dispute whether he received it volume by volume or complete as a whole (Gitt. 60 a). But on the question of its inspiration not the smallest doubt could be tolerated. Thus, to admit generally, that the Torah as a whole was from heaven, except this (one) verse, which the Holy One, blessed be He, did not speak, but Moses of himself was to become an infidel and a blasphemer (Sanh. 99 a). Even the concluding verses in Deuteronomy had been dictated by God to Moses, and he wrote them down, not repeating them, however, as before, but weeping as he wrote. It will readily be understood in what extravagant terms Moses himself was spoken of. It is not only that the expression man of God was supposed to imply, that while as regarded the lower part of his nature Moses was man, as regarded the higher he was Divine, but that his glorification and exaltation amount to blasphemy. So far as inspiration or revelation is concerned, it was said that Moses saw in a clear glass, the prophets in a dark one, or, to put it otherwise: he saw through one glass, they through seven. Indeed, although the opening words of Psalm 75: showed, that the Psalms were as much revelation as the Law, yet, if Israel had not sinned, they would have only received the Pentateuch, and the Book of Joshua, and, in the time to come, of all Scripture the Pentateuch alone would retain its place. It was somewhat contemptuously remarked, that the Prophets uttered nothing as regarded practice that had not already been told in the Pentateuch (Taan. 9 a). It was but natural for Rabbinism to declare that the Law alone fully explained its meaning (at least according to their interpretation of it), while the Prophets left much in obscurity. To mark the distinction, it was forbidden to put the Law in the same wrapper with the Prophets, so as not to place perhaps the latter on the top of the former (Tos. Meg. 4:20). Among the Prophets themselves there was a considerable difference, not only in style and training but even in substance (Sanh. 89 a), although all of them had certain common qualifications (comp. Ab. de R. Nathan, 37). Of all the prophets Isaiah was greatest, and stood next to Moses. Ezekiel saw all that Isaiah saw, but the former was like a villager, the latter like a townsman who saw the king (Chag. 13 b). Jeremiah and Amos were, so to speak, scolding, owing to the violence of their temperament, while Isaiah's was the book of consolation, especially in response to Jeremiah.

The Hagiographa or Kethubhim also bear in the Talmud the general designation of Chokhmah, wisdom. It has been asserted that, as the Prophetic Books, so the Hagiographa, were distinguished into anterior (Psalms, Proverbs, Job) and posterior, or else into great and small. But the statement rests on quite insufficient evidence. Certain, however, it is, that the Hagiographa, as we possess them, formed part of the Canon in the time of Jesus the son of Sirach, that is, even of the latest computation of his authorship, about the year 130 BC. Even so, it would not be easy to vindicate, on historical grounds, the so called Maccabean authorship of the Book of Daniel, which would fix its date about 105 BC. For, if other considerations did not interfere, few students of Jewish history would be disposed to assert that a book, which dated from 104 BC, could have found a place in the Jewish Canon. But, as explained in Volume 1, we would assign a much earlier date to the Book of Sirach. The whole question in its bearing on the New Testament is so important, that one or two further remarks may be allowed. Leaving aside most serious critical objections, and the unquestionable fact, that no amount of ingenuity can conciliate the Maccabean application of Daniel 9:24-27 with the chronology of that period, while the Messianic interpretation fits in with it, other, and seemingly insuperable difficulties are in the way of the theory impugned. It implies, that the Book of Daniel was not an Apocryphal, but a Pseudepigraphic work; that of all such works it alone has come down to us in its Hebrew or Chaldee original; that a Pseudepigraphic work, nearly contemporary with the oldest portion of the Book of Enoch, should not only be so different from it, but that it should find admission into the Canon, while Enoch was excluded; that a Pseudepigraphon younger that Jesus the Son of Sirach should have been on the Khethubhim; and, finally, that it should have passed the repeated revision of different Rabbinic Colleges, and that at times of considerable theological activity, without the suspicion being even raised that its authorship dated from so late a period as a century an a half before Christ. And we have evidence that since the Babylonian exile, at least four revisions of the Canon took place within periods sufficiently distant from each other.

The question up to this point treated has been exclusively of the date of the composition of the Book of Daniel, without reference to who may have been its author, whether its present is exactly the same as its original form, and finally, whether it ever belonged to those books whose right to canonicity, or their age, was in controversy, that is, whether it belonged, so to speak, to the Old Testament ntilegmena. As this is not the place for a detailed discussion of the canonicity of the Book of Daniel, or of any other in the Old Testament canon, we shall only add, to prevent misunderstanding, that no opinion is here expressed as to possible, greater or less, digressions on the Book of Daniel, or in any other part of the Old Testament. We must here bear in mind that the moral view taken of such digressions, as we would call them, was entirely different in those times from ours; and it may perhaps be an historically and critically no unwarranted proposition, that such digressions were, to speak moderately, not all unusual in ancient documents. In each case the question must be separately critically examined in the light of internal and (if possible) external evidence. But it would be a very different thing to suggest that there may be an interpretative influence, or, it may be, a re-arrangement in a document (although at present we make no assertions on the subject, one way or the other), and to pronounce a whole document a fabrication dating from a much later period. The one would, at any rate, be quite in the spirit of those times; the other implies, beside insuperable critical difficulties, a deliberate religious fraud, to which no unprejudiced student could seriously regard the so called Pseudepigrapha as forming any real enlargement.

But as regards the Book of Daniel, it is an important fact that the right of the Book of Daniel to canonicity was never called in question in the ancient Synagogue. The fact that it was distinguished as visions (Chezyonoth) from the other prophecies has no bearing on the question, any more than the circumstance that later Rabbinism, which, naturally enough, could not find its way through the Messianic prophecies of the book, declare that even Daniel was mistaken in, and could not make anything of the predictions concerning the latter days (Ber. R. 98). On the other hand, Daniel was elevated to almost the same pinnacle as Moses, while it was said that, as compared with pagan sages, if they were all placed in one scale, and Daniel in the other, he would outweigh them all. We can readily understand that, in times of national sorrow or excitement, these prophecies would be eagerly resorted to, as pointing to a glorious future.

But although the Book of Daniel was not among the Antilegomena, doubts were raised, not indeed about the age, but about the right to canonicity of certain other portions of the Bible. Thus, certain expressions in the prophecies of Ezekiel were questioned as apparently incompatible with statements in the Pentateuch (Men. 45 a), and although a celebrated Rabbi, Chananyah, the son of Chizkuyah, the son of Garon (about the time of Christ), with immense labor, sought to placate them, and thus preserved the Book of Ezekiel (or, at least, part of it) from being relegated among the Apocrypha, it was deemed safest to leave the final exposition of the meaning of Ezekiel, until Elijah come, as the restorer of all things.

The other objections to canonicity apply exclusively to the third division of the Old Testament, the Kethubhim or Hagiographa. Here even the Book of Proverbs seems at one time to have been called in question (Ab. R. Nathan 1), partly on the ground of its secular contents, and partly as containing supposed contradictory statements (Shabb. 30 b). Very strong doubts were raised on the Book of Ecclesiastes (Yad. 3:5; Eduy. v. 3), first, on that ground of its contradiction to some of the Psalms (Shabb. 30 a); secondly, on that of its inconsistencies (Shabb. 30 b); and thirdly, because it seemed to countenance the denial of another life, and, as in Ecclesiastes 11:1, 3, 9, other heretical views (Vayyikra R. 28, at the beginning). But these objections were finally answered by great ingenuity, while an appeal to Ecclesiastes 12:12, 13, was regarded as removing the difficulty about another life and future rewards and punishments. And as the contradictions in Ecclesiastes had been conciliated, it hopefully argued deeper study would equally remove those in the Book of Proverbs (Shabb. 30 b). Still, the controversy about the canonicity of Ecclesiastes continue so late as the second century of our era (comp. Yad. 3:5). That grave doubts also existed about the Song of Solomon, appears even from the terms in which its canonicity is insisted upon (Yad. u. s.), not to speak of express statements in opposition to it (Ab. de. R. Nathan 1). Even when by an allegorical interpretation it was shown to be the wisdom of all wisdom, the most precious gem, the holy of holies, tradition still ascribed its composition to the early years of Solomon (Shir haSh. R. 1). It had been his first work, and was followed by Proverbs, and finally by Ecclesiastes. But perhaps the greatest objections were those taken to the Book of Esther (Meg. 7 a). It excited the hostility of other nations against Israel, and it was outside the canon. Grave doubts prevailed whether it was canonical or inspired by the Holy Spirit (Meg. u. s.; Yoma 29 a). The books of Ezra and Nehemiah were anciently regarded as one, the name of the latter author being kept back on account of his tendency to self exaltation (Sanh. 93 b). Lastly, the genealogical parts of the Book of Chronicles were made the subject of very elaborate secret commentary (Pes. 62 b).

Two points still require brief mention. Even from a comparison of the LXX Version with our Hebrew text, it is evident that there were not only many variations, but that spurious additions (as Daniel) were eliminated. This critical activity, which commenced with Ezra, whose copy of the Pentateuch was, according to tradition, placed in the Temple, that the people might correct their copies by it, must have continued for many centuries. There is abundant evidence of frequent divergences, though perhaps minute, and although later Rabbinism laid down the most painfully minute directions about the mode of writing and copying the rolls of the Law, there is such discrepancy, even where least it might be expected, as to show that the purification of the text was by no means settled. Considering the lack of exegetical knowledge and historical conscientiousness, and keeping in view how often the Rabbis, for Haggadic purposes, alter letters, and thus change the meaning of words, we may well doubt the satisfactory character of their critical labors. Lastly, as certain omissions were made, and as the Canon underwent (as will be shown) repeated revision, it may have been certain portions were added as well as left out, and words changed as well as restored.

For, ancient tradition ascribes a peculiar activity to certain Colleges, as they are termed, in regard to the Canon. In general, the well known Baraita (Baba B. 14 b, 15 a) bears, that Moses wrote the Pentateuch, the book (Prophecies?) of Balaam, and Job; Joshua the work that bears his name, and the last eight verses of Deuteronomy; Samuel the corresponding books, Judges and Ruth; David with the ten Elders, Adam, Melchizedek, Abraham, Moses, Heman, Jeduthun, Asaph, and the three sons of Korah, the Psalter; Jeremiah wrote his prophecies, Lamentations, and Kings; King Hezekiah and his Sanhedrin compiled, or edited, the Prophecies of Isaiah, Proverbs, the Song, and Ecclesiastes; and the men of the Great Synagogue the Prophecies of Ezekiel, of the twelve Minor Prophets, and the books of Daniel and Esther; Ezra wrote his own book and Chronicles, the work being completed by Nehemiah, the son of Chakaliah. The last verse of Joshua were written by Eleazar and Phinehas; the last chapters of Samuel by Gad and Nathan.

Loose and uncritical as these statements may appear, they so far help our investigations as to show that, according to tradition, certain portions of Scripture were compiled or edited by one or another Rabbinic College, and that there were several Colleges which successively busied themselves with the codification and revision of the Canon. By these Colleges, we are not to understand gatherings of certain members, who discussed and decided a question at one or more of their meetings. They rather indicate the learned activity of the authorities during a certain period, which are respectively designed by the generic names of the Sanhedrin of Hezekiah, The men of the Synagogue, the Legal Court of the Maccabees, and finally, Chananayah and his College, We have thus somewhat firmer historical ground. If in Proverbs 25:1, we read of the activity about the Canon of the Men of Hezekiah, and bear in mind the Scriptural account of the religious revival of that reign (for Exodus 2 Chronicles 29:25-30; 2 Chronicles 30:1), we scarcely required the frequent and elaborate glorification of tradition to lead us to infer that, if the collection of the Book of Proverbs was due to their activity, they must have equally collated the other portions of Scripture then existing, and fixed the Canon as their time. Again, if we are to credit the statement that they equally collected and edited the Prophecies of Isaiah, we are obliged to infer that the continuance of that College was not limited to the life of Hezekiah, since the latter died before Isaiah (Tos. Baba Bathra; Yeb. 49 b).

What has just been indicated is fully confirmed by what we know of the activity of Ezra (Ezra 5:6, 10), and of his successors in the great

Synagogue. If we are to attach credit to the notice in 2 Maccabees 2:13, it points to such literary activity as tradition indicates. That the revision and determination of the Canon must have been among the main occupations of Ezra and his successors of the Great Synagogue, whatever precise meaning may be attached to that institution, seems scarcely to require proof. The same remark applies to another period of religious reformation, that of the so called Asmonean College. Even if we had not the evidence of their exclusion of such works as those of Ben Sirach and others, there could be no rational doubt that in their time the Canon, as now existing, was firmly fixed, and that no work of comparatively late date could have found admission into it. The period of their activity is sufficiently known, and too near what may be called the historical times of Rabbinism, for any attempt in that direction, without leaving traces of it. Lastly, we come to the indications of a critical revision of the text by Chananyah and his College, shortly before the time of Jesus. Thus we have, in all, a record of four critical revisions of the Canon up to time of Christ.

3. Any attempt to set forth in this place a detailed exposition of the Exegetical Canon of the Rabbis, or of their application, would manifestly be impossible. It would require almost a treatise of its own; and a cursory survey would neither be satisfactory to the writer nor instructive to the general reader. Besides, on all subjects connected with Rabbinic exegesis, a sufficient number of learned treatises exists, which are easily accessible to students, while the general reader can only be interested in such general results as have been frequently indicated throughout these volumes. Lastly, the treatment of certain branches of the subject, such as a criticism of the Targumim, really belongs to what is known as the science of Introduction, either to the Old Testament, in manuals of which, as well as in special treaties, all such subjects are fully discussed. Besides these the student may be referred, for a general summary, to the labors of Dr. Hamburger (Real Encycl.). Special works on various branches of the subject cannot here be named, since this would involve an analysis and critical investigation. But for a knowledge of the Rabbinic statements in regard to the Codices and the text of the Old Testament, reference may here be made to the short but masterly analysis of Professor Strack (Prolegomena Critica), in which, first, the various codices of the Old Testament, and then the text as existing in Talmudical times, are discussed, and the literature of the subject fully and critically given. The various passages are also mentioned in which

the Biblical quotations in the Mishnah and Gemara differ from our present text. Most of them are, however, of no exegetical importance. On the exegesis of the Rabbis generally, I would take leave to refer to sketch of it given in the History of the Jewish Nation, Chapter 11, and especially in App. V., on Rabbinical Exegesis, where all its canons are enumerated. Some brief notices connected with Rabbinic Commentaries quoted in this work will be found at the beginning of Volume 1.

4. Somewhat similar observations must be made in regard to the mystical Theology of the Synagogue, or the so called Kabbalah. Its beginning must certainly be traced to, and before, the times described in these volumes. For a discussion of its origin and doctrines I must once more take leave to refer to the account given in the History of the Jewish Nation (pp. 435, etc.). The whole modern literature of the subject, besides much illustrative matter, is given in the Italian text annexed to David Castellis edition of Sabbatai Donnolos Hebrew Commentary on the Book Yetsirah, or the Book of Creation. For, the Kabbalah busies itself with these two subjects: the History of the Creation (Yetsirah, perhaps rather formation than Creation), and the Merkabhah, or the Divine apparition as described by Ezekiel. Both refer to the great question, underlying all theosophic speculation: that of God's connection with His creature. They treat the mystery of Nature and of Providence, with especial bearing on Revelation; and the question, how the Infinite God can have any connection or intercourse with finite creatures, is attempted to be answered. Of the two points raised, that of Creation is of course the first in the order of thinking as well as of time, and the book Yetsirah is the oldest Kabbalistic document.

The Sepher Yetsirah is properly a monologue on the part of Abraham, in which, by the contemplation of all that is around him, he ultimately arrives at the conviction of the Unity of God.

We distinguish the substance and the form of creation; that which is, and the mode in which it is. We have already indicated that the original of all that exists is Divine. 1st, We have God; 2nd, God manifest, or the Divine entering into form; 3rd, That Divine in its form, from which in turn all original realities are afterwards derived. In the Sepher Yetsirah, these Divine realities (the substance) are represented by the ten numerals, and their form by the twenty two letters which constitute the Hebrew alphabet, language being viewed as the medium of connection between the spiritual and the material; as the form in which the spiritual appears. At the same time, number and language indicate also the arrangement and the mode of creation, and, in general, its boundaries. "By thirty two wonderful paths," so begins the Sepher Yetsirah, "the Eternal, the Lord of Hosts, the God of Israel, the Living God, the King of the World, the merciful and gracious God, the glorious One, He that inhabits eternity, Whose Name is high and holy, has created the world." But these ten numerals are in reality the ten Sephiroth, or Divine emanations, arranged in triads, each triad consisting of two opposites (flowing or emanating from a superior triad until the Divine Unity is reached), and being reconciled in a middle point of connection. These ten Sephiroth, in the above arrangement, recur everywhere, and the sacred number ten is that of perfection. Each of these Sephiroth flows from its predecessor, and in this manner the Divine gradually evolves. This emanation of the ten Sephiroth then constitutes the substance of word; we may add, it constitutes everything else. In God, in the world, in man, everywhere we meet these ten Sephiroth, at the head of which is God manifest, or the Memra (Logos, the Word). If the ten Sephiroth give the Substance, the twenty two letters are the form of creation and of revelation. "By giving them form and shape, and by interchanging them, God has made the soul of everything that has been made, or shall be made." "Upon those letters, also, has the Holy One, Whose Name be praised, founded His holy and glorious Name." These letters are next subdivided, and their application in all the departments of nature is shown. In the unit creation, the triad; world, time and man are found. Above all these is the Lord. Such is a very brief outline of the rational exposition of the Creation, attempted by the Sepher Yetsirah.

We append a translation of the book Yetsirah, only adding that much, not only as regards the meaning of the expressions but even their translation, is in controversy. Therefore, not infrequently, our rendering must be regarded as our interpretation of the mysterious original.

Appendix 6

The Book Yetsirah

Pereq. I.

Mishnah 1. In thirty two wonderful paths of wisdom, Jah, Jehovah Tsebhaoth, the God of Israel, the Living God, and King of the World, God merciful and gracious, High and Exalted, Who dwells to Eternity, high and holy is His Name, has ordered [established, created?] (the world) by three Sepharim [books]: by Sepher [the written Word], Sephar [number, numeral] and Sippur [spoken word]. Others, pointing the world's differently, render these mysterious terms: Number, Word, Writing; others Number, Numberer, Numbered; while still other see in it a reference to the threefold division of the letters of the Hebrew alphabet, of which more afterwards.

Mishnah 2. Ten Sephiroth [emanations] belimah [without anything, i.e. before these, the sole elements out of which all else evolved], twenty two letters of foundation (these constitute the Hebrew Alphabet, and the meaning seems that the Sephiroth manifest themselves in that which is uttered): three mothers (Aleph, the first letter of Avveyr, air; Mem, the first letter of Mayim, water; and Shin, the last letter of Esh, fire, although this may represent only one mystical aspect of the meaning of the term mothers, as applied to these letters), seven duplex (Pronounced soft or hard, namely Beth, Gimel, Daleth, Kaph, Pe, Resh, Tau, which are, or where in Hebrew capable of modification by a Dagesh, but this also must be mystically understood) and twelve simple ones (the simple letters of the Hebrew Alphabet).

Mishnah 3. Ten Sephiorth belimah (the analogy is now further traced in God and in man), the number of the ten fingers, five against five, and the covenant of the One Only (God) placed between them (the covenant relationship between God and man in the midst, even as it is symbolized in the person of man which is between the twice five fingers) by the word of the tongue (this, the relation Godward) and by the word of sexualness [nuditas] (the relation earthwards, the one has become dual.)

Mishnah 4. Ten Sephiroth belimah, ten and not nine, ten and not eleven, be informed in wisdom, and be wise in information; examine in them, search out from them, and put the thing in its reality (certitude, proper state?), and place again the Creator in His place.

Mishnah 5. Ten Sephiroth belimah, their measurement ten, which have no end (limitation): depth of beginning (past) and depth of ending (future), depth of good and depth of evil, depth of height and depth of profundity (or, above and beneath), depth of east and depth of west, depth of north and depth of south, One only Lord, God, the true (approved) King, Who reigns over all from His holy dwelling and to all eternity.

Mishnah 6. Ten Sephiroth belimah, their appearance like the sheen of lightning (reference here to Ezekiel 1:14), and their outgoings (goal) that they have no end, His word is in them (the Logos manifest in the Sephiroth), in running and in returning, and at His word like storm wind they pursue (follow), and before His throne they bend (in worship).

Mishnah 7. Ten Sephiroth belimah, their end is joined to their beginning, like the flame that is bound up with the coal, for the Lord is One only, and there is no second to Him, and before him what count you?

Mishnah 8. Ten Sephiroth belimah, shut your mouth, that is speak not, and your heart, that it think not, and if your heart run away, bring it back to its place, for on this account is it said (Ezekiel 1:14) they run and return, and on this condition has the Covenant been made.

Mishnah 9 and 10. Ten Sephiroth belimah, One: the Spirit of the living God, blessed and again blessed be the Name of Him Who lives forever, Voice and Spirit and Word, and this is the Holy Spirit.

Two: Wind (air, spirit?) from (out of) Spirit, thereby ordered and shaped He the twenty two letters of foundation, three mothers, and 7 duplicate, and 12 simple ones, and one Spirit from (among) them. Three: Water from beneath (wind), He designed and shaped in them tohu vavohu, slime and dung, designed them like a bed (a garden bed), shaped them like a wall, covered them like pavement. Four: Fire from water, He designed it and shaped in it the throne of glory, the Ophanim and Seraphim, the sacred living creatures, and the angels of service, and of these three He founded His dwelling place, as it is said, He makes His angels breaths (winds), and His ministers a flaming fire.

Mishnah 11. Five: Three letters from out the simple ones: He sealed spirit on the three, and fastened them in His Great Name (Jehovah, of which these three letters are the abbreviation; what follows shows how the permutation of these three letters makes the varied relationship of God to creation in time and space, and at the same time, so to speak, the immanence of His manifestation in it). And He sealed with them six outgoings (ends, terminations): He turned upwards, and He sealed it with. Six: He sealed below, turned downwards, and sealed it with. Seven: He sealed eastward, He turned in front of Him, and sealed it with. Eight: He sealed westward, and turned behind, and sealed it with. Nine: He sealed southward, and turned to His right, and sealed it with. Ten: He sealed northward, and turned to His left, and sealed it with.

Mishnah 12. These are the Sephiroth belimah, one: Spirit of the living God, and wind (air, spirit? the word ruach means all these), water, and fire; and height above and below, east and west, north and south.

Pereq II.

Mishnah 1. Twenty and two letters of foundation: three mothers, seven duplex, and twelve simple ones, three mothers, their foundation the scale of merit and the scale of guilt, and the tongue of statute trembling (deciding) between them. (This, to be mystically carried out, in its development, and application to all things: the elements, man, etc.)

Mishnah 2. Twenty two letters of foundation: He drew them, shaped them, weighed them, and interchanged them, melted them together (showing how in the permutation of letters all words, viewed mystically as the designation of things, arose), He formed by them the nephesh of all that is formed (created), and the nephesh of everything that is to be formed (created).

Mishnah 3. Two and twenty letters of foundation: drawn in the voice, hewn in the wind (air, spirit?) fastened on the mouth in five places: (the gutturals among the Hebrew letters), (the labials), (the palatals), (the linguals), (the dentals).

Mishnah 4. Twenty two letters of foundation, fastened in a circle in 231 gates (marking how these letters are capable of forming, by the permutation of two of them, in all 231 permutations); and the circle turns forwards and backwards, and this is the indication of the matter: as regards what is good, there is nothing higher than (oneg), delight, and nothing lower than (negah), plague (stroke). In such manner He weighed them and combined them, with them all, and them all with them all, and them all with, and thus the rest, so that it is found that all that is formed and all that is spoken proceeds from one Name (the name of God being, as it were, the fundamental origin of everything).

Mishnah 5. He formed from Tohu that which has substance, and made that which is not into being, and shaped great pillars from the air, which cannot be handled; and this is the indication: beholding and speaking He made all that is formed and all words by one Name, and the indication of the matter: twenty two numbers and one body.

Pereq III.

Mishnah 1. Three mothers: their foundation, the scale of guilt and the scale of merit, and the tongue of the statue trembling (deciding) between them.

Mishnah 2. Three mothers: a great mystery, marvelous and hidden, and sealed with six signets, and from them go forth fire and water, and divide themselves into male and female. Three mothers, their foundation, and from them were born the fathers (rerum naturae semina), from which everything is created (fire is regarded as the male principle, water as the female principle, and air as combining the two: is the first letter of the Hebrew word for air, for that of water, the last for that of fire).

Mishnah 3. Three letters, in the world: air, water, fire; the heavens were created in the beginning from fire, and the earth was created from water, and the air trembles (the same word as that in regard to the tongue between the scales of the balance, indicating the intermediate, inclining to the one or the other) between the fire and the water.

Mishnah 4. Three mothers, in the year: fire, and water, and wind. Heat is created from fire, cold from water, and moderate from the wind (air) that is intermediate between them. Three mothers, in the nephesh: fire, water, and wind. The head was created from fire, and the belly from water, and the body from wind that is intermediate between them.

Mishnah 5. Three mothers, He drew them, and shaped them, and melted them together, and sealed with them the three mothers in the world, the three mothers in the year, and three mothers in the nephesh, male and female.

(Now follows a further mystical development and application.) The letter He made King in the Spirit, and bound upon him the crown (this refers to farther mystical signs indicated in the Kabbalistic figure drawn on p. 438 of the History of the Jewish Nation), and melted them one with the other, and sealed with them: in the world the air, in the soul life, and in the nephesh (living thing) body, the male with, the female with. He made King in the waters, and bound on it the crown, and melted them one with the other, and sealed: in the world earth, and in the year cold, and in the nephesh the belly, male and female, male in, and female in. He made King in the fire, and bound on it the crown, and melted them one with the other, and sealed with it: in the upper world the heavens, in the year heat, in the nephesh the head, male and female.

Pereq IV.

Mishnah 1. Seven duplex letters, (it will here be observed that we now proceed from the numeral 3 to the further mystic numeral 7), accustomed (habituated, adapted, fitted) for two languages (correlate ideas); life, and peace, and wisdom, and riches, grace, and seed, and government (the mystic number 7 will here he noted), and accustomed (fitted) for two tongues (modes of pronunciation), the formation of soft and hard, the formation of strong and weak (the dual principle will here be observed); duplicate, because they are opposites: the opposites, life and death; the opposites, peace and evil; the opposites, wisdom and folly; the opposites, riches and poverty; the opposites, grace and ugliness; the opposites—fertility and desolation; the opposites, rule and servitude.

Mishnah 2. Seven duplex letters; corresponding to the seven out goings; from them seven outgoings: above and below, east and west, north and south, and the holy Temple in the middle, and it upholds the whole.

Mishnah 3. Seven duplex; He drew them, and shaped them, and melted them, and from them, in the world the stars (the planets), in the year the days, in the nephesh the issues, and with them He drew seven firmaments, and seven earth's, and seven Sabbaths, therefore He loves the seventh under all heavens.

Mishnah 4. Two letters build two houses (here the number of possible permutations are indicated). Three letters build six houses, four build twenty four houses, five build 120 houses, six build 720 houses, and from there go onward and think what the mouth is not able to speak, and the ear not able to hear. And these are the in the world, seven: the Sun, Venus, Mercury, the Moon, Saturn, Jupiter, Mars. And these are the days in the year; the seven days of creation; and the seven gates of issue in the nephesh: two eyes, two ears, and a mouth, and the two nostrils. And with them were drawn the seven above all that is delight under the heavens.

Pereq V.

Mishnah 1. The properties of the twelve simple letters (or their attributes), their foundation: sight, hearing, smell, speech, eating, lying together, working, walking, anger, laughter, thinking, sleep. Their measurement twelve boundaries in the hypotenuse (points in transverse lines), the boundary N. E., the boundary S. E., the boundary E. upwards, the boundary E. downwards; the boundary N. upwards, the boundary N. downwards, the boundary S. W., the boundary N. W., the boundary W. upwards, the boundary W. downwards, the boundary S. upwards, the boundary S. downwards, and they extended and go on into the eternal (boundless space), and they are the arms of the world.

Mishnah 2. Twelve simple letters., He drew them, and melted them, and formed of them the twelve constellations in the world (sign of the Zodiac): Aries, Taurus, Gemini, Cancer, Leo, Virgo, Libra, Scorpio, Sagattarius, Capricornus, Aquarius, Pisces (these are expressed in the original in an abbreviated, contracted form). These are the twelve months of the year: Nisan, Iyar, Sivan, Tammuz, Abh, Elul, Tishri, Marcheshvan, Kislev, Tebheth, Shebhat, Adar (thus the number twelve is marked, first in the functions of man, then in the points of the compass, then in the starry skies, and then in the year). And these are the twelve leaders in nephesh (living beings): two hands, and two feet, and two kidneys, the spleen, the liver, the gall, the intestine, the upper stomach, the lower stomach (perhaps gullet, stomach, and intestine, at any rate, three organs connected with deglutition and digestion). He made them like a land (province), and set them in order like war, and also, this as against that, ordered God. Three mothers, which are three fathers, because from them issue fire, wind, and water. Three mothers, and seven duplicate, and twelve simple ones.

Mishnah 3. These are the twenty two letters with which the Holy One has founded (all), blessed be He, Jah, Jehovah Tsebhaoth, the living God of Israel, high and lifted up, dwelling eternally, and holy is His Name, exalted and holy is He.

Pereq VI.

Mishnah 1. Three fathers and their generations, seven subduers and their hosts (planets?), seven boundaries of hypotenuse, and the proof of matter: faithful witnesses are the world, the year, and the nephesh. The law (statute, settled order) of the twelve, and of the seven, and of the three, and they are appointed over the heavenly dragon, and the cycle, and the heart. Three: fire, and water, and wind (air); the fire above, the water below, and the wind (air) the statute intermediate between them. And the demonstration of the matter: the fire bears the water, is silent, hisses, and is the statute intermediate between them (all these have further mystic meaning and application in connection with words and ideas).

Mishnah 2. The dragon is in the world like a king on his throne; the cycle is in the year like a king in his land; the heart is in the nephesh like a king in war. Also in all that is pursued God has made the one against the other (opposite poles and their reconciliation): the good against the evil; good from good, and evil from evil; the good trying the evil, and the evil trying the good the good is kept for the good, and the evil is kept for the evil.

Mishnah 3. Three are one, that stands alone; seven are divided, there as against three, and the statute intermediate between them. Twelve are in war: three loving, three hating, three giving life, three giving death. The three loving ones: the heart, the ears, and the mouth; the three hating ones: the liver, the gall, and the tongue, and God a faithful king reigning over all: one (is) over three, three over seven, seven over twelve, and they are all joined together, the one with the other.

Mishnah 4. And when Abraham our father had beheld, and considered, and seen, and drawn, and hewn, and obtained it, then the Lord of all revealed Himself to him, and called him His friend, and made a covenant with him and with his seed: and he believed in Jehovah, and it was imputed to him for righteousness. He made with him a covenant between the ten toes, and that is circumcision; between the ten fingers of his hand, and that is the tongue; and He bound two and twenty letters on his tongue, and showed him their foundation. He drew them with water, He kindled them with fire, He breathed them with (air); He burnt them in seven; He poured them forth in the twelve constellations.

The views expressed in the Book Yetsirah are repeatedly referred to in the Mishnah and in other of the most ancient Jewish writings. They represent, as stated at the outset, a direction long anterior to the Mishnah, and of which the first beginnings and ultimate principles are of deepest interest to the Christian student. The reader who wishes to see the application to Christian metaphysics and theology of the Kabbalah, of which Yetsirah is but the first word, is referred to a deeply interesting and profound work, strangely unknown to English scholars: Molitor, Philosophie d. Gesch. oder uber d. Tradition, 4 vols. English readers will find much to interest them in the now somewhat rare work of the Revelation John Oxley: The Christian Doctrine of the Trinity and Incarnation (London, 1815, 2 vols.)

The principles laid down in the Book Yetsirah are further carried out and receive their fullest (often most remarkable) development and application in the book Zohar (Splendor, the edition used by us is the 8 vol. edition, Amsterdam, 1805, in 3 vols, with the Amsterdam edition of the Tikkune Zohar; other Kabbalistic books used by us need not here be mentioned). The main portion of the Zohar is in the form of a Commentary on the Pentateuch, but other tractates are interspersed throughout the volumes.

5. Dogmatic Theology., This is fully treated of in the text of these volumes.
6. Historic Theology., To describe and criticize the various works which come under this designation would require the expansion of this Appendix into a Tractate. Some of these compositions have been referred to in the text of these volumes. For a general account and criticism of them I must again refer to the History of the Jewish Nation (see especially the chapters on The Progress of Arts and Sciences among the Jews, and Theological Science and Religious Belief in Palestine). For the historical and critical account of Rabbinic historical works the student is referred to Zunz, Gottesd. Vortr. d. Juden, Chapter 8: The only thing which we shall here attempt is a translation of the so called Megillath Taanith, or Roll of Fast; rather, a Calendar of the days on which fasting

and mourning was prohibited. The oldest part of the document (referred to in the Mishnah, Taan. 2:8) dates from the beginning of the second century AD, and contains elements of even much greater antiquity. That which has come down of it is here given in translation:

MEGILLATH TAANITH, OR ROLL OF FASTS

These are the days on which it is not lawful to fast, and during some of them mourning must also be intermitted.

I. Nisan.
1. From the 1st day of the month Nisan, and to the 8th of it, it was settled about the daily sacrifice (that it should be paid out of the Temple treasury), mourning is prohibited.
2. And from the 8th to the end of the Feast (the 27th) the Feast of Weeks was re-established, mourning is interdicted.

II. Iyar.
1. On the 7th Iyar the dedication of the wall of Jerusalem—mourning is prohibited.
2. On the 14th is the day of the little (the second) Passover, mourning is prohibited.
3. On the 23rd the sons of Acra issued from Jerusalem.
4. On the 27th the imposts were removed from Judea and Jerusalem.

III. Sivan.
1. On the 17th Sivan the tower of Zur was taken.
2. On the15th and 16th men of Bethshean and of the plain were exiled.
3. On the 25th the tax gatherers were withdrawn from Judah and Jerusalem.

IV. Tammuz.
1. On the 14th Tammuz the Book of Decisions (aggravating ordinances) was abolished, mourning is prohibited.

V. Abh.
1. On the 15th Abh the season of wood offerings (for the Temple use) of priests (comp. Jos. War 2:17. 6), mourning is prohibited.
2. On the 24th we returned to our Law.

VI. Elul.
  1. On the 7th of Elul the day of the Dedication of Jerusalem—mourning prohibited.
  2. On the 17th the Romans withdrew from Judea and Jerusalem.
  3. On the 22nd we returned to kill the apostates.

VII. Tisri.
  1. On the 3rd Tishri the mention of the Divine Name was removed from public deeds.

VIII. Marcheshvan.
  1. On the 23rd Marcheshvan the Sorigah (a partition wall in the Temple, supposed to have been erected by the pagan, comp. 1 Maccabees iv. 43-46) was removed from the Temple court.
  2. On the 25th the wall of Samaria was taken.
  3. On the 27th the meat offering was again brought on the altar.

IX. Kislev.
  1. On the 3rd the Simavatha (another pagan structure) was removed from the court or the Temple,
  2. On the 7th is a feast day.
  3. On the 21st is the day of Mount Garizim, mourning is prohibited.
  4. On the 25th the eight days of the Feast of Lights (Chanukah) begin, mourning is prohibited.

X. Tebheth.
  1. On the 28th the congregation was re-established according to the Law. (This seems to refer to the restoration of the Sanhedrin after the Sadducean members were removed, under the rule of Queen Salome. See the historical notes in Appendix 4)

XI. Shebhat.
  1. On the 2nd a feast day, mourning is prohibited.
  2. On the 22nd the work, of which the enemy said that it was to be in the Temple, was destroyed, mourning is interdicted. (This seems to refer to the time of Caligula, when, on the resistance of the Jews, the statute of the Emperor was at last not allowed to be in the Temple.)

3. On the 28th King Antiochus was removed from Jerusalem (supposed to refer to the day of the death of Antiochus, son of Antiochus Epiphanes, in his expedition against the Parthians).

XII. Adar.
1. On the 8th and the 9th, days of joy on account of rain fall.
2. On the 12th is the day of Trajan.
3. On the 13th is the day of Nicanor (his defeat).
4. On the 14th and on the 15th are the days of Purim (Feast of Esther), mourning is prohibited.
5. On the 16th was begun the building the wall of Jerusalem—mourning is prohibited.
6. On the 17th rose the pagans against the remnant of the Scribes in the country of Chalcis and of the Zabedaeans, and Israel was delivered.
7. On the 20th the people fasted for rain, and it was granted to them.
8. On the 28th the Jews received good news that they would no longer be hindered from the sayings of the Law, mourning is prohibited.

On these days everyone who has before made a vow of fasting is to give himself to prayer.

(In extenuation of the apparent harshness and literality of our renderings, it should be stated, that both the Sepher Yetsirah and the Megillath Taanith are here for the first time translated into English.)

End Notes:

[12] Erub. 4 a; Nidd. 72 b; Ab. d. R. N. 19, 25; Tos. Chall. 1:6; Shabb 70 a; Bekh. 16 a; Naz. 28 b; Chull. 27 a, 28 a; 42 a, 43 a; Moed Q 3 b. Of these, the most interesting to the Christian reader are about the 11 ingredients of the sacred incensed (Ker. 6 b); about the 26 kinds of work prohibited on the Sabbath (Shabb. 70 a); that the father, but not the mother, might dedicate a child under age to the Nazirate (Naz. 28 b); the 7 rules as to slaughtering animals; to cut the neck; to cut through the trachea, and, in the case of four footed animals, also through the gullet; not to pause while slaughtering; to use a knife perfectly free of all notches, and quite sharp; not to strike with the knife; not to cut too near the head; and not to

stick, the knife into the throat; certain determinations about the Feast of Tabernacles, such as about the pouring out of the water, etc.

[13]   Eduy. v3:7; Tanch. 60 a. The first of these Halakhoth speaks of the activity of Elijah in preparation for the coming of the Messiah (Mal. 3:23, 24, KJV iv. 5, 6), as directed to restore those of pure Israelite descent who had been improperly extruded, and to extrude those who had been improperly admitted.

[14]   Baba K. 81 a; Tos. Baba M. 11; Jeremiah Baba K. 3:2. Among the police regulations is this curious one, that all were allowed to fish in the Lake of Galilee, but not to lay down nets, so as not to impede the navigation.

[15]   At first the priests in the Temple were habit to deposit the Terumah near the copy of the Law there kept (Shabb 14 a). But as mice were thereby attracted, and damage to the Sacred Roll was apprehended, it was enacted that the Sacred Roll in the Temple rendered all meat that touched it unclean. This decree gave rise to another, by way of further precaution, that even the hands which touched the Sacred Roll, or any other part of the Bible became unclean (so that, having touched the latter, they could not touch the Terumah). Then followed (in the course of development) a third decree, that such touch defiled also outside the Temple. Finally, the first decree was modified to the effect that the Sacred Roll in the Temple did not defile the hands, while all other Scriptures (anywhere else) defiled them (Chel 15:6) The explanation offered to the Sadducees by R. Jochanan b. Zakkai is evidently intended to mislead (Yad iv. 6), Comp. Levy, Neuhebr Woerterb. Volume 2: pp. 163, 164.

[16]   The difference in the degree of inspiration between the Prophetic and the Hagiographic books is not accurately defined. Later Jewish theologians rather evade it by describing the former as given by the spirit of prophecy, the latter by the Holy Spirit. It must, however, be admitted that in Jewish writings the Holy Spirit is not only not a Personality, but an influence very inferior to what we associate with the designation.

[17]   In Meg. 31 b the formulation of the curses by Moses in Leviticus 25: is said to have been (from God directly), while that in Deuteronomy 10:6: was (from Moses himself).

[18]   The school of Shammai was against, that of Hillel in favor of the Canonicity of Ecclesiastes (Eduy. v. 3). In Tos. Yad. 2 Ecclesiastes is said to be uninspired, and to contain only the wisdom of Solomon.

Appendix 7

The Date of the Nativity

At the outset it must be admitted, that absolute certainty is impossible as to the exact date of Christ's Nativity, the precise year even, and still more the month and the day. But in regard to the year, we possess such data as to invest it with such probability, as almost to amount to certainty.

1. The first and most certain date is that of the death of Herod the Great. Jesus was born before the death of Herod, and, as we judge from the Gospel history, very shortly before that event. Now the year of Herod's death has been ascertained with absolute certainty, as shortly before the Passover of the year 750 A.U.C., which corresponds to about the 12th of April of the year 4 BC, according to our common reckoning. More particularly, shortly before the death of Herod there was a lunar eclipse (Jos. Ant. 15:6. 4), which, it is astronomically ascertained, occurred on the night from the 12th to the 13th of March of the year 4 BC. Thus the death of Herod must have taken place between the 12th of March and the 12th of April, or, say, about the end of March (comp. Ant. 15:8. 1). Again, the Gospel history necessitates an interval of, at the least, seven or eight weeks before that date for the birth of Christ (we have to insert the purification of the Virgin, at the earliest, six weeks after the Birth, The Visit of the Magi, and the murder of the children at Bethlehem, and, at any rate, some days more before the death of Herod). Thus the Birth of Christ could not have possibly occurred after the beginning of February 4 BC, and most likely several weeks earlier. This brings us close to the ecclesiastical date, the 25th of December, in confirmation of which we refer to what has been stated in Volume

1. At any rate, the often repeated, but very superficial objection, as to the impossibility of shepherds tending flocks in the open at that season, must now be dismissed as utterly untenable, not only for the reasons stated in Volume 1, but even for this, that if the question is to be decided on the ground of rain fall, the probabilities are in favor of December as compared with February, later than which it is impossible to place the birth of Christ.

2. No certain inference can be drawn from the appearance of the star that guided the Magi: That, and on what grounds, our investigations have pointed to a confirmation of the date of the Nativity, as given above, has been fully explained in Volume 1: Chapter 6.

3. On the taxing of Quirinius, see Volume 1.

4. The next historical datum furnished by the Gospels is that of the beginning of John the Baptist's ministry, which, according to Luke, was in the fifteenth year of Tiberius, and when Jesus was about thirty years old (Luke 3:23). The accord of this with our reckoning of the date of the Nativity has been shown in Volume 1.

5. A similar conclusion would be reached by following the somewhat vague and general indication furnished in John 2:20.

6. Lastly, we reach the same goal if we follow the historically somewhat uncertain guidance of the date of the Birth of the Baptist, as furnished in this notice (Luke 1:5) of his annunciation to his father, that Zacharias officiated in the Temple as on of the course of Abia (see here Volume 1). In Taan. 29 a we have the notice, with which Josephus agrees (War 6:4. 1. 5), that at the time of the destruction of the Temple the course of Jehoiarib, which was the first of the priestly courses, was on duty. That was on the 9-10 Ab of the year 823 A.U.C., or the 5th August of the year 70 of our era. If this calculation be correct (of which, however, we cannot feel quite sure), then counting the courses of priests backwards, the course of Abia would, in the year 748 A.U.C. (the year before the birth of Christ) have been on duty from the 2nd to the 9th of October. This also would place the birth of Christ in the end of December of the following year (749 A.U.C.), taking the expression sixth month in Luke 1:26, 36, in the sense of the running month (from the 5th to the 6th month, comp. Luke 1:24). But we repeat that absolute reliance cannot be placed on such calculations, at least so far as regards month and day. (Comp. here generally Wieseler, Synopse, and his Beitraege.)

Appendix 8

Rabbinic Traditions about Elijah, The Forerunner

To complete the evidence, presented in the text, as to the essential difference between the teaching of the ancient Synagogue about the Forerunner of the Messiah and the history and mission of John the Baptist, as described in the New Testaments, we append a full, though condensed, account of the earlier Rabbinic traditions about Elijah.

Opinions differ as to the descent and birthplace of Elijah. According to some, he was from the land of Gilead (Bemid. R. 14), and of the tribe of Gad (Tanch. on Genesis 49:19). Others describe him as a Benjamite, from Jerusalem, one of those who sat in the Hall of Hewn Stones (Tanch. on Exodus 30:2), or else as paternally descended from Gad and maternally from Benjamin. Yet a third opinion, and to which apparently most weight attaches, represents him as a Levite, and a Priest, as the great High Priest of Messianic days. This is expressly stated in the Targum Pseudo-Jon, on Exodus 40:10, where it also seems implied that he was to anoint the Messiah with the sacred oil, the composition of which was among the things unknown in the second Temple, but to be restored by Elijah (Tanch. on Exodus 23:20, ed. Warsh. p. 91 a, lines 4 and 5 from the top). Another curious tradition identifies Elijah with Phinehas (Targum Pseudo-Jon, on Exodus 6:18). The same expression as in the Targum (Phinehas, that is Elijah) occurs in that great storehouse of Rabbinic tradition, Yalkut (Volume 1: p. 245 b, last two lines, and col. c). From the pointed manner in which reference is made to the parallelism between the zeal of Phinehas and that of Elijah, and between their work in reconciling God and Israel, and bringing the latter to repentance, we may gather the origin of this tradition and its deeper meaning.

For (as fully explained in Book II, Chapter 5) it is one of the principles frequently expressed by the ancient Synagogue, in its deeper perception of the unity and import of the Old Testament, that the miraculous events and Divine interruption of Israel's earlier history would be re-enacted, only with wider application, in Messianic days. If this idea underlay the parallelism between Phinehas and Elijah, it is still more fully carried out in that between Elijah and Moses. On comparing the Scriptural account of these two messengers of God we are struck with the close correspondence between the details of their history. The Synagogue is careful to trace this analogy step by step (Yalkut, Volume 2: p. 32 d) the final deliverance of Israel of Egypt, so would the final deliverance by Elijah forever break the yoke of all foreign rule. The allusion here is to the part which Elijah was expected to take in the future wars of Gog and Magog (Seder Olam R. 100:17) This parallelism is carried so far, that tradition has it, that, when Moses was commissioned by God to go to Pharaoh, he pleaded that God should rather send by him whom He designed to send for the far greater deliverance in the latter days. On this it was told him that Elijah's mission would be to Israel, while he(Moses) was sent to Pharaoh (Pirqe de R. Eliez. 40). Similarly, it is asserted that the cave from which Moses beheld the Divine Presence passing before him (Exodus 33:22) was the same as that in which Elijah stood under similar circumstances, that cave having been created with the rest of the world, but especially on the eve of the world's first Sabbath (Siphre on Deuteronomy ed. Friedmann, p. 147 a, last line). Considering this parallelism between them, the occurrence of the somewhat difficult expression will scarcely surprise us, that in the days of the Messiah Moses and Elijah would come together, as one (Debar. R. 3, at the end).

It has been noted in the text that the activity of Elijah, from the time of his appearance in the days of Ahab to that of his return as the forerunner of the Messiah, is represented in Jewish tradition as continuous, and that he is almost constantly introduced on the scene, either as in converse with some Rabbi, or else as busy about Israel's welfare, and connected with it. Thus Elijah chronicles in heaven the deeds of man (Seder Olam R. 17), or else writes down the observances of the commandments by men, and then the Messiah and God seal it (Midrast on Ruth 2:14, last line, ed. Warsh. p. 43 b). In general, he is ever interested in all that concerns Israel's present state or their future deliverance (Sanh. 98 a). Indeed, he is connected with the initiatory rite of the covenant, in acknowledgement of his zeal in the restoration of circumcision, when, according to tradition, it had been abolished by the ten tribes after their separation from Judah. God accordingly had declared: Israel shall not make the covenant of circumcision, but you shall see it, and the sages decreed that (at circumcision) a seat of honor shall be placed for the Angel of the Covenant (Mal. 3:2; Pirqe de R. Eliez. 29, end). Tradition goes even further. Not only was he the only ambassador to whom God had delegated His three special keys: of birth, of the rainfall, and of waking the dead (Yalkut, Volume 2:32 c), but his working was almost Divine (Tanch. Bereshith 7; ed. Warsh. p. 6 b, last line, and 7 a).

We purposely pass over the activity of Elijah in connection with Israel, and especially its Rabbis and saints, during the interval between the Prophet's death and his return as the Forerunner of the Messiah, such as Jewish legend describes it. No good purpose could be served by repeating what so frequently sounds not only utterly foolish and superstitious, but profane. In Jewish legend Elijah is always introduced as the guardian of the interests of Israel, whether theologically or personally, as it were the constant living medium between God and his people, the link that binds the Israel of the present, with its pursuits, wants, difficulties and interests, to the bright Messianic future of which he is the harbinger. This probably is the idea underlying the many, often grotesque, legends about his sayings and doings. Sometimes he is represented as, in his well meant zeal, going so far as to bear false witness in order to free Rabbis from danger and difficulty (Berach. 58 a). In general, he is always ready to instruct, to comfort, or to heal, condescending even to so slight a malady as a toothache (Ber. R. 96, end). But most frequently is he the adviser and friend of the Rabbis, in whose meetings and studies he delights. Thus he was a frequent attendant in Rabh Academy, and his indiscretion in divulging to his friends the secrets of heaven had once procured for him in heaven the punishment of fiery stripes (Babha Mets. 85 b). But it is useless to do more than indicate all this. Our object is to describe the activity of Elijah in connection with the coming of the Messiah.

When, at length, the time of Israel's redemption arrived, then would Elijah return. Of two things only are we sure in connection with it. Elijah will not come yesterday, that is, he will be revealed the same day that he comes, and he will not come on the eve of either a Sabbath or feast day, in order not to interrupt the festive rest, nor to break the festive laws (Erub. 43 b, Shabb. 33 a). Whether he came one day (Er. 43 b) or three days before the Messiah (Yalkut, Volume 2: p. 53 c, about the middle) his advent would be close to that of that Messiah (Yalkut, Volume 1: p. 310 a, line 21 from bottom). The account given of the three days between the advent of Elijah and of the Messiah is peculiar (Yalkut, Volume 2: p.53 c). Commenting on Isaiah 52:7, it is explained, that on the first of those three days Elijah would stand on the mountains of Israel, lamenting the desolateness of the land, his voice being heard from one end of the world to the other, after which he would proclaim: Peace comes to the world; peace comes to the world! Similarly on the second day he would proclaim, Good comes to the world; good comes to the world! Lastly, on the third day, he would, in the same manner as the two previous days, make proclamation: Jeshuah (salvation) comes to the world; Jeshuah (salvation) comes to the world, which, in order to mark the difference between Israel and the Gentiles, would be further explained by this addition: Saying to Zion, Your King comes!

The period of Elijah's advent would, according to one opinion (Pirqe de R. Eliez. 43), be a time of genuine repentance by Israel, although it is not stated that this change would be brought about by his ministry. On the other hand, his peculiar activity would consist in settling ceremonial and ritual questions, doubts, and difficulties, in making peace, in restoring those who by violence had been wrongfully excluded from the congregation and excluding those who by violence had been wrongfully introduced (Bab. Mets. 1:8; 2:8; 3:4, 5; Eduy. 7:7). He would also restore to Israel these three things which had been lost: the golden pot of Manna (Exodus 15:33), the vessel containing the anointing oil, and that with the waters of purification, according to some, also Aarons rod that budded and bore fruit. Again, his activity is likened to that of the Angel whom God had sent before Israel to drive out and to vanquish the hostile nations (Tanch. on Exodus 23:20, S: 18 at the close; ed. Warsh. p. 106 b). For Elijah was to appear, then to disappear, and to appear again in the wars of Gog and Magog (Seder Olam R. xvii.). But after that time general peace and happiness would prevail, when Elijah would discharge his peculiar functions. Finally, to the ministry of Elijah some also ascribed the office of raising the dead (Sotah ix. 15, closing words).

Such is a summary of ancient Jewish tradition concerning Elijah as the forerunner of the Messiah. Comparing it with the New Testament description of John the Baptist, it will at least be admitted that, from whatever source the sketch of the activity and mission of the Baptist be derived, it cannot have been from the ideal of the ancient Synagogue, nor yet from popularly current Jewish views. And could there be a greater contrast than between the Jewish forerunner of the Messiah and him of the New Testament?

End Notes:

[19] The question has been raised whether Jeremiah (or even Isaiah) was also to appear in Messianic days. In favor of this view 2 Maccabees 2:1-8 and 15:14-16 afford, to say the least, presumptive evidence. We do not refer to 4 Esdras 2:18, because the two first and the two last chapters of that book in our Apocrypha (2 Esdras) are spurious, being from much later, probably Christian authorship. Gfroerer thinks that 4 Esdras v. (2 Esdras 5:28) refers to Jeremiah and Isaiah (Urchrist Volume 2: p. 230). But I cannot draw the same inference from it. On the other hand, there is a remarkable passage in Mechilta on Exodus 15:33 (ed. Weiss, p. 59 b), which not only seems to conjoin Jeremiah with the Messiah (though the inaccurate rendering of Wetstein, Nov. Tevol. 1: p. 430 conveys an exaggerated and wrong impression of this), but reminds us of 2 Mac. 2:1-18.

[20] Reference is made to the zeal of Phinehas as corresponding to that of Elijah.

[21] The reader will find, in our remarks on Psalm Exodus 2 in Append. IX the curious traditions about this rod of Aaron, as given in Bemid. R. 18 and Yalkut on Psalm 110:2. The story of the wonder working rod is told somewhat differently in the Targum Pseudo-Jon. on Exodus 2:20, 21 and 4:20; and again, with other variations, in Pirke de R. Eliez. 40. In the latter passage we are told, that this rod had passed from the possession of Joseph (after his death) into the palace of Pharaoh. Then Jethro, who was one of the magicians of Egypt, had removed it to his own home. The ability of Moses to read the writing on the rod, according to other traditions, to uproot it out of the garden, indicated him to Jethro as the future deliverer of Israel, and determined him to give to Moses Zipporah for his wife (in preference to all other suitors). According to other traditions, Moses had been for many years imprisoned, and ministered to by Zipporah, who loved him. It may be added, that, according to very ancient tradition, the rod of Aaron was one of the things created on the eve of the world's first Sabbath (Siphre, ed. Friedmann, p. 147 a, last line).

[22] We have purposely omitted all reference to the connection between Elijah and the second Messiah, the son of Ephraim, because that line of tradition belongs to a later period than that of Christ.

[23] The view of the Apocrypha on the Mission of Elijah may be gathered from Ecclus. 48:1-12. Some additional Talmudic notices about Elijah will be found at the close of Append. IX. The Sepher Eliyahu (Apocalypse of Elijah), published in Jellineks Beth haMidr. part 2: pp. 65-68, adds

nothing to our knowledge. It professes to be a revelation by the Angel
Michael to Elijah of the end and the last days, at the close of the fourth
monarchy. As it is simply an Apocalyptic account of the events of those
days, it cannot here find a place, however interesting the Tractate. I have
purposely not referred to the abominable story about Elijah told in Yoma
19 b, last lines.

Appendix 9

Old Testament Passages Messianically Applied In Ancient Rabbinic Writings

The following list contains the passages in the Old Testament applied to the Messiah or to Messianic times in the most ancient Jewish writings. They amount in all to 456, thus distributed: 75 from the Pentateuch, 243 from the Prophets, and 138 from the Hagiographa, and supported by more than 558 separate quotations from Rabbinic writings. Despite all labor care, it can scarcely be hoped that the list is quite complete, although, it is hoped, no important passage has been omitted. The Rabbinic references might have been considerably increased, but it seemed useless to quote the same application of a passage in many different books. Similarly, for the sake of space, only the most important Rabbinic quotations have been extensively translated. The Rabbinic works from which quotations have been made are: the Targumim, the two Talmuds, and the most ancient Midrashim, but neither the Zohar (as the date of its composition is in dispute), nor any other Kabbalistic work, nor yet the younger Midrashim, nor the writings of later Rabbis. I have, however, frequently quoted from the well known work Yalkut, because, although of comparatively late date, it is really, as its name implies, a collection and selection from more than fifty older and accredited writings, and adduces passages now not otherwise accessible to us. And I have the more readily availed myself of it, as I have been reluctantly forced to the conclusion that even the Midrashim preserved to us have occasionally been tampered with for controversial purposes. I have quoted from the best edition of Yalkut (Frankfort a. M., 1687), but in the case of the other Midrashim I have been obliged to content myself with such more recent reprints as I possessed, instead of the older and more expensive editions. In quoting from the Midrashim, not only the Parashah, but mostly also the folio, the page, and frequently even the lines are referred to. Lastly, it only remains to acknowledge in general that, so far as possible, I have availed myself of the labors of my predecessors, especially of those of Schoettgen. Yet, even so, I may, in a sense, claim these references also as the result of my own labors, since I have not availed myself of quotations without comparing them with the works from which they were cited, a process in which not a few passages quoted had to be rejected. And if any student should arrive at a different conclusion from mine in regard to any of the passages hereafter quoted, I can at least assure him that mine is the result of the most careful and candid study I could give to the consideration of each passage. With these prefatory remarks I proceed to give the list of Old Testament passages Messianically applied in ancient Rabbinic writings.

In Genesis 1:2, the expression, Spirit of God, is explained of the Spirit of the King Messiah, with reference to Isaiah 10:2, and the moving on the face of the deep of repentance, according to Lamentations 2:19. So in Ber. R. 2, and in regard to the first point also in Ber. R. 8, in Vayyik. R. 14, and in other places. Genesis 2:4: These are the generations, of the heavens and of the earth, taken in connection with Genesis 3:15 and Ruth 4:18. Here we note one of the most curious Messianic interoperations in Ber. R. 12 (ed. Warsh. p. 24 b). It is noted that the word generations is always written in the Bible without which is the equivalent for the numeral 6, except in Genesis 2:4 and Ruth 4:18. This to indicate that subsequent to Genesis 2:4 the Fall took place, in which Adam lost, six, things: his glorious sheen (Job xiv. 20); life (Genesis 3:19)); his stature (Genesis 3:8, either by 100, by 200, by 300, or even by 900 cubits); the fruit of the ground; the fruits of the trees (Genesis 3:17); and the heavenly lights. We have now seen why in Genesis 2:4, that is, previous to the Fall—the is still in, since at that time these six things were not yet lost. But the reappears in the word in Ruth 4:18, because these six things are to be restored to man by the son of Pharez, or the Messiah (comp. for each of these six things: Judg. v. 31 b; Isaiah 66:22; Leviticus 25:13; Zechariah 8:12; Isaiah 300:26). It is added that although, according to the literal rendering of Psalm 49:12 (in Hebrews ver. 13), man did not remain unfallen one single night, yet, for the sake of the Sabbath, the heavenly lights were not extinguished until after the close of the Sabbath. When Adam saw the darkness, it is added, he was greatly afraid, saying: Perhaps he, of whom it is written, he shall bruise your head, and you shall bruise his heel, comes to molest and attack me, and he said, Surely the darkness shall cover me. This curious extract at least shown in what context the Synagogue applied Genesis 3:15. The same occurs substantially in Shem. R. 30.

Gen 3:15. This well known passage is paraphrased, with express reference to the Messiah, in the Targum Pseudo Jonathan and the so called Jerusalem Targum. Schoettgen conjectures that the Talmudic designation of heels of the Messiah (Sot. 49 b, line 2 from top) in reference to the near Advent of the Messiah in the description of the troubles of those days (comp. Matthew 10:35, 36) may have been chosen partly with a view to this passage.

Genesis 4:25. The language of Eve at the birth of Seth: another seed, is explained as meaning seed which comes from another place, and referred to the Messiah in Ber. R. 23 (ed. Warsh. p. 45 b, lines 8, 7 from the bottom). The same explanation occurs twice in the Midrash on Ruth 4:19 (in the genealogy of David, ed. Warsh. p. 46 b), the second time in connection with Psalm 40:8 (in the volume of the book it is written of me, bimgillath sepher, Ruth belonging to the class).

In connection with Genesis 5:1 it is noted in Ber. R. 24, that King Messiah will not come until all souls predestined for it have appeared in human bodies on earth.

In Genesis v3:11 the Targum Pseudo Jonathan notes that the olive leaf, brought by the dove, was taken from the Mount of the Messiah.

Genesis 9:27. The promise, that Japhet shall dwell in the tents of Shem, is paraphrased in the Targum Pseudo Jon, as meaning, that his descendants should become proselytes, and dwell in the school of Shem, which seems to refer to Messianic times.

In connection with Genesis 14:1, we are reminded in Ber. R. 42, that when we see the nations warring together, we may expect the coming of the Messiah.

The promise in Genesis 15:18 is expected to be finally fulfilled in the time of Messiah, in Ber. R. 44.

In connection with Genesis 16:4, 5 it is noted (Ber. R. 48, ed. Warsh. p. 87 b) that the words of Abraham to his Angelic guests were to be returned in blessing to Abraham's descendants, in the wilderness, in the land of Canaan, and in the latter (Messianic) days. Referring only to this last point, the words let a little water be fetched, is paralleled with the living waters in Zechariah 14:8; wash your feet, with Isaiah 4:4 (the washing away of the filth of the daughters of Zion); rest under the tree, with Isaiah

4:6: there shall be a tabernacle for a shadow in the daytime from the heat; I will fetch a morsel of bread, with the provision, Psalm 72:16: there shall be a handful of grain in the earth, etc. So also the words: Abraham ran to the herd, are paralleled with Isaiah 5:21 (which is most significantly here applied to Messianic times); and lastly, the words, he stood by them, with Mic. 2:13: the breaker is come up before them. The same interpretation occurs in Bemid. R. 14 (ed. Warsh. p. 55 a), the references to Messianic days there being to Isaiah 14:2; 30:25; 41:18; 6:4; and 4:6.

The last clause of Genesis 19:32 is interpreted (Ber. R. 51, ed. Warsh. p. 95 a), as referring, like the words of Eve about Seth, to the Messiah, the sin of the daughters of Lot being explained on the ground of their believing that all mankind had been destroyed in the judgment that overthrew Sodom.

The promise in Genesis 22:18 is also explained Messianically in Bemid. R. 2 (ed. W. P. 5 b), in connection with Numbers 2:32 where it is somewhat curiously shown in what sense Israel is to be like the sand of the sea.

Genesis 33:1. The Midrash conjoins this with Isaiah 65:7, and notes that, before the first oppressor was born, the last Redeemer was already born.

In Genesis 35:21 the Targum Pseudo Jon, paraphrases the tower of Eder (at Bethlehem) as the place from which the Messiah would be revealed.

On Genesis 36:1, 2 there are very remarkable Messianic comments in Ber. R. 85.

Genesis 49:1. The Targum Pseudo Jon. notes, that the end for which the Meshuah would come was not revealed to Jacob. A similar statement is found in the Midrash on the passage (Ber. R. 98, ed. Warsh. p. 173 a), where it is said of Jacob and Daniel that they saw the end, and yet it was afterwards hid from them. The passage quoted in the case of Daniel is Daniel 12:4.

Genesis 49:9. The expression lion's whelp, is explained of the Messiah in Yalkut 160 (Volume 1: p. 49 c), no less than five times; while the term he couched, is referred to the Messiah in Ber. R. 98.

Genesis 49:10. This well known prediction (on which see the full and interesting discussion in Raym. Martini, Pugio Fidei) is in Yalkut, u. s., applied to the Messiah, with a quotation of Psalm 2:9. This expression Shiloh is also applied to the Messiah, with the curious addition, that in the latter days all nations would bring gifts to Him. The Targum Onkelos, Pseudo Jonathan, and the Jerusalem Targum, as well as Sanh. 98 b, the Midrash on the passage, and that on Proverbs 19:21, and on

Lamentations 1:16, where it is rendered shelo, whose it is, refer the expression Shiloh, and the whole passage, to the Messiah; the Midrah Ber. R. (99, ed. Warsh. p. 178 b) with special reference to Isaiah 10:10, while the promise with reference to the donkey's colt is brought into connection with Zechariah 9:9, the fulfillment of this prophecy being expected along with that in Ezekiel 35:25 (I will sprinkle clean water). Another remarkable statement occurs in the Midrash on the passage (Ber. R. 98, ed. Warsh. p. 174 b), which applies the verse to the coming of Him of Whom it is written, Zechariah 9:9. Then He would wash his garment in wine (Genesis 49:11), which is explained as meaning the teaching of the Law to Israel, and His clothes in the blood of grapes, which is explained as meaning that He would bring them back from their errors. One of the Rabbis, however, remarks that Israel would not require to be taught by the King Messiah in the latter days, since it was written (Isaiah 10:10), to it shall the Gentiles seek. If so, then why should the Messiah come, and what will He do to the congregation of Israel? He will redeem Israel, and give them thirty commandments, according to Zechariah 10:12. The Targum Pseudo Jon. and the Jeremiah Targum also apply verse 11 to the Messiah. Indeed, so general was this interpretation, that, according popular opinion, to see a palm tree in ones dreams was to see the days of the Messiah (Berach. 57 a).

Genesis 49:12 is also applied to the Messiah in the Targum Pseudo Jon. and the Jerusalem Targum. So also is verse 18, although not in express words.

In Genesis 48:17, last clause, in its connection with ver. 18, the Midrash (Ber. R. 98) sees a reference to the disappointment of Jacob in mistaking Samson for the Messiah.

In the prophecy of Gad in Genesis 49:19 there is an allusion to Messianic days, as Elijah was to be of the tribe of Gad (Ber. R. 99, ed. Warsh. p. 179 a). There is, however, in Ber. R. 71, towards the close, a dispute whether he was of the tribe of Gad, or of the tribe of Benjamin, at the close of which Elijah appears, and settles the dispute in a rather summary manner.

On Genesis 50:10 the Midrash, at the close of Ber. R., remarks that as they had mourned, so in Messianic days God would turn their mourning into joy, quoting Jeremiah 30:13 and Isaiah 51:3.

Exodus 4:22 is referred to the Messiah in the Midr. on Psalm 2:7.

On Exodus 12:2, let this be the beginning of months, it is remarked in Shem.R. 15 (ed. Warsh. p. 24 b) that God would make new ten things in the latter days, these being marked by the following passages: Is 60:19;

Ezekiel 45:9; 45:12; Ezekiel 15:55; Is 54:11; Isaiah 11:7; Hos. 2:20; Isaiah 65:19; Isaiah 35:8; Isaiah 35:10. Similarly on Numbers 12:1 we have, in Shem. R. 51, a parallelism between Old Testament times and their institutions and those of the latter days, to which Isaiah 49:12 and 60:8 are suppose to apply.

On Exodus 12:42 the Jerus. Targum notes that there were 4 remarkable nights: those of creation, of the covenant with Abraham, of the first Passover, and of the redemption of the world; and that as Moses came out of the desert, so would the Messiah come out of Rome.

On Exodus 15:1. It is noted in Mekhilta (ed. Weiss, p. 41 a) that this song would be taken up in Messianic days, only with far wide reach, as explained in Isaiah 60:5; 58:8; 35:5, 6; Jeremiah 30:13; and Psalm 145:2.

Exodus 15:25 is applied to the Messiah, it being said that, if Israel only kept one Sabbath according to the commandment, the Messiah would immediately come (Jeremiah Taan. 64 a).

Exodus 15:33. This manna, it is noted in Mechil. ed. Weiss, p. 59 b, was to be preserved for the days of the Messiah. Isaiah 30:15 is similarly explained in Jeremiah Taan. 1:1.

Exodus 15:16 the Targum Pseudo Jonathan refers to Messianic times.

Exodus 20:1. Shem. R. 30, ed Warsh. p. 44. b, 45 a, notes on the word judgments a number of things connected with judgment, showing how Balaam could not have wished the advent of the future deliverance (Numbers 24:17), since he was to perish in it; but that Israel should stick to the great hope pressed in Genesis 49:18; Isaiah 56:1; 59:16; and especially Zechariah 9:9, of which a different rendering is proposed.

On Exodus 40:9, 11 there is in the Targum Pesudo Jon. Distinct reference to the King Messiah, on whose account the anointing oil was to be used.

The promise (Leviticus 25:12) is also referred to the latter, or Messianic, days in Yalkut 62 (Volume 1: p. 17 b).

Leviticus 25:13 is applied to Messianic times. See our remarks on Genesis 2:4.

The promise of peace in the Aaronic benediction Numbers 6:26 is referred to the peace of the Kingdom of David, in accordance with Isaiah 9:7 (Siphre on Numbers par. 42, ed. Friedmann, p. 12 b).

Numbers 5:12. In connection with this it is marked that the six blessings which were lost by the Fall are to be restored by the son of Nahshon, i.e. the Messiah (Bem. R. 13, ed. W. p. 51 a).

In the Jerusalem Targum on Numbers 10:26 the prophecy of Eldad and Medad is supposed to have been with regard to the war of the later days against Jerusalem and to the defeat of Gog and Magog by the Messiah.

In Numbers 23:21 the term King is expressly referred to the Messiah in Targum Pseudo Jon. So also Numbers 24:7 in the Jeremiah Targum.

In Numbers 24:17 Balaam's prediction of the Star and Scepter is referred to the Messiah in the Targum Onkelos and the Targum Pessudo Jonathan, as well as in Jeremiah Taan. 4:8; Deb. R. 1; Midr. On Lament. 2:2. Similarly verses 20 and 24 of that prophecy are ascribed in the Targum Pseudo Jon. to the Messiah.

Numbers 25:16. In connection with this verse it is noticed that His one Spirit is worth as much as all other spirits, according to Isaiah 11:1 (Yalkut, Volume 1: p. 247 a).

Deuteronomy 1:8 is applied to the days of the Messiah in Sphre, 67 a.

In the comments of Tanchuma on Deuteronomy v3:1. (ed. Warsh. p. 104 b, 105 a) there are several allusions to Messianic days.

Deuteronomy 10:21 is applied in Siphre Par. 47 (ed. Friedmann, p. 83 a) to the days of the Messiah.

In Deuteronomy 15:3 the record of the deliverance from Egypt is supposed to be carried on to the days of the Messiah, in Spihre, Par. 130 (ed. Friedmann, p. 101 a). See, also, Ber. 1:5.

On Deuteronomy 19:8, 9 it is noted, in Siphre on Deuteronomy, Par. 185 (ed. Friedm. p. 108 b), that as three of these cities were in territory never possessed by Israel, this was to be fulfilled in Messianic times. See also Jeremiah Maccabees 2:7.

In Tanchuma on Deuteronomy 20:10 (Par. 19, ed. Warsh. p. 114 b) the offer of peace to a hostile city is applied to the future action of Messiah to the Gentiles, in accordance with Zechariah 9:10; Isaiah 2:4; and Ps 56:32; while, on the other hand, the resistance of a city to the offer of peace is likened to rebellion against the Messiah, and consequent judgment, according to Isaiah 10:4.

Deuteronomy 23:11 is typically applied to the evening of time, when God would wash away the filth of the daughters of Zion (Isaiah 4:4); and the words: when the sun is down to when King Messiah would come (Tanchuma on Par. Ki Thetse 3, ed. Warsh. p. 115 b).

Deuteronomy 25:19 and Deuteronomy 30:4 are referred by the Targum Pesudo Jon. the Messianic times. In the latter passage the gathering of dispersed Israel by Elijah, and their being brought back by Messiah, are spoken of. Comp. also Bem. R., last three lines.

On Deuteronomy 32:7 Siphre (Par. 210, ed. Friedm. p. 134 a) makes the beautiful observation, that in all Israel's afflictions they were to remember the good and comfortable things which God had promised them for the future world, and in connection with this there is special reference to the time of the Messiah.

On Deuteronomy 32:30 Siphre (p. 138 a) marks its fulfillment in the days of the Messiah.

On Deuteronomy 33:5 the Jeremiah Targum speaks of a king whom the tribes of Israel shall obey, this being evidently the King Messiah.

Deuteronomy 33:17. Tanchuma on Genesis 1:Par. 1 (ed. Warsh. p. 4 a) applies this to the Messiah. So also in Benidb. R. 14.

Deuteronomy 33:12. The expression, he shall cover him, is referred to this world; all the day long, to the days of the Messiah; and he shall dwell between his shoulders, to the world to come (Sebach. 118 b).

Judg. 5:31: let them that love Him be as the sun when he goes forth in his might, is applied to Messianic times in Ber. R. 12. See our remarks on Genesis 2:4.

On Ruth 2:14: come hither at the time of meat, the Midr. R. Ruth 5 (ed. Warsh. p. 43 a and b), has a very remarkable interpretation. Besides the application of the word eat, as beyond this present time, to the days of the Messiah, and again to the world to come, which is to follow these days, the Midrash applies the whole of it mystically to the Messiah, namely, Come hither, that is, draw near to the kingdom, and eat of the bread, that is, the bread of royalty, and dip your morsel in vinegar, these are the sufferings, as it is written in Isaiah 53:5, He was wounded for our transgression. And she sat beside the reapers, because His Kingdom would in the further be put aside from Him for a short time, according to

Zechariah 14:2; and he reached her parched grain, because He will restore it to Him, according to Isaiah 10:4. R. Berachiah, in the name of R. Levi, adds, that the second Redeemer should be like the first. As the first

Redeemer (Moses) appeared, and disappeared, and reappeared after three months, so the second Redeemer would also appear, and disappear, and again become manifest, Daniel 12:11, 12 being brought into connection with it. Comp. Midr. on Song of Solomon 2:9; Pesik. 49 a, b. Again, the words, she ate, and was sufficed, and left, are thus interpreted in Shabb. 113 b: she ate, in this world; and was sufficed, in the days of the Messiah; and left, for the world to come.

Again, the Targum on Ruth 1:1 speaks of the Messiah; and again on Ruth 3:15 paraphrases the six measures of barley as referring to six righteous ones, of which the last was the Messiah, and who were each to have six special blessings.

Ruth 4:18. The Messiah is called the son of Pharez, who restores what had been lost to humanity through the fall of Adam. See our remarks on Genesis 2:4.

The Messianic interpretation of Ruth 4:20 has already been given under Genesis 4:25.

1 Samuel 2:10. The latter clause of this promise is understood by the Targum (and also is some of the Medrashim) as applying to the Kingdom of the Messiah.

2 Samuel 22:28. In a Talmudic passage (Sanh. 98 a, line 19, etc., from the bottom), which contains many references to the coming of the Messiah, His advent is predicted in connection with this passage.

2 Samuel 23:1 is applied by the Targum to the prophecy of David concerning the latter Messianic days.

2 Samuel 23:3. The ruling in the fear of God is referred in the Targum to the future raising up of the Messiah.

In 2 Samuel 23:4 the morning light at sunrise is explained in the Midrash on the passage (par. 29, ed. Lemberg, p, 56 b, lines 7-9 from the top), as applying to the appearance of the Messiah.

The expression, 1 Kings 4:33, that Solomon spoke of trees, is referred in the Targum to his prophecy concerning kings that were to reign in this age, and in that of the Messiah.

On the name Anani, in 1 Chr. 3:24, the Targum remarks that this is the Messiah, the interpretation being that the word anani is connected with the word similarly written (not punctuated) in Deuteronomy 5:13, and there translated clouds, of which the explanation is given in Tanchuma (Par. Toledoth 14, p. 27 b).

Psalm 2: as might be expected, is treated as full of Messianic references. To begin with, Psalm 2:1 is applied to the wars of Gog and Magog in the Talmud (Berach. 7 b and Abhod. Zarah 3 b), and also in the Midrash on Psalm 2: Similarly, verse 2 is applied to the Messiah in Abhod. Zach, u. s., in the Midrash on Psalm 82:11 (ed. Warsh. p. 70 b, line 8 from the top); in Pirque de R. Eliez. c. 28 (ed. Lemberg, p. 33 b, line 9 from top). In Yalkut (Volume 2: par. 620, p. 90 a, line 12 from the bottom), we have the following remarkable simile on the words, against God, and His Messiah, likening them to a robber who stands defiantly behind the palace of the king, and says, If I shall find the son of the king, I shall lay hold on him, and crucify him, and kill him with a cruel death. But the

Holy Spirit mocks at him, He that sits in the heavens shall laugh. On the same verse the Midrashon Psalm 2 has a curious conceit, intended to show that each who rose against God and His people thought he was wiser than he who had preceded him. If Cain had killed his brother while his father was alive, forgetful that there would be other sons, Esau proposed to wait until after his father's death. Pharaoh, again, blamed Esau for his folly in forgetting that in the meantime Jacob would have children, and therefore proposed to kill all the male children, while Haman, ridiculing Pharaoh's folly in forgetting that there were daughters set himself to destroy the whole people; and, in turn, Gog and Magog, ridiculing the shortsightedness of all, who had preceded them, in taking counsel against Israel so long as they had a Patron in heaven, resolved first to attack their heavenly Patron, and after that Israel. To which apply the words, against the Lord, and against His Anointed.

But to return Psalm 2:4 is Messianically applied in the Talmud (Abhod. Z. u. s.). Psalm 2:6 is applied to the Messiah in the Midrash on 1 Samuel 15:1 (Par. 19, ed, Lemberg, p. 45 a and b), where it is said that of the three measures of sufferings one goes to the King Messiah, of whom it is written (Isaiah 53) He was wounded for our transgression. They say to the King Messiah: Where do You seek to dwell? He answers: Is this question also necessary? In Zion My holy hill (Psalm 2:6). (Comp. also Yalkut 2: p. 53 c.)

Psalm 2:7 is quoted as Messianic in the Talmud, among a number of other Messianic quotations (Sukk. 52 a). There is a very remarkable passage in the Midrash on Psalm 2:7 (ed. Warsh p. 5 a), in which the unity of Israel and the Messiah in prophetic vision seems clearly indicated. Tracing the decree through the Law, the Prophets, and the Hagiograph, the first passage quoted in Exodus 4:22: Israel is My first born son; the second, from the Prophets, Isaiah 52:13: Behold My servants shall deal prudently, and Isaiah 42:1: Behold My servant, whom I uphold; the third, from the Hagiographa, Psalm 110:1: The Lord said to my Lord, and again, Psalm 2:7: The Lord said to Me, You are My Son, and yet this other saying (Daniel 5:13): Behold, one like the Son of Man came with the clouds of heaven. Five lines further down, the same Midrash, in reference to the words You are My Son, observes that, when that hour comes, God speaks to Him to make a new covenant, and thus He speaks: This day have I begotten You, this is the hour in which He become His Son.

Psalm 2:8 is applied in Ber. R. 44 (ed. Warsh. p. 80 a) and in the Midrash on the passage, to the Messiah, with the curious remark that there were three of whom it was said Ask of Me, Solomon, Ahaz, and the Messiah. In the Talmud (Shukk. 52 a) the same passage is very curiously applied, it being suggested that, when the Messiah, the Son of David, saw that the Messiah, the Son of Joseph, would be killed, He said to the Almighty, I seek nothing of You except life. To which the reply was: Life before You has spoken, as David Your father prophesied of You, Psalm 20:4.

Psalm 2:9 will be referred to in our remarks on Psalm 120.

Psalm 15:5 is discussed in Ber. R. 88, in connection with the cup which Pharaoh's butler saw in his dream. From this the Midrash proceeds to speak of the four cups appointed for the Passover night, and to explain their meaning in various manners, among others, contrasting the four cups of fury, which God would make the nations drink, with the four cups of salvation which He would give Israel in the latter days, namely Psalm 15:5; Psalm 115:13; Psalm 23:5. The expression, Psalm 115:13, rendered the cup of salvation in the KJV, is in the original, the cup of salvations, and is explained as implying on one for the days of the Messiah, and the other for the days of Gog.

On verse 9, the Midrash on the passage says: My glory shall rejoice in the King Messiah, Who in the future shall come forth from me, as it is written in Isaiah 4:5: "upon all the glory a covering." And the Midrash continues my flesh also shall dwell in safety, i.e. after death, to teach us that corruption and the worm shall not rule over it.

Psalm 16:31 (in the Hebrews verse 32). The Targum explains this in reference to the works and miracles of the Messiah.

Psalm 16:50 is referred in Jeremiah Talmud (Ber. 2:4, p. 5 a, line 11 from the top), and in the Midr. on Lamentations 1:16, to the Messiah, with this curious remark, implying the doubt whether He was alive or dead: The king Messiah, whether He belong to the living or the dead, His Name is to be David, according to Psalm 16:50.

Psalm 20:1 (2 in the Hebrew), the King there spoken of is explained by the Targum to be King Messiah. The Midrash on the passage identifies him with Isaiah 10:10, on which Rabbi Chanina adds that the object of the Messiah is to give certain commandments to the Gentiles (not to Israel, who are to learn from God Himself), according to the passage in Isaiah above quoted, adding that the words his rest shall be glorious mean that God gives to the King Messiah from the glory above, as it is said: In Your strength shall the king rejoice, which strength is a little afterwards explained as the Kingdom (ed. Warsh. p. 30 a and b).

Verse 3 is Messianically applied in the Midrash on the passage.

Psalm 20:3 (4 in the Hebrew). Only a few lines farther down in the same Midrash, among remarkable Messianic applications, is that of this verses to the Messiah, where also the expression Jehovah is a man of war, and Jehovah Zidkenu, are applied to the Messiah. Comp. also Shemoth R. 8, where it is noted that God will crown Him with His own crown.

Verse 4 is Messianically applied in Sukk. 52 a.

Psalm 20:5 (6 in the Hebrew). The first clause of this verse. Yalkut on Numbers 25:20 (Volume 1: p. 248 a, line 10 from the bottom) applies to the glory of the King Messiah, immediately quoting the second clause in proof of its Messianic application. This is also done in the Midrash on the passage. But perhaps one of the most remarkable applications of it is in Bemidbar R. 15, p. 63 b, where the passage is applied to the Messiah.

Finally in Psalm 20:7 (8 in the Hebrew), the expression king is applied in the Targum to the Messiah.

On the whole, then, it may be remarked that Psalm 20: was throughout regarded as Messianic.

On Psalm 22:7 (8 in the Hebrew) a remarkable comment appears in Yalkut on Isaiah 60, applying this passage to the Messiah (the second, or son of Ephraim), and using almost the same words in which the Evangelists describe the mocking behavior of the Jews at the Cross.

Psalm 22:15 (16 in the Hebrew). There is a similarly remarkable application to the Messiah of this verse in Yalkut.

The promise in Psalm 23:5 is referred in Benid. R. 21 to the spreading of the great feast before Israel in the latter days.

Psalm 30:19 (20 in the Hebrew) is in the Midrash applied to the reward that in the latter days Israel would receive for their faithfulness. Also in Pesiqta, p. 149 b, to the joy of Israel in the presence of the Messiah.

The expression in Psalm 35:9, In Your light shall we see light, is applied to the Messiah in Yalkut on Isaiah lx. (Volume 2: p. 56 c, line 22 from the bottom).

The application of Psalm 40:7 to the Messiah has already been noted in our remarks on Genesis 4:25.

Psalm 45 is throughout regarded as Messianic. To begin with; the Targum renders verse 2 (3 in the Hebrew): Your beauty, O King Messiah, is greater than that of the sons of men.

Verse 3 (4 in the Hebrew) is applied in the Talmud (Shabb 63 a) to the Messiah, although other interpretations of that verse immediately follow.

The application of verse 6 (7 in the Hebrew), to the Messiah in a MS. copy of the Targum has already been referred to in another part of his book, while the words, Your throne is forever and ever are brought into connection with the promise that the scepter would not depart from Judah in Ber. R. 99, ed. Warsh. p. 178 b, line 9 from the bottom.

On verse 7 the Targum though not in the Venice edition (1568), has: You O King Messiah because You love righteousness, etc. Comp. Levy, Targum. Woerterb. Volume 2: p. 41 a.

The Midrash on the Psalm deals exclusively with the inscription (of which it has several and significant interpretations) with the opening words of the Psalm, and with the words (ver. 16), Instead of your fathers shall be your children, but at the same time it clearly indicates that the Psalm applies to the latter, or Messianic, days.

On Psalm 50:2 Siphre (p. 143 a) notes that four times God would appear, the last being in the days of King Messiah.

Psalm 60:7. Bemidbar R. on Numbers 5:48, Parash. 14 (ed. Warsh p. 54 a) contains some very curious Haggadic discussion on this verse. But it also broaches the opinion of its reference to the Messiah.

Psalm 110:6 (7 in the Hebrew). You shall add days to the days of the king, is rendered by the Targum: You shall add days to the days of King Messiah. There is a curious gloss on this in Pirqe d. R. Eliez. c. 19 (ed. Lemberg, p. 24 b), in which Adam is supposed to have taken 70 of his years, and added them to those of King David. According to another tradition, this accounts for Adam living 930 years, this is, 70 less than 1,000, which constitute before God one day, and so the threatening had been literally fulfilled: In the day you eat thereof, you shall die.

Psalm 110:8 (9 in the Hebrew). The expression, that I may daily perform my vows, is applied in the Targum to the day in which the Messiah is anointed King.

Psalm 116:31 (32 in the Hebrew). On the words Princes shall come out of Egypt, there is a very remarkable comment in the Talmud (Pes. 118 b) and in Shemoth R. on Exodus x15:15, etc. (ed. Warsh. p. 50 b), in which we are told that in the latter days all nations would bring gifts to the King Messiah, beginning with Egypt. And for fear that it be thought that He (Messiah) would not accept it from them, the Holy One says to the Messiah: Accept from them hospitable entertainment, or it might be rendered, Accept it from them; they have given hospitable entertainment to My son.

Psalm 72: This Psalm also was viewed by the ancient Synagogue as throughout Messianic, as indicated by the fact that the Targum renders the very first verse: Give the sentence of Your judgment to the King Messiah, and Your justice to the Son of David the King, which is re-echoed by the Midrash on the passage (ed. Warsh. p. 55 b) which applies it explicitly to the Messiah, with reference to Isaiah 10:1. Similarly, the Talmud applies ver. 16 to Messianic times (in a very hyperbolical passage, Shabb. 30 b, line 4 from the bottom). The last clause of verse 16 is applied, in Keth. 111 b, line 21 from top, and again in the Midr. on Ecclesiastes 1:9, to the Messiah sending down manna like Moses.

Verse 17. In Sanh. 98 b; Pes. 54 a; Ned. 39 b, the various names of the Messiah are discussed, and also in Ber. R. 1; in Midr. on Lamentations 1:16, and in Pirqe de R. Eliez. c. 3. One of these is stated to be Jinnon, according to Psalm 72:17.

Verse 8 is applied in Pirqe de R. El. c. 11, to the Messiah. Yalkut (Volume 2).on Isaiah 55:8 (p. 54 c), speaks of the other Redeemer as the Messiah, applying to him Psalm 72:8.

In commenting on the meeting of Jacob and Esau, the Midr. Ber. R. (78, ed. Warsh. p. 141 b) remarks that all the gifts which Jacob gave to Esau, the nations of the world would return to the King Messiah, proving it by a reference to Psalm 72:10; while in Midrash Bemidbar R. 13 it is remarked that as the nations brought gifts to Solomon, so they would bring them to the King Messiah.

In the same place, a little higher up, Solomon and the Messiah are likened as reigning over the whole world, the proof passages being, besides others, Psalm 72:8, Daniel 5:13, and 2:35.

On the application to the Messiah of verse 16 we have already spoken, as also on that of verse 17.

Psalm 80:17 (in the Hebrew 18). The Targum paraphrases the Son of Man by King Messiah.

Psalm 89:22-25 (23-26 in the Hebrew). In Yalkut on Isaiah 60:1 (Volume 2: p. 56 c) this promise is referred to the future deliverance of Israel by the Messiah.

Again, verse 27 (28 in the Hebrew) is applied in Shemoth R. 19, towards the end, to the Messiah, special reference being made to Exodus 4:22, Israel is My first born son.

Verse 51 (52 in the Hebrew). There is a remarkable comment on this in the Midrash on the inscription of Psalm 16: (ed. Warsh. p. 24 a, line 2 from the bottom), in which it is set forth that as Israel and David did not sing until the hour of persecution and reproach, so when the Messiah shall come, speedily, in our days, the song will not be raised until the Messiah is put to reproach, according to Psalm 89:52 (51), and until there shall fall before Him the wicked idolaters referred to in Daniel 2:42, and the four kingdoms referred to in Zechariah 14:2. In that hour shall the song be raised, as it is written Psalm 98:1.

In the Midr. on Song of Solomon 2:13 it is said: If you see one generation after another blaspheming, expect the feet of the King Messiah, as it is written, Psalm 89:53.

Psalm 90:15. The Midr. (ed. Warsh. p. 67 b) remarks: The days wherein You have afflicted us, that is, the days of the Messiah. Upon which follows a discussion upon the length of days of the Messiah, R.

Eliezer holding that they are 1,000 years, quoting the words as yesterday, one day being 1,000 years. R. Joshua holds that they were 2,000 years, the words the days implying that there were two days. R. Berachiah holds that they were 600 years, appealing to Isaiah 65:22, because the root of the tree perishes in the earth in 600 years. R. Jose thinks that they are 60 years, according to Psalm 72:5, the words throughout all generations (dor dorim) being interpreted: Dor = 20 years; Dorim = 40 years: 20 + 40 = 60. R. Akiba says: 40 years, according to the years in the wilderness. The Rabbis say: 354 years, according to the days in the lunar year. R. Abahu thinks 7,000 years, reckoning the 7 according to the days of the bridegroom.

On Psalm 90 the Midrash concludes by drawing a contrast between the Temple which men built, and which was destroyed, and the Temple of the latter or Messianic days, which God would build, and which would not be destroyed.

Psalm 92, verses 8, 11, and 13 (7, 10, and 12 in our A. V.), are Messianically interpreted in Pirqe de R. El. c. 19. In the Midrash on verse 13 (12 in our A. V.), among other beautiful applications of the figure of the Psalm, is that to the Messiah the Son of David. The note of the Midrash on the expression like a cedar of Lebanon, as applied to Israel, is very beautiful, likening it to the cedar, which, although driven and bent by all the winds of heaven, cannot be rooted up from its place.

Psalm 95:7, last clause. In Shem. R. 25 and in the Midrash on Song of Solomon 5:2 (ed. Warsh. p. 26 a), it is noted that, if Israel did penitence only one day [or else properly observed even one Sabbath], the Messiah the Son of David would immediately come. [The whole passage from which this reference is taken is exceedingly interesting. It introduces God as saying to Israel: My son, open to Me a door of penitence only as small as a needles eye, and I will open to you doors through which carriages and wagons shall come in. It almost seems a counterpart to Jesus' words (Revelation 3:20): Behold, I stand at the door and knock; if any man hear My voice and open the door, I will come in to Him.] Substantially the same view is taken in Sanh. 98 a, where the tokens of the coming of the Messiah are described, and also in Jeremiah Taan. 64 a.

Psalm 102:16 (17 in the Hebrew) is applied in Bereshith R. 56 (ed. Warsh. p. 104 b) to Messianic times.

Psalm 106:44. On this there is in the Midrash a long Messianic discussion, setting forth the five grounds on which Israel is redeemed: through the sorrows of Israel through prayer, through the merits of the patriarchs, through repentance towards God, and in the time of the end.

Psalm 110 is throughout applied to the Messiah. To begin with, it evidently underlies the Targumic of ver. 4. Similarly, it is propounded in the Midr. on Psalm 2: (although there the chief application of it is to Abraham). But in the Midrash on Psalm 16:36 (35 in our A. V.), Psalm 110 verse 1, Sit you at My right hand is especially applied to the Messiah, while Abraham is said to be seated at the left.

Verse 2, The rod of Your strength. In a very curious mystic interpretation of the pledges which Tamar had, by the Holy Spirit, asked of Judah, the seal is interpreted as signifying the Kingdom, the bracelet as the Sanhedrin, and the staff as the King Messiah, with special reference to Isaiah 10: and Psalm 110:2 (Beresh. R. 85, ed. Warsh. p. 153 a) Similarly in Bemid. R. 18, last line, the staff of Aaron, which is said to have been in the hands of every king until the Temple was destroyed, and since then to have been hid, is to be restored to King Messiah, according to this verse; and in Yalkut on this Psalm (Volume 2: Par. 869, p. 124 c) this staff is supposed to be the same as that of Jacob with which he crossed Jordan, and of Judah, and of Moses, and of Aaron, and the same which David had in his hand when he slew Goliath, it being also the same which will be restored to the Messiah.

Verse 7 is also applied in Yalkut (u. s. col. d) to Messianic times, when streams of the blood of the wicked should flow out, and birds come to drink of that flood.

Psalm 115:9 is in Ber. R. 96 supposed to indicate that the dead of Palestine would live first in the days of the Messiah.

Psalm 115:13 has been already commented upon.

On Psalm 119:33 the Midrash remarks that there were three who asked wisdom of God: David, Solomon, and the King Messiah, the latter according to Psalm 72:1.

Psalm 120:7 is applied to the Messiah in the Midrash (p. 91 a, ed. Warsh.), the first clause being brought into connection with Isaiah 57:19, with reference to the Messiahs dealings with the Gentiles, the resistance being described in the second clause, and the result in Psalm 2:9.

Psalm 120:1 is applied in Tanchuma (Par. Toledoth 14, ed. Warsh. p. 37 b. See also Yalkut, Volume 2:878, p. 127 c) to the Messiah, with special reference to Zechariah 4:7 and Isaiah 52:7.

Psalm 125:2. In Tanchuma on Exodus 15:1: (ed. Warsh. p. 87 a) this verse is applied to Messianic times in a absorbed description, in which successively Isaiah 60:5, Isaiah 58:8, Isaiah 35:5, 6, Jeremiah 30:13, and Psalm 125:2, are grouped together as all applying to these latter days.

The promise in Psalm 132:18 is applied in Pirke de R. El. c. 28 to Messianic times, and verse 14 in Ber. R. 56.

So is Psalm 133:3 in Ber. R. 65 (p. 122 a), closing lines.

The words in Psalm 122:5 are applied in Ber. R. 74 to the resurrection of Israel in Palestine in the days of Messiah.

The words, When you awaken, in Proverbs v1:22 are Messianically applied in Siphre on Deuteronomy (ed. Friedmann, p. 74 b).

In Midr. on Ecclesiastes 1:9 it is shown at great length that the Messiah would re-enact all the miracles of the past.

The last clause of Ecclesiastes 1:11 is applied to the days of the Messiah in the Targum.

Ecclesiastes 5:24 is thus paraphrased in the Targum: Behold, it is remote from the sons of men that they should know what was done from the beginning of the world, but a mystery is the day of death, and the day when shall come King Messiah, who can find it out by his wisdom?

In the Midr. on Ecclesiastes 10:8 it is noted that, however many years a man might study, his learning would be empty before the teaching of Messiah. In the Midr. on Ecclesiastes 12:1 it is noted that the evil days are those of the woes of Messiah.

Canticles. Here we have first the Talmudic passage (Sheb. 35 b) in which the principle is laid down, that whenever throughout that book Solomon is named, except in Chapter 8:12, it applies, not to Solomon, but to Him Who was His peace (there is here a play on these words, and on the name Solomon).

To Song of Solomon 1:8 the Targum makes this addition: They shall be nourished in the captivity, until the time that I shall send to them the King Messiah, Who will feed them in quietness.

So also on verse 17 the Targum contrasts the Temple built by Solomon with the far superior Temple to be built in the days of the Messiah, of which the beams were to be made of the cedars of Paradise.

Song of Solomon 2:8, although applied by most authorities to Moses, is by others referred to the Messiah (Shir haShirim R., ed. Warsh., p. 15 a, about the middle; Pesiqta, ed. Buber, p. 47 b). Song of Solomon 2:9 is Messianically applied in Pesiqta, ed. Buber, p. 49, a and b.

The same may be said of verse 10; while in connection with verse 12, in similar application, Isaiah 52:7 is quoted.

In connection with verse 13, in the same Midrash (p. 17 a), Rabbi Chija bar Abba speaks of a great matter as happening close to the days of the Messiah, namely, that the wicked should be destroyed, quoting in regard to it Isaiah 4:3.

Song of Solomon 3:11, the day of his espousals. In Yalkut on the passage (Volume 2: p. 178 d) this is explained: the day of the Messiah, because the Holy One, blessed be His name, is likened to a bridegroom; "as the bridegroom rejoices over the bride", and the day of the gladness of his heart, as the day when the Sanctuary is rebuilt, and Jerusalem is redeemed.

On Song of Solomon 4:5 the Targum again introduces the twofold Messiah, the one the son of David, and the other the son of Ephraim.

Song of Solomon 4:16. According to one opinion in the Midrash (p. 25 b, line 13 from the bottom) this applies to the Messiah, Who comes from the north, and builds the Temple, which is in the south. See also Bemidbar R. 13, p. 48 b.

On Song of Solomon 5:10 Yalkut remarks that He is white to Israel, and red to the Gentiles, according to Isaiah 63:2.

On Song of Solomon 6:10 Yalkut (Volume 2: p. 184 b) has some beautiful observations, first, likening Israel in the wilderness, and God's mighty deeds there, to the morning; and then adding that, according to another view, this morning light is the redemption of the Messiah: For as, when the morning rises, the darkness flees before it, so shall darkness fall upon the kingdoms of this world when the Messiah comes. And yet again, as the sun and moon appear, so will the Kingdom of the Messiah also appear, the commentary going on to trace farther illustrations.

Song of Solomon 5:6. The Midrash thus comments on it (among other explanations): How fair in the world to come, how pleasant in the days of the Messiah!

On Song of Solomon 5:13, the Targum has it: When it shall please God to deliver His people from captivity, then shall it be said to the Messiah: The time of captivity is past, and the merit of the just shall be sweet before Me like the odor of balsam.

Similarly on Song of Solomon 8:1, the Targum has it: And at that shall the King Messiah be revealed to the congregation of Israel, and the children of Israel shall say to Him, Come and be a brother to us, and let us go up to Jerusalem, and there suck with you the meaning of the Law, as an infant its mother's breast.

On Song of Solomon 8:2 the Targum has it: I will take You, O King Messiah, and make you go up into my Temple, there You shall teach me to tremble before the Lord, and to walk in His ways. There we shall hold the feast of leviathan, and drink the old wine, which has been kept in its grapes from the day the world was created, and of the pomegranates and of the fruits which are prepared for the just in the Garden of Eden.

On verse 4 the Targum says: The King Messiah shall say: I adjure you, My people, house of Israel, why should you rise against the Gentiles, to go out of captivity, and why should you rebel against the might of Gog and Magog? Wait a little, until those nations are consumed which go up to fight against Jerusalem, and then shall the Lord of the world remember you, and it shall be His good will to set you free.

Chap. 8:11 is applied Messianically in the Talmud (Shebhu. 35 b), and so is verse 12 in the Targum.

(It should, however, be remarked that there are many other Messianic references in the comments on the Song of Solomon.)

Isaiah 50:25, 26, is thus explained in the Talmud (Sanh. 98 a): The Son of David shall not come until all the judges and rulers in Israel shall have ceased.

Similarly Isaiah 2:4 is Messianically interpreted in Shabb. 63 a.

Isaiah 4:2 the Targum distinctly applies to the times of the Messiah.

Isaiah 4:4 has been already commented upon in our remarks on Genesis 18:4, 5, and again on Deuteronomy 23:11.

Verses 5 and 6 are brought into connection with Israel's former service in contributing to, and making the Tabernacle in the wilderness, and it is remarked that in the latter days God would return it to them by covering them with a cloud of glory. This, in Yalkut (Volume 1: p. 99 c), and in the Midrash on Psalm 13, as also in that on Psalm 15:9.

Isaiah 6:13 is referred in the Talmud (Keth. 112 b) to Messianic times.

The reference of Isaiah 5:21 to Messianic times has already been discussed in our notes on Genesis 16:7.

Isaiah 8:14 is also Messianically applied in the Talmud (Sanh. 38 a).

Isaiah 9:6 is expressly applied to the Messiah in the Targum, and there is a very curious comment in Debarim R. 1 (ed. Warsh., p. 4 a) in connection with a Haggadic discussion of Genesis 43:14, which, however fanciful, makes a Messianic application of this passage, also in Bemidbar R. 11.

Verse 7, Of the increase of his government and peace there shall be no end, has already been referred to in our comments on Numbers 6:26.

Isaiah 10:27 is in the Targum applied to the destruction of the Gentiles before the Messiah. Isaiah 10:34, is quoted in the Midrash on Lamentations 1:16, in evidence that somehow the birth of the Messiah was to be connected with the destruction of the Temple.

Isaiah 11, as will readily be believed, is Messianically interpreted in Jewish writings. Thus, to begin with in the Targum on verses 1 and 6; in the Talmud (Jeremiah Berach. 5 a and Sanh. 93 b); and in a number of passages in the Midrashim. Thus, verse 1 in Bereshith R. 85 on Genesis 26:18, where also Psalm 110:2 is quoted, and in Ber. R. 99, ed. Warsh., p, 178 b. In Yalkut (Volume 1: p. 247 d, near the top), where it is described how God had shown Moses all the spirits of the rulers and prophets in Israel, from that time forward to the Resurrection, it is said that all these had one knowledge and one spirit, but that the Messiah had one spirit which was equal to all the others put together, according to Isaiah 10:1.

On the 2nd verse see our remarks on Genesis 1:2, while in Yalkut on Proverbs 3:19, 20 (Volume 2: p. 133 a) the verse is quoted in connection with Messianic times, when by wisdom, understanding, and knowledge the Temple will be built again. On that verse see also pirq. d. R. El. 3.

On Isaiah 10:3 the Talmud (Sanh. 93 b, lines 21 etc. from the top) has a curious explanation. After quoting Chapter 10:2 as Messianic, it makes a play on the words, of quick understanding, or scent, as it might be rendered, and suggest that this word is intended to teach us that God has laden Him with commandments and sufferings like millstones. Immediately afterwards, from the expression He shall not judge after the sight of His eyes, but reprove with equity for the meek of the earth, it is inferred that the Messiah knew the thoughts of the heart, and it is added that, as Bar Kokhabh was unable to do this, he was killed.

Verse 4, he shall strike the earth with the rod of his mouth, is Messianically applied in the Midrash on Psalm 2:2, and in that on Ruth 2:14, also in Yalkut on Isaiah 60.

Verse 7 has been already noticed in connection with Exodus 12:2.

On verse 10 see our remarks on Genesis 49:10 and Psalm 20:1.

Verse 11 is Messianically applied in Yalkut (Volume 1: p. 31 b and Volume 2:38 a), as also in the Midrash on Psalm 105:2.

Verse 12 is Messianically applied in that curious passage in the Midrash on Lamentations 1:2, where it is indicated that, as the children of Israel sinned from to, so God would in the latter days comfort them from to (i.e. through the whole alphabet), Scripture passages being in each case quoted.

The Messianic application of Isaiah 12:3 is sufficiently established by the ancient symbolic practice of pouring out the water on the Feast of Tabernacles.

In connection with Isaiah 10:5 the Midrash on Psalm 116:23 first speak of the wonderment of the Egyptians when they saw the change in Israel from servitude to glory of their Exodus, and then adds, that the words were intended by his Holy Spirit to apply to the wonders of the latter days (ed. Warsh. p. 85 b).

On Isaiah 14:2, see our comments on Genesis 16:4, 5.

Isaiah 14:29, 15:2, 15:1, and 15:5 are Messianically applied in the Targum.

Isaiah 16:5 is similarly applied in the Talmud (Sanh. 98 a); and Isaiah 23:15 in Sanh. 99 a.

Isaiah 20:11, 12 is in Jeremiah Taan. 64 a, and in Shem. R. 18, applied to the manifestation of Messiah.

Isaiah 23:8 the Midr. on Ecclesiastes 1:7 sees a curious reference to the return of this world's wealth to Israel in Messianic days.

Isaiah 23:15 is Messianically applied in the Talmud (Sanh 99 a) where the expression a king is explained as referring to the Messiah.

Isaiah 24:23 is Messianically applied in the curious passage in Bemidbar R. quoted under Genesis 22:18; also in Bemidbar R. 13 (ed. Warsh. p. 51 a).

The remarkable promise in Isaiah 25:8 is applied to the times of the Messiah in the Talmud (Moed Q. 28 b), and in that most ancient commentary Siphra, (Yalkut 1: p. 190 d applies the passage to the world to come). But the most remarkable interpretation is that which occurs in connection with Isaiah 60:1 (Yalkut 2:56 c, line 16 from the bottom), where the passage (Isaiah 25:8) is after an challenge on the part of Satan with regard to the Messiah, applied to the casting into Gehenna of Satan and of the Gentiles. See also our remarks on Exodus 12:2. In Debar.

R. 2, Isaiah 25:8 is applied to the destruction of the Jetser ha Ra and the abolishing of death in Messianic days; in Shem. R. 30 to the time of the Messiah.

Verse 9. Tanchuma on Deuteronomy opens with a record of how God would work all the miracles, which He had shown in the wilderness, in a fuller manner for Zion in the latter days, the last passage quoted in that section being Isaiah 25:9. (Tanchuma on Deuteronomy ed. Warsh. p. 99 a, line 5 from the bottom).

Of Isaiah 25:19 there is Messianic application in the Midrash on Ecclesiastes 1:7.

Of Isaiah 25:10 Shem. R. 1, and Tanchuma on Exodus 2:5 (ed. Warsh. p. 64 b) remark that, like Moses, the Messiah, Who would deliver His own from the worshippers of false gods, should be brought up with the latter in the land.

Verse 13 is quoted in the Talmud (Rosh. haSh. 11 b) in connection with the future deliverance. So also in Yalkut, 1: p. 217 d, and Pirqe de R. El. c. 31.

Isaiah 106:5 is thus paraphrased in the Targum: At that time shall the Messiah of the Lord of hosts be a crown of joy.

Isaiah 106:16 the Targum apparently applies to the Messiah. At least, so Rashi (on the passage) understands it.

Isaiah 30:18 is Messianically applied in Sanh 97 b; verse 15 Jeremiah Taan. 1:1.

The expression in Isaiah 30:19, he shall be very gracious to you, is applied to the merits of the Messiah in Yalkut on Zeph. 3:8 (p. 84 c).

On verse 25 see our remarks on Genesis 16:4.

Verse 26 is applied to Messianic times in the Talmud (Pes. 68 a, and Sanh. 91 b), and similarly in Pirqe de R. El. 51, and Shemoth R. 50. So also in Ber. R. 12. see our remarks on Genesis 2:4.

Isaiah 32:14, 15. On this passage the Midrash of Lamentations 3:49 significantly remarks that it is one of the three passage in which mention of the Holy Spirit follows upon mention of redemption, the other two passages being Isaiah 22, followed by 60:1, and Lamentations 3:49.

Isaiah 32:20. The first clause is explained by Tanchuma (Par. 1. ed. Warsh. p. 4 a, first three lines) to apply to the study of the Law, and the second to the two Messiahs, the son of Joseph being likened to the ox, and the son of David to the donkey, accordingly to Zechariah 9:9; and similarly the verse is Messianically referred to in Deb. R. 6 (ed. Warsh.

Vol. 3: p. 15 b), in a very curious play on the words in Deuteronomy 22:6, 7, where the observance of that commandment is supposed to hasten the coming of King Messiah.

Isaiah 35:1. This is one of the passages quoted in Tanchuma on Deuteronomy 1:1. (ed.Warsh. p. 99 a) as among the miracles which God would do to redeem Zion in the latter days. So also is verse 2 in this chapter.

Isaiah 35:5, 6 is repeatedly applied to Messianic times. Thus, in Yalkut 1:78 c, and 157 a; in Ber. R. 95; and in Midrash on Psalm 146:8.

Verse 10 is equally applied to Messianic times in the Midrash on Psalm 105:1, while at the same time it is noted that this deliverance will be accomplished by God Himself, and not either by Elijah, nor by the King Messiah. A similar reference occurs in Yalkut (Volume 2: p. 162 d), at the close of the Commentary on the Book of Chronicles, where it is remarked that in this world the deliverance of Israel was accomplished by man, and was followed by fresh captivities, but in the latter or Messianic days their deliverance would be accomplished by God, and would no more be followed by captivity. See also Shemoth R. 15 and 23.

Isaiah 40:1 is one of the passages referred to in our note on Isaiah 10:12, and also on Isaiah 35:1.

The same remark applies to verses 2 and 3.

Verse 5 is also Messianically applied in Vayyikra R. 1; Yalk. 2:77 b about the middle.

On verse 10 Yalkut, in discussing Exodus 32:6 (Volume 1: p. 108 c) broaches the opinion, that in the days of the Messiah Israel would have a double reward, on account of the calamities which they had suffered, quoting Isaiah 40:10.

Isaiah 41:18 has been already noted in remarks on Genesis 16:4, 5.

Verse 25 is Messianically applied in Bem. R. 13, p. 48 b.

The expression The first, in Chapter 41:27, is generally applied to the Messiah; in the Targum, according to Rashi; in Bereshith R. 63; in Vayyikra R. 30; and in the Talmud (Pes. 5 a); so also in Pesiqta (ed. Buber) p. 185 b.

Isaiah 42:1 is applied in the Targum to the Messiah, as also in the Midrash or Psalm 2; and in Yalkut 2: p. 104 d. See also our comments on Psalm 2:7.

On Isaiah 43:10, the Targum renders My servant by My servant the Messiah.

The promise in Isaiah 45:22 is also among the future things mentioned in the Midrash on Lamentations, to which we have referred in our remarks on Isaiah 10:12.

Isaiah 49:8. There is a remarkable comment on this in Yalkut on the passage, to the effect that the Messiah suffers in every age for the sins of that generation, but that God would in the day of redemption repair it all (Yalk. 2: p. 52 b).

Isaiah 49:9 is quoted as the words of the Messiah in Yalkut (Volume 2, p. 52 b).

Verse 10 is one of the passages referred to in the Midrash on Lamentations, quoted in connection with Isaiah 10:12.

Verse 12 has already been noticed in our remarked on Exodus 12:2.

From the expression comfort in verse 13, the Messianic title Menachem is derived. Comp. the Midrash on Proverbs 19:21.

Verse 14 is Messianically applied in Yalkut 2: p. 52 c.

Verse 21 is also one of the passages referred to in the Midrash of Lamentations, quoted under Psalm 10:12.

On verse 23 it is remarked in Vayyikra R. 27 (ed. Warsh. p. 42 a), that Messianic blessings were generally prefigured by similar events, as for example, the passage here quoted in the case of Nebuchadnezzar and Daniel.

A Messianic application of the same passage also occurs in Par. 33 and 36, as a contrast to the contempt that Israel experiences in this world.

The second clause of verse 23 is applied to the Messiah in the Midrash on Psalm 2:2, as to be fulfilled when the Gentiles shall see the terrible judgments.

Verse 26 is similarly applied to the destruction of the Gentiles in Vayyikra R.33 (end).

Isaiah 51:12 is one of the passages referred to in the Midrash of Lamentations, quoted in our comments in Isaiah 10:12.

Isaiah 51:12 and 17 are among the passages referred to in our remarks on Isaiah 25:9

Isaiah 12:3 is Messianically applied in the Talmud (Sanh. 97 b), while the last clause of verse 2 is one of the passages quoted in the Midrash on Lamentations (see Isaiah 10:12).

The well known Evangelic declaration in Isaiah 52:7 is thus commented upon in Yalkut (Volume 2: p. 53 c): In the hour when the Holy One, blessed be His Name, redeems Israel, three days before Messiah comes Elijah, and stands upon the mountains of Israel, and weeps and mourns for them, and says to them: Behold the land of Israel, how long shall you stand in a dry and desolate land? And his voice is heard from the world's end to the world's end, and after that it is said to them: Peace has come to the world, peace has come to the world, as it is said: How beautiful upon the mountains, etc. And when the wicked hear it, they rejoice, and they say one to the other: Peace has come to us. On the second day he shall stand upon the mountains of Israel, and shall say: Good has come to the world, good has come to the world, as it is written: That brings good news of good. On the third day he shall come and stand upon the mountains of

Israel, and say: Salvation has come to the world, salvation has come to the world, as it is written: That publishes salvation.

Similarly, this passage is quoted in Yalkut on Psalm 102:1. See also our remarks on Song of Solomon 2:13.

Verse 8 is one of the passages referred to in the Midrash on Lamentations quoted above, and frequently in other places as Messianic.

Verse 12 is Messianically applied in Shemoth R. 15 and 19.

Verse 13 is applied in the Targum expressly to the Messiah. On the words He shall be exalted and extolled we read in Yalkut 2: (Par. 338, p. 53 c, lines 7 etc. from the bottom): He shall be higher than Abraham, to whom applies Genesis 14:22; higher than Moses, of whom Numbers 10:12 is predicated; higher than the ministering angels, of whom Ezekiel 1:18 is said. But to Him there applies this in Zechariah iv. 7: Who are you, O great mountain? And He was wounded for our transgressions, and bruised for our iniquities, and the chastisement of our peace was upon Him, and with His stripes we are healed. R. Huma says, in the name of R. Acha: All sufferings are divided into three parts; one part goes to David and the Patriarchs, another to the generation of the rebellion (rebellious Israel), and the third to the King Messiah, as it is written (Psalm 2:7), Yet have I set My King upon My holy hill of Zion. Then follows a curious quotation from the Midrash on Samuel, in which the Messiah indicates that His dwelling is on Mount Zion, and that guilt is connected with the destruction of its walls.

In regard to Isaiah 53:we remember, that the Messianic name of Leprous (Sanh. 98 b) is expressly based upon it. Isaiah 53:10 is applied in the Targum on the passage to the Kingdom of the Messiah.

Verse 5 is Messianically interpreted in the Midrash on Samuel (ed. Lemberg, p. 45 a, last line), where it is said that all sufferings are divided into three parts, one of which the Messiah bore, a remark which is brought into connection with Ruth 2:14. (See our comments on that passage.)

Isaiah 54:2 is expected to be fulfilled in Messianic times (Vayyikra R. 10).

Isaiah 54:5. In Shemoth R. 15 this is expressly applied to Messianic days.

Isaiah 54:11 is repeatedly applied to the Messianic glory, as, for example, in Shemoth R. 15. (See our comments on Exodus 12:2.)

So is verse 13, as in Yalkut (Volume 1:78 c); in the Midrash on Psalm 21:1; and in other passages.

Isaiah 55:12 is referred to Messianic times, as in the Midrash on Psalm 13.

Isaiah 56:1. See our comments on Exodus 20:1.

Verse 7 is one of the passages in the Midrash on Lamentations which we have quoted under Isaiah 10:12.

On Isaiah 55:14 Bemidhar R. 15 (ed. Warsh. p. 64 a) expresses a curious idea about the stumbling block, as mystically the evil inclination, and adds that the promise applies to God's removal of it in the world to come, or else it may be in Messianic days.

Verse 16 receives in the Talmud (Yeb. 62 a and 63 b) and in the Midr. on Eccl. 1:6 the following curious comment: The Son of David shall not come until all the souls are completed which are in the Guph, (i.e. the pre-existence of souls is taught, and that they are kept in heaven until one after another appears in human form, and that the Messiah is kept back until all these shall have appeared), proof of this being derived from Isaiah 55:16.

Similarly Chapter 59:15 is applied to Messianic times in Sanh. 97 a, and Midr. on Song of Solomon 2:13; and verse 19 in Sanh. 98 a.

Verse 17 is applied to Messianic times in Pesiqta, ed. Buber, p. 149 a.

Verse 20 is one of the passages mentioned in the Midrash on Lamentations quoted above. (See Isaiah 10:12.)

Isaiah 59:19, 20, is applied to Messianic times in Sanh. 98 a. In Pesiqta 166 b it is similarly applied, the peculiar form (plene) in which the word Goel (Redeemer) is written being taken to indicate the Messiah as the Redeemer in the full sense.

Isaiah 60:1. This is applied in the Targum to Messianic times. Similarly, it is explained in Ber. R. 1:with reference to Daniel 2:2; in Ber. R. 2; and also in Bemidbar R. 15 and 21. In Yalkut we have some very interesting remarks on the subject. Thus (Volume 1:Par. 363, p. 99 c), commenting on Exod 25:3 etc., in a very curious description of how God would in the world to come return to Israel the various things which they had offered for the Tabernacle, the oil is brought into connection with the Messiah, with reference to Psalm 132:17 and Isaiah 60:1. Again, on p. 215 c (at the beginning of the Parashah Behaalothekha) we have, first, a very curious comparison between the work of the Tabernacle and that of the six days of Creation, after which the question is put: Why Moses made seven lights, and Solomon seventy? To this the reply is given, that Moses rooted up seven nations before Israel, while Solomon reigned over all the seventy nations which, according to Jewish ideas, constitute the world.

Upon this it is added, that God had promised, that as Israel had lighted for His glory the lights in the Sanctuary, so would He in the latter days fill

Jerusalem with His glory, according to the promise in Isaiah 60:1, and also set up in the midst of it lights, according to Zeph. 1:12. Still more clearly is the Messianic interpretation of Isaiah 60. brought out in the comments in Yalkut on that chapter. One part of it is so curious that it may here find a place. After explaining that this light for which Israel is looking is the light of the Messiah, and that Genesis 1:4 really referred to it, it is added that this is intended to teach us that God looked forward to the age of the Messiah and His works before the Creation of the world, and that He hid that light for the Messiah and His generation under His throne of glory. On Satan's questioning Him for whom that light was destined, the answer is: For Him Who in the latter days will conquer you, and cover your face with shame. On which Satan requests to see Him, and when he is shown Him, falls on his face and says: I confess that this is the Messiah Who will in the latter days be able to cast me, and all the Gentiles, into Gehenna, according to Isaiah 25:8. In that hour all the nations will tremble, and say before God: Who is this into Whose hand we fall, what is His Name, and what is His purpose? On which God replies: This is Ephraim, the Messiah [the second Messiah, the son of Joseph]; My Righteousness is His Name. And so the commentary goes on to touch on Psalm 89:23, 24, and 26, in a manner most deeply interesting, but which it would be impossible here fully to give (Yalkut, Volume 2: Par. 359, p. 56 c). In col. d there are farther remarkable discussions about the Messiah, in connection with the wars in the days when Messiah should be revealed, and about Israel's final safety. But the most remarkable passage of all, reminding us almost of the history of the Temptation, is that which reads as follows (line 22 etc. from the top): It is a tradition from our Rabbis that, in the hour when King Messiah comes, He stands on the roof of the Temple, and proclaims to them, that the hour of their deliverance has come, and that if they believed they would rejoice in the light that had risen upon them, as it is written (Isaiah 60:1), Arise, shine, for your light is come. This light would be for them alone, as it is written (ver. 2), For darkness shall cover the earth. In that hour also would God take the light of the Messiah and of Israel, and all should walk in the light of Messiah and of Israel, as it is written (ver. 3), The Gentiles shall come to your light, and kings to the brightness of your rising. And the kings of the nations should lick the dust from under the feet of the Messiah, and should all fall on their faces before Him and before Israel, and say: Let us be servants to You and to Israel. And so the passage goes on to describe the glory of the latter days. The whole of this chapter may be said to be full of Messianic interpretations.

After this it will scarcely be necessary to say that verses 2, 3, and 4 are similarly applied in the Midrashim. But it is interesting to notice that verse 2 is specifically applied to Messianic times in the Talmud (Sanh. 99 a), in answer to the question when the Messiah should come.

On verse 4 the Midrash on Song of Solomon 1:4, on the words we will be glad and rejoice in you, has the following beautiful illustration. A Queen is introduced whose husband and sons and sons-in-law go to a distant country. Tidings are brought to her: Your sons are come back. On which she says: Cause for gladness have I, my daughters-in-law will rejoice. Next, news are brought her that her sons-in-law are coming, and she is glad that her daughters will rejoice. Lastly, news are brought: The king, your husband, comes. On which she replies: This is indeed perfect joy, joy upon joy. So in the latter days would the prophets come, and say to Jerusalem: Your sons shall come from far (verse 4), and she will say: What gladness is this to me!, and your daughters shall be nursed at your side, and again she will say: What gladness is this to me! But when they shall say to her (Zechariah 9:9): Behold, your king comes to you; he is just, and having salvation, then shall Zion say: This indeed is perfect joy, as it is written (Zechariah 9:9), Rejoice greatly, O daughter of Zion, and again (Zechariah 2:10), Sing and rejoice, O daughter of Zion. In that hour she will say (Isaiah 61:10): I will greatly rejoice in the Lord, my soul shall be joyful in my God.

Verse 7 is Messianically applied in the Talmud (Abod. Sar. 24 a).

Verse 8 is Messianically applied in the Midrash on Psalm 45:13.

In connection with verse 19 we read in Yalkut (Volume 1: p. 103 b) that God said to Israel: In this world you are engaged (or busied) with the light for the Sanctuary, but in the world to come, for the merit of this light, I send you the King Messiah, Who is likened to a light, according to Psalm 132:17 and Isaiah 60:19, the Lord shall be to you an everlasting light.

Verse 21 is thus alluded to in the Talmud (Sanh. 98 a): Rabbi Jochanan said, The Son of David shall not come, until all be either just or all be unjust: the former according to Isaiah 60:21, the latter according to Isaiah 59:16.

Verse 22 is also Messianically applied in the Talmudic passage above cited.

Isaiah 60:1 has already been mentioned in our remarks on Isaiah 32:14, 15.

On verse 5 there is a curious story related (Yalkut, Volume 1: Par. 212, p. 64 a, lines 23-17 from the bottom) in which, in answer to a question, what was to become of the nations in the days of the Messiah, the reply is given that every nation and kingdom that had persecuted and mocked Israel would see, and be confounded, and have no share in life; but that every nation and kingdom which had not so dealt with Israel would come and be husbandmen and vinedressers to Israel in the days of the Messiah. A similar statement to this is found in the Midrash on Ecclesiastes 2:7.

Verse 9 is also applied to Messianic times.

Verse 10 is one of the passages referred to in Tanchuma on Deuteronomy 1:1 quoted under Isaiah 25:9. In Pesiqta, ed. Buber, p. 149 a, the verse is explained as applying to the glory of Messiahs appearance.

Isaiah 62:10 has already been referred to in our remarks on Isaiah 57:14.

Isaiah 63: is applied to the Messiah, Who comes to the land after having seen the destruction of the Gentiles, in Pirqe de R. Eliez. c. 30.

Verse 2 has been referred to in our comments on Song of Solomon v. 10. It is also quoted in reference to Messianic days in Pesiqta, ed. Buber, p. 149 a.

Verse 4 is explained as pointing to the days of the Messiah, which are supposed to be 365 years, according to the number of the solar days (Sanh. 99 a); while in other passages of the Midrashim, the destruction of Rome and the coming of the Messiah are connected with the day of vengeance. See also the Midr. on Ecclesiastes 12:10.

Isaiah 64:4 (3 in the Hebrew). In Yalkut on Isaiah 60. (Volume 2: p. 56 d, line 6, etc., from the bottom) Messianic application is made of this passage in a legendary account of the seven tabernacles which God would make for the Messiah, out of each of which proceed four streams of wine, milk, honey, and pure balsam. Then God is represented as speaking of the sufferings which Messiah was to undergo, after which the verse in question is quoted.

Isaiah 65:17 is quoted in the Midrash on Lamentations, referred to in our remarks on Isaiah 10:12.

Verse 19 is one of the passages referred to in Tanchuma on Deuteronomy 1:1. See Isaiah 25:9.

To verse 25 we have the following curious illustrative reference in Ber. R. 20 (ed. Warsh. p. 38 b, line 6 from the bottom) in connection with the Fall: In the latter days everything shall be healed again (restored again) except the serpent (Isaiah 65:25) and the Gibeonites (Ezekiel 48:19). But a still more strange application of the verse occurs in the same Midrash (Par. 95, ed. Warsh. p. 170 a), where the opening clauses of it are quoted with this remark: Come and see all that the Holy One, blessed be His Name, has struck in this world, He will heal in the latter days. Upon which a curious disquisition follows, to prove that every man would appear after death exactly as he had been in life, whether blind, dumb, or halting, even in the same dress, as in the case of Samuel when Saul saw him, but that afterwards God would heal the diseased.

Isaiah 65:7 is applied to Messianic times in Vayyikra R. 14 (last line), and so are some of the following verses in the Midrashim, notably on Genesis 33:1.

Isaiah 66:22 is applied to Messianic times in Ber. R. 12. See our remarks on Genesis 2:4.

Jeremiah 3:17 is applied to Messianic days in Yalkut on Joshua 3:9 etc. (Volume 2: p. 3 c, line 17 from the top),and so is verse 18 in the commentary on the words in Song of Solomon 1:16 our bed is green, the expression being understood of the ten tribes, who had been led captive beyond the river Sabbayon; but when Judah's deliverance came, Judah and Benjamin would go to them and bring them back, that they might be worthy of the days of the Messiah (Volume 2: p., 176 d, line 9 etc. from the bottom).

Jeremiah 5:19 is mentioned in the Introd. to Echa R. as one of three passages by which to infer from the apostasy of Israel the near advent of Messiah.

The expression speckled bird in Jeremiah 12:9 is applied to the Messiah in Pirqe de R. Eliez. c. 28.

The last word in Jeremiah 15:13 is made the basis of the name Chaninah, given to the Messiah in the Talmud (Sanh. 98 b), and in the Midr. On Lamentations 1:16.

On verse 14 Mechilta has it, that in the latter days the Exodus would no more be mentioned on account of the greater wonders then experienced.

On Jeremiah 23:5, 6, the Targum has it: And I will raise up for David the Messiah the Just. This is one of the passages from which according to Rabbinic views, one of the Names of the Messiah is derived, viz: Jehovah our Righteousness. So in the Talmud (Babba Bathra 75 b), in the Midrash on Psalm 20:1, Proverbs 19:21, and in that on Lamentations 1:16.

On verse 7 see our remarks on Jeremiah 16:14. In the Talmud (Ber. 12 b) this verse is distinctly applied to Messianic days. Jeremiah 30:9 is Messianically applied in the Targum on the passage.

Jeremiah 30:21 is applied to the Messiah in the Targum, and also in the Midrash on Psalm 20:7.

On Jeremiah 30:8, 3rd clause, Yalkut has a Messianic interpretation, although extremely far fetched. In general, the following verses are Messianically interpreted in the Midrashim.

Verse 20 is Messianically applied in Yalkut (2: p. 66 c, end), where it is supposed to refer to the Messiah when imprisoned, when all the nations mock and shake their heads at Him. A more remarkable interpretation still occurs in the passage on Isaiah 60:1, to which we have already referred. Some farther extracts from it may be interesting. Thus, when the enemies of the Messiah flee before Him. God is supposed to make an agreement with the Messiah to this effect: The sins of those who are hidden with You will cause You to be put under an iron yoke, and they will do with You as with this calf, whose eyes are covered, and they will choke Your spirit under the yoke, and on account of their sins Your tongue shall stick to Your mouth. On which the Messiah inquires whether these troubles are to last for many years, and the Holy replies that He has decreed a week, but that if His soul were in sorrow, He would immediately dispel these sorrows. On this the Messiah says: Lord of the world, with gladness and joy of heart I take it upon Me, on condition that not one of Israel should perish, and that not only those alone should be saved who are in My days, but also those who are hid in the dust; and that not only the dead should be saved who are in My days, but also those who have died from the days of the first Adam until now; and not those, but also those who have been prematurely born. And only these, but also those who have come into Your knowledge to create them, but have not yet been created. Thus I agree, and thus I take all upon Me. In the week when the Son of David comes, they shall bring beams of iron, and shall make them a yoke to His neck, until His stature is bent down. But He cries and weeps, and lifts up His voice on high, and says before Him: Lord of the world, what is My strength, My spirit, and My soul, and My members? Am I not flesh and blood? In that honor David (the Son of David) weeps, and says: My strength is dried up like a potsherd. In that hour the Holy One, blessed be His Name, says: Ephraim the Messiah, My righteous one, You have already taken this upon You before the six days of the world, now Your anguish shall be like My anguish; for from the time that Nebuchadnezzar, the wicked one, has come up and destroyed My house, and burned My Sanctuary, and I have sent into captivity My children among the children of the Gentiles, by My life, and by the life of Your head, I have not sat down on My throne. And if You will not believe Me, see the dew which is on My head, as it is said (Song of Solomon 5:2) My head is filled with dew. In that hour the Messiah answers

Him: Lord of the world, now I am quieted, for it is enough for the servant that he is as his Master (his reminding us of Jesus' saying, Matthew 10:25). R. Isaac then remarks that in the year when the King Messiah shall be revealed, all nations shall rise up against each other (we have already quoted this passage in another place, as also that about the Messiah standing upon the roof of the Temple). Then follows this as a tradition of the Rabbis: In the latter days the Father's shall stand up in the month of Nisan, and say to Him:

Ephraim, the Messiah, our Righteousness, though we are Your Father's, yet You are better than we, because You have borne all the sins of our sons, and hard and evil measure has passed upon You, such as has not been passed either upon those before or upon those after. And You have been for laughter and derision to the nations for the sake of Israel, and You have dwelt in darkness and in mist, and Your eyes have not seen light, and Your light clung to You alone, and Your body was dried up like wood, and Your eyes were darkened through fasting, and Your strength was dried up like a potsherd. And all this on account of the sins of our children. Is it Your pleasure that our sons should enjoy the good thing which God had displayed to Israel? Or perhaps on account of the anguish which You have suffered for them, because they have bound You in the prison house, will You not give to them thereof? He says to them: Father's of the world, whatever I have done I have done for your sakes, and for the sake of your children, that they may enjoy that goodness which the Holy One, blessed be He, has displayed to Israel. Then say to Him the Father's of the world: Ephraim, Messiah, our Righteousness, be You reconciled to us, because You have reconciled Your Maker and us. R. Simeon, the son of Pasi, In that hour the Holy One, blessed be His Name, exalts the Messiah to the heaven of heavens, and spreads over Him the splendor of His glory, because of the nations of the world, and because of the wicked Persians. Then the Father's of the world say to Him: Ephraim, Messiah, our Righteousness, be You their judge, and do to them what Your soul desires. For unless mercies had been multiplied on You, they would long ago have exterminated You suddenly from the world, as it is written (Jeremiah 30:20) Is Ephraim my dear son? And why is the expression: I will surely have mercy [in the Hebrew reduplicated: having mercy I will have mercy], but that the first expression mercy refers to the hour when He was bound in prison, when day by day they gnashed with their teeth, and winked with their eyes, and nodded with their heads, and wide opened their mouths, as it is written in Psalm 22:7 [8 in Hebrew]; while the second expression I will have mercy refers to the hour when He came out of the prison house, when not only one kingdom, not two, came against Him, but 140 kingdoms came round about Him, and the Holy One, blessed be His Name, says to Him: Ephraim, Messiah, My righteous one, do not be afraid, for all these shall perish by the breath of Your mouth, as it is written (Isaiah 10:4). As long as this quotation may be, its interest seems sufficient to warrant its insertion.

Jeremiah 30:31, 33, and 34 are applied to Messianic times in Yalkut (Volume 1: p. 196 c; 78 c; and in Volume 2: p. 54 b, and p. 66 d).

Jeremiah 33:13. The close of the verse is thus paraphrased in the Targum: The people shall yet learn by the hands of the Messiah, while in Yalkut (Volume 1: p.105 d) mention is made of a tenfold gathering of Israel, the last, in connection with this verse, in the latter days.

On Lamentations 1:16 there is in the Midrash R. (ed. Warsh. p. 64 b) the curious story about the birth of the Messiah in the royal palace of Bethlehem, which also occurs in the Jeremiah Talmud.

Lamentations 2:22, first clause. The Targum here remarks: You will proclaim liberty to Your people, the house of Israel, by the hand of the Messiah.

Lamentations 4:22, first clause. The Targum here remarks: And after these things your iniquity shall cease, and you shall be set free by the hands of the Messiah and by the hands of Elijah the Priest.

Ezekiel 10:19 is applied to the great spiritual change that was to take place in Messianic days, when the evil desire would be taken out of the heart (Deb. R. 6, at the end; and also in other Midrashic passages).

Ezekiel 15:55 is referred to among the ten things which God would renew in Messianic days, the rebuilding of ruined cities, inclusive of Sodom and Gomorrah, being the fourth (Shem. R. 15, ed. Warsh. p. 24 b).

Ezekiel 15:22 and 23 is distinctly and very beautifully referred to the Messiah in the Targum.

Ezekiel 25:14 is applied to the destruction of all the nations by Israel in the days of the Messiah in Bemidbar R. on Numbers 2:32 (Par. 2, ed. Warsh. p. 5 b).

Ezekiel 29:21 is among the passages applied to the time when the Messiah should come, in Sanh. 98 a.

So is Ezekiel 32:14.

Ezekiel 35:25 is applied to Messianic times in the Targum and in Yalkut (Volume 1: p. 235 a), as our in the Talmud (Kidd. 72 b).

On verse 27 see our remarks on Chapter 10:19.

Ezekiel 39:2 is Messianically applied in Bemidbar R. 13, Warsh. p. 48 b.

Ezekiel 45:9 and 12 are quoted as the second and the third things which God would renew in the latter days (Shem. R. 15), the second being, that living waters should go forth out of Jerusalem, and the third, that trees should bear fruit every month, and the sick be healed by them.

On Ezekiel 48:19 the Talmud (Baba B. 122 a) has the following curious comment, that the land of Israel would be divided into thirteenth tribes, the thirteenth belonging to the Prince, and this verse is quoted as proof.

Daniel 2:22 is Messianically applied in Ber. R. 1, and in the Midr. on Lament. 1:16, where it gives rise to another name of the Messiah: the Light giver.

Verse 35 is similarly applied in the Pirqe de R. Eliez. c. 11, and verse 44 in c. 30.

Daniel 5:9. This passage was interpreted by R. Akiba as implying that one throne was set for God, and the other for the Messiah (Chag. 14 a).

Daniel 5:13 is curiously explained in the Talmud (Sanh. 98 a), where it is said that, if Israel behaved worthily, the Messiah would come in the clouds of heaven; if otherwise, humble, and riding upon a donkey.

Daniel 5:27 is applied to Messianic times in Bem. R. 11.

Daniel 8:13, 14. By a very curious combination these verses are brought into connection with Genesis 3:22 (man has become like one of us), and it is argued, that in Messianic days man's primeval innocence and glory would be restored to him, and he become like one of the heavenly beings, Ber. R. 21 (ed. Warsh. p. 41 a).

Daniel 9:24. In Naz. 32 b it is noted as that referred to the time when the second Temple was to be destroyed. So also in Yalkut, Volume 2: p. 79 d, lines 16etc. from the bottom.

Daniel 12:3 is applied to Messianic times in a beautiful passage in Shem. R. 15 (at the end).

Daniel 12:11, 12. These two verses receive a peculiar Messianic interpretation, and that by the authority of the Rabbis. For it is argued that, as Moses, the first Redeemer, appeared, and was withdrawn for a time, and then reappeared, so would the second Redeemer; and the interval between His disappearance and reappearance is calculated at 45 days, arrived at by deducting the 1,290 days of the cessation of the sacrifice (Daniel 12:11) from the 1,335 days of Daniel 12:12 (Midr. On Ruth 2:14, ed. Warsh. p. 43 b).

Hos. 2:2 is explained in the Midr. on Psalm 45:1 as implying that Israel's redemption would be when they were at the lowest.

Hos. 2:13 is one of the three passages referred to on Jeremiah 5:19.

Hos. 2:18 is quoted in Shem. R. 15 (on Exodus 12:2) as the seventh of the ten things which God would make new in Messianic days.

Hos. 3:5 is applied to the Messiah in the Targum, and from it the Jeremiah Talm.(Ber. 5 a) derives the name David as one of those given to the Messiah.

Hos. 6:2 is Messianically applied in the Targum.

Hos. 13:14 is applied to the deliverance by the Messiah of those of Israel who are in Gehinnom, whom He sets free;, the term Zion being understood of Paradise. See Yalk. on Isaiah Par. 269, comp. Maas. de R. Joshua in Jellineks Beth ha Midr. 2: p. 50.

Hos. 14:7 is Messianically applied in the Targum.

Joel 2:28 is explained in the Midrashim as referring to the latter days, when all Israel will be prophets (Bemidbar R. 15; Yalkut 1: p. 220 c, and other places).

Joel 3:18 is similarly applied in the Midrashim, as in that on Psalm 13: and in others. The last clause of this verse is explained in the Midr. on Ecclesiastes 1:9 to imply that the Messiah would cause a fountain miraculously to spring up, as Moses did in the wilderness.

Amos 4:7 is in Midr. on Song of Solomon 2:13 applied to the first of the seven years before Messiah come.

Amos 5:18 is one of the passages cited in the Talmud (Sanh. 98 b) to explain why certain Rabbis did not wish to see the day of the Messiah.

Amos 8:11 is applied to Messianic times in Ber. R. 25.

Amos 9:11 is a notable Messianic passage. Thus, in the Talmud (Sanh. 96 b) where the Messiah is called the Son of the Fallen, the name is explained by a reference to this passage. Again, in Ber. R. 88, last three lines (ed. Warsh. p. 157 a) after enumerating the unexpected deliverances which Israel had formerly experienced, it is added: Who could have expected that the fallen tabernacle of David should be raised up by God, as it is written (Amos 9:11) and who should have expected that the whole world should become one bundle (be gathered into one Church)? Yet it is written Zeph. 3:9. Comp. also the long discussion in Yalkut on this passage (Volume 2: p. 80 a and b).

Obadiah verses 18 and 21 are applied to the Kingdom and time of the Messiah in Deb. R. 1.

Micah 2:13. See our remarks on Genesis 16:4, 5. The passage is also Messianically quoted in the Midrash on Proverbs 6: (ed. Lemberg, p. 5 a, first two lines).

The promise in Micah 4:3 is applied to the times of the Messiah in the Talmud (Shabb. 63 a).

So is the prediction in verse 5 in Shemoth R. 15; while verse 8 is thus commented upon in the Targum: And you Messiah of Israel, Who shall be hidden on account of the sins of Zion, to you shall the Kingdom come.

The well know passage, Micah 5:2, is admittedly Messianic. So in the Targum, in the Pirqe de R. Eliez. c. 3, and by later Rabbis.

Verse 3 is applied in the Talmud to the fact that the Messiah was not to come until the hostile kingdom had spread for nine months over the whole world (Yoma 10 a), or else, over the whole land of Israel (Sanh. 98 b).

Similarly Micah 5:6 is applied to Messianic times in Sanh. 97 a, and in Sotah 49 b; also in the Midr. on Song of Solomon 2:13. And so is verse 15 in Yalkut (Volume 2: p. 112 b.)

In Micah 5:8, the expression, Jehovah shall be light to me, is referred to the days of the Messiah in Deb. R. 11, ed. Warsh. Volume v. p. 22 a.

Nahum 2:1. See our remarks on Isaiah 52:7.

Habakkuk 2:3. This is applied to Messianic times in a remarkable passage in Sanh. 97 b, which will be quoted in full at the close of this Appendix; also in Yalkut, Volume 2: p. 83 b.

Habakkuk 3:18 is applied to Messianic times in the Targum.

Zephaniah 3:8. The words rendered in our KJV the day that I rise up to the prey are translated for testimony and applied to God's bearing testimony for the Messiah (Yalkut, Volume 2: p. 84 c, line 6 from the top).

Verse 9 is applied to the voluntary conversion of the Gentiles in the days of the Messiah in the Talmud (Abhod. Zarah, 24 a); and in Ber. R. 88; and verse 11 in Sanh. 98 a.

Haggai 2:6 is expressly applied to the coming redemption in Deb. R. 1 (ed. Warsh. p. 4 b, line 15 from the top).

Zechariah 1:20. The four carpenters there spoken of are variously interpreted in the Talmud (Sukk. 52 b), and in the Midrash (Bemidbar R. 14). But both agree that one of them refers to the Messiah.

Zechariah 2:10 is one of the Messianic passages to which we have referred in our remarks on Isaiah 60:4. It has also a Messianic cast in the Targum.

Zechariah 3:8. The designation Branch is expressly applied to King Messiah in the Targum. This is one of the Messiahs peculiar names.

Verse 10 is quoted in the Midrash on Psalm 72:(ed. Warsh. p. 56 a, at the top) in a description of the future time of universal peace.

Zechariah 4:7 is generally applied to the Messiah, expressly in the Targum, and also in several of the Midrashim. Thus, as regards both clauses of it, in Tanchuma (Par. Toledoth 14, ed. Warsh. p. 37 b and 38 a).

Verse 10 is Messianically explained in Tanchuma (u. s.).

Zechariah 6:12 is universally admitted to be Messianic. So in the Targum, the Jerusalem Talmud (Ber. 5 a), in the Pirqe de R. Eliez. c. 48, and in the Midrashim.

Zechariah 5:13 is one of the three passages supposed to mark the near advent of Messiah. See our remarks on Jeremiah 5:19.

Zechariah 8:12 is applied to Messianic times in Ber. R. 12. See our remarks on Genesis 2:4.

Zechariah 8:23 is one of the predictions expected to be fulfilled in Messianic days, it being however noted that it refers to instruction in the Law in that remarkable passage on Isaiah 60:1 in Yalkut 2: p. 56 d, to which we have already referred.

In Zechariah 9:1 the name Chadrakh is mystically separated into Chad, sharp, and rakh, gentle, the Messiah being the one to the Gentiles and the other to the Jews (Siphre on Deuteronomy p. 65 a, Yalkut 1: p. 258 b).

Verse 9. The Messianic application of this verse in all its parts has already repeatedly been indicated. We may here add that there are many traditions about this donkey on which the Messiah is to ride; and so firm was the belief in it, that, according to the Talmud, if anyone saw a donkey in his dreams, he will see salvation (Ber. 56 b). The verse is also Messianically quoted in Sanh. 98 a, in Pirqe de R. Eliez. c. 31, and in several of the Midrashim.

On verse 10 see our remarks on Deuteronomy 20:10.

Zechariah 10:4 is Messianically applied in the Targum.

Zechariah 10:12 is Messianically explained in Ber. R. 98, but with this remark, that the 30 pieces of silver apply to 30 percepts, which the Messiah is to give to Israel.

Zechariah 12:10 is applied to the Messiah the Son of Joseph in the Talmud (Sukk. 52 a), and so is verse 12, there being, however, a difference of opinion whether the mourning is caused by the death of the Messiah the Son of Joseph, or else on account of the evil concupiscence (Yetser haRa).

Zechariah 14:2 will be readily understood to have been applied to the wars of Messianic times, and this in many passages of the Midrashim, as are verses 3, 4, 5, and 6.

Verse 7. The following interesting remark occurs in Yalkut on Psalm 139:16, 17 (Volume 2: p. 129 d) on the words none of them. This world is to last 6,000 years; 2,000 years it was waste and desolate, 2,000 years mark the period under the Law, 2,000 years that under the Messiah. And because our sins are increased, they are prolonged. As they are prolonged, and as we make one year in seven a Sabbatic year, so will God in the latter days make one day a Sabbatic year, which day is 1,000 years, to which applies the verse in Zechariah just quoted. See also Pirqe de R. Eliez. c. 28.

Verse 8 is Messianically applied in Ber. R. 48. See our remarks on Genesis 18:4, 5.

Verse 9 is applied to Messianic times, as in Yalkut 1: p. 76 c, 266 a, and Volume 2: p. 33 c, Midr. on Song of Solomon 2:13, and in other passages.

Malachi 3:1 is applied to Elijah as forerunner of the Messiah in Pirqe de R.Eliez. c. 29.

Verse 4. In Bemidbar R. 17, a little before the close (ed. Warsh. p. 69 a), this verse seems to be applied to acceptable sacrifices in Messianic days.

On verse 16 Vayyikra R. 34 (ed. Warsh. p. 51 b, line 4 from the bottom) has the following curious remark: If anyone in former times did the Commandment, the prophets wrote it down. But now when a man observes the Commandment, who writes it down? Elijah and the King Messiah and the Holy One, blessed be His Name, seal it at their hands, and a memorial book is written, as it is written Mal. 3:16.

The promise in verse 17 is extended to Messianic days in Shemoth R. 18.

On Mal. 4:1 (in Hebrew 3:19) the following curious comment occurs in Bereshith R. 6 (p. 14 b, lines 15 etc. from the bottom): The globe of the sun is encased, as it is said, He makes a tabernacle for the sun (Psalm 19). And a pool of water is before it. When the sun comes out, God cools its heat in the water for fear that it should burn up the world. But in the latter days the Holy One takes it out of its sheath, and with it burns up the wicked, as it is written Mal. 4:1.

Verse 2 (3:20 in Hebrew) is in Shemoth R. 31 quoted in connection with Exodus 22:26, and explained until the Messiah comes.

Verse 5 is applied to the forerunner of the Messiah. So in many places, as in the Pirqe de R. Eliez. c. 40; Debarm R. 3; in the Midrash on Song of Solomon 1:1; in the Talmud, and in Yalkut repeatedly.

To the above passages we add some from the Apocryphal Books, partly as indicating the views concerning the Messiah which the Jews had derived from the Old Testament, and partly because of their agreement with Jewish traditionalism as already expounded by us. These passages must therefore be judged in connection with the Rabbinical ideas of the Messiah and of Messianic days. It is in this sense that we read, for example, the address to Jerusalem, Tobit 13:9 to the end. Comp. here, for example, our quotations on Amos 9:11.

Similarly Tobit 14:5-7 may be compared with our quotations on Psalm 90, Isaiah 60:3, and especially on Zechariah 8:23, also on Genesis 49:11.

Wisdom of Solomon 3:7, 8 may be compared with our remarks on Isaiah 60:1.

Ecclus. 44:21 etc. and 45:11 may be compared with our quotations on Psalm 89:22-25; Psalm 132:18; Ezekiel 29:21.

Ecclus. 48:10, 11. See the comments on Isaiah 52:7, also our references on Mal. 3:1; Mal. 4:5; Deuteronomy 25:19 and 30:4; Lamentations 2:22. In Sotah 9:15 Elijah is represented as raising the dead.

Baruch 2:34, 35; 4:29 etc.; and Chapter 5 are so thoroughly in accordance with Rabbinic, and with Scriptural views, that it is almost impossible to enumerate special references.

The same may be said of 1 Maccabees 2:57; while such passages as 4:46 and 14:41 point forward to the ministry of Elijah as resolving doubts, as this is frequently described in the Talmud (Shekalim 2:5; Men. 45 a, Pes. 13 a; and in other places).

Lastly, 2 Maccabees 2:18 is fully enlarged on in the Rabbinic descriptions of the gathering of Israel.

Perhaps it may be as well here to add the Messianic discussion in the Talmud, to which such frequent reference has been made (Sanhedrin, beginning at the two last lines of p. 96 b, and ending at p. 99 a). The first question is that asked by one Rabbi of the other, whether he knew when the Son of the Fallen would come? Upon which follows an explanation of that designation, based on Amos 9:11, after which it is added that it would be a generation in which the disciples of the sages would be diminished, and the rest of men consume their eyes for sorrow, and terrible sorrows so follow each other, that one had not ceased before the other began. Then a description is given of what was to happen during the week when the Son of David would come. In the first year it would be according to Amos 4:7; in the second year there would be darts of famine; in the third year great famine and terrible mortality, in consequence of which the Law would be forgotten by those who studied it. In the fourth year there would be abundance, and yet no abundance; in the fifth year great abundance and great joy, and return to the study of the Law; in the sixth year voices (announcements); in the seventh wars, and at the end of the seventh the Son of David would come. Then follows some discussion about the order of the sixth and seventh year, when Psalm 89:51 is referred to. Next we have a description of the general state during those days. Sacred places (Academies) would be used for the vilest purposes, Galilee be desolated,

Gablan laid waste, and the men of Gebul wander from city to city, and not find mercy. And the wisdom of the scribes would be corrupted, and they who fear sin be abhorred, and the face of that generation would be like that of a dog, and truth should fail, according to Isaiah 59:15. (Here a side issue is raised.) The Talmud then continues in much the same terms to describe the Messianic age as one, in which children would rebel against their parents, and as one of general lawlessness, when Sadduceeism should universally prevail, apostasy increase, study of the Law decrease; and, generally, universal poverty and despair of redemption prevail, the growing disregard of the Law being pointed out as especially characterizing the last days. R. Kattina said: The world is to last 6,000 years, and during one millennium it is to lie desolate, according to Isaiah 2:17. R. Abayi held that this state would last 2,000 years, according to Hosea 6:2. The opinion of R. Kattian was however, regarded as supported by this, that in each period of seven there is a Sabbatic year, the day here = 1,000 years of desolateness and rest, the appeal being to Isaiah 2:17; Psalm 92:1, and 90:4. According to another tradition the world was to last 6,000 years: 2,000 in a state of chaos, 2,000 under the Law, and 2,000 being the Messianic age. But on account of Israel's sins those years were to be deducted which had already passed. On the authority of Elijah it was stated that the world would not last less than eighty five jubilees, and that in the last jubilee the Son of David would come. When Elijah was asked whether at the beginning or at the end of it, he replied that he did not know. Being further asked whether the whole of that period would first elapse or not, he similarly replied, his meaning being supposed to be that until that term people were not to hope for the Advent of Messiah, but after that term they were to look for it. A story is related of a man being met who had in his hands a writing in square Hebrew characters, and in Hebrew, which he professed to have got from the Persian archives, and in which it was written that after 4,290 years from the Creation the world would come to an end. And then would be the wars of the great sea monsters, and those of Gog and Magog, and the rest of the time would be the time of the Messiah, and that the Holy One, blessed be His Name, would only renew His world after the 7,000 years; to which, however, one Rabbi objects, making it 5,000 years. Rabbi Nathan speaks of Habakkuk 2:3 as a passage so deep as to go down to the abyss, reproving the opinion of the Rabbis who sought out the meaning of Daniel 5:25, and of Rabbi Samlai, who similarly busied himself with Psalm 80:5, and of Rabbi Akiba, who dwelt upon Haggai 2:6. But the first kingdom (Babylonian?) was to last seventy years; the second (Asmonean?) fifty two years; and the rule of the son of Kozebhah (Bar Kakhabh, the false Messiah) two and a half years. According to Rabbi Samuel, speaking in the name of Rabbi Jonathan: Let the bones of those be broken who calculate the end, because they say, The end has come, and the Messiah has not come, therefore He will not come at all. But still expect Him, as it is said (Hab. 2:3), Though it wait, wait for it. Perhaps you will say: We wait for Him, but He does not wait for it. On this point read Isaiah 30:18. But if so, what hinders it? The quality of judgment. But in that case, why should we wait? In order to receive the reward, according to the last clause of Isaiah 30:18. On which follows a further discussion. Again, Rabh maintains that all the limits of time as regards the Messiah are past, and that it now only depends on repentance and good works when He shall come. To this Rabbi Samuel objected, but Rabh's view was supported by Rabbi Eliezer, who said that if Israel repented they would be redeemed, but if not they would not be redeemed. To which Rabbi Joshua added, that in the latter case God would raise over them a King whose decrees would be hard like those of Haman, when Israel would repent. The opinion of Rabbi Eliezer was further supported by Jeremiah 3:22, to which Rabbi Joshua objected by quoting Isaiah 52:3, which seemed to imply that Israel's redemption was not dependent on their repentance and good works. On this Rabbi Joshua retorted by quoting Mal. 3:7, to which again Rabbi Joshua replied by quoting Jeremiah 3:14, and Rabbi Eleizer by quoting Isaiah 30:15. To this Rabbi Joshua replied from Isaiah 49:7. Rabbi Eliezer then urged Jeremiah 4:1, upon which Rabbi Joshua retorted from Daniel 12:7, and so effectually silenced Rabbi Eliezer. On this Rabbi Abba propounded that there was not a clearer mark of the Messianic term than that in Isaiah 35:8. To which Rabbi Eliezer added Zechariah 8:10. On this the question is raised as to the meaning of the words neither was there any peace to him that went out or came in. To this Rabh gave answer that it applied to the disciples of the sages, according to Psalm 119:165. On which Rabbi Samuel replied that at that time all the entrances would be equal (i.e. that all should be on the same footing of danger). Rabbi Chanina remarked that the Son of David would not come until after fish had been sought for the sick and not found, according to Ezekiel 32:14 in connection with Ezekiel 29:21. Rabbi Chamma, the son of Rabbi Chaina, said that the Son of David would not come until the vile dominion over Israel had ceased, appealing to Isaiah 16:5, 7. R. Seira said that Rabbi Chanina said: The Son of David would not come until the proud had ceased in Israel, according to Zeph. 3:11, 12. Rabbi Samlai, in the name of Rabbi Eliezer the son of Rabbi Simeon, said that the Son of David would not come until all judges and rulers had ceased in Israel, according to Isaiah 1:26. Ula said Jerusalem is not to be redeemed, except by righteousness, according to Isaiah 1:27. We pass over the remarks of Rabbi Papa, as not adding to the subject. Rabbi Jochanan said: If you see a generation that increasingly diminishes, expect Him, according to 2 Samuel 22:28. He also added: If you see a generation upon which many sorrows come like a stream, expect Him, according to Isaiah 59:19, 20. He also added: The son of David does not come except in a generation where all are either righteous, or all guilty, the former idea being based on Isaiah 60:21, the latter on Isaiah 59:16 and 48:11. Rabbi Alexander said, that Rabbi Joshua the son of Levi referred to the contradiction in Isaiah 60:22 between the words in his time and again I will hasten it, and explained it thus: If they are worthy, I will hasten it, and if not, in His time. Another similar contradiction between Daniel 5:13 and Zechariah 9:9 is thus reconciled: if Israel deserve it, He will come in the clouds of heaven; if they are not deserving, He will come poor, and riding upon a donkey. Upon this it is remarked that Sabor the King sneered at Samuel, saying: You say that the Messiah is to come upon a donkey: I will send Him my splendid horse. To which the Rabbi replied: Is it of a hundred colors, like His donkey? Rabbi Joshua, the son of Levi, saw Elijah, who stood at the door of Paradise. He said to him: When shall the Messiah come? He replied: When that Lord shall come (meaning God). Rabbi Joshua, the son of Levi, said: I saw two (himself and Elijah), and I heard the voice of three (besides the former two the Voice of the son of Jochai, and said to him: Shall I attain the world to come? Elijah replied: If it pleases the Lord. Upon which follows the same remark: I have seen the Messiah come? To which the answer is: Go and ask Him yourself. And where does He abide? At the gate of the city (Rome). And what is His sign? He abides among the poor, the sick and stricken. And all unbind, and bind up again the wounds at the same time, but He undoes (namely the bandage) and rebinds each separately, so that if they call for Him they may not find him engaged. He went to meet Him and said: peace be to You, my Rabbi and my Lord. He replied to him: Peace be to you, you son of Levi: he said to Him: When will You come, my Lord? He replied to him: Today. Then he turned to Elijah, who said to him: What has He said to you? He said to me: Son of Levi, peace be to you. Elijah said to him: He has assured you and your Father of the world to come. He said to him: But He has deceived me in that He said: I come today, and he has not come. He said to him that by the words today He meant: Today if you will hear My voice (Psalm 95:7). Rabbi Jose was asked by his disciples: When will the Son of David come? To this he replied: I am afraid you will ask me also for a sign. Upon which they assured him they would not. On this he replied: When this gate (namely of Rome) shall fall, and be built, and again fall, and they shall not have time to rebuild it until the Son of David comes. They said to him: Rabbi, give us a sign. He said to them: Have you not promised me that you would not seek a sign? They said to him: Notwithstanding do it. He said to them: If so, the waters from the cave of Pamias (one of the sources of the Jordan) shall be changed into blood. In that moment they were changed into blood. Then the Rabbi goes on to predict that the land would be overrun by enemies, every stable being filled with their horses. Rabh said that the son of David would not come until the kingdom (i.e foreign domination) should extend over Israel for nine months, according to Micah 5:3. Ula said: Let Him come, but may I not see Him, and so said Raba. Rabbi Joseph said: Let Him come, and may I be found worthy to stand in the shadow of the dung of His donkey (according to some: the tail of his donkey). Abayi said to Raba: Why has this been the bearing of your words? If on account of the sorrows of the Messiah, we have the tradition that Rabbi Eliezer was asked by his disciples, what a man should do to be freed from the sorrows of the Messiah; on which they were told: By busying yourselves with the Torah, and with good works. And you are a master of the Torah, and you have good works. He answered: Perhaps sin might lead to occasion of danger. To this comforting replies are given from Scripture, such as Genesis 16:15, and other passages, some of them being subjected to detailed commentary.

Rabbi Jochanan expressed a similar dislike of seeing the days of the Messiah, on which Resh Lakish suggested that it might be on the ground of Amos 5:19, or rather on that of Jeremiah 30:6. Upon this, such fear before God is accounted for by the consideration that what is called service above is not like what is called service below (the family above is not like the family below), so that one kind may outweigh the other. Rabbi Giddel said, that Rabh said, that Israel would rejoice in the years of the Messiah. Rabbi Joseph said: Surely, who else would rejoice in them? Chillak and Billak? (two imaginary names, meaning no one). This, to exclude the words of Rabbi Hillel, who said: There is no Messiah for Israel, seeing they have had Him in the time of Hezekiah. Rabh said: The world was only created for David; Samuel, for Moses; and Rabbi Jochanan, for the Messiah. What is His Name? The school of Rabbi Shila said: Shiloh is His Name, according to Genesis 49:10. The school of Rabbi Jannai said: Jinnon, according to Psalm 72:17. The school of Rabbi Chanina said: Chaninah, according to

Jeremiah 15:13. And some say Menachem, the son of Hezekiah, according to Lamentations 1:16. And our Rabbis say: The Leprous One of the house of Rabbi, is His Name, as it is written Isaiah 53:4. Rabbi Nachman said: If He is among the living, He is like me, according to Jeremiah 30:21. Rabh said: If He is among the living, He is like Rabbi Jehudah the Holy, and if among the dead he is like Daniel, the man greatly beloved. Rabbi Jehudah said, Rabh said: God will raise up to them another David, according to Jeremiah 30:9, a passage which evidently points to the future. Rabbi Papa said to Abaji: But we have this other Scripture Ezekiel 35:25, and the two terms (Messiah and David) stand related like Augustus and Caesar. Rabbi Samlai illustrated Amos 5:18, by a parable of the rooster and the bat which were looking for the light. The rooster said to the bat: I look for the light, but of what use is the light to you? So it happened to a Sadducee who said to Rabbi Abahu: When will the Messiah come? He answered him: When darkness covers this people. He said to him: Dost you intend to curse me? He replied: It is said in Scripture Isaiah 60:2. Rabbi Eliezer taught: The days of the Messiah are forty years according to Psalm 95:10. Rabbi Eleazar, the son of Asariah, said: Seventy years, according to Isaiah 23:15, according to the days of a King, the King there spoken of being the unique king, the Messiah. Rabbi said: Three generations, according to Psalm 72:5. Rabbi Hillel said: Israel shall have no more Messiah, for they had him in the days of Hezekiah. Rabbi Joseph said: May God forgive Rabbi Hillel: when did Hezekiah live? During the first Temple. And Zechariah prophesied during the second Temple, and said Zechariah 10:9. We have the tradition that Rabbi Eliezer said: The days of the Messiah are forty years. It is written Deuteronomy 8:3, 4, and again in Psalm 90:15 (showing that the days of rejoicing must be like those of affliction in the wilderness). Rabbi Dosa said: Four hundred years quoting Genesis 15:13 in connection with the same Psalm. Rabbi thought it was 365 years, according to the solar year, quoting Isaiah 63:4. He asked the meaning of the words: The day of vengeance is in My heart, Rabbi Jochanan explained them: I have manifested it to My heart, but not to My members, and Rabbi Simon benLakish: To My heart, and not to the ministering angels. Abimi taught that the days of the Messiah were to last for Israel 7,000 years (a Divine marriage week), according to Isaiah 62:5. Rabbi Jehudah said, that Rabbi Samuel said, that the days of the Messiah were to be as from the day that the world was created until now, according to Deuteronomy 11:21. Rabbi Nacham said: As from the days of Noah until now, according to Isaiah 54:9. Rabbi Chija said, that Rabbi Jochanan said: All the prophets have only prophesied in regard of the days of the Messiah; but in regard to the world to come, eye has not seen, O God, beside You, what He has prepared for him that waits for Him (Isaiah 64:4). And this is opposed to what Rabbi Samuel said, that there was no differences between this world and the days of the Messiah, except that foreign domination would cease. Upon which the Talmud goes off to discourse upon repentance, and its relation to perfect righteousness.

Lengthy as this extract may be, it will at least show the infinite differences between the Rabbinic expectation of the Messiah, and the picture of him presented in the New Testament. Surely the Messianic idea, as realized in Christ, could not have been derived from the views current in those times!

End Notes:

[24]   Signor Castelli remarks in his learned treatise (Il Messia, p. 164) that redemption is always ascribed to God, and not to the Messiah. But the distinction is of no importance, seeing that this is indeed the work of God, but carried out by the Messiah, while, on the other hand, Rabbinic writings frequently refer Israel's deliverance to the agency of the Messiah.

[25]   From the above review of Old Testament passages, all reference to sacrifices has been omitted, because, although the Synagogue held the doctrine of the vicariousness and atoning character of these sacrifices, no mention occurs of the Messiah in connection with them.

Appendix 10

The Supposed Temple Synagogue

Putting aside, as quite untenable, the idea of a regular Beth ha Midrash in the Temple (though advocated even by Wuenche), we have to inquire whether any historical evidence can be cited for the existence of a Synagogue within the bounds of the Temple buildings. The notice (Sot. 5:8) that on every Sabbatic year lection of certain portions was made to the people in the Court, and that a service was conducted there during public fasts on account of dry weather (Taan. 2:5), can not be cited as proving the existence of a regular Temple Synagogue. On the other hand, it is expressly said in Sanh. 88 b, lines 19, 20 from top, that on the Sabbaths and feast days the members of the Sanhedrin went out upon the Chel of Terrace of the temple, when questions were asked of them and answered. It is quite true that in Tos. Sanh. 5:(p. 158, col. d) we have an inaccurate statement about the second of the Temple Sanhedrin as sitting on the Chel (instead of at the entrance of the Priests Court, as in Sanh. 88 b), and that there the Sabbath and festive discourses are loosely designated as a Beth haMidrash which was on the Temple Mount. But since exactly the same description in the same words—of what took place is given in the Tosephta as in Talmud itself, the former must be corrected by the latter, or rather the term Beth ha Midrahs must be taken in the wider and more general sense as the place of Rabbinic exposition, and not as indicating any permanent Academy. But even if the words in the Tosephta were to be taken in preference to those in the Talmud itself, they contain no mention of any Temple Synagogue.

Equally inappropriate are the other arguments in favor of this supposed Temple Synagogue. The first of them is derived from a notice in Tos. Sukkah. 4:4, in which R. Joshua explains how, during the first night of the Feast of

Tabernacles, the pious never saw sleep since they went, first to the Morning Sacrifice, then of the Synagogue, then the Beth ha Midrash, then to the Evening Sacrifice, and then to the "joy of the house of water drawing" (the night feast and services in the Temple Courts). The only other argument is that from Yoma 5:1, 2 where we read that while the bullock and the goat were burned the High Priest read to the people certain portions of the Law, the roll of which was handed by the Chazzan of the Synagogue (it is not said which Synagogue) to the head of the Synagogue, by him to the Sagan, and by the Sagan to the High Priest. How utterly inconclusive inference from these notices are, need not be pointed out. More than this—the existence of a Temple Synagogue seems entirely incompatible with the remark in Yoma 5:2, that it was impossible for anyone present at the reading of the High Priest to witness the burning of the bullock and goat, and that, not because the former took place in a regular Temple Synagogue, but because the way was far and the two services were exactly at the same time. Such, so far as I know, are all the Talmudical passages from which the existence of a regular Temple Synagogue has been inferred, and with what reason, the reader may judge for himself.

It is indeed easy to understand that Rabbinism and later Judaism should have wished to locate a Synagogue and a Beth ha Midrash within the sacred precincts of the Temple itself. But it is difficult to account for the circumstance that such Christian scholars as Reland, Carpzov, and Lightfoot should have been content to repeat the statement without subjecting its grounds to personal examination. Vitringa (Synag. p. 30) almost grows indignant at the possibility of any doubt, and that, although he himself quotes passages from Maimonides to the effect that the reading of the Law by the High Priest on the Day of Atonement took place in the Court of the Women, and therefore not in any supposed Synagogue. Yet commentators generally, and writers on the Life of Christ have located the sitting of Jesus among the Doctors in the Temple in this supposed Temple Synagogue.

End Notes:

[26]   A similar arrangement is described in Sot. 5:8 as connected with the reading of the Law by the kings of Israel to the people according to Duet 30:10. Will it be argued from this that there was a Synagogue in the temple in the early days of the kings?

[27]   In a former book (Sketches of Jewish Life in the Time of Jesus) I had expressed hesitation and misgivings on the subject. These (as explained in

the text), a fuller study has converted into absolute certitude against the popularly accepted hypothesis. And what could have been the meaning of a Synagogue, which, after all, stood as substitute for the Temple and its Services, within the precincts of the Temple; or how could the respective services be so arranged as not to clash; or, lastly, have not the prayers of the Synagogue, admittedly, taken the place of the Services and Sacrifices of the Temple?

Appendix 11

The Prophecy

According to the Synoptic Gospels, the public appearance and preaching of John was the fulfillment of the prediction with which the second part of the prophecies of Isaiah opens, called by the Rabbis, the book of consolations. After a brief general preface (Isaiah 40:1, 2), the words occur which are quoted by Matthew and Mark (Isaiah 40:3), and more fully by Luke (Isaiah 40:3-5). A more appropriate beginning of the book of consolations could scarcely be conceived.

The quotation of Isaiah 50:3 is made according to the LXX, the only difference being the change of paths of our God into His paths. The divergences between the LXX and our Hebrew text of Isaiah 40:4, 5 are somewhat more numerous, but equally unimportant, the main difference from the Hebrew original lying in this, that, instead of rendering all flesh shall see it together, we have in the LXX and the New Testament, all flesh shall see the salvation of God. As it can scarcely be supposed that the LXX read for, we must regard their rendering as Targumic. Lastly, although according to the accents in the Hebrew Bible we should read, The Voice of one crying: In the wilderness prepare, etc., yet, as the LXX, the Targum, and the synoptists render, The Voice of one crying in the wilderness: Prepare, their testimony must be regarded as outweighing the authority of the accents, which are of so much later date.

But the main question is, whether Isaiah 40:3, etc., refers to Messianic times or not. Most modern interpreters regard it as applying to the return of the exiles from Babylon. This is not the place to enter on a critical discussion of the passage; but it may be remarked that the insertion of the word salvation in v.5 by the LXX seems to imply that they had viewed it as Messianic. It is, at any rate, certain that the Synopists so understood the rendering of the LXX. But this is not all. The quotation from Isaiah 40 was regarded by the Evangelists as fulfilled, when John the

Baptist announced the coming Kingdom of God. We have proof positive that, on the supposition of the correctness of the announcement made by John, they only took the view of their contemporaries in applying Isaiah 40:3, etc., to the preaching of the Baptist. The evidence here seems to be indisputable, for the Targum renders the close of v. 9 (say to the cities of Judah, Behold your God!) by the words: Say to the cities of the House of Judah, the Kingdom of your God shall be manifested.

In fact, according to the Targum, the good news are not brought by Zion nor by Jerusalem, but to Zion and to Jerusalem.

Appendix 12

The Baptism of Proselytes

Only those who have made study of it can have any idea how large, and sometimes bewildering, is the literature on the subject of Jewish Proselytes and their Baptism. Our present remarks will be confined to the Baptism of Proselytes.

1. Generally, as regards proselytes (Gerim) we have to distinguish between the Ger ha Shaar (proselyte of the gate) and Ger Toshabh (sojourner, settled among Israel), and again the Ger hatstsedeq (proselyte of righteousness) and Ger habberith (proselyte of the covenant). The former are referred to by Josephus (Ant. 14:7. 2), and frequently in the New Testament, in the KJV under the designation of those who fear God, Acts 13:16, 26; are religious, Acts 13:43; devout, Acts 13:50; 15:4, 17; worship God, Acts 15:14; 16:7. Whether the expression devout and feared God in Acts 10:2, 7 refers to proselytes of the gates is doubtful. As the proselytes of the gate only professed their faith in the God of Israel, and merely bound themselves to the observance of the so called seven Noachic commandments (on which in another place), the question of baptism need not be discussed in connection with them, since they did not even undergo circumcision.

2. It was otherwise with the proselytes of righteousness, who became children of the covenant, perfect Israelites, Israelites in every respect, both as regarded duties and privileges. All writers are agreed that three things were required for the admission of such proselytes: Circumcision (Milah), Baptism (Tebhilah), and a Sacrifice (Qorban, in the case of women: baptism and sacrifice), the latter consisting of a burnt offering

of a heifer, or of a pair of turtle doves or of young doves (Maimonides, Hilkh. Iss. Biah 13:5). After the destruction of the Temple promise had to be made of such a sacrifice when the services of the Sanctuary were restored. On this and the ordinances about circumcision it is not necessary to enter further. That baptism was absolutely necessary to make a proselyte is so frequently stated as not to be disputed (See Maimonides, u. s.; the tractate Massekheth Gerim in Kirchheims Septem Libri Talm. Parvi, pp. 38-44 [which, however, adds little to our knowledge]; Targum on Exodus 12:44; Ber. 47 b; Kerith. 9 a; Jeremiah Yebam. p. 8 d; Yebam. 45 b, 46 a and b, 48 b, 76 a; Ab. Sar. 57 a, 59 a, and other passages). There was, indeed a difference between Rabbis Joshua and Eliezer, the former maintaining that baptism alone without circumcision, the latter that circumcision alone without baptism, sufficed to make a proselyte, but the sages decided in favor of the necessity of both rites (Yebam. 46 a and b). The baptism was to be performed in the presence of three witnesses, ordinarily Sanhedrists (Yebam. 47 b), but in case of necessity others might act. The person to be baptized, having cut his hair and nails, undressed completely, made fresh profession of his faith before what were the fathers of the baptism (our Godfathers, Kethub. 11 a; Erub. 15 a), and then immersed completely, so that every part of the body was touched by the water. The rite would be accompanied by exhortations and benedictions (Maimonides, Hilkh. Milah 3:4; Hilkh. Iss. Biah 14:6). Baptism was not to be administered at night, nor on a Sabbath or feast day (Yebam. 46 b). Women were attended by those of their own sex, the Rabbis standing at the door outside. Yet unborn children of proselytes did not require to be baptized, because they were born in holiness (Yebam. 78 a). In regard to the little children of proselytes opinions differed. A person under age was indeed received, but not regarded as properly an Israelite until he had attained majority. Secret baptism, or where only the mother brought a child, was not acknowledged. In general, the statements of a proselyte about his baptism required attestation by witnesses. But the children of a Jewess or of a proselyte were regarded as Jews, even if the baptism of the father was doubtful.

It was indeed a great thing when, in the words of Maimonides, a stranger sought shelter under the wings of the Shechinah, and the change of condition which he underwent was regarded as complete. The waters of baptism were to him in very truth, though in a far different from the

Christian sense, the bath of regeneration (Titus 3:5). As he stepped out of these waters he was considered as born anew, in the language of the Rabbis, as if he were a little child just born (Yeb. 22 a; 48 b; 97 b), as a child of one day (Mass. Ger. 102). But this new birth was not a birth from above in the sense of moral or spiritual renovation, but only as implying a new relationship to God, to Israel, and to his own past, present, and future. It was expressly enjoined that all the difficulties of his new citizenship should first be set before him, and if, after that, he took upon himself the yoke of the law, he should be told how all those sorrows and persecutions were intended to convey a greater blessing, and all those commandments to redound to greater merit. More especially was he to regard himself as a new man in reference to his past. Country, home, habits, friends, and relation were all changed. The past, with all that had belonged to it, was past, and he was a new man, the old, with its defilements, was buried in the waters of baptism. This was carried out with such pitiless logic as not only to determine such questions as those of inheritance, but that it was declared that, except, for the sake of not bringing proselytism into contempt, a proselyte might have wedded his own mother or sister (comp. Yeb. 22 a; Sanh. 58 b). It is a curious circumstances that marriage with a female proselyte was apparently very popular (Horay. 13 a, line 5 from bottom; see also Shem. R. 27), and the Talmud names at least three celebrated doctors who were the offspring of such unions (comp. Derenbourg, Hide la Palest., p. 223, note 2). The praises of proselytism are also sung in Vayy. R. 1.

If anything could have further enhanced the value of such proselytism, it would have been its supposed antiquity. Tradition traced it up to Abraham and Sarah, and the expression (Genesis 12:5) the souls that they had gotten was explained as referring to their proselytes, since everyone that makes a proselyte is as if he made (created) him (Ber. R. 39, comp also the Targums Pseudo Jon. and Jerus. and Midr. on Song of Solomon 1:3). The Talmud, differing in this from the Targumim, finds in Exodus 2:5 a reference to the baptism of Pharoahs daughter (Sotah 12 b, line 3; Megill. 13 a, line 11). In Shem. R. 27 Jethro is proved to have been a convert, from the circumstances that his original name had been Jether (Exodus 4:18), an additional letter (Jethro), as in the case of Abraham, having been added to his name when became a proselyte (comp. also Zebhach. 116 a and Targum Psalm Jon. on Exodus 16:6, 27, Numbers 24:21. To pass over other instances, we are pointed to Ruth (Targum on Ruth 1:10, 15). and to Nebuzaradan, who is also described as a proselyte (Sanh. 96 b, line 19 form the bottom). But is said that in the days of David and Solomon proselytes were not admitted by the Sanhedrin because their motives were suspected (Yeb. 76 a), or that at least they were closely, watched.

But although the baptism of proselytes seems thus far beyond doubt, Christian theologians have discussed the question, whether the rite was practiced at the time of Christ, or only introduced after the destruction of the Temple and its Services, to take the place of the Sacrifice previously offered. The controversy, which owed its origin chiefly to dogmatic prejudices on the part of Lutherans, Calvinists, and Baptist's, has since been continued on historical or quasi-historical grounds. The silence of Josephus and Philo can scarcely be quoted in favor of the later origin of the rite. On the other hand, it may be urged that, as Baptism did not take the place of sacrifices in any other instance, it would be difficult account for the origin of such a rite in connection with the admission of proselytes.

Again, if a Jew who had become Levitically defiled, required immersion, it is difficult to suppose that a pagan would have been admitted to all the services of the Sanctuary without a similar purification. But we have also positive testimony (which the objections of Winer, Keil, and Leyrer, in my opinion do not invalidate), that the baptism of proselytes existed in the time of Hillel and Shammai: For, whereas the school of Shammai is said to have allowed a proselyte who was circumcised on the eve of the Passover, to partake after baptism of the Passover, the school of Hillel prohibitted it. This controversy must be regarded as providing that at that time (previous to Christ) the baptism of proselytes was customary (Pes. 8:8, Eduy. 5:2).

Apendix 13

Jewish Angelology and Demonology the Fall of the Angels

Without here entering on a discussion of the doctrine of Angels and devils as presented in Holy Scripture, the Apocrypha, and the Pseudepigrapha, it will be admitted that considerable progression may be marked as we advance from even the latest Canonical to Apocryphal, and again from these to the Pseudepigraphic Writings. The same remark applies even more strongly to a comparison of the later with Rabbinic literature. There we have comparatively little of the Biblical in its purity. But, added to it, we now find much that is the outcome of Eastern or of desiring imagination, of national conceit, of ignorant superstition, and of foreign, especially Persian, elements. In this latter respect it is true, not as regards the doctrine of good and evil Angels, but much of its Rabbinic elaboration, that the names of the Angels (and of the months) were brought form Babylon (Jeremiah Rosh. haSh. 56 d; Ber. r. 48), and with the names, not a few of the notions regarding them. At the same time, it would be unjust to deny that mush of the symbolism which it is evidently intended to convey is s singularly beautiful.

I. ANGELOLOGY

1. Creation, Number, Duration and Location of the Angels. We are now considering, not the Angel Princes but that vast unnumbered Host generally designated as the ministering Angels. Opinions differ (Ber. R. 3) whether they were created on the second day as being spirit, winds

(Psalm 104:4), or on the fifth day (Isaiah 6:2) in accordance with the words of Creation on those days. Viewed in reference to God's Service and Praise, they are a flaming fire: in regard to their office, winged messengers (Pirqe de R. El. 4). But not only so: every day ministering Angels are created, whose apparent destiny is only to raise the praise of God, after which they pass away into the fiery stream (Nahar deNur) from which they originally issued (Chag. 14 a; Ber. R. 78). More than this, a new Angel is created to execute to every command of God, and then passes away (Chag. u. s.). This continual new creation of Angels, which is partly a beautiful allegory, partly savors of the doctrine of emanation, is Biblical supported by an appeal to Lament. 3:23. Thus it may be said that daily a Kath, or company, of Angels is created for daily service of God, and that every word which proceeds from His mouth becomes an Angel [Messenger, mark here the ideal unity of Word and Deed], (Chang. 14 a).

The vast number of that Angelic Host, and the consequent safety of Israel as against its enemies, was described in the most hyperbolic language. There were 12 Mazzaloth (signs of the Zodiac), each having 30 chiefs of armies, each chief with 30 legions, each legion with 30 leaders, each leader with 30 captains, each captain with 30 under him, and each of these things with 365,000 stars, and all were created for the sake of Israel! (Ber. 32. b.) Similarly, when Nebuchadnezzar proposed to ascend into heaven, and to exalt his throne above the stars, and be like the Most High, the Bath Qol replied to this grandson of Nimrod that man's age was 70, or at most 80 years, while the way from earth to the firmament occupied 500 years, a thickness of the firmament was 500 years, the feet of the living creatures were equal to all that had preceded, and the joints of their feet to as many as had preceded them, and so on increasingly through all their members up to their horns, after which came the Throne of Glory, the feet of which again equaled all that had preceded, and so on (Chag. 13 a). In connection with this we read in Chag. 12 b that there are seven heavens: the Vdon, in which there is the sun; Riqia, in which the sun shines, and the moon, stars, and planets are fixed; Shechaqim, in which are the millstones to make the manna for the pious; Zebhul, in which the Upper Jerusalem, and the Temple and the Altar, and in which Michael, the chief Angel Prince, offers sacrifices; Maon, in which the Angels of the Ministry are, who sing by night and are silent by day for the sake of the honor of Israel (who now have their services); Machon, in which are the treasuries of snow, hail, the chambers of noxious dews, and of the receptacles of water, the chamber of wind, and the cave of mist, and their doors are of fire; lastly, Araboth, wherein Justice, Judgment and Righteousness are, the treasures of Life, of Peace and of Blessing, the soul of the righteous, and the spirits and souls of those who are to be born in the future, and the dew by which the dead are to be raised. There also are the Ophanim, and the Seraphim, and the living creatures and the ministering Angels, and the Throne of Glory and over them is enthroned the Great King. [For a description of this Throne and of the Appearance of its King, see Pirqe de R. Eliez. 4.] On the other hand, sometimes every power and phenomenon in Nature is hypostatized into an Angel, such as hail, rain, wind, sea etc.; similarly, every occurrence, such as life, death, nourishment, poverty, as it is expressed: there is not stalk of grass upon earth but it has its Angels in heaven (Ber R. 10). This seems to approximate the views of Alexandrian Mysticism. So also, perhaps, the idea that certain Biblical heroes became after death Angels. But as this may be regarded as implying their service as messengers of God. We leave it for the present.

2.   The Angel Princes, their location, names, and offices. Any limitation, as to duration or otherwise, of the Ministering Angels does not apply either to the Ophanim (or wheel angels), the Seraphim, the Cayoth (or living creatures), nor to the Angel Princes (Ber. R. 78). In Chag. 13 a, b the name Chashamal is given to the living creatures. The word is explained as composed of two others which mean silence and speech, it being beautifully explained, that they keep silence when the Word proceeds out of the mouth of God, and speak when He has ceased. It would be difficult exactly to state the number of the Angel Princes. The 70 nations, of which the world is composed, had each their Angel Prince (Targ. Jeremiah on Gen 11:7, 8; comp. Ber. R. 56; Shem. R. 21; Vayy1:R. 29; Ruth R. ed. Warsh. p. 36 b), who plead their cause with God. Therefore these Angels are really hostile to Israel, and may be regarded as not quite good Angels, and are cast down when the nationality which they represent is destroyed. It may have been as a reflection on Christian teaching that Israel was described as not requiring any representative with God, like the Gentiles. For, as will soon appear, this was not the general view entertained. Besides these Gentile Angel Princes there were other chiefs, whose office will be explained in the sequel. Of these 5 are especially mentioned, of whom four surrounded the Throne of God: Michael, Gabriel, Rephael, and

Uriel. But the greatest of all is Metatron, who is under the Throne, and before it. These Angels are privileged to be within the Pargod, or cloudy veil, while the others only hear the Divine commands or counsels outside this curtain (Chag. 16 a, Pirqe d. R. El. iv.). It is a slight variation when the Targum Pseudo Jonathan on Deuteronomy 34:6 enumerates the following as the 6 principal Angels: Michael, Gabriel, Metatron, Yopheil, Uriel, and Yophyophyah. The Book of Enoch (Chapter 20) speaks also of 6 principal Angels, while Pirqe d. R. Eliez. 4 mentions seven. In that very curious passage (Berakhoth 51 a) we read of three directions given by Suriel, Prince of the Face, to preserve the Rabbis from the Techaspith (company of Evil Angels), or according to others, form Istalganith (another company of Evil Angels). In Chag. 13 b we read of an Angel called Sandalpon, who stands upon the earth, while his head reaches 500 years way beyond the living creatures. He is supposed to stand behind the Merkabah (the throne chariot), and make crowns for the Creator, which rise of their own accord. We also read of Sagsagel, who taught Moses the sacred Name of God, and was present at his death. But, confining ourselves to the five principal Angel chiefs, we have, a. Metaron, who appears most closely to correspond to the Angel of the Face, or the Logos. He is the representative of God. In the Talmud (Sanh. 38 b) a Christian is introduced as clumsily starting a controversy on this point, that, according to the Jewish contention, Exodus 24:1 should have read, Come up to Me. On this R. Idith explained that the expression referred to the Metatron (Exodus 33:21), but denied the inference that Metatron was either to be adored, or had power to forgive sins, or that he was to be regarded as a Mediator. In continuation of this controversy we are told (Chang. 15 a, b) that, when an apostate Rabbi had seen Metatron sitting in heaven, and would have interfered from it that there were two supreme powers, Metatron received from another Angel 60 fiery stripes so as to prove his inferiority! In Targ. Psalm Jon. on Genesis 5:24 he is called the Great Scribe, and also the Prince of this world. He is also designated as the Youth, and in the Kabbalah as the Little God, who had 7 names like the Almighty, and shared His Majesty. He is also called the Prince of the Face, and described as the Angel who sits in the innermost chamber (Chag. 5 b), while the other Angels hear their commands outside the Veil (Chag. 16 a). He is represented as showing the unseen to Moses (Siphre, p. 141 a), and as instructing infants who have died without receiving knowledge (Abhod. Zar. 3 b). In the Introduction to the

Midrash on Lamentations there is a revolting story in which Metatron is represented as proposing to shed tears in order that God might not have to weep over the destruction of Jerusalem, to which, however, the Almighty is made to refuse His assent. We hesitate to quote further from the passage. In Siphre on Deuteronomy (ed. Freidm. p. 141 a) Metatron is said to have shown Moses the whole of Palestine. He is also said to have gone before Israel in the Wilderness. b. Michael (who is like God?), or the Great Prince (Chag. 12 b). He stands at the right hand of the throne of God. According to Targ. Psalm Jon. on Exodus 24:1, he is the Prince of Wisdom. According to the Targum on Psalm 135:7, 8, the Prince of Jerusalem, the representative of Israel. According to Sebach. 62 a he offers upon the heavenly Altar; according to some, the soul of the pious; according to others, lambs of fire. But, although Michael is the Prince of Israel, he is not to be invoked by them (Jeremiah Ber. ix. 13 a). In Yoma 77 a we have an instance of his ineffectual advocacy for Israel before the destruction of Jerusalem. The origin of his name as connected with the Song of Moses at the Red Sea is explained in Bemidb. R. 2. Many instances of his activity are related. Thus, he delivered Abraham from the fiery oven of Nimrod, and afterwards, also, the Three Children out of the fiery furnace. He was the principal or middle Angel of the three who came to announce to Abraham the birth of Isaac, Gabriel being at his right, and Rephael at his left. Michael also saved Lot. Michael and Gabriel wrote down that the primogeniture belonged to Jacob, and God confirmed it. Michael and Gabriel acted as friends of the bridegroom in the nuptials of Adam. Yet they could not bear to look upon the glory of Moses. Michael is also supposed to have been the Angel in the bush (according to others, Gabriel). At the death of Moses, Michael prepared his bier, Gabriel spread a cloth over the head of Moses, and Sagsagel over his feet. In the world to come Michael would pronounce the blessing over the fruits of Eden, then hand them to Gabriel, who would give them to the patriarchs, and so on to David. The superiority of Michael over Gabriel is asserted in Ber. 4 b, where, by an ingenious combination with Daniel 10:13, it is shown that Isaiah 6:6 applies to him (both having the word, one). It is added that Michael flies in one fight, Gabriel in two, Elijah in four, and the Angel of death in eight flights (no doubt to give time for repentance). c. Gabriel (the Hero of God) represents rather judgment, while Michael represents mercy. Thus he destroyed Sodom (Bab. Mez. 86 b, and other places). He restored to Tamar the pledges of Judah, which Sammael had taken away (Sot. 10 b). He struck the servants of the Egyptian princess, who would have kept their mistress from taking Moses out of the water (Sot. 12 b); also Moses, that he might cry and so awaken pity. According to some, it was he who delivered the Three Children; but all are agreed that he killed the men that were standing outside the furnace. He also smote the army of Sennacherib. The passage in Ezekiel 10:2, 7 was applied to Gabriel, who had received from the Cherub two coals, which, however, he retained for six years, in the hope that Israel might repent. He is supposed to be referred to in Ezekiel 9:4 as affixing the mark on the forehead which is a, drawn, in the wicked, in blood (Shabb. 55 a). We are also told that he had instructed Moses about making the Candlestick, on which occasion he had put on an apron, like a goldsmith; and that he had disputed with Michael about the meaning of a word. To his activity the bringing of fruits to maturity is ascribed, perhaps because he was regarded as made of fire, while Michael was made of snow (Deb. R. 5). These Angels are supposed to stand beside each other, without the fire of the one injuring the snow of the other. The curious legend is connected with him (Shabb. 56 b, Sanh. 21 b), that, when Solomon married the daughter of Pharaoh, Gabriel descended into the sea, and fixed a reed in it, around which a mud bank gathered, on which a forest sprang up. On this site imperial Rome was built. The meaning of the legend, or perhaps rather allegory, seems (as explained in other parts of this book) that, when Israel began to turn from God, the punishment through its enemies was prepared, which culminated in the dominion of Rome. In the future age Gabriel would hunt and slay Leviathan. This also may be a parabolic representation of the destruction of Israel's enemies. d. Of Uriel (God is my light) and Rephael (God heals) it need only be said, that the one stands at the left side of the Throne of glory, the other behind it.

3. The Ministering Angels and their Ministry. The ministry of the Angels may be divided into two parts, that of praising God, and that of executing His commands. In regard to the former, there are 684,000 myriads who daily praise the Name of God. From sunrise to sundown they say: Holy, holy, holy, and from sundown to sunrise: Blessed be the Glory of God from its place. In connection with this we may mention the beautiful allegory (Shem. R. 21) that the Angel of prayer weaves crowns for God out of the prayer of Israel. As to the execution of the Divine commands by the Angels, it is suggested (Aboth d. R. Nathan

8) that their general designation as ministering Angels might have led to jealousy among them. Accordingly, their names were always a composition of that of God with the special commission entrusted to them (Shem. r. 29), so that the name of each Angel depended in Yalkut (Volume 2: Par. 797), where we are told that each Angel has a tablet on his heart, in which the Name of God and that of the Angel is combined. This change of names explained the answer of the Angel to Manoah (Bemidb. R. 10). It is impossible to enumerate all the instances of Angelic activity recorded in Talmudic writings. Angels had performed the music at the first sacrifice of Adam; they had announced the consequences of his punishment; they had cut off the hands and feet of the serpent; they had appeared to Abraham in the form of a baker, a sailor, and an Arab. 120,000 of them had danced before Jacob when he left Laban; 4,000 myriads of them were ready to fight for him against Esau; 22,000 of them descended on Sinai and stood beside Israel when, in their terror at the Voice of God, they fled for twelve miles. Angels were directed to close the gates of heaven when the prayer of Moses with the All powerful, Ineffable Name in it, which he had learn from Sagsagel, would have prevented his death. Finally, as they were pledged to help Israel, so would they also punish every apostate Israelite. Especially would they execute that most terrible punishment of throwing souls to each other from one world to another. By the side of these debasing superstitions we come upon beautiful allegories, such as that a good and an evil Angel always accompanied man, but especially on the eve of the Sabbath when he returned from the Synagogue, and that for every precept he observed God sent him a protecting Angel. This is realistically developed in Pirke d. R. El. 15, where the various modes and time which the good Angels keep man from destruction are set forth.

It is quite in accordance with what we know of the system of Rabbinism, that the heavenly host should be represented as forming a sort of consultative Sanhedrin. Since God never did anything without first taking counsel with the family above (Sanh. 38 b), it had been so when He resolved to create man. Afterward the Angels had interceded for Adam, and, when God pointed to his disobedience, they had urged that thus death would also come upon Moses and Aaron, who were sinless, since one fate must come to the just and the unjust. Similarly, they had interceded for Isaac, when Abraham was about to offer him and finally dropped three tears on the sacrificial knife, by which its edge became blunted. And so through the rest of Israel's history, where on all critical occasions Jewish legend introduces the Angels on the scene.

4. Limitation of the power of the Angels. According to Jewish ideas, the faculties, the powers, and even the knowledge of Angels were limited. They are pure spiritual beings (Vayyikra R. 24), without sensuous requirements (Yoma 75 b), without hatred, envy, or jealousy (Chag. 14), and without sin (Pirqe d. R. El. 46). They know much, notably the future (Ab. d. R. Nath. 37), and have part in the Divine Light. They live on the beams of the Divine Glory (Bem. R. 21), are not subject to our limitations as to movement, see but are not seen (A b. d. R. Nath. u. s.), can turn their face to any side (Ab. d. R. Nath. 37), and only appear to share in our ways, such as in eating (Bar. R. 48). Still, in many respects they are inferior to Israel, and had been employed in ministry (Ber. R. 75). They were unable to give names to the animals, which Adam did (Priqe d. R. El. 13). Jacob had wrestled with the Angel and prevailed over him when the Angel wept (Chull. 92 a). Thus it was rather their nature than their powers or dignity which distinguished them from man. No angel could do two messages at the same time (Ber. R. 50). In general they are merely instruments blindly to do a certain work, not even beholding the Throne of Glory (Bemidb. R. 14), but needed mutual assistance (Vayyikia R. 31). They are also liable to punishments (Chag. 16 a). Thus, they were banished from their station for 138 years, because they had told Lot that God would destroy Sodom, while the Angel Princes of the Gentiles were kept in chains until the days of Jeremiah. As regards their limited knowledge, with the exception of Gabriel, they do not understand Chaldee or Syriac (Sot. 33 a). The realistic application of their supposed ignorance on this score need not here be repeated (see Shabb. 12 b). As the Angels are inferior to the righteous, it follows that they are so to Israel. God had informed the Angels that the creation of man was superior to theirs, and it had excited their envy. Adam attained a place much nearer to God than they, and God loved Israel more than the Angels. And God had left all the ministering Angels in order to come to Moses, and when He communicated with him it was directly, and the Angels standing between them did not hear what passed. In connection with this ministry of the Angels on behalf of Biblical heroes a curious legend may here find its place. From a combination of Exodus 16:4 with

Exodus 2:15 the strange inference was made that Moses had actually been seized by Pharaoh. Two different accounts of how he escaped from his power are given. According to the one, the sword with which he was to be executed rebounded from the neck of Moses, and was broken, to which Song of Solomon 5:5 was supposed to refer, it being added that the rebound killed the would be executioner. According to another account, an Angel took the place of Moses, and thus enabled him to fly, his flight being facilitated by the circumstances that all the attendants of the king were miraculously rendered either dumb, deaf, or blind, so that they could not execute the command of their master. Of this miraculous interjection Moses is supposed to have been reminded in Exodus 4:11, for his encouragement in undertaking his mission to Pharaoh. In the exaggeration of Jewish boastfulness in the Law, it was said that the Angels had wished to receive the Law, but that they had not been granted this privilege (Job 16:21). And sixty myriads of Angels had crowned with two crowns every Israelite who at Mount Sinai had taken upon himself the Law (Shabb. 88 a). In view of all this we need scarcely mention the Rabbinic prohibition to address to the Angels prayers, even although they bore them to heaven (Jeremiah Ber. ix. 1), or to make pictorial representations of them (Targ. Ps Jon. on Exodus 20:23; Mechilta on the passage, ed. Weiss, p. 80 a).

5. The Angels are not absolutely good. Strange as it may seem, this is really the view expressed by the Rabbis. Thus it is said that, when God consulted the Angels, they opposed the creation of man, and that, for this reason, God had concealed from them that man would sin. But more than this, the Angels had actually conspired for the fall of man (the whole of this is also related in Pirqe d. R. El. 13). Nor had their jealous and envy been confined to that occasion. They had accused Abraham, that, when he gave a great feast at the weaning of Isaac, he did not even offer to God a bullock or a goat. Similarly, they had laid charges against Ishmael, in the hope that he might be left to perish of thirst. They had reasoned earnestly against Jacob, because he went to sleep at Bethel. But especially had they, from envy, opposed Moses ascension into heaven; they had objected to his being allowed to write down the Law, falsely urging that Moses would claim the glory of it for himself, and they are represented, in a strangely blasphemous manner, as having been with difficulty appeased by God. In Shabb. 88 b we have an account of how Moses pacified the Angels, by showing that the Law was not suitable for them, since they were not subject to sinful

desires, upon which they became the friends of Moses, and each taught him some secret, among others the Angel of death how to arrest the pestilence. Again, it is said, that the Angels were prone to bring charges against Israel, and that, when Manasseh wished to repent, the Angels shut the entrance to heaven, so that his prayer might not penetrate into the presence of God.

Equally profane, though in another direction, is the notion that Angels might be employed for magical purposes. This had happened at the siege of Jerusalem under Nebuchadnezzar, when, after the death of that mighty hero Abika, the son of Gaphteri, Chananeel, the uncle of Jeremiah, had conjured up ministering Angels, who frightened the Chaldees into flight. On this God had changed their names, when Chananee, unable any longer to command their services, had summoned up the Prince of the World by using the Ineffable Name, and lifted Jerusalem into the air, but God had trodden it down again, to all which Lamentations 2:1 referred (Yalk. Volume 2: p. 166 c and d, Par. 1001). The same story is repeated in another place (p. 167, last line of col. c, and col. d), with the addition that the leading inhabitants of Jerusalem had proposed to defend the city by conjuring up the Angels of Water and Fire, and surrounding their city with walls of water, of fire, or of iron; but their hopes were disappointed when God assigned to the Angel names different from those which they had previously possessed, so that when called upon they were unable to do what was expected of them.

6. The Names of the Angels. Besides those already enumerated, we may here mention, the Sar ha Olam, or Prince of the World (Yeb. 16 b); the Prince of the Sea, whose name is supposed to have been Rahab, and whom God destroyed because he had refused to receive the waters which had covered the world, and the smell of whose dead body would kill everyone if it were not covered by water. Dumah is the Angel of the realm of the dead (Ber. 18 b). When the soul of the righteous leaves the body, the ministering Angels announce it before God, Who sends them to meet it. Three hosts of Angels then proceed on this errand, each quoting successively one clause of Isaiah 15:2. On the other hand, when the wicked leave the body, they are met by three hosts of destroying Angels, one of which repeats Isaiah 48:22, another Isaiah 1:11, and the third Ezekiel 32:19 (Keth. 104 a). Then the souls

of all the dead, good or bad, are handed over to Dunah. Yorqemi is the Prince of hail. He had proposed to cool the fiery furnace into which the Three Children were cast, but Gabriel had objected that this might seem a deliverance by natural means, and being himself the Prince of the fire, had proposed, instead of this, to make the furnace cold within and hot without, in order both to deliver the Three Children and to destroy those who watched outside (Pes. 118 a and b) Ridya, or Rayda is the Angel of rain. One of the Rabbis professed to describe him from actual vision as like a calf whose lips were open, standing between the Upper and the Lower Deep, and saying to the Upper Deep, Let your waters run down, and to the Lower, Let your waters spring up. The representation of this Angel as a calf may be due to the connection between rain and plowing, and in connection with this observe that Ryda means both a plough and plowing (Taan. 25 b). Of other Angels we will only name the Ruach Pisqonith, or Spirit of decision, who is supposed to have made most daring objection to what God had said, Ezekiel 15:3, in which he is defended by the Rabbis, since his activity had been on behalf of Israel (Sanh. 44 b); Naqid, the Angel of Food; Nabhel, the Angel of Poverty; the two Angels of Healing; the Angel of Dreams, Lailah; and even the Angel of Lust.

It is not asserted that all these grossly materialistic superstitious and profane views were entertained in Palestine, or at the time of Jesus, still less that they are shared by educated Jews in the West. But they certainly date from Talmudic times; they embody the only teaching of Rabbinic writings about the Angels which we possess, and therefore, how ever introduced or developed, their roots must be traced back to far earlier times than those when they were taught in Rabbinic Academies. All the more that modern Judaism would indignantly repudiate them, do they bear testimony against Rabbinic teaching. And one thing at least must be evident, for the sake of which we have undertaken the task of recording at such length views and statements repugnant to all reverent feeling. The contention of certain modern writers that the teaching about Angels in the New Testament is derived from, and represents Jewish notions must be perceived to be absolutely groundless and contrary to fact. In truth, the teaching of the New Testament on the subject of Angels represents, as compared with that of the Rabbis, not only a return to the purity of Old Testament teaching, but, we might almost say, a new revelation.

II. SATANOLOGY AND FALL OF THE ANGELS.

The difference between the Satanology of the Rabbis and of the New Testament is, if possible, even more marked than that in their Angelology. In general we note that, with the exception of the word Satan, none of the names given to the great enemy in the New Testament occurs in Rabbinic writing. More important still, the latter contain no mention of a Kingdom of Satan. In other words, the power of the evil is not contrasted with that of good, nor Satan with God. The devil is presented rather as the enemy of man, than of God and of good. This marks a fundamental difference. The New Testament sets before us two opposing kingdoms, or principles, which exercise absolute sway over man. Christ is the Stronger one who overcomes the strong man armed, and taken from him not only his spoils, but his armor (Luke 11:21, 22). It is a moral contest in which Satan is vanquished, and the liberation of his subjects is the consequence of his own subdual. This implies the deliverance of man from the power of the enemy, not only externally but internally, and substitution of a new principle of spiritual life for the old one. It introduces a moral element, both as the ground and as the result of the contest. From this point of view the difference between the New Testament and Rabbinism cannot be too much emphasized, and it is no exaggeration to say that this alone—the question here being one of principle not of details, would mark the doctrine of Christ as fundamentally divergent from, and incomparably superior to, that of Rabbinism. From where has this Man this wisdom? Assuredly, it may be answered, not from His contemporaries.

Since Rabbinism viewed the great enemy only as the envious and malicious opponent of man, the spiritual element was entirely eliminated. Instead of the personified principle of Evil, to which there is response in us, and of which all have some experience, we have only a clumsy and, to speak plainly, often a stupid hater. This holds equally true in regard to the threefold aspect under which Rabbinism presents the devil: as Satan (also called Sammael); as the Yetser haRa, or evil impulse personified; and as the Angel of death, in other words, as the Accuser, Tempter, and Punisher. Before explaining the Rabbinic views on each of these points, it is necessary to indicate them in regard to:

1. The Fall of Satan and of his Angels. This took place, not before, but subsequently to the creation of man. As related in Pirqe de R. Eliezer, Chapter 13, the primary cause of it was jealously and envy on the part of the Angels. Their opposition to man's creation is also described in

Ber. R. 8, although there the fall of man is not traced to Satanic agency. But we have (as before stated) a somewhat blasphemous account of the discussions in the heavenly Sanhedrin, whether or not man should be created. While the dispute was still proceeding God actually created man, and addressed the ministering Angels: Why dispute any longer? Man is already created. In the Pirqe de R. Eliezer, we are only told that the Angels had in vain attempted to oppose the creation of man. The circumstance that his superiority was evidenced by his ability to give names to all creatures, induced them to lay a plot against Adam, so that by his fall they might obtain supremacy. Now of all Angel Princes in heaven Sammael was the first, distinguished above. Taking the company of Angels subject to him, he came down upon earth, and selected as the only fit instrument for his designs the serpent, which at that time had not only speech, but hands and feet, and was in stature and appearance like the camel. In the language of the Pirqe de R. Eliezer, Sammael took complete possession of the serpent, even as demoniacs act under the absolute control of evil spirits. Then Sammael, in the serpent, first deceived the woman, and next imposed on her by touching the tree of life (although the tree cried out), saying, that he had actually touched the tree, of which he pretended the touch had been forbidden on pain of death (Genesis 3:3), and yet he had not died! Upon this Eve followed his example, and touched the tree when she immediately saw the Angel of death coming against her. Afraid that she would die and God give another wife to Adam, she led her husband into sin of disobedience. The story of the Fall is somewhat differently related in Ber. R. 18, 19. No mention is there earlier of Sammael or of his agency, and the serpent is represented as beguiling Eve from a wish to marry her, and for that purpose to compass the death of Adam.

Critical ingenuity may attempt to find a symbolic meaning in many of the details of the Jewish legend of the Fall, although, to use moderate language, they seem equally profane and repulsive. But this will surely be admitted by all, that the Rabbinic account of the fall of the Angels, as connected with fall of man, equally contrasts with the reverent silence of the Old Testament narrative and the magnificent teaching of the New Testament about sin and evil.

2. Satan, or Sammael, as the accuser of man. And clumsy are his accusations. Thus the statement (Genesis 22:1) that God tempted Abraham is, in

Jewish legend, transformed (Sanh. 89 b) into a scene, where, in the great upper Sanhedrin (Ber. R. 56), Satan brings accusation against the Patriarch. All his previous piety had been merely interested; and now when, at the age of one hundred, God had given him a son, he had made a great feast and not offered anything whatever to the Almighty. On this God is represented as answering, that Abraham was ready to sacrifice not only an animal but his own son; and this had been the occasion of the temptation of Abraham. That this legend is very ancient, indeed pre-Christian (a circumstance of considerable importance to the student of this history) appears from its occurrence, though in more general form, in the Book of Jubilees, Chapter 15:In Ber.R. 55 and in Tacchuma (ed. Warsh p. 29 a and b), the legend is connected with a dispute between Isaac and Ishmael as to their respective merits, when former declares himself ready to offer up his life to God. In Tanchuma (u. s.) we are told that this was one of the great merits of man, to which the Almighty and pointed when the Angels made objection to his creation.

3. Satan, or Sammael, as the seducer of man. This statement in Baba B. 16 a which identifies Satan with the Yetser haRa, or evil impulse in man, must be regarded are a rationalistic attempt to gloss over the older teaching about Sammael, by representing him as a personification of the evil inclination within us. For, the Talmud not only distinguishes between a personal Satan without, and evil inclination within man, but expressly ascribes to God the creation of the Yetser haRa in man as he was before the Fall, the occurrence of two in the word (and He formed, Genesis 2:7) being supposed to indicate the existence of two impulses in us, the Yetser Tobh and the Yetser haRa (Ber. 61 a). And it is stated that this existence of evil in man's original nature was infinite comfort in the fear which would otherwise beset us in trouble (Ber. R. 14). More than this (as will now be shown), the existence of this evil principle within us was declared to be absolutely necessary for the continuance of the world (Yoma 69 b, Sanh. 64 a).

Satan, or Sammael, is introduced as the seducer of man in all the great events of Israel's history. With varying legendary additions the story of Satan's attempts to prevent the obedience of Abraham and the sacrifice of Isaac is told in Sanh. 89 b, Ber. R. 56, and Tanchuma, p. 30 a and b. Yet there is nothing even astute, only a coarse realism, about the description of the clumsy attempts of Satan to turn Abraham from, or to hinder him in, his purpose; to influence Isaac; or to frighten Sarah. Nor are the other personages in the legend more successfully sketched. There is an absence of all higher conception in the references to the Almighty, a painful amount of downright untruthfulness about Abraham, lamentable boastfulness and petty spite about Isaac, while the Sarah of the Jewish legend is rather a weak old Eastern woman than the mother in Israel. To hold perversions of the Old Testament by the side of the New Testament conception of the motives of lives of the heroes of old, or the doctrinal inferences and teaching of the Rabbis by those of Christ and His Apostles, were to compare darkness with light.

The same remarks apply to the other legends in which Satan is introduced as seducer. Anything more childish could scarcely be invented than this, that, when Sammael could not otherwise persuade Israel that Moses would not return from Mount Sinai, he at last made his bier appear before them in the clouds (Shab. 89 a), unless it be this story, that when Satan would seduce David he assumed the form of a bird, and that, when David shot at it, Bath Sheba suddenly looked up, thus gaining the king by her beauty (Sanh. 107 a). In both these instances the obvious purpose is to offer excuses for the guilt whether of Israel or of David, which is in other places entirely explained away as not due to disobedience or to lust.

4. As the Enemy of man, Satan seeks to hurt and destroy him; and he is the Angel of death. Thus, when Satan had failed in shaking the constancy of Abraham and Isaac, he attacked Sarah (Yalkut, 1:Par. last lines p. 28 b). To his suggestions, or rather false reports, her death had been due, either from fright at being told that Isaac had been offered (Pirqe de R. El. 32, and Targum Psalm Jon.), or else from the shock, when after all she learned that Isaac was not dead (Ber. R. 58). Similarly, Satan had sought to take from Tamar the pledges which Judah had given her. He appeared as an old man to show Nimrod how to have Abraham cast into the fiery oven, at the same time persuading Abraham not to resist it, etc. Equally silly are the representations of Satan as the Angel of death. According to Abod. Zar. 20 b, the dying sees his enemy with a drawn sword, on the point of which a drop of gall trembles. In his fright he opens his mouth and swallows this drop, which accounts for the paleness of the face and the corruption that follows. According to another Rabbi, the Angel of death really uses his sword, although, on account of the dignity of humanity, the wound which he inflicts is not allowed to be visible. It is difficult to imagine a narrative more repulsive

than that of the death of Moses according to Deb. R. 11. Beginning with the triumph of Sammael over Michael at the expected event, it tells how Moses had asked rather to be changed into a beast or a bird than to die; how Gabriel and Michael had successively refused to bring the soul of Moses; how Moses, knowing that Sammael was coming for the purpose, had armed himself with the Ineffable Name; how Moses had in boastfulness recounted to Sammael all his achievements, real and legendary; and how at last Moses had pursued the Enemy with the Ineffable Name, and in his anger taken off one of his horns of glory and blinded Satan in one eye. We must be excused from following this story through its revolting details.

But, whether as the Angel of death or as the seducer of man, Sammael does not have absolute power. When Israel took the Law upon themselves at Mount Sinai, they became entirely free from his sway, and would have remained so, but for the sin of the Golden Calf. Similarly, in the time of Ezra, the object of Israel's prayer (Nehemiah 7) was to have Satan delivered to them. After a three days fast it was granted, and the Yetser haRa of idolatry, in the shape of a young lion, was delivered up to them. It would serve no good purpose to repeat the story of what was done with the bound enemy, or how his cries were rendered inaudible in heaven. Suffice it that, in view of the requirements of the present world, Israel liberated him from the ephah covered with lead (Zechariah 5:8), under which, by advice of the prophet Zechariah, they had confined him, although for precaution they first put out his eyes (Yoam, 69 b). And yet, in view, or probably, rather, in ignorance, of such teaching, modern criticism would derive the Satanology of the New Testament and the history of the Temptation from Jewish sources!

Over these six persons, Abraham, Isaac, Jacob, Moses, Aaron, and Miriam, with whom some apparently rank Benjamin, the Angel of death, had no power (Baba. B. 17 a). Benjamin, Amram, Jesse, and Chileb (the son of David) are said to have died (only) through the sin of the serpent. In other cases, also, Sammael may not be able to exercise his sway until, for example, he has by some ruse diverted a theologian from his sacred study. Thus he interrupted the pious meditations of David by going up into a tree and shaking it, when, as David went to examine it, a rung of the ladder, on which he stood, broke, and so interrupted David's holy thoughts. Similarly, Rabbi Chasda, by occupation with sacred study, warded off the Angel of death until the crackling of a beam diverted his attention. Instances of the awkwardness of the Enemy are related, and one rabbi, Joshua, actually took away his sword, only returning it by direct command of God. Where such views of Satan could even find temporary expression, superstitious fears may have been excited; but the thought of moral evil and of a moral combat with it could never have found lodgment.

III. EVIL SPIRITS (Shedim, Ruchin, Rucoth, Lilin).

Here also, as throughout, we mark the presence of Parsee elements of superstition. In general, these spirits resemble the gnomes, hobgoblins, elves, and sprites of our fairy tales. They are cunning and malicious, and contact with them is dangerous; but they can scarcely be described as absolutely evil. They often prove kind and useful; and may at all times be rendered innocuous, and even made serviceable.

1. Their origin, nature, and numbers. Opinions differ as to their origin, in fact, they variously originated. According to Ab. 12 b, Ber. R. 7, they were created on the eve of the first Sabbath. But since that time their numbers have greatly increased. For, according to Erub. 18 b, Ber. R. 20, multitudes of them were the offspring of Eve and of male spirits, and of Adam with female spirits, or with Lillith (the queen of the female spirits), during the 130 years that Adam had been under the ban, and before Seth was born (Genesis 5:3): comp. Erub. 18 b. Again, their number can scarcely be limited, since they propagate themselves, resembling men in this as well as in their taking of nourishment and dying. On the other hand, like the Angels they have wings, pass unhindered through space, and know the future. Still further, they are produced by a process of transformation from vipers, which, in the course of four times seven years, successively pass through the forms of vampires, thistles and thorns, into Shedim, perhaps a parabolic form of indicating the origination of Shedim through the fall of man. Another parabolic idea may be implied in the saying that Shedim spring from the backbone of those who have not bent in worship.

Although Shedim bear, when they appear, the form of human beings, they may assume any other form. Those of their number who are identified with dirty places are represented as themselves black. But the reflection of their likeness is not the same as that of man. When conjured up, their position (whether with the head or the feet uppermost) depends on the mode of conjuring. Some of the Shedim have defects. Thus, those of them who lodge in the caper bushes are blind, and an instance is related when one of their number, in pursuit of a Rabbi, fell over the root of a tree and perished. Trees, gardens, vineyards, and also ruined and desolate houses, but especially dirty places, were their favorite habitation, and the night time, or before rooster crowing, their special time of appearance. Therefore the danger of going alone into such places. A company of two escaped the danger, while before three the Shed did not even appear. For the same reason it was dangerous to sleep alone in a house, while the man who went out before rooster crow, without at least carrying for protection a burning torch (though moonlight was far safer) had his blood on his own head. If you greeted anyone in the dark you might unawares bid Godspeed to a Shed. Nor was the danger of this inconsiderable, since one of the worst of these Shedim, especially hurtful to Rabbis, was like a dragon with seven heads, each of which dropped off with every successive lowly bending during Rabbi Achas devotions. Especially dangerous times were the days of Wednesday and of the Sabbath. But it was a comfort to know that the Shedim could not create or produce anything; nor had they power over that which had been counted, measured, tied up and sealed; they could be conquered by the Ineffable Name; and they might be banished by the use of certain formulas, which, when written and worn, served as amulets.

The number of these spirits was like the earth that is thrown up around a bed that is sown. Indeed, no one would survive it, if he saw their number. A thousand at your right hand and ten thousand at your left, such crowding in the Academy or by the side of a bride; such weariness and faintness through their malignant touch, which rent the very dress of the wearers! The queen of the female spirits had no less a following than 180,000. Little as we imagine it, these spirits lurk everywhere around us: in the crumbs on the floor, in the oil in the vessels, in the water which we would drink, in the diseases which attack us, in the even numbered cups of our drinking, in the air in the room, by day and by night.

2. Their arrangement. Generally, they may be arranged into male and female spirits, the former under their king Ashmedai, the latter under their queen Lilith probably the same as Agrath bath Machlath—only that the latter may more fully present hurtful aspect of the demoness. The hurtful spirits are especially designated as Ruchin, Mazziqin (harmers), Malakhey Chabbalath (angels of damage), etc. From another aspect they are arranged into four classes: the Tsaphrire, or morning

spirits; the Tihare, or midday spirits; the Telane, or evening spirits; and the Lilin, or night spirits. a. Ashmedai (perhaps a Parsee name), Ashmodi, Ashmedon, or Shamdon, the king of the demons. It deserves notice, that this name does not occur in the Jerusalem Talmud nor in older Palestinian sources. He is represented as of immense size and strength, as cunning, malignant, and dissolute. At times, however, he is known also to do works of kindness, such as lead the blind, or to show the road to a drunken man. Of course, he foreknows the future, can do magic, but may be rendered serviceable by the use of the Ineffable Name, and especially by the signet of King Solomon, on which it was graven. The story of Solomon's power over him is well known and can here only be referred to in briefest outline. It is said, that as no iron was to be used in the construction of the Temple, Solomon was anxious to secure the services of the worm Shamir, which possessed the power of cutting stones. By advice of the Sanhedrin, Solomon conjured up for this purpose a male and a female Shed, who directed him to Ashmedai: The latter lived at the bottom of a deep cistern on a high mountain. Every morning on leaving it to go into heaven and hear the decrees of the Upper Sanhedrin, he covered the cistern with a stone, and sealed it. On this Benayah, armed with a chain, and Solomon's signet with the Ineffable Name, went and filled the cistern with wine, which Ashmedai, as all other spirits, hated. But as he could not otherwise quench his thirst, Ashmedai became drunk, when it was easy, by means of the magical signet, to secure the chain around him. Without entering on the story of his exploits, or how he indicated the custody of Shamir, and how ultimately the worm (which was in the custody of the male swamp bird) was secured, it appears that, by his cunning, Ashmedai finally got released, when he immediately hurled Solomon to a great distance, assumed his form, and reigned in his stead; until at last, after a series of adventures, Solomon recovered his signet, which Ashmedai had flung away, and a fish swallowed. Solomon was recognized by the Sanhedrin and Ashmedai fled at sight of the signet. [Possibly the whole of this is only a parabolic form for the story of Solomon's spiritual falling away, and final repentance.] b. Lilith, the queen of female spirits, to be distinguished from the Lilin or night spirits, and from Lela or Laila, an Angel who accompanied Abraham on his expedition against Chedorlaomer. Here we recognize still more distinctly the Parsee elements. Lillith is the queen of Zemargad—Zemargad representing all green crystals, malachite, and emerald, and the land of Zemargad being Sheba. Lillith is described as the mother of Hormiz or Hormuz. Sometimes she is represented as a very fair woman, but mostly with long, wild flowing hair, and winged. In Pes. 111 a we have a formula for exorcising Lillith. In Pes 112 b (towards the end) we are told how Agrath bath Machlath (probably the Zend word Agra, smiting, very wicked, bath Machlath the dancer) threatened Rabbi Chanina with serious mischief, had it not been that his greatness had been proclaimed in heaven, on which the Rabbi would have shown his power by banning her from all inhabited places, but finally gave her liberty on the eve of the fourth day and of the Sabbath, which nights accordingly are the most dangerous seasons.

3.   Character and habits of the Shedim. As many of the Angels, so many of the Shedim, are only personifications. Thus, as diseases were often ascribed to their agency, there were Shedim of certain diseases, as of asthma, croup, canine rabies, madness, stomachic diseases, etc. Again, there were local Shedim, as of Samaria, Tiberias, etc. On the other hand, Shedim might be employed in the magic cure of diseases. In fact, to conjure up and make use of demons was considered lawful although dangerous, while a little knowledge of the subject would enable a person to avoid any danger from them. Thus, although Chamath, the demon of oil, brings eruptions on the face, yet the danger is avoided if the oil is used out of the hollow of the hand, and not out of a vessel. Similarly, there are formulas by which the power of the demons can be counteracted. In these formulas, where they are not Biblical verses, the names of the demons are inserted. This subject will be further treated in another Appendix.

In general, we may expect to find demons on water, oil, or anything else that has stood uncovered all night; on the hands before they have been washed for religious purposes, and on the water in which they have been washed; and on the breadcrumbs on the floor. Demons may imitate or perform all that the prophets or great men of old had performed. The magicians of Egypt had imitated the miracles of Moses by demoniacal power. So general at the time of Jesus was the belief in demons and in the power of employing them, that even Josephus contended that the power of conjuring up, and driving out demons, and of magical cures had been derived from King Hezekiah, to whom God had given it. Josephus declares himself to have been an eye witness of such a wonderful cure by the repetition of a magical formula. This illustrates the contention of the Scribes that the miraculous cures of Jesus were due to demoniac agency.

Legions of demons lay in waiting for any error or falling on the part of man. Their power extended over all even numbers. Therefore, care must be had not to drink an even number of cups, except on the Passover night, when the demons have no power over Israel. On the other hand, there are demons who might almost be designated as familiar spirits, who taught the Rabbis, Shed Joseph and the Shed Jonathan. Rabbi Papa had a young Shed to wait upon him. There can, however, be no difficulty in making sure of their real existence. As Shedim have rooster's feet, nothing more is required than to strew ashes by the side of ones bed, when in the morning their marks will be perceived. It was by the shape of his feet that the Sanhedrin hoped to recognize, whether Ashmedai was really Solomon, or not, but it was found that he never appeared with his feet uncovered. The Talmud describes the following as an infallible means for actually seeing these spirits: Take the afterbirth of a black cat which is the daughter of a black cat, both mother and daughter being firstborn, burn it in the fire, and put some of the ashes in your eyes. Before using them, the ashes must be put into an iron tube, and sealed with an iron signet. It is added, that Rabbi Bibi successfully tried this experiment, but was hurt by the demons, on which he was restored to health by the prayers of the Rabbis.

Other and kindred questions, such as those of amulets, etc., will be treated under demoniac possessions. But may we not here once more and confidently appeal to impartial students whether, in view of this sketch of Jewish Angelology and Satanology, the contention can be sustained that the teaching of Christ on this subject has been derived from Jewish sources?

End Notes:

[28]   The following notice from Josephus is not only interesting in itself, but for the view which it presents of baptism. It shows what views rationalizing Jews took of the work of the Baptist, and how little such were able to enter into the real meaning of his baptism. But to some of the Jews it appeared, that the destruction of Herod's army came from God, and as a righteous punishment on account of what had been done to John, who was surnamed the Baptist. For Herod ordered him to be killed, a good man, and who commanded the Jews to exercise virtue, both as to righteousness towards one another, and piety towards God, and so to come to baptism. For that the baptizing would be acceptable to Him, if they made use of it, not for

the putting away (remission) of some sins, but for the purification of the body, after that the soul had been previously cleansed by righteousness. And when others had come in crowds, for they were exceedingly moved by hearing these words, Herod, fearing for fear that such influence of his over the people might lead to some rebellion, for they seemed ready to do any thing by his council, deemed it best, before anything new should happen through him, to put him to death, rather than that, when a change should arise in affairs, he might have to repent, etc.

[29]   This stream issued from under the throne of God, and is really the sweat of the living creatures in their awe at the glory of God.

[30]   According to Jer Ber. ix. 1, the abode of the living creatures was to an extent of 515 years journey, which is proved from the numerical value of the word straight (Ezekiel 1:7).

[31]   Gabriel was also designated Itmon, because he stops up the sins of Israel.

[32]   According to Jeremiah Ber. ix. 7, God only takes counsel with His Sanhedrin when He takes away, not when He gives (Job 1:21), and it is argued that, wherever the expression and Jehovah occurs, as in the last clause of 1 Kings 22:23, it means God His Sanhedrin.

[33]   Akhtariel, perhaps the crown of God, seems to be a name given to the Deity.

[34]   As a curious illustration how extremes meet, we append the following from Jonathan Edwards. After describing how Satan, before his fall, was the chief of all the angels . . . . the Messiah or Christ (!), as he was the Anointed, so that in the respect, Jesus Christ is exalted to his place in heaven; and that Lucifer or Satan, while a holy angel . . . was a type of Christ, the great American divine explains his fall as follows: But when it was revealed to him, high and glorious as he was, that he must be a ministering spirit to the race of mankind which he had seen newly created, which appeared so feeble, mean, and despicable, of vastly inferior not only to him, the prince of the angels, and head of the created universe, but also to the inferior angels, and that he must be subject to one of that race which should hereafter be born, he could not bear it, This occasioned his fall. Could Jonathan Edwards have heard of the Rabbinic legends, or is this only a strange coincidence? The curious reader will find much quaint information, though, I fear, little help, in Prof. W. Scotts Volume The Existence of Evil Spirits, London, 1843.

[35]   The Rabbis point out, how Eve had added to the words of God. He had only commanded them not to eat of the tree, while Eve added to it, that they were not to touch it. Thus adding to the words of God had led to the first sin with all the terrible consequences connected with it.

[36]   From the expression a son in his own likeness, etc., it is inferred that Adam's previous offspring during the 138 years was not in his likeness.

[37]   The following Haggadah will illustrate both the power of the evil spirits at night and how amenable they are to reasoning. A Rabbi was distributing his gifts to the poor at night when he was confronted by the Prince of the Ruchin with the quotation Deuteronomy 19:34 (You shall not remove your neighbors landmark), which seemed to give the spirit a warrant for attacking him. But when the Rabbi replied by quoting Proverbs 20:14 (a gift in secret appeases wrath), the spirit fled in confusion.

[38]   The Tarnegol Bera, a mythical animal reaching from earth to heaven, also called Naggar Tura from his activity in cleaving mountains.

Appendix 14

The Law in Messianic Times

The question as to the Rabbinic views in regard to the binding character of the Law, and its imposition on the Gentiles, in Messianic times, although, strictly speaking, not forming part of this history, is of such vital importance in connection with recent controversies as to demand special consideration. In the text to which this Appendix refers it has been indicated, that a new legislation was expected in Messianic days. The ultimate basis of this expectancy must be sought in the Old Testament itself, not merely in such allusions as to the intrinsic worthlessness of sacrifices, but in such passages as Deuteronomy 16:15, 18, and its prophetic commentary in Jeremiah 30:31, etc. It was with a view to this that the Jewish deputation inquired whether John the Baptist was that Prophet. For, as has been shown, Rabbinism associated certain reformatory and legislative functions with the appearance of the Forerunner of the Messiah.

There were in this, as in most respects, diverging opinions according to the different standpoints of the Rabbis, and, as we infer, not without controversial bearing on the teaching of Christianity. The strictest tendency may be characterized as that which denied the possibility of any change in the ceremonial Law, as well as the abrogation of festivals in the future. Even the destruction of the Temple and with it the necessary cessation of sacrifices, if which is a moot question, all sacrifices did at once and absolutely cease, only caused a gap; just as exile from the land could only free from such laws as attached to the soil of Israel. The reading of the sacrificial sections in the Law, at any rate, in conjunction with prayers, but especially study of the Law, took in the meantime the place of the sacrifices. And as regarded the most sacred of all sacrifices, that of the Day of Atonement, it was explained that the day rather than the sacrifices brought reconciliation. This party held the principle that not only those Divine, but even those Rabbinic, ordinances, which apparently had been intended only for a certain time or for a certain purpose, were of eternal duration. The law is never to cease; there are the commandments, since there is no prophet who may change a word in them.

So far were these views carried, that it was asserted: Israel needs not the teaching of the King Messiah, but that He only comes to gather the dispersed, and to give to the Gentiles thirty commandments, as it is written (Zechariah 10:12), "they weighed me my price, thirty pieces of silver". But even these extreme statements seem to imply that keen controversy had raged on the subject. Besides, the most zealous defenders of the Law admitted that the Gentiles were to receive laws in Messianic times. The smallest and most extreme section held that, the laws, as Israel observed them, would be imposed on the Gentiles; others that only thirty commandments, the original Noachic ordinances supposed to be enumerated in Leviticus 19, would become obligatory, while some held, that only three ordinances would be binding on the new converts: two connected with the Feast of Tabernacles, the third, that of the phylacteries. On the other hand, we have the most clear testimony that the prevailing tendency of teaching was in a different direction. In a very curious passage, in which the final restitution of the sinners of Israel and of the righteous of the Gentiles who are all in Gehinnom, is taught in very figurative language, we are told of a new Law which God will give by the Messiah in the age to come, thanksgiving for which calls forth that universal Amen, not only on earth but in Gehinnom, which leads to the deliverance of those who are in the latter. But as this may refer to the time of the final consummation, we turn to other passages. The Midrash on Song 2:13, applying the passage in conjunction with Jeremiah 30:31, expressly states that the Messiah would give Israel a new law, and the Targum, on Isaiah 12:3, although perhaps not quite so clearly, also speaks of a new instruction. It is needless to multiply proofs. But the Talmud goes even further, and lays down the two principles, that in the age to come the whole ceremonial Law and all the feasts were to cease. And although this may be regarded as merely a general statement, it is definitely applied to the effect, that all sacrifices except the thank offering, and all fasts and feasts except the Day of Atonement, or else the Feast of Esther, were to come to an end, that what had formerly been bound or forbidden would be loosed or allowed, notably that the distinctions between clean and unclean animals would be removed.

There is the less need for apology for any digression here, that, besides the intrinsic interest of the question, it casts light on two most important subjects, For, first, it illustrates the attempt of the narrowest Judaic party in the Church to force on Gentile believers the yoke of the whole Law; the bearing of Paul in this respect; his relation to Peter; the conduct of the latter; and the proceedings of the Apostolic Synod in Jerusalem (Acts 15). Paul, in his opposition to that party, stood even on Orthodox Jewish ground. But when he asserted, not only a new law of liberty, but the typical and preparatory character of the whole Law, and its fulfillment in Christ, he went far beyond the Jewish standpoint. Further, the favorite modern theory as to fundamental opposition in principle between Pauline and Petrine theology in this respect, has, like many kindred theories, no support in the Jewish views on that subject, unless we suppose that Peter had belonged to the narrowest Jewish school, which his whole history seems to forbid. We can also understand, how the Divinely granted vision of the abrogation of the distinction between clean and unclean animals (Acts 10:9-16) may, though coming as a surprise, have had a natural basis in Jewish expectancy, and it explains how the Apostolic Synod, when settling the question, ultimately fell back on the so called Noachic commandments, though with very wider reaching principles underlying their decision (Acts 15:13-21). Lastly, it seems to cast even some light on the authorship of the Fourth Gospel; for, the question about that prophet evidently referring to the possible alteration of the Law in Messianic times, which is reported only in the Fourth Gospel, shows such close acquaintance with the details of Jewish ideas on this subject, as seems to us utterly incompatible with its supposed origination as The Ephesian Gospel towards the end of the second century, the outcome of Ephesian Church teaching, an esoteric and eclectic book, designed to modify the impressions produced by the tradition previously recorded by the Synoptists.

Appendix 15

The Location of Sychar and the Date of Jesus' Visit to Samaria

I. The Location of Sychar.

Although modern writers are now mostly agreed on this subject, it may be well briefly to put before our readers the facts of the case.

Until comparatively lately, the Sychar of John 4 was generally as representing the ancient Shechem. The first difficulty here was the name, since Shechem, or even Sichem, could scarcely be identified with Sychar, which is undoubtedly the correct reading. Accordingly, the latter term was represented as one of infamy, and derived from Shekhar (in Aramean Shikhra), as it were, drunken town, or else from Sheqer (in Aramean Shiqra), lying town. But, not to mention other objections, there is no trace of such as alteration of the name Sychar in Jewish writings, while its employment would seem wholly incongruous in such a narrative as John 4. Moreover, all the earliest writers distinguished Sychar from Shechem. Lastly, in the Talmud the name of Sokher, also written Sikhra, frequently occurs, and that not only as distinct from Schechem, but in a connection which renders the hypothesis of a shameful by-name impossible. Professor Delitzch has collected seven passages from the Babylon Talmud to that effect, in five of which Sichra, is mentioned as the birthplace of celebrated Rabbis, the town having at a later period apparently been left by the Samaritans, and occupied by Jews. If further proof were required, it would be sufficient to say that a woman would scarcely have gone a mile and a half from Shechem

691

to Jacobs well to fetch water, when there are so many springs about the former city. In these circumstances, later writers have generally fixed upon the village of Askar, half a mile from Jacobs Well, and within sight of it, as the Sychar of the New Testament, one of the earliest to advocate this view having been the late learned Canon Williams. Little more than a third of a mile from Askar is the reputed tomb of Joseph. The transformation of the name Sychar into Askar is explained, either by a contraction of Ain Askar the well of Sychar, or else by the fact that in the Samaritan Chronicle the place is called Iskar, which seems to have been the vernacular pronunciation of Sychar.

II. Time of Jesus' Visit to Sychar.

Jesus spent some time after the Feast of Passover (John 2:23) in the province of Judea. But it can scarcely be supposed that this was a long period, for, 2ndly, in John 4:45 the Galileans have evidently a fresh remembrance of what had taken place at the Passover in Jerusalem, which would scarcely have been the case if a long period and other festivals had intervened. Similarly, the King's Offer (John 4:47) seems also to act upon a recent report. 3rdly, the unnamed Feast of John 5:1 forms an important element in our computations. Some months of Galilean ministry must have intervened between it and the return of Jesus to Galilee. Therefore it could not have been Pentecost. Nor could it have been the Feast of Tabernacles, which was in autumn, nor yet the feast of the Dedication, which took place in winter, since both are expressly mentioned by their names (John 5:2, 10:22). The only other feasts were: the Feast of Wood Offering, the Feast of Trumpets, or New Years Day, the Day of Atonement, and the feast of Esther, or Purim.

To begin with the latter, since of late it has found most favor. The reasons against Christ's attendance in Jerusalem at Purim seem to me irresistible. Canon Westcott urges that the discourse of Christ at the unnamed Feast has not, as is generally the case, any connection with the thoughts of that festival. To this I would add, that I can scarcely conceive Jesus going up to a feast observed with such boisterous merriment as Purim was, while the season of the year in which it falls would scarcely tally with the statement of John 5:3, that a great multitude of sick people were laid down in the porches of Bethesda.

But if the unnamed Feast was not Purim, it must have been one of these three, the Feast of the Ingathering of Wood, the Feast of Trumpets, or Day of Atonement. In other words, it must have taken place late in summer, or in the very beginning of autumn. But if so, then the Galilean ministry intervening between the visit to Samaria and this Feast leads to the necessary inferences that the visit to Sychar had taken place in early summer, probably about the middle or end of May. This would allow ample time for Christ's stay in Jerusalem during the Passover and for His Judean ministry.

As we are discussing the date of the unnamed Feast, it may be as well to bring the subject here to a close. We have seen that the only three Feasts to which reference could have been are to the Feast of Wood Offering, the Feast of Trumpets, and the Day of Atonement. But the last of those could not be meant, since it is designated, not only by Philo, but in Acts 25:9, as the fast, not the feast nestea, or ort. As between the Feast of the Wood Offering and that of Trumpets I feel at considerable loss. Canon Westcott has urged on behalf on the latter reasons which I confess are very weighty. On the other hand, the Feast of Trumpets was not one of those on which people generally resorted to Jerusalem, and as it took place on the 1st of Tishri (about the middle of September), it is difficult to believe that anyone going up to it would not rather have chosen, or at least remained over, the Day of Atonement and the Feast of Tabernacles, which followed respectively, on the 10th and 15th days of that month. Lastly, the Feast of Wood Offering, which took place on the 15th Ab (in August), was a popular and joyous festival, when the wood needed for the altar was brought up from all parts of the country. As between these two feasts, we must leave the question undecided, only noticing that barely six weeks intervened between the one and the other feast.

End Notes:

[39] I must here correct the view expressed in my book on The Temple due to a misunderstanding of John 4:35. Of course, if latter had implied that Jesus was at Sychar in December, the unnamed feast must have been Purim.

Appendix 16

Jewish Views About Demons and the Demonized, Interaction Between Jews and Jewish Christians in the First Centuries

It is not our purpose here to attempt an exhaustive account of the Jewish views on demons and the demonized. A few preliminary strictures were, however, necessary on a work upon which writers on this subject have too implicitly relied. I refer to Gfroerers Jahrhundert des Heils. Gfroerer sets out by quoting a passage in the Book of Enoch on which he lays great stress, but which critical inquiries of Dillmann and other scholars have shown to be of no value on the argument. This disposes of many pages of negative criticism on the New Testament which Gfroerer founds on this quotation. Similarly, 4 Esdras would not in our days be cited in evidence of pre-Christian teaching. As regards Rabbinic passages, Gfroerer uncritically quotes from Kabalistic works which he mixes with quotations from the Talmud and from writings of a later date. Again, as regards the two quotations of Gfroerer from the Mishah, it has already been stated that neither of these passages bears any reference to demoniac possessions. Further, Gfroerer appeals to two passages in Sifre which may here be given in extenso. The first of these is on Deuteronomy 16:12, and reads thus: He who joins himself (cleaves) to uncleanness, on him rests the spirit of uncleanness; but he who cleaves to the Shechinah, it is meet that the Holy Spirit should rest on him. The second occurs in explanation of Deuteronomy 32:16, and reads as follows: What is the way of a "demon" (Shed)? He enters into a man and subjects him. It will be observed that in both these quotations

694

reference is made to certain moral, not to a physical effects, such as in the case of the demonized. Lastly, although one passage from the Talmud which Gfroerer adduces (though not quite exactly) applies to demonical possessions, but is given in an exaggerated and embellished form.

If from these incorrect references we turn to what Jewish authorities really state on the subject, we have:

1. To deal with the Writings of Josephus in Aniq. 6:8. 2, Josephus ascribes Saul's disorder to demonic influence, which brought upon him such suffocations as were ready to choke him. In Antiq. 8:2. 5, Josephus describes the wisdom, learning, and achievements of Solomon, referring especially to his skill in expelling demons who caused various diseases. According to Josephus, Solomon had exercised this power by incantations, his formulae and words of exorcism being still known in Josephus' days. In such manner a certain Eleazar had healed a demoniac in the presence of Vespasian, his officers, and troops, by putting to his nostrils a ring that held a root of one of those mentioned by Solomon, by which the demon was drawn out amid convulsions of the demoniac, when the demon was further adjured not to return by frequent mention of the name of Solomon, and by incantations which he [Solomon] had composed. To show the reality of this, a vessel with water had been placed at a little distance, and the demon had, in coming out, overturned it. It is probably to this root that Josephus refers in War. 5:6. 3, where he names it Baaras, which I conjecture to be the equivalent of the form, boara, the burning, since he describes it as of color like a flame, and as emitting at even a ray like lightning, and which it would cost a man's life to take up otherwise than by certain magical means which Josephus specifies. From all this we infer that Josephus occupied the later Talmudical standpoint, as regards exorcism, magical cures, and magical preventions. This is of great importance as showing that these views prevailed in New Testament times. But when Josephus adds, that the demons expelled by Baaras were the spirits of the wicked, he represents a superstition which is not shared by the earlier Rabbis, and may possibly be due to a rationalizing attempt to account for the phenomenon. It is true that the same view occurs in comparatively late Jewish writings, and that in Yalkuat on Isaiah 46 b there appears to be a reference to it, at least in connection with the spirits of those who had perished in the flood; but this seems to belong to a different cycle of legends.

2. Rabbinic views. Probably the nearest approach to the idea of Josephus that demons were the souls of the wicked, is the (perhaps allegorical) statement that the backbone of a person who did not bow down to worship God became a Shed, or demon. The ordinary names for demons are evil spirits, or unclean spirits (ruach raah, ruach tumeah), Seirim (lit. goats). Shedim (Sheyda, a demon, male or female, either because their chief habitation is in desolate places, or from the word to fly about, or else from to rebel), and Mazzikin (the hurtful ones). A demoniac is called Gebher Shediyin. Even this, that demons are supposed to eat and drink, to propagate themselves, and to die, distinguishes them from the demons of the New Testament. The food of demons consists of certain elements in fire and water, and of certain odors. Therefore the mode of incantation by incense made of certain ingredients. Of their origin, number, habitation, and general influence, sufficient has been said in the Appendix on Demonology. It is more important here to notice these two Jewish ideas: that demons entered into, or took possession of, men; and that many diseases were due to their agency. The former is frequently expressed. The evil spirit constrains a man to do certain things, such as to pass beyond the Sabbath boundary, to eat the Passover bread, etc. But it reads more like a caustic than a serious remark when we are informed that these three thing deprive a man of his free will and make him transgress: the Cutheans, an evil spirit, and poverty. Diseases, such as rabies, angina, asthma, or accidents, such as an encounter with a wild bull, are due to their agency, which, happily, is not unlimited. As stated in Appendix 13, the most dangerous demons are those of dirty (secret) places. Even numbers (2, 4, 6, etc.) are always dangerous, so is anything that comes from unwashed hands. For such, or similar oversights, a whole legion of demons is on the watch. On the evening of the Passover the demons are bound, and, in general, their power has now been restricted, chiefly to the eves of Wednesday and of the Sabbath. Yet there are, as we shall see, circumstances in which it would be foolhardiness to risk their encounter. Without here entering on the views expressed in the Talmud about prophecy, visions, and dreams, we turn to the questions germane to our subject.

A. Magic and Magicians. We must here bear in mind that the practice of magic was strictly prohibited to Israelites, and that, as a matter of principle at least, witchcraft, or magic, was supposed to have no power over Israel, if they owned and served their God. But in this matter also, as will now appear, theory and practice did not accord. Thus, under certain circumstances, the repetition of magical formulas was declared lawful even on the Sabbath. Egypt was regarded as the home of magic. In connection with this, it deserves notice that the Talmud ascribes the miracles of Jesus to magic, which He had learned during His stay in Egypt having taken care, when He left, to insert under His skin its rules and formulas, since every traveler, on quitting the country, was searched, for fear that he should take to other lands the mysteries of magic.

Here it may be interesting to refer to some of the strange ideas which Rabbinism attached to the early Christians, as showing both the intercourse between the two parties, and that the Jews did not deny the gift of miracles in the Church, only ascribing its exercise to magic. Of the existence of such intercourse with Jewish Christians there is abundant evidence. Thus, R. Joshua, the son of Levi (at the end of the second century), was so hard pressed by their quotations from the Bible that, unable to answer, he pronounced a curse on them, which, however, did not come. We gather, that in the first century Christianity had widely spread among the Jews, and R. Ishmael, the son of Elisha, the grandson of that High Priest who was executed by the Romans, seems in vain to have contended against the advance of Christianity. At last he agreed with R. Tarphon that nothing else remained but to burn their writings. It was this R. Ishmael who prevented his nephew Ben Dama from being cured of the bite of a serpent by a Christian, preferring that he should die rather than be healed by such means. Similarly, the great R. Eliezer ben Hyrcanus, also in the first century, was so suspected of the prevailing heresy that he was actually taken up as a Christian in the persecution of the later. Though he cleared himself of the suspicion, yet his contemporaries regarded him for a time doubtfully, and all agreed that the troubles which befell him were in punishment for having listened with pleasure to the teaching of the heretics. The following may be mentioned as instances of the magic practiced by these heretics. In Jeremiah Sanh. 25 d, we are told about two great Rabbis who were banned by a heretic to the beam of a bath. In return the Rabbis, by similar means, fastened the heretic to the door of the bath. Having mutually agreed to set each other free, the same parties next met on board a ship. Here the heretic by magical means divided the sea, by way of imitating Moses. On this the Rabbis called upon him to walk through the sea, like Moses, when he was immediately overwhelmed through the ban of R. Joshua! Other stories of a similar and even more absurd character might be quoted. But if such opinions were entertained of Jewish Christians, we can scarcely wonder that all their books were ordered to be burnt, that even a roll of the Law written by a heretic was to be destroyed, and that Jewish Christians were consigned to eternal punishment in Gehinnom, from which even the token of circumcision should not deliver them since an Angel would convert it into uncircumcision.

But to return. Talmudic writings distinguishing several classes of magicians. The Baal Obh, or conjuror of the dead, evoked a voice from under the armpit, or from other members of the dead body, the arms or other members being struck together, for the purpose of eliciting the sound. Necromancy might be practiced in two different ways. The dead might be called up, in which case they would appear with the feet upwards. But this must not be practiced on the Sabbath. Or again, a skull might, by magical means, be made to answer. This might be done on the Sabbath also. Or a demon might be conjured up by a certain kind of incense, and then employed in magic. A second class of magicians (called Yideoni) uttered oracles by putting a certain bone into their mouth. Thirdly, there was the Chabar, or serpent charmer, a distinction being made between a great and small Chabar, according as larger or smaller serpents were charmed. Fourthly, we have the Meonen, who could indicate what days or hours were lucky and unlucky. Fifthly, there was the searcher after the dead, who remained fasting on graves in order to communicate with an unclean spirit; and, lastly, the Menachesh, who knew what omens were lucky and what unlucky. And if they were treated only as signs and not as omens, the practice was declared lawful.

In general the black are might be practiced either through demons, or else by the employment of magical means. Among the latter we reckon, not only incantations, but magic by means of the thumb, by a knife with a black handle, or by a glass cup, or by a cup of incantation. But there was danger here, since, if all proper rules and cautions were not observed the magician might be hurt by the demon. Such an instance is related, although the Rabbi in question was mercifully preserved by being swallowed by a cedar, which afterwards burst and set him free. Women were especially suspected of witchcraft, and great caution was accordingly enjoined. Thus, it might even be dangerous to lift up loaves of bread (though not broken pieces) for fear that they should be bewitched. A number of instances are related in which persons were in imminent danger from magic, in some of which they suffered not only damage but death, while in others the Rabbis knew how to turn the impending danger against their would be assailants. A very peculiar idea is that about the Teraphim of Scripture. It occurs already in the Targum Psalm Jon. on Genesis 30:19, and is found also in the Pirqe de R. Eliez. c. 36. It is stated that the Teraphim were made in the following manner: a first born was killed, his head cut off, and prepared with salt and spices, after which a gold plate, upon which magical formulas had been graven, was placed under his tongue, when the head was supposed to give answer to whatever questions might be addressed to it.

B. After this we can scarcely wonder, that so many diseases should have been imputed to magical or else demoniac influences, and cured either by magical means or by exorcism. For our present purpose we leave aside not only the question, whether and what diseases were regarded as the punishment of certain sins, but also all questions as to their magical causes and means of cure. We confine our remarks to the supposed power of evil spirits in the production of diseases. Four things are mentioned as dangerous on account of demons, of which we shall only mention three: To walk between two palm trees, if the space is wider than four cubits; to borrow drinking water; and to walk over water that has been poured out, unless it have been covered with earth, or spat upon, or you have taken off your shoes. Similarly, the shadow of the moon, of certain trees, and of other objects, is dangerous, because demons love to hide there. Much caution must also be observed in regard to the water with which the hands are washed in the morning, as well as in regard to oil for anointing, which must never be taken from a strange vessel which might have been bewitched.

Many diseases are caused by direct demoniac agency. Thus, leprosy, rabies, heart disease, madness, asthma, croup, and other diseases, are ascribed to special demons. And although I cannot find any notices of demoniac possession in the sense of permanent indwelling, yet an evil spirit may seize and influence a person. The nearest approach to demoniac possession is in a legend of two Rabbis who went to Rome to procure the repeal of a persecuting edict, when they were met on board ship by a demon, Ben Temalion, whose offer of company they accepted, in hope of being able to do some miracle through him. Arrival in Rome, the demon took possession of the daughter of Caesar. On this he was exorcised by the Rabbis (Ben Temalion, come out! Ben Temalion, come out), when they were rewarded by the offer of anything they might choose from the Imperial Treasury, on which they removed from it the hostile decree.

As against this one instance, many are related of cures by magical means. By the latter we mean the superstitious and irrational application of means which could in no way affect any disease, although they might sometimes be combined with what might be called domestic remedies. Thus, for a bad cold in the head this remedy is proposed: Pour slowly a quart of the milk of a white goat over three cabbage stalks, keep the pot boiling and stir with a piece of Marmehon wood. The other remedy proposed is the excrement of a white dog mixed with balsam. It need scarcely be said, that the more intractable the disease, the more irrational are the remedies proposed. Thus against blindness by day it is proposed to take of the spleen of seven calves and put it on the basin used by surgeons for bleeding. Next, someone outside the door is to ask the blind man to give him something to eat, when he is to reply: How can I open the door—come in and eat, on which the latter obeys, taking care, however, to break the basin, as else the blindness might strike him. We have here an indication of one of the favorite modes of healing disease, that by its transference to another. But if the loss of the power of vision is greater at night than by day, a cord is to be made of the hair of some animal, one end of which is to be tied to the foot of the patient the other to that of a dog. The children are to strike together pieces of crockery behind the dog, while the patient repeats these words: The dog is old and the rooster is foolish. Next seven pieces of meat are to be taken from seven different houses, and hung up on the doorposts, and the dog must afterwards eat the meat on a dunghill in an open place. Lastly, the cord is to be untied when one is to repeat: Let the blindness of M. the son of N. leave M. the son of N. and pierce the eyeballs of the dog!

We have next to refer to strictly magical cures. These were performed by amulets, either preventive, or curative or disease, or else by exorcism. An amulet was regarded as probate, if three cures had been performed by it. In such case it might be put on even on the Sabbath. It consisted either of a piece of parchment, on which certain magical words were written, or of small bundles of certain plants or herbs. However, even probate amulets might fail, owing to the adverse constellation under which a person was. In any case the names and numbers of the demons, whose power it was wished to counteract, required to be expressly stated. Sometimes the amulet contained also a verse from the Bible. It need scarcely be said, that the other words written on the amulet had, at least, in their connection, little if any sensible meaning. But those learned in these arts and the Rabbis had the secret of discovering them, so that there was at least no mystery about them, and the formulas used were well known. If the mischief to be counteracted was due to demoniac agency, it might be prevented or removed by a kind of incantation, or by incantation along with other means, or in difficult cases by exorcism. As instances of the first we may quote the following. To ward off any danger from drinking water on a Wednesday or Sabbath Evening, when evil spirits may rest on it, it is advised either to repeat a passage of Scripture in which the world Qol (Voice) occurs seven times (Psalm 29:3-9), or else to say this: Lul, Shaphan, Anigron, Anirdaphin, between the stars I sit, between the lean and the fat I walk! Against flatulence, certain remedies are recommended (such as drinking warm water), but they are to be accompanied by the following formula: Qapa, Qapa, I think of you, and of your seven daughters, and eight daughters-in-law! Many similar prescriptions might be quoted. As the remedy against blindness has been cited to point the contrast to Jesus' mode of treatment, it may be mentioned that quite a number of remedies are suggested for the cure of a bloody flux, of which perhaps wine in which Persian onions, or anise and saffron, or other plants have been boiled, seem the most rational—the medicament being, however, in each case accompanied by this formula: Be cured of your flux!

Lastly, as regards incantation and exorcism, the formulas to be used for the purpose are enumerated. These mostly consist of words which have little if any meaning (so far as we know), but which form a rhyme or alliteration when a syllable is either omitted or added in successive words. The following, for example, is the formula of incantation against boils: Baz, Baziyah, Mas, Masiya, Kas, Kasiyah, Sharlai and Amarlai, you Angels that come from the land of Sodom to heal painful boils! Let the color not become more red, let it not farther spread, let its seed be absorbed in the belly. As a mule does not propagate itself, so let not this evil propagate itself in the body of M. the son of M. In other formulas the demons are not invoked for the cure, but threatened. We have the following as against another skin disease: A sword drawn, and a sling outstretched! His name is not Yokhabh, and the disease stand still! Against danger from the demon of foul places we have the following: On the head of the cast him into a bed of lettuce, and beat him with the jawbone of a donkey. On the other hand, it is recommended as a precaution against the evil eye to put ones right thumb into the left hand and ones left thumb into the right hand, and to say: I, M. N. belong to the house of Joseph over whom the evil eye has no power. A certain Rabbi gave this as information derived from one of the chief of the witches, by which witchcraft might be rendered harmless. The person in danger should thus address the witches: Hot filth into your mouths from baskets with holes, you witching women! Let your head become bald, and the wind scatter your breadcrumbs. Let it carry away your spices, let the fresh saffron which you carry in your hands be scattered. You witches, so long as I had grace and was careful, I did not come among you, and now I have come, and you are not favorable to me. To avoid the danger of two or more persons being separated by a dog, a palm tree, a woman, or a pig, we are advised to repeat a verse from the Bible which begins and ends with the word El (Almighty)). Or in passing between women suspected of witchcraft it may be well to repeat this formula: Agrath, Azelath, Asiya, Belusiya are already killed by arrows. Lastly, the following may be quoted as a form of exorcism of demons: Burst, curst, dashed, banned be Bar Tit, Bar Tema, Bar Tena, Chashmagoz, Merigoz, and Isteaham!

It has been a weary and unpleasant task to record such abject superstitions, mostly the outcome of contact with Parsee or other pagan elements. Brief though our sketch has been, we have felt as if it should have been even more curtailed. But it seemed necessary to furnish these unwelcome details in order to remove the possibility of comparing what is reported in the New Testament about the demonized and demons with Jewish notions on such subjects. Greater contrast could scarcely be conceived than between what we read in the New Testament and the views and practices mentioned in Rabbinic writings, and if this, as it is hoped, has been firmly established, even the ungrateful labor bestowed on collecting these unsavory notices will have been sufficiently repaid.

End Notes:

[40]   The practice of some early Christians to make themselves eunuchs is alluded to in the Talmud. In general palm trees and their fruit are dangerous, and you should always wash your hands after eating dates.

Appendix 17

The Ordinances and Law of the Sabbath in The Mishnah and The Jerusalem Talmud

The terribly exaggerated views of the Rabbis, and their endless, burdensome rules about the Sabbath may best be learned from a brief analysis of the Mishnah, as further explained and enlarged in the Jerusalem Talmud. For this purpose a brief analysis of what is, confessedly, one of the most difficult tractates may here be given.

The Mishnic tractate Sabbath stands at the head of twelve tractates which together form the second of the six sections into which the Mishnah is divided, and which addresses Festive Seasons. Properly to understand the Sabbath regulations, it is, however, necessary also to take into account the second tractate in that section, which addresses what are called commixtures or connections. Its object is to make the Sabbath Laws more bearable. For this purpose, it is explained how places, beyond which it would otherwise have been unlawful to carry things, may be connected together, so as, by a legal fiction, to convert them into a sort of private dwelling. Thus, supposing a number of small private houses to open into a common court, it would have been unlawful on the Sabbath to carry anything from one of these houses into the other. This difficulty is removed if all the families deposit before the Sabbath some food in the common court, when a connection is established between the various house, which makes them one dwelling. This was called the Erubh of Courts. Similarly, an extension of what was allowed as a Sabbath journey might be secured by another commixture, the Erubh or connection of boundaries. An ordinary Sabbath day's journey extended 2,000 cubits beyond ones dwelling. But if at the boundary of that journey a man deposited on the Friday food for two meals, he thereby constituted it his dwelling, and therefore might go on for other 2,000 cubits. Lastly, there was another Erubh, when narrow streets or blind alleys were connected into a private dwelling by laying a beam over the entrance, or extending a wire or rope along such streets and alleyways. This, by a legal fiction, made them a private dwelling, so that everything was lawful there which a man might do on the Sabbath in his own house.

Without discussing the possible and impossible questions about these Erubin raised by the most ingenious misleading reasoning, let us see how Rabbinism taught Israel to observe its Sabbath. In not less than twenty four chapters, matters are seriously discussed as of vital religious importance, which one would scarcely imagine a sane intellect would seriously entertain. Through 64 1/2 folio columns in the Jerusalem, and 156 double pages of folio in the Babylon Talmud does the enumeration and discussion of possible cases, drag on, almost unrelieved even by Haggadah. The Talmud itself bears witness to this, when it speaks (no doubt exaggeratedly) of a certain Rabbi who had spent no less than two and a half years in the study of only one of those twenty four chapters! And it further bears testimony to the unprofitableness of these endless discussions and determinations. The occasion of this is so curious and characteristic, that it might here find mention. The discussion was concerning a beast of burden. A donkey might not be led out on the road with its covering on, unless such had been put on the animal previous to the Sabbath, but it was lawful to lead the animal about in this fashion in ones courtyard. The same rule applied to a packsaddle, provided it were not fastened on by girth and back strap. Upon this one of the Rabbis is reported as bursting into the declaration that this formed part of those Sabbath Laws which were like mountains suspended by a hair! And yet in all these wearisome details there is not a single trace of anything spiritual, not a word even to suggest higher thoughts of God's holy day and its observance.

The tractate on the Sabbath begins with regulations extending its provisions to the close of the Friday afternoon, so as to prevent the possibility of infringing the Sabbath itself, which commenced on the Friday evening. As the most common kind of labor would be that of carrying, this is the first point discussed. The Biblical Law prohibitted such labor in simple terms (Exodus 35:6; comp. Jeremiah 17:22). But Rabbinism developed the prohibition into eight special ordinances, by first dividing the bearing of a burden into two separate acts, lifting it up and putting it down, and then arguing, that it might be lifted up or put down from two different places, from a public into a private, or from a private into a public place. Here there are discussions as to what constituted a private place; a public place; a wide space, which belongs neither to a special individual nor to a community, such as the sea, a deep wide valley, or else the corner of a property leading out on the road or fields, and, lastly, a legally free place. Again, a burden meant, as the lowest standard of it, the weight of a dried fig. But if half a fig were carried at two different times, lifted or deposited from a private into a public place, or vice versa, were these two actions to be combined into one so as to constitute the sin of Sabbath desecration? And if so, under what conditions as to state of mind, locality, etc.? And, lastly, how many different sins might one such act involve? To give an instance of the kind of questions that were generally discussed the standard measure for forbidden food was the size of an olive, just as that for carrying burdens was the weight of a fig. If a man swallowed forbidden food of the size of half an olive, rejected it, and again eaten of the size of half an olive, he would be guilty, because the palate had altogether tasted food to the size of a whole olive; but if one had deposited in another locality a burden of the weight of a half a fig, and removed it again, it involved no guilt, because the burden was altogether only of half a fig, nor even if the first half figs burden had been burnt and then a second half fig introduced. Similarly, if an object that was intended to be worn or carried in front had slipped behind it involved no guilt, but if it had been intended to be worn or carried behind, and it slipped forward, this involved guilt, as involving labor.

Similar difficulties were discussed as to the reverse. Whether, if an object were thrown from a private into a public place, or the reverse. Whether, if an object was thrown into the air with the left, and caught again in the right hand, this involved sin, was a nice question, though there could be no doubt a man incurred guilt if he caught it with the same hand which it had been thrown, but he was not guilty if he caught it in his mouth, since, after being eaten, the object no longer existed, and therefore catching with the mouth was as if it had been done by a second person. Again, if it rained, and the water which fell from the sky was carried, there was no sin in it; but if the rain had run down from a wall it would involve sin. If a person were in one place and his hand filled with fruit stretched into another, and the Sabbath overtook him in this attitude, he would have to drop the fruit, since if he withdrew his full hand from one locality into another, he would be carrying a burden on the Sabbath.

It is needless to continue to analysis of this misleading reasoning. All discussions to which we have referred turn only on the first of the legal canons in the tractate Sabbath. They will show what a complicated machinery of merely external ordinances traditionalism set in motion, how utterly unspiritual the whole system was, and how it required no small amount of learning and ingenuity to avoid committing grievous sin. In what follows we shall only attempt to indicate the leading points in the Sabbath legislation of the Rabbis.

Shortly before the beginning of the Sabbath (late on Friday afternoon) nothing new was to be begun; the tailor might no longer go out with his needle, nor the scribe with his pen; nor were clothes to be examined by lamp light. A teacher might not allow his pupils to read, if he himself looked on the book. All these are precautionary measures. The tailor or scribe carrying his ordinary means of employment, might forget the advent of the holy day; the person examining a dress might kill insects, which is strictly forbidden on the Sabbath, and the teacher might move the lamp to see better, while the pupils were supposed to be so zealous as to do this.

These latter rules, we are reminded, were passed at a certain celebrated discussion between the schools of Hillel and Shammai, when the latter were in the majority. On that occasion also opposition to the Gentiles was carried to its farthest length, and their food, their language, their testimony, their presence, their intercourse, in short, all connection with them denounced. The school of Shammai also prohibitted making any mixture, the ingredients of which would not be wholly dissolved and assimilated before the Sabbath. The Sabbath law was declared to apply even to lifeless objects. Thus, wool might not be dyed if the process was not completed before the Sabbath. Nor was it even lawful to sell anything to a pagan unless the object would reach its destination before the Sabbath, nor to give to a pagan workman anything to do which might involve him in Sabbath work. Thus, Rabbi Gamaliel was careful to send his linen to be washed three days before Sabbath. But it was lawful to leave olives or grapes in the olive or wine press. Both schools were agreed that, in roasting or baking, a crust must have been formed before the Sabbath, except in case of the Passover lamb. The Jerusalem Talmud, however, modifies certain of these rules. Thus the prohibition of work to a pagan only implies, if they work in the house of a Jew, or at least in the same town with him. The school of Shammai, however, went so far as to forbid sending a letter by a pagan, not only a Friday or on a Thursday, but even sending on a Wednesday, or to embark on the sea on these days.

It being assumed that the lighting of the Sabbath lamp was a law given to Moses on Mount Sinai, the Mishnah proceeds, in the second chapter of the tractate on the Sabbath, to discuss the substances of which respectively the wick and the oil may be composed, provided always that oil which feeds the wick is not put in a separate vessel, since the removal of that vessel would cause the extinction of the lamp, which would involve a breach of the Sabbath law. But if the light were extinguished from fear of the Gentiles, of robbers, or of an evil spirit, or in order that one dangerously ill might go to sleep, it involved no guilt. Here, many points in misleading reasoning are discussed, such as whether twofold guilt is incurred if in blowing out a candle its flame lights another. The Mishnah here diverges to discuss the other commandments, which, like that of lighting the Sabbath lamp, especially devolve on women, on which occasion the Talmud broaches some curious statements about the heavenly Sanhedrin and Satan, such as that it is in moments of danger that the Great Enemy brings accusations against us, in order to ensure our ruin; or that on three occasions he especially lies in ambush: when one travels alone, when one sleeps alone in a dark house, and when one crosses the sea. In regard to the latter we may note as illustrative of Paul's warning not to travel after the fast (Day of Atonement), that the Jewish proverb had it: When you bind your Lulabh (at the Feast of Tabernacles) bind also your feet, as regards a sea voyage.

The next two chapters in the tractate on the Sabbath discuss the manner in which food may be kept warm for the Sabbath, since no fire might be lighted. If the food had been partially cooked, or was such as would improve by increased heat, there would be temptation to attend to the fire, and this must be avoided. Therefore the oven was immediately before the Sabbath only to be heated with straw or chaff; if otherwise, the coals were to be removed or covered with ashes. Clothes ought not to be dried by the hot air of a stove. At any rate, care must be taken that neighbors do not see it. An egg may not be boiled by putting it near a hot kettle, nor in a cloth, nor sand heated by the sun. Cold water might be poured on warm, but not the reverse (at least such was the opinion of the school of Shammai), nor was it lawful to prepare either cold or warm compresses. A Rabbi went so far as to forbid throwing hot water over ones self, for fear of spreading the vapor, or of cleaning the floor thereby! A vessel might be put under a lamp to catch the falling sparks, but no water might be put into it, because it was not lawful to extinguish a light. Nor would it have been allowed on the Sabbath to put a vessel to receive the drops of oil that might fall from the lamp. Among many other questions raised was this: whether a parent might take his child in his arms. Happily Rabbinic literally went so far as not only to allow this, but even in the supposed case that the child might happen to have a stone in its hands, although this would involve the labor of carrying that stone! Similarly, it was declared lawful to lift seats, provided they had not, as it were, four steps, when they must be considered as ladders. But it was not allowed to draw along chairs, as this might produce a rut of cavity, although a little carriage might be moved, since the wheels would only compress the soil but not produce a cavity.

Again, the question is discussed, whether it is lawful to keep the food warm by wrapping around a vessel certain substances. Here the general rule is, that all must be avoided which would increase the heat: since this would be to produce some outward effect, which would be equivalent to work.

In the fifth chapter of the tractate we are supposed to begin the Sabbath morning. Ordinarily, the first business of the morning would, have been to take out the cattle. Accordingly, the laws are now laid down for ensuring Sabbath rest to the animals. The principle underlying these is, that only what serves as ornament, or is absolutely necessary for leading out or bringing back animals, or for safety, may be worn by them; all else is regarded as a burden. Even such things as might be put on to prevent the rubbing of a wound, or other possible harm, or to distinguish an animal, must be left aside on the day of rest.

Next, certain regulations are laid down to guide the Jew when dressing on the Sabbath morning, so as to prevent his breaking its rest. Therefore he must be careful not to put on any dress which might become burdensome, nor to wear any ornament which he might put off and carry in his hand, for this would be a burden. A woman must not wear such headgear as would require unloosing before taking a bath, nor go out with such ornaments as could be taken off in the street, such as a frontlet, unless it is attached to the cap, nor with a gold crown, nor with a necklace or nose ring, nor with rings, nor have a pin in her dress. The reason for this prohibition of ornaments was, that in their vanity women might take them off to show them to their companions, and then, forgetful to the day, carry them, which would be a burden. Women are also forbidden to look in the glass on the Sabbath, because they might discover a white hair and attempt to pull it out, which would be a grievous sin; but men ought not to use looking glasses even on weekdays, because this was undignified. A woman may walk about her own court, but not in the streets, with false hair. Similarly, a man was forbidden to wear on the Sabbath wooden shoes studded with nails, or only one shoe, as this would involve labor; nor was he to wear phylacteries nor amulets, unless they had been made by competent persons (since they might lift them off in order to show the novelty). Similarly, it was forbidden to wear any part of a suit of armor. It was not lawful to scrape shoes, except perhaps with the back of a knife, but they might be touched with oil or water. Nor should sandals be softened with oil, because that would improve them. It was a very serious question, which led to much discussion, what should be done if the tie of a sandal had broken on the Sabbath. A plaster might be worn, provided its object was to prevent the wound from getting worse, not to heal it, for that would have been a work. Ornaments which could not easily be taken off might be worn in ones courtyard. Similarly, a person might go about with wadding in his ear, but not with false teeth nor with a gold plug in the tooth. If the wadding fell out of the ear, it could not be replaced. Some indeed, thought that its healing virtues lay in the oil in which it had been soaked, and which had dried up, but others ascribed them to the warmth of the wadding itself. In either case there was danger of healing—of doing anything for the purpose of a cure, and therefore wadding might not be put into the ear on the Sabbath, although if worn before it might be continued. Again, as regarded false teeth: they might fall out, and the weary might then lift and carry them, which would be sinful on the Sabbath. But anything which formed part of the ordinary dress of a person might be worn also on the Sabbath, and children whose ears were being bored might have a plug put into the hole. It was also allowed to go about on crutches, or with a wooden leg, and children might have bells on their dresses; but it was prohibited to walk on stilts, or to carry any pagan amulet.

The seventh chapter of the tractate contains the most important part of the whole. It opens by laying down the principle that, if a person has either not known, or forgotten, the whole Sabbath law, all the breaches of it which he has committed during ever so many weeks are to be considered as only one error or one sin. If he has broken the Sabbath law by mistaking the day, every Sabbath thus profaned must be atoned for; but he has broken the law because he thought that what he did was permissible, then every separate infringement constitutes a separate sin, although labors which stand related as species to the genus are regarded as only one work. It follows, that guilt attaches to the state of mind rather than to the outward deed. Next, forty less one chief or fathers of work (Aboth) are enumerated, all of which are supposed to be forbidden in the Bible. They are: sowing, plowing reaping, binding sheaves, threshing, winnowing, sifting (selecting), grinding, sifting in a sieve, kneading, baking; shearing the wool, washing it, beating it, dyeing it, spinning, putting it on the weavers beam, making a knot, undoing a knot, sewing two stitches, tearing in order to sew two stitches; catching deer, killing; skinning, salting it, preparing its skin, scraping off its hair, cutting it up, writing two letters, scraping in order to write two letters; building, pulling down, extinguishing fire, lighting fire, beating with the hammer, and carrying from one possession into the other.

The number thirty nine is said to represent the number of times that the word labor occurs in the Biblical text, and all these Aboth or fathers of work are supposed to be connected with some work that had been done about the Tabernacle, or to be kindred to such work. Again, each of these principal works involved the prohibition of a number of others which were derived from them, and therefore called their descendants (toledoth). The thirty nine principal works have been arranged in four groups: the first (1-11) referring to the preparation of bread; the second (12-24) to all connected with dress; the third (25-33) to all connected with writing; and the last (34-39) to all the work necessary for a private house. Another Rabbi derives the number thirty nine (of these Aboth) from the numerical value of the initial word in Exodus 35:1, although in so doing he has to change the last letter. Further explanations must here be added. If you scatter two seeds, you have been sowing. In general, the principle is laid down, that anything by which the ground may be benefited is to be considered a work or labor, even if it were to sweep away or to break up a clod of earth. To pluck a blade of grass was a sin. Similarly, it was sinful labor to do anything that would promote the ripening of fruits, such as to water, or even to remove a withered leaf. To pick fruit, or even to lift it from the ground, would be like reaping. If for example, a mushroom were cut, there would be twofold sin, since by the act of cutting, a new one would spring in its place. According to the Rabbis of Caesarea, fishing, and all that put an end to life, must be ranked with harvesting. In connection with the conduct of the disciples in rubbing the ears of grain on the Sabbath, it is interesting to know that all work connected with food would be classed as one of the toledoth, of binding into sheaves. If a woman were to roll wheat to take away the husks, she would be guilty of sifting with a sieve. If she were rubbing the ends of the stalks, she would be guilty of threshing. If she were cleaning what adheres to the side of a stalk, she would be guilty of sifting. If she were brushing the stalk, she would be guilty of grinding. If she were throwing it up in her hands, she would be guilty of winnowing. Distinctions like the following are made: A radish may be dipped into salt, but not left in it too long, since this would be to make pickle. A new dress might be put on, irrespective of the danger that in so doing it might be torn. Mud on the dress might be crushed in the hand and shaken off, but the dress must not be rubbed (for fear of affecting the material). If a person took a bath, opinions are divided, whether the whole body should be dried at once, or limb after limb. If water had fallen on the dress, some allowed the dress to be shaken but not wrung; other, to be wrung but not shaken. One Rabbi allowed to spit into the handkerchief, and that although it may necessitate the compressing of what had been wetted; but there is a grave discussion whether it was lawful to spit on the ground, and then to rub it with the foot, because thereby the earth may be scratched. It may, however, be done on stones. In the labor of grinding would be included such an act as crushing salt. To sweep, or to water the ground, would involve the same sin as beating out the grain. To lay on a plaster would be a grievous sin; to scratch out a big letter, leaving room for two small ones, would be a sin, but to write one big letter occupying the room of two small letters was no sin. To change one letter into another might imply a double sin. And so on through endless details!

The Mishnah continues to explain that, in order to involve guilt, the thing carried from one locality to another must be sufficient to be entrusted for safekeeping. The quantity is regulated: as regards the food of animals, to the capacity of their mouth; as regards man, a dried fig is the standard. As regards fluids, the measure is as much wine as is used for one cup, that is, the measure of the cup being a quarter of a log, and wine being mixed with water in the proportion of three parts water to one of wine, one sixteenth of a log. As regards milk, a mouthful; of honey, sufficient to lay on a wound; of oil, sufficient to anoint the smallest member; of water, sufficient to wet eye salve; and of all other fluids, a quarter of a log.

As regarded other substances, the standard as to what constituted a burden was whether the thing could be turned to any practical use, however trifling. Thus, two horses hairs might be made into a bird trap; a scrap of clean paper into a custom house notice; a small piece of paper written upon might be converted into a wrapper for a small flagon. In all these cases, therefore, transport would involve sin. Similarly, ink sufficient to write two letters, wax enough to fill up a small hole, even a pebble with which you might aim at a little bird, or a small piece of broken earthenware with which you might stir the coals, would be burdens!

Passing to another aspect of the subject, the Mishnah lays it down that, in order to constitute sin, a thing must have been carried from one locality into another entirely and immediately, and that it must have been done in the way in which things are ordinarily carried. If an object which one person could carry is carried by two, they are not guilty. Finally, like all labor on the Sabbath, that of cutting ones nails or hair involves moral sin, but only if it is done in the ordinary way, otherwise only the lesser sin of the breach of the Sabbath rest. A very interesting notice in connection with John 5, is that in which it is explained how it would not involve sin to carry a living person on a pallet, the pallet being regarded only as an accessory to the man; while to carry a dead body in such manner, or even the smallest part of a dead body, would involve guilt.

From this the Mishnah proceeds to discuss what is analogous to carrying, such as drawing or throwing. Other labors are similarly made the subject of inquiry, and it is shown how any approach to them involves guilt. The rule here is that anything that might prove of lasting character must not be done on the Sabbath. The same rule applies to what might prove the beginning of work, such as letting the hammer fall on the anvil; or to anything that might contribute to improve a place, to gathering as much wood as would boil an egg, to uprooting weeds, to writing two letters of a word, in short, to anything that might be helpful in, or contribute towards, some future work.

The Mishnah next passes to such work in which not quantity, but quality, is in question, such as catching deer. Here it is explained that anything by which an animal might be caught is included in the prohibition. So far is this carried that, if a deer had run into a house, and the door were shut upon it, it would involve guilt, and this, even if, without closing the door, persons seated themselves at the entry to prevent the exit of the animal.

Passing over the other chapters, which similarly illustrate what are supposed to be Biblical prohibitions of labor as defined in the thirty nine Aboth and their toledoth, we come, in the sixteenth chapter of the tractate, to one of the most interesting parts, containing such Sabbath laws as, by their own admission, were imposed only by the Rabbis. These embrace: 1. Things forbidden, because they might lead to a transgression of the Biblical command; 2. Such as are like the kind of labor supposed to be forbidden in the Bible; 3. Such as are regarded a sin compatible with the honor due to the Sabbath. In the first class are included a number of regulations in case of a fire. All portions of Holy Scripture, whether in the original or translated, and the case in which they are laid; the phylacteries and their case, might be rescued from the flames. Of food or drink only what was needful for the Sabbath might be rescued; but if the food were in a cupboard or basket the whole might be carried out. Similarly, all utensils needed for the Sabbath meal, but of dress only what was absolutely necessary, might be saved, it being, however, provided, that a person might put on a dress, save it, to go back and put on another, and so on. Again, anything in the house might be covered with skin so as to save it from the flames, or the spread of the flames might be arrested by piling up vessels. It was not lawful to ask a Gentile to extinguish the flame, but not duty to hinder him, if he did so. It was lawful to put a vessel over a lamp, to prevent the ceiling from catching fire; similarly, to throw a vessel over a scorpion, although on that point there is doubt. On the other hand, it is allowed, if a Gentile has lighted a lamp on the Sabbath, to make use of it, the fiction being, however, kept up that he did it for himself, and not for the Jew. By the same fiction the cattle may be watered, or, in fact, any other use made of his services.

Before passing from this, we should point out that it was directed that the Hagiographa should not be read except in the evening, since the daytime was to be devoted to more doctrinal studies. In the same connection it is added, that the study of the Mishnah is more important than that of the Bible, that of the Talmud being considered the most meritorious of all, as enabling one to understand all questions of right and wrong. Liturgical pieces, though containing the Name of God might not be rescued from the flames. The Gospels, and the writings of Christians, or of heretics, might not be rescued. If it be asked what should be done with them on weekdays, the answer is, that the Names of God which they contain ought to be cut out, and then the books themselves burned. One of the Rabbis, however, would have had them burnt at once he would rather have fled into an idolatrous temple than into a Christian church: for the idolaters deny God because they have not known Him, but the apostates are worse. To them applied Psalm 139:21, and, if it was lawful to wash out in the waters of jealousy the Divine Name in order to restore peace, much more would it be lawful to burn such books, even though they contained the Divine Name, because they led to hostility between Israel and their Heavenly Father.

Another chapter of the tractate deals with the question of the various pieces of furniture, how far they may be moved and used. Thus, curtains, or a lid, may be regarded as furniture, and therefore used. More interesting is the next chapter (18), which deals with things forbidden by the Rabbis because they resemble those kinds of labor supposed to be interdicted in the Bible. Here it is declared lawful, for example, to remove quantities of straw or grain in order to make room for guests, or for a assembly of students, but the whole barn must not be emptied, because in so doing the floor might be injured. Again, as regards animals, some assistance might be given if an animal was about to have its young, though not to the same amount as to a woman in childbirth, for whose sake the Sabbath might be desecrated. Lastly, all might be done on the holy day needful for circumcision. At the same time, every preparation possible for the service should be made the day before. The Mishnah proceeds to enter here on details not necessarily connected with the Sabbath law.

In the following chapter (20) the tractate goes on to indicate such things as are only allowed on the Sabbath on condition that they are done differently from ordinary days. Thus, for example, certain solutions ordinarily made in water should be made in vinegar. The food for horses or cattle must not be taken out of the manger, unless it is immediately given to some other animal. The bedding straw must not be turned with hand, but with other part of the body. A press in which linen is smoothed may be opened to take out napkins, but must not be screwed down again, etc.

The next chapter proceeds upon the principle that, although everything is to be avoided which resembles the labors referred to in the Bible, the same prohibition does not apply to such labors as resemble those interdicted by the Rabbis. The application of this principle is not, however, of interest to general readers.

In the twenty second chapter the Mishnah proceeds to show that all the precautions of the Rabbis had only this object: to prevent an ultimate breach of a Biblical prohibition. Therefore, where such was not to be feared, an act might be done. For example, a person might bathe in mineral waters, but not carry home the linen with which he had dried himself. He might anoint and rub the body, but not to the degree of making himself tired; but he might not use any artificial remedial measures, such as taking a shower bath. Bones might not be set, nor substances which cause vomiting up poison given, nor any medical or surgical operation performed.

In the last two chapters the Mishnah points out those things which are unlawful as derogatory to the dignity of the Sabbath. Certain things are here of interest as bearing on the question of purchasing things for the feast day. Thus, it is expressly allowed to borrow wine, or oil, or bread on the Sabbath, and to leave ones upper garment in pledge, though one should not express it in such manner as to imply it was a loan. Moreover, it is expressly added that if the day before the Passover falls on a Sabbath, one may in this manner purchase a Paschal lamb, and, presumably, all else that is needful for the feast. This shows how Judas might have been sent on the eve of the Passover to purchase what was needful, for the law applying to a feast day was much less strict than that of the Sabbath. Again, to avoid the possibility of effacing anything written, it was forbidden to read from a tablet the names of ones guests, or the menu. It was lawful for children to cast lots for their portions at table, but not with strangers, for this might lead to a breach of the Sabbath, and to games of chance. Similarly, it was improper on the Sabbath to engage workmen for the following week, nor should one be on the watch for the close of that day to begin ones ordinary work. It was otherwise if religious obligations awaited one at the close of the Sabbath such as attending to a bride, or making preparation for a funeral. On the Sabbath itself it was lawful to do all that was absolutely necessary connected with the dead, such as to anoint or wash the body, although without moving the limbs, nor might the eyes of the dying be closed, a practice which was generally denounced.

In the last chapter of the tractate the Mishnah returns to the discussion of thorough details. Supposing a traveler to arrive in a place just as the Sabbath commenced, he must only take from his beast of burden such objects are allowed to be handled on the Sabbath. As for the rest, he may loosen the ropes and let them fall down of themselves. Further, it is declared lawful to unloose bundles of straw, or to rub up what can only be eaten in that condition; but care must be taken that nothing is done which is not absolutely necessary. On the other hand, cooking would not be allowed, in short, nothing must be done but what was absolutely necessary to satisfy the cravings of hunger or thirst. Finally, it was declared lawful on the Sabbath to absolve from vows, and to attend to similar religious calls.

Detailed as this analysis of the Sabbath law is, we have not by any means exhausted the subject. Thus, one of the most curious provisions of the Sabbath law was, that on the Sabbath only such things were to be touched or eaten as had been expressly prepared on a weekday with a view to the Sabbath. Anything not so destined was forbidden, as the expression is on account of Muqtsah, i.e. as not having been the intention. Jewish dogmatists enumerate nearly fifty cases in which that theological term finds its application. Thus, if a hen had laid on the Sabbath, the egg was forbidden, because, evidently, it could not have been destined on a weekday for eating, since it was not yet laid, and did not exist; while if the hen had been kept, not for laying but for fattening, the egg might be eaten as forming a part of the hen that had fallen off! But when the principle of Muqtsah is applied to the touching of things which are not used because they have become ugly (and therefore are not in ones mind), so that, for example, an old lamp may not be touched, or raisins during the process of drying them (because they are not eatable then), it will be seen how complicated such a law must have been.

Chiefly from other tractates of the Talmud the following may here be added. It would break the Sabbath rest to climb a tree, to ride, to swim, to clap ones hands, to strike ones side, or to dance. All judicial acts, vows, and tilling were also prohibited on that day. It has already been noted that aid might be given or promised for a woman in her bed. But the Law went further. While it prohibited the application or use on the Sabbath of any remedies that would bring improvement or cure to the sick, all actual danger to life, superseded the Sabbath law, but nothing short of that. Thus, to state an extreme case, if on the Sabbath a wall had fallen on a person, and it were doubtful whether he was under the ruins or not, whether he was alive or dead, a Jew or Gentile, it would be duty to clear away the rubbish sufficiently to find the body. If life were not extinct the labor would have to be continued; but if the person were dead nothing further should be done to extricate the body. Similarly, a Rabbi allowed the use of remedies on the Sabbath in throat diseases, on the express ground that he regarded them as endangering life. On a similar principle a woman with child or a sick person was allowed to break even the fast of the Day of Atonement, while one who had a maniacal attack of morbid craving for food = bolimos might on that sacred day have even unlawful food.

End Notes:

[41]   The Lulabh consisted of a palm with myrtle and willow branch tied on either side of it, which every worshipper carried on the Feast of Tabernacles.
[42]   A log = 0.36 of a liter; six hens eggs.
[43]   An Israelite may be buried in the coffin and grave originally destined for a Gentile, but not vice versa.

Appendix 18

Haggadah of Simeon Kepha
(Legend of Simon Peter)

This Haggadah exists in four different edition. The first of these, reproduce by Jellinek was first published by Wagenseil in his collection of Antichristian writings, the Tela Ignea Satanae, at the close that blasphemous production, the Sepher Toledoth Jeshu. The second edition is that by Huldrich; the third has been printed, as is inferred, at Breslau in 1824; while the fourth exists only in MS. Dr. Jellinek has substantially reproduced (without the closing sentences) the text of Wagenseils, and also editions III. and IV. He regards edition IV as the oldest; but we infer from its plea against the abduction of Jewish children by Christians and against forced baptisms, as well as from the use of certain expressions, that edition IV is younger than the text of Waggenseil, which seems to present the legend in its most primitive form. Even this, however, appears a mixture of several legends; or perhaps the original may afterwards have been edited. It was impossible to fix even approximately the age of this Christianity in Rome, and that of the Papacy, though it seems to contain older elements. It may be regarded as embodying certain ancient legends among the Jews about Peter, but adapted to later times, and cast in an apologetic form. A brief criticism of the document will best follow an abstract of the text, according to the first or earlier edition.

The text begins by a notice that the strife between the Nazarenes and the Jews had grown to such proportions that they separated, since any Nazarene who saw a Jew would kill him. Such became the misery for thirty years, that the Nazarenes increased to thousands and myriads, and prevented the Jew from going up to the feast of Jerusalem. And distress was as great as at the time of the Golden Calf. And still the opposing faith increased, and twelve wicked men went out, who traversed the twelve kingdoms. And they prophesied false prophecies in the camp, and they misled Israel, and they were men of reputation, and strengthened the faith of Jesus, for they said that they were the Apostles of the Crucified. And they drew to themselves a large number from among the children of Israel. On this the text describes, how the sages in Israel were afflicted and humbled themselves, each confessing to his neighbor the sins which had brought this evil, and earnestly asking of God to give them direction how to arrest the advance of Nazarene doctrine and persecution. As they finished their prayer, up rose an elder from their midst, whose name was Simeon Kepha, who had formerly put into requisition the Bath Kol and said: Listen to me, my brethren and my people! If my words are good in your sight, I will separate those sinners from the congregation of the children of Israel, and they will have neither part nor inheritance in the midst of Israel, if only you take upon you the sin. And they all answered and said: We will take upon us the sin, if only you will do what you have said. Upon this, the narrative proceeds, Peter went into the Sanctuary, wrote the Ineffable Name, and inserted it in his flesh. Having learned the Ineffable Name, he went to the metropolis (metroplin) of the Nazarenes, and proclaimed that every believer in Christ should come to him, since he was an Apostle. The multitudes required that he should prove his claim by a sign (oath) such as Jesus had done while He was alive, when Peter, through the power of the Ineffable Name, restored a leper, by laying on of hands, and raised the dead. When the Nazarenes saw this, they fell on their faces, and acknowledged his Apostolate. Then Peter delivered this as his message, first inviting them swear to do as he would command: know (said he) that the Crucified hated Israel and their law, as Isaiah prophesied: "Your new moons and your feasts my soul hates;" know also, that he delights not in Israel, as Hosea prophesied, "You are not my people." And although it is in His power to exterminate them from the world in a moment, from out of every place, yet He does not purpose to destroy them, but intends to leave them, in order that they be in memory of His Crucifixion and death by stoning to all generations. Besides, know that He bore all those great sufferings and afflictions to redeem you from Gehenna. And now He admonishes and commands you, that you should do no evil to the Jews: and if a Jews says to a Nazarene, "Go with me one parasang" (Persian mile about three English miles), let him go with him two parasangs. And if a Jew smites him on the left check, let him present to him also the right cheek, in order that they may have their reward in this world, while in the next they will be punished in Gehenna. And if you do thus, you will deserve to sit with Him in Feast of the Passover, but observe the day of His death. And instead of the Feast of Pentecost observe the forty days from the time that He was slain to when He went up into heaven. And instead of the Feast of Tabernacles observe the day of His birth, and on the eighth day after His birth observe that on which He was circumcised.

To these commands all agreed, on condition that Peter should remain with them. This he consented to do, on the understanding that he would not eat anything except bread of misery and water of affliction, presumably not only to avoid forbidden food, but in atoning suffering for his sin, and that they should build him a tower in the midst of the city, in which he would remain to the day of his death, all which provisions were duly carried out. It is added, that in this tower he served the God of his fathers, Abraham, Isaac, and Jacob. What is still stranger, it is added, that he wrote many Piutim, a certain class of liturgical poems which form apart of the Synagogue service, and that he sent these throughout all Israel to be in perpetual memory of him, and especially that he dispatched them to the Rabbis. The remark is the more noteworthy, as other Jewish writers also describe the Apostle Peter as the author of several liturgical poems, of which one is still repeated in the Synagogue on Sabbaths and Feast days. But to return, Peter is said to have remained in that tower for six years, when he died, and by his direction was buried within the tower. But the Nazarenes raised there a great fabric, and this tower may be seen in Rome, and they call it Peter, which is the word for a stone, because he sat on a stone until the day of his death. But after his death another person named Elijah came, in the wickedness and cunning of his heart to mislead them. And he said to them Simon had deceived them, for that Jesus had commanded him to tell them: it had not come into His heart to despise the Law of Moses; that if anyone wished to circumcise, he should circumcise; but if anyone did not wish to be circumcised, let him be immersed in foul waters. And even if he were not immersed, he would not thereby be in danger in the world. And he commanded that they should not observe the seventh day, but only the first day, because on it were created the heavens and the earth. And he made to them many statutes which were not good. But the people asked him: Give us a true sign that Jesus has sent you. And he said to them: What is the sign that you seek? And the word had not been out of his own mouth when a great stone of immense weight fell and crushed his head. So perish all Your enemies, O God, but let them that love You be as the sun when he goes forth in his strength!

Thus far what we regard as the oldest edition. The chief variations between this and the others are, that in the third edition the opponent of Peter is called Abba Shaul, while in the fourth edition, which consists of nineteen chapters, this opponent is called Elijah. In the latter edition there is mention of Antioch and Tiberias, and other places connected with the lives of Peter and Paul, and the early history of the Church. But the occurrence of certain Romanic words, such as Papa, Vescova, etc., shows its later date. Again, we mark that, according to edition III. and IV., Peter sent his liturgical pieces to Babylon, which may either indicate that at the time of the document Babylon was the center of the Jewish population, or else be a legendary reminiscence of Peter's labors in the Church that is in Babylon (1 Peter 5:13). In view of modern controversies it is of special interest that, according to the Jewish legend, Peter, secretly a Jew, advised the Christians to throw off completely the Law of Moses, while Paul, in opposition to him, stands up for Israel and the Law, and insists that either circumcision or baptism may be practiced. It will be further noted, that the object of the document seems to be: 1st, to serve as an apology for Judaism, by explaining how it came that so many Jews, under the leadership of Apostles, embraced the new faith. This seems to be traced to the continued observance of Jewish legal practices by the Christians. Simon Peter is supposed to have arrested the progress of Christianity by separating the Church from the Synagogue, which he did by proclaiming that Israel was rejected, and the Law of Moses abolished. On the other hand, Paul is represented as the friend of the Jews, and as proclaiming that the question of circumcision or baptism, of legal observances or Christian practices, was a matter of influences. This attempt to heal the breach between the Church and the Synagogue had been the cause of Divine judgment on him. 2ndly, the legend is intended as an apology for the Jews, with a view to ward off persecution. 3rdly, it is intended to show that the leaders of the Christians remained in heart Jews. It will perhaps not be difficult, at least, hypothetically, to separate the various legends mixed up, or perhaps edited in the tractate. From the mention of the Piutim and the ignorance as to their origin, we might be disposed to assign the composition of the legend in its present form to about the eighth century AD.

Appendix 19

Eternal Punishment, According to the Rabbis and The New Testament

The Parables of the Ten Virgins and of the Unfaithful Servant close with a discourse on the Last Things, the final Judgment, and the fate of those at Christ's Right Hand and at His Left (Matthew 25:31-46). This final Judgment by Jesus forms a fundamental article in the Creed of the Church. It is the Christ Who comes, accompanied by the Angelic Host, and sits down on the throne of His Glory, when all nations are gathered before Him. Then the final separation is made, and joy or sorrow awarded in accordance with the past of each man's history. And that past, as in relationship to the Christ, whether it has been with Him or not with Him, which latter is now shown to be equivalent to against Him. And while, in the deep sense of a love to Christ which is utterly self forgetful in its service and utterly humble in its realization to Him to Whom no real service can be done by man, to their blessed surprise, those on the Right find work and acknowledgement where they had never thought of its possibility, every ministry of their life, however small, is now owned of Him as rendered to Himself, partly, because the new direction, from which all such ministry sprang, was of Christ in them, and partly, because of the identification of Christ with His people. On the other hand, as the lowest service of him who has the new inner direction if Christ-ward, so does ignorance, or else feigned ignorance, of Christ issue in neglect of service and labor of love, and neglect of service proceed from neglect and rejection of Christ. And so is life either to Christ or not to Christ, and necessarily ends in the Kingdom prepared from the foundation of the world or in the eternal fire which is prepared for the Devil and his angels.

Thus far the meaning of Jesus' Words, which could only be impaired by any attempt at commentary. But they also raise questions of the deepest importance, in which not only the head, but perhaps much more the heart, is interested, as regards the precise meaning of the term everlasting and eternal in this and other connections, so far as those on the Left Hand of Christ are concerned. The subject has of late attracted renewed attention. The doctrine of the Eternity of Punishments, with the proper explanations and limitations given to it in the teaching of the Church, has been set forth by Dr. Pusey in his Treatise: What is of Faith as to Everlasting Punishment? Before adverting, however briefly, to the New Testament teaching, it seems desirable with some fullness to set forth the Jewish views on this subject. For the views held at the time of Christ, whatever they were must have been those which the hearers of Christ entertained; and whatever views, Christ did not at least directly, contradict or, so far as we can infer, intend to correct them. And here we have happily sufficient materials for a history of Jewish opinions at different periods on the Eternity Punishment; and it seems the more desirable carefully to set it forth, as statements both inaccurate and incomplete have been put forward on the subject.

Leaving aside the teaching of the Apocrypha and Pseudepigraphic Writing, the first Rabbinic utterances come to us from the time immediately before that of Christ, from the Schools of Shammai and Hillel. The former arranged all mankind into three classes: the perfectly righteous, who are immediately written and sealed to eternal life; the perfectly wicked, who are immediately written and sealed to Gehenna; and an intermediate class. who go down to Gehinnom, and moan, and come up again, according to Zechariah 13:9, and which seemed also indicated in certain words in the Song of Hannah (1 Samuel 2:6). The careful reader will notice that this statement implies belief in Eternal Punishment on the part of the School of Shammai: For (1) The perfectly wicked are spoken of as written and sealed to Gehenna; (2) The school of Shammai expressly quotes, in support of what it teaches about these wicked, Daniel 12:2, a passage which undoubtedly refers to the final judgment after the Resurrection; (3) The perfectly wicked, so punished, are expressly distinguished from the third, or intermediate class, who merely go down to Gehinnom, but are not written and sealed, and come up again.

Substantially the same, as regards Eternity of Punishment, is the view of the School of Hillel. In regard to sinners of Israel and of the Gentiles it teaches that they are tormented in Gehenna for twelve months, after which their bodies and souls are burnt up and scattered as dust under the feet of the righteous; but it significantly excepts from this number certain classes of transgressors who go down to Gehinnom and are punished there to ages of ages. That the Niphal form of the verb used,; must mean punished and not judged, appears, not only from the context, but from the use of the same word and form in the same tractate, when it is said of the generation of the Flood that they were punished surely not judged, by hot water. However, therefore the School of Hillel might accentuate the mercy of God, or limit the number of those who would suffer Eternal Punishment, it did teach Eternal Punishment in the case of some. And this is the point in question.

But, since the Schools of Shammai and Hillel represented the theological teaching in the time of Christ and His Apostles, it follows, that the doctrine of Eternal Punishment was that held in the days of Jesus, however it may afterwards have been modified. Here, so far as this book is concerned, we might rest the case. But for completeness sake it will be better to follow the historical development of Jewish theological teaching, at least a certain distance.

The doctrine of the Eternity of Punishments seems to have been held by the Synagogue throughout the whole first century of our era. This will appear from the sayings of the Teachers who flourished during its course. The Jewish Parable of the fate of those who had not kept their festive garments in readiness or appeared in such as were not clean has been already quoted in our exposition of the Parables of the Man without the Wedding garment and of the Ten Virgins. But we have more than this. We are told that, when that great Rabbinic authority of the first century, Rabbi Jochanan ben Zakkai, the light of Israel, the right hand pillar, the mighty hammer, lay a dying and wept, he accounted for his tears by fear as to his fate in judgment, illustrating the danger by the contrast of punishment by an earthly king whose bonds are not eternal bonds nor his death eternal death, while as regarded God and His judgment: if He is angry with me, His Wrath is an Eternal Wrath, if He binds me in fetters, His fetters are Eternal fetters, and if He kills me, His death is an Eternal death. In the same direction is this saying of another great Rabbi of the first century, Elieser, to the effect that the souls of the righteous are hidden under the throne of glory, while those of the wicked were to be bound and in unrest, one Angel hurling them to another from one end of the world to the other, of which latter strange idea he saw confirmation in 1 Samuel 25:29. To the fate of the righteous applied, among other beautiful passages, Isaiah 55:2, to that of the wicked Isaiah 55:21. Evidently, the views of the Rabbis of the first century were in strict accordance with those Shammai and Hillel.

In the second century of our era, we mark a decided difference in Rabbinic opinion. Although it was said that, after the death of Rabbi Meir, the ascent of smoke from the grave of his apostate teacher had indicated that the Rabbis prayers for the deliverance of his matter from Gehenna had been answered, most of the eminent teachers of that period propounded the idea, that in the last day the sheath would be removed which now covered the sun, when its fiery heat would burn up the wicked. One Rabbi maintained that there was no hell at all, but that that day would consume the wicked, and yet another, that even this was not so, but that the wicked would be consumed by a sort of internal uncontrolled burning.

In the third century of our era we have once more a reaction, and a return to the former views. Thus Rabbi Eleasar speaks of the three bands of Angels, which successively go forth to meet the righteousness, each with a welcome of their own, and of the three bands of Angels of sorrow, which similarly receive the wicked in their death, and this, in terms which leave no doubt as to the expected fate of the wicked. And here Rabbi Jose informs us, that the fire of Gehenna which was created on the second day is not extinguished forever. With this view accord the seven designations which according to Rabbi Joshua ben Levi, attach to Gehenna. This doctrine was only modified, when Ben Lakish maintained, that the fire of Gehenna did not hurt sinners from among the Jews. Nor does even this other saying of his necessarily imply that he denied the eternity of punishment: There is no Gehinnom in the world to come, since it is qualified by the expectation that the wicked would be punished, not annihilated, by the heat of the sun, which would be felt as healing by the righteous. Lastly, if not universal sainthood, yet a kind of universal moral restoration seems implies in the teaching of Rabbi Jehudah to the effect that in the soeculum futurum God would destroy the Yetser haRa.

Tempting as the subject is, we must here break off this historical review, for lack to space, not of material. Dr. Pusey has shown that the Targumim also teach the doctrine of Eternal Punishment, though their date is matter of discussion, and to the passage quoted by him in evidence others might be added. And if on the other side the saying of Rabbi Akiba should be quoted to the effect that the judgment of the wicked in Gehenna was one of the five things that lasted for twelve months, it must be remembered that, even if this be taken seriously, it does not necessarily imply more than the teaching of Hillel concerning that intermediate class of sinners who were in Gehenna for a year, while there was another class the duration of whose punishment would be for ages of ages. Even more palpably inapt is the quotation from Baba Mez. 58 b. For, if that passage declares that all are destined to come up again from Gehenna, it expressly excepts from this these three classes of persons: adulterers, those who put their fellow men publicly to shame, and those who apply an evil name to their neighbors.

But there can at least be no question that the passage which has been quoted at the outset of these remarks, proves beyond the possibility of controdiction that both the Great Schools, in which Rabbinic teaching at the time of Christ was divided, held the doctrine of Eternal Punishments. This entirely apart from the question who, how many, or rather, how few, were to suffer this terrible fate. And here the cautions and limitations, with which Dr. Pusey has shown that the Church has surrounded her teaching, cannot be too often or earnestly repeated. It does seem painfully strange that, if the meaning of it be all realized, some should seem so anxious to contend for the extension to so many of a misery from which our thoughts shrink in awe. Yet of this we are well assured, that the Judge of all the Earth will judge, not only righteously, but mercifully. He alone knows all the secrets of heart and life, and He alone can apportion to each the due need. And in this assured conviction may the mind trustfully rest as regards those who have been dear to us.

But if on such grounds we shrink from narrow and harsh dogmatism, there are certain questions which we cannot quite evade, even although we may answer them generally rather than specifically. We put aside, as an unhealthy and threatening sign of certain religious movements, the theory, lately broached, of a so called Conditional Immortality. So far as the readings of the present writer extends, it is based on bad philosophy and even worse exegesis. But the question itself, to which this rough and ready kind of answer has been attempted, is one of the most serious. In our view, an impartial study of the Words of the Lord, recorded in the Gospels, as repeatedly indicated in the text of these volumes, leads to the impression that His teaching in regard to reward and punishment should be taken in the ordinary and obvious sense, and not in that suggested by some. And this is confirmed by what is now quite clear to us, that the Jews, to whom He spoke, believed in Eternal Punishment, however few they might consign to it. And yet we feel that this line of argument is not quite convincing. For might not Jesus, as in regard to the period of His Second

Coming, in this also have intended to leave His hearers in incertitude? And is it really necessary to be quite sure of this aspect of eternity?

And here the question arises about the precise meaning of the words which Christ used. It is maintained that the terms anios and similar expression always refer to eternity in the strict sense. But of this I cannot express myself convinced, although the balance of evidence is in favor of such meaning. But it is at least conceivable that the expressions might refer to the end of all time, and the merging of the mediatorial regency (1 Corinthians 15:24) in the absolute kingship of God.

In further thinking on this most solemn subject, it seems to the present writer that exaggerations have been made in the argument. It has been said that, the hypothesis of annihilation being set aside, we are practically shut up to what is called Universalism. And again, that Universalism implies, not only the final restoration of all the wicked, but even of Satan and his angels. And further, it has been argued that the metaphysical difficulties of the question ultimately resolve themselves into this: why the God of all foreknowledge had created beings, be they men or fallen angels, who, as He foreknew, would ultimately sin? Now this argument has evidently no force as against absolute Universalism. But even otherwise, it is rather specious than convincing. For we only possess data for reasoning in regard to the sphere which falls within our cognition, which the absolutely Divine, the pre-human and the pre-created, does not, except so far as it has been the subject of Revelation. This limitation excludes from the sphere of our possible comprehension all questions connected with the Divine foreknowledge and its compatibility with that which we know to be the fundamental law of created intelligences, and the very condition of their moral being: personal freedom and choice. To quarrel with this limitation of our sphere of reasoning, were to rebel against the conditions of human existence. But if so, then the question of Divine foreknowledge must not be raised at all, and the question of the fall of angels and of the sin of man must be left on the (to us) alone intelligible basis: that of personal choice and absolute moral freedom.

Again, it seems least an exaggeration to put the alternatives thus: absolute eternity of punishment, and, with it, of the state of rebellion which it implies, since it is unthinkable that rebellion should absolutely cease, and yet punishment continue; annihilation; or else universal restoration. Something else is at least thinkable, that may not lie within these hard and fast lines of demarcation. It is at least conceivable that there may be a quartum quid, that there may be a purification or transformation of all who are capable of such, or, if it is preferred, an unfolding of the germ of grace, present before death, invisible though it may have been to other men, and that in the end of what we call time or dispensation, only that which is morally incapable of transformation, be it men or devils, shall be cast into the lake of fire and brimstone (Revelation 20:10, 14, 15; 20:8). And here, if, perhaps just, exception is taken to the terms purification or transformation (perhaps spiritual development), I would refer in explanation to what Dr. Pusey has so beautifully written, although my reference is only to this point, not to others on which he touches. And, in connection with this, we note that there is quite a series of Scripture statements, which teach the final reign of God (that God may be all in all), and the final putting of all things under Christ, and all this in connection with blessed fact that Christ has tasted death for every man, that the world through Him might be saved, and, in consequence, to draw all to Himself, comp. Colossians 1:19, 20 (comp. John 3:17; 12:32; Romans 5:18-24; 1 Corinthians 15:20-28; Ephesians 1:10; Colossians 1:19, 20; 1 Timothy 2:4, 6; 4:10; Hebrews 2:9; 1 John 2:2; 4:14, all which passages must, however, be studied in their connection).

Thus far it has been the sole aim of the present writer to set before the reader, so far as he can, all the elements to be taken into consideration. He has pronounced no definite conclusion, and he neither wishes nor purposes to do so. This only he will repeat, that to his mind the Words of Jesus, as recorded in the Gospels, convey this impression, that there is an eternity of punishment; and further, that this was the accepted belief of the Jewish schools in the time of Christ. But of these things does he feel fully assured: that we may absolutely trust in the loving kindness of our God; that the Word of Christ is for all and of infinite value, and that its outcome must correspond to its character; and lastly, for practical purposes, that in regard to those who have departed (whether or not we know of grace in them) our views and our hopes should be the widest (consistent with Scripture teaching), and that as regards ourselves, personally and individually, our views as to the need of absolute and immediate faith in Christ as the Savior, of holiness of life, and of service of the Lord Jesus, should be the closest and most rigidly fixed.

Ingram Content Group UK Ltd.
Milton Keynes UK
UKHW011835140323
418553UK00001B/77